MASTER THE CLEP

2004

Leo Lieberman

THOMSON™

ARCO

Australia • Canada • Mexico • Singapore • Spain • United Kingdom • United States

An ARCO Book

ARCO is a registered trademark of Thomson Learning, Inc., and is used herein under license by Peterson's.

About The Thomson Corporation and Peterson's

With revenues of US$7.8 billion, The Thomson Corporation (www.thomson.com) is a leading global provider of integrated information solutions for business, education, and professional customers. Its Learning businesses and brands (www.thomsonlearning.com) serve the needs of individuals, learning institutions, and corporations with products and services for both traditional and distributed learning.

Peterson's, part of The Thomson Corporation, is one of the nation's most respected providers of lifelong learning online resources, software, reference guides, and books. The Education Supersite[SM] at www.petersons.com—the Internet's most heavily traveled education resources—has searchable databases and interactive tools for contacting U.S.-accredited institutions and programs. In addition, Peterson's serves more than 105 million education consumers annually.

For more information, contact Peterson's, 2000 Lenox Drive, Lawrenceville, NJ 08648; 800-338-3282; or find us on the World Wide Web at: www.petersons.com/about

ISBN: 0-7689-1201-6

Printed in the United States of America

10 9 8 7 6 5 4 3 2 1   05 04 03

Contents

Introduction

WHAT THIS BOOK WILL DO FOR YOU

This book is for people who have attained the college level of education in nontraditional ways. It is for those who have gained their education outside the classroom. It tells about examinations that help you show what you know. These examinations give you the opportunity to:

1. Have your educational attainment validated, thereby establishing the fact that you possess college-level skills and knowledge

2. Attain college credit for the knowledge you have acquired outside the classroom and help you progress toward a degree

3. Avoid classroom attendance in subjects you already know and obtain advanced placement in a college curriculum

4. Qualify for jobs in an industry that requires college training as a prerequisite for employment or advancement

5. Demonstrate for your own satisfaction the college-level ability that you have gained

If you want to take the CLEP exams but are reluctant for fear they may be too difficult, this book is for you. Here you will find out all about the CLEP General Examinations, including:

1. How to register for the examinations

2. Where and when they are given

3. How to prepare for the exams with hundreds of questions and answers typical of those found on the actual tests

4. How to interpret your scores and use the results to your best advantage

Used correctly, this "self-tutor" will show you what to expect and will give you a speedy brush-up on the subjects particular to your exam. Even if your study time is very limited, you will:

- Become familiar with the type of examination you can expect

- Improve your general examination-taking skill

- Improve your skill in answering questions involving reasoning, judgment, comparison, and evaluation

- Improve your speed and skill in reading and understanding what you read— an important part of your ability to learn and an important part of most tests

- Prepare yourself in the particular fields covered by the CLEP General Examinations

In fact, this guide will tell you exactly what to study by presenting in full every type of question you will get on the actual exam. You will do better merely by familiarizing yourself with them.

It will help you find your weaknesses and find them fast. Once you know where you are weak, you will know how best to use your study time in preparing for your exam.

In addition, this book will give you the feel of the exam. Since previous CLEP exams are not available for inspection, the sample test questions are invaluable to you.

Finally, this book will give you confidence now, while you are preparing for the exam. It will build your self-confidence as you proceed and help to ward off the pre-test jitters that have undermined so many test takers.

THE COLLEGE-LEVEL EXAMINATION PROGRAM

Do you have know-how that was gained from other than accredited college training? Have you read widely or had life experiences that qualify you for jobs you can't get because you don't have the college credits? Or are you disqualified for advanced placement in college simply because you don't have the course credits from an accredited institution? If so, you are among the large number of people for whom the College-Level Examination Program is designed.

The College-Level Examination Program (CLEP) offers you an opportunity to show a college admissions officer, or a prospective employer, or just yourself, what you know in a variety of subject areas. Some employers in business, industry, professional groups, and government use the results of CLEP examinations to assess a potential employee's educational level, regardless of the credits listed on his resume. Many college admissions officers use CLEP scores to determine where to place college applicants in their traditional four-year programs.

There have long been tests to assess the achievement of students who progress from high school to college in the usual way. However, for those who have gained their education through correspondence courses, television courses, home-study courses via records or tapes, on-the-job training or life experiences, no widely recognized evaluation test has been available until CLEP.

The CLEP Examinations are sponsored by the College Entrance Examination Board. The Board employs the services of the Educational Testing Service (ETS) to develop and administer the exams. ETS is a nonprofit corporation specializing in test development and educational research. The College Board, with the support of the Carnegie Corporation of New York, developed the CLEP program to aid students who wish to gain college credit for achievement outside the classroom. CLEP examinations are open to anyone who desires to demonstrate college-level proficiency no matter how or where that proficiency was gained.

Two Kinds of CLEP Examinations

The College-Level Examination Program comprises two types of examinations: the General Examinations and the Subject Examinations.

The General Examinations measure college-level achievement in five basic areas of the liberal arts: English Composition, Humanities, Mathematics, Natural Sciences, and Social Sciences and History. These examinations test material usually covered in the first two years of college and often referred to as the general or liberal education requirement. The General Examinations are not intended to measure specialized knowledge of a particular discipline, nor are they based on a particular curriculum or course of study. Rather, they are designed to evaluate broad-based ability that can be acquired in a number of ways, through personal reading, employment, television, radio, adult classes, or advanced high school work.

Each General Examination is 90 minutes long and, except for English Composition with Essay, consists entirely of multiple-choice questions presented in two separately timed sections. The content and format of each General Examination is fully detailed in the chapters that follow.

The Subject Examinations measure achievement in specific college courses and are used to grant exemption from and credit for these courses. Like the General Examinations, each Subject Examination is 90 minutes long and consists of multiple-choice questions presented in two separately timed sections. The four Subject Exams in Composition and Literature also include an optional 90-minute essay section. Check with the college you are planning to attend to see if the essay section is required.

Twenty-nine Subject Examinations are offered. More detailed information about the Subject Examinations is available at the College Board Web site: www.collegeboard.com or in *The Official Handbook for the CLEP Examinations* published by the College Board.

College Board Offices

New York Office: 45 Columbus Avenue, New York, NY 10023-6992
Middle States Regional Office: 3440 Market Street, Suite 410, Philadelphia, PA 19104-3338
Midwestern Regional Office: 1800 Sherman Avenue, Suite 401, Evanston, IL 60201-3715
New England Regional Office: 470 Totten Pond Road, Waltham, MA 02154-1982
Puerto Rico Office: P.O. Box 71101, San Juan, PR 00936-7001
Southern Regional Office: 2970 Clairmont Road, Suite 250, Atlanta, GA 30329-1639
Southwestern Regional Office: 701 Brozos, Suite 400, Austin, TX 78701-3253
Western Regional Office: 2099 Gateway Place, Suite 480, San Jose, CA 95110-1017

When and Where CLEP Tests Are Given

CLEP tests are administered throughout the year at more than 1,200 test centers throughout the United States. These centers, usually located on college and university campuses, are listed in the publication *CLEP Colleges*, which you may obtain

by writing: CLEP, P.O. Box 6600, Princeton, NJ 08541-6600
by e-mailing: clep@info.collegeboard.com
or by calling: (609) 771-7865

When you register, you may ask to take the test at the most convenient location for you. If you live more than 150 miles from the nearest listed test center, the College Board may be able to arrange a special test location that is closer to your home. If you require special arrangements, you must pay an extra fee. Arrangements for a special testing center take about five weeks. If you live outside the United States, you may request a special administration of the CLEP exams. You must list at least three cities where you could be tested and you must submit your request at least four months before the date on which you wish to be tested.

You may register for one or more examinations on a given testing date. No matter which examination you take, you must arrive at the start of the test session. Late arrivals will usually not be admitted as they may disturb those who have begun to work.

How to Register for the Examinations

The first thing to do if you are considering the possibility of utilizing your life experiences to obtain college credit is write for the booklets *CLEP Colleges* and *Information for Candidates and Registration Form*. These publications are available at College Board offices or from the Princeton address given on the previous page.

The Registration Form must be completed and sent with your test fee to the test center you select no later than three weeks before the test is scheduled. Be sure to send your Registration Form and fee to the test center, not to the College Board. Consult the *Information for Candidates* booklet for detailed instructions on registration procedures and for directions for filling out your application form.

If you wish to obtain college credit for participating in the CLEP program, it is important that you contact your college guidance department to learn what regulations govern the use of the tests at your school. College credit is awarded only by the colleges and universities that participate in the program. Although the tests are devised and administered by the College Entrance Examination Board, the Board is not a college and does not give college credit. Each college and university has its own policy regarding CLEP scores, and it is up to you to find out the requirements of the school to which you are applying for credit.

Computer-Based Testing (CBT)

All CLEP exams are now administered on computer. The exam is preceded by a tutorial that explains how to take the exam on computer. The CLEP CBT exams are fixed-length exams, like the paper-and-pencil version. There are advantages of the CLEP CBT. Your score report will be generated immediately after taking the test and you will be able to take those scores with you. The English Composition with Essay test will be separately scored. Once you send your essay electronically to CLEP, you will receive your score within two weeks.

How the Tests Are Scored

In the CLEP CBT version, only the right answers will count toward your score.

Your score is then converted to a scaled score that ranges from 200 to 800 for the General Exams and from 20 to 80 for the Subject Exams. The scaled score provides a uniform indicator of performance no matter which edition of a particular test you take.

There are no passing or failing scores on the General Examinations. Each college or university determines how and to what extent it will use CLEP examinations to award credit, including which tests it recognizes and what scores it requires.

How Scores Are Reported

Your scores will be sent to any institutions you designated at the time of your examination. Test scores are kept on file for twenty years. You may request that your test score reports be sent to any institution at any time during this period by completing the Transcript Request Form included in your score report.

Since the optional essay section of the Subject Examination is graded by the institution receiving the score, there is no transcript service on Subject Examination essay answers.

If, after registering for an exam, you decide not to take it, you may cancel your registration and obtain a refund. Fill out the appropriate space on the bottom of your Admission Form and send the form to the test center where you were scheduled to take the test. Your request must be mailed no later than two days before the testing date. In this case, you will receive a refund check for one half your testing fee.

You may retake any CLEP examination provided that six months have elapsed since you last took that examination. If you retake an exam within fewer than six months, your score will be cancelled and your fees will not be refunded.

STUDY HINTS

1. Be confident. It is important to know that you are not expected to answer every question correctly on the CLEP Examinations. The questions have a range of difficulty and differentiate among several levels of skill.

2. Read each question carefully. The questions on the General Examinations are not designed to trick you through misleading or ambiguous alternative choices. On the other hand, they are not all direct questions of factual information. Some are designed to elicit responses that reveal your ability to reason, or to interpret a fact or idea. It's up to you to read each question carefully so you know what is being asked. The exam authors have tried to make the questions clear. Do not go too far astray in looking for hidden meanings.

3. Become familiar with the test's scope, format, and purpose. It is important to discover how the test is organized, what material is covered, where the concentration is, and how the questions are phrased.

4. Review past examinations, or, if these tests are not available, become familiar with practice tests based on the examination. Test yourself and analyze your strong points as well as your weaknesses. Try to find the underlying reasons for the correct answer to each question.

5. Long-range studying is more effective than last-minute cramming. As soon as possible, plan a program to prepare yourself for the test.

6. Develop regular study habits. It is far better to study for an hour three times a week for five weeks than to attempt to study for 15 hours during the two or three days preceding the actual examination. However, there is value in last-minute cramming as a means of reviewing material prior to the test.

7. Lengthy study periods can be counterproductive. Short, intensive study periods are usually more effective than unrealistically long ones. If you begin to drift away from the material or resent studying, the time will become valueless.

8. Frequent short reviews of material have great value. In addition to a regimen of study sessions, you may find that a 5- or 10-minute brush-up will help to fix and consolidate material studied the previous day.

9. Be an active participant in the study process. Sitting in a comfortable chair, listening to the stereo, and munching on a cookie may be pleasant, but this is certainly not an effective way to study important material. It is better to sit at a well-lighted desk in a quiet place with pencil and paper, underlining key phrases, taking notes, and recording items that you want to remember. Students are often told to keep notebooks of material they wish to remember and to reread their notes whenever they have spare time.

10. Don't burden yourself with unnecessary material. Many colored markers, slide rules, and Scotch tape can prove to be a distraction if not needed.

11. Analyze the questions carefully. Sometimes a word such as *never, always,* or *not* can change the question and its resulting response. Before you answer a question, you must know what the question is.

12. Be positive! Approach the examination with an optimistic attitude. Know that your studying will help you to do well.

Test-Taking Tips for the Day of the Examination

1. Get to the room at least 10 to 15 minutes before exam time. Allow yourself ample time to settle down so that you are familiar with the room and relatively comfortable.

2. Make certain that the test conditions are favorable. If there are distractions or any adverse conditions, inform the proctor. Don't be a martyr. The test will require all your energy. Don't be distracted unnecessarily.

3. Follow all the directions given by the proctor. If you do not understand what to do or are uncertain how to proceed, don't hesitate to ask the proctor for assistance.

4. Budget your time wisely. Be certain you understand the directions for each examination. Don't spend too much time on any one question. Proceed from question to question without needless worry regarding how you answered a previous question. If a question thoroughly confuses you, omit it and move on to the next one.

5. If you find yourself becoming tense, a few deep breaths will help. Some people close their eyes for a few seconds and then continue to work.

6. It is better not to answer a question than to take a wild guess. But an educated guess is better than a complete omission.

7. If you take the essay component, you will have 45 minutes to write a composition. You should allow yourself 5 or 10 minutes to proofread, but you will probably not have enough time to rewrite the entire essay.

8. If you have used this book wisely, you will be at ease with the general format of the exam and the types of questions asked. As a result, there will be no surprises for you and you will be free to concentrate on giving correct responses. To get the most out of this book, read each section thoroughly and complete all the exercises.

English Composition

ABOUT THE GENERAL EXAMINATION IN ENGLISH COMPOSITION

The CLEP General Examination in English Composition is designed to determine how well you can handle the kind of writing that is appropriate for students on a college level. In a sense, it tests your ability to manage college writing with fluency and adequacy. Since there is no one course of study or even one special text that is used in colleges throughout the country, the examination cannot focus on any one approach or even on a narrow selection of material. The examination emphasizes what is called "standard written English." This is the language that students are expected to use in academic or classroom situations and the language that is usually found in textbooks and reference works. Standard written English tends to be rather formal and contrasts with slang or colloquial usage.

There are two editions of the General Examination in English Composition: one multiple-choice examination and one that includes an essay. Both editions start with a 45-minute section covering logical and structural relationships within the sentence and ability to revise a work in progress. The 55 questions in this section are divided among three question types.

Section I (for both editions of this exam):

1. *Identifying Sentence Errors*. These questions require you to determine which of four underlined parts of a sentence needs correction or whether the sentence is correct as written.

2. *Improving Sentences*. These questions require you to decide which of five alternatives best conveys the intended meaning of the underlined part of a given sentence.

3. *Revising Work in Progress*. These questions present an early draft of a student essay and ask you to identify ways of improving the draft.

In the multiple-choice examination, Section II consists of a 45-minute test that measures your ability to recognize sentence errors, to revise sentences for emphasis or clarity, to improve a work in progress, and to analyze prose passages. The 50 questions in this section are apportioned among the following four question types.

7

Section II (for the multiple-choice edition of this exam):

1. *Identifying Sentence Errors*. Same as Section I above.

2. *Restructuring Sentences*. These questions require you to reword a sentence according to specific directions and then choose the word or phrase that will appear in your revised sentence.

3. *Revising Work in Progress*. Same as in Section I above.

4. *Analyzing Writing*. These questions present two prose passages and ask you to answer questions about the structure of each passage and the strategies used by each author.

In the essay version of the General Examination in English Composition, Section II is devoted to an expository essay. You will be allowed 45 minutes to organize and write an essay on a specified topic. The topic is usually presented in the form of a short paragraph, which you are to support or refute. In addition to providing a demonstration of your writing skill, your essay should indicate your ability to present a point of view, develop an argument logically, and provide relevant supporting evidence from reading or personal experience. The essay is scored by English faculty members who are more concerned with the quality of the writing as a whole than with the number of spelling errors committed or commas omitted.

It is important to know which examination is required by the academic institution to which you are applying for credit. You must find out whether to take the all multiple-choice or the essay edition of the English Composition Exam. If you plan to take the edition with the essay, it is essential that you check the dates on which it is offered since this version is not available at every administration.

A Study Plan

Start your preparation for the General Examination in English Composition by taking the mini-exam that follows. The 27 sample questions represent every question type included on both the multiple-choice and the essay version of the English Composition exam. Explanations of each answer will be found at the end of the examination along with suggestions for answering the essay question and two sample essay responses.

Following the mini-exam are three complete Practice Examinations. Two of these exams follow the pattern of the multiple-choice CLEP exam. The third exam is similar to the CLEP exam with essay.

Take the first Practice Examination, following the directions given and adhering to the time limits set. When you have completed the exam, compare your answers to the explanations provided. Your responses should indicate your strengths and weaknesses in English Composition.

In the bibliography that follows, you will find a listing of college-level English texts to which you may refer for additional study. Look over the suggested texts at a library or bookstore and choose the one you like best for your study guide. Concentrate your study on those areas of English Composition in which your scores indicated weakness.

Now turn to the second and third Practice Exams. Take each one as if it were the actual CLEP exam. Check your answers with the answer key at the end of each exam and score yourself honestly. The explanations provided for each question should help you to evaluate your own strengths and weaknesses because they indicate not only which answers are correct, but also why they are correct. Consult your reference text for further study where you feel you need it.

Following this plan of attack will enable you to handle the actual examination with greater facility, to score higher, and perhaps most important of all, to become a better college student in the area of English Composition.

Selected Bibliography

There are literally thousands of English texts and manuals available. The following five books have been chosen because students have found them to be effective both in preparing for examinations and as resource texts. The exercises are helpful, the drills provided are useful, and the explanatory material is clear. It is suggested that you browse among the texts and then make your own choice.

If a book has a table of contents or an index, use these to facilitate your studying. For example, if you know that you find it difficult to isolate and avoid clichés, check the indexes of a few of these books to discover which ones contain material on clichés. You might want to master this subject before moving on to another. Try to select a variety of materials, including books that emphasize English mechanics as well as those that stress composition. Both areas are important. It might be wise to select and skim at least one book from each general area.

Although current books are emphasized, this bibliography also includes texts that have been in use for a while and have proved effective. In addition, newspapers and weekly news magazines are excellent sources of current information and should be used as part of a continuing study process.

1. *Chicago Manual of Style.* 14th ed. Chicago: University of Chicago Press, 1993.
2. Kane, Thomas S, *New Oxford Guide to Writing.* New York: Oxford University Press, 1994.
3. Kirszner, Laurie G., *The Holt Handbook.* 5th ed. Orlando, FL: Harcourt College Publishers, 1999.
4. Kramer, Melinda, et al. *Prentice-Hall Handbook for Writers.* 12th ed. Englewood Cliffs, NJ: Prentice Hall, 1994.
5. *Oxford Companion to the English Language.* Ed. Tom McArthur. Oxford, England: Oxford University Press, 1992.

MINI-EXAM IN ENGLISH COMPOSITION

The CLEP exam in English Composition includes five different question types. On the multiple-choice exam all five types will appear. On the essay version of the exam only three multiple-choice question types appear—Identifying Sentence Errors, Improving Sentences, and Revising Work in Progress. In the Mini-Exam that follows, we'll take a look at all five multiple-choice question types. At the end of the exam you'll find explanations for every question as well as techniques for answering the essay question.

Identifying Sentence Errors

This type of question tests your knowledge of English usage and grammar as well as proper word choice and idiom. You will have to determine if the sentence is correct as written or if there is a part of the sentence that requires a correction. Try these three sample questions:

Directions: Some of the sentences below contain an error in grammar, usage, word choice, or idiom. Other sentences are correct. Parts of each sentence are underlined and lettered. The error, if there is one, is contained in one of the underlined parts of the sentence. Assume that all other parts of the sentence are correct and cannot be changed. For each sentence, select the one underlined part that must be changed to make the sentence correct. If there is no error in a sentence, choose choice (E). No sentence has more than one error.

1. The second speaker was the <u>most amusing</u> of
   A
   the two, <u>though</u> he had <u>little</u> <u>of substance</u> to
   B   C   D
   add. <u>No error</u>
   E

2. Anyone <u>dissatisfied with</u> the board's decision
   A
   <u>should make</u> <u>their</u> objections <u>known</u>. <u>No error</u>
   B   C   D   E

3. All that <u>he added</u> as extra equipment on the
   A
   new car <u>was</u> two <u>speakers, a</u> cassette <u>deck, and</u>
   B   C   D
   a retractable antenna. <u>No error</u>
   E

Improving Sentences

In this section you must decide which of five alternatives provides the best phrasing of a sentence. Here again you may choose to leave the sentence exactly as it was written if you think the original wording best conveys the intended meaning. Here are three samples to try:

Directions: The sentences below may contain problems in grammar, usage, word choice, sentence construction, and punctuation. Part or all of each sentence is underlined. Following each sentence you will find five ways of expressing the underlined part. Choice (A) always repeats the original underlined section. The other four choices are all different. You are to select the lettered answer that produces the most effective sentence. If you think the original sentence is best, choose choice (A) as your answer. If one of the other choices makes a better sentence, select the letter of that choice. Do not choose an answer that changes the meaning of the original sentence.

4. <u>There is evidence how</u> THC, the psychoactive chemical in marijuana, is useful in treating glaucoma, an eye disease.
   (A) There is evidence how
   (B) They're is evidence how
   (C) Their is evidence how
   (D) It is evident that
   (E) There is evidence that

5. The road test for a driver's license measures a person's knowledge of traffic rules and <u>their skill in handling</u> an automobile.
   (A) their skill in handling
   (B) skill in handling
   (C) a person's skill in handling
   (D) their skill to handle
   (E) their skilled handling of

6. In the event that she is dissuaded by her parents from leaving home, it will be a shame.

    (A) In the event that she is dissuaded by her parents from leaving home, it will be a shame.

    (B) It will be a shame if her parents dissuade her from leaving home.

    (C) It will be shameful if her parents dissuade her from leaving home.

    (D) In the event that her parents are dissuading her from leaving home, it will be a shame.

    (E) If in the event that she is dissuaded she leaves home, it will be a shame.

Restructuring Sentences

This section appears only in Section II of the multiple-choice exam. It is not included in the essay exam. Here you are asked to rephrase a sentence to change its emphasis or improve its clarity. The rephrased sentence must preserve the meaning of the original sentence and must not violate the rules of standard written English. Try the sample questions that follow:

Directions: Below each of the following sentences are directions for revising the sentence and a choice of five words or phrases that may occur in your revised sentence. Mentally rephrase each sentence according to the directions given. Then choose the lettered word or phrase that is included in your revised sentence. If you think of a sentence that has none of the words listed in the choices, rephrase the sentence again to include one of the words or phrases listed. Take care to make only those changes that the directions require and to choose an answer that is part of a complete and grammatically correct sentence.

7. "Taxes will not be raised," according to the revenue collector, but I'm not sure he's correct in stating this.

    Begin with The revenue collector and eliminate the direct quotation.

    (A) according to

    (B) and

    (C) therefore

    (D) that taxes

    (E) Taxes

8. Sally was unable to fly kites, to blow bubbles with her gum, and to climb trees.

    Substitute could neither for was unable.

    (A) kites, blow

    (B) kites and blow

    (C) kites nor climb

    (D) kites, to blow

    (E) kites blowing

9. Walking in the rain, he noticed an umbrella lying unused in the trash can.

    Change walking in to He walked.

    (A) and then he began to notice

    (B) and so he noticed

    (C) before he noticed

    (D) and noticed

    (E) and then noticing

Revising Work in Progress

In this section, you will be presented with what appears to be the early draft of a student essay. Following the essay are questions that offer various ways to improve the draft. You must demonstrate that you know how to join sentences, achieve variety, develop coherence, employ logic, and organize the essay in an effective and relevant way. Read the sample draft that follows and then answer the questions about it.

Directions: The selection that follows is an early draft of a student essay in which each sentence has been numbered for easy reference. Following the passage are questions that direct you to a part of the essay or to the entire essay. The questions focus upon improving sentence structure and word choice, organization and development of the essay, and effectiveness of language for the intended purpose and audience of the work. For each question, choose the letter of the answer you consider to be correct and mark the corresponding oval on your answer sheet.

(1) We really are very lucky to be living in a country where there are so many newspapers. (2) There are many countries in the world where there are only one or two newspapers and even

these papers are under strict government control. (3) People living in these countries do not have access to newspapers the way we have. (4) They are not so fortunate as we are.

(5) Now there are times when we do not like what is on the editorial page. (6) We can disagree with what the editor or the publisher feels about a certain issue. (7) If we want we do not have to support the paper and we don't have to continue buying them. (8) There are other papers that may be more to our liking or may conform to our philosophy. (9) Whereas those living in countries where the press is under the government's thumb have to be satisfied with reading the one point of view. (10) This is what makes a democracy so very special.

(11) Now there is a problem with school news-papers and freedom of the press as it concerns high school and college students. (12) But that is another matter.

10. In sentence (2), the phrase where there are only one or two
    (A) should remain the way it is written.
    (B) should be changed to *where there is only one or two.*
    (C) should be changed to *only where there are one or two.*
    (D) should read *where there's only one or two.*
    (E) should be changed to *where there's only a couple of.*

11. Sentence (7) can best be linked to sentence (8) by adding which word after sentence (7)?
    (A) And
    (B) Although
    (C) However
    (D) Since
    (E) When

12. Sentence (9)
    (A) is a fragment and should be linked to sentence (8).
    (B) is correct as it stands.
    (C) is too lengthy.
    (D) contains incorrect information.
    (E) is not consistent with the rest of the essay.

13. The first word in sentence (10)
    (A) is correct.
    (B) should be changed to *It.*
    (C) should be changed to *However, this.*
    (D) should be changed to *But this.*
    (E) should be changed to *but it* and joined to sentence (8).

14. The concluding paragraph
    (A) provides a suitable frame for the essay.
    (B) presents material not germane to the essay.
    (C) should be added to the second paragraph.
    (D) provides excellent emphasis.
    (E) is different in tone and diction from the rest of the essay.

Analyzing Writing

This section appears only in the all multiple-choice examination. A prose passage is given, which is assumed to be part of a larger work. The questions that follow each passage ask you to examine the strategies used by the author. You will be asked about the author's style, the purpose of the writing, and the relationship of each sentence to the work as a whole. Read this sample passage and answer the questions about it.

Directions: This section presents two prose passages. Following each passage are questions that test how well you recognize the purpose of the writer and the characteristics of good writing. As you read each passage, bear in mind that it may be part of a longer piece of writing and it might not, as a result, present a complete analysis or discussion of the issues under consideration. Read each passage carefully, then answer each question by selecting the letter of the answer choice you consider to be correct.

(1) When television is good, nothing—not the theater, not the magazines or newspapers—nothing is inferior. (2) But when television is bad, nothing is worse. (3) I invite you to sit down in front of your television set when your station

goes on the air and stay there without a book, magazine, newspaper, or anything else to distract you. (4) Keep your eyes glued to that set until the station signs off. (5) There are many people in this great country, and radio stations must serve all of us. (6) I can assure you that you will observe a vast wasteland. (7) They are game shows, violence, audience participation shows and formula comedies about totally unbelievable families. (8) Followed by blood and thunder, mayhem, more violence, sadism, murder, Western badmen, Western goodmen, private eyes, gangsters, still more violence, cartoons. (9) And, endlessly, there are commercials that scream and cajole and offend without end. (10) True, you will see a few things you will enjoy. (11) And most of all, there is boredom. (12) But they will be very, very few. (13) And if you think I exaggerate and overstate the matter, try it.

15. The word inferior in sentence (1) should be
    (A) left as it is.
    (B) changed to *worse.*
    (C) changed to *the best.*
    (D) changed to *anterior.*
    (E) changed to *better.*

16. What should be done with sentence (5)?
    (A) It should be left as it is.
    (B) It should follow sentence (1).
    (C) It should be omitted entirely.
    (D) It should be made into two separate sentences.
    (E) It should follow sentence (8).

17. The word wasteland in sentence (6) should be
    (A) left as it is.
    (B) changed to *baseball park.*
    (C) changed to *ocean.*
    (D) changed to *alley.*
    (E) changed to *football field.*

18. The meaning of sentence (7) would be clearest if
    (A) left as it is.
    (B) the phrase *They are* were changed to *You will see.*
    (C) the phrase *They are* were changed to *They will see.*
    (D) the word *totally* were omitted.
    (E) everything after *comedies* were omitted.

19. What should be done with sentence (8)?
    (A) It should be left as is.
    (B) It should be joined to sentence (7).
    (C) It should be divided into 2 sentences.
    (D) It should begin with *Thus.*
    (E) It should end with *therefore.*

20. Sentence (9) would be most improved if
    (A) *and offend* were omitted.
    (B) *without end* were omitted.
    (C) *and advertisements* were added after commercials.
    (D) *ceaselessly* were substituted for *endlessly.*
    (E) *cajole* were changed to *cavort.*

21. Sentence (11) is best placed after
    (A) sentence (6).
    (B) sentence (13).
    (C) sentence (9).
    (D) sentence (5).
    (E) sentence (12).

22. Sentence (13) would be best if the phrase *exaggerate and overstate the matter* were
    (A) left as it is.
    (B) changed to *exaggerate and understate the matter.*
    (C) changed to *magnify and overstate.*
    (D) changed to *multiply the matter.*
    (E) changed to *exaggerate.*

Monseigneur, one of the great lords in power at the court, held his fortnightly reception in his grand hotel in Paris. Monseigneur was in his inner room, his sanctuary of sanctuaries, the Holiest of Holiests to the crowd of worshippers in the suite of rooms without. Monseigneur took his royal chocolate at this time. Monseigneur could swallow a great many things with ease, and was by some few sullen minds supposed to be rather rapidly swallowing France.

23. The locale of this passage is
    (A) the opera.
    (B) a sweet shop.
    (C) the field of battle.
    (D) an apartment.
    (E) a church.

24. The tone of the selection is
    (A) sarcastic.
    (B) inquiring.
    (C) objective.
    (D) informative.
    (E) serious.

25. Monseigneur represents a(n)
    (A) person who elicits sympathy.
    (B) simpleton who cannot provide for himself.
    (C) profligate who cares little about others.
    (D) intellectual who dabbles in business matters.
    (E) miser who has moments of extravagance.

26. The style of the passage suggests that it is part of a(n)
    (A) theoretical document.
    (B) textbook on sociology.
    (C) essay against political prisoners.
    (D) magazine article on good etiquette.
    (E) story about greed and the abuse of power.

27. The paragraph is set in which of the following types of political structures?
    (A) Democracy
    (B) Monarchy
    (C) Communist state
    (D) Matriarchy
    (E) Republic

Answer Key

1.	A	6.	B	11.	D	16.	C	21.	C	26. E
2.	C	7.	D	12.	A	17.	A	22.	E	27. B
3.	B	8.	A	13.	A	18.	B	23.	D	
4.	E	9.	D	14.	B	19.	B	24.	A	
5.	B	10.	A	15.	E	20.	B	25.	C	

Explanatory Answers

1. **The correct answer is (A).** When comparing only two people or things, use the comparative forms *more* or *-er: more amusing* or *funnier.*

2. **The correct answer is (C).** A singular pronoun (*his* or *her*) is required to agree with the antecedent *Anyone.*

3. **The correct answer is (B).** The plural verb *were* is required to agree with the compound subject that follows.

4. **The correct answer is (E).** Choice (A) is incorrect because the sentence says nothing about *how* THC is useful; it simply says "*that* THC. . . is useful.*" Choices (B) and (C) confuse the homonyms *there* (introductory expletive), *they're* (contraction for *they are*) and *their* (possessive form). Choice (D) changes the meaning, omitting the crucial information that evidence exists.

5. **The correct answer is (B).** The plural form of *their* cannot refer back to a singular noun such as *person.* But no possessive adjective is needed before *skill in handling: a person's* can modify both *knowledge of traffic rules* and *skill in handling.*

6. **The correct answer is (B).** The original sentence uses the passive voice (*she is dissuaded*) where the active voice would be shorter, simpler, and more effective (*her parents dissuade her*). It uses the wordy phrase *in the event that* where *if* will suffice. The construction makes us regard it as a pronoun that refers to something (*home? leaving?*) instead of using it as an intro-

ductory expletive. Choice (B) says well in 13 words what choice (A) says poorly in 18. Choice (C) departs needlessly from *it will be a shame.* Choice (D) uses the active but retains other faults of choice (A). Choice (E) confuses the meaning.

7. **The correct answer is (D).** The revenue collector said *that taxes* will not be raised, but I'm not sure he's correct in stating this.

8. **The correct answer is (A).** Sally could not fly *kites, blow* bubbles with her gum, or climb trees.

9. **The correct answer is (D).** He walked in the rain *and noticed* an umbrella lying unused in the trash can.

10. **The correct answer is (A).** Choices (B), (D), and (E) violate subject-verb agreement since the subject *newspapers* is plural and requires the plural verb *are.* In choice (C) the adverb *only* is misplaced.

11. **The correct answer is (D).** The subordinating conjunction *since* works best as sentence (8) is dependent upon sentence (7).

12. **The correct answer is (A).** This is not a complete sentence and must be joined to a main idea. It is a subordinate clause and could well be linked to the previous sentence.

13. **The correct answer is (A).** The sentence is good the way it stands, and the initial word *This,* referring to the previous idea, is satisfactory.

14. **The correct answer is (B).** Although the tone and diction of the last paragraph is not inconsistent with the rest of the essay, the content has nothing to do with Paragraphs 1 and 2. The fact that the writer tells us that this is *another matter* does not help. Therefore, choice (B) is accurate.

15. **The correct answer is (E).** *Inferior*, which is an adjective meaning poor in quality or below average, should be changed to *better*, a comparative adjective meaning more excellent.

16. **The correct answer is (C).** The subject of sentence (5) is radio stations and since the subject of the passage is *television*, the sentence should be omitted.

17. **The correct answer is (A).** *Wasteland*, a noun defined as barren land or unproductive activity, accurately completes the meaning of sentence (6).

18. **The correct answer is (B).** *You will see* is consistent with the imperative tone of the passage.

19. **The correct answer is (B).** Sentence (8) is not a complete sentence and, since it completes the train of thought of sentence (7), should be joined to sentence (7).

20. **The correct answer is (B).** *Without end*, which carries the same meaning as *endlessly*, should be omitted to make sentence (9) less wordy.

21. **The correct answer is (C).** Sentence (11) completes the train of thought running throughout sentences (7), (8), and (9), and thus should follow sentence (9).

22. **The correct answer is (E).** The phrase, *exaggerate and overstate the matter*, is verbose and should be simply *exaggerate*.

23. **The correct answer is (D).** The first line states that Monseigneur is in his "grand hotel" in Paris.

24. **The correct answer is (A).** "Sarcasm" is a taunting or caustic tone that is generally ironic.

25. **The correct answer is (C).** The allusion in the last line of the paragraph to the fact Monseigneur may be "rather rapidly swallowing France," ultimately reveals his "profligate" or dissolute character.

26. **The correct answer is (E).** The wealthy, greedy lifestyle of Monseigneur illustrates his misuse of his powerful station.

27. **The correct answer is (B).** Monseigneur is a lord in the court of a monarch.

THE ESSAY QUESTION

If you are planning to take the essay version of the CLEP General Examination in English Composition, the second section of your examination will allow you 45 minutes to write an expository essay on a given topic. Your writing will be evaluated by two college English instructors; the sum of their ratings will be combined with your multiple-choice score.

We have included in this section of the book some important material on how to organize and write an essay. These techniques will help you to become a better writer and to develop a successful essay on the examination.

In scoring your essay, readers will look for a work that is competently organized and logically developed. They will expect you to present a point of view and to support your position with appropriate examples drawn from reading or personal experience. In addition, your work must demonstrate command of the conventions of standard written English and a sufficiently extensive vocabulary to convey your ideas precisely and effectively. Your sentences should indicate a command of punctuation, syntax, grammatical inflection, and agreement. You should take care to avoid monotony, oversimplification, awkward expressions, and incoherence.

How to Write a Good Essay

There are many approaches to any composition, and each individual possesses his own style. The writer should always bear in mind that he is writing for an audience, in this case a group of instructors with knowledge and experience different from his. Although the writer is not trying to impress his reader, he does want to make certain that the message of his essay is understood and that its style elicits a positive reaction. There is no single way to achieve this result, but if the writer keeps the following three rules in mind, he will be on the way to becoming a successful writer.

1. *Practice.* The more you write, the more at ease you will be with the writing experience. It is far more valuable to write many short essays than a few longer ones.

2. *Read* as much as you can, observing the techniques and style of professional writers. Editorials in newspapers and magazines are particularly good to examine. Notice how the professional writer organizes his ideas, how he concludes the essay, and what level of vocabulary and originality of expression he employs. When you discover a piece of writing that impresses you, try to analyze it to discover why it is so effective.

3. *Remember* that for the purpose of this examination you should avoid informal or colloquial expressions. Try to be formal without writing in a stilted, artificial fashion.

Five Positive Aims

1. Originality of approach
2. Clarity of organization
3. Freshness of expression
4. Logical development
5. Variety of sentence patterns

Five Errors to Avoid

1. Technical problems such as mistakes in sentence structure; frequent misspellings; errors in agreement, punctuation, and capitalization; and misuse of words
2. Poor paragraphing
3. Unnecessary repetition of material
4. Poor level of English—illiteracies, mixed metaphors, trite expressions, or overuse of colloquialisms
5. Stylistic problems such as oversimplification, incoherent writing, wordiness, and restating the obvious

Prewriting

Before you begin to write your essay, you should read the question several times so that you are familiar with the material. You might wish to underline key words or phrases. Do not spend too much time—only a few minutes—on this planning. What you hope to accomplish during this prewriting state is to

1. gain familiarity with the essay question.

2. develop a point of view, deciding perhaps whether you are in agreement or disagreement with the statement given.

3. develop a thesis statement to express the essential idea of your essay.

Organizing the Essay

Decide how many paragraphs you are going to write. There is no set rule concerning length. We are often told that "length is not a valid substitute for strength." Therefore, do not write furiously to fill up several pages so that it will appear that you have many ideas. This approach can actually result in needless repetition, rambling, lack of organization, and muddled thinking. By the same token, you don't want your essay to appear skimpy. Obviously, if you write only five or six sentences, the examiner may not be able to get an adequate picture of your writing ability and may penalize you as a result. Many college instructors indicate that a development of at least three paragraphs is desirable, considering that the student is allotted 45 minutes to think through, write, and proofread his essay. This is not to say that some students may not wish to attempt more in the designated time. Here is where practice before the examination can be of great help. Remember to time yourself during the practice sessions.

The Introductory Paragraph

Start right in. You have analyzed the question in your prewriting. Now, in your introduction you want to set down in clear sentences the topic you are going to write about, indicating to the reader perhaps why the topic has value or is cause for concern, giving if you can some background to the situation and pointing the reader in the general direction that your essay is going to move.

Since you have only 5 or 10 minutes for this introduction, it is often sufficient to accomplish one or two of these tasks in three to six sentences.

Five Items to Bear in Mind

1. In writing your introduction, keep in mind the key words of the question.

2. Avoid being cute or funny, ironic or satiric, or overly emotional or dramatic. Set the tone or attitude in your first sentence. You may well

wish to appear sincere, clear, and straightforward.

3. Don't bother repeating the question word for word. Paraphrasing is far better than just copying.

4. Let the reader know in your first paragraph what your essay is going to deal with and what your controlling idea is. This can be accomplished in a clear topic sentence.

5. Each sentence should advance your topic and should provide interest to your reader.

The Development

The heart of the essay is the development, or the middle paragraph of paragraphs. Here you must attempt to support the main idea of your essay through illustrations, details, and examples. The developmental paragraphs must serve as a link in the chain of ideas and contribute directly to the essay's central thought. All the sentences of the development must explain the essential truth of the thesis or topic sentence without digression. You may do this through a style that is descriptive, narrative, or expository, using a factual approach or an anecdotal one. Whatever approach and style you choose, your writing should be coherent, logical, unified, and well-ordered.

Avoid the following pitfalls:

1. Sentences that are irrelevant and contain extraneous material

2. Sentences that follow no sequence of thought but seem to jump from one idea to another

3. Sentences that do not relate to the topic sentence or do not flow from the preceding sentence

The good writer makes use of transitional words or phrases to connect thoughts and to provide for a logical sequence of ideas. Examine the following list of transitional words and phrases. They can help make your method of development clear to your reader.

therefore	*first of all*	*then*
moreover	*secondly*	*indeed*
however	*for example*	*in any case*
consequently	*for instance*	*nevertheless*
of course	*finally*	

Many other good linking expressions can be added to the above list, but if you choose judiciously from these fourteen, you will find that your development will be more coherent and well-ordered.

The Conclusion

The successful writer, like the wise guest, knows that he must not prolong his stay; when he comes to the end of his essay, he must draw his comments together in a strong, clear concluding paragraph.

A good concluding paragraph should give the reader the feeling that the essay has made its point, that the thesis has been explained, and that a point of view has been established. This can be accomplished in about four to six sentences in one of the following ways:

1. Through a *restatement* of the main idea
2. Through a *summary* of the material covered in the essay
3. Through a clear *statement of the writer's opinion* of the issue(s) involved

Just as there are good techniques, there are also some very ineffective methods that students are tempted to use in drawing a composition to a close. Avoid falling into the following traps:

1. Apologizing for your inability to discuss all the issues in the allotted time
2. Complaining that the topics did not interest you or that you don't think it was fair to be asked to write on so broad a topic
3. Introducing material that you will not develop, rambling on about nonpertinent matters, or using trite material

Keep in mind that a good conclusion is integrally related to the thesis of the essay. Whether it reviews, restates, or leads the reader to think on his own, the conclusion must be strong, clear, and effective.

Illustrative Examples
Essay A

Directions: You will have 45 minutes to plan and write an essay on the topic specified below. Do not write on a topic other than the one specified. Consider the topic and organize your thoughts before you begin to write.

Take care to express your thoughts clearly and exactly and to make them of interest. Be specific and use examples to support your position whenever appropriate. Remember that how well you write is much more important than how much you write.

Assignment:

Although there are those who feel that there should be strict gun control laws, these laws would certainly curtail the freedom of the majority and prove ineffective. Violence comes about because our society has many violent members, not because we have allowed people to possess weapons. Actually, allowing our citizens to possess guns would offer a means of protection and preserve law and order.

The passage states that gun control laws are valueless and can even prove harmful. Do you agree or disagree? In a well-organized essay of approximately 300 to 400 words, explain and illustrate your answer.

Sample Essay:

Those people who oppose gun control laws state, "Guns don't kill; people kill." They point out that many crimes of passion are committed with "weapons" other than guns, such as knives, tools, and bats; even a person's hands can be used to hurt, maim, and destroy a human life. Why then should we make it so difficult for law-abiding citizens to obtain guns that could be used for self-defense?

Certainly this issue is a complicated one. However, we must remember that if we make it easy for people to purchase guns and remove all controls, then soon teenagers and even younger children will be playing cops and robbers with loaded weapons. Nervous storekeepers will keep guns in drawers, ready for use at the slightest provocation. Angry citizens will attend meetings armed and the excuse will be, "just in case. . . ." Unfortunately, we live in a volatile society. People no longer turn the other cheek. This has been demonstrated in the frequent marches, sit-ins, and demonstrations. We are not arguing over the value of the marches and demonstrations; what should concern us is what might occur if even a handful of "trigger-happy" marchers came with pistols in their pockets. Or, even worse, what could take place if a group of counterdemonstrators appeared armed to the teeth as well?

We can appreciate the fact that people do harm and not objects; but we must bear in mind as well that people with guns are potential killers and to remove all "stops" and place guns in the hands of the great majority of people may be causing a potential danger. Therefore, I strongly feel that only those who are trained and licensed should be permitted to own guns.

Comment:

The writer states a position clearly and organizes his essay in a clear three-paragraph form. He recognizes that the issue is a complex one (sentence 1, paragraph 2) but supports his position through specific and concrete details in his second paragraph, which is used as the development of the essay. Although the essay is a bit short, it still accomplishes what the writer has set out to do, to present a case for gun control. This is always clear. The writing is neither too formal nor too colloquial, a happy balance being achieved.

Essay B

Directions: You will have 45 minutes to plan and write an essay on the topic specified below. Do not write on a topic other than the one specified. Consider the topic and organize your thoughts before you begin to write.

Take care to express your thoughts clearly and exactly and to make them of interest. Be specific and use examples to support your position whenever appropriate. Remember that how well you write is much more important than how much you write.

Assignment:

There are those who contend that children learn more about life from the television programs they watch than from their parents. The television hero becomes the role model and children often imitate the violence and hostility depicted on the television screen.

Do you agree or disagree? Explain and illustrate your answer from your own experience or from your observation of others.

Sample Essay:

The most important influence in a child's life should be the influence exerted by his parents. After all, his mother and father are his prime source of love and affection, the people who first fulfill the infant's needs and provide him with the means to exist in the world at a time when he is too young and weak to fend for himself. It, therefore, should follow that the parents should be the most effective role models for their children, and that from them children should learn either how to live harmoniously or to vent with anger and hostility when they are frustrated.

But this is not always the case. In recent years, another more powerful influence has intruded upon the family scene. The television has become the center of the family home and many precious hours are spent watching programs. If this was not serious enough, a greater problem has resulted. In many homes, the children are supplied with their personal television set and permitted—in fact, encouraged—to watch programs indiscriminately. The television has become the babysitter and the pacifier. Many parents tell their children, "Don't you have anything to do? Go watch T.V." And that is exactly what they do. They watch and are fascinated by programs depicting crimes, murders, and acts of violence. The television hero, and not the parent, becomes the role model. Even cartoons show the hero indulging in violent behavior and solving problems by the use of force. Is it any wonder, therefore, that young people learn at an early age that one effective means of dealing with anger and frustration is by kicking the dog or lashing out at others?

Parents have a responsibility. They must supervise the idle moments of their children and control television viewing. They must also actively teach their children to handle their frustration not by imitating television heroes who respond with violence but rather utilizing means that are socially acceptable.

Comment:

The writer presents a point of view in the first paragraph that he attacks in the second. In the third paragraph, the writer concludes with a strong point of view. Sentences are of varying length and ideas are subordinate in different ways. Transitional words and phrases (yet, after all, therefore) are used effectively. In the final sentence of paragraph 2, an interrogative sentence provides a good conclusion.

Paragraph 3 begins with a short but strong sentence and is followed by two sentences, both of which begin with "They must." This is an effective and judicious use of repetition to achieve emphasis.

Answer Sheet for Practice Examination I

Section I

1 Ⓐ Ⓑ Ⓒ Ⓓ Ⓔ 12 Ⓐ Ⓑ Ⓒ Ⓓ Ⓔ 23 Ⓐ Ⓑ Ⓒ Ⓓ Ⓔ 34 Ⓐ Ⓑ Ⓒ Ⓓ Ⓔ 45 Ⓐ Ⓑ Ⓒ Ⓓ Ⓔ

2 Ⓐ Ⓑ Ⓒ Ⓓ Ⓔ 13 Ⓐ Ⓑ Ⓒ Ⓓ Ⓔ 24 Ⓐ Ⓑ Ⓒ Ⓓ Ⓔ 35 Ⓐ Ⓑ Ⓒ Ⓓ Ⓔ 46 Ⓐ Ⓑ Ⓒ Ⓓ Ⓔ

3 Ⓐ Ⓑ Ⓒ Ⓓ Ⓔ 14 Ⓐ Ⓑ Ⓒ Ⓓ Ⓔ 25 Ⓐ Ⓑ Ⓒ Ⓓ Ⓔ 36 Ⓐ Ⓑ Ⓒ Ⓓ Ⓔ 47 Ⓐ Ⓑ Ⓒ Ⓓ Ⓔ

4 Ⓐ Ⓑ Ⓒ Ⓓ Ⓔ 15 Ⓐ Ⓑ Ⓒ Ⓓ Ⓔ 26 Ⓐ Ⓑ Ⓒ Ⓓ Ⓔ 37 Ⓐ Ⓑ Ⓒ Ⓓ Ⓔ 48 Ⓐ Ⓑ Ⓒ Ⓓ Ⓔ

5 Ⓐ Ⓑ Ⓒ Ⓓ Ⓔ 16 Ⓐ Ⓑ Ⓒ Ⓓ Ⓔ 27 Ⓐ Ⓑ Ⓒ Ⓓ Ⓔ 38 Ⓐ Ⓑ Ⓒ Ⓓ Ⓔ 49 Ⓐ Ⓑ Ⓒ Ⓓ Ⓔ

6 Ⓐ Ⓑ Ⓒ Ⓓ Ⓔ 17 Ⓐ Ⓑ Ⓒ Ⓓ Ⓔ 28 Ⓐ Ⓑ Ⓒ Ⓓ Ⓔ 39 Ⓐ Ⓑ Ⓒ Ⓓ Ⓔ 50 Ⓐ Ⓑ Ⓒ Ⓓ Ⓔ

7 Ⓐ Ⓑ Ⓒ Ⓓ Ⓔ 18 Ⓐ Ⓑ Ⓒ Ⓓ Ⓔ 29 Ⓐ Ⓑ Ⓒ Ⓓ Ⓔ 40 Ⓐ Ⓑ Ⓒ Ⓓ Ⓔ 51 Ⓐ Ⓑ Ⓒ Ⓓ Ⓔ

8 Ⓐ Ⓑ Ⓒ Ⓓ Ⓔ 19 Ⓐ Ⓑ Ⓒ Ⓓ Ⓔ 30 Ⓐ Ⓑ Ⓒ Ⓓ Ⓔ 41 Ⓐ Ⓑ Ⓒ Ⓓ Ⓔ 52 Ⓐ Ⓑ Ⓒ Ⓓ Ⓔ

9 Ⓐ Ⓑ Ⓒ Ⓓ Ⓔ 20 Ⓐ Ⓑ Ⓒ Ⓓ Ⓔ 31 Ⓐ Ⓑ Ⓒ Ⓓ Ⓔ 42 Ⓐ Ⓑ Ⓒ Ⓓ Ⓔ 53 Ⓐ Ⓑ Ⓒ Ⓓ Ⓔ

10 Ⓐ Ⓑ Ⓒ Ⓓ Ⓔ 21 Ⓐ Ⓑ Ⓒ Ⓓ Ⓔ 32 Ⓐ Ⓑ Ⓒ Ⓓ Ⓔ 43 Ⓐ Ⓑ Ⓒ Ⓓ Ⓔ 54 Ⓐ Ⓑ Ⓒ Ⓓ Ⓔ

11 Ⓐ Ⓑ Ⓒ Ⓓ Ⓔ 22 Ⓐ Ⓑ Ⓒ Ⓓ Ⓔ 33 Ⓐ Ⓑ Ⓒ Ⓓ Ⓔ 44 Ⓐ Ⓑ Ⓒ Ⓓ Ⓔ 55 Ⓐ Ⓑ Ⓒ Ⓓ Ⓔ

Section II

56 Ⓐ Ⓑ Ⓒ Ⓓ Ⓔ 66 Ⓐ Ⓑ Ⓒ Ⓓ Ⓔ 76 Ⓐ Ⓑ Ⓒ Ⓓ Ⓔ 86 Ⓐ Ⓑ Ⓒ Ⓓ Ⓔ 96 Ⓐ Ⓑ Ⓒ Ⓓ Ⓔ

57 Ⓐ Ⓑ Ⓒ Ⓓ Ⓔ 67 Ⓐ Ⓑ Ⓒ Ⓓ Ⓔ 77 Ⓐ Ⓑ Ⓒ Ⓓ Ⓔ 87 Ⓐ Ⓑ Ⓒ Ⓓ Ⓔ 97 Ⓐ Ⓑ Ⓒ Ⓓ Ⓔ

58 Ⓐ Ⓑ Ⓒ Ⓓ Ⓔ 68 Ⓐ Ⓑ Ⓒ Ⓓ Ⓔ 78 Ⓐ Ⓑ Ⓒ Ⓓ Ⓔ 88 Ⓐ Ⓑ Ⓒ Ⓓ Ⓔ 98 Ⓐ Ⓑ Ⓒ Ⓓ Ⓔ

59 Ⓐ Ⓑ Ⓒ Ⓓ Ⓔ 69 Ⓐ Ⓑ Ⓒ Ⓓ Ⓔ 79 Ⓐ Ⓑ Ⓒ Ⓓ Ⓔ 89 Ⓐ Ⓑ Ⓒ Ⓓ Ⓔ 99 Ⓐ Ⓑ Ⓒ Ⓓ Ⓔ

60 Ⓐ Ⓑ Ⓒ Ⓓ Ⓔ 70 Ⓐ Ⓑ Ⓒ Ⓓ Ⓔ 80 Ⓐ Ⓑ Ⓒ Ⓓ Ⓔ 90 Ⓐ Ⓑ Ⓒ Ⓓ Ⓔ 100 Ⓐ Ⓑ Ⓒ Ⓓ Ⓔ

61 Ⓐ Ⓑ Ⓒ Ⓓ Ⓔ 71 Ⓐ Ⓑ Ⓒ Ⓓ Ⓔ 81 Ⓐ Ⓑ Ⓒ Ⓓ Ⓔ 91 Ⓐ Ⓑ Ⓒ Ⓓ Ⓔ 101 Ⓐ Ⓑ Ⓒ Ⓓ Ⓔ

62 Ⓐ Ⓑ Ⓒ Ⓓ Ⓔ 72 Ⓐ Ⓑ Ⓒ Ⓓ Ⓔ 82 Ⓐ Ⓑ Ⓒ Ⓓ Ⓔ 92 Ⓐ Ⓑ Ⓒ Ⓓ Ⓔ 102 Ⓐ Ⓑ Ⓒ Ⓓ Ⓔ

63 Ⓐ Ⓑ Ⓒ Ⓓ Ⓔ 73 Ⓐ Ⓑ Ⓒ Ⓓ Ⓔ 83 Ⓐ Ⓑ Ⓒ Ⓓ Ⓔ 93 Ⓐ Ⓑ Ⓒ Ⓓ Ⓔ 103 Ⓐ Ⓑ Ⓒ Ⓓ Ⓔ

64 Ⓐ Ⓑ Ⓒ Ⓓ Ⓔ 74 Ⓐ Ⓑ Ⓒ Ⓓ Ⓔ 84 Ⓐ Ⓑ Ⓒ Ⓓ Ⓔ 94 Ⓐ Ⓑ Ⓒ Ⓓ Ⓔ 104 Ⓐ Ⓑ Ⓒ Ⓓ Ⓔ

65 Ⓐ Ⓑ Ⓒ Ⓓ Ⓔ 75 Ⓐ Ⓑ Ⓒ Ⓓ Ⓔ 85 Ⓐ Ⓑ Ⓒ Ⓓ Ⓔ 95 Ⓐ Ⓑ Ⓒ Ⓓ Ⓔ 105 Ⓐ Ⓑ Ⓒ Ⓓ Ⓔ

PRACTICE EXAMINATION I

Section I

55 Questions
Time—45 minutes

Directions: Some of the sentences below contain an error in grammar, usage, word choice, or idiom. Other sentences are correct. Parts of each sentence are underlined and lettered. The error, if there is one, is contained in one of the underlined parts of the sentence. Assume that all other parts of the sentence are correct and cannot be changed. For each sentence, select the one underlined part that must be changed to make the sentence correct and mark its letter on your answer sheet. If there is no error in a sentence, mark answer choice (E). No sentence contains more than one error.

Example:

Being that it's such a lovely day, we are having a
  A   B   C

difficult time concentrating on our assignment.
            D

No error
 E

Sample Answer:

● Ⓑ Ⓒ Ⓓ Ⓔ

1. Some people think Hamlet's "To be or not to be"
               A   B
    soliloquy is one of the most unique speeches
    C   D
    in literature. No error
           E

2. If the game went into extra innings, the
          A   B
    relief pitcher would have won it for the visiting
    C   D
    team. No error
       E

3. It is all together too early to forecast accurately
          A   B
    what the rate of inflation will be by year's end.
  C   D
    No error
   E

4. My girlfriend and myself plan to get married
   A   B   C
    next year, if we are able to finish our education
               D
    by that time. No error
          E

5. Even after Richard Cory killed himself (in the
    famous poem), many of the townspeople who
       A   B
    had envied him probably still wished they
    C   D
    could have lived in his situation. No error
                    E

6. When my mother first learned to knit, she
    made a beautiful sweater for my father; it only
                      A   B
    didn't fit him too well. No error
  C   D   E

7. Hardly no one is able to compete in
       A   B
    professional sports after the age of 40.
       C   D
    No error
  E

8. He was <u>around</u> 3 years <u>of age</u> when his
        A   B

  father <u>became</u> ill and <u>was taken</u> to the hospital.
           C   D

  <u>No error</u>
    E

9. Most students <u>who auditioned</u> for the special
               A

  program were accompanied <u>by their parents</u>,
                        B

  but a few <u>who lived nearby</u> were able to travel
            C

  <u>by theirselves</u>. <u>No error</u>
     D   E

10. <u>During the winter recess</u>, I <u>plan to study</u> for
         A   B

  final examinations in the library <u>since it is</u> very
                         C

  quiet <u>there</u>. <u>No error</u>
     D   E

11. The pension fund officials said <u>they</u> would
                      A

  be willing to <u>loan</u> him $500 if he would
          B

  sign a statement <u>promising to repay</u> the sum
                C

  <u>within a year</u>. <u>No error</u>
     D   E

12. Bill, not to mention his friends, <u>are</u> <u>to be held</u>
                      A   B

  <u>accountable</u> for the damage <u>done</u> to the student
     C   D

  lounge. <u>No error</u>
        E

13. Everyone was asked, <u>in fact ordered</u>, <u>to take</u>
                A   B

  <u>their</u> coat to the locker room <u>prior to</u> the game.
   C   D

  <u>No error</u>
    E

14. She <u>could hardly</u> <u>accept</u> the invitation <u>since</u> it
       A   B   C

  was extended in <u>so halfhearted</u> a manner.
                D

  <u>No error</u>
    E

15. <u>In regards to</u> the problem <u>presented</u>, I feel that
     A   B

  all <u>aspects</u> must be considered <u>carefully</u>.
     C   D

  <u>No error</u>
    E

Improving Sentences

Directions: The sentences below may contain problems in grammar, usage, word choice, sentence construction, and punctuation. Part or all of each sentence is underlined. Following each sentence, you will find five ways of expressing the underlined part. Answer choice (A) always repeats the original underlined section. The other four answer choices are all different. You are to select the letter answer that produces the most effective sentence. If you think the original sentence is best, choose choice (A) as your answer. If one of the other choices makes a better sentence, mark your answer sheet for the letter of that choice. Do not choose an answer that changes the meaning of the original sentence.

Example:

I have always enjoyed <u>singing as well as to dance</u>.

  (A) singing as well as to dance

  (B) singing as well as dancing

  (C) to sing as well as dancing

  (D) singing in addition to dance

  (E) to sing in addition to dancing

Sample Answer:

Ⓐ ● Ⓒ Ⓓ Ⓔ

16. <u>Noticing how close the other car was to him,</u> his hands began to shake and he broke out in a sweat.

(A) Noticing how close the other car was to him,

(B) Noticing how closely the other car was following him,

(C) When he noticed how close the other car was to him,

(D) After noticing how close the other car was to him,

(E) He noticed how close the other car was near to him,

17. The money <u>had been split equally between the four gang members.</u>

(A) had been split equally between the four gang members.

(B) was split equally between the four gang members.

(C) had been split into equal shares between the four gang members.

(D) had been split equally among the four gang members.

(E) had been split equal by the four gang members.

18. Hardcover books usually last longer <u>than paperbacks; of course,</u> paperbacks usually are less expensive to purchase.

(A) than paperbacks; of course,

(B) then paperbacks of course,

(C) then paperbacks. Of course,

(D) than paperbacks, of course,

(E) than paperbacks, of course

19. In the six months since the truce was declared, <u>several minor skirmishes occurring along the border</u>.

(A) several minor skirmishes occurring along the border

(B) several minor skirmishes breaking out along the border

(C) there have been several minor skirmishes along the border

(D) along the border there has been several minor skirmishes

(E) the several skirmishes along the border have been minor

20. I have a fever of 101°, <u>so I have lain</u> in bed all day.

(A) so I have lain

(B) so I laid

(C) but I lay

(D) so I have laid

(E) but I lied

21. The desire for public acclaim and recognition is universal, <u>yet it is rarely achieved.</u>

(A) yet it is rarely achieved.

(B) yet its rarely achieved.

(C) yet it is rarely satisfied.

(D) however it is rarely achieved.

(E) yet it is achieved rarely.

22. The computer <u>has the capability for processing</u> all the relevant data within a half hour.

(A) has the capability for processing

(B) has the capacity for processing

(C) has the capability in processing

(D) can process

(E) processes

23. <u>Neither one of the twins has been</u> inoculated against polio.

    (A) Neither one of the twins has been
    (B) Neither one nor the other of the twins has been
    (C) Neither one or the other twin has been
    (D) Neither one of the twins have been
    (E) Neither one of the twins been

24. <u>Not only reading in poor light but she warned that sitting</u> too close to the television can strain the eyes.

    (A) Not only reading in poor light but she warned that sitting
    (B) Not only reading in poor light she warned, but sitting
    (C) She warned that not only reading in poor light but also sitting
    (D) In addition to reading in poor light, she warned that sitting
    (E) Not only reading in poor light, but she also warned that sitting

25. <u>If I would have realized how much</u> the music disturbed her, I would have turned the volume down.

    (A) If I would have realized how much
    (B) If I realize how much
    (C) Had I realized how much
    (D) When I realized how much
    (E) If I would have realized to what extent

26. I prefer <u>him singing his own material</u> to his performances of other people's songs.

    (A) him singing his own material
    (B) him when he is singing his own material
    (C) him to sing his own material
    (D) him singing his own material himself
    (E) his singing his own material

27. The geometrical design of the quilt was traditional, but <u>using strikingly modern fabrics.</u>

    (A) using strikingly modern fabrics.
    (B) strikingly modern fabrics were used.
    (C) using striking modern fabrics.
    (D) making use of strikingly modern fabrics.
    (E) the fabrics used were strikingly modern.

28. <u>He handwrote his application sloppily and filled with spelling errors.</u>

    (A) He handwrote his application sloppily and filled with spelling errors.
    (B) He sloppily wrote his application by hand and it was filled with spelling errors.
    (C) His application was sloppily handwritten and filled with spelling errors.
    (D) He handwrote his application, it was sloppy and filled with spelling errors.
    (E) His application was handwritten sloppy and filled with spelling errors.

29. Only Congress can declare <u>war officially however</u> the Commander-in-Chief of the armed forces has the power to order a military action without consulting Congress.

    (A) war officially however
    (B) war, officially; however,
    (C) war, officially, however,
    (D) war. Officially, however,
    (E) war officially. However

30. <u>For one to accept constructive criticism without getting resentful is a sign that one is mature.</u>

    (A) For one to accept constructive criticism without getting resentful is a sign that one is mature.
    (B) It is a sign that one is mature when one accepts constructive criticism without getting resentful.
    (C) Accepting constructive criticism without one getting resentful is a sign of maturity.
    (D) A mature sign is to accept constructive criticism without resentment.
    (E) Accepting constructive criticism without resentment is a sign of maturity.

31. Neither the boys nor their teacher are responsible for causing the situation.
    (A) Neither the boys nor their teacher are
    (B) Neither the boys nor their teacher is
    (C) Neither the boys or their teacher are
    (D) Neither the boys or their teacher is
    (E) Neither the boys nor there teacher is

32. Over the loudspeaker, the principle announced that the school was going to change its attendance policy.
    (A) the principle announced that the school was going to change its attendance policy
    (B) the principle announced that the school was going to change their attendance policy
    (C) the principal announced that the school was going to change it's attendance policy
    (D) the principal that the school was going to change its attendance policy
    (E) the principal announced that the school was going to change its attendance policy

33. If we had left the house earlier, we might of been on time for the plane.
    (A) might of been on time
    (B) could of been on time
    (C) should of been on time
    (D) might have been on time
    (E) might of made it in time

34. They arrived on time and were able to witness the entire graduation ceremony.
    (A) arrived on time and were able
    (B) have arrived on time and were able
    (C) were arriving on time in order
    (D) arrived in time
    (E) arrived on time being able

35. He was more aggravated than us by the boy's behavior.
    (A) more aggravated than us
    (B) more aggravated than we
    (C) more annoyed then us
    (D) more annoyed than we
    (E) more annoyed than us

Revising Work in Progress

Directions: The selections that follow are early drafts of student essays in which each sentence has been numbered for easy reference. Following each essay are questions that direct you to a part of the essay or to the entire essay. The questions focus upon improving sentence structure and word choice, organization and development of the essay, and effectiveness of language for the intended purpose and audience of the work. For each question, choose the letter of the answer you consider to be correct, and mark the corresponding oval on your answer sheet.

Questions 36–40 are based on the following essay.

(1) Breaking a habit is no easy matter. (2) Especially old habits are very difficult to break. (3) I know because I became addicted to smoking several years ago, when I was much younger. (4) When I first started to smoke, I thought that it was the thing to do. (5) All of my friends encouraged me to smoke. (6) They told me that I would look more grown up, more mature. (7) They never mentioned all the negative aspects.

(8) Now that I am older, I hope that I have become wiser as well. (9) I have decided to quit the habit and give up smoking. (10) I know that it will take a lot of willpower to stop. (11) I think that in the long run it will be worth it. (12) I have decided to start to break this habit at once and once and for all. (13) My decision is made. (14) If I am offered a cigarette, I shall say, "No!" (15) I am also aware secondhand smoke can be dangerous.

36. Which of the following ways best revises and combines sentences (1) and (2) shown below?
    Breaking a habit is no easy matter. Especially old habits are very difficult to break.
    (A) Breaking a habit is no easy matter; it is difficult to break.
    (B) Breaking habits are difficult when they are present.
    (C) Breaking habits, especially old ones, is no easy matter.
    (D) Breaking old habits are not an easy matter.
    (E) Breaking an old habit is more difficult when it has been well established.

37. Sentence (3) serves basically to

    (A) personalize the essay.

    (B) provide a straw man.

    (C) present an opposing point of view.

    (D) offer a light touch to a serious topic.

    (E) furnish an opposing point of view.

38. Which of the following is the best way to revise the underlined portion of sentences (5) and (6) (shown below) so that the two sentences are combined into one?

    All of my friends encouraged me to smoke. They told me that I would look more grown up and mature.

    (A) to smoke when they told me

    (B) to smoke since they told me

    (C) to smoke having told me

    (D) to smoke, telling me

    (E) to smoke; however, they told me

39. Which of the following is the best change to sentence (13) (shown below)?

    My decision is made.

    (A) Omit the sentence.

    (B) Allow the sentence to stand as is.

    (C) Move the sentence to the end of the essay.

    (D) Place the sentence after sentence 1.

    (E) Change the sentence to *I have made my decision.*

40. The last sentence

    (A) provides an effective conclusion.

    (B) should be the opening sentence.

    (C) is not necessary.

    (D) is a strong personal statement germane to the topic.

    (E) provides statistical evidence.

Questions 41–45 are based on the following essay.

(1) At one time, New Yorkers pointed with pride to the fact that the United Nations had as its headquarters their home city and this gave them a sense of being a special place. (2) One reason for this sense of pride was that our city was the mecca for people of all backgrounds, from all countries and from all diverse cultures to come together to work in our backyard. (3) Another is because we felt that the United Nations had a lofty purpose: to foster peace and to be above the petty political squabbles of people and nations.

(4) But now this is not the case. (5) I, for one, have become terribly disillusioned. (6) For example, I see foreign diplomats literally getting away with murder. (7) They park cars illegally and commit petty crimes. (8) They violate laws that the rest of us must obey. (9) They claim that they have diplomatic immunity. (10) In addition, the diplomats use the United Nations as a forum to vent their anger and to ridicule their host country, taking their money and their hospitality and showing only disrespect to us. (11) And when we try to solve the problems of other nations, they accuse us of trying to be the policemen of the world.

(12) Perhaps it is about time for us to step back and take a long hard look at the United Nations. (13) As long as you are paying the bill, perhaps you should call the tune as well. (14) Unless the diplomats of the United Nations begin to show respect for the city which houses them, they might consider that one day, they will no longer be welcome guests in our house. (15) Perhaps that will be an unpleasant day for us. (16) But it will be a sad and costly one for those diplomats who felt that they were being given a free ride.

41. Which of the following is the best revision of the underlined portion of sentence (1) below.

    At one time, New Yorkers pointed with pride to the fact that the United Nations had as its headquarters their home <u>city and this gave them a sense of being a special place.</u>

    (A) city, this gave them a sense of being a special place.

    (B) city, giving it a sense of being a special place.

    (C) city, and giving them a sense of being a special place.

    (D) city; giving it a sense of being special.

    (E) city and this gives them a feeling of being a special place.

42. Which of the following is the best way to combine sentences (8) and (9)?

    (A) They violate laws and they claim that they have diplomatic immunity, laws that we have to obey.

    (B) They violate laws that the rest of us must obey having diplomatic immunity.

    (C) They violate laws that the rest of us must obey, they claim that they have diplomatic immunity.

    (D) They violate laws that the rest of us must obey and claiming that they have diplomatic immunity.

    (E) Claiming that they have diplomatic immunity, they violate laws that the rest of us must obey.

43. In relation to the passage as a whole, which of the following best describes the writer's intention in the second paragraph?

    (A) To convince the reader that the position set forth in the introductory paragraph is no longer valid

    (B) To propose a possible solution

    (C) To indicate that the problem may be insoluble

    (D) To provide examples to substantiate the position set forth in the previous paragraph

    (E) To show the dilemma faced by the writer

44. Which of the following is the best revision of the underlined portion of sentence (10) below?

    In addition, the diplomats use the United Nations as a forum to vent their anger and to ridicule their host country, <u>taking their money and their hospitality and showing only disrespect to us.</u>

    (A) taking their money and hospitality, showing disrespect

    (B) by taking their money and hospitality as well as showing disrespect to us

    (C) taking their money and their hospitality and showing us their disrespect

    (D) having taken their money and hospitality and then showing disrespect to us

    (E) taking its money and hospitality and showing us disrespect

45. In the context of the sentences preceding and following sentence (13), which of the following is the best revision of sentence (13)?

    (A) As long as we are paying the bill perhaps we should also call the tune.

    (B) As long as the bill is being paid, perhaps the time should be called.

    (C) If you pay the bill, you should call the tune.

    (D) Since you are paying the bill, you can also call the tune.

    (E) Those who call the tune, should also pay the bill.

Questions 46–50 are based on the following essay.

(1) Sex education should be the province of the parent and not left to the school. (2) I don't believe that it should be left to the professionals. (3) The argument that the highly trained professional is best able to handle such a delicate matter of instruction, teaching young children about matters relating to sex, is not valid. (4) Parents know their children and know best how to teach them about moral and personal issues.

(5) There are people who will say that if we put the responsibility of sex education in the hands of parents, many of them will not take it or will not

do it well. (6) Perhaps we could offer parent workshops led by professionals who could help parents and teach them how to deal with this sensitive matter. (7) Perhaps then parents could be trained so that they would know how to instruct their children. (8) A parent could be given the appropriate knowledge and skills so that they could help their children.

(9) Parents are really role models. (10) Ethics and morals begin in the home. (11) A strong sense of family is needed today. (12) Parents could be helped to become positive role models and they must assume the responsibility of sex instruction in accordance with their religious and personal beliefs.

46. Which of the following is the best way to revise the underlined portion of sentence (2) below?

I don't believe that it should be left to the professionals.

(A) leaving it to the professional works.

(B) that we should leave it to those who are teachers.

(C) that sex education is best placed in the hands of educators.

(D) that it should be left in the province of those who educate our children.

(E) leaving it with those who are professionally trained.

47. Which of the following best describes the writer's purpose in the first paragraph?

(A) To present a solution to a problem

(B) To state the topic and to give the writer's position

(C) To indicate that the writer has no definite opinion since there are two sides to the issue

(D) To provide a good backup argument by way of examples

(E) To indicate that the problem presented has no clear-cut solutions

48. Which of the following is the best revision of the underlined portion of sentence (5) below?

There are people who will say that if we put the responsibility of sex education in the hands of parents, many of them will not take it or will not do it well.

(A) will neither take nor do it well.

(B) will not take it well and not do it.

(C) will not take it or will not perform the job well.

(D) will not be able to take it or do it.

(E) will not do or take the responsibility correctly.

49. Which of the following choices below is the best way to revise the underlined portion of sentence (8) below?

A parent could be given the appropriate knowledge and skills so that they could help their children.

(A) to provide help for the children.

(B) in order that their children could be helped.

(C) to provide assistance for their children.

(D) so that they could have their children be helped.

(E) in order for their children to receive proper instruction.

50. Which of the following is the most effective way to combine sentences (9), (10), and (11)?

(A) Parents are really role models and ethics and morals begin in the home, therefore a strong sense of family is needed today.

(B) A strong sense of family with ethics and morals is needed for parents.

(C) Since a strong sense of family is needed today, ethics and morals begin in the home and parents will see them as role models.

(D) A strong sense of family, with ethics and morals starting in the home, and parents serving as role models.

(E) A strong sense of family is needed today, since ethics and morals start in the home with parents serving as role models.

Questions 51–55 are based on the following essay.

(1) Today more and more people are losing their respect for authority. (2) A reason for this may be because there is corruption in high places. (3) Those whom we have put our trust in and who should have faith in our society have not earned it. (4) As a result, our society is in a turmoil.

(5) In many cities, riots have broken out and there has been looting and vandalism. (6) What has precipitated this you may ask. (7) Sometimes this has resulted from an unpopular decision in the courts. (8) Groups then complain that they are being disenfranchised and that justice is not equal for all. (9) They, then, in their anger and frustration, seek to break the fabric of our society apart. (10) Because they feel that they have nothing to lose, they seek to destroy.

(11) We may agree or disagree with the methods being used by those who feel neglected and shut out. (12) Whatever our opinion, we must agree that there is a real problem. (13) Young people are taking matters into their own hands. (14) They feel that they cannot trust their elders and so they lash out against society.

51. Which of the following is the best revision of the underlined portion of sentence (2) below?

    A reason for this <u>may be because there is</u> corruption in high places.

    (A) may be that there is
    (B) is because there may be
    (C) may be possibly there is
    (D) may possibly be there is
    (E) may be because possibly there is

52. Which of the following is the best way to combine sentences (6) and (7)?

    (A) Has this been precipitated by an unpopular court decision?
    (B) Sometimes an unpopular court decision has precipitated this.
    (C) You may well ask if an unpopular court decision precipitated this.
    (D) Have court decisions precipitated this?
    (E) You may ask if court decisions that precipitated this were unpopular.

53. Which of the following is the best revision of the underlined portion of sentence (9) below?

    They, then, in their anger and frustration, <u>seek to break the fabric of our society apart.</u>

    (A) seek to break the fabric of our society apart.
    (B) seek the breaking of the fabric of our society.
    (C) seek to destroy the fabric of our society apart.
    (D) seek to break apart the fabric of our society.
    (E) seek to rend the fabric of our society.

54. In relation to the passage as a whole, which of the following is the best description of the writer's intention in the third paragraph?

    (A) To change the position of the reader
    (B) To indicate that a problem exists and should be addressed
    (C) To present contradictory viewpoints
    (D) To provide additional examples or illustrations
    (E) To suggest a solution to a serious situation

55. Which is the best way to combine sentences (13) and (14)?

    (A) Young people are taking matters into their own hands, they lash out against society, feeling they cannot trust their elders.
    (B) They take matters into their own hands when they lash out against society, feeling they can put no trust in their elders.
    (C) Because they feel that they cannot trust their elders, they take matters into their own hands and lash out against society.
    (D) Feeling that they cannot trust their elders, young people take matters into their own hands and lash out against society.
    (E) When they feel that they cannot trust their elders or society and take matters into their own hands.

Section II

50 Questions

Time—45 minutes

Directions: Some of the sentences below contain an error in grammar, usage, word choice, or idiom. Other sentences are correct. Parts of each sentence are underlined and lettered. The error, if there is one, is contained in one of the underlined parts of the sentence. Assume that all other parts of the sentence are correct and cannot be changed. For each sentence, select the one underlined part that must be changed to make the sentence correct and mark its letter on your answer sheet. If there is no error in a sentence, mark answer choice (E). No sentence contains more than one error.

56. I hope you do not feel <u>too</u> <u>badly</u> but I must
             A   B

    <u>inform</u> you that it is quite <u>likely</u> your applica-
     C   D

    tion will be rejected. <u>No error</u>
                    E

57. <u>There is</u> certainly sufficient reasons <u>for</u>
       A   B

    <u>his being rejected</u> by the <u>group's membership</u>.
         C   D

    <u>No error</u>
     E

58. <u>All the members</u> of the group <u>were required</u>
         A   B

    to swear that they would tell <u>the honest truth</u>
                              C

    even though they disliked <u>the concept</u> of an
                        D

    investigation. <u>No error</u>
               E

59. <u>"My Last Duchess"</u> is one of the most interesting
         A

    poems <u>that was written</u> by <u>Robert Browning</u>,
           B   C

    <u>a Victorian poet</u>. <u>No error</u>
        D   E

60. <u>In order to produce</u> <u>a more effective</u> opening
        A   B

    <u>paragraph, sentences</u> three and four should be
              C

    <u>combined together</u>. <u>No error</u>
          D   E

61. Is it <u>their</u> contention that the set of dishes
     A B

    <u>were broken</u> <u>in transit?</u> <u>No error</u>
       C   D   E

62. They drove out to the construction <u>sight</u> to see
                                   A

    <u>how far</u> the work <u>had</u> <u>progressed</u>. <u>No error</u>
      B   C   D   E

63. <u>As</u> people <u>have been</u> moving into the reno-
     A   B

    vated building, the volume of business in the
    <u>neighborhood</u> stores <u>have been</u> growing. <u>No error</u>
         C   D   E

64. The couple <u>upstairs</u> insinuated <u>them to be</u>
             A   B

    <u>undesirable</u> <u>tenants</u>. <u>No error</u>
       C   D   E

65. Most people <u>successful</u> in business find <u>that you</u>
             A   B

    can't <u>exercise authority</u> without <u>sometimes</u>
          C   D

    inspiring discontent. <u>No error</u>
                  E

Restructuring Sentences

Directions: Below each of the following sentences are directions for revising the sentence and a choice of five words or phrases that may occur in your revised sentence. Mentally rephrase each sentence according to the directions given. Then choose the lettered word or phrase that is included in your revised sentence and blacken the corresponding space on your answer sheet.

If you think of a sentence that contains none of the words listed in the choices, rephrase the sentence again to include a word or phrase that is listed. Take care to make only those changes that the directions require and to choose an answer that is part of a complete and grammatically correct sentence.

Example:

Arriving at the airport late, he went directly to the departure gate.

Change <u>Arriving</u> to <u>He arrived</u>.

(A) and should have gone

(B) and went

(C) and going

(D) and then going

(E) and had gone

Revised sentence: He arrived at the airport late and went directly to the departure gate. Therefore, you should blacken answer space (B) for this question.

Sample Answer:

Ⓐ ● Ⓒ Ⓓ Ⓔ

66. There are times when the medical profession appears to be a mystical cabal and not a scientific field.

Substitute <u>appears more</u> for <u>appears to be</u>.

(A) than a scientific field

(B) being a scientific field

(C) rather than a mystical cabal

(D) and less than scientific

(E) and being mystical as well as

67. Having joined the armed forces as soon as he graduated from high school, he spent the next decade of his life taking orders and obeying commands, feeling that he was an automaton.

Change <u>Having joined</u> to <u>He joined</u>.

(A) then he spent the next decade of his life

(B) he had spent the next decade of his life

(C) after graduating high school

(D) spending the next decade of his life

(E) before his high school graduation

68. Responsibility for completing the assigned task could not be placed on either the workers or the supervisor.

Begin with <u>Neither the workers</u>.

(A) was responsible for completing

(B) were responsible for completing

(C) have responsibility for the completion

(D) responsibility for having completed

(E) are responsible for completing

69. When we spoke to the group, they were receptive to our ideas.

Change <u>When we spoke</u> to <u>Speaking</u>.

(A) group, they were

(B) group; they were found to be

(C) group, it was found

(D) group, we found they were

(E) group which was

70. He exhibits sensitivity which is certainly an asset.

Change <u>exhibits sensitivity</u> to <u>is sensitive</u>.

(A) which can be an asset

(B) something which is certainly an asset

(C) that which is certainly an asset

(D) an asset he certainly exhibits

(E) and this is certainly an asset

71. A good politician cannot be elected without first developing a broad base of supporters.

Change <u>without</u> to <u>unless</u>.

(A) he will have first developed

(B) he first develops

(C) having first developed

(D) they first develop

(E) first developing

72. The errors in timing and sequence of ideas can easily be detected by an astute reader.

    Begin with <u>An astute reader</u>.

    (A) can be detected easily
    (B) can have detection
    (C) can reveal errors in timing
    (D) will have detected
    (E) can easily detect

73. When we lived with our parents and depended on them for all our needs, life was much simpler and our daily routine more circumscribed.

    Begin with <u>Living with our parents</u>.

    (A) when we depended on them
    (B) and having depended on them
    (C) depending on them
    (D) since we depended on them
    (E) having to depend on them

74. That he had wide popular appeal was clearly evidenced by the number of eligible voters who turned out.

    Begin with <u>The number of eligible voters</u>.

    (A) turned out to evidence
    (B) was clearly evidenced
    (C) clearly evidenced
    (D) was appealed by
    (E) was a show of support

75. During my leisure hours I like reading the latest novel or simply turning on the radio and listening to a call-in program.

    Change <u>reading</u> to <u>to read</u>.

    (A) or I simply turn on the radio, listening
    (B) or to simply turn on the radio, while listening
    (C) or simply turn on the radio and listen
    (D) by simply turning on the radio and listen
    (E) simply turning on the radio and listening

76. It delights my students when the principal of the school and I disagree on an issue.

    Begin with <u>My students approve</u>.

    (A) of the principal of the school and me disagreeing
    (B) of the school principal's and my disagreeing
    (C) of the school principal and I disagreeing
    (D) when the principal of the school and me disagree
    (E) of I and the principal of the school disagreeing

77. Although they were very poor, the Moores were a warm and loving family.

    Begin with <u>Despite</u>.

    (A) having been very poor
    (B) to be very poor
    (C) of the poverty
    (D) their poverty
    (E) that they were very poor

78. It is not often that students are so enthralled by a lecture.

    Begin with <u>Seldom</u>.

    (A) that students are
    (B) are students so
    (C) are students often
    (D) students can be
    (E) students that are

79. Certainty that the students alone were to blame for the discipline problems in the high school caused the school board to retain the principal.

    Change <u>certainty</u> to <u>sure</u>.

    (A) was retained
    (B) will retain
    (C) retained
    (D) has been retained
    (E) had retained

80. Walking down the street, Phyllis immediately located a bookstore.

    Begin with <u>Phyllis walked</u>.

    (A) and then immediately had located

    (B) and immediately located

    (C) and immediately she had located

    (D) and immediately she locates

    (E) which immediately located

Revising Work in Progress

Directions: The selections that follow are early drafts of student essays in which each sentence has been numbered for easy reference. Following each essay are questions that direct you to a part of the essay or to the entire essay. The questions focus upon improving sentence structure and word choice, organization and development of the essay, and effectiveness of language for the intended purpose and audience of the work. For each question, choose the letter of the answer you consider to be correct, and mark the corresponding oval on your answer sheet.

Questions 81–86 are based on the following essay.

(1) Jazz is still my favorite! (2) I spent my vacation studying rock and roll, folk, classical, rhythm and blues, and reggae, even a few minutes of punk and heavy metal, and I enjoyed nearly everything I heard, but when all was said and done, the winner was jazz, which I have listened to for many years now, ever since I was a youngster. (3) Rolling Stones, Beatles, Dylan, Baez, Bach, Brahms, B.B. King, Bob Marley, Jimmy Cliff. (4) I love them all! (5) But in the final analysis, truth be told, I'd choose Miles, Brubeck, Coltrane, and Monk over them all. (6) Or maybe Bird and Diz, Wynton, Branford, Modern Jazz Quartet.

(7) Especially late at night, I enjoy turning on the radio to catch a show or two. (8) I also enjoy going downtown to a club to hear live music. (9) Recently I spent a lovely Sunday eating lunch while being entertained by a group of excellent young artists. (10) They were just beginning to make a name for themselves. (11) Their playing was very exciting. (12) College radio stations often program an hour or two of jazz daily, and so does several of the local public radio networks.

(13) I have a number of hobbies—playing sports, traveling, and exercising, for example—but my favorite and most relaxing is listening to music. (14) As I suggested earlier, my taste is eclectic; therefore, I sometimes find it hard to choose between jazz and rock and roll, folk, classical, rhythm and blues, and reggae. (15) But when it comes right down to it, jazz is still my favorite type of music.

81. Which of the following is the best way to improve the structure of sentence (2)?

    (A) I spent my vacation studying rock and roll, folk, classical, rhythm and blues, and reggae; even a few minutes of punk and heavy metal; and I enjoyed nearly everything I heard; but when all was said and done, the winner was jazz; which I have listened to for many years now, ever since I was a youngster.

    (B) I spent my vacation studying rock and roll, folk, classical, rhythm and blues, and reggae, even a few minutes of punk and heavy metal and I enjoyed nearly everything I heard, but when all was said and done, the winner was jazz, which I have listened to for many years now ever since I was a youngster.

    (C) I spent my vacation studying rock and roll, folk, classical, rhythm and blues, and reggae I even listened to a few minutes of punk and heavy metal; and I enjoyed nearly everything I heard; but when all was said and done the winner was jazz; I have listened to it for many years now ever since I was a youngster.

    (D) I spent my vacation studying rock and roll, folk, classical, rhythm and blues and reggae, punk and heavy metal, and I enjoyed nearly everything I heard, but when all was said and done, the winner was jazz, which I have listened to for many years now, since I was a youngster.

    (E) I spent my vacation studying rock and roll, folk, classical, rhythm and blues, reggae and even a few minutes of punk and heavy metal. I enjoyed nearly everything I heard, but when all was said and done, the winner was jazz, which I have listened to for many years now, ever since I was a youngster.

82. Which of the following would be the best way to improve the first paragraph?
    (A) Add and develop one or two examples
    (B) Eliminate one or two examples
    (C) Revise to eliminate clichés and be more concise
    (D) Correct spelling errors
    (E) Add a thesis statement

83. The second paragraph should be revised in order to
    (A) eliminate the inappropriate analogy.
    (B) improve the organization.
    (C) make the tone more consistent.
    (D) make the vocabulary more sophisticated.
    (E) discuss the tunes played by the young artists.

84. Which of the following is the best way to combine sentences (9) and (10)?
    (A) While being entertained at lunch by a group of young artists who were just beginning to make a name for themselves.
    (B) Recently I spent a lovely Sunday eating lunch while being entertained by a group of excellent young artists who were just beginning to make a name for themselves.
    (C) Recently at Sunday lunch, a group of young artists entertained me, beginning to make a name for themselves.
    (D) A group of young artists entertained me recently at lunch beginning to make a name for themselves.
    (E) While at lunch recently, a group of young artists making a name for themselves entertained me.

85. Which of the following is the best way to revise the underlined portion of sentence (12) below?

    College radio stations often program an hour or two of jazz <u>daily, and so does several of the local public radio networks</u>.
    (A) daily; and so does several of the local public radio networks.
    (B) daily; as well as several of the local public radio networks.
    (C) daily, as well as several of the local public radio networks.
    (D) daily, and so do several of the local public radio networks.
    (E) on a daily basis, and so does several of the local public radio networks.

86. Which of the following is the best revision of the underlined portion of sentence (14) below?

    As I suggested earlier, <u>my taste is eclectic; therefore, I sometimes find it hard to choose between</u> jazz, rock and roll, folk, classical, rhythm and blues, and reggae.
    (A) my taste is eclectic; therefore, I sometimes find it hard to choose among
    (B) my tastes are eclectic; therefore I sometimes find it hard to choose between
    (C) my taste is eclectic, therefore, I sometimes find it hard to choose among
    (D) my taste is eclectic, so I sometimes find it hard to choose between
    (E) since my taste is eclectic, therefore I sometimes find it hard to choose between

Questions 87–91 are based on the following essay.

(1) Voting is not a privilege, it is also a responsibility. (2) There are people who say that it doesn't really make any difference whether or not you vote. (3) They say that it is almost predetermined who will win an election. (4) They claim that only those with a good deal of money are chosen to run for office. (5) They further state that poor people are never selected to run for office.

(6) In many countries, a free and open election is unheard of. (7) There is a one-party system.

(8) As a result, the average citizen's right to vote is nonexistent. (9) To vote in an unchallenged way, to exercise free speech, and enjoy open political debate are all forbidden by the state. (10) How they must envy us when they see what we enjoy in our country. (11) Even if our choice is limited, at least we can vote for whomever we feel has the best qualifications.

(12) And yet, there are those who ignore this situation. (13) They don't realize how fortunate we are, they are like the pessimists who see only the half-empty glass, not the half-full one. (14) For years, women and minorities have struggled for the right to vote. (15) Now that we have it, you shouldn't waste it.

87. Which of the following best describes the writer's intention in sentence (1)?

    (A) To present two points of view
    (B) To suggest that a solution is needed
    (C) To present a "straw man"
    (D) To change a reader's opinion
    (E) To present the main thesis of the essay

88. Which of the following is the best way to combine sentences (3), (4), and (5)?

    (A) Claiming that only the wealthy are chosen to run for office, they say that winning an election is almost predetermined.
    (B) They claim that only the rich can afford to run and poor people are never chosen.
    (C) Since it requires a good deal of money to run for public office, the choice of candidates is determined in advance.
    (D) Election results are predetermined since only the rich are chosen to run and the poor are disenfranchised.
    (E) Since it is predetermined who will win an election, they claim only the wealthy, and never the poor, are selected.

89. Which of the following best characterizes sentence (5)?

    (A) It provides an alternate viewpoint.
    (B) It restates sentence (4), without adding anything new.
    (C) It provides a summary to the introductory paragraph.
    (D) It provides a bridge between paragraph one and paragraph two.
    (E) It adds further proof that the system is not working.

90. Which of the following is the best revision of the underlined portion of sentence (11) below?

    Even if our choice is limited, at least we can vote for <u>whomever we feel has the best qualifications</u>.

    (A) for whomever we feel is the best qualified.
    (B) the candidate whom we feel has the best qualifications.
    (C) for whoever we feel has the best qualifications.
    (D) for whomever we feel have the best qualifications.
    (E) for the candidates who we feel have the best qualifications.

91. In light of the sentence that precedes it, which is the best way to revise sentence (15)?

    (A) Now that the right to vote has been achieved, it shouldn't be wasted.
    (B) You shouldn't waste the vote, if you have it.
    (C) Now that this important right has been gained, work for it.
    (D) Since other nations are not so lucky, we shouldn't waste our right to vote.
    (E) You shouldn't waste the right, once you have the vote.

Analyzing Writing

Directions: This section presents two prose passages. Following each passage are questions that test how well you recognize the purpose of the writer and the characteristics of good writing. As you read each passage, bear in mind that it may be part of a longer piece of writing and it might not, as a result, present a complete analysis or discussion of the issues under consideration. Read each passage carefully, then answer each question by selecting the letter of the answer choice you consider to be correct.

Questions 92–98 refer to the following paragraph.

(1) Regarding physical changes that have been and are now taking place on the surface of the earth. (2) The sea and its shores have been the scene of the greatest stability. (3) The dry land has seen the rise, the decline, and even the disappearance and vanishing, of vast hordes of various types and forms. (4) This has occurred within comparatively recent times, geologically talking. (5) But life in the sea is today virtuously what it was when many of the forms now extinct on land had not yet been evolved. (6) Many of these have a marked capacity to cling closely to the substratum. (7) Also, it may be parenthetically stated here, the marine habitat has been biologically the most important in the evolution and development. (8) Its rhythmic influence can still be traced in those animals whose ancestors have long since left the water. (9) It is now generally held as an accepted fact that the shore area of an ancient sea was the birthplace of life.

92. What should be done with sentence (1)?
    (A) It should be left as it is.
    (B) It should be joined to the beginning of sentence (3) with *since*.
    (C) It should be joined to the beginning of sentence (2).
    (D) It should begin with *Regardless of physical changes.*
    (E) The part after *place* should be omitted.

93. Sentence (3) would be best if
    (A) it were left as it is.
    (B) the word *disappearance* were changed to *disappearing*.
    (C) The phrase *and even the disappearance and vanishing* were omitted entirely.
    (D) the words *and vanishing* were omitted.
    (E) it were joined to sentence (4) with a comma.

94. In sentence (4), the word *talking* should be
    (A) left as it is.
    (B) omitted entirely.
    (C) changed to *chatting.*
    (D) changed to *conversing.*
    (E) changed to *speaking.*

95. The word *virtuously* in sentence (5) should be
    (A) left as it is.
    (B) changed to *virtuous.*
    (C) changed to *virtually.*
    (D) changed to *a lot like.*
    (E) changed to *arduously.*

96. What should be done with sentence (6)?
    (A) It should be left as it is.
    (B) It should be omitted entirely.
    (C) It should be placed at the end of the passage.
    (D) It should be placed at the beginning of the passage.
    (E) It should be placed after the first sentence.

97. Sentence (7) would be clearest if
    (A) it were left as it is.
    (B) it began with *Thusly and also.*
    (C) it began *This is the way of things also.*
    (D) the part after *important* were omitted.
    (E) it ended with *of life on this planet.*

98. Sentence (8) is best placed
    (A) where it is now.
    (B) before sentence (1).
    (C) after sentence (1).
    (D) after sentence (3).
    (E) after sentence (9).

Questions 99–105 refer to the following paragraph.

(1) With increasing prosperity, West European youth is having a fling that is creating distinctive consumer and cultural patterns. (2) The increasing emergence in Europe of that phenomenon well-known in America as the "youth market." (3) This is a market in which enterprising businesses cater to the demands of teenagers and older youths. (4) The Norwegians have simply adopted the English word "teenager." (5) In the United States, the market is large, successful, wide-ranging and well established. (6) Moreover, in Western Europe, the youth market may appropriately be said to be in its infancy. (7) In some countries, such as Britain, West Germany, and France, it is more advanced than in the others. (8) Some manifestations of the market, chiefly sociological, have been recorded. (9) But they are only just beginning to be the subject of organized consumer research and promotion.

99. In sentence (1), *having a fling* should be

  (A) left as it is.
  (B) changed to *making an ascent.*
  (C) changed to *throwing a party.*
  (D) changed to *racing with time.*
  (E) changed to *having a flight.*

100. The meaning of sentence (2) would be clearest if the sentence is (was)

  (A) left as it is.
  (B) begun with *The hope will be.*
  (C) ended with *and often grandparents.*
  (D) begun with *The result has been.*
  (E) ended with *and that is all.*

101. What should be done with sentence (4)?

  (A) It should be left as it is.
  (B) It should be joined to sentence (5).
  (C) It should be the topic sentence of the second paragraph.
  (D) The word *simply* should be omitted.
  (E) It should be omitted entirely.

102. Sentence (5) would be most improved if

  (A) it were left as it is.
  (B) *In the United States* were omitted.
  (C) *large, successful* were omitted.
  (D) the entire sentence were joined to the end of sentence (4).
  (E) the entire sentence were joined to the end of sentence (3) with *and.*

103. Sentence (6) should begin

  (A) the way it begins now.
  (B) with *Western Europe.*
  (C) with *Outside of Western Europe.*
  (D) with *In Western Europe.*
  (E) with *In Western Europe, therefore.*

104. Sentence (7) is best placed

  (A) where it is now.
  (B) after sentence (3).
  (C) before sentence (3).
  (D) after sentence (9).
  (E) after sentence (8).

105. If the passage is to be divided into three paragraphs, the third paragraph should begin with

  (A) sentence (6).
  (B) sentence (8).
  (C) sentence (4).
  (D) sentence (2).
  (E) sentence (7).

End of Practice Examination I

Answer Key

Section I

1.	D	12.	A	23.	A	34.	A	45.	A
2.	A	13.	C	24.	C	35.	D	46.	C
3.	A	14.	E	25.	C	36.	C	47.	B
4.	B	15.	A	26.	E	37.	A	48.	C
5.	E	16.	C	27.	E	38.	D	49.	A
6.	B	17.	D	28.	C	39.	A	50.	E
7.	A	18.	A	29.	D	40.	C	51.	A
8.	A	19.	C	30.	E	41.	B	52.	B
9.	D	20.	A	31.	B	42.	E	53.	E
10.	E	21.	C	32.	E	43.	A	54.	B
11.	B	22.	D	33.	D	44.	E	55.	D

Section II

56.	B	66.	A	76.	B	86.	A	96.	B
57.	A	67.	D	77.	D	87.	E	97.	E
58.	C	68.	A	78.	B	88.	A	98.	A
59.	E	69.	D	79.	C	89.	B	99.	A
60.	D	70.	E	80.	B	90.	C	100.	D
61.	C	71.	B	81.	E	91.	A	101.	E
62.	A	72.	E	82.	C	92.	C	102.	C
63.	D	73.	C	83.	B	93.	D	103.	D
64.	B	74.	C	84.	B	94.	E	104.	A
65.	B	75.	C	85.	D	95.	C	105.	B

Explanatory Answers

Section I

1. **The correct answer is (D).** Since *unique* is an absolute, it is not used in the superlative (or comparative) form; eliminate *most*.

2. **The correct answer is (A).** The past subjunctive *had gone* is needed in the first clause to coordinate with the past conditional in the second clause (*would have won*).

3. **The correct answer is (A).** *All together,* which means everybody or everything together, should be *altogether,* which means entirely or completely.

4. **The correct answer is (B).** As part of the compound subject, the correct pronoun is *I,* not *myself.*

5. **The correct answer is (E).** The sentence is correct.

6. **The correct answer is (B).** *Only* should precede *it.*

7. **The correct answer is (A).** *Hardly no one* is a double negative and is incorrect. The correct phrase is *Hardly any one.*

8. **The correct answer is (A).** The correct word is *about.*

9. **The correct answer is (D).** *Theirselves* is illiterate; *themselves* is correct.

10. **The correct answer is (E).** The sentence is correct.

11. **The correct answer is (B).** The noun *loan* is incorrect. The correct word is the verb *lend.*

12. **The correct answer is (A).** The singular subject *Bill* requires the singular verb *is.*

13. **The correct answer is (C).** The singular pronoun *his* (or *her*) is required to agree with the singular antecedent *everyone.*

14. **The correct answer is (E).** The sentence is correct.

15. **The correct answer is (A).** The correct phrase is *In regard to.*

16. **The correct answer is (C).** The sentence should be rephrased so that it does not seem as if *his hands* were *noticing.* Although choice (E) corrects the misplaced modifier, it creates a run-on sentence.

17. **The correct answer is (D).** The correct word is *among* (not *between*) the four gang members.

18. **The correct answer is (A).** No error.

19. **The correct answer is (C).** The original sentence lacks a verb in the main clause. Both choices (C) and (E) provide a verb that agrees with the subject, but choice (E) changes the meaning of the original sentence.

20. **The correct answer is (A).** No error. *So* establishes the cause-effect relationship; *have lain* is the present perfect form of *to lie.*

21. **The correct answer is (C).** The *it* does not refer to acclaim and recognition, which could be *achieved.* It refers to *desire,* which is either *satisfied* or *not satisfied.*

22. **The correct answer is (D).** The original uses five words where two will do, eleven syllables where three suffice.

23. **The correct answer is (A).** *Neither one* is singular and takes the singular verb form *has been.*

24. **The correct answer is (C).** The original idea poses two problems in a parallel structure: (1) The two warnings must branch off grammatically from the subject that warns. (2) If the *not only* correlative form is used, it should be balanced by a phrase like *but also.* Only choice (C) meets both requirements.

25. **The correct answer is (C).** The sentence deals with a condition that is not a fact but a possibility. The verb used to express the condition contrary to fact should be in the subjunctive mood; the verb used to explain the possible conclusion should be in the conditional mood. The first clause should read: *Had I realized* or *If I had realized.*

26. **The correct answer is (E).** If the *material* and the *performances* are his, so is the singing: *his* singing.

27. **The correct answer is (E).** The design and the fabrics are being compared. The first is traditional, the second, modern. The inevitable form is parallel structure, as in choice (E). Choice (B) only appears to be parallel: It would put the second clause in the passive voice instead of in a simple linking-verb construction like the first clause.

28. **The correct answer is (C).** Parallel ideas should be expressed in parallel form. If a man produced an application that had two faults, they should be expressed in similar grammar. Choice (B) only seems to be parallel: The first clause is active voice, the second passive. Choice (D) creates a comma splice. Choice (E) fails to use commas.

29. **The correct answer is (D).** The original, choice (A), is a run-on sentence. Choice (B) correctly separates the clauses but incorrectly adds a comma before *officially*. Choice (C) creates a comma splice. Choice (E) omits the comma required after *however*. Choice (D) resolves all problems. It assigns *officially* to the president's powers, puts *however* in the right place, and uses the punctuation required when such an adverb is tucked inside the sentence.

30. **The correct answer is (E).** The original sentence takes 16 words to say what choice (E) says in 10 words.

31. **The correct answer is (B).** In a neither-nor construction, the verb agrees with the closest subject. In this example, the singular *is* should agree with *teacher*.

32. **The correct answer is (E).** The correct word for the head of a school is *principal*; therefore, choices (A) and (B) are wrong. Choice (C) uses the contraction for *it is* instead of the possessive *its*. Choice (D) has no verb in the main clause.

33. **The correct answer is (D).** *Might of, could of,* and *should of* are nonstandard English. The correct form is might *have* (or, informally, *might've*).

34. **The correct answer is (A).** The sentence is correct. Both verbs should be in the past tense.

35. **The correct answer is (D).** The correct word is *annoyed*, meaning made angry; *aggravated* means made worse. The completed comparison is *than we (were)*. Only choice (D) meets both of these requirements.

36. **The correct answer is (C).** Choice (C) is the best response, since it avoids the lack of clarity or redundancy in choices (A), (B), and (E). Subject-verb agreement is violated in choice (D).

37. **The correct answer is (A).** Choice (A) is best because the essayist relates the topic to his own experience.

38. **The correct answer is (D).** The sentence would now read *All my friends encouraged me to smoke, telling me that I would look more grown up and mature*.

39. **The correct answer is (A).** Choice (A) is best since this sentence just repeats what has been stated in sentence (12).

40. **The correct answer is (C).** Choice (C) is best since a new idea is being introduced and the writer does not elaborate on this new area of the dangers of second-hand smoke.

41. **The correct answer is (B).** Choice (B) is best since it corrects the awkward use of *them*. People are not a special place; a city is special. Therefore, *them* should be replaced by *it*. Choice (D) is not correct because the semicolon is used incorrectly.

42. **The correct answer is (E).** The best way to combine the two sentences is to subordinate sentence (9) by making it a participle phrase modifying *they*.

43. **The correct answer is (A).** The introductory paragraph presents the position that New Yorkers formerly were happy that their city housed the United Nations. The second paragraph shows why New Yorkers no longer feel this way.

44. **The correct answer is (E).** In the underlined portion, the antecedent of *their* is not clear. The sense of the sentence indicates that it should be *host country*, a singular noun, making *their*, a plural, incorrect. The pronoun *its* is better; therefore, choice (E) is correct.

45. **The correct answer is (A).** Sentences (12), (14), and (15) use the first-person plural pronouns *us* and *our*. Sentence (13) changes to *you*. Choice (A) is correct since the pronoun used is consistent with the one in the previous and following sentences.

46. **The correct answer is (C).** In the second sentence, the antecedent of the pronoun *it* is vague. Grammatically, the antecedent appears to be *school*, but this does not make sense.

47. **The correct answer is (B).** In the first paragraph, the writer indicates that the topic of the essay is sex instruction and states the belief that this area of education should be the province of parents, not professionals.

48. **The correct answer is (C).** The antecedent of *it*, which appears twice in the underlined portion, is apparently *responsibility*. Although it is correct to *take responsibility*, it is not correct to *do responsibility*. Therefore, choices (A), (B), (D), and (E) do not correct the error. Choice (C) corrects the error by substituting the phrase *perform the job*.

49. **The correct answer is (A).** The problem presented is that the antecedent of the plural pronoun *they* is the singular noun *parent*. Only choice (A) addresses this error and corrects it.

50. **The correct answer is (E).** Choice (A) contains a comma splice error, and choice (D) is a fragment. Choice (B) omits sentence (9), and choice (C) changes the meaning of the three original sentences. Choice (E) is best.

51. **The correct answer is (A).** Idiomatic construction requires that the word *that*—not *because*—should be used. Therefore, choices (B) and (E) are poor. Choices (C) and (D) are awkward since the word *possibly* following *may* is not necessary. Choice (A) is best.

52. **The correct answer is (B).** Asking a question is contrived here and providing an answer makes the essay unnecessarily wordy. To add strength to the paragraph, a simple declarative statement as shown in choice (B) is best.

53. **The correct answer is (E).** The metaphor *fabric of our society* should be consistent with its accompanying verb. The verb *break* is not appropriate because one does not *break fabric* as stated in the original sentence as well as in choices (B) and (D). Choice (C) is incorrect because the preposition *apart* at the end of the sentence is wrong. The correct choice is (E).

54. **The correct answer is (B).** Sentence (12) states that a problem exists, and the two sentences that follow present this problem, which requires a solution.

55. **The correct answer is (D).** Choice (A) contains a comma splice error. Choices (B) and (C) are poor since the antecedent of *they* is not clear in either sentence. Choice (E) is a fragment and is incorrect. Choice (D) is best.

Section II

56. **The correct answer is (B).** The adjective *bad* is required after the verb *feel*.

57. **The correct answer is (A).** The verb *is*, a singular form, is incorrect; the correct form is *are* to agree with the plural subject *reasons*.

58. **The correct answer is (C).** *Honest truth* is redundant, since, by its very definition, *truth* is *honest*.

59. **The correct answer is (E).** The sentence is correct as is.

60. **The correct answer is (D).** The phrase *combined together* is redundant; *together* should be deleted.

61. **The correct answer is (C).** The subject of the verb is *set*, a singular; *were broken*, a plural, should be changed to *was broken*.

62. **The correct answer is (A).** Substitute *site*, meaning *place*, for *sight*, meaning vision.

63. **The correct answer is (D).** The subject of the main clause is *volume*, which takes a singular verb: *has been* growing.

64. **The correct answer is (B).** The correct idiom would be *that they are*.

65. **The correct answer is (B).** Not *you*, but *they*, referring back to *people*.

66. **The correct answer is (A).** There are times when the medical profession appears more a mystical cabal *than a scientific field*.

67. **The correct answer is (D).** He joined the armed forces as soon as he graduated from high school, *spending the next decade of his life* taking orders and obeying commands, feeling that he was an automaton.

68. **The correct answer is (A).** Neither the workers nor the supervisor *was responsible for completing* the assigned task.

69. **The correct answer is (D).** Speaking to the *group, we found* they were receptive to our ideas.

70. **The correct answer is (E).** He is sensitive *and this is certainly an asset*.

71. **The correct answer is (B).** A good politician cannot be elected unless *he first develops* a broad base of supporters.

72. **The correct answer is (E).** An astute reader *can easily detect* the errors in timing and sequence of ideas.

73. **The correct answer is (C).** Living with our parents and *depending on them* for all our needs, we found life much simpler and our daily routine more circumscribed.

74. **The correct answer is (C).** The number of eligible voters who turned out *clearly evidenced* that he had wide popular appeal.

75. **The correct answer is (C).** During my leisure hours, I like to read the latest novel *or simply turn on the radio and listen* to a call-in program.

76. **The correct answer is (B).** My students approve *of the school principal's and my disagreeing* on an issue.

77. **The correct answer is (D).** Despite *their poverty*, the Moores were a warm and loving family.

78. **The correct answer is (B).** Seldom *are students so* enthralled by a lecture.

79. **The correct answer is (C).** Sure that the students alone were to blame for the discipline problems in the high school, the school board *retained* the principal.

80. **The correct answer is (B).** Phyllis walked down the street *and immediately located* a bookstore.

81. **The correct answer is (E).** The best way to improve sentence (2) is to break it up into two shorter and more manageable sentences as in choice (E). Choice (A) uses semicolons incorrectly. Choices (B), (C), and (D) are all unnecessarily long and complicated. Also, choices (B) and (C) need a comma between *now* and *ever since I was a youngster*.

82. **The correct answer is (C).** Such phrases as "all was said and done," "in the final analysis," and "truth be told," are clichés and should be eliminated. Choice (C) is correct.

83. **The correct answer is (B).** The organization of the second paragraph is weak. Sentence (12) does not necessarily follow the preceding sentences. The entire paragraph should be strengthened and more tightly organized. Choice (B) is correct.

84. **The correct answer is (B).** Choice (A) is a fragment. Choice (C) is awkward because of the placement of the final phrase. Choices (D) and (E) are also clumsily phrased and garbled. Choice (B) is best.

85. **The correct answer is (D).** There is a problem of subject-verb agreement here. The subject *networks* is plural and requires a plural verb, *do*. Choices (A) and (E) do not correct this error. Choices (B) and (C) are awkward and ungrammatical. Choice (D) is correct.

86. **The correct answer is (A).** The transitional adverb *therefore* should be followed by a comma; therefore, choices (B) and (E) are incorrect. Choices (B), (D), and (E) use the preposition *between* rather than *among*. When three or more objects follow, the preposition should be *among*. Choice (A) is correct.

87. **The correct answer is (E).** Since the entire essay concerns the concept that in a free and open society like ours, the citizenry has both the right and the obligation to participate in the election process, sentence (1) presents the main thesis of the essay.

88. **The correct answer is (A).** Choices (C), (D), and (E) omit the concept that these ideas are only *claims*, not statements of fact. Choice (B) omits the claim that the winner is almost predetermined. Therefore, choice (A) is best.

89. **The correct answer is (B).** Sentence (4) offers the claim that only those with money are selected; sentence (5) claims that poor people are never selected. Thus, sentence (5) is merely a negative restatement of sentence (4) and offers no new information.

90. **The correct answer is (C).** *Whomever* is incorrect usage. The sentence requires a subject pronoun, the subject of the verb *has*. *Whom* and *whomever* are object pronouns. Choice (C) is best since it provides the subject pronoun *whoever*.

91. **The correct answer is (A).** Choice (A) is best since it is both clear and consistent with the tone of the passage.

92. **The correct answer is (C).** Sentence (1) is not a complete sentence. When joined to sentence (2), its meaning is fully revealed.

93. **The correct answer is (D).** *Disappearance and vanishing* mean essentially the same thing. Thus, the omission of *and vanishing* prevents sentence (3) from being verbose.

94. **The correct answer is (E).** The gerund *speaking* preceded by a certain type of adverb, such as *geologically,* forms a figure of speech.

95. **The correct answer is (C).** *Virtuously* is an adverb meaning "in a manner indicating moral excellence." *Virtually,* an adverb meaning being so in effect, is the appropriate choice for sentence (5).

96. **The correct answer is (B).** Sentence (6) has no place in the thought pattern of the passage and should be omitted.

97. **The correct answer is (E).** It is not clear what is *evolving* and *developing.* The addition of *life on this planet* solves this problem.

98. **The correct answer is (A).** Sentence (8) in its current position logically develops the train of thought of the passage.

99. **The correct answer is (A).** The phrase, *having a fling,* is defined as having a brief time of wild pleasures. It most accurately completes the meaning of the sentence.

100. **The correct answer is (D).** Sentence (2) is not a complete sentence. The addition of the phrase, *The result has been,* completes the sentence and integrates it into the passage.

101. **The correct answer is (E).** The Norwegian word for teenagers is irrelevant to the topic of the paragraph, which is the Western European youth market. Thus, the sentence should be omitted.

102. **The correct answer is (C).** *Large, successful, wide-ranging, and well established* are all adjectives that convey approximately the same meaning. The elimination of *large* and *successful* prevents redundancy.

103. **The correct answer is (D).** *Moreover* is an adverb that means "in addition to what has been said." It is inappropriate in sentence (6). The sentence should begin with *In Western Europe.*

104. **The correct answer is (A).** Sentence (7) accurately completes the train of thought of sentence (6).

105. **The correct answer is (B).** The second paragraph should begin with sentence (5). The third paragraph, which introduces the research done on the subject explained in the first two paragraphs, must begin with sentence (8).

Practice Examination I Diagnostic Chart

Question Type	Approx. % of Section	Question Numbers	Number of Questions	Number Wrong
Section I:				
Identifying Sentence Errors	28%	1–15	15	_____
Improving Sentences	36%	16–35	20	_____
Revising Work in Progress	36%	36–55	20	_____
Section II:				
Identifying Sentence Errors	20%	56–65	10	_____
Restructuring Sentences	30%	66–80	15	_____
Revising Work in Progress	20%	81–90	10	_____
Analyzing Writing	30%	91–105	15	_____

Answer Sheet for Practice Examination II

Section I

1 Ⓐ Ⓑ Ⓒ Ⓓ Ⓔ   12 Ⓐ Ⓑ Ⓒ Ⓓ Ⓔ   23 Ⓐ Ⓑ Ⓒ Ⓓ Ⓔ   34 Ⓐ Ⓑ Ⓒ Ⓓ Ⓔ   45 Ⓐ Ⓑ Ⓒ Ⓓ Ⓔ

2 Ⓐ Ⓑ Ⓒ Ⓓ Ⓔ   13 Ⓐ Ⓑ Ⓒ Ⓓ Ⓔ   24 Ⓐ Ⓑ Ⓒ Ⓓ Ⓔ   35 Ⓐ Ⓑ Ⓒ Ⓓ Ⓔ   46 Ⓐ Ⓑ Ⓒ Ⓓ Ⓔ

3 Ⓐ Ⓑ Ⓒ Ⓓ Ⓔ   14 Ⓐ Ⓑ Ⓒ Ⓓ Ⓔ   25 Ⓐ Ⓑ Ⓒ Ⓓ Ⓔ   36 Ⓐ Ⓑ Ⓒ Ⓓ Ⓔ   47 Ⓐ Ⓑ Ⓒ Ⓓ Ⓔ

4 Ⓐ Ⓑ Ⓒ Ⓓ Ⓔ   15 Ⓐ Ⓑ Ⓒ Ⓓ Ⓔ   26 Ⓐ Ⓑ Ⓒ Ⓓ Ⓔ   37 Ⓐ Ⓑ Ⓒ Ⓓ Ⓔ   48 Ⓐ Ⓑ Ⓒ Ⓓ Ⓔ

5 Ⓐ Ⓑ Ⓒ Ⓓ Ⓔ   16 Ⓐ Ⓑ Ⓒ Ⓓ Ⓔ   27 Ⓐ Ⓑ Ⓒ Ⓓ Ⓔ   38 Ⓐ Ⓑ Ⓒ Ⓓ Ⓔ   49 Ⓐ Ⓑ Ⓒ Ⓓ Ⓔ

6 Ⓐ Ⓑ Ⓒ Ⓓ Ⓔ   17 Ⓐ Ⓑ Ⓒ Ⓓ Ⓔ   28 Ⓐ Ⓑ Ⓒ Ⓓ Ⓔ   39 Ⓐ Ⓑ Ⓒ Ⓓ Ⓔ   50 Ⓐ Ⓑ Ⓒ Ⓓ Ⓔ

7 Ⓐ Ⓑ Ⓒ Ⓓ Ⓔ   18 Ⓐ Ⓑ Ⓒ Ⓓ Ⓔ   29 Ⓐ Ⓑ Ⓒ Ⓓ Ⓔ   40 Ⓐ Ⓑ Ⓒ Ⓓ Ⓔ   51 Ⓐ Ⓑ Ⓒ Ⓓ Ⓔ

8 Ⓐ Ⓑ Ⓒ Ⓓ Ⓔ   19 Ⓐ Ⓑ Ⓒ Ⓓ Ⓔ   30 Ⓐ Ⓑ Ⓒ Ⓓ Ⓔ   41 Ⓐ Ⓑ Ⓒ Ⓓ Ⓔ   52 Ⓐ Ⓑ Ⓒ Ⓓ Ⓔ

9 Ⓐ Ⓑ Ⓒ Ⓓ Ⓔ   20 Ⓐ Ⓑ Ⓒ Ⓓ Ⓔ   31 Ⓐ Ⓑ Ⓒ Ⓓ Ⓔ   42 Ⓐ Ⓑ Ⓒ Ⓓ Ⓔ   53 Ⓐ Ⓑ Ⓒ Ⓓ Ⓔ

10 Ⓐ Ⓑ Ⓒ Ⓓ Ⓔ   21 Ⓐ Ⓑ Ⓒ Ⓓ Ⓔ   32 Ⓐ Ⓑ Ⓒ Ⓓ Ⓔ   43 Ⓐ Ⓑ Ⓒ Ⓓ Ⓔ   54 Ⓐ Ⓑ Ⓒ Ⓓ Ⓔ

11 Ⓐ Ⓑ Ⓒ Ⓓ Ⓔ   22 Ⓐ Ⓑ Ⓒ Ⓓ Ⓔ   33 Ⓐ Ⓑ Ⓒ Ⓓ Ⓔ   44 Ⓐ Ⓑ Ⓒ Ⓓ Ⓔ   55 Ⓐ Ⓑ Ⓒ Ⓓ Ⓔ

Section II

56 Ⓐ Ⓑ Ⓒ Ⓓ Ⓔ   66 Ⓐ Ⓑ Ⓒ Ⓓ Ⓔ   76 Ⓐ Ⓑ Ⓒ Ⓓ Ⓔ   86 Ⓐ Ⓑ Ⓒ Ⓓ Ⓔ   96 Ⓐ Ⓑ Ⓒ Ⓓ Ⓔ

57 Ⓐ Ⓑ Ⓒ Ⓓ Ⓔ   67 Ⓐ Ⓑ Ⓒ Ⓓ Ⓔ   77 Ⓐ Ⓑ Ⓒ Ⓓ Ⓔ   87 Ⓐ Ⓑ Ⓒ Ⓓ Ⓔ   97 Ⓐ Ⓑ Ⓒ Ⓓ Ⓔ

58 Ⓐ Ⓑ Ⓒ Ⓓ Ⓔ   68 Ⓐ Ⓑ Ⓒ Ⓓ Ⓔ   78 Ⓐ Ⓑ Ⓒ Ⓓ Ⓔ   88 Ⓐ Ⓑ Ⓒ Ⓓ Ⓔ   98 Ⓐ Ⓑ Ⓒ Ⓓ Ⓔ

59 Ⓐ Ⓑ Ⓒ Ⓓ Ⓔ   69 Ⓐ Ⓑ Ⓒ Ⓓ Ⓔ   79 Ⓐ Ⓑ Ⓒ Ⓓ Ⓔ   89 Ⓐ Ⓑ Ⓒ Ⓓ Ⓔ   99 Ⓐ Ⓑ Ⓒ Ⓓ Ⓔ

60 Ⓐ Ⓑ Ⓒ Ⓓ Ⓔ   70 Ⓐ Ⓑ Ⓒ Ⓓ Ⓔ   80 Ⓐ Ⓑ Ⓒ Ⓓ Ⓔ   90 Ⓐ Ⓑ Ⓒ Ⓓ Ⓔ   100 Ⓐ Ⓑ Ⓒ Ⓓ Ⓔ

61 Ⓐ Ⓑ Ⓒ Ⓓ Ⓔ   71 Ⓐ Ⓑ Ⓒ Ⓓ Ⓔ   81 Ⓐ Ⓑ Ⓒ Ⓓ Ⓔ   91 Ⓐ Ⓑ Ⓒ Ⓓ Ⓔ   101 Ⓐ Ⓑ Ⓒ Ⓓ Ⓔ

62 Ⓐ Ⓑ Ⓒ Ⓓ Ⓔ   72 Ⓐ Ⓑ Ⓒ Ⓓ Ⓔ   82 Ⓐ Ⓑ Ⓒ Ⓓ Ⓔ   92 Ⓐ Ⓑ Ⓒ Ⓓ Ⓔ   102 Ⓐ Ⓑ Ⓒ Ⓓ Ⓔ

63 Ⓐ Ⓑ Ⓒ Ⓓ Ⓔ   73 Ⓐ Ⓑ Ⓒ Ⓓ Ⓔ   83 Ⓐ Ⓑ Ⓒ Ⓓ Ⓔ   93 Ⓐ Ⓑ Ⓒ Ⓓ Ⓔ   103 Ⓐ Ⓑ Ⓒ Ⓓ Ⓔ

64 Ⓐ Ⓑ Ⓒ Ⓓ Ⓔ   74 Ⓐ Ⓑ Ⓒ Ⓓ Ⓔ   84 Ⓐ Ⓑ Ⓒ Ⓓ Ⓔ   94 Ⓐ Ⓑ Ⓒ Ⓓ Ⓔ   104 Ⓐ Ⓑ Ⓒ Ⓓ Ⓔ

65 Ⓐ Ⓑ Ⓒ Ⓓ Ⓔ   75 Ⓐ Ⓑ Ⓒ Ⓓ Ⓔ   85 Ⓐ Ⓑ Ⓒ Ⓓ Ⓔ   95 Ⓐ Ⓑ Ⓒ Ⓓ Ⓔ   105 Ⓐ Ⓑ Ⓒ Ⓓ Ⓔ

PRACTICE EXAMINATION II

Section I

55 Questions
Time—45 minutes

Identifying Sentence Errors

Directions: Some of the sentences below contain an error in grammar, usage, word choice, or idiom. Other sentences are correct. Parts of each sentence are underlined and lettered. The error, if there is one, is contained in one of the underlined parts of the sentence. Assume that all other parts of the sentence are correct and cannot be changed. For each sentence, select the one underlined part that must be changed to make the sentence correct and mark its letter on your answer sheet. If there is no error in a sentence, mark answer space (E). No sentence contains more than one error.

Example:

Being that it's such a lovely day, we are having a
A   B   C
difficult time concentrating on our assignment.
                    D
No error
E

Sample Answer:
● Ⓑ Ⓒ Ⓓ Ⓔ

1. She poured over the travel brochure as if she
            A   B
    had never seen photographs of snowcapped
            C
    mountains before. No error
                D   E

2. At the heart of the New England town was the
    A
    common, a public pasture for the citizens'
    B   C   D
    sheep and cattle. No error
                    E

3. Being a real estate agent it requires passing a
    A   B   C   D
    licensing examination. No error
                        E

4. These oranges taste more sweetly than any
                    A   B
    others I've ever tried. No error
    C   D   E

5. In applying for the loan, one is required
    A   B
    to supply copies of your federal income tax
    C   D
    return. No error
            E

6. Coming from the rainy forests, we never dreamed
    A   B
    that the desert could be so beautiful. No error
                    C   D   E

7. <u>On</u> the following day the blizzard <u>grew</u> even
     A   B

   <u>worst</u>, <u>surpassing</u> all previous records.
     C   D

   <u>No error</u>
     E

8. All <u>but</u> seven passengers, three crewmen, and
       A

   a small dog <u>was</u> lost <u>when</u> the ship <u>sank</u>.
            B   C   D

   <u>No error</u>
     E

9. <u>Everybody</u> in the choir <u>except for</u> Meryl and <u>I</u>
     A   B   C

   <u>had sung</u> the hymn previously. <u>No error</u>
     D   E

10. She wrote <u>that</u> they had visited Chartres and
             A

    <u>saw</u> the <u>cathedral</u> <u>there</u>. <u>No error</u>
      B   C   D   E

11. Quickly and <u>in a brusque way</u>, the press agent
                 A

    <u>informed</u> the reporters that the tour <u>had had</u>
      B   C

    <u>to be canceled</u>. <u>No error</u>
        D   E

12. Traditionally, the <u>street number</u> of a house in
                  A

    a Japanese town reflected the relative antiq-
    uity of the building <u>rather than</u> <u>its location</u>; the
                     B   C

    oldest house was number one, the next oldest
    number two, <u>and so forth</u>. <u>No error</u>
                D   E

13. Please ask <u>she</u> and the other applicant <u>to call</u>
             A   B

    on Friday <u>to arrange</u> <u>interviews</u>. <u>No error</u>
            C   D   E

14. One must organize <u>their</u> time efficiently
                    A

    <u>in order to</u> complete <u>all</u> the assignments
      B   C

    <u>promptly</u>. <u>No error</u>
      D   E

15. Though <u>well-intentioned</u>, his <u>advise</u> was
            A   B

    <u>usually</u> <u>ineffectual</u>. <u>No error</u>
      C   D   E

Improving Sentences

Directions: The sentences below may contain problems in grammar, usage, word choice, sentence construction, and punctuation. Part or all of each sentence is underlined. Following each sentence you will find five ways of expressing the underlined part. Answer choice (A) always repeats the original underlined section. The other four answer choices are all different. You are to select the lettered answer that produces the most effective sentence. If you think the original sentence is best, choose (A) as your answer. If one of the other choices makes a better sentence, mark your answer sheet for the letter of that choice. Do not choose an answer that changes the meaning of the original sentence.

Example:

I have always enjoyed <u>singing as well as to dance</u>.

(A) singing as well as to dance

(B) singing as well as dancing

(C) to sing as well as dancing

(D) singing in addition to dance

(E) to sing in addition to dancing

Sample Answer:

Ⓐ ● Ⓒ Ⓓ Ⓔ

16. It is perfectly satisfactory to give the sample test <u>to whomever you think needs it.</u>

    (A) to whomever you think needs it.
    (B) to whomsoever has a need for it.
    (C) to whosoever you think has a need of it.
    (D) to whoever you think needs it.
    (E) to who you think has need of it.

17. The painting titled "Solitude" is certainly one of the most remarkable studies <u>that was done by Gauguin.</u>

    (A) that was done by Gauguin.
    (B) that has been done.
    (C) that is done by Gauguin.
    (D) which Gauguin done.
    (E) that Gauguin done.

18. <u>Due to the pressure being placed</u> on the workers to meet the deadline, all leaves had to be cancelled.

    (A) Due to the pressure being placed
    (B) Due to the pressure placed
    (C) Due to the pressure having been placed
    (D) Notwithstanding the pressure being placed
    (E) Because of the pressure being placed

19. He plays the violin with ease and <u>with skill; hardly taking time</u> to glance at the score.

    (A) skill; hardly taking time
    (B) skill, hardly taking time
    (C) skill; scarcely taking time
    (D) skill. Hardly taking time
    (E) skill, he hardly takes time

20. When I was riding on the bus to school, my best friend <u>comes and sits beside me.</u>

    (A) comes and sits beside me.
    (B) comes and sits besides me.
    (C) came and sat beside me.
    (D) came and sat besides me.
    (E) comes to sit beside me.

21. If the highway is widened, the maple trees <u>that give such beauty to the summer and the fall</u> will have to be cut down.

    (A) that give such beauty to the summer and the fall
    (B) that had given such beauty to the summer and the fall
    (C) that makes the summer and fall so beautiful
    (D) which makes it so beautiful in the summer and the fall
    (E) that makes it so beautiful all summer and fall

22. He sings better <u>then any tenor</u> in the men's chorus.

    (A) then any tenor
    (B) than any other tenor
    (C) then any other tenor
    (D) of all the tenors
    (E) then the tenors

23. When the first quarter ended, the home team <u>were leading by ten points.</u>

    (A) were leading by ten points
    (B) leads by ten points
    (C) is leading by ten points
    (D) was leading by ten points
    (E) has a ten-point lead

24. Avoiding fatty foods, exercising regularly, <u>and visits to the doctor for annual blood tests were recommended</u> as an important regimen.

    (A) and visits to the doctor for annual blood tests were recommended
    (B) and visits to the doctor for annual blood testing was recommended
    (C) and visiting the doctor for annual blood tests were recommended
    (D) and annual visits to the doctor for blood tests were recommended
    (E) and visiting the doctor for annual blood tests was recommended

25. In the second act, <u>it shows very clearly that</u> her motivation is greed.

(A) it shows very clearly that

(B) it very clearly shows that

(C) the author shows very clearly that

(D) it is showed very clearly how

(E) the author showed how

26. <u>Between you and me, it is no longer so important as it once was</u> for you to pay cash for your supplies.

(A) Between you and me, it is no longer so important as it once was

(B) Between you and me, it is no longer as important as it once was

(C) Between you and I, it is no longer so important as it once was

(D) Between you and I, it is no longer as important as it once was

(E) Between us, it is not as important as it once was

27. Playing ball, swimming in the pool, and <u>a diet without starchy foods help</u> keep his weight down.

(A) a diet without starchy foods help

(B) avoiding starchy foods help

(C) dieting without starchy foods helps

(D) avoiding starchy foods helps

(E) a diet without starchy foods helped

28. According to the Farmer's Almanac, <u>it looks like this will be the coldest winter in many years.</u>

(A) it looks like this will be the coldest winter in many years.

(B) it looks like this winter will be colder than many other years.

(C) it looks like a cold winter is coming this year.

(D) this may be the coldest winter in many years.

(E) this year will be a cold winter.

29. To decipher the instructions for assembling this tuner <u>it demands the clairvoyance of genius</u>.

(A) it demands the clairvoyance of genius

(B) the clairvoyance of genius are demanded

(C) the clairvoyance of genius is demanded

(D) it demands genius clairvoyance

(E) demands the clairvoyance of genius

30. If <u>the stage sets were to be designed by him</u>, I would have more confidence in the production.

(A) the stage sets were to be designed by him

(B) he were designing the stage sets

(C) he were to be designing the stage sets

(D) the stage sets are designed by him

(E) the stage sets by him were to be designed

31. Jennifer lined the walls of her room with shelves, <u>making them straight by means of using a level.</u>

(A) making them straight by means of using a level.

(B) straightening them up by means of using a level.

(C) using a level to make them straight.

(D) making them, by means of a level, straight.

(E) using the means of a level to make them straight.

32. <u>Because the drug had been proved to cause cancer</u> in mice, the FDA banned its use as a food additive.

(A) Because the drug had been proved to cause

(B) Since the drug had been proved to cause

(C) Seeing as how the drug was proved to cause

(D) Because the drug had been proven to be a cause of

(E) Because the drug, as it proved, was a cause of

33. Some gardeners put dead leaves or straw be-tween the rows of seedlings so that the ground doesn't dry out and <u>you don't have to weed as much.</u>

   (A) you don't have to weed as much.

   (B) they don't have to weed as much.

   (C) they don't have weeding as much as before.

   (D) your weeding is less.

   (E) you don't have as much weeding to do.

34. If <u>all of this bickering were to be stopped by you children</u>, we might be able to reach an equitable solution.

   (A) all of this bickering were to be stopped by you children

   (B) all this bickering were stopped by you children

   (C) all of you children had stopped this bickering

   (D) all of this bickering stopped you chil-dren

   (E) you children stopped all of this bicker-ing

35. Perched on the roof like a fantastic mechanical bird, <u>electricity is generated by the windmill to light the classroom building.</u>

   (A) electricity is generated by the windmill to light the classroom building.

   (B) the classroom building is lit by electric-ity generated by the windmill.

   (C) the windmill's electricity is generated to light the classroom building.

   (D) the windmill generates electricity and lights the classroom building.

   (E) the windmill generates electricity to light the classroom building.

Revising Work in Progress

Directions: The selections that follow are early drafts of student essays in which each sentence has been numbered for easy reference. Fol-lowing each essay are questions that direct you to a part of the essay or to the entire essay. The questions focus upon improving sentence struc-ture and word choice, organization and devel-opment of the essay, and effectiveness of lan-guage for the intended purpose and audience of the work. For each question, choose the letter of the answer you consider to be correct, and mark the corresponding oval on your an-swer sheet.

Questions 36–40 are based on the following essay.

(1) I feel very strongly that it is important for everyone to protect the environment. (2) When I see people littering or graffiti on the streets, it really makes me mad. (3) Don't people realize what damage they are doing to the environment? (4) And what makes me even more infuriated is when I make a comment to one of these litterbugs and they tell me that I should mind my own business. (5) Indeed this is my business. (6) It is everybody's business.

(7) I once heard a story. (8) It is about an old man who was planting a tree. (9) When he was asked why he was planting a tree since he was so old. (10) He wouldn't be around probably to enjoy the shade of the tree since he was so elderly. (11) He told the person who criticized him that his fathers planted for him. (12) Now he was enjoy-ing the shade of those trees planted by those who came before. (13) He was planting so that his children and those who came after him would enjoy the fruits of his labor.

(14) To me this was a very wise comment. (15) I think that we should think of our children and those who come after us. (16) We must take care of our environment for their sake as well as for us. (17) And we should not be so quick to question the elderly.

36. Which of the following best describes sentence (1)?

    (A) It is too opinionated.

    (B) It introduces the topic effectively.

    (C) It may be deleted.

    (D) It is not consistent with the rest of the essay.

    (E) It is redundant.

37. Which of the following is true of sentence (3)?

    (A) It is rhetorical in nature.

    (B) It is too sarcastic.

    (C) It is not consistent with the rest of the paragraph.

    (D) It should be placed after sentence (6).

    (E) It is a fragment.

38. Which of the following best describes the purpose of the second paragraph?

    (A) To prove an illustrative story

    (B) To show a differing point of view

    (C) To give a historical basis

    (D) To show that there are good people as well as bad

    (E) To give needed facts

39. Sentence (11) can be joined to sentence (12) by adding which of the following words after sentence (11)?

    (A) but

    (B) however

    (C) although

    (D) thusly

    (E) and

40. The final sentence of the essay

    (A) is an excellent conclusion.

    (B) reinforces the writer's point of view.

    (C) can be deleted.

    (D) is the main idea of the essay.

    (E) could link paragraph 2 and paragraph 3.

Questions 41–45 are based on the following essay.

(1) Almost every time you pick up a newspaper or turn on a radio, you hear a report of child abuse. (2) Personally, I am appalled by this situation. (3) I think there is no excuse for adults to hurt poor, defenseless children, whether they hurt them psychologically, emotionally, or physically.

(4) The story of Paul for example. (5) Paul came to the shelter where I work. (6) Paul was an abused, 5-year-old little boy. (7) Paul was abused by his parents both physically and mentally. (8) He was actually abandoned. (9) He had scars and burns all over his body. (10) These were the outward signs of the physical abuse his parents had used as a means of discipline. (11) But worse than it were the scars he carried that no one could see. (12) Those were the scars that he had on his soul.

(13) I say we must pass stricter laws to punish parents who abuse their children. (14) Before they strike a child, parents must be made to think of all the harm they will be doing. (15) Parents who cannot help themselves must turn to agencies which can help you. (16) Child abuse is an evil that must be eliminated from our society.

41. Which of the following is the best revision of the underlined portion of sentence (3) below?

    I think there is no excuse for adults to hurt poor, defenseless children, whether <u>they hurt them</u> psychologically, emotionally, or physically.

    (A) either they injure them

    (B) injuring them

    (C) no one should hurt them

    (D) even if they hurt them

    (E) they must not be allowed to hurt them

42. Which of the following is the best revision of sentence (4)?

    (A) For example, the story of Paul.

    (B) Paul's story for example.

    (C) An example of Paul's story.

    (D) The story of Paul provides a good example.

    (E) Paul's story, for example, is a good one.

43. Which of the following is the best way to combine sentences (6), (7), and (8)?

    (A) Paul was an abused boy by his parents, who later abandoned him when he was 5 years old.

    (B) Paul's parents abandoned him and then abused him both physically and mentally, as a 5-year-old little boy.

    (C) Paul was abandoned by his parents who left him in the shelter after abusing him.

    (D) His parents abused and abandoned Paul, a 5-year-old little boy, both physically and mentally.

    (E) A 5-year-old little boy, Paul was abandoned by his parents who had abused him both physically and mentally.

44. In relation to the passage as a whole, which of the following best describes the writer's intention in the second paragraph?

    (A) To provide an illustrative anecdote

    (B) To present the problem

    (C) To provide a summary

    (D) To present contradictory evidence

    (E) To convince the reader to change his or her opinion

45. In the context of the sentences preceding and following sentence (15), which of the following is the best revision of sentence (15)?

    (A) If parents cannot be helped, we must turn to agencies that can help.

    (B) Parents who cannot help themselves must turn to agencies that can help them.

    (C) Agencies can provide help to parents who cannot be helped.

    (D) If parents are to be helped, you must turn to agencies that can help.

    (E) If you cannot help yourself, then we must seek the help of outside agencies.

Questions 46–50 are based on the following essay.

(1) Advocates of a student dress code maintain that proper attire and proper behavior are interrelated. (2) If a student dresses correctly, they will also behave correctly. (3) At least, that's what is claimed.

(4) I do not believe that this is a valid assumption. (5) I know many young people who come to class in a very informal fashion. (6) They wear sweat suits or cut-off jeans. (7) Sometimes they dress so sloppily that teachers or their peers make remarks to them. (8) And yet their grades are quite acceptable, or often even more than acceptable. (9) I feel that as long as a person performs well academically, the way they dress should be of no concern to others.

(10) I suppose that one day psychologists will conduct studies to test whether or not attire affects behavior. (11) If these studies prove that poor attire results in poor behavior, then school administrators will be justified in trying to establish and enforce a dress code. (12) But until that day comes, dress the way you feel most comfortable.

46. Which of the following is the best way to combine sentences (2) and (3)?

    (A) If you dress well, you will behave well, at least so they say.

    (B) They claim that if student dresses correctly, they will also behave correctly.

    (C) They claim that students who dress well also behave well.

    (D) As claimed by them, correct dress and correct behavior go hand-in-hand.

    (E) At least they claim that to dress correctly means you will behave correctly.

47. Which of the following best describes the chief purpose of sentence (4)?

    (A) To change the opinion of the reader

    (B) To prepare the reader for a second point of view

    (C) To offer an illustration or example

    (D) To provide a partial summary

    (E) To help the reader evaluate paragraph one

48. Which of the following is the best way to combine sentences (5) and (6)?
    - (A) I know many people who come to class dressed very informally in sweats or cut-off jeans.
    - (B) I know many students who dress informally, they even wear sweat suits or cut-off jeans.
    - (C) Many students I know come to class in sweats or jeans, this is informal dress.
    - (D) Students come to class dressed in sweats or other ways.
    - (E) If there are students who come to class dressed informally, wearing sweat suits or cut-off jeans.

49. Which of the following best describes the purpose of paragraph two?
    - (A) To provide a transition
    - (B) To continue the philosophy of the first paragraph
    - (C) To summarize the material previously offered
    - (D) To present material opposing that already presented
    - (E) To offer two diametrically opposing opinions

50. Which of the following is the best revision of the underlined portion of sentence (9) below?

    I feel that as long as a person performs well academically, the way they dress should be of no concern to others.
    - (A) how they dress should be of no concern to others.
    - (B) the way they dress should not concern others.
    - (C) their dress should be of no concern to others.
    - (D) what they wear or how they dress should be their own concern.
    - (E) the way he dresses should be of no concern to others.

Questions 51–55 are based on the following essay.

(1) Everybody is talking about gun control. (2) Some people say that according to the Bill of Rights, every person is allowed to carry a gun. (3) Others say that if you allow guns to be placed in the hands of every citizen, the crime rate will go up.

(4) I think that each person should be thoroughly investigated before they are allowed to own a gun. (5) I know that the rifle associations and all the hunting groups would not agree, but I do. (6) Just think what would happen if each family had a gun. (7) Children and teenagers would begin to experiment with these weapons. (8) At first, it would be fun. (9) But then they would put these guns to use, to commit armed robberies, petty thievery, murdering, and killing. (10) We would soon turn all our major cities into a replica of Dodge City and there would be chaos and lawlessness.

(11) If a person had legitimate need to own a gun, then he should get a permit. (12) This would allow the authorities time to investigate the background of the person who wants to own a gun. (13) Don't put guns in the hands of potential criminals, but screen each person carefully. (14) Perhaps this way we will lessen the number of crimes that plague our cities and also do away with many accidental shootings.

51. Which of the following choices below is the best way of combining sentences (2) and (3)?

    (A) There are some people who say that every person is entitled because of the Bill of Rights to possess a gun, others say that the crime rate will go up if guns are placed in the hands of every citizen.

    (B) There are those who say that the Bill of Rights entitles every person to bear firearms; others maintain that the crime rate will rise if guns are placed in the hands of every citizen.

    (C) Allowing guns in the hands of every citizen, contrary to the Bill of Rights, which states that every person should be allowed to bear arms, will cause the crime rate to rise.

    (D) Some people say that the Bill of Rights gives each person the ability to bear arms, others say that the crime rate will go up if this happens.

    (E) There are some who say that the crime rate will be affected by allowing us to bear arms, while others claim that the Bill of Rights addresses this issue.

52. Which of the following is the best revision of the underlined portion of sentence (4) below?

    I think that each person should be thoroughly investigated <u>before they are allowed to own a gun.</u>

    (A) prior to their owning a gun.

    (B) before a gun is issued to them.

    (C) before receiving permission to own a gun.

    (D) prior to the receipt of permission for them to own a gun.

    (E) before they may possess a gun.

53. Which of the following best describes the purpose of paragraph one?

    (A) To state the writer's opinion on the issue

    (B) To propose possible solutions to a difficult problem

    (C) To cause the reader to alter his opinion

    (D) To show two different points of view

    (E) To offer two cogent illustrations

54. Which of the following is the best revision of the underlined portion of sentence (9) below?

    But then they would put these guns to use, <u>to commit armed robberies, petty thievery, murdering, and killing.</u>

    (A) to commit armed robbery, petty thieving, and killing.

    (B) committing armed robbery, petty thieving, and for murdering.

    (C) to commit robbery, thievery, murder, and killing.

    (D) for robbing, thieving, and murder.

    (E) to commit armed robberies, petty thievery, and murder.

55. In the context of the sentences preceding and following sentence (13), which of the following is the best revision of sentence (13)?

    (A) Don't allow potential criminals to own guns, but let each person be screened carefully.

    (B) Guns should not be placed in the hands of potential criminals, each person being carefully screened.

    (C) Instead of putting guns in the hands of potential criminals, screen each person carefully.

    (D) Guns should not be put in the hands of potential criminals; rather, each person should be screened carefully.

    (E) Guns should not be placed in the hand of a potential criminal; but they should be carefully screened.

Section II

50 Questions

Time—45 minutes

Identifying Sentence Errors

Directions: Some of the sentences below contain an error in grammar, usage, word choice, or idiom. Other sentences are correct. Parts of each sentence are underlined and lettered. The error, if there is one, is contained in one of the underlined parts of the sentence. Assume that all other parts of the sentence are correct and cannot be changed. For each sentence, select the one underlined part that must be changed to make the sentence correct and mark its letter on your answer sheet. If there is no error in a sentence, mark answer choice (E). No sentence contains more than one error.

Example:

Being that it's such a lovely day, we are having
  A   B   C

a difficult time concentrating on our assignment.
             D

No error
E

Sample Answer:

● Ⓑ Ⓒ Ⓓ Ⓔ

56. The publisher said he would be happy to sup-
                          A

ply you with a new copy of the book, since its
           B   C

definitely better than the copy you already
                               D

own. No error
      E

57. He clearly saw you coming here as tangible
             A   B   C

evidence of your involvement in the

criminal act. No error
    D   E

58. When my grandfather comes to visit us, he
                  A   B

takes off his shoes and sets in the easy chair all
                 C   D

day. No error
      E

59. It is all ready too late for us to do our Christmas
   A   B   C

shopping in an uncrowded atmosphere. No error
        D   E

60. Lacking the idiomatic vocabulary necessary
   A

for true fluency, many students who study a
                 B

foreign language in school are unable to con-
                      C

verse comfortably in the language. No error
         D   E

61. As soon as he saw me, the interviewer's
                     A

attitude changed drastically; obviously he was
            B

prejudice against me for one reason or another.
   C   D

No error
E

62. Before they could adjourn for the day they
              A   B

must consider the group's petition. No error
C   D   E

63. The children <u>who</u> <u>I</u> observed at the theater
             A B
    seemed <u>enchanted</u> by the <u>antics</u> of the puppets.
               C   D
    <u>No error</u>
       E

64. Most animals cannot recognize <u>their</u> reflection
                                      A
    in a mirror <u>as themselves</u>; they usually react <u>as if</u>
                    B   C
    confronted by another member of <u>their species</u>.
                                         D
    <u>No error</u>
       E

65. Of the two candidates applying for the <u>position</u>,
                                               A
    we have <u>no doubt</u> that Jim is <u>likely</u> to be the
                B   C
    <u>most favored</u>. <u>No error</u>
        D   E

Restructuring Sentences

Directions: Below each of the following sentences are directions for revising the sentence and a choice of five words or phrases that may occur in your revised sentence. Mentally rephrase each sentence according to the directions given. Then, choose the lettered word or phrase that is included in your revised sentence and blacken the corresponding space on your answer sheet.

If you think of a sentence that contains none of the words listed in the choices, rephrase the sentence again to include a word or phrase that is listed. Take care to make only those changes that the directions require and to choose an answer that is part of a complete and grammatically correct sentence.

66. Every one of the nurses was awarded her credentials with honors.
    Begin with <u>All of the nurses</u>.
    (A) should have been awarded her
    (B) were awarded their
    (C) was awarded their
    (D) had been awarded their
    (E) had been awarded its

67. Faulkner's novels' language resembles the language of Proust.
    Begin with <u>The language of Faulkner's novels</u>.
    (A) is somewhat as Proust.
    (B) is somewhat like Proust.
    (C) is somewhat like that of Proust's.
    (D) is somewhat as Proust's.
    (E) is somewhat like Proust's novels.

68. I spent many hours at work in the library, and, therefore, I expected to be paid accordingly.
    Begin with <u>Because</u>.
    (A) I should spend
    (B) ; and, therefore,
    (C) . Therefore,
    (D) library, I
    (E) accordingly; I

69. Were they really the students who cheated on the test?

    Begin with <u>Was it really</u>.

    (A) they who
    (B) them who
    (C) they which
    (D) them that
    (E) they whom

70. If you can pinpoint your errors, you will at least have a chance to correct them.

    Begin with <u>Pinpoint</u>.

    (A) errors, you
    (B) had a chance
    (C) having a chance
    (D) errors, then
    (E) errors, and

71. Considerable energy has been expended by those who criticize the present system.

    Begin with <u>Those who</u>.

    (A) had expended
    (B) had to expend
    (C) have expended
    (D) expenditure
    (E) in expenditure

72. The chairperson was unable to draw conclusions and to make recommendations.

    Substitute <u>could neither</u> for <u>was unable</u>.

    (A) conclusions or make
    (B) conclusions and make
    (C) conclusions nor make
    (D) conclusions making
    (E) conclusions to make

73. My father, my mother, my sister, and I were invited to the cookout.

    Begin with <u>They invited</u>.

    (A) and I to
    (B) and myself to
    (C) and I for
    (D) and me to
    (E) and me too

74. My father's old Ford is a very early model. It should be restored and treasured as an antique.

    Combine the sentences.

    (A) model; should
    (B) Ford a
    (C) model should
    (D) restored and treasured;
    (E) model, should

75. That he was bitterly disappointed was clearly indicated by his tone.

    Begin with <u>His tone</u>.

    (A) clearly implied
    (B) clearly inferred
    (C) clearly remarked
    (D) implied a clear inference
    (E) clearly implied and inferred

76. Our former professor was a brilliant speaker and an able writer.

    Change <u>was</u> to <u>was not only</u>.

    (A) speaker and as well
    (B) speaker as well as
    (C) speaker, was a
    (D) speaker but also
    (E) speaker, and in addition

77. We could find no precedent for the judge's outrageous ruling in this case.

    Begin with <u>No precedent</u>.

    (A) can be found
    (B) could be found
    (C) is being found
    (D) cannot be found
    (E) can find

78. Ultimately, the President is responsible for deciding how each branch of the armed forces will operate, since he is the commander-in-chief of the military.

    Omit <u>since he is</u>.

    (A) President, the
    (B) operate; the
    (C) operate. The
    (D) , military ultimately
    (E) responsibility,

79. Because of her lovely personality, Josie had many friends.

    Begin with <u>Friends</u>.

    (A) flocked to Josie because of

    (B) flaunted Josie because of

    (C) flocked to Josie while

    (D) flocked to Josie although

    (E) congregated around Josie and

80. Here in New York City, we have people of various ethnic backgrounds.

    Begin with <u>We have</u>.

    (A) New York City people

    (B) backgrounds; here in New York City

    (C) with various New York City backgrounds

    (D) people in New York City here

    (E) ethnic backgrounds here

Revising Work in Progress

Directions: The selections that follow are early drafts of student essays in which each sentence has been numbered for easy reference. Following each essay are questions that direct you to a part of the essay or to the entire essay. The questions focus upon improving structure and word choice, organization and development of the essay, and effectiveness of language for the intended purpose and audience of the work. For each question, choose the letter of the answer you consider to be correct, and mark the corresponding oval on your answer sheet.

Questions 81–85 are based on the following essay.

(1) It seems that every time I pick up a newspaper today, I hear about young children committing crimes. (2) I mean serious crimes like murder and robbery, not small ones like shoplifting or vandalism. (3) Not that I approve of these crimes either because I think all crimes are wrong.

(4) I think that the main trouble is that parents do not take a big enough interest in their children. (5) I feel that it is the responsibility of the parents to show an interest and to watch over them even beginning when they are very young. (6) Chil-dren must feel that they can't get away with murder as they are growing up. (7) They must have the careful supervision that only their parents can give them. (8) They must also know that if they do something wrong they will be punished. (9) I feel too that the punishment should fit the crime.

(10) If a child or teenager is arrested for speeding then he should lose the privilege of driving the family car. (11) If a young person stays out past his curfew, then he should be grounded. (12) I think that perhaps this may be a beginning to keep people under control. (13) I really feel that everything starts with supervision and that supervision begins in the home. (14) I also feel that adults must be good role models.

81. Which is the most effective way of revising the underlined portions of sentences (1) and (2) (shown below) so that the two sentences are combined?

    It seems that every time I pick up a newspaper today, I hear about young children committing <u>crime. I mean serious crimes</u> like murder and robbery, not small ones like shoplifting or vandalism.

    (A) crimes that involve serious matters like crimes

    (B) serious crimes

    (C) felonies or serious crimes

    (D) major crimes, I mean serious crimes

    (E) crimes, I mean serious crimes

82. In sentence (1) the words *I hear about*

    (A) should be changed to *I have heard about.*

    (B) should be deleted entirely.

    (C) should be changed to *we read about.*

    (D) should be changed to *it speaks about.*

    (E) should be changed to *I read about.*

83. Which of the following is true of sentence (9)?

    (A) It should be the opening sentence of the third paragraph.

    (B) It is perfect where it is.

    (C) It should be deleted.

    (D) It provides a good thesis statement.

    (E) It is a rhetorical statement.

84. One of the main criticisms of this essay is that it

    (A) does not present a definite point of view.
    (B) is too radical in content.
    (C) is subject to criticism by young people.
    (D) tends to be repetitive.
    (E) has no relevance.

85. The concluding sentence of this essay

    (A) should be deleted.
    (B) is too repetitive.
    (C) is inconsistent with the tone of the writer.
    (D) is better used as the opening sentence of the final paragraph.
    (E) is excellent as it stands.

Questions 86–90 are based on the following essay.

(1) Prayer has no place in public schools. (2) Traditionally, we have always had a separation between church and state. (3) Recognizing the dangers of having a state religion, our founding fathers framed our Constitution in such a way so as to insure that there would be no one official religion.

(4) Now there are many municipalities that are attempting to change this policy. (5) I recently read that one small town wanted each class in its public school system to start each day with a reading from the Bible. (6) Many residents felt that reading a biblical passage, perhaps a psalm, would set a positive spiritual tone for the students, some objected.

(7) They said that this violated separation between church and state. (8) They pointed out that it was unfair to students who might not believe in the Bible and who were not part of any religious upbringing.

(9) I feel that a wholesome atmosphere can be created in our schools without coating it with religion. (10) It should be free of partisan spirituality which is likely to occur if prayer is introduced into the classroom. (11) Religious training is best left up to the parents. (12) Schools should stick with academics.

86. Which of the following best describes the main purpose of sentence (1)?

    (A) To clearly and strongly state the writer's opinion on the issue
    (B) To present the problem
    (C) To introduce the idea that this is a controversial issue
    (D) To show a fair-minded and unbiased point of view
    (E) To indicate that a problem exists and must be addressed

87. Which of the following is the best revision of the underlined portion of sentence (3) below?

    Recognizing the dangers of having a state religion, our founding fathers framed our Constitution in such a way so as to insure that there would be no one official religion.

    (A) religion. Our founding fathers framed our Constitution in such a way as to insure that there would be no one official religion.
    (B) religion; our founding fathers framed our Constitution to avoid this.
    (C) religion, our founding fathers fashioned a Constitution that would prevent having one official religion.
    (D) religion and framing our Constitution in such a way as to insure that there would be no one official religion.
    (E) religion, our Constitution was framed in such a way as to avoid this.

88. Which of the following is the best revision of the underlined portion of sentence (6) below?

Many residents felt that reading a biblical passage, perhaps a psalm, would set a positive spiritual tone for the <u>students, some objected.</u>

(A) students, some had objections.

(B) students, some others objected.

(C) students; however, they objected.

(D) students. However, some townspeople objected.

(E) students; however, some were objections.

89. Which of the following is the best way to combine sentences (7) and (8)?

(A) They said this violated the separation between church and state, and they pointed out that it was unfair to some students.

(B) They said this violated the separation between church and state, and it was unfair to students who did not believe in religion.

(C) They said that Bible reading in school violated the separation between church and state and was unfair to those students who did not believe in the Bible or belong to any religious group.

(D) They said that Bible reading violated the separation between church and state and was unfair to students who might not believe in the Bible or belong to any religious group.

(E) Saying that this violated separation between church and state and pointing out that it was unfair to students who might not believe in the Bible and who were not part of any religious upbringing.

90. Which of the following is the best revision of the underlined portion of sentence (10) below?

<u>It should be free of partisan spirituality</u>, which is likely to occur if prayer is introduced into the classroom.

(A) The school should be free of partisan spirituality

(B) It should be freed from partisan spirituality

(C) Partisan spirituality should be eliminated

(D) The school should free partisan spirituality

(E) It should eliminated partisan spirituality

Analyzing Writing

Directions: This section presents two prose passages. Following each passage are questions that test how well you recognize the purpose of the writer and the characteristics of good writing. As you read each passage, bear in mind that it may be part of a longer piece of writing and it might not, as a result, present a complete analysis or discussion of the issues under consideration. Read each passage carefully, then answer each question by selecting the letter of the answer choice you consider to be correct.

Questions 91–98 refer to the following paragraph.

(1) A Polish proverb claims that fish, to taste right, should swim three times. (2) To taste right it should swim in water, in butter, and in wine. (3) The early efforts of scientists in the food industry were directed at improving the preparation, preservation, and distribution. (4) Our memories of certain foodstuffs eaten during the Second World War suggest that, although these might have been nutritious. (5) They certainly did not taste good nor were they particularly appealing in appearance or smell. (6) With regard to touch, systems of classification are of little value because of the extraordinary sensitivity of the skin. (7) This neglect of the sensory appeal of foods is happily becoming a thing of the past. (8) A book grew out of this course. (9) Indeed, in 1957, the

University of California considered the subject of such main importance to set up a course in the analysis of foods by sensory methods. (10) The authors hope that it will be useful to food technologists in industry. (11) They also hope to help others researching the problem of the sensory evaluation of foods according to sight, taste, and smell.

91. Sentence (2) would be best if

    (A) it were left as it is.

    (B) the first 6 words were omitted and the remainder of the sentence joined to sentence (1).

    (C) the part after *water* were omitted.

    (D) it were joined to sentence (1) with *since*.

    (E) it were omitted entirely.

92. Sentence (3) would be most improved if

    (A) it began with *At that time*.

    (B) it ended with *of fish in butter and wine*.

    (C) it ended with *of nutritious food*.

    (D) the part after *preparation* were omitted.

    (E) the word *preservation* were omitted.

93. What should be done with sentence (4)?

    (A) It should be left as it is.

    (B) It should be joined to sentence (3) with *since*.

    (C) It should be joined to sentence (2) with *and*.

    (D) It should begin with *Thus*.

    (E) It should be joined to sentence (5).

94. What should be done with sentence (6)?

    (A) It should be left as it is.

    (B) It should follow sentence (3).

    (C) It should be made into two separate sentences.

    (D) The part after *value* should be omitted.

    (E) It should be omitted entirely.

95. Sentence (8) is best placed

    (A) after sentence (6).

    (B) after sentence (3).

    (C) after sentence (9).

    (D) after sentence (11).

    (E) after sentence (12).

96. In sentence (9), *such main* should be

    (A) left as it is.

    (B) changed to *charitable*.

    (C) changed to *sufficient*.

    (D) changed to *insufficient*.

    (E) changed to *such suffering*.

97. What should be done with sentence (11)?

    (A) It should be left as it is.

    (B) It should begin with *Thus*.

    (C) The part after *foods* should be omitted.

    (D) It should end with *forever*.

    (E) The part after *sight* should be omitted.

98. If the passage is to be divided into two paragraphs, the second paragraph should begin with

    (A) sentence (7).

    (B) sentence (6).

    (C) sentence (11).

    (D) sentence (5).

    (E) sentence (3).

Questions 99–105 refer to the following paragraph.

(1) What is to happen to transportation in the future? (2) Evidently there are gargantuan and important changes in prospect. (3) A decade or so from now, there will have been yet another transformation in the way in which people and their goods. (4) This occurs because better methods of travelling have come along or simply because the old methods have become intolerable. (5) Old techniques are being faced with extinction, destruction, and annihilation. (6) The development of recent decades most likely to be continued is the tendency for alternative methods of travel to co-exist. (7) Instead, potential travelers have a choice. (8) Within large cities, for example, un-

derground transport is usually an alternative to several ways of travelling on the surface. (9) This, after all, is how the great oil companies organize their affairs. (10) Choices between coexisting alternatives are usually made on the grounds of speed, cost, and comfort.

99. In sentence (2), the word *gargantuan* would be best

   (A) left as it is.

   (B) changed to *vastly*.

   (C) changed to *huge*.

   (D) changed to *implication*.

   (E) changed to *hugeness*.

100. The meaning of sentence (3) would be clearest if

   (A) the sentence were left as it is.

   (B) the sentence were begun with *Nevertheless, only a decade*.

   (C) the phrase *are moved from place to place* were added after *goods*.

   (D) everything in the sentence after *transformation* were omitted.

   (E) it were made into two sentences.

101. Sentence (4) is best placed

   (A) where it is now.

   (B) after sentence (1).

   (C) before sentence (1).

   (D) after sentence (7).

   (E) after sentence (5).

102. Sentence (5) would be best if

   (A) it were left as it is.

   (B) it were made into two sentences.

   (C) the part after *extinction* were omitted.

   (D) the part after *faced* were omitted.

   (E) if were joined to sentence (4) with *since*.

103. What should be done with sentence (9)?

   (A) It should be left as it is.

   (B) It should be made into two sentences.

   (C) It should be moved to the end of the passage.

   (D) It should be lengthened to give more information about *oil companies*.

   (E) It should be omitted entirely.

104. Sentence (7) should begin

   (A) the way it begins now.

   (B) with *Potential travelers, however*.

   (C) with *This happens because*.

   (D) with *This potential*.

   (E) with *Anyway potential*.

105. If the passage is to be divided into two paragraphs, the second paragraph should begin with

   (A) sentence (6).

   (B) sentence (10).

   (C) sentence (7).

   (D) sentence (4).

   (E) sentence (3).

End of Practice Examination II

Answer Key

Section I

1.	A	12.	E	23.	D	34.	E	45.	B
2.	E	13.	A	24.	C	35.	E	46.	C
3.	C	14.	A	25.	C	36.	B	47.	B
4.	A	15.	B	26.	A	37.	A	48.	A
5.	B	16.	D	27.	B	38.	A	49.	D
6.	E	17.	A	28.	D	39.	E	50.	E
7.	C	18.	E	29.	E	40.	C	51.	B
8.	B	19.	B	30.	B	41.	B	52.	C
9.	C	20.	C	31.	C	42.	D	53.	D
10.	B	21.	A	32.	A	43.	E	54.	E
11.	A	22.	B	33.	B	44.	A	55.	D

Section II

56.	C	66.	B	76.	D	86.	A	96.	C
57.	A	67.	C	77.	B	87.	C	97.	C
58.	C	68.	D	78.	A	88.	D	98.	A
59.	B	69.	A	79.	A	89.	C	99.	C
60.	E	70.	E	80.	E	90.	A	100.	C
61.	C	71.	C	81.	B	91.	B	101.	E
62.	C	72.	C	82.	E	92.	C	102.	C
63.	A	73.	D	83.	A	93.	E	103.	E
64.	E	74.	E	84.	D	94.	E	104.	D
65.	D	75.	A	85.	A	95.	C	105.	A

Explanatory Answers

Section I

1. **The correct answer is (A).** The correct verb is to *pore over*, meaning to study carefully. To *pour* means to flow continuously.

2. **The correct answer is (E).** The sentence is correct.

3. **The correct answer is (C).** The subject is *being a real estate agent.* The pronoun *it* is superfluous.

4. **The correct answer is (A).** *Taste* is a linking verb that should be modified by an adjective (*sweeter*), not an adverb (*more sweetly*).

5. **The correct answer is (B).** *You are required* is needed to agree with *your federal tax return.*

6. **The correct answer is (E).** The sentence is correct.

7. **The correct answer is (C).** To compare weather conditions for two days use the comparative *worse.*

8. **The correct answer is (B).** When *all* refers to the total number of persons or things in a group, it takes a plural verb: *All were lost.*

9. **The correct answer is (C).** The preposition *except for* takes an objective pronoun *except for Meryl and me.*

10. **The correct answer is (B).** *Wrote* is past tense. The events that preceded the writing must be described in the past perfect: *had visited* and *had seen.*

11. **The correct answer is (A).** Use the adverb *brusquely* to parallel the adverb *quickly.*

12. **The correct answer is (E).** The sentence is correct.

13. **The correct answer is (A).** The object of the verb *ask* must be in the objective case; *she* is the nominative case and must be replaced by *her.*

14. **The correct answer is (A).** A singular possessive pronoun (*one's, his,* or *her*) is required to agree with the singular subject *one.*

15. **The correct answer is (B).** The sentence requires the noun *advice,* not the verb *advise.*

16. **The correct answer is (D).** The nominative *whoever* is required as the subject of the verb *need.* Nothing is gained by changing the simple *need* to the more cumbersome *has need of.*

17. **The correct answer is (A).** The verb agrees with *one*, which is outside of the prepositional phrase. Choices (B), (C), (D), and (E) are ungrammatical.

18. **The correct answer is (E).** The subordinate clause should be introduced by a subordinating conjunction, such as *Because,* and not by the phrase *Due to.*

19. **The correct answer is (B).** The semicolon is incorrect since a comma is required to separate the independent clause from the dependent clause. Choice (E) is incorrect since a comma cannot be employed to separate two independent clauses.

20. **The correct answer is (C).** The first verb (*was riding*) sets the time for the verbs to follow (*came* and *sat*). Choices (A), (B), and (E) shift from past to present tense. Choice (C) incorrectly used *besides,* which means *in addition to,* in place of *beside,* which means *close to.*

21. **The correct answer is (A).** The sentence is correct. The antecedent of *that* is *trees,* so the verb must be plural.

22. **The correct answer is (B).** In the comparison, the correct phrase is "than any *other*. . ."

23. **The correct answer is (D).** The collective noun *team* when thought of as a unit takes a singular verb. Since the first verb (*ended*) is past tense, the second must also reflect past time (*was leading*). Choice (A) is a plural verb form. Choices (B), (C), and (E) are all present tense.

24. **The correct answer is (C).** Correct parallel structure requires all of the phrases to begin with *-ing* verb forms as in choices (C) and (E). However, the compound subject requires a plural verb (*were recommended*), which is found only in choice (C).

25. **The correct answer is (C).** The pronoun *it* is unclear; the verb *shows* requires a more definite subject. Both choices (D) and (E) provide a suitable subject. However, the author showed *that*, not *how*, her motivation is greed.

26. **The correct answer is (A).** The sentence is correct.

27. **The correct answer is (B).** To maintain parallel structure, the participle *avoiding* is required. The verb must be the plural *help* to agree with the compound subject.

28. **The correct answer is (D).** The original sentence uses *like* where *as if* is required. Choices (B) and (C) have the same problem. Choice (E) is not idiomatic. Choice (D) is both correct and concise.

29. **The correct answer is (E).** The use of *it* in the original sentence is awkward and unnecessary.

30. **The correct answer is (B).** Avoid the awkward use of the passive.

31. **The correct answer is (C).** *By means of* means the same as *using*; the use of the two together is redundant.

32. **The correct answer is (A).** The sentence is correct.

33. **The correct answer is (B).** Do not switch from the third person (*gardeners*) to the second person (*you*) in the middle of a sentence.

34. **The correct answer is (E).** Avoid the awkward use of the passive as in choices (A) and (B) and unnecessary shifts in tense as in (C).

35. **The correct answer is (E).** The original sentence contains a dangling phrase. Since *perched* must refer to *windmill, windmill* should be made the subject of the sentence.

36. **The correct answer is (B).** The first sentence effectively introduces the topic, the protection of the environment. It gives the point of view of the writer, and this point of view is consistent with the remainder of the essay.

37. **The correct answer is (A).** The question posed does not seek an answer since the answer is an obvious one. It is simply a literary device known as a rhetorical question.

38. **The correct answer is (A).** The second paragraph tends to back up the author's view by giving an illustrative fable.

39. **The correct answer is (E).** Sentence (12) naturally follows sentence (11), and thus the coordinating conjunction *and* is the best choice.

40. **The correct answer is (C).** The final sentence has no real relevance to the rest of the essay, an essay that deals with the environment and not with our relationship with older people.

41. **The correct answer is (B).** As written, the sentence contains two pronouns that lack clear antecedents. Choices (A) and (D) have the same problem. Choices (C) and (E) have comma splice errors. Only choice (B) correctly eliminates the pronoun confusion.

42. **The correct answer is (D).** Sentence (4) is a fragment. Choices (A), (B), and (C) have the same problem. Both choices (D) and (E) are complete sentences, but only choice (D) makes sense in the passage.

43. **The correct answer is (E).** Only choice (E) contains all the essential information from sentences (6), (7), and (8) and places it in the proper tense sequence. The other choices are awkward rephrasings or, as in the case of choice (C), omit material, changing the meaning of the sentences.

44. **The correct answer is (A).** Paragraph two presents an example to illustrate the main position of the writer, that child abuse is terrible.

45. **The correct answer is (B).** Sentence (14) is in the third person (before *they* strike...*parents* must be). Sentence (15) starts out in the same third person, but it ends up with a second person pronoun (*you*). Choice (B) starts and ends in the third person, thus avoiding the shifts apparent in choices (A), (D), and (E). Choice (C) makes no sense.

46. **The correct answer is (C).** Choice (A) switches unnecessarily to the second person (*you*). Choice (B) has an agreement problem, using the plural pronoun *they* to refer to the singular noun *student*. Choices (D) and (E) are awkward. Choice (C) is best.

47. **The correct answer is (B).** Sentence (4) states that the material presented in the first paragraph, that a dress code is important, may not be valid. This paves the way for the presentation of another point of view.

48. **The correct answer is (A).** Choices (B) and (C) contain comma splice errors. Choice (E) is a fragment. Choice (D) is awkward and omits details. Choice (A) is best.

49. **The correct answer is (D).** Paragraph one presents the opinion of those who favor a dress code. Paragraph two presents arguments against a dress code. Since paragraph two offers material opposing that already presented, choice (D) is best.

50. **The correct answer is (E).** The antecedent of *they* appears to be *a person,* but *they* is a plural pronoun, and *person* is a singular noun. Choices (A), (B), (C), and (D) do not address this problem. Choice (E) does and is correct.

51. **The correct answer is (B).** Choices (A) and (D) are incorrect since they contain comma splice errors. Choices (C) and (E) change the facts given in the essay and are, therefore, poor choices. Choice (B) is best.

52. **The correct answer is (C).** The pronoun agreeing with *each person* should be singular. Choices (A), (B), (D), and (E) contain plural pronouns and are, therefore, wrong. Choice (C) is best.

53. **The correct answer is (D).** In the first paragraph, the writer states that there are two camps, one believing in gun control and the other opposed to it. Choice (D) is correct.

54. **The correct answer is (E).** There is a problem with parallel structure in the underlined portion. In addition, *murdering* and *killing* are redundant. Only choice (E) corrects these two problems.

55. **The correct answer is (D).** Sentence (13) is phrased as a direct command and is not in keeping with the tone of the other sentences. Choices (A) and (C) do not correct this and are poor choices. Choice (B) is awkward grammatically, and choice (E) is poor since the antecedent of the plural pronoun *they* is *criminal,* a singular noun.

Section II

56. **The correct answer is (C).** The contraction for *it is* is written *it's.*

57. **The correct answer is (A).** The gerund *coming* is preceded by the possessive *your.*

58. **The correct answer is (C).** The standard form is *sits.*

59. **The correct answer is (B).** The correct word is *already.*

60. **The correct answer is (E).** The sentence is correct.

61. **The correct answer is (C).** The correct word is *prejudiced.*

62. **The correct answer is (C).** The verb form *could adjourn* establishes the action as past tense. Therefore the second clause must also be in the past tense: not *must* consider but *had to* consider.

63. **The correct answer is (A).** As the object of *I observed, who* must be in the objective case: *whom.*

64. **The correct answer is (E).** The sentence is correct.

65. **The correct answer is (D).** The comparative *more* is required since two people are mentioned.

66. **The correct answer is (B).** All of the nurses *were awarded their* credentials with honors.

67. **The correct answer is (C).** The language of Faulkner's novels *is somewhat like that of* Proust's.

68. **The correct answer is (D).** Because I spent many hours at work in the *library, I* expected to be paid accordingly.

69. **The correct answer is (A).** Was it really *they who* cheated on the test?

70. **The correct answer is (E).** Pinpoint your *errors,* and you will at least have a chance to correct them.

71. **The correct answer is (C).** Those who criticize the present system *have expended* considerable energy.

72. **The correct answer is (C).** The chairperson could neither draw *conclusions nor make* recommendations.

73. **The correct answer is (D).** They invited my mother, my father, my sister, *and me* to the cookout.

74. **The correct answer is (E).** My father's old Ford, a very early *model, should* be restored and treasured as an antique.

75. **The correct answer is (A).** His tone *clearly implied* that he was bitterly disappointed.

76. **The correct answer is (D).** Our former professor was not only a brilliant *speaker but also* an able writer.

77. **The correct answer is (B).** No precedent *could be found* for the judge's outrageous ruling in this case.

78. **The correct answer is (A).** Ultimately, the *President, the* commander-in-chief of the military, is responsible for deciding how each branch of the armed forces will operate.

79. **The correct answer is (A).** Friends *flocked to Josie because of* her lovely personality.

80. **The correct answer is (E).** We have people of various *ethnic backgrounds here* in New York City.

81. **The correct answer is (B).** The words *I mean serious crimes* repeats what has been indicated and therefore can easily be deleted.

82. **The correct answer is (E).** We *read* newspapers and therefore, for clarity and consistence, it would be best to select choice (E). Choice (C) changes the pronoun from singular to plural and is therefore not correct.

83. **The correct answer is (A).** Sentence (9) introduces the idea of the final paragraph and would therefore be a good opening sentence of the third paragraph.

84. **The correct answer is (D).** The only valid response is choice (D) since the writer tends to be wordy and repetitive. The other suggestions are not valid criticisms.

85. **The correct answer is (A).** The final sentence introduces a completely new concept, one which the writer never develops. It would best be omitted.

86. **The correct answer is (A).** Sentence (1) is a clear and forceful statement of the writer's position on the subject of prayer in the public school.

87. **The correct answer is (C).** Sentence (3) is wordy. Choice (C) offers a better version of the same thought. Choice (A) makes a fragment out of the first part of the sentence. Choice (B) contains an incorrect use of the semicolon. Choice (D) makes the entire sentence a fragment, and choice (E) creates a dangling modifier.

88. **The correct answer is (D).** Sentence (6) has a comma splice error and an ambiguous *some*. Choices (A) and (B) have the same problems. Choice (C) corrects the comma splice, but introduces an ambiguous *they*. Choice (E) does not make sense. Choice (D) corrects both the comma splice and the ambiguity.

89. **The correct answer is (C).** Sentences (7) and (8) contain ambiguous pronouns (*this* and *it*). Choices (A) and (B) have the same problem. Choice (D) changes the intended meaning. It is not *Bible reading* that the townspeople object to, but rather Bible reading in *school*. Choice (E) is a fragment. Choice (C) is best.

90. **The correct answer is (A).** *It* in sentence (10) has no clear antecedent. Choice (A) corrects this error. Either the other choices do not address this error or they change the meaning of the sentence.

91. **The correct answer is (B).** The repetition of the words "to taste right it should swim" makes an awkward transition between sentences (1) and (2). Omitting this phrase and adding the remainder of sentence (2) to sentence (1) eliminates this clumsiness.

92. **The correct answer is (C).** As sentence (3) stands, it is not clear exactly what is being prepared, preserved, and distributed. The addition "of nutritious food" clarifies this.

93. **The correct answer is (E).** Sentence (4) is not a complete sentence until joined with sentence (5).

94. **The correct answer is (E).** Sentence (6) discusses the sense of "touch," which is largely irrelevant to the sensory evaluation of food, the subject of the paragraph.

95. **The correct answer is (C).** Sentence (8) is an extension of the train of thought in sentence (9) and thus should follow it.

96. **The correct answer is (C).** The adjective "sufficient" is defined as enough or adequate and most accurately completes the meaning of sentence (9).

97. **The correct answer is (C).** The adjective "sensory" and the phrase "according to sight, taste, and smell" convey the same meaning. Thus, the elimination of the phrase makes this a better sentence.

98. **The correct answer is (A).** Sentence (7) introduces the research currently being done on the theme set forth in the first six sentences.

99. **The correct answer is (C).** *Gargantuan* is an adjective defined as giant in size. *Huge,* an adjective defined as very large or immense, is less dramatic and thus more appropriate to the factual tone of the passage.

100. **The correct answer is (C).** The addition of *are moved from place to place* is necessary to complete sentence (3).

101. **The correct answer is (E).** Sentence (4) completes the train of thought of sentence (5) and thus should follow it. The subject of sentence (4), *this,* refers to the extinction of old techniques described in sentence (5).

102. **The correct answer is (C).** *Extinction, destruction, and annihilation* mean essentially the same thing. Thus, the elimination of the latter two prevents wordiness.

103. **The correct answer is (E).** Sentence (9) discusses *oil companies* in a passage whose theme is transportation. It is irrelevant and should be omitted.

104. **The correct answer is (D).** *Instead,* an adverb which means in place of the one mentioned, should be replaced with *Thus.*

105. **The correct answer is (A).** Sentence (6), which introduces the most recent developments in transportation, is the most appropriate spot to begin a new paragraph.

Practice Examination II Diagnostic Chart

Question Type	Approx. % of Section	Question Numbers	Number of Questions	Number Wrong
Section I:				
Identifying Sentence Errors	28%	1–15	15	_____
Improving Sentences	36%	16–35	20	_____
Revising Work in Progress	36%	36–55	20	_____
Section II:				
Identifying Sentence Errors	20%	56–65	10	_____
Restructuring Sentences	30%	66–80	15	_____
Revising Work in Progress	20%	81–90	10	_____
Analyzing Writing	30%	91–105	15	_____

Answer Sheet for Practice Examination III

Section I

1 Ⓐ Ⓑ Ⓒ Ⓓ Ⓔ	12 Ⓐ Ⓑ Ⓒ Ⓓ Ⓔ	23 Ⓐ Ⓑ Ⓒ Ⓓ Ⓔ	34 Ⓐ Ⓑ Ⓒ Ⓓ Ⓔ	45 Ⓐ Ⓑ Ⓒ Ⓓ Ⓔ
2 Ⓐ Ⓑ Ⓒ Ⓓ Ⓔ	13 Ⓐ Ⓑ Ⓒ Ⓓ Ⓔ	24 Ⓐ Ⓑ Ⓒ Ⓓ Ⓔ	35 Ⓐ Ⓑ Ⓒ Ⓓ Ⓔ	46 Ⓐ Ⓑ Ⓒ Ⓓ Ⓔ
3 Ⓐ Ⓑ Ⓒ Ⓓ Ⓔ	14 Ⓐ Ⓑ Ⓒ Ⓓ Ⓔ	25 Ⓐ Ⓑ Ⓒ Ⓓ Ⓔ	36 Ⓐ Ⓑ Ⓒ Ⓓ Ⓔ	47 Ⓐ Ⓑ Ⓒ Ⓓ Ⓔ
4 Ⓐ Ⓑ Ⓒ Ⓓ Ⓔ	15 Ⓐ Ⓑ Ⓒ Ⓓ Ⓔ	26 Ⓐ Ⓑ Ⓒ Ⓓ Ⓔ	37 Ⓐ Ⓑ Ⓒ Ⓓ Ⓔ	48 Ⓐ Ⓑ Ⓒ Ⓓ Ⓔ
5 Ⓐ Ⓑ Ⓒ Ⓓ Ⓔ	16 Ⓐ Ⓑ Ⓒ Ⓓ Ⓔ	27 Ⓐ Ⓑ Ⓒ Ⓓ Ⓔ	38 Ⓐ Ⓑ Ⓒ Ⓓ Ⓔ	49 Ⓐ Ⓑ Ⓒ Ⓓ Ⓔ
6 Ⓐ Ⓑ Ⓒ Ⓓ Ⓔ	17 Ⓐ Ⓑ Ⓒ Ⓓ Ⓔ	28 Ⓐ Ⓑ Ⓒ Ⓓ Ⓔ	39 Ⓐ Ⓑ Ⓒ Ⓓ Ⓔ	50 Ⓐ Ⓑ Ⓒ Ⓓ Ⓔ
7 Ⓐ Ⓑ Ⓒ Ⓓ Ⓔ	18 Ⓐ Ⓑ Ⓒ Ⓓ Ⓔ	29 Ⓐ Ⓑ Ⓒ Ⓓ Ⓔ	40 Ⓐ Ⓑ Ⓒ Ⓓ Ⓔ	51 Ⓐ Ⓑ Ⓒ Ⓓ Ⓔ
8 Ⓐ Ⓑ Ⓒ Ⓓ Ⓔ	19 Ⓐ Ⓑ Ⓒ Ⓓ Ⓔ	30 Ⓐ Ⓑ Ⓒ Ⓓ Ⓔ	41 Ⓐ Ⓑ Ⓒ Ⓓ Ⓔ	52 Ⓐ Ⓑ Ⓒ Ⓓ Ⓔ
9 Ⓐ Ⓑ Ⓒ Ⓓ Ⓔ	20 Ⓐ Ⓑ Ⓒ Ⓓ Ⓔ	31 Ⓐ Ⓑ Ⓒ Ⓓ Ⓔ	42 Ⓐ Ⓑ Ⓒ Ⓓ Ⓔ	53 Ⓐ Ⓑ Ⓒ Ⓓ Ⓔ
10 Ⓐ Ⓑ Ⓒ Ⓓ Ⓔ	21 Ⓐ Ⓑ Ⓒ Ⓓ Ⓔ	32 Ⓐ Ⓑ Ⓒ Ⓓ Ⓔ	43 Ⓐ Ⓑ Ⓒ Ⓓ Ⓔ	54 Ⓐ Ⓑ Ⓒ Ⓓ Ⓔ
11 Ⓐ Ⓑ Ⓒ Ⓓ Ⓔ	22 Ⓐ Ⓑ Ⓒ Ⓓ Ⓔ	33 Ⓐ Ⓑ Ⓒ Ⓓ Ⓔ	44 Ⓐ Ⓑ Ⓒ Ⓓ Ⓔ	55 Ⓐ Ⓑ Ⓒ Ⓓ Ⓔ

PRACTICE EXAMINATION III

Section I

55 Questions

Time—45 minutes

Identifying Sentence Errors

Directions: Some of the sentences below contain an error in grammar, usage, word choice, or idiom. Other sentences are correct. Parts of each sentence are underlined and lettered. The error, if there is one, is contained in one of the underlined parts of the sentence. Assume that all other parts of the sentence are correct and cannot be changed. For each sentence, select the one underlined part that must be changed to make the sentence correct and mark its letter on your answer sheet. If there is no error in a sentence, mark answer space (E). No sentence contains more than one error.

Example:

<u>Being that</u> <u>it's</u> such a lovely day, we <u>are having</u>
A   B   C

a difficult time <u>concentrating</u> on our assignment.
                      D

<u>No error</u>
E

Sample Answer:

● Ⓑ Ⓒ Ⓓ Ⓔ

1. The office was <u>so overheated</u> <u>that</u> every man
                          A   B

    <u>present</u> removed <u>their jackets</u>. <u>No error</u>
    C   D   E

2. She <u>had</u> never played tennis <u>well</u> on <u>no</u> surface
           A   B   C

    <u>but</u> grass. <u>No error</u>
    D   E

3. I had delayed <u>too long</u> <u>talking</u> on the phone;
                      A   B

    the shop <u>was</u> <u>close</u> by the time I arrived.
              C   D

    <u>No error</u>
    E

4. While it <u>comprises</u> only a small <u>percentage</u>
                 A   B

    of the student population, the club,

    <u>numbering some</u> 150 members, <u>are</u> very vocal.
    C   D

    <u>No error</u>
    E

5. Besides George and <u>her</u>, no one <u>I know</u> seems
                          A   B

    <u>distressed about</u> the <u>prospect of</u> war. <u>No error</u>
    C   D   E

6. The clothes were <u>jumbled</u> <u>altogether</u> in the
                          A   B

    suitcase; <u>obviously</u>, she had packed <u>hurriedly</u>.
              C   D

    <u>No error</u>
    E

7. It's unfair to expect Rob and <u>I</u> to pay <u>all bills</u>
                                      A   B

    when <u>you're</u> working <u>also</u>. <u>No error</u>
    C   D   E

8. The previous commander was a <u>personable</u>
                                      A
    man <u>too concerned</u> with being liked;
              B
    <u>as a leader</u>, he was <u>ineffectual</u>. <u>No error</u>
          C   D   E

9. The athlete <u>dove</u> <u>smooth</u> into the lake, creating
                    A   B
    <u>hardly</u> a ripple on <u>its</u> glassy surface. <u>No error</u>
        C   D   E

10. One must <u>be sure of</u> the facts <u>before</u> <u>you make</u>
                  A   B   C
    <u>such a</u> serious accusation. <u>No error</u>
        D   E

11. Neither the <u>dilemma</u> <u>nor</u> the solution <u>are</u> as
                    A   B   C
    simple as that editorial <u>would lead</u> one to
                                  D
    believe. <u>No error</u>
                 E

12. Few freshmen <u>these days</u> are <u>as</u> ingenuous
                      A   B
    <u>as him</u> <u>that</u> first year. <u>No error</u>
        C   D   E

13. The Sudan, the <u>largest</u> country in Africa, is
                        A
    <u>near</u> one million <u>square miles</u> of desert,
        B   C
    savanna, <u>and</u> papyrus swamp. <u>No error</u>
                 D   E

14. On the issue of human rights, the candidate
    <u>vowed</u> to vote <u>according to</u> his <u>conscious</u> and
        A   B   C
    to resist the pressure of <u>political expediency</u>.
                                    D
    <u>No error</u>
        E

15. <u>Listening to</u> another student's question, I
        A
    frequently discover that <u>they are</u> confused
                                  B
    <u>about</u> the same points that <u>I am</u>. <u>No error</u>
        C   D   E

16. The anthology <u>was comprised</u> of modern
                        A
    American poems <u>and</u> included a <u>varied</u>
                        B   C
    selection of <u>lesser known</u> works by Stevens
                      D
    and Williams. <u>No error</u>
                      E

17. It is not <u>I</u> <u>to whom</u> you <u>ought to</u> <u>complain</u>.
                  A   B   C   D
    <u>No error</u>
        E

18. We planned to <u>canvas</u> the neighborhood,
                      A
    <u>going</u> <u>door to door</u> to get signatures <u>on</u> the
        B   C   D
    petition. <u>No error</u>
                  E

19. The conditions of the contract <u>by which</u> the
                                        A
    strike <u>has been</u> settled <u>has not yet</u> been
              B   C
    <u>made public</u>. <u>No error</u>
        D   E

20. Myths are often <u>marked by</u> anthropomorphism,
                        A
    the concept <u>where</u> animals and <u>inanimate</u> forces
                    B   C
    are <u>invested with</u> human characteristics. <u>No error</u>
            D   E

Improving Sentences

Directions: The sentences below may contain problems in grammar, usage, word choice, sentence construction, and punctuation. Part or all of each sentence is underlined. Following each sentence you will find five ways of expressing the underlined part. Answer choice (A) always repeats the original underlined section. The other four answer choices are all different. You are to select the lettered answer that produces the most effective sentence. If you think the original sentence is best, choose choice (A) as your answer. If one of the other choices makes a better sentence, mark your answer sheet for the letter of that choice. Do not choose an answer that changes the meaning of the original sentence.

Example:

I have always enjoyed singing as well as to dance.

(A) singing as well as to dance

(B) singing as well as dancing

(C) to sing as well as dancing

(D) singing in addition to dance

(E) to sing in addition to dancing

Sample Answer:

Ⓐ ● Ⓒ Ⓓ Ⓔ

21. The committee requested that there be input from all the staff before a vote was taken.

(A) from all the staff before a vote was taken

(B) from all the staff taking a vote

(C) before the staff took a vote on the input

(D) from all the staff before having taken a vote

(E) from all the staff who would take a vote

22. She could not scarcely but be affected by the plight of the homeless.

(A) could not scarcely but be affected

(B) could hardly help being effected

(C) could not help being affected

(D) could not help being effected

(E) could not scarcely be affected

23. With regards to examining the union contract, the staff spent several days discussing the various sections and then voted on it.

(A) With regards to examining the union contract, the staff spent several days discussing the various sections and then voted on it.

(B) As concerns the contract, the staff spent several days on a discussion which resulted in a vote.

(C) An examination of the contract resulted in several days of voting and discussing the various sections.

(D) After several days of discussing the various sections of the union contract, the staff voted on it.

(E) A vote followed a discussion of the union contract by the staff which examined the sections and followed it with a vote.

24. There are, of course, three possible alternatives that we have in order to reach an equitable solution.

(A) There are, of course, three possible alternatives that

(B) There is, of course three possible alternatives that

(C) There are, of course, three possible choices that

(D) There are, of course, three possible alternatives which

(E) There are of course three possible choices that

25. In the dictionary, it indicates how words should be pronounced.

(A) In the dictionary, it indicates

(B) In the dictionary, it has

(C) The dictionary indicates

(D) There in the dictionary, it indicates

(E) In the dictionary, it has an indication

26. The actor <u>was apparently unaware or unconcerned by the small audience.</u>

   (A) was apparently unaware or unconcerned by the small audience.

   (B) was apparently unaware or unconcerned, by the small audience.

   (C) was not aware or unconcerned by the small audience.

   (D) seemed to ignore the fact that there was a small audience.

   (E) was apparently unaware of or unconcerned by the small audience.

27. The main pipe broke, and they were without water for a <u>week, which created many problems for them.</u>

   (A) week, which created many problems for them.

   (B) week; this situation created many problems for them.

   (C) week; which situation created many problems for them.

   (D) week, which is creating many problems for them.

   (E) week, this created many problems for them.

28. If we ever have the <u>watch inscribed; we will ask the jewelers</u> to use italic lettering for the quotation.

   (A) watch inscribed; we will ask the jewelers

   (B) watch inscribed; we'll ask the jeweler's

   (C) watch inscribed, we will ask the jewelers

   (D) watch inscribed, we will ask the jewelers'

   (E) watch inscribed, we will ask for the jewelers

29. <u>No one, including Walter and I, have the ability</u> to cash this check for her.

   (A) No one, including Walter and I, have the ability

   (B) No one, including Walter and I, had the ability

   (C) No one, including Walter and me, have the ability

   (D) No one, including Walter and me, has the ability

   (E) No one including Walter and me, has the ability

30. <u>Recognizing the expense of the repairs,</u> the plumbing mishap created a great deal of consternation.

   (A) Recognizing the expense of the repairs,

   (B) Recognizing the expensive repairs,

   (C) Recognizing that the repairs are expensive

   (D) Due to the repairs are going to be expensive

   (E) Recognizing the expense of the repairs, he noted that

31. <u>Seatbelts, while unquestionably a good idea, it's sometimes a nuisance to use them.</u>

   (A) Seatbelts, while unquestionably a good idea, it's sometimes a nuisance to use them.

   (B) Seatbelts, while unquestionably a good idea, are sometimes a nuisance.

   (C) Seatbelts are unquestionably a good idea and also they are sometimes a nuisance.

   (D) Seatbelts, while unquestionably a good idea, but sometimes a nuisance to use.

   (E) Seatbelts, while it's unquestionably a good idea to have them, it's sometimes a nuisance to use them.

32. Your application for a scholarship <u>arriving late, however; it will still be considered by the committee.</u>

   (A) arriving late, however; it will still be considered by the committee.

   (B) arrived late, however the committee will consider it still.

   (C) arrived late; however, the committee will still consider it.

   (D) will be considered by the committee which arrived late.

   (E) arriving late and being considered by the committee.

33. When I travel, <u>I most always enjoy seeing sights that differ from the typical tourist traps.</u>

   (A) I most always enjoy seeing sights that differ from the typical tourist traps.

   (B) I almost always enjoy to see sights other than the typical tourist traps.

   (C) I most always enjoy seeing sights that are different than the typical tourist traps.

   (D) I almost always enjoy seeing sights that are different than the typical tourist traps.

   (E) I almost always enjoy seeing sights other than the typical tourist traps.

34. Unless treated and rewarmed, <u>hypothermia causes death.</u>

   (A) hypothermia causes death.

   (B) death results from hypothermia.

   (C) hypothermia kills.

   (D) the victim of hypothermia will die.

   (E) hypothermia will cause death.

35. First choose a recipe; <u>then you should make a list of the ingredients needed.</u>

   (A) then you should make a list of the ingredients needed.

   (B) then a list can be made of the ingredients needed.

   (C) then you can make a list of the ingredients needed.

   (D) then you should list the ingredients needed.

   (E) then make a list of the ingredients needed.

Revising Work in Progress

Directions: The selections that follow are early drafts of student essays in which each sentence has been numbered for easy reference. Following each essay are questions that direct you to a part of the essay or to the entire essay. The questions focus upon improving sentence structure and word choice, organization and development of the essay, and effectiveness of language for the intended purpose and audience of the work. For each question, choose the letter of the answer you consider to be correct, and mark the corresponding oval on your answer sheet.

Questions 36–40 are based on the following essay.

(1) Recently I heard a discussion about telling the truth and that you should never lie. (2) Is a "little white lie" ever justified? (3) Is it always essential to tell the honest truth at all times?

(4) I believe that there are occasions when one can stretch the truth. (5) For example, if someone asks you if she's wearing too much makeup, do you always have to tell the truth? (6) Even if you know that their feelings will be hurt? (7) Certainly in a court of law you must tell the truth since you took an oath and swore to do it. (8) And I don't believe that you should lie to people who are important to you when you are asked to tell what happened.

(9) On minor matters, when you are sparing someone's feelings, then I think it is time for the little white lie. (10) If telling the whole truth and nothing but the truth will cause damage, then perhaps we can stretch the truth. (11) In other words, I think all the mitigating circumstances must be considered.

(12) There is no black or white on many issues. (13) There are various shades of gray. (14) And all this should be considered when you think of telling the truth always, at all times.

36. Which of the following is the most effective way to revise the underlined section of sentence 1 (shown below)?

    Recently I heard a discussion about telling the <u>truth and that</u> you should never lie.

    (A) truth when
    (B) truth indicating that
    (C) people that
    (D) truth if
    (E) me that

37. The best way to change *honest truth* in sentence (3) is to

    (A) let it stand.
    (B) change it to *all the truth.*
    (C) omit *honest.*
    (D) change it to *the truth as you see it.*
    (E) delete it entirely.

38. Which of the following best describes sentence (6)?

    (A) It is a fragment and should be combined with sentence (4).
    (B) It shows genuine feeling on the part of the writer.
    (C) It provides an effective example.
    (D) It need not be changed.
    (E) It provides a thesis statement.

39. In sentence (6), the phrase *their feelings*

    (A) is effective.
    (B) should be changed to *her feelings.*
    (C) should be changed to *his or her feelings.*
    (D) should be changed to *his feelings.*
    (E) should be changed to *their sensitivities.*

40. In sentence (14) the final words *always, at all times*

    (A) provide a strong conclusion.
    (B) may be deleted.
    (C) are used for emphasis effectively.
    (D) provide the writer's thesis.
    (E) are too strong.

Questions 41–45 are based on the following essay.

(1) A few weeks ago I read a short story about a group of people who meet every year to conduct a lottery. (2) But this is no ordinary lottery in which people can win large sums of money. (3) Instead, someone is selected to be stoned to death by fellow townspeople. (4) One of the authors points, as I interpret them, is that some traditions should not be followed, or at least should be reevaluated when they no longer make sense. (5) The woman who wrote the tale found a very disturbing way to get the reader's interest.

(6) The story begins on a lovely, peaceful June day. (7) The only hint that something unusual may be about to happen is that children are busily collecting rocks and placing them in neat piles. (8) Then, one by one, people leave their jobs and head for the center of town where they all meet at noon. (9) Everyone is very friendly. (10) Everything is very organized. (11) It is evidently a time-honored ritual. (12) Heads of families pick pieces of paper from a box. (13) One paper has a special mark on it. (14) Whichever family picks the marked paper must have every family member select a piece of paper. (15) Male or female, adult or child doesn't matter. (16) The one who gets the marked paper this time is the victim.

(17) Of course, the "winner" of this lottery is actually a terrible "loser." (18) The author hints at primitive beginnings to the whole thing. (19) Whatever made them do it, no one speaks out forcefully enough against this. (20) The tradition will continue, the story suggests, and only if the young do not throw stones—refuse to participate, in other words—will things change. (21) There are similar things you should think about in your own life.

41. Which of the following is the best revision of the underlined portion of sentence (4) below?

    <u>One of the authors points, as I interpret them,</u> is that some traditions should not be followed, or at least should be reevaluated when they no longer make sense.

    (A) One of the authors points in my interpretation,

    (B) One of the author's points, as I interpret them

    (C) The author's point, as I interpret them,

    (D) One of the authors point, as I interpret it,

    (E) One of the author's points, as I interpret it,

42. Which of the following is the best way to combine sentences (9) to (12)?

    (A) Everyone is very friendly, everything is very organized. It is evidently a time-honored ritual, heads of families pick pieces of paper from a box.

    (B) Everyone is very friendly; everything is very organized. In what is evidently a time-honored ritual, heads of families pick pieces of paper from a box.

    (C) Everyone is very friendly, everything is very organized. Evidently a time-honored ritual is that heads of families pick pieces of paper from a box.

    (D) Everyone is very friendly and organized, in a time-honored ritual of heads of families picking pieces of paper from a box.

    (E) In a friendly, organized, time-honored ritual; heads of families pick pieces of paper from a box.

43. Which of the following is the best way to combine sentences (14) and (15)?

    (A) Male or female, adult or child—whichever family picks it must have every family member select a piece of paper.

    (B) Whichever family picks it—male or female, adult or child—must have every family member select a piece of paper.

    (C) Whichever family picks it must have every family member—male or female, adult or child—select a piece of paper.

    (D) Whichever family picks it, must have every family member select a piece of paper—whether male or female, adult or child.

    (E) Male or female, adult or child—the family that picks it must have every member select a piece of paper.

44. Which of the following is the best reason to revise sentences (17) to (19)?

    (A) To eliminate the two sets of quotation marks

    (B) To improve organization

    (C) To use more exact language

    (D) To include the author and title of the story

    (E) To eliminate incorrect punctuation

45. In light of the sentences that precede it, which of the following is the best way to revise sentence (21)?

    (A) There may be similar customs in our own lives that need to be thought about and changed.

    (B) There are but a few of the things that you should think about in your own lives.

    (C) There are many customs like this one that you should think about in your own lives.

    (D) You should think about things like this in your own life.

    (E) Think about this and similar things that affect our lives.

Questions 46–50 are based on the following essay.

(1) Hopefully the government of the United States will soon make sure that all their citizens are able to have good, affordable health care. (2) If legislation is enacted and national coverage is assured, we will truly be ready to enter a new age in America. (3) It will be one in which all people—rich or poor, working or unemployed—will be provided for when they are ill.

(4) The significance of a national health-care plan cannot be overstated. (5) Recently, for instance, my aunt and uncle were involved in an automobile accident. (6) Although their injuries were pretty serious, yet after some emergency treatment they didn't get a lot of medical attention. (7) Due to the fact that they didn't have much coverage. (8) So doctors and hospital staff didn't want to treat them. (9) It's hard to believe that good, hardworking people like my relatives, now they are being neglected by society.

(10) And this is only one example of a situation in which people without adequate protection are mistreated by the medical profession, there are many other stories that could be told. (11) That's why I sincerely hope that our government will soon provide for all those needy people, like my aunt and uncle, who presently lack adequate health-care coverage.

46. Which of the following is the best revision of the underlined portion of sentence (1) below?

    Hopefully the government of the United States will soon make sure that all their citizens are able to have good, affordable health care.

    (A) Hopefully the government of the United States will soon provide all citizens with

    (B) It is hoped that the government of the United States will soon make sure that all its citizens are able to have

    (C) Hopefully the government of the United States will soon make sure that all citizens would be able to have

    (D) I hope that the government of the United States will soon make sure that all its citizens will be able to have

    (E) I hope that the government of the United States soon makes sure that all their citizens would be able to have

47. Which of the following is the best way to combine sentences (2) and (3)?

    (A) If legislation is enacted and national coverage is assured, we will truly be ready to enter a new age in America, being one in which all people, rich or poor, will be provided for when they are ill.

    (B) If legislation is enacted and national coverage is assured, we will truly be able to enter a new age, one in which all Americans—rich or poor, working or unemployed—will be provided for when they are ill.

    (C) If legislation is enacted and national coverage is assured, we will truly be ready to enter a new age in America, it will be one in which all people, rich or poor, working or unemployed, will be provided for when they are ill.

    (D) If legislation is enacted then all people, no matter what their abilities will be provided for by their government at all times.

    (E) If we enact legislation and assure national coverage, we will be able to enter a new age in America; in which all—rich or poor, working or unemployed—will be provided for when they are ill.

48. Which of the following is the best way to revise sentences (6), (7), and (8)?

    (A) Although their injuries were serious, after some emergency treatment, they received very little medical attention. Since they did not have much coverage, doctors and hospital staff did not want to treat them.

    (B) Although their injuries were serious, yet after some emergency treatment, they didn't get a lot of medical attention. Due to the fact they didn't have much coverage, doctors and hospital staff didn't want to treat them.

    (C) Their injuries were pretty serious although after some emergency treatment they didn't get a lot medical attention, due to the fact that they didn't have much coverage. So doctors and hospital staff didn't want to treat them.

    (D) Their injuries were pretty serious, yet after some emergency treatment, they did not get much medical attention. Due to the fact that they did not have much coverage, so doctor and hospitals did not want to treat them.

    (E) Although their injuries were serious, after some emergency treatment, they didn't get a lot of attention because of the fact that they didn't have much coverage so doctors and hospital staff didn't want to treat them.

49. Which of the following is the best revision of the underlined portion of sentence (9) below?

    It's hard to believe that good, hardworking people like my <u>relatives, now they are being neglected by society.</u>

    (A) relatives. Now they are being neglected by society.

    (B) relatives and being neglected by society now.

    (C) relatives are now being neglected by society.

    (D) relatives and now they are being neglected by society.

    (E) relatives have neglected society.

50. Which of the following is the reason sentence (10) should be revised?

    (A) To provide another example

    (B) To correct an error in usage

    (C) To correct a sentence structure error

    (D) To correct an error in verb agreement

    (E) To correct a pronoun reference error

Questions 51–55 are based on the following essay.

(1) When my family came to the United States to live, we spoke no English. (2) My parents luckily got a job and my sister and I were very young and we did what many other immigrant children did. (3) We learned English in public school and learned our native language and culture at home with our family. (4) It was not long before we all realized that success in the United States would depend on our ability to be fluent in English.

(5) Because of my own case I think that bilingual education is not as good as English in school, native language at home. (6) But I know of other people who found a bilingual education to be just what they needed, in fact it was essential to their progress since their English was so limited. (7) However, some people I knew did drop out of school later on. (8) Some of them had been labeled learning disabled. (9) It was really just a language problem. (10) And some of my friends' parents felt that their children's bilingual education was ineffective or harmful, while others felt it was very good for them.

(11) As a result, I cannot decide for certain whether English is being taught better to foreigners today than it was in the past. (12) But I think that I would like to see small groups of nonnative speakers taught in English by caring, well-trained professionals. (13) Then I would like them to be moved into regular classrooms as soon as possible. (14) In that way, I think they would be best served by a school system that has not always done justice to their needs. (15) Perhaps that would be one way to solve the problem of how to help them to succeed in school and in their life in the United States.

51. Which of the following is the best way to revise sentence (2)?

    (A) My parents luckily got a job. My sister and I were young. We did what many other immigrated children did.

    (B) My parents luckily got a job and my sister and I were very young so we did what many other immigrants did.

    (C) My parents got jobs, luckily; my very young sister and I did what many others did.

    (D) Luckily, my parents got jobs. My sister and I, who were very young, did what many other immigrant children did.

    (E) Luckily, my parents got jobs and my sister and I were very young. We did what many other immigrant children did.

52. Which of the following is the best way to revise sentence (5)?

    (A) Because of my own experience, I think that a bilingual education is not so good as learning English in school and the family's native language at home.

    (B) In my own case, bilingual education is not so good as English in school and native language at home.

    (C) I think that because of my own experience, English in school, native language at home is better than bilingual education.

    (D) As a result of my own case, I think that bilingual education is not as good as students who learn English in school and their native language at home.

    (E) Because of my own case, I consider bilingual education less effective than learning English in school and their native language at home.

53. Which of the following is the best revision of the underlined portion of sentence (6) below? But I know of other people who found a bilingual education to be just what they <u>needed, in fact it was essential</u> to their progress since their English was so limited.

    (A) needed; in fact it being essential

    (B) needed, being that it was essential

    (C) needed; in fact it was essential

    (D) needed; essential as it was in fact

    (E) needed. In fact essential

54. Which of the following is the best way to combine sentences (8) and (9)?

    (A) Although it was really just a language problem; some had been labeled learning disabled.

    (B) Some of them were labeled learning disabled, it was really just a language problem.

    (C) Some of them had been labeled learning disabled, even though what they really had was a language problem.

    (D) Some of them were learning disabled with a language problem.

    (E) Some of them had a language problem that made them learning disabled.

55. Which of the following is the best revision of sentence (10)?

    (A) Some of my friend's parents felt that their children's bilingual education was ineffective or harmful, while others felt it was very good for them.

    (B) Some felt that their child's bilingual education was ineffective or harmful, but other of my friends' parents felt it was very good for them.

    (C) Though some of my friends' parents felt it was very good for them, some felt that bilingual education was ineffective or harmful.

    (D) Although some of my friends' parents felt it was very good, some felt that their children's bilingual education was ineffective or harmful.

    (E) Ineffective or harmful though it may have been to some, others of my friends' parents felt that their children's bilingual education has been very good.

Section II

1 Essay
Time—45 minutes

Directions: You will have 45 minutes to plan and write an essay on the specified topic. Do not write on a topic other than the one specified. Consider the topic and organize your thoughts before you begin to write.

Take care to express your thoughts clearly and exactly and to make them of interest. Be specific and use examples to support your position whenever appropriate. Remember that how well you write is much more important than how much you write.

Assignment:

The public schools have been criticized for being too lenient with students who break rules concerning proper dress and behavior. Some critics of the system say that students should be given strict punishment when they are found guilty of violating school rules.

Do you agree or disagree? Explain and illustrate your answer from your own experience, your observation of others, or your reading.

End of Practice Examination III

Answer Key

Section I

1.	D	12.	C	23.	D	34.	D	45.	A
2.	C	13.	B	24.	C	35.	E	46.	D
3.	D	14.	C	25.	C	36.	B	47.	B
4.	D	15.	B	26.	E	37.	C	48.	A
5.	E	16.	A	27.	B	38.	A	49.	C
6.	B	17.	E	28.	C	39.	B	50.	C
7.	A	18.	A	29.	D	40.	B	51.	D
8.	E	19.	C	30.	E	41.	E	52.	A
9.	B	20.	B	31.	B	42.	B	53.	C
10.	C	21.	A	32.	C	43.	C	54.	C
11.	C	22.	C	33.	E	44.	C	55.	D

Explanatory Answers

Section I

1. **The correct answer is (D).** Since *every man* is singular, the pronoun referring back to it should be *his*, not *their*.

2. **The correct answer is (C).** The combination of *never. . . on no surface* is a double negative. Standard English is *never. . . on any surface*.

3. **The correct answer is (D).** There's a big difference between a shop's being *close* and its being *closed*.

4. **The correct answer is (D).** As a collective noun discussed as a single entity, *club* takes a singular verb: *is* very vocal.

5. **The correct answer is (E).** The sentence is correct.

6. **The correct answer is (B).** *Altogether* means entirely or utterly. This sentence needs *all together*, implying unity or proximity.

7. **The correct answer is (A).** *Rob and I* is a phrase in the nominative case. But the verb *expect* takes an object, so the phrase should be in the objective case: Rob and *me*.

8. **The correct answer is (E).** The sentence is correct.

9. **The correct answer is (B).** The adjective *smooth* should be the adverb *smoothly*, since it modifies the verb *dove*.

10. **The correct answer is (C).** Consistency is important in standard written English; it's either *one must be, one makes*, or *you must be, you make*.

11. **The correct answer is (C).** The subject is singular (either *dilemma* or *solution*), and so the verb should be *is*, not *are*.

12. **The correct answer is (C).** The verb is understood, so the phrase should read, "ingenuous as *he [was]* that first year."

13. **The correct answer is (B).** The sense is that the Sudan is *almost* a million square miles, hence *nearly* (not *near*) that area.

14. **The correct answer is (C).** He vowed to vote according to his *conscience*.

15. **The correct answer is (B).** It's one student's question: Hence, *he is* or *she is* (not *they are*) confused.

16. **The correct answer is (A).** *Is (or was) comprised of* is always wrong. *Comprised* means embraced, included; it is not a synonym for *composed*.

17. **The correct answer is (E).** The sentence is correct.

18. **The correct answer is (A).** Canvas is the name of a coarse fabric. This sentence requires the verb *to canvass*, meaning "to go through (an area) to solicit votes, orders, or opinions."

19. **The correct answer is (C).** The subject of the main clause is *conditions*, a plural noun taking a plural verb: *have not*. The subject of the subordinate clause is the *strike*, which properly takes the singular verb *has been settled*.

20. **The correct answer is (B).** A *concept* is not a *place* to be referred back to as *where*. A concept is an idea, which we can refer to by using such expressions as *according to which*.

21. **The correct answer is (A).** The sentence is correct.

22. **The correct answer is (C).** The double negative (*could not scarcely*) is incorrect. *Affected* (meaning *influenced*) is correct.

23. **The correct answer is (D).** *With regards to* is unacceptable for *in regard to*. Choice (B) is awkward and wordy, choice (C) is illogical, and choice (E) is gibberish. Choice (D) offers the best expression of the thought.

24. **The correct answer is (C).** *Choices* is used for three or more items, *alternatives* for two. The *commas* separating *of course* are correct.

25. **The correct answer is (C).** There is no antecedent for the pronoun *it*; the subject of *indicates* should be *dictionary* as in choice (C).

26. **The correct answer is (E).** *Unaware* should be followed by the preposition *of*. Choice (D) alters the sense of the sentence.

27. **The correct answer is (B).** The original sentence, choice (A), is awkward, since *which* seems to refer to *week*, rather than the *situation*, which created the problem. Choices (D) and (C) have the same problem, and choice (C) uses the semicolon incorrectly. Choice (E) is a comma splice.

28. **The correct answer is (C).** A dependent clause introduced by a subordinating conjunction is separated from the main clause by a comma. Choice (D) is incorrect since *jewelers* is not possessive and does not require an apostrophe; choice (E) is awkward because of the preposition *for* following *ask*.

29. **The correct answer is (D).** The preposition *including* takes the objective case, *me*. Choice (C) is incorrect since the correct singular verb *has* (the subject is *no one*) is changed to the plural *have*. Choice (E) omits the comma after *one*.

30. **The correct answer is (E).** As the sentence stands there is a dangling participle, *recognizing,* so that the meaning conveyed is that the plumbing mishaps recognized the expense of the repairs. A subject must be added in the main clause.

31. **The correct answer is (B).** The original includes the superfluous pronoun *it* and leaves *seatbelts* without a verb. Choices (D) and (E) do nothing to correct these problems. Choice (C) provides the verb needed to make a complete sentence, but it is awkward and wordy. Choice (B) is both correct and concise.

32. **The correct answer is (C).** When used as a conjunctive adverb, *however* is preceded by a semicolon and followed by a comma. In addition, a semicolon is used to join closely related *independent* clauses. Choice (B) is a comma splice, choice (E) is a fragment, and choice (D) changes the meaning of the original sentence.

33. **The correct answer is (E).** The correct expressions are *almost always* (not *most always*) and *different from* (not *different than*).

34. **The correct answer is (D).** The *victim* is the one who must be treated and rewarmed. Only choice (D) correctly places the subject next to the phrase that modifies it.

35. **The correct answer is (E).** The original sentence shifts needlessly from the imperative (*choose*) to the indicative mood (*you should make*). Choices (C) and (D) do the same. Choice (B) shifts subjects (from *you* to *a list*). Choice (E) is consistent in both subject and mood.

36. **The correct answer is (B).** The sentence is awkward and clumsily stated. It could be improved through choice (B), now reading *Recently I heard a discussion about telling the truth indicating that you should never lie.*

37. **The correct answer is (C).** The phrase *honest truth* is a redundancy since truth must be honest; therefore, choice (C) is correct.

38. **The correct answer is (A).** Sentence (5) is not a complete sentence, but a fragment, and should be joined to the previous sentence.

39. **The correct answer is (B).** The antecedent of *their* is *she*; therefore, choice (B) is best.

40. **The correct answer is (B).** The phrase is redundant, simply repeating what has already been indicated. It adds nothing to the conclusion and should be deleted.

41. **The correct answer is (E).** The word *authors* needs an apostrophe to indicate that it is possessive, not plural. The singular possessive form is *author's* as in choices (B) and (E). However, choice (B) uses the plural pronoun *them* to refer to the singular subject *one*. Choice (E) corrects both problems.

42. **The correct answer is (B).** Choices (A) and (C) contain comma splice errors. Choice (D) is awkward, and choice (E) contains an incorrect use of the semicolon. Choice (B) is best.

43. **The correct answer is (C).** *Male or female, adult or child* is best placed next to the noun described, *every family member.* This occurs only in choice (C).

44. **The correct answer is (C).** More specific language is needed. *The whole thing* in sentence (18) is vague and inexact; also, there is no clear reference for *them* or *this* in sentence (19).

45. **The correct answer is (A).** There is no good reason to switch to the second person in sentence (21). Also the imprecise word *thing* should be changed. Only choice (A) corrects both of these errors.

46. **The correct answer is (D).** To start the sentence with the adverb *hopefully* is poor since *hopefully* does not modify government. Therefore, choices (A) and (C) are weak. Choice (B) is vague, and choice (E) has a problem of reference (*their* should be *its*). Choice (D) is best because the entire essay is written from the first person point of view, and the pronoun is correct.

47. **The correct answer is (B).** Choice (A) is weak since the phrase *being one* is poor. Choice (C) contains a comma splice error following *America*. Choice (D) does not convey the sense of the original sentence. Choice (E) is poor since the semicolon following *America* is incorrect punctuation.

48. **The correct answer is (A).** The only choice that is clear and grammatically sound, with proper punctuation and good word choice, is choice (A).

49. **The correct answer is (C).** Choice (A) makes a fragment of the first part of the sentence, and choice (B) makes a fragment of the entire sentence. Choice (D), like the original sentence, includes the extra pronoun *they*. Choice (E) changes the meaning.

50. **The correct answer is (C).** The error in sentence (10) is a comma splice error. A comma cannot separate two main clauses. A period or a semicolon should be used after *profession*. This type of error is an error in sentence structure.

51. **The correct answer is (D).** What is required is a grammatically sound and precisely worded revision. The adverb *luckily* is best placed at the beginning of the sentence. Choice (D) is best.

52. **The correct answer is (A).** The only choice that is not awkward and does not misrepresent the material given is choice (A).

53. **The correct answer is (C).** A comma cannot join two independent clauses as in sentence

(6). Choice (C) corrects this error by replacing the comma with a semicolon. In choices (A) and (D), the words following the semicolon do not form an independent clause. The use of *being that* in choice (B) is incorrect. Choice (E) creates a fragment.

54. **The correct answer is (C).** The word *it* in sentence (9) has no clear reference. Choices (A) and (B) have the same problem. In addition, choice (A) has a fragment, and choice (B) has a comma splice error. Choices (D) and (E) change the intended meaning. Choice (C) correctly eliminates the vague *it* and makes it clear that these students had a language problem, not a learning disability.

55. **The correct answer is (D).** Choices (A), (B), and (C) are poor since the antecedent of the pronoun *them* is not clear. Choice (E) is wrong since the sentence is awkwardly phrased. Choice (D) is best.

Section II

Sample Essay 1:

It is certainly true that effective learning cannot take place in a chaotic situation. All groups of people live in a society in which sensible rules are established and followed. Schools, too, are part of our society and should, therefore, operate under clear regulations.

But all too often we punish students who break foolish rules that they have had no part in setting up. School administrators claiming that if we force pupils to abide by outmoded regulations, they will learn more because their classroom will be quiet and orderly. As a result, teachers insist that everyone dress in a regulated manner, that everyone in class maintain strict silence, that obedience be the absolute rule. When students depart from these patterns, they are forced back with threats and punishments.

What is the result? We are developing a group of noncreative adults who are afraid to break out of a mode and try something new. What we need are sensible and flexible rules that will allow us to become thinking individuals. Then rules will not be broken, because they will be seen as measures to help us to live life in a more exciting and effective way.

Analysis of Sample Essay 1:

This essay answers the question in an interesting and intelligent manner, with a mature vocabulary and a minimum of technical errors. Using a three-paragraph format, the writer proceeds from a clear introduction to a thought-provoking conclusion. More careful proof-reading might have helped the student to eliminate the fragment in paragraph 2 (*claiming* should be changed to *claim*). In paragraph 3, *mode* should be changed to *mold*. On the whole, however, this is an excellent response to the topic.

Sample Essay 2:

Of course students that act bad in school should be treated strict. Its ridiculous how teachers are being hit and robbed and disrespected all over. Therefore students do bad work and go out into the world not known how to read and write or even count their change. And the clothes they wear are sometimes disgraceful. No wonder theres no more respect for people in our society.

School is where young kids should be taught to behave and dress clean and neat. If not they should be punish. Not just a note home. But they should rules made on how to enforce a schools dress and behavior code.

The old saying, "Spare the rod and spoil the child." In my opinion, I feel that students should know that they will be disciplined for fractures of the rules. Also good students will do better when they feel safe and sound in our schools.

Analysis of Sample Essay 2:

Many writing errors appear in this essay. The writer is confused about the correct use of punctuation, omitting the commas after *of course* and *therefore*. Since *It's* and *there's* are contractions, an apostrophe is required. There is adjective-adverb confusion in the first sentence (bad-badly, strict-strictly). Fragments need correction in paragraph 2 ("Not just a note home." "The old saying. . ."). In addition, there are ending and tense errors, and a cliché is used in the last sentence.

Despite these many grammatical weaknesses there is some degree of organization. A three-paragraph development is attempted and the indignant tone is maintained throughout the essay.

Practice Examination III Diagnostic Chart

Question Type	Approx. % of Section	Question Numbers	Number of Questions	Number Wrong
Section I:				
Identifying Sentence Errors	36%	1–20	20	_____
Improving Sentences	28%	21–35	15	_____
Revising Work in Progress	36%	36–55	20	_____
Section II:				
Essay	100%			

The Humanities

ABOUT THE GENERAL EXAMINATION IN THE HUMANITIES

The CLEP General Examination in the Humanities is a 90–minute, 140–question test of your knowledge of literature, art, and music. The questions are divided about equally between literature and the fine arts. Since the exam covers a broad range of subjects, you may expect questions on all periods from classical to contemporary, and in a wide variety of fields—such as drama, poetry, fiction, nonfiction, philosophy, painting, sculpture, architecture, film, the mass media, dance, classical music, opera, and jazz. Some questions call for factual information, some test your skill as an observer, and some challenge your ability to comprehend excerpts from literature or to analyze reproductions of works of art or architecture.

Because the test is long and varied, it provides many opportunities for you to demonstrate what you know and understand about the humanities. The two separately timed 45-minute sections are divided approximately as follows:

50% Literature:

    Drama— 5–10%

    Poetry— 15–20%

    Fiction— 10–15%

    Nonfiction— 5–10%

    Philosophy— 5%

50% Fine Arts:

    Visual arts—(painting, sculpture) 25%

    Music—15%

    Performing Arts—(film, dance) 5%

    Architecture—5%

The General Examination in the Humanities is a wide–ranging test of your knowledge of literature and fine arts. No special course or list of readings is available to prepare you for the exam. The best preparation for the General Examination in the Humanities consists of studying the practice examinations, reading widely, examining appropriate categories on the Internet, going to museums and concerts, seeing films, and attending theater.

ROAD MAP

- *About the General Examination in the Humanities*
- *Mini-Exam in the Humanities*
- *Practice Examination I*
- *Practice Examination II*
- *Practice Examination III*

The three complete practice exams that follow indicate the nature and scope of the General Examination in the Humanities. Try the following study strategy:

1. Take the first Practice Exam, adhering to the time limits given and answering every question to the best of your ability.

2. Check your answers against the Answer Key to see where you stand.

3. Seek out books in the areas in which your scores indicated you are weak.

4. After shoring up those weak spots, take the other Practice Exams.

5. Be sure to read the explanations provided at the end of each exam—even for the questions you answered correctly. These explanatory answers are full of the kind of background information that can add points to your exam score.

The mini-exam that follows will give you a good idea of the kinds of questions you may expect.

MINI–EXAM IN THE HUMANITIES

Directions: For each question, choose the best answer from the five choices offered. Explanations for each answer will be found at the end of the test.

1. The phrase "Fourscore and seven years ago" begins a famous speech by
   - (A) Daniel Webster.
   - (B) Winston Churchill.
   - (C) Abraham Lincoln.
   - (D) Martin Luther King, Jr.
   - (E) Franklin Delano Roosevelt.

2. Technical terms such as "soffit," "pediment," and "clerestory" might be used most often by a(n)
   - (A) painter.
   - (B) dancer.
   - (C) musician.
   - (D) poet.
   - (E) architect.

3. Isaac Stern and Pinchas Zuckerman are world–famous
   - (A) violinists.
   - (B) composers of electronic music.
   - (C) German lieder singers.
   - (D) cellists.
   - (E) innovators in twelve–tone music.

4. The illustrations of Oscar Wilde's *Salome* are by
   - (A) Auguste Rodin.
   - (B) Aubrey Beardsley.
   - (C) Milton Glaser.
   - (D) Peter Max.
   - (E) Pablo Picasso.

5. All of the following accurately describe Elizabethan drama EXCEPT
   - (A) female roles were portrayed by men.
   - (B) the producers competed for royal patronage.
   - (C) the plays were performed in churches by monks.
   - (D) the acting companies operated by royal charter.
   - (E) significant events often happened offstage.

6. "They shall beat their swords into plowshares, and their spears into pruning hooks" is a statement from
   - (A) The Bible.
   - (B) *War and Peace.*
   - (C) The United Nations Charter.
   - (D) Shakespeare.
   - (E) *The Farmer's Almanac.*

7. In motion pictures and the theater, the names Gower Champion and Twyla Tharp are associated with
   - (A) acting.
   - (B) choreography.
   - (C) set design.
   - (D) lighting.
   - (E) singing.

8. Highly respected in the field of drawing, Auguste Rodin was even more talented in the area of
   - (A) oil painting.
   - (B) enameling.
   - (C) philosophy.
   - (D) sculpture.
   - (E) poetry.

Questions 9 and 10 refer to the following.

"Tis education forms the common mind, Just as the twig is bent the tree's inclin'd."

9. Which term describes the form of the lines above?
   - (A) Free verse
   - (B) Blank verse
   - (C) A quatrain
   - (D) A couplet
   - (E) A tercet

10. The lines were written by
    - (A) John Donne.
    - (B) Alexander Pope.
    - (C) Marge Piercy.
    - (D) Ezra Pound.
    - (E) Emily Dickinson.

Answer Key

1. C	2. E	3. A	4. B	5. C
6. A	7. B	8. D	9. D	10. B

Explanatory Answers

1. **The correct answer is (C).** The words begin "The Gettysburg Address," delivered in 1863 by Abraham Lincoln, sixteenth president of the United States ("Fourscore and seven years ago, our fathers brought forth upon this continent a new nation, conceived in liberty and dedicated to the proposition that all men are created equal. . .").

2. **The correct answer is (E).** "Soffit" refers to the underside of a subordinate part of a building, such as a staircase, archway, or cornice. "Pediment" describes the triangular space forming the gable of a two–pitched roof, or the form used as decoration over porticoes, doors, or windows. "Clerestory" is that part of a church (or *any* building, in common usage) that rises clear of the roof and whose wall contains windows for lighting or ventilation.

3. **The correct answer is (A).** Isaac Stern (1920–2001) has been president of New York's Carnegie Hall since 1960, and for over forty years he has been recognized as one of the world's master violinists. Pinchas Zukerman (1948–), a child prodigy and protégé of Isaac Stern, is considered one of the most accomplished violinists of his generation.

4. **The correct answer is (B).** Aubrey Beardsley (1872–1898) was an English artist who became famous with the publication of his illustrations for the English version of Oscar Wilde's *Salome.* He was associated with the Art Nouveau style.

5. **The correct answer is (C).** In Elizabethan times, plays were performed by professional actors (Will Kempe and Richard Burbage are noted examples).

6. **The correct answer is (A).** The words appear in *Isaiah 2:4* ("He shall judge between the nations, and shall decide for many peoples;/ and they shall beat their swords into plowshares, and their spears into pruning hooks;/ nation shall not lift up sword against nation, neither shall they learn war anymore.")

7. **The correct answer is (B).** Gower Champion (1921–1980) was a celebrated dancer who choreographed many films and plays, such as *Bye Bye Birdie* and *42nd Street.* Twyla Tharp (1941–) has choreographed for the Joffrey Ballet, the American Ballet Theatre, and the film version of *Hair,* and she appeared with her dance company in the Broadway production based on A.A. Milne's *When We Were Very Young.*

8. **The correct answer is (D).** Auguste Rodin (1840–1917), creator of such works as "The Kiss," "The Thinker," and the "Balzac" monument, was the most important sculptor of the French Romantic school.

9. **The correct answer is (D).** *Couplet* refers to a pair of lines of the same meter and length, usually rhyming. *Couplet* also may be used to describe a two–line stanza.

10. **The correct answer is (B).** Alexander Pope (1688–1744) is associated with the couplet form. The lines cited appear in his *Moral Essays (Epistle I).* He is also known for *An Essay on Criticism, The Rape of the Lock, An Essay on Man,* and *The Dunciad.*

Answer Sheet for Practice Examination I

Section I

1 Ⓐ Ⓑ Ⓒ Ⓓ Ⓔ   16 Ⓐ Ⓑ Ⓒ Ⓓ Ⓔ   31 Ⓐ Ⓑ Ⓒ Ⓓ Ⓔ   46 Ⓐ Ⓑ Ⓒ Ⓓ Ⓔ   61 Ⓐ Ⓑ Ⓒ Ⓓ Ⓔ

2 Ⓐ Ⓑ Ⓒ Ⓓ Ⓔ   17 Ⓐ Ⓑ Ⓒ Ⓓ Ⓔ   32 Ⓐ Ⓑ Ⓒ Ⓓ Ⓔ   47 Ⓐ Ⓑ Ⓒ Ⓓ Ⓔ   62 Ⓐ Ⓑ Ⓒ Ⓓ Ⓔ

3 Ⓐ Ⓑ Ⓒ Ⓓ Ⓔ   18 Ⓐ Ⓑ Ⓒ Ⓓ Ⓔ   33 Ⓐ Ⓑ Ⓒ Ⓓ Ⓔ   48 Ⓐ Ⓑ Ⓒ Ⓓ Ⓔ   63 Ⓐ Ⓑ Ⓒ Ⓓ Ⓔ

4 Ⓐ Ⓑ Ⓒ Ⓓ Ⓔ   19 Ⓐ Ⓑ Ⓒ Ⓓ Ⓔ   34 Ⓐ Ⓑ Ⓒ Ⓓ Ⓔ   49 Ⓐ Ⓑ Ⓒ Ⓓ Ⓔ   64 Ⓐ Ⓑ Ⓒ Ⓓ Ⓔ

5 Ⓐ Ⓑ Ⓒ Ⓓ Ⓔ   20 Ⓐ Ⓑ Ⓒ Ⓓ Ⓔ   35 Ⓐ Ⓑ Ⓒ Ⓓ Ⓔ   50 Ⓐ Ⓑ Ⓒ Ⓓ Ⓔ   65 Ⓐ Ⓑ Ⓒ Ⓓ Ⓔ

6 Ⓐ Ⓑ Ⓒ Ⓓ Ⓔ   21 Ⓐ Ⓑ Ⓒ Ⓓ Ⓔ   36 Ⓐ Ⓑ Ⓒ Ⓓ Ⓔ   51 Ⓐ Ⓑ Ⓒ Ⓓ Ⓔ   66 Ⓐ Ⓑ Ⓒ Ⓓ Ⓔ

7 Ⓐ Ⓑ Ⓒ Ⓓ Ⓔ   22 Ⓐ Ⓑ Ⓒ Ⓓ Ⓔ   37 Ⓐ Ⓑ Ⓒ Ⓓ Ⓔ   52 Ⓐ Ⓑ Ⓒ Ⓓ Ⓔ   67 Ⓐ Ⓑ Ⓒ Ⓓ Ⓔ

8 Ⓐ Ⓑ Ⓒ Ⓓ Ⓔ   23 Ⓐ Ⓑ Ⓒ Ⓓ Ⓔ   38 Ⓐ Ⓑ Ⓒ Ⓓ Ⓔ   53 Ⓐ Ⓑ Ⓒ Ⓓ Ⓔ   68 Ⓐ Ⓑ Ⓒ Ⓓ Ⓔ

9 Ⓐ Ⓑ Ⓒ Ⓓ Ⓔ   24 Ⓐ Ⓑ Ⓒ Ⓓ Ⓔ   39 Ⓐ Ⓑ Ⓒ Ⓓ Ⓔ   54 Ⓐ Ⓑ Ⓒ Ⓓ Ⓔ   69 Ⓐ Ⓑ Ⓒ Ⓓ Ⓔ

10 Ⓐ Ⓑ Ⓒ Ⓓ Ⓔ   25 Ⓐ Ⓑ Ⓒ Ⓓ Ⓔ   40 Ⓐ Ⓑ Ⓒ Ⓓ Ⓔ   55 Ⓐ Ⓑ Ⓒ Ⓓ Ⓔ   70 Ⓐ Ⓑ Ⓒ Ⓓ Ⓔ

11 Ⓐ Ⓑ Ⓒ Ⓓ Ⓔ   26 Ⓐ Ⓑ Ⓒ Ⓓ Ⓔ   41 Ⓐ Ⓑ Ⓒ Ⓓ Ⓔ   56 Ⓐ Ⓑ Ⓒ Ⓓ Ⓔ   71 Ⓐ Ⓑ Ⓒ Ⓓ Ⓔ

12 Ⓐ Ⓑ Ⓒ Ⓓ Ⓔ   27 Ⓐ Ⓑ Ⓒ Ⓓ Ⓔ   42 Ⓐ Ⓑ Ⓒ Ⓓ Ⓔ   57 Ⓐ Ⓑ Ⓒ Ⓓ Ⓔ   72 Ⓐ Ⓑ Ⓒ Ⓓ Ⓔ

13 Ⓐ Ⓑ Ⓒ Ⓓ Ⓔ   28 Ⓐ Ⓑ Ⓒ Ⓓ Ⓔ   43 Ⓐ Ⓑ Ⓒ Ⓓ Ⓔ   58 Ⓐ Ⓑ Ⓒ Ⓓ Ⓔ   73 Ⓐ Ⓑ Ⓒ Ⓓ Ⓔ

14 Ⓐ Ⓑ Ⓒ Ⓓ Ⓔ   29 Ⓐ Ⓑ Ⓒ Ⓓ Ⓔ   44 Ⓐ Ⓑ Ⓒ Ⓓ Ⓔ   59 Ⓐ Ⓑ Ⓒ Ⓓ Ⓔ   74 Ⓐ Ⓑ Ⓒ Ⓓ Ⓔ

15 Ⓐ Ⓑ Ⓒ Ⓓ Ⓔ   30 Ⓐ Ⓑ Ⓒ Ⓓ Ⓔ   45 Ⓐ Ⓑ Ⓒ Ⓓ Ⓔ   60 Ⓐ Ⓑ Ⓒ Ⓓ Ⓔ   75 Ⓐ Ⓑ Ⓒ Ⓓ Ⓔ

Section II

76 Ⓐ Ⓑ Ⓒ Ⓓ Ⓔ	91 Ⓐ Ⓑ Ⓒ Ⓓ Ⓔ	106 Ⓐ Ⓑ Ⓒ Ⓓ Ⓔ	121 Ⓐ Ⓑ Ⓒ Ⓓ Ⓔ	136 Ⓐ Ⓑ Ⓒ Ⓓ Ⓔ
77 Ⓐ Ⓑ Ⓒ Ⓓ Ⓔ	92 Ⓐ Ⓑ Ⓒ Ⓓ Ⓔ	107 Ⓐ Ⓑ Ⓒ Ⓓ Ⓔ	122 Ⓐ Ⓑ Ⓒ Ⓓ Ⓔ	137 Ⓐ Ⓑ Ⓒ Ⓓ Ⓔ
78 Ⓐ Ⓑ Ⓒ Ⓓ Ⓔ	93 Ⓐ Ⓑ Ⓒ Ⓓ Ⓔ	108 Ⓐ Ⓑ Ⓒ Ⓓ Ⓔ	123 Ⓐ Ⓑ Ⓒ Ⓓ Ⓔ	138 Ⓐ Ⓑ Ⓒ Ⓓ Ⓔ
79 Ⓐ Ⓑ Ⓒ Ⓓ Ⓔ	94 Ⓐ Ⓑ Ⓒ Ⓓ Ⓔ	109 Ⓐ Ⓑ Ⓒ Ⓓ Ⓔ	124 Ⓐ Ⓑ Ⓒ Ⓓ Ⓔ	139 Ⓐ Ⓑ Ⓒ Ⓓ Ⓔ
80 Ⓐ Ⓑ Ⓒ Ⓓ Ⓔ	95 Ⓐ Ⓑ Ⓒ Ⓓ Ⓔ	110 Ⓐ Ⓑ Ⓒ Ⓓ Ⓔ	125 Ⓐ Ⓑ Ⓒ Ⓓ Ⓔ	140 Ⓐ Ⓑ Ⓒ Ⓓ Ⓔ
81 Ⓐ Ⓑ Ⓒ Ⓓ Ⓔ	96 Ⓐ Ⓑ Ⓒ Ⓓ Ⓔ	111 Ⓐ Ⓑ Ⓒ Ⓓ Ⓔ	126 Ⓐ Ⓑ Ⓒ Ⓓ Ⓔ	
82 Ⓐ Ⓑ Ⓒ Ⓓ Ⓔ	97 Ⓐ Ⓑ Ⓒ Ⓓ Ⓔ	112 Ⓐ Ⓑ Ⓒ Ⓓ Ⓔ	127 Ⓐ Ⓑ Ⓒ Ⓓ Ⓔ	
83 Ⓐ Ⓑ Ⓒ Ⓓ Ⓔ	98 Ⓐ Ⓑ Ⓒ Ⓓ Ⓔ	113 Ⓐ Ⓑ Ⓒ Ⓓ Ⓔ	128 Ⓐ Ⓑ Ⓒ Ⓓ Ⓔ	
84 Ⓐ Ⓑ Ⓒ Ⓓ Ⓔ	99 Ⓐ Ⓑ Ⓒ Ⓓ Ⓔ	114 Ⓐ Ⓑ Ⓒ Ⓓ Ⓔ	129 Ⓐ Ⓑ Ⓒ Ⓓ Ⓔ	
85 Ⓐ Ⓑ Ⓒ Ⓓ Ⓔ	100 Ⓐ Ⓑ Ⓒ Ⓓ Ⓔ	115 Ⓐ Ⓑ Ⓒ Ⓓ Ⓔ	130 Ⓐ Ⓑ Ⓒ Ⓓ Ⓔ	
86 Ⓐ Ⓑ Ⓒ Ⓓ Ⓔ	101 Ⓐ Ⓑ Ⓒ Ⓓ Ⓔ	116 Ⓐ Ⓑ Ⓒ Ⓓ Ⓔ	131 Ⓐ Ⓑ Ⓒ Ⓓ Ⓔ	
87 Ⓐ Ⓑ Ⓒ Ⓓ Ⓔ	102 Ⓐ Ⓑ Ⓒ Ⓓ Ⓔ	117 Ⓐ Ⓑ Ⓒ Ⓓ Ⓔ	132 Ⓐ Ⓑ Ⓒ Ⓓ Ⓔ	
88 Ⓐ Ⓑ Ⓒ Ⓓ Ⓔ	103 Ⓐ Ⓑ Ⓒ Ⓓ Ⓔ	118 Ⓐ Ⓑ Ⓒ Ⓓ Ⓔ	133 Ⓐ Ⓑ Ⓒ Ⓓ Ⓔ	
89 Ⓐ Ⓑ Ⓒ Ⓓ Ⓔ	104 Ⓐ Ⓑ Ⓒ Ⓓ Ⓔ	119 Ⓐ Ⓑ Ⓒ Ⓓ Ⓔ	134 Ⓐ Ⓑ Ⓒ Ⓓ Ⓔ	
90 Ⓐ Ⓑ Ⓒ Ⓓ Ⓔ	105 Ⓐ Ⓑ Ⓒ Ⓓ Ⓔ	120 Ⓐ Ⓑ Ⓒ Ⓓ Ⓔ	135 Ⓐ Ⓑ Ⓒ Ⓓ Ⓔ	

PRACTICE EXAMINATION I

Section I: Literature

75 Questions

Time—45 minutes

Directions: Each of the questions or incomplete statements below is followed by five suggested answers or completions. Select the one that is best in each case and blacken your answer sheet (A), (B), (C), (D), or (E) accordingly.

1. *Canterbury Tales,* an unfinished poetic work, was written by
   (A) John Donne.
   (B) Lord Byron.
   (C) Geoffrey Chaucer.
   (D) John Milton.
   (E) William Langland.

2. It deals with "the lost generation" of Americans who had fought in France during World War I and then had expatriated themselves from the America of Calvin Coolidge. The sentence above discusses
   (A) Dreiser's *An American Tragedy.*
   (B) Mailer's *The Deer Park.*
   (C) Hemingway's *The Sun Also Rises.*
   (D) James' *The Ambassadors.*
   (E) Faulkner's *Sanctuary.*

3. All of the following were American essayists EXCEPT
   (A) Jonathan Edwards.
   (B) Ralph Waldo Emerson.
   (C) Langston Hughes.
   (D) John Adams.
   (E) John Stuart Mill.

4. The person most associated with New York City's Public Theater is
   (A) Arthur Miller.
   (B) Cecil B. DeMille.
   (C) Robert Brustein.
   (D) Joseph Papp.
   (E) Joseph Losey.

5. Crazy Jane is the heroine of a series of poems by the author of "Sailing to Byzantium," who is
   (A) T.S. Eliot.
   (B) Alfred Tennyson.
   (C) Dylan Thomas.
   (D) William Butler Yeats.
   (E) W.H. Auden.

6. Which author in such works as *The Kandy Kolored Tangerine–Flake Streamline Baby* presents current issues in a fictional form in which apparently random detail is arranged kaleidoscopically around a subject?
   (A) Truman Capote
   (B) Tom Wolfe
   (C) e.e. cummings
   (D) Joseph Heller
   (E) Thomas Tryon

7. Which of the following plays was NOT written by Eugene O'Neill?
   (A) *Long Day's Journey Into Night*
   (B) *Anna Christie*
   (C) *The Iceman Cometh*
   (D) *Streetcar Named Desire*
   (E) *The Emperor Jones*

8. Which author is out of chronological order?
   (A) Plato
   (B) Horace
   (C) Spinoza
   (D) Mailer
   (E) Paine

9. Which of the following poems was written by Hart Crane?

    (A) "The Bridge"
    (B) "Trees"
    (C) "Fog"
    (D) "Maud"
    (E) "The Charge of the Light Brigade"

10. Which of the following short stories was NOT written by Edgar Allan Poe?

    (A) "The Murders in the Rue Morgue"
    (B) "The Tell–Tale Heart"
    (C) "The Pit and the Pendulum"
    (D) "The Killers"
    (E) "The Fall of the House of Usher"

11. Harlequin and Pierrot are players in

    (A) T.V. melodrama.
    (B) Italian opera.
    (C) commedia dell'arte.
    (D) French cinema.
    (E) Swedish cinema.

12. Which of the following is a part–social, part–literary phenomenon of the mid–1950s centered in Greenwich Village in New York, the North Beach district of San Francisco, and Venice West, a suburb of Los Angeles?

    (A) Transcendentalism
    (B) Socialist realism
    (C) The Beat Movement
    (D) The lost generation
    (E) The New Wave

Questions 13 and 14 refer to the following passage.

"Where, like a pillow on a bed,

  A pregnant bank swelled up to rest

The violet's reclining head,

  Sat we two, one another's best."

13. These lines employ the technique of

    (A) blank verse.
    (B) simile.
    (C) apostrophe.
    (D) onomatopoeia.
    (E) refrain.

14. The rhyme scheme employed in these lines follows a pattern of

    (A) ABAB.
    (B) ABBA.
    (C) AABB.
    (D) ABCD.
    (E) ABCB.

15. Which of the following characters is incorrectly paired with the novel in which he appears?

    (A) Jake Barnes . . . *The Sun Also Rises*
    (B) Ishmael . . . *Moby Dick*
    (C) Dean Moriarty . . . *On the Road*
    (D) Jean Valjean . . . *Les Misérables*
    (E) Leopold Bloom . . . *Steppenwolf*

16. Which of the following plays was NOT written by Arthur Miller?

    (A) *Death of A Salesman*
    (B) *The Crucible*
    (C) *Who's Afraid of Virginia Woolf?*
    (D) *The Price*
    (E) *The Fall*

17. *All the President's Men,* which concerns major events in U.S. presidential history and in investigative journalism, was written by

    (A) Comden and Green.
    (B) Sulzberger and Ochs.
    (C) Redford and Hoffman.
    (D) Woodward and Bernstein.
    (E) Pearson and Anderson.

Questions 18 and 19 refer to the following passage.

"Full fathom five thy father lies;

  Of his bones are coral made;

Those are pearls that were his eyes:

  Nothing of him that doth fade. . ."

18. The opening line employs the technique of

    (A) symbolism.
    (B) anthropomorphism.
    (C) metaphor.
    (D) caesura.
    (E) alliteration.

19. The lines relate to which setting?

    (A) Desert
    (B) Mountain
    (C) Urban
    (D) Sea
    (E) Tropical

20. *A Sportsman's Sketches,* a collection of short stories, was written by

    (A) John Rechy.
    (B) Ernest Hemingway.
    (C) Ivan Turgenev.
    (D) Norman Mailer.
    (E) Kurt Vonnegut, Jr.

21. It is a tragicomedy about two tramps, in which nothing happens except trivial events and conversations that suggest the meaninglessness of life.

    The sentence above discusses

    (A) Synge's *The Playboy of the Western World.*
    (B) Ionesco's *The Chairs.*
    (C) Beckett's *Waiting for Godot.*
    (D) Albee's *The Sandbox.*
    (E) Stoppard's *Rosencrantz and Guildenstern Are Dead.*

22. All of the following were written by Charles Lamb EXCEPT

    (A) "Dream Children."
    (B) "A Dissertation on Roast Pig."
    (C) "Old China."
    (D) "A Modest Proposal."
    (E) "The Superannuated Man."

23. All of the following were Greek playwrights, EXCEPT

    (A) Aeschylus.
    (B) Thucydides.
    (C) Sophocles.
    (D) Euripides.
    (E) Aristophanes.

24. An old lighthouse keeper, preparing to die, invites a group of guests to a gathering where his final words of wisdom will be delivered. In a scene that is both a dramatic and a symbolic *tour de force,* he and his wife rush desperately about to seat an enormous crowd of imaginary guests.

    The passage above discusses

    (A) Ionesco's *The Chairs.*
    (B) Beckett's *Waiting for Godot.*
    (C) Pinter's *The Dumbwaiter.*
    (D) Crowley's *The Boys In The Band.*
    (E) Ibsen's *The Master Builder.*

25. The American who won a Nobel Prize for work that includes *The Adventures of Augie March, Herzog,* and *Mr. Sammler's Planet* is

    (A) William Styron.
    (B) Norman Mailer.
    (C) Philip Roth.
    (D) Saul Bellow.
    (E) Joseph Heller.

26. It reveals the absurd as the condition of man, who feels himself a stranger in his world. Meursault refuses to "play the game," by telling the conventional social white lies demanded of him or by believing in human love or religious faith.

    The passage above discusses

    (A) Camus' *The Stranger.*
    (B) Ellison's *Invisible Man.*
    (C) Lewis' *Main Street.*
    (D) London's *The Sea Wolf.*
    (E) Miller's *Tropic of Cancer.*

27. "And so, all the night–tide, I lie down by the side

    Of my darling, my darling, my life and my bride,

    In her sepulchre there by the sea—

    In her tomb by the side of the sea."

    These lines were composed by

    (A) William Faulkner.
    (B) D.H. Lawrence.
    (C) Sylvia Plath.
    (D) Edgar Allan Poe.
    (E) John Masefield.

28. The book is a radical experiment in form and technique. Three of the novel's four sections are the interior monologues of the three Compson brothers. With their hypochondriac mother and their vanished sister, Caddy, they are the sole surviving members of a decaying aristocratic family in Mississippi.

    The passage above discusses

    (A) Lewis' *Main Street.*
    (B) Wright's *Native Son.*
    (C) Steinbeck's *The Grapes of Wrath.*
    (D) Wolfe's *Of Time and the River.*
    (E) Faulkner's *The Sound and the Fury.*

Questions 29 and 30 refer to the following poem.

"so much depends

upon

a red wheel

barrow

glazed with rain

water

beside the white

chickens."

29. These lines were composed by
    (A) William Shakespeare.
    (B) John Donne.
    (C) William Carlos Williams.
    (D) John Milton.
    (E) William Blake.

30. The main figure of speech employed in the poem is
    (A) allusion.
    (B) simile.
    (C) personification.
    (D) imagery.
    (E) alliteration.

31. The poor student Raskolnikov, after a long period of brooding over his poverty and the helpless position of his mother and young sister, plans and carries out the murder of an old woman moneylender.

    The sentence above discusses

    (A) Sholokhov's *And Quiet Flows the Don.*
    (B) Hamsun's *Hunger.*
    (C) Dostoyevski's *Crime and Punishment.*
    (D) Turgenev's *Fathers and Sons.*
    (E) Tolstoy's *Anna Karenina.*

32. A piece of verse consisting of fourteen 10-syllable lines, expressing a single idea, with rhymes arranged according to a certain definite scheme is a(n)
    (A) sonnet.
    (B) ode.
    (C) ballad.
    (D) stanza.
    (E) epic.

Questions 33 and 34 refer to the following.
    (A) *Anatomy of Melancholy*—Burton
    (B) *Interpretation of Dreams*—Freud
    (C) *My Life and Hard Times*—Thurber
    (D) *Utopia*—More
    (E) *Wealth of Nations*—Smith

33. Which of the above is humorous in tone?

34. Which of the above is concerned with how to fashion a better world for people to live in?

35. Which of the following poets was an important figure in the "San Francisco Renaissance"?
    (A) Edgar Lee Masters
    (B) Robert Frost
    (C) Robert Penn Warren
    (D) Carl Sandburg
    (E) Lawrence Ferlinghetti

36. Which of the following short stories was written by F. Scott Fitzgerald?

    (A) "The Killers"
    (B) "The Fox"
    (C) "A Rose for Emily"
    (D) "The Death of Ivan Ilyich"
    (E) "Babylon Revisited"

37. It is the story of Constance, the wife of an English aristocrat who runs away with her gamekeeper. Her husband, Sir Clifford, is a physical and emotional cripple.

    The passage above discusses

    (A) Greene's *The Heart of the Matter.*
    (B) Woolf's *To the Lighthouse.*
    (C) Lawrence's *Lady Chatterley's Lover.*
    (D) Faulkner's *Sanctuary.*
    (E) Mitchell's *Gone with the Wind.*

38. Which of the following is NOT an examination of religious thought?

    (A) *The Imitation of Christ*
    (B) *Leviathan*
    (C) *Peace of Mind*
    (D) *Divine Love and Wisdom*
    (E) *Letter to the Corinthians*

39. "Ain't got nobody in all this world
    Ain't got nobody but ma self.
    I's gwine to quit ma frownin'
    And put ma troubles on the shelf."

    These lines are found in a poem by

    (A) Shirley Jackson.
    (B) Edgar Allan Poe.
    (C) William Empson.
    (D) Langston Hughes.
    (E) Edna St. Vincent Millay.

40. How is the character of Don Quixote best described?

    (A) Stupid and blundering
    (B) Comically insane
    (C) Extravagantly chivalrous and impractically idealistic
    (D) Deceptively clever
    (E) Pathetic

41. Which of the following novels was not written by Thomas Mann?

    (A) *Confessions of Felix Krull: Confidence Man*
    (B) *Buddenbrooks*
    (C) *The Magic Mountain*
    (D) *Doktor Faustus*
    (E) *Steppenwolf*

42. "O where ha' you been, Lord Randal, my son?
    And where ha' you been, my handsome young man?"

    "I ha' been at the greenwood; mother, mak my bed soon,
    For I'm wearied wi' huntin', and fain wad lie down."

    The form of these lines is

    (A) ballad.
    (B) sonnet.
    (C) limerick.
    (D) epic.
    (E) villanelle.

43. Set in a Sicilian community on the Gulf Coast, the play deals with Serafina Delle Rose, a passionate and warmhearted dressmaker, whose truck driver husband has just been killed.

    This sentence describes

    (A) Osborne's *Look Back in Anger.*
    (B) Ionesco's *The Bald Soprano.*
    (C) Williams' *The Rose Tattoo.*
    (D) O'Neill's *Beyond the Horizon.*
    (E) Beckett's *Waiting for Godot.*

44. Which of the following plays is NOT paired with its correct author?

    (A) *The Maids* . . . Jean Genet
    (B) *Motel* . . . Jean–Claude van Italie
    (C) *The Alchemist* . . . Ben Jonson
    (D) *A Woman of No Importance* . . . Oscar Wilde
    (E) *Hedda Gabler* . . . Anton Chekhov

45. Who created the character of Walter Mitty?

    (A) James Thurber
    (B) O. Henry
    (C) George Ade
    (D) E.B. White
    (E) S.J. Perelman

46. Which of the following novels was NOT written by Charles Dickens?

    (A) *Pickwick Papers*
    (B) *Treasure Island*
    (C) *David Copperfield*
    (D) *Great Expectations*
    (E) *A Tale of Two Cities*

47. *Walden; Or, Life in the Woods* was written by

    (A) Henry David Thoreau.
    (B) Theodore Dreiser.
    (C) Walt Whitman.
    (D) Ralph Waldo Emerson.
    (E) Mark Twain.

48. The work that is an elegy for a drowned friend is

    (A) *The Dunciad.*
    (B) *The Wasteland.*
    (C) *The Prelude.*
    (D) *Hero and Leander.*
    (E) *Lycidas.*

49. Who delivered the famous "I Have A Dream" speech of the 1960s?

    (A) Martin Luther King, Jr.
    (B) Robert Kennedy
    (C) John Lennon
    (D) John F. Kennedy
    (E) Medgar Evers

50. "The curfew tolls the knell of parting day,

    The lowing herd wind slowly o'er the lea,

    The plowman homeward plods his weary way,

    And leaves the world to darkness and to me."

    These are the opening lines of a poem about

    (A) farming.
    (B) marriage.
    (C) death.
    (D) parting lovers.
    (E) parent-child relationships.

51. He is known for the eccentricity of his typography and punctuation, which he employed to indicate the rhythmic pattern and interwoven meaning of his poems. His work includes lyrical love poems, humorous character sketches, and bitter satires on the foibles and institutions of his time.

    The passage above discusses

    (A) Robinson Jeffers.
    (B) Robert Penn Warren.
    (C) Wallace Stevens.
    (D) e.e. cummings.
    (E) Richard Howard.

52. *Madame Bovary* made Gustave Flaubert the leading figure of what school of writing in France?

    (A) Symbolic
    (B) Realistic
    (C) Romantic
    (D) Lyric
    (E) Classic

53. Which of the following is an American philosophic and literary movement centered in New England during the nineteenth century?

    (A) Formalism
    (B) Transcendentalism
    (C) The New Wave
    (D) The Agrarian group
    (E) Surrealism

54. Joan of Arc, Eugene Marchbanks, and Eliza Doolittle are all characters in plays by

    (A) Shakespeare.
    (B) Marlowe.
    (C) Shaw.
    (D) Ibsen.
    (E) Miller.

55. A poem NOT written by Robert Frost is

    (A) "Mending Wall."
    (B) "Birches."
    (C) "Stopping by Woods on a Snowy Evening."
    (D) "The Gift Outright."
    (E) "Chicago."

56. The author of *The Children's Hour, The Little Foxes,* and *Julia,* who also earned a considerable reputation for speaking out against the McCarthyism of the 1950s, is

    (A) Mary McCarthy.
    (B) Susan Sontag.
    (C) Marilyn French.
    (D) Lillian Hellman.
    (E) Renata Adler.

57. Which of the following wrote *The Legend of Sleepy Hollow?*

    (A) Walt Whitman
    (B) Washington Irving
    (C) Edgar Allen Poe
    (D) Lewis Carroll
    (E) Nathaniel Hawthorne

58. Which is a series of essays of Joseph Addison and Richard Steele?

    (A) *New Masses*
    (B) *The Dial*
    (C) *The Spectator*
    (D) *Transition*
    (E) *The Federalist Papers*

59. Though *A Season in Hell* and *Illuminations* had great influence on the poetic schools of Symbolism and Surrealism, the author of these works abandoned literature forever at the age of nineteen. He is

    (A) Paul Verlaine.
    (B) Ezra Pound.
    (C) Arthur Rimbaud.
    (D) Jean Genet.
    (E) William Blake.

60. Which of the following poets wrote the line, "I hear America singing"?

    (A) Robert Frost
    (B) Walt Whitman
    (C) Stephen Vincent Benet
    (D) Joyce Kilmer
    (E) Francis Scott Key

61. The British writer known for work in film and for plays such as *The Homecoming* and *The Birthday Party* is

    (A) Edward Albee.
    (B) George Bernard Shaw.
    (C) Harold Pinter.
    (D) Tom Stoppard.
    (E) Virginia Woolf.

62. The author of *The Feminine Mystique,* who is often credited with inspiring the woman's movement of the 1960s in the United States, is

    (A) Adrienne Rich.
    (B) Marjorie Morningstar.
    (C) Elizabeth Holtzman.
    (D) Lorraine Hansberry.
    (E) Betty Friedan.

63. Which of the following wrote *Tess of the D' Urbervilles?*

    (A) Guy de Maupassant
    (B) Alexander Dumas
    (C) Wilkie Collins
    (D) Thomas Hardy
    (E) Aldous Huxley

64. Which of the following Shakespearean characters is incorrectly paired with the play in which he appears?

    (A) Prospero—*The Tempest*
    (B) Shylock—*The Merchant of Venice*
    (C) Laertes—*Hamlet*
    (D) Iago—*Othello*
    (E) Polonius—*The Tempest*

65. Written without any beginning or ending, the book extensively details the fears, fantasies, and reflections of a lower–class laborer through the use of elaborate wordplays in a number of languages. The sentence above discusses

    (A) *The Grapes of Wrath.*
    (B) *Finnegan's Wake.*
    (C) *The Brothers Karamazov.*
    (D) *Ulysses.*
    (E) *Manhattan Transfer.*

66. *Howl and Other Poems* was written by
    - (A) Kenneth Rexroth.
    - (B) Walt Whitman.
    - (C) Allen Ginsberg.
    - (D) Charles Baudelaire.
    - (E) Carl Sandburg.

67. Which novel is NOT paired with its correct author?
    - (A) *Death Comes to the Archbishop*—Willa Cather
    - (B) *Babbit*—Sinclair Lewis
    - (C) *This Side of Paradise*—F. Scott Fitzgerald
    - (D) *Invisible Man*—Richard Wright
    - (E) *Catch–22*—Joseph Heller

68. Which of the following characters is incorrectly paired with the play in which he/she appears?
    - (A) Willy Loman—*The Caretaker*
    - (B) Abbie—*Desire Under the Elms*
    - (C) King Creon—*Antigone*
    - (D) Maggie Pollitt—*Cat on a Hot Tin Roof*
    - (E) Claire—*The Maids*

69. "But suicides have a special language.

    Like carpenters they want to know which tools.

    They never ask *why build*."

    These lines were written by
    - (A) Elizabeth Barrett Browning.
    - (B) Anne Sexton.
    - (C) Daphne du Maurier.
    - (D) Gertrude Stein.
    - (E) Ogden Nash.

70. The author of the statement, "I think, therefore I am," is
    - (A) Socrates.
    - (B) Kant.
    - (C) Einstein.
    - (D) Descartes.
    - (E) Buber.

71. "His true Penelope was Flaubert,

    He fished by obstinate isles;

    Observed the elegance of Circe's hair

    Rather than the mottoes on sundials."

    In lines 1 and 3, the poet makes use of
    - (A) alliteration.
    - (B) allusion.
    - (C) personification.
    - (D) metaphor.
    - (E) simile.

72. John Bunyan's *Pilgrim's Progress* deals with the subject of
    - (A) the sailing of the Mayflower.
    - (B) allegorical enlightenment.
    - (C) Oliver Cromwell.
    - (D) a journey to Canterbury.
    - (E) the Plymouth Colony.

73. *The Status Seekers* by Vance Packard is a work dealing mainly with
    - (A) social classes in the United States.
    - (B) teenagers and their problems.
    - (C) the struggle of underprivileged nations for recognition.
    - (D) the changing role of the doctor in American society.
    - (E) alcoholism in the United States.

74. Which of the following groups is most associated with the philosophy of existentialism?
    - (A) Camus, Marcel, Whitehead, Darwin
    - (B) Jaspers, Croce, Unamuno, Chomsky
    - (C) Kierkegaard, Nietzsche, Sartre, Heidegger
    - (D) Whitehead, Russell, Smith, James
    - (E) Bellamy, Popper, Camus, DeBeauvoir

75. Which of the following was a member of the Bloomsbury Group?
    - (A) Upton Sinclair
    - (B) John Crowe Ransom
    - (C) Virginia Woolf
    - (D) Theodore Dreiser
    - (E) Sherwood Anderson

Section II: Fine Arts

65 Questions

Time—45 minutes

Directions: For each question, choose the best answer from the five choices offered. Blacken your answer sheet for the letter of the correct answer.

76. The concert–overture *Eighteen Twelve* (1812) was composed by

    (A) Frédéric Chopin.
    (B) Igor Stravinsky.
    (C) Claude–Achille Debussy.
    (D) Piotr Ilyich Tchaikovsky.
    (E) Richard Wagner.

77. The American designer who created many fine works of glass was

    (A) Tiffany.
    (B) Thonet.
    (C) Gaudi.
    (D) Sullivan.
    (E) Arp.

78. The Union Army's official photographer who created a detailed and unique visual history of one side's participation in the War Between the States was

    (A) Louis Daguerre.
    (B) Edward Steichen.
    (C) Will Soule.
    (D) Lewis Carroll.
    (E) Mathew Brady.

79. A piece of orchestral music preceding an opera or oratorio is a(n)

    (A) fugue.
    (B) aria.
    (C) interlude.
    (D) madrigal.
    (E) overture.

80. All are Beatles' works EXCEPT

    (A) "Yellow Submarine."
    (B) "Hard Day's Night."
    (C) "I Heard It Through the Grapevine."
    (D) "Sergeant Pepper's Lonely Hearts Club Band."
    (E) "Lucy in the Sky with Diamonds."

81. The film *Rashomon*, starring Toshiro Mifune, was directed by

    (A) Peter Bogdanovich.
    (B) Isamu Noguchi.
    (C) Akira Kurosawa.
    (D) Red Buttons.
    (E) S.I. Hayakawa.

82. Although he had no professional training as an architect or engineer, he invented the geodesic dome. He is

    (A) Gordon Bunshaft.
    (B) Buckminster Fuller.
    (C) Raymond Skorupa.
    (D) Phillip Johnson.
    (E) I.M. Pei.

83. Why is it often misleading to refer to a painting of Peter Paul Rubens as "genuine"?

    (A) Most are modern forgeries.
    (B) Most were begun by Rubens but detailed or completed by others.
    (C) Rubens never actually painted anything but only managed a painting workshop.
    (D) Only copies of Rubens' work by his pupils now exist.
    (E) "Rubens" was one of Rembrandt's pseudonyms.

84. His art of free fantasy is best defined in his own words as "taking a line for a walk."

    The painter referred to in the sentence above is

    (A) Manet.
    (B) Gauguin.
    (C) Klee.
    (D) Degas.
    (E) Courbet.

Questions 85 and 86 refer to the following operas.

(A) *Lucia di Lammermoor*
(B) *Pagliaci*
(C) *Don Giovanni*
(D) *Fidelio*
(E) *La Bohème*

85. In which opera does the drama on a mimic stage become the player's real–life tragedy?

86. Which opera was composed by Puccini?

87. The *Campbell's Soup* painting and this *Green Coca Cola Bottles* canvas were created by

(A) Georgia O'Keeffe.
(B) Georges Seurat.
(C) Tom Wesselmann.
(D) Andy Warhol.
(E) Roy Lichtenstein.

88. Which of the following groups is associated with the Minimalist movement?

(A) Philip Johnson, Louis Kahn, Frank Lloyd Wright, Edward Durrell Stone
(B) Sol LeWitt, Robert Rauschenberg, Michelangelo Pistoletto, Eva Hesse
(C) Robert Morris, Dan Flavin, Donald Judd, Tony Smith
(D) Lynda Benglis, Jannis Kounellis, Louise Bourgeois, Cy Twombly
(E) Nicolas de Stael, Karel Appel, Mark Rothko, Barnett Newman

89. Albrecht Dürer is best known for his skill with

(A) oils.
(B) water colors.
(C) woodcuts and engravings.
(D) charcoal and pastels.
(E) pen and ink.

90. The film *Citizen Kane* was directed by which of the following pioneers in the American film industry?

(A) D.W. Griffith
(B) Charlie Chaplin
(C) Orson Welles
(D) John Ford
(E) Busby Berkeley

91. Jimmy Cliff, Bob Marley, and Peter Tosh are associated with the style of music called

(A) punk.
(B) reggae.
(C) country–western.
(D) calypso.
(E) jazz.

92. His works include the operas *Four Saints in Three Acts* and *The Mother of Us All* (both to librettos of Gertrude Stein).

The sentence above refers to

(A) Pierre Boulez.
(B) Erik Satie.
(C) Benjamin Britten.
(D) Béla Bartók.
(E) Virgil Thomson.

93. Which of the following is opaque watercolor paint?

(A) Acrylic
(B) Encaustic wax
(C) Fresco
(D) Gouache
(E) Pastel

94. Which of the following is a celebrated Gothic monastery built on a high rock over the sea?

(A) Lourdes
(B) Mont–Saint–Michel
(C) Saint–Riquier
(D) Vierzehnheiligen
(E) Compostela

95.	The great composer–bandleader of New Or-leans jazz was

(A)	Edward "Duke" Ellington.
(B)	Ferdinand "Jelly Roll" Morton.
(C)	William "Count" Basie.
(D)	Scott Joplin.
(E)	James Scott.

96.	The outstanding composer of German opera was

(A)	Arnold Schoenberg.
(B)	Gustav Mahler.
(C)	Richard Wagner.
(D)	Franz Liszt.
(E)	Johann Sebastian Bach.

97.	All of the following films starred Humphrey Bogart EXCEPT

(A)	*Casablanca.*
(B)	*African Queen.*
(C)	*Petrified Forest.*
(D)	*High Noon.*
(E)	*To Have and Have Not.*

98.	Most of Beethoven's compositions are written in which of the following forms?

(A)	Sectional form
(B)	Variation form
(C)	Fugal form
(D)	Sonata form
(E)	Free form

99.	A pioneer in the production of animated cartoons is

(A)	Charles Adams.
(B)	Diego Rivera.
(C)	Walt Kelly.
(D)	Paul Terry.
(E)	Shel Silverstein.

100.	The Bauhaus was founded in Weimar, Ger-many in 1919 by

(A)	Mies van der Rohe.
(B)	Peter Behrens.
(C)	Louis Kahn.
(D)	Walter Gropius.
(E)	Otto Wagner.

101.	A musical about youth and love that was based on a Shakespearean play was

(A)	*Hair.*
(B)	*My Fair Lady.*
(C)	*Grease.*
(D)	*West Side Story.*
(E)	*Annie.*

102.	The Russian Ballet was an important force in music under the control of

(A)	Nijinsky.
(B)	Diaghilev.
(C)	Pavlova.
(D)	Satie.
(E)	Dufy.

103.	Which of the following was a school of Ameri-can landscape painting, highly Romantic in feeling and glorifying the wonders of nature as visible in the American landscape?

(A)	Hudson River School
(B)	Barbizon School
(C)	Les Nabis
(D)	Pre–Raphaelite Brotherhood
(E)	Euston Road

104.	"The Moldau," one of a cycle of symphonic poems entitled "My Country," was composed by

(A)	Smetana.
(B)	Dvorák.
(C)	Goldmark.
(D)	Spohr.
(E)	Copland.

105.	A song about the syllable tones of the musical scale comes from the musical comedy

(A)	*My Fair Lady.*
(B)	*The Most Happy Fella.*
(C)	*The Sound of Music.*
(D)	*The Music Man.*
(E)	*Bye Bye Birdie.*

106.	The television set installation pictured below is the work of

(A)	Nam June Paik.
(B)	Michael Heizer.
(C)	Robert Smithson.
(D)	Joseph Beuys.
(E)	Yves Klein.

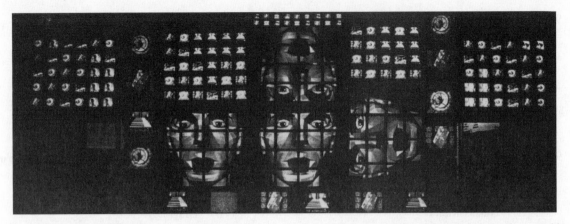

107. Jean Arp was one of the cofounders of

    (A) Art Nouveau.
    (B) Dada.
    (C) Cubism.
    (D) Fauvism.
    (E) Futurism.

108. What American painter is known for her use of exquisite colors and abstract representations of flower forms?

    (A) Lillian Westcott Hale
    (B) Violet Oakley
    (C) Georgia O'Keeffe
    (D) Marie Danforth Page
    (E) Jessie Wilcox Smith

109. The leader of a modern dance company whose work is influenced by gospel and soul music is

    (A) Jose Limon.
    (B) Martha Graham.
    (C) Alvin Ailey.
    (D) Doris Humphrey.
    (E) Merce Cunningham.

110. The musical instrument below was invented by

    (A) Richard Wagner.
    (B) John Philip Sousa.
    (C) Johann Strauss.
    (D) George Gershwin.
    (E) Charles Ives.

111. Which of the following architects is also known for his furniture designs?

(A) Charles Eames
(B) I.M. Pei
(C) Paul McKim
(D) Inigo Jones
(E) Christopher Wren

112. Some of the most incisive portrayals of the horrors and brutality of war are the work of

(A) Titian.
(B) Stuart.
(C) Velasquez.
(D) Goya.
(E) Constable.

113. Frontality and formal, rather rigid figures are characteristic of the sculptures of

(A) Rome.
(B) Egypt.
(C) Greece.
(D) Renaissance France.
(E) the Aztecs.

114. The singer of "Heartbreak Hotel" and "Jailhouse Rock" who was notorious for his long sideburns and controversial gyrations was

(A) Jerry Lee Lewis.
(B) Fats Domino.
(C) Perry Como.
(D) Elvis Presley.
(E) Hank Williams.

Questions 115 and 116 refer to the following ballets.

(A) *The Judgment of Paris*
(B) *Orpheus*
(C) *The Age of Anxiety*
(D) *Dark Elegies*
(E) *Illuminations*

115. Which ballet was inspired by Leonard Bernstein's Second Symphony and the poem by W.H. Auden on which the symphony is based?

116. Which ballet is a contemporary treatment of the ancient myth of the Greek musician who descended into Hades in search of his dead wife?

117. The three classical architectural orders are the Ionic, Corinthian, and

(A) Doric.
(B) Mycenean.
(C) Minoan.
(D) Hellenistic.
(E) Etruscan.

118. His *Rhapsody in Blue* was an attempt to combine the languages of jazz and classical music. He is

(A) George Gershwin.
(B) Ralph Vaughan Williams.
(C) Erik Satie.
(D) Virgil Thomson.
(E) Arnold Schoenberg.

119. Which of the following sought to free artists from the normal association of pictorial ideas and from all accepted means of expression, so that they might create according to the irrational dictates of their subconscious mind and vision?

(A) Cubism
(B) Pop Art
(C) Impressionism
(D) Futurism
(E) Surrealism

120. *The Gamble,* mixed media and collage on board pictured below, was created by

(A) Stuart Davis.
(B) Romare Bearden.
(C) Fairfield Porter.
(D) Alex Katz.
(E) Alice Neel.

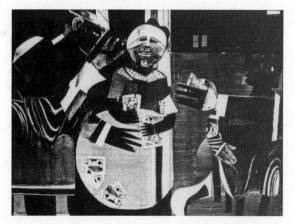

121. All of the following are/were popular recording and film artists EXCEPT

    (A) Donna Summer.
    (B) Frank Sinatra.
    (C) Olivia Newton John.
    (D) Elizabeth Taylor.
    (E) Barbra Streisand.

122. The source of the film *Blow Up* is

    (A) *The Daybooks of Edward Weston.*
    (B) a short story by Julio Cortázar.
    (C) a series of photographs by Man Ray.
    (D) a short story by Jean Kerr.
    (E) a song by Bob Dylan.

123. They combined several views of any given object all more or less superimposed, expressing the idea of the object rather than any one view of it.

    The sentence above discusses the

    (A) Fauvists.
    (B) Impressionists.
    (C) Cubists.
    (D) Surrealists.
    (E) Symbolists.

124. A Florentine sculptor and goldsmith who lived in the sixteenth century was

    (A) Giovanni Bellini.
    (B) Benvenuto Cellini.
    (C) Giovanni Cimabue.
    (D) Leonardo Da Vinci.
    (E) Michelangelo.

125. An outstanding jazz pianist is

    (A) "Count" Basie.
    (B) Charlie Parker.
    (C) Sonny Rollins.
    (D) Scott Joplin.
    (E) "Doc" Sevarinson.

126. The raised design on a cameo is an example of

    (A) bas–relief.
    (B) intaglio.
    (C) modeling.
    (D) sculpture.
    (E) sgraffito.

127. Which of the following painters is incorrectly paired with the group or movement with which he was associated?

    (A) Beardsley . . . Mannerism
    (B) Klimt . . . *Jugendstil*
    (C) Kandinsky . . . *Der Blaue Reiter*
    (D) Rauschenberg . . . Pop Art
    (E) Balla . . . Futurism

128. James Agee's *Let Us Now Praise Famous Men* contained a series of photographs by

    (A) Paul Strand.
    (B) Walker Evans.
    (C) Ansel Adams.
    (D) Imogen Cunningham.
    (E) Edward Weston.

129. Chiaroscuro is a technique involving the use of

    (A) light and shade.
    (B) color.
    (C) pictorial illusionism.
    (D) geometric forms.
    (E) biomorphic forms.

130. The blind musicians Stevie Wonder, Ray Charles, and George Shearing all play the

    (A) harmonica.
    (B) guitar.
    (C) saxophone.
    (D) piano.
    (E) clarinet.

131. Which of the following painters was NOT an Impressionist?

    (A) Monet
    (B) Pissarro
    (C) Morisot
    (D) Sisley
    (E) Chirico

132. All of the following are popular dances that originated in either Central America, the Caribbean, or South America, EXCEPT the

    (A) marimba.
    (B) samba.
    (C) conga.
    (D) mambo.
    (E) cha–cha.

Questions 133–136 refer to the following pictures.

133.   Which is by Grant Wood?

134.   Which is by Rembrandt?

135.   Which is an Impressionist painting?

136.   Which is by Alexander Calder?

(A)

(C)

(B)

(D)

(E)

137. Who played three roles in *Dr. Strangelove* and starred in the *Pink Panther* films?

    (A) George C. Scott
    (B) Peter Sellers
    (C) The Marx Brothers
    (D) Albert Finney
    (E) Richard Attenborough

138. Which of the following was a great Renaissance sculptor?

    (A) Donatello
    (B) Gianlorenzo Bernini
    (C) Clodion
    (D) Jean Baptiste Carpeaux
    (E) Medardo Rosso

139. Once famous for performing in fancy sunglasses and outlandish costumes, this singer–pianist later changed his style. He is

    (A) Kiss.
    (B) Elton John.
    (C) Jimmy Hendrix.
    (D) Rod Stewart.
    (E) John Lennon.

140. All of the following works are by Michelangelo EXCEPT

    (A) the painting, "The Last Judgment."
    (B) the portal of the baptistery in Florence, "The Gates of Paradise."
    (C) the statue of Moses.
    (D) the fresco on the ceiling of the Sistine Chapel.
    (E) the Pieta.

End of Practice Examination I

Answer Key

Section I

1.	C	16.	C	31.	C	46.	B	61.	C
2.	C	17.	D	32.	A	47.	A	62.	E
3.	E	18.	E	33.	C	48.	E	63.	D
4.	D	19.	D	34.	D	49.	A	64.	E
5.	D	20.	C	35.	E	50.	C	65.	B
6.	B	21.	C	36.	E	51.	D	66.	C
7.	D	22.	D	37.	C	52.	B	67.	D
8.	D	23.	B	38.	B	53.	B	68.	A
9.	A	24.	A	39.	D	54.	C	69.	B
10.	D	25.	D	40.	C	55.	E	70.	D
11.	C	26.	A	41.	E	56.	D	71.	B
12.	C	27.	D	42.	A	57.	B	72.	B
13.	B	28.	E	43.	C	58.	C	73.	A
14.	A	29.	C	44.	E	59.	C	74.	C
15.	E	30.	D	45.	A	60.	B	75.	C

Section II

76.	D	91.	B	106.	A	121.	D	136.	C
77.	A	92.	E	107.	B	122.	B	137.	B
78.	E	93.	D	108.	C	123.	C	138.	A
79.	E	94.	B	109.	C	124.	B	139.	B
80.	C	95.	B	110.	B	125.	A	140.	B
81.	C	96.	C	111.	A	126.	A		
82.	B	97.	D	112.	D	127.	A		
83.	B	98.	D	113.	B	128.	B		
84.	C	99.	D	114.	D	129.	A		
85.	B	100.	D	115.	C	130.	D		
86.	E	101.	D	116.	B	131.	E		
87.	D	102.	B	117.	A	132.	A		
88.	C	103.	A	118.	A	133.	E		
89.	C	104.	A	119.	E	134.	D		
90.	C	105.	C	120.	B	135.	A		

Explanatory Answers

Section I

1. **The correct answer is (C).** Geoffrey Chaucer (1343–1400) describes in *The Canterbury Tales* a group of pilgrims who amuse themselves by telling stories as they travel ("The Nun's Tale," "The Priest's Tale," "The Pardoner's Tale," and "The Miller's Tale," for instance).

2. **The correct answer is (C).** Ernest Hemingway (1898–1961) wrote *The Sun Also Rises* in 1926. (It was called *Fiesta* in England.) The novel takes place in Paris and Pamplona in the 1920s and tells of Jake Barnes, who has been emasculated in World War I.

3. **The correct answer is (E).** John Stuart Mill (1806–1873) was an Englishman who developed the Utilitarian movement; he was known for his philosophical essay *On Liberty* (1859), a defense of individuality against all authoritarianism, and for *The Subjection of Women* (1869), an early treatise in the struggle for equal rights for women.

4. **The correct answer is (D).** Joseph Papp (1921–1991) was founder of the New York Public Theater and producer of the Shakespeare Festival in New York's Delacorte Theatre in Central Park; he was associated with many productions of Shakespeare's works and with the award–winning plays *Sticks and Bones, In the Boom Boom Room, A Chorus Line, Short Eyes,* and *That Championship Season.*

5. **The correct answer is (D).** William Butler Yeats (1865–1939) was the great Irish poet and playwright who cofounded the Irish National Theatre Society, which became Dublin's famous Abbey Theatre. He is known for "Leda and the Swan," "The Second Coming," and many other works and was awarded the Nobel Prize in literature in 1923.

6. **The correct answer is (B).** Tom Wolfe (1931–) is the journalist and pop critic who developed his style in the 1960s, when he produced *The Electric Kool–Aid Acid Test.* He should not be confused with the novelist, Thomas Wolfe, who died in 1938.

7. **The correct answer is (D).** *A Streetcar Named Desire* was written in 1947 by Tennessee Williams (1911–1983), who is also known for *The Glass Menagerie, Cat on a Hot Tin Roof, Orpheus Descending, Sweet Bird of Youth,* and *The Night of the Iguana.*

8. **The correct answer is (D).** Norman Mailer (1923–), the twentieth–century novelist and essayist who once ran for the office of Mayor of New York City, lived *after* Thomas Paine (1735–1809), the author of *Common Sense, The Age of Reason,* and *The Rights of Man,* who urged the American colonies to seek independence from England ("These are the times that try men's souls").

9. **The correct answer is (A).** Hart Crane (1899–1932) wrote *The Bridge* in 1930. It has been called a "triumph of the use of the principle of 'objective correlative,'" in which the images are arranged for emotional rather than logical effect, with the meaning emerging for the careful reader at the work's conclusion.

10. **The correct answer is (D).** "The Killers" is a short story from the collection *Men Without Women,* published by Ernest Hemingway in 1927.

11. **The correct answer is (C).** Commedia dell'arte (comedy of the guild, or by professionals in the art) developed in sixteenth-century Italy and spread throughout Europe, shaping seventeenth- and eighteenth-century comedy and influencing twentieth-century drama. Basically, it is comedy that follows a scenario rather than written dialogue.

12. **The correct answer is (C).** The Beat Movement, a bohemian rebellion against established society, involved such writers as Allen Ginsberg, Gregory Corso, Lawrence Ferlinghetti, and Jack Kerouac.

13. **The correct answer is (B).** *Simile* is a figure of speech that makes a comparison between essentially unlike things by using "like" or "as"; in this case, "A pregnant bank" (of a stream or river) is compared to "a pillow on a bed."

14. **The correct answer is (A).** Rhyme scheme is determined by the final sounds in lines of

poetry. In this case, "bed" (A) and "head" (A) rhyme, as do "rest" (B) and "best" (B), so the scheme is said to be ABAB.

15. **The correct answer is (E).** Leopold Bloom appears in James Joyce's *Ulysses,* which depicts a single day in the lives of Bloom, his wife Molly, and Stephen Dedalus (who also appears in *A Portrait of the Artist as a Young Man*).

16. **The correct answer is (C).** *Who's Afraid of Virginia Woolf?* was the first full–length play written by Edward Albee (1928–). It won the Drama Critics Circle Award and the Antoinette Perry Award as best play of the 1962 season.

17. **The correct answer is (D).** Bob Woodward and Carl Bernstein worked together on *The Washington Post* and also coauthored *The Final Days*. They won a Pulitzer Prize for their investigative journalism that produced the series concerning the 1972 Watergate scandal.

18. **The correct answer is (E).** *Alliteration* is a literary device involving the repetition of initial sounds, in this case "f".

19. **The correct answer is (D).** The lines are from Shakespeare's *The Tempest,* which is set on an island in the distant seas; "fathom," "coral," and "pearls" cue the reader to think of the sea.

20. **The correct answer is (C).** Ivan Turgenev (1818–1883) is the Russian author who is also known for *Fathers and Sons.*

21. **The correct answer is (C).** Samuel Beckett (1906–1989) wrote *Waiting for Godot* in 1952. He is also known for the novels *Murphy, Molloy,* and *Malone Dies* and the plays *Endgame* and *Krapp's Last Tape,* among others.

22. **The correct answer is (D).** *A Modest Proposal for Preventing the Children of Poor People of Ireland from Being a Burden to Their Parents* is the masterpiece of satire and irony written in 1729 by Jonathan Swift (1667–1745), who also wrote *Gulliver's Travels.*

23. **The correct answer is (B).** Thucydides (455(?) B.C.E.–400 B.C.E.) was the Greek historian who wrote *History of the Peloponnesian War.*

24. **The correct answer is (A).** Eugene Ionesco (1909–1994), who wrote *The Chairs* in 1952, is also known for other works against the conventional theater of his time: *The Bald Soprano, The Lesson,* and *Rhinoceros.*

25. **The correct answer is (D).** Saul Bellow (1915–) also authored *Dangling Man, The Victim, Henderson the Rain King, Seize the Day, The Last Analysis,* and *Humboldt's Gift.*

26. **The correct answer is (A).** Albert Camus (1913–1960) wrote *The Stranger* in 1942 as an expression of his existentialist philosophy. He also wrote *The Plague, The Fall, The Myth of Sisyphus,* and *The Rebel* and was awarded the Nobel Prize in literature in 1957.

27. **The correct answer is (D).** Edgar Allan Poe (1809–1849) wrote many poems concerning the death of a loved one. The lines cited are the conclusion of "Annabel Lee." "The Raven," "To Helen," and "The Bells" are some of his other poems.

28. **The correct answer is (E).** William Faulkner (1897–1962) sets *The Sound and the Fury* in Mississippi between the years 1910 and 1928. He accepted the Nobel Prize in literature in 1949 for work that includes *As I Lay Dying, Sartoris, Light in August, Absalom, Absalom!, Requiem for a Nun,* and *Intruder in the Dust.*

29. **The correct answer is (C).** William Carlos Williams (1883–1963) was a physician who became one of America's leading contemporary poets, the author of the Paterson poems and of short poems of the world he knew and lived in.

30. **The correct answer is (D).** Influenced by Ezra Pound and the imagists, Williams was also determined to show the inseparability of vivid imagery and thought; as he created a picture in words (to create in the lines cited, for example, the "reality" of the wheelbarrow), Williams also sought to write as Americans *spoke.*

31. **The correct answer is (C).** Fyodor Dostoyevsky (1821–1881) wrote *Crime and Punishment* in 1866. Among other works by this great Russian novelist are *Notes from the Underground, The Gambler, The Idiot, The Possessed,* and *The Brothers Karamazov.*

32. **The correct answer is (A).** The Italian (or Petrarchan) sonnet is divided into two parts, an *octave* (the first eight lines) and a *sestet* (the last six), usually rhyming *abbaabba cdecde.* The English (or Shakespearean) sonnet is usually divided into three *quatrains* (four–line stanzas) and a *couplet,* rhyming *abab cdcd efef gg.*

33. **The correct answer is (C).** The American humorist James Thurber (1894–1961) is known for essays, line drawings, and short stories (*The Male Animal, The Thurber Carnival,* and *The Seal in the Bedroom and Other Predicaments*).

34. **The correct answer is (D).** Sir Thomas More (1478–1535) was an English writer and statesman known for his humanistic treatise, *Utopia*; nowadays he is better known as the central character of the play and film, *A Man for All Seasons.*

35. **The correct answer is (E).** Lawrence Ferlinghetti (1919–) is known as a member of the San Francisco beat movement, as publisher of Allen Ginsberg and Gregory Corso, and as owner of San Francisco's City Lights Bookshop. His poetry has been collected in *Pictures of the Gone World, A Coney Island of the Mind,* and *Starting from San Francisco.*

36. **The correct answer is (E).** F. Scott Fitzgerald (1896–1940) published "Babylon Revisited" in his last story collection, *Taps at Reveille.* He is known also for *The Great Gatsby* and *Tender is the Night,* among other works.

37. **The correct answer is (C).** When D. H. Lawrence (1885–1930) published *Lady Chatterley's Lover* in 1928, the novel's frankness of language and detail was received with charges of obscenity, with seizures and threats of prosecution by government agencies.

38. **The correct answer is (B).** *Leviathan* is a political treatise written in 1651 by Thomas Hobbes (1588–1679). According to Hobbes, life in the "state of nature" is "solitary, poor, nasty, brutish, and short."

39. **The correct answer is (D).** Langston Hughes (1902–1967) is the author of "The Weary Blues," "The Negro Speaks of Rivers," and "Harlem" ("What happens to a dream deferred? . . . Does it dry up like a raisin in the sun?"), among many others.

40. **The correct answer is (C).** The term "quixotic" has come to mean "caught up in the romance of noble deeds or unreachable ideals; romantic without regard to practicality"—after the hero of the novel by Miguel de Cervantes (1547–1616).

41. **The correct answer is (E).** *Steppenwolf* was written in 1927 by Hermann Hesse (1877–1962), who is also the author of *Demian, Siddhartha,* and *Narcissus and Goldmund.*

42. **The correct answer is (A).** Ballads, stories told in song passed down by word of mouth from singer to singer, were especially common in the fifteenth century. In Francis J. Child's comprehensive collection, *The English and Scottish Popular Ballads,* 1892–98, "Lord Randal" is listed as No. 12.A.

43. **The correct answer is (C).** Tennessee Williams (1911–1983) wrote *The Rose Tattoo* in 1951; many of his plays are set in the southern part of the United States and involve themes of passion and violence.

44. **The correct answer is (E).** *Hedda Gabler* was written in 1890 by the Norwegian playwright Henrik Ibsen (1828–1906); the work depicts the destruction of a woman who seeks to control the lives of those around her but who ultimately cannot even control her own life.

45. **The correct answer is (A).** James Thurber's *The Secret Life of Walter Mitty* introduced the title character whose name is popularly taken to refer to any impotent daydreamer or ineffectual escapist. The role of Walter Mitty was portrayed on the screen by Danny Kaye.

46. **The correct answer is (B).** *Treasure Island* was written in 1883 by Robert Louis Stevenson (1850–1894), who is also known for *Kidnapped, The Strange Case of Dr. Jekyll and Mr. Hyde,* and *A Child's Garden of Verses.*

47. **The correct answer is (A).** In *Walden,* a masterpiece of nature writing, Henry David Thoreau (1812–1862) tells of the two years he spent in a small cabin he built at Walden Pond,

near Concord, Massachusetts. Thoreau is also remembered for his essay "On the Duty of Civil Disobedience," which influenced Mahatma Gandhi and Martin Luther King, Jr.

48. **The correct answer is (E).** *Lycidas* was written by John Milton (1608–1674) when his friend Edward King drowned in 1637. Milton called the poem a "monody," an elegy or dirge sung by a single voice.

49. **The correct answer is (A).** Martin Luther King, Jr. (1929–1968) was the clergyman and civil rights leader who founded the Southern Christian Leadership Conference and was awarded the Nobel Peace Prize in 1964. He was assassinated in 1968.

50. **The correct answer is (C).** The lines begin *Elegy in a Country Churchyard*, written in 1751 by Thomas Gray (1716–1771). The bell tolling "parting day" and the "darkness" cue the reader to think of the theme of *death*.

51. **The correct answer is (D).** e. e. cummings (1894–1962) wrote *Tulips and Chimneys, XLI Poems, Is 5, Him, The Enormous Room, Eimi,* and *i: six nonlectures.*

52. **The correct answer is (B).** Gustave Flaubert (1821–1880) is known for his novels of psychological realism. *Madame Bovary* tells of a sentimental young woman whose foolishly romantic view of life and love causes her to leave her physician husband and ultimately destroy her life.

53. **The correct answer is (B).** The Transcendentalists, such as Thoreau, Emerson, and Margaret Fuller, believed that knowledge of reality is acquired from intuitive sources rather than from objective experience.

54. **The correct answer is (C).** George Bernard Shaw (1856–1950) presented Joan of Arc in *St. Joan*, Eugene Marchbanks in *Candida*, and Eliza Doolittle in *Pygmalion.*

55. **The correct answer is (E).** "Chicago" is found in Carl Sandburg's (1878–1967) *Chicago Poems.*

56. **The correct answer is (D).** Lillian Hellman (1905–1984) is also known as the author of

Watch on the Rhine, Another Part of the Forest, and *Pentimento.*

57. **The correct answer is (B).** *The Legend of Sleepy Hollow,* by Washington Irving (1783–1859), tells of Ichabod Crane and his adventure with The Headless Horseman.

58. **The correct answer is (C).** Joseph Addison (1672–1719) and Richard Steele (1672–1729) wrote *The Spectator*, a daily paper that Dr. Samuel Johnson called "the best, the most humorous, urbane and decorous" of all their writings.

59. **The correct answer is (C).** Arthur Rimbaud (1854–1891) was associated for a time with the poet Paul Verlaine and led a troubled existence for most of his life.

60. **The correct answer is (B).** Walt Whitman (1819–1892) liked to be known as the spokesman of democracy. He is best known for *Leaves of Grass, Democratic Vistas,* and two poems about Abraham Lincoln: "O Captain! My Captain!" and "When Lilacs Last in the Dooryard Bloom'd."

61. **The correct answer is (C).** The work of Harold Pinter (1930–) ranges from avant-garde theatre (*The Dumbwaiter, The Caretaker*) to mass media (the films *Accident* and *The Quiller Memorandum*).

62. **The correct answer is (E).** Betty Friedan (1921–) wrote *The Feminine Mystique* in 1963 and *It Changed My Life* in 1976. She was founder and first president of NOW, the National Organization of Women.

63. **The correct answer is (D).** Thomas Hardy (1840–1928) was a Victorian architect who became a writer known for such novels as *Far From the Madding Crowd, The Return of the Native, Jude the Obscure, The Mayor of Casterbridge,* as well as for *Tess of the D'Urbervilles* and a very large body of poetry.

64. **The correct answer is (E).** Polonius, father of Ophelia and Laertes, appears in Shakespeare's *Hamlet.*

65. **The correct answer is (B).** *Finnegans Wake* is the most complex novel of James Joyce (1882–

1941), in which the author practically invented a new language in telling the story of H. C. Earwicker (Everyman) and his wife Anna Livia Plurabelle (the feminine life force).

66. **The correct answer is (C).** Allen Ginsberg (1926–1997) was associated with Jack Kerouac and Lawrence Ferlinghetti in the Beat Movement in American literary history and is also known for "Kaddish," "America," "Wichita Vortex Sutra," and *Indian Journals.*

67. **The correct answer is (D).** *Invisible Man* was written in 1952 by Ralph Ellison (1914–1994). It is considered by many critics to be the finest American novel of the postwar period.

68. **The correct answer is (A).** Willie Loman appears as the main character in Arthur Miller's (1915–) *Death of A Salesman,* which won the Pulitzer Prize in drama in 1949.

69. **The correct answer is (B).** Anne Sexton (1928–1974) was much concerned in her work with themes of separation, death, and suicide, as the titles of a few of her poems indicate: "Suicide Note," "Wanting to Die," and "Live."

70. **The correct answer is (D).** René Descartes (1596–1650), a French mathematician and philosopher, is probably best remembered today for his statement, "*Cogito, ergo sum.*"

71. **The correct answer is (B).** *Allusion* is the literary device of making reference to something outside of the work. In this case, the poet *alludes* to Penelope and Circe of *The Odyssey* and to the writer Flaubert.

72. **The correct answer is (B).** Published in 1678, John Bunyan's (1628–1688) *The Pilgrim's Progress* is an allegorical account of a journey of a man named "Christian" and includes characters named Simple, Hypocrisy, Mistrust, and Mr. Worldly Wiseman.

73. **The correct answer is (A).** Vance Packard (1914–1996) subtitled *The Status Seekers* "An Exploration of Class Behavior in America and the Hidden Barriers That Affect You, Your Community, Your Future." He also wrote *The Hidden Persuaders,* concerning the development of psychological techniques geared toward persuading and manipulating modern Americans.

74. **The correct answer is (C).** Soren Kierkegard (1813–1855) believed that religion is an individual matter and the relation of the individual to God involves suffering (*Either/Or; The Concept of Dread*). Friedrich Nietzsche (1844–1900) is often cited ("God is Dead") in discussions of how modern people attempt to find meaning in life (*Beyond Good and Evil; The Birth of Tragedy*). Jean Paul Sartre (1905–1980) wrote *Being in Nothingness*, sometimes referred to as the existentialist manifesto. Martin Heidegger (1889–1976) wrote *Being and Time* and is known for his discussions of *da sein*, proper being.

75. **The correct answer is (C).** The daughter of the eminent editor, biographer, and critic Sir Leslie Stephen, Virginia Woolf (1882–1941) lived with her husband Leonard Woolf in the Bloomsbury district of London, where they met regularly with other intellectuals of their time, such as John Maynard Keynes, Roger Fry, and Lytton Strachey—known as the "Bloomsbury Group."

Section II

76. **The correct answer is (D).** The Russian composer Piotr Ilyich Tchaikovsky (1840–1893) is also known for the ballets *The Swan Lake* and *The Sleeping Beauty,* the fantasy–overture *Romeo and Juliet,* the opera *Eugene Onegin,* and the "Pathetique" Symphony.

77. **The correct answer is (A).** Louis Comfort Tiffany (1848–1933) was internationally known for his "Favrile glass," which reproduced the opalescent sheen found on long–buried ancient glass and also provided an iridescent appearance.

78. **The correct answer is (E).** Matthew Brady (1823–1896) accompanied Union armies (1861–65), taking photographs that became the basis for a pictorial history of the Civil War.

79. **The correct answer is (E).** An overture is often used as preparation for the mood of the

opening scene of the work it precedes; or it might be composed of a collection of the work's most prominent melodies.

80. **The correct answer is (C).** "I Heard It Through the Grapevine" was introduced by Gladys Knight and the Pips in 1967 and covered by numerous recording artists.

81. **The correct answer is (C).** Akira Kurosawa (1910–1998) directed *Rashomon* in 1950. An examination of the nature of truth, the work awakened Western interest in Japanese cinema.

82. **The correct answer is (B).** R. Buckminster Fuller (1895–1983), who has been described as "a philosopher of structure," designed the American Pavilions in Moscow in 1959 and in Montreal at Expo 67.

83. **The correct answer is (B).** Peter Paul Rubens (1577–1640), the great Flemish painter of the Baroque period, received a special appointment to the Spanish regent and established a workshop in Antwerp, where he was aided by numerous assistants.

84. **The correct answer is (C).** For Paul Klee (1879–1940), a German–Swiss painter influenced by Cubism and by primitive art, "art" was a concise pictorial language with simple lines, a language of signs. He was also interested in hieroglyphics, hex signs, and cave markings.

85. **The correct answer is (B).** *Pagliacci (Clowns)* by Ruggiero Leoncavallo (1858–1919), first performed in Milan in 1892, utilizes the "play within a play" device in which a comic scene enacted by a group of players for a village audience becomes a tragic drama of real life. After the actor who portrays Pagliaccio stabs his wife and her lover, he turns to the audience with the famous statement, "La commedia è finita." ("The comedy is ended.")

86. **The correct answer is (E).** *La Bohème (Bohemian Life)* by Giacomo Puccini (1858–1924), first performed in 1896, is one of the most successful operas ever written. It tells of the love of Mimi (a frail woman who embroiders artificial flowers) and Rudolfo (a painter) and of Mimi's death of consumption.

87. **The correct answer is (D).** Andy Warhol: *Green Coca Cola Bottles* (1962).

88. **The correct answer is (C).** Morris (1931–), Flavin (1933–1996), Judd (1928–1994), and Smith (1912–1980) are known for minimalist sculptures made of painted steel, galvanized iron, fluorescent lights, and gray fiberglass, for example.

89. **The correct answer is (C).** The woodcuts and engravings of the German artist Albrecht Dürer (1471–1528) had great influence on sixteenth-century Western art. He is noted for *Self-portrait, Adam and Eve,* and *Four Horsemen of the Apocalypse,* among many others.

90. **The correct answer is (C).** *Citizen Kane* was the very impressive first film by Orson Welles (1915–1985). He is also remembered for his radio version of H.G. Wells' *The War of the Worlds* (which caused quite a scare, as listeners believed it was an actual newscast) and for *Othello, The Third Man,* and *Jane Eyre,* among others.

91. **The correct answer is (B).** Peter Tosh and Bob Marley were part of the original "Wailers." Tosh's Jamaican reggae style is evident in "Legalize It" and "Till Your Well Runs Dry." Reggae developed in the slums of Kingston, Jamaica. Marley is known for "I Shot the Sheriff (But I Didn't Shoot the Deputy)," "Burnin' and Lootin'," and "Roots Rock Reggae." Jimmy Cliff starred in the film *The Harder They Come,* which is set in a Jamaican shantytown and contains the popular reggae title song.

92. **The correct answer is (E).** Virgil Thomson (1896–1989) scored a great success with *Four Saints in Three Acts* in Paris in the late 1920s and on Broadway in 1934. He also wrote so perceptively about music for the *New York Herald Tribune* that he has been called the greatest music critic that the Western Hemisphere has produced.

93. **The correct answer is (D).** Gouache is a method of painting with opaque colors that have been ground in water and incorporated with a preparation of gum.

94. **The correct answer is (B).** Mont–St.–Michel, a French islet crowned by a medieval abbey church, was a famous pilgrimage site in the middle ages and is now a historical monument.

95. **The correct answer is (B).** Ferdinand "Jelly Roll" Morton (1885–1941) was a pianist–composer–arranger who performed in New Orleans around the turn of the twentieth century and played for nearly fifty years throughout the United States, with the legendary W.C. Handy, among others.

96. **The correct answer is (C).** Richard Wagner (1813–1883), the genius of German opera, is noted for *The Ring of the Nibelung*, 1853–74 (*Das Rheingold, Die Walkure, Siegfried, Gotterdammerung), Tannhauser, Lohengrin, Tristan and Isolde, Die Meistersinger,* and *Parsifal.*

97. **The correct answer is (D).** Gary Cooper (1901–1961) won an Academy Award in 1952 for his portrayal of the marshall of a small frontier town in *High Noon* (with Grace Kelly).

98. **The correct answer is (D).** Ludwig van Beethoven (1770–1827) created nine symphonies, eleven overtures, six concertos, sixteen string quartets, nine piano trios, nearly fifty sonatas (including the popular *Moonlight Sonata*), and a variety of other music. The sonata is a composition for piano or for violin, cello, or flute, (usually with piano accompaniment), which consists of three or four separate sections called movements.

99. **The correct answer is (D).** Paul Terry (1887–1971) was an early developer of the technique of animation in film, and his "Terrytoons" were seen for more than thirty years in moviehouse programs.

100. **The correct answer is (D).** Walter Gropius (1883–1969) directed a curriculum embracing all of the visual arts, linked by the root concept of "structure," *Bau.* He chaired the Department of Architecture at Harvard from 1938–52 and designed with an emphasis on clarity, cleanliness, and light.

101. **The correct answer is (D).** The plot of this musical of rival street gangs was loosely based on the story of Romeo and Juliet.

102. **The correct answer is (B).** Sergei Diaghilev (1872–1929) first presented Russian music to Western Europe in 1907, and, in 1909, he founded Ballets Russes, with Anna Pavlova and Vaslaw Nijinsky as dancers.

103. **The correct answer is (A).** The Hudson River School encompassed several generations of landscape painters, including John James Audubon (1785?–1851) and Thomas Cole (1801–1848).

104. **The correct answer is (A).** Bedrich Smetana (1824–1884), the Czech composer who is also known for the opera *The Bartered Bride,* planned a cycle of symphonic poems to extol the glories of his nation. *Moldau* depicts the great Czech river, which Smetana follows from its source to the city, describing the life along its banks.

105. **The correct answer is (C).** "Do Re Mi" is one of the most popular light songs from the musical *The Sound of Music.*

106. **The correct answer is (A).** This installation, *Fin de Siecle II* (1989), is typical of the work of Nam June Paik (1932–), who is known for using video and sound in his creations.

107. **The correct answer is (B).** Jean Arp (1887–1966) created a newspaper collage with woodcut for the cover of a journal, *Dada 4–5.* He also attempted to substitute the random effects of chance for traditional values of creation in his collages entitled *Squares Arranged According to the Laws of Chance* (papers falling onto a horizontal surface).

108. **The correct answer is (C).** Georgia O'Keeffe (1887–1986) is known for her natural forms presented in large close–ups, such as *Black Iris* or other flowers, shells or clouds found on her many posters for concerts or environmental causes. She was married to the photographer Alfred Stieglitz.

109. **The correct answer is (C).** Alvin Ailey (1931–1989), choreographer–director of the Alvin Ailey Dance Theatre, one of the first genuine modern–dance repertory companies, was associated early in his career with Lester Horton, a pioneer of modern dance. Ailey's masterwork, *Revelations,* is described in its program note as a suite exploring the "motivations and emotions of American Negro religious music."

110. **The correct answer is (B).** John Philip Sousa (1854–1932) is known for marches (*The Stars and Stripes Forever, Hands Across The Sea*). The Sousaphone, a helicon bass tuba with bell opening directly upward, was made for his band in 1899 and named in Sousa's honor. The bell–front type was developed in 1909.

111. **The correct answer is (A).** Charles Eames (1907–1978) was virtually self–taught in architecture. With Eero Saarinen he designed a pioneer plywood and aluminum chair and is known for other chair designs. His work was the subject of the first one–man furniture exhibition at New York City's Museum of Modern Art.

112. **The correct answer is (D).** Francisco Goya (1746–1828) was highly esteemed as a portrait painter (as in *The Family of Charles IV*), but the occupation of Spain by Napoleon's troops in 1808 resulted in many of Goya's best works, which depicted the ugliness of war (such as *The Third of May,* commemorating the execution of a group of people in Madrid).

113. **The correct answer is (B).** The cubic character of Egyptian statuary was not determined by aesthetics but by the sculptor's method of approach. Sketches were made on two or more sides of a cuboid block, which was reduced until the finished piece was a combination of a profile and a frontal view. Most Egyptian statues face straight ahead.

114. **The correct answer is (D).** Elvis Presley (1935–1979) was once known as "the Pelvis" because of his swivel–hipped style. He is known for the songs "Love Me Tender" and "Blue Suede Shoes" and for a number of films shot around his singing.

115. **The correct answer is (C).** *The Age of Anxiety,* a dramatic ballet in six scenes, with music by Leonard Bernstein, choreography by Jerome Robbins, and scenery by Oliver Smith, was first presented in New York in 1950. It is concerned with the attempts of four people to find themselves and to find faith in their daily lives.

116. **The correct answer is (B).** *Orpheus,* a ballet in three scenes, with music by Igor Stravinsky, choreography by George Balanchine, scenery and costumes by Isamu Noguchi, was first presented in New York in 1948. In it, Orpheus uses his music to charm the God of the Dead into returning his wife, Eurydice, promising not to look at her until they have reached earth again. She unknowingly persuades him to break this promise and, thus, brings about her irrevocable death. The ballet also depicts the death of Orpheus.

117. **The correct answer is (A).** The Doric (from the Greek mainland) is older and more sharply defined than the Ionic (which developed on the Aegean islands and the Asia Minor coast); the Corinthian is a variant of the Ionic.

118. **The correct answer is (A).** George Gershwin (1898–1937) attempted to bridge the gap between popular music and the concert–hall audience. In addition to *Rhapsody in Blue,* he is known for *Of Thee I Sing, Porgy and Bess,* and *An American In Paris.*

119. **The correct answer is (E).** André Breton (1896–1966) called Surrealism "pure psychic automatism" and thought that a "superior reality" could be produced by the juxtaposition of unrelated objects. Some major surrealists: Giorgio de Chirico, Max Ernst, Salvador Dali, René Magritte, Yves Tanguy, and Roberto Matta.

120. **The correct answer is (B).** This 1968 piece is by Romare Bearden (1914–1988), whose work is known for its depiction of life in black America.

121. **The correct answer is (D).** Elizabeth Taylor has been successful in the worlds of perfume advertising and film, but not popular music.

122.   **The correct answer is (B).** Julio Cortazar (1914–1984) was an Argentine novelist and short–story writer, author of *Bestiario, End of the Game,* and *Hopscotch.* His work entitled "Blow Up" was filmed by Michelangelo Antonioni in 1967.

123.   **The correct answer is (C).** See, for examples, Picasso's *Les Demoiselles d' Avignon* or *The Three Musicians,* Braque's *Man With Guitar,* or Léger's *Three Women.*

124.   **The correct answer is (B).** Benvenuto Cellini (1500–1571) is remembered for his gold salt-cellar made for Francis I of France and for his autobiography.

125.   **The correct answer is (A).** William "Count" Basie (1904–1984) studied for a while with Fats Waller, became known with the "Hippity Hop" show, recorded with the Benny Goodman Sextet, and toured throughout the United States and Europe in numerous engagements.

126.   **The correct answer is (A).** In sculpture, *relief* describes the projection of figures, ornaments, and such from a background. In *bas–relief* (low relief), the degree of projection is slight, no part being entirely detached.

127.   **The correct answer is (A).** Aubrey Beardsley (1872–1898) is associated with Art Nouveau.

128.   **The correct answer is (B).** Walker Evans (1903–1975) joined James Agee in the study of Alabama sharecroppers in 1941. His photos are bleak, spare, motionless studies; they are collected in *American Photographs, Many Are Called,* and *Message From The Interior.*

129.   **The correct answer is (A).** *Chiaroscuro* is the style of pictorial art that employs light and shade, or gradations between brightness and darkness, for its effect. The master of chiaroscuro was Rembrandt.

130.   **The correct answer is (D).** Blind from birth, Stevie Wonder was successful at the age of twelve, and won five Grammy awards in 1977. His music includes rock, jazz, and soul, in such albums as *Journey Through the Secret Life of Plants* and *Songs in the Key of Life.* George Shearing is the celebrated pianist famous for his *Black Satin* album and his jazz renditions of popular old favorites. It has been said of Ray Charles that he performs with a "gospel fervor that brings to his concerts the atmosphere of a revival meeting." His first hit was a rasping "Georgia On My Mind." (Others: "I Can't Stop Loving You" and "Let The Good Times Roll.")

131.   **The correct answer is (E).** Giorgio de Chirico (1888–1980) is associated with Surrealism.

132.   **The correct answer is (A).** *Marimba* is a xylophone of southern Africa and central America, with resonators beneath each bar.

133.   **The correct answer is (E).** Grant Wood: *American Gothic* (1930).

134.   **The correct answer is (D).** Rembrandt van Rijn: *The Syndics of the Draper's Guild* (1662).

135.   **The correct answer is (A).** Alfred Sisley: *Flood at Port Marley* (1876).

136.   **The correct answer is (C).** Alexander Calder: *Aluminum Leaves, Red Post* (1941).

The other work shown is:

(B) Nicolas Poussin: *Dance to the Music of Time* (c. 1640).

137.   **The correct answer is (B).** Peter Sellers (1925–1980) also appeared in *Being There, The Mouse That Roared, Lolita,* and *The World of Henry Orient.*

138.   **The correct answer is (A).** Donatello (1386–1466) is known for sculptures of *St. Mark, David, St. George and the Dragon,* and for *The Feast of Herod.*

139.   **The correct answer is (B).** Elton John, popularizer of "Goodbye Yellow Brick Road," "Daniel," and "Island Girl," among many others, played for hundreds of thousands of his fans at a 1980 concert in New York's Central Park.

140.   **The correct answer is (B).** The Florentine sculptor Lorenzo Ghiberti (1378–1455) created ten large reliefs in square frames on these magnificient bronze doors.

Answer Sheet for Practice Examination II

Section I

1 Ⓐ Ⓑ Ⓒ Ⓓ Ⓔ   16 Ⓐ Ⓑ Ⓒ Ⓓ Ⓔ   31 Ⓐ Ⓑ Ⓒ Ⓓ Ⓔ   46 Ⓐ Ⓑ Ⓒ Ⓓ Ⓔ   61 Ⓐ Ⓑ Ⓒ Ⓓ Ⓔ

2 Ⓐ Ⓑ Ⓒ Ⓓ Ⓔ   17 Ⓐ Ⓑ Ⓒ Ⓓ Ⓔ   32 Ⓐ Ⓑ Ⓒ Ⓓ Ⓔ   47 Ⓐ Ⓑ Ⓒ Ⓓ Ⓔ   62 Ⓐ Ⓑ Ⓒ Ⓓ Ⓔ

3 Ⓐ Ⓑ Ⓒ Ⓓ Ⓔ   18 Ⓐ Ⓑ Ⓒ Ⓓ Ⓔ   33 Ⓐ Ⓑ Ⓒ Ⓓ Ⓔ   48 Ⓐ Ⓑ Ⓒ Ⓓ Ⓔ   63 Ⓐ Ⓑ Ⓒ Ⓓ Ⓔ

4 Ⓐ Ⓑ Ⓒ Ⓓ Ⓔ   19 Ⓐ Ⓑ Ⓒ Ⓓ Ⓔ   34 Ⓐ Ⓑ Ⓒ Ⓓ Ⓔ   49 Ⓐ Ⓑ Ⓒ Ⓓ Ⓔ   64 Ⓐ Ⓑ Ⓒ Ⓓ Ⓔ

5 Ⓐ Ⓑ Ⓒ Ⓓ Ⓔ   20 Ⓐ Ⓑ Ⓒ Ⓓ Ⓔ   35 Ⓐ Ⓑ Ⓒ Ⓓ Ⓔ   50 Ⓐ Ⓑ Ⓒ Ⓓ Ⓔ   65 Ⓐ Ⓑ Ⓒ Ⓓ Ⓔ

6 Ⓐ Ⓑ Ⓒ Ⓓ Ⓔ   21 Ⓐ Ⓑ Ⓒ Ⓓ Ⓔ   36 Ⓐ Ⓑ Ⓒ Ⓓ Ⓔ   51 Ⓐ Ⓑ Ⓒ Ⓓ Ⓔ   66 Ⓐ Ⓑ Ⓒ Ⓓ Ⓔ

7 Ⓐ Ⓑ Ⓒ Ⓓ Ⓔ   22 Ⓐ Ⓑ Ⓒ Ⓓ Ⓔ   37 Ⓐ Ⓑ Ⓒ Ⓓ Ⓔ   52 Ⓐ Ⓑ Ⓒ Ⓓ Ⓔ   67 Ⓐ Ⓑ Ⓒ Ⓓ Ⓔ

8 Ⓐ Ⓑ Ⓒ Ⓓ Ⓔ   23 Ⓐ Ⓑ Ⓒ Ⓓ Ⓔ   38 Ⓐ Ⓑ Ⓒ Ⓓ Ⓔ   53 Ⓐ Ⓑ Ⓒ Ⓓ Ⓔ   68 Ⓐ Ⓑ Ⓒ Ⓓ Ⓔ

9 Ⓐ Ⓑ Ⓒ Ⓓ Ⓔ   24 Ⓐ Ⓑ Ⓒ Ⓓ Ⓔ   39 Ⓐ Ⓑ Ⓒ Ⓓ Ⓔ   54 Ⓐ Ⓑ Ⓒ Ⓓ Ⓔ   69 Ⓐ Ⓑ Ⓒ Ⓓ Ⓔ

10 Ⓐ Ⓑ Ⓒ Ⓓ Ⓔ   25 Ⓐ Ⓑ Ⓒ Ⓓ Ⓔ   40 Ⓐ Ⓑ Ⓒ Ⓓ Ⓔ   55 Ⓐ Ⓑ Ⓒ Ⓓ Ⓔ   70 Ⓐ Ⓑ Ⓒ Ⓓ Ⓔ

11 Ⓐ Ⓑ Ⓒ Ⓓ Ⓔ   26 Ⓐ Ⓑ Ⓒ Ⓓ Ⓔ   41 Ⓐ Ⓑ Ⓒ Ⓓ Ⓔ   56 Ⓐ Ⓑ Ⓒ Ⓓ Ⓔ   71 Ⓐ Ⓑ Ⓒ Ⓓ Ⓔ

12 Ⓐ Ⓑ Ⓒ Ⓓ Ⓔ   27 Ⓐ Ⓑ Ⓒ Ⓓ Ⓔ   42 Ⓐ Ⓑ Ⓒ Ⓓ Ⓔ   57 Ⓐ Ⓑ Ⓒ Ⓓ Ⓔ   72 Ⓐ Ⓑ Ⓒ Ⓓ Ⓔ

13 Ⓐ Ⓑ Ⓒ Ⓓ Ⓔ   28 Ⓐ Ⓑ Ⓒ Ⓓ Ⓔ   43 Ⓐ Ⓑ Ⓒ Ⓓ Ⓔ   58 Ⓐ Ⓑ Ⓒ Ⓓ Ⓔ   73 Ⓐ Ⓑ Ⓒ Ⓓ Ⓔ

14 Ⓐ Ⓑ Ⓒ Ⓓ Ⓔ   29 Ⓐ Ⓑ Ⓒ Ⓓ Ⓔ   44 Ⓐ Ⓑ Ⓒ Ⓓ Ⓔ   59 Ⓐ Ⓑ Ⓒ Ⓓ Ⓔ   74 Ⓐ Ⓑ Ⓒ Ⓓ Ⓔ

15 Ⓐ Ⓑ Ⓒ Ⓓ Ⓔ   30 Ⓐ Ⓑ Ⓒ Ⓓ Ⓔ   45 Ⓐ Ⓑ Ⓒ Ⓓ Ⓔ   60 Ⓐ Ⓑ Ⓒ Ⓓ Ⓔ   75 Ⓐ Ⓑ Ⓒ Ⓓ Ⓔ

Section II

76 Ⓐ Ⓑ Ⓒ Ⓓ Ⓔ　　91 Ⓐ Ⓑ Ⓒ Ⓓ Ⓔ　　106 Ⓐ Ⓑ Ⓒ Ⓓ Ⓔ　　121 Ⓐ Ⓑ Ⓒ Ⓓ Ⓔ　　136 Ⓐ Ⓑ Ⓒ Ⓓ Ⓔ

77 Ⓐ Ⓑ Ⓒ Ⓓ Ⓔ　　92 Ⓐ Ⓑ Ⓒ Ⓓ Ⓔ　　107 Ⓐ Ⓑ Ⓒ Ⓓ Ⓔ　　122 Ⓐ Ⓑ Ⓒ Ⓓ Ⓔ　　137 Ⓐ Ⓑ Ⓒ Ⓓ Ⓔ

78 Ⓐ Ⓑ Ⓒ Ⓓ Ⓔ　　93 Ⓐ Ⓑ Ⓒ Ⓓ Ⓔ　　108 Ⓐ Ⓑ Ⓒ Ⓓ Ⓔ　　123 Ⓐ Ⓑ Ⓒ Ⓓ Ⓔ　　138 Ⓐ Ⓑ Ⓒ Ⓓ Ⓔ

79 Ⓐ Ⓑ Ⓒ Ⓓ Ⓔ　　94 Ⓐ Ⓑ Ⓒ Ⓓ Ⓔ　　109 Ⓐ Ⓑ Ⓒ Ⓓ Ⓔ　　124 Ⓐ Ⓑ Ⓒ Ⓓ Ⓔ　　139 Ⓐ Ⓑ Ⓒ Ⓓ Ⓔ

80 Ⓐ Ⓑ Ⓒ Ⓓ Ⓔ　　95 Ⓐ Ⓑ Ⓒ Ⓓ Ⓔ　　110 Ⓐ Ⓑ Ⓒ Ⓓ Ⓔ　　125 Ⓐ Ⓑ Ⓒ Ⓓ Ⓔ　　140 Ⓐ Ⓑ Ⓒ Ⓓ Ⓔ

81 Ⓐ Ⓑ Ⓒ Ⓓ Ⓔ　　96 Ⓐ Ⓑ Ⓒ Ⓓ Ⓔ　　111 Ⓐ Ⓑ Ⓒ Ⓓ Ⓔ　　126 Ⓐ Ⓑ Ⓒ Ⓓ Ⓔ　　141 Ⓐ Ⓑ Ⓒ Ⓓ Ⓔ

82 Ⓐ Ⓑ Ⓒ Ⓓ Ⓔ　　97 Ⓐ Ⓑ Ⓒ Ⓓ Ⓔ　　112 Ⓐ Ⓑ Ⓒ Ⓓ Ⓔ　　127 Ⓐ Ⓑ Ⓒ Ⓓ Ⓔ　　142 Ⓐ Ⓑ Ⓒ Ⓓ Ⓔ

83 Ⓐ Ⓑ Ⓒ Ⓓ Ⓔ　　98 Ⓐ Ⓑ Ⓒ Ⓓ Ⓔ　　113 Ⓐ Ⓑ Ⓒ Ⓓ Ⓔ　　128 Ⓐ Ⓑ Ⓒ Ⓓ Ⓔ　　143 Ⓐ Ⓑ Ⓒ Ⓓ Ⓔ

84 Ⓐ Ⓑ Ⓒ Ⓓ Ⓔ　　99 Ⓐ Ⓑ Ⓒ Ⓓ Ⓔ　　114 Ⓐ Ⓑ Ⓒ Ⓓ Ⓔ　　129 Ⓐ Ⓑ Ⓒ Ⓓ Ⓔ　　144 Ⓐ Ⓑ Ⓒ Ⓓ Ⓔ

85 Ⓐ Ⓑ Ⓒ Ⓓ Ⓔ　　100 Ⓐ Ⓑ Ⓒ Ⓓ Ⓔ　　115 Ⓐ Ⓑ Ⓒ Ⓓ Ⓔ　　130 Ⓐ Ⓑ Ⓒ Ⓓ Ⓔ　　145 Ⓐ Ⓑ Ⓒ Ⓓ Ⓔ

86 Ⓐ Ⓑ Ⓒ Ⓓ Ⓔ　　101 Ⓐ Ⓑ Ⓒ Ⓓ Ⓔ　　116 Ⓐ Ⓑ Ⓒ Ⓓ Ⓔ　　131 Ⓐ Ⓑ Ⓒ Ⓓ Ⓔ　　146 Ⓐ Ⓑ Ⓒ Ⓓ Ⓔ

87 Ⓐ Ⓑ Ⓒ Ⓓ Ⓔ　　102 Ⓐ Ⓑ Ⓒ Ⓓ Ⓔ　　117 Ⓐ Ⓑ Ⓒ Ⓓ Ⓔ　　132 Ⓐ Ⓑ Ⓒ Ⓓ Ⓔ　　147 Ⓐ Ⓑ Ⓒ Ⓓ Ⓔ

88 Ⓐ Ⓑ Ⓒ Ⓓ Ⓔ　　103 Ⓐ Ⓑ Ⓒ Ⓓ Ⓔ　　118 Ⓐ Ⓑ Ⓒ Ⓓ Ⓔ　　133 Ⓐ Ⓑ Ⓒ Ⓓ Ⓔ　　148 Ⓐ Ⓑ Ⓒ Ⓓ Ⓔ

89 Ⓐ Ⓑ Ⓒ Ⓓ Ⓔ　　104 Ⓐ Ⓑ Ⓒ Ⓓ Ⓔ　　119 Ⓐ Ⓑ Ⓒ Ⓓ Ⓔ　　134 Ⓐ Ⓑ Ⓒ Ⓓ Ⓔ　　149 Ⓐ Ⓑ Ⓒ Ⓓ Ⓔ

90 Ⓐ Ⓑ Ⓒ Ⓓ Ⓔ　　105 Ⓐ Ⓑ Ⓒ Ⓓ Ⓔ　　120 Ⓐ Ⓑ Ⓒ Ⓓ Ⓔ　　135 Ⓐ Ⓑ Ⓒ Ⓓ Ⓔ　　150 Ⓐ Ⓑ Ⓒ Ⓓ Ⓔ

PRACTICE EXAMINATION II

Section I: Literature

75 Questions

Time—45 minutes

Directions: Each of the questions or incomplete statements below is followed by five suggested answers or completions. Select the one that is best in each case and blacken your answer sheet (A), (B), (C), (D), or (E) accordingly.

1. His essays and works of criticism are almost as important as his poetic output. During World War II, he started to broadcast fascist propaganda to the United States from Rome, an act which led to his arrest in May, 1945, by American forces, his confinement at Pisa (where he wrote *The Pisan Cantos*), and his trial in the United States.

    The passage above discusses

    (A) D.H. Lawrence.
    (B) Ezra Pound.
    (C) T.S. Eliot.
    (D) Dylan Thomas.
    (E) e.e. cummings.

2. The character Sherlock Holmes was created by

    (A) Agatha Christie.
    (B) Leslie Charteris.
    (C) Arthur Conan Doyle.
    (D) H.G. Wells.
    (E) Ellery Queen.

3. The plot concerns a beautiful youth who has his portrait painted by Basil Hallward. Hallward introduces him to Lord Henry Wotton, who initiates the youth into a life of vice. The painting, it turns out, has supernatural powers, and while the hero remains young and beautiful throughout his deterioration, the portrait changes, reflecting his real state of degeneracy.

    The passage above discusses

    (A) Kosinski's *The Devil Tree.*
    (B) Gide's *The Immoralist.*
    (C) Joyce's *A Portrait of the Artist as a Young Man.*
    (D) Wilde's *The Picture of Dorian Gray.*
    (E) Stevenson's *The Strange Case of Dr. Jekyll and Mr. Hyde.*

4. "Piers Plowman" is a(n)

    (A) unfinished poetic work by Geoffrey Chaucer.
    (B) unfinished epic satire by Lord Byron.
    (C) narrative poem in blank verse.
    (D) Old English (Anglo–Saxon) epic in alliterative verse.
    (E) Middle English poem in alliterative verse.

5. The author of a series of books concerning "The Making of the President" is

    (A) Thomas Jefferson.
    (B) V.O. Key.
    (C) Theodore White.
    (D) Walter Cronkite.
    (E) Arthur Schlesinger.

6. The novel *Don Quixote* was the inspiration for the musical

   (A) *The Wiz.*
   (B) *West Side Story.*
   (C) *Man of La Mancha.*
   (D) *Evita.*
   (E) *The House of Bernarda Alba.*

7. "Death, be not proud, though some have called thee / Mighty and dreadful, for thou are not so"

   A technique employed in these lines is

   (A) simile.
   (B) alliteration.
   (C) refrain.
   (D) apostrophe.
   (E) terza rima.

8. Which of the following characters is incorrectly paired with the novel in which he/she appears?

   (A) Professor Humbert Humbert . . . *Lolita*
   (B) Madame Defarge . . . *A Tale of Two Cities*
   (C) Stephen Dedalus . . . *The Sun Also Rises*
   (D) Queequeg . . . *Moby Dick*
   (E) Man Friday . . . *Robinson Crusoe*

9. The writer associated with the *Lyceum* and *Poetics* is

   (A) Plato.
   (B) Norman Mailer.
   (C) Sigmund Freud.
   (D) Aristotle.
   (E) Langston Hughes.

10. Sheltered, petted, and expected to behave like an amiable nitwit by first her father and then her husband, Nora Helmer commits forgery in order to get money to save her husband's life.

    The sentence above discusses

    (A) Albee's *The Sandbox.*
    (B) Ibsen's *A Doll's House.*
    (C) Pinter's *The Dumbwaiter.*
    (D) Shaw's *Pygmalion.*
    (E) Wilde's *A Woman of No Importance.*

Questions 11 and 12 refer to the following lines.

"Summer is i–cumen in—

 Lhude sing, cuccu!

Groweth sed and bloweth med

 And springth the wude num

  Sing, cuccu!"

11. These lines were written in the

    (A) thirteenth or fourteenth century.
    (B) sixteenth or seventeenth century.
    (C) eighteenth century.
    (D) nineteenth century.
    (E) twentieth century.

12. These lines are an example of

    (A) a sonnet.
    (B) an early lyric.
    (C) a dramatic monologue.
    (D) blank verse.
    (E) a ballad.

13. Which of the following are considered the leading theorists of the New Wave?

    (A) Jack Kerouac and Allen Ginsberg
    (B) Virginia Woolf and Leonard Woolf
    (C) Allen Tate and Robert Penn Warren
    (D) Alain Robbe–Grillet and Nathalie Sarraute
    (E) Yvor Winters and Cleanth Brooks

14. Who is known as a science–fiction writer?

    (A) S.J. Perelman
    (B) Ellery Queen
    (C) Ray Bradbury
    (D) George Wilbur Peck
    (E) John Dickson Carr

15. Henry Higgins, a teacher of phonetics, takes on Eliza Doolittle, a Cockney flower girl, as his student. She is transformed from a guttersnipe into an elegant woman.

    The passage above discusses

    (A) Williams' *A Streetcar Named Desire.*
    (B) Shaw's *Pygmalion.*
    (C) Eliot's *The Cocktail Party.*
    (D) Osborne's *Look Back in Anger.*
    (E) O'Neill's *Beyond the Horizon.*

16. The novel is an appallingly grim account of life in the Chicago stockyards. It depicts with vivid and brutal realism the experiences of a Baltic immigrant, Jurgis Rudkus, and his wife, Ona.

    The passage above discusses

    (A) Huxley's *Brave New World.*
    (B) Hemingway's *To Have and Have Not.*
    (C) Sartre's *Nausea.*
    (D) Sinclair's *The Jungle.*
    (E) James' *The Turn of the Screw.*

17. In which of the following works was the theory of the *Ubermensch* (superman) developed?

    (A) Nietzsche's *Thus Spake Zarathustra*
    (B) Machiavelli's *The Prince*
    (C) Darwin's *The Origin of Species*
    (D) Camus' *The Myth of Sisyphus*
    (E) Toynbee's *The World and the West*

18. "By the rude bridge that arched the flood,

    Their flag to April's breeze unfurled,

    Here once the embattled farmers stood

    And fired the shot heard round the world."

    These lines describe a battle of

    (A) the Russian Revolution.
    (B) the American Revolution.
    (C) the American Civil War.
    (D) World War I.
    (E) the French and Indian War.

19. "The Divine Comedy," an epic poem, was written by

    (A) Dante.
    (B) John Milton.
    (C) John Donne.
    (D) Geoffrey Chaucer.
    (E) Homer.

20. Set in New England, it deals with Ephraim Cabot and his new young wife, Abbie. Abbie seduces Eben, the youngest son of Ephraim, hoping to bear a son she can claim is Ephraim's. When it appears to Eben that Abbie has used him only for her own ends, he threatens to expose her infidelity; to prove her love for him, she smothers the child.

    The passage above discusses

    (A) Behan's *Borstal Boy.*
    (B) Osborne's *Look Back in Anger.*
    (C) Miller's *The Crucible.*
    (D) Shaw's *The Devil's Disciple.*
    (E) O'Neill's *Desire Under the Elms.*

21. "And her channeled muscles

    are cluster grapes of sorrow

    purple in the evening sun

    nearly ripe for worms"

    The main figure of speech employed in these lines is

    (A) metaphor.
    (B) simile.
    (C) allusion.
    (D) alliteration.
    (E) personification.

22. The story concerns the middle–class household of the Bennets. The empty–headed and garrulous Mrs. Bennet has but one aim in life: to find a good match for each of her five daughters.

    The passage above discusses

    (A) de Beauvoir's *The Coming of Age.*
    (B) Hawthorne's *The House of the Seven Gables.*
    (C) Austen's *Pride and Prejudice.*
    (D) Wolfe's *Of Time and the River.*
    (E) Dickens' *Bleak House.*

23. Mark Twain is the pen name of

    (A) C. Day Lewis.
    (B) William Sydney Porter.
    (C) Eric Blair.
    (D) Samuel Clemens.
    (E) Upton Sinclair.

24. The novel records the events of one average day, June 16, 1904, in the lives of its three leading characters: Leopold Bloom, his wife Molly, and Stephen Dedalus.

    The sentence above discusses

    (A) Wolfe's *Of Time and the River.*
    (B) Lawrence's *Sons and Lovers.*
    (C) Hemingway's *The Sun Also Rises.*
    (D) Joyce's *Ulysses.*
    (E) Lowry's *Under the Volcano.*

25. All of the following are records of travel EXCEPT

    (A) *Roughing It*—Mark Twain.
    (B) *Two Years Before the Mast*—Richard Dana.
    (C) *Down These Mean Streets*—Piri Thomas.
    (D) *The Voyage of the Beagle*—Charles Darwin.
    (E) *The Oregon Trail*—Francis Parkman.

26. Which is NOT associated with Greek theater?

    (A) Masks
    (B) Deus ex machina
    (C) Chorus
    (D) Scene changes
    (E) Proscenium

Questions 27 and 28 refer to the following poem.

"The fog comes

on little cat feet.

It sits looking

over harbor and city

on silent haunches

and then moves on."

27. The lines above were written by

    (A) Allen Ginsberg.
    (B) Robert Frost.
    (C) Ezra Pound.
    (D) e.e. cummings.
    (E) Carl Sandburg.

28. Which of the following describes the lines in the poem?

    (A) A sestina
    (B) An epic
    (C) A sonnet
    (D) Alliteration
    (E) Free verse

29. A satirical novel set in the year 632 AF (After Ford), it is a grim picture of the world that the author thinks our scientific and social developments have already begun to create.

    The passage above discusses

    (A) Baldwin's *Another Country.*
    (B) Mann's *The Magic Mountain.*
    (C) Orwell's *1984.*
    (D) Huxley's *Brave New World.*
    (E) Ellison's *Invisible Man.*

30. In American history, they were a group of reformers whose writings drew public attention to corruption in politics and business and to other social ills.

    (A) The Muckrakers
    (B) The Agrarians
    (C) The New Wave
    (D) The Bloomsbury Group
    (E) The Beat novelists

31. All of the following were written by Plato EXCEPT

    (A) Confessions.
    (B) Crito.
    (C) Laws.
    (D) Republic.
    (E) Apology.

32. "in Just—

    spring when the world is mud—

    luscious the little

    lame balloonman

    whistles far and wee"

    The poet who wrote these lines is

    (A) Edna St. Vincent Millay.
    (B) e.e. cummings.
    (C) Carl Sandberg.
    (D) Vachel Lindsay.
    (E) Ezra Pound.

33. Which of the following plays is NOT paired with its correct author?

    (A) *Streamers* . . . David Rabe
    (B) *The Wild Duck* . . . Henrik Ibsen
    (C) *The Dutchman* . . . Tom Stoppard
    (D) *The Importance of Being Earnest* . . . Oscar Wilde
    (E) *Our Town* . . . Thornton Wilder

34. Which of the following characters is incorrectly paired with the novel in which he/she appears?

    (A) Tom Joad . . . *The Grapes of Wrath*
    (B) Hester Prynne . . . *The Scarlet Letter*
    (C) Brett Ashley . . . *Crime and Punishment*
    (D) Ishmael . . . *Moby Dick*
    (E) Des Esseintes . . . *Against the Grain (or Against Nature)*

35. Which of the following works is NOT paired with its correct author?

    (A) *Pygmalion* . . . George Bernard Shaw
    (B) *The Zoo Story* . . . Edward Albee
    (C) *The Threepenny Opera* . . . Brecht and Weill
    (D) *The Plough and the Stars* . . . Jules Feiffer
    (E) *The Prisoner of Second Avenue* . . . Neil Simon

36. Which of the following novels is NOT included among Lawrence Durrell's *The Alexandria Quartet?*

    (A) *Lolita*
    (B) *Justine*
    (C) *Balthazar*
    (D) *Mountolive*
    (E) *Clea*

37. Which of the following is a satire on the development of the Russian Revolution under Stalin?

    (A) Sholokhov's *And Quiet Flows the Don*
    (B) Orwell's *Animal Farm*
    (C) Malraux's *Man's Fate*
    (D) London's *The Iron Heel*
    (E) Gide's *Strait Is the Gate*

38. A landmark in the history of American journalism was the right of a certain newspaper to publish "The Pentagon Papers." That newspaper was

    (A) The *New York Times.*
    (B) The *Village Voice.*
    (C) The *Boston Globe.*
    (D) The *Wall Street Journal.*
    (E) The *San Francisco Chronicle.*

39. "Here, in this little Bay,

    Full of tumultuous life and great repose,

    Where, twice a day,

    The purposeless, glad ocean comes and goes,

    Under high cliffs, and far from the huge town,

    I sit me down."

    In the context of the lines quoted above, "glad" means

    (A) resolute.
    (B) steadfast.
    (C) noisy.
    (D) lapping.
    (E) recurrent.

40. Which of the following Shakespearean heroines is INCORRECTLY matched with the hero of the play in which she appears?

    (A) Ophelia—Hamlet
    (B) Cordelia—Macbeth
    (C) Cressida—Troilus
    (D) Cleopatra—Antony
    (E) Beatrice—Benedict

Questions 41 and 42 refer to the following lines.

"Beside the idle summer sea,

And in the vacant summer days,

Light Love came fluting down the ways

Where you were loitering with me."

41. The rhyme scheme of the lines is

    (A) ABAB
    (B) AABB
    (C) ABBA
    (D) ABCD
    (E) ABBC

42. Which of the following describes the lines in the poem?

    (A) Onomatopoeia
    (B) Blank verse
    (C) A quatrain
    (D) A tercet
    (E) A simile

43. Which of the following characters is incorrectly paired with the play in which he/she appears?

    (A) Blanche DuBois . . . *A Streetcar Named Desire*
    (B) Rizzo . . . *Grease*
    (C) Stanley Kowalski . . . *Who's Afraid of Virginia Woolf?*
    (D) Robert Mayo . . . *Beyond the Horizon*
    (E) Eteocles . . . *Seven Against Thebes*

44. *Songs of Innocence* and *Songs of Experience*, two series of poems, were written by

    (A) Robert Burns.
    (B) Walt Whitman.
    (C) Rainer Maria Rilke.
    (D) William Blake.
    (E) Henry Wadsworth Longfellow.

45. Which of the following is often a symbol of the hero of the absurd?

    (A) Prometheus
    (B) A unicorn
    (C) Sisyphus
    (D) Persephone
    (C) The phoenix

Questions 46 and 47 refer to the following.

    (A) *Utopia*—Sir Thomas More
    (B) *Walden*—Henry David Thoreau
    (C) *Life on the Mississippi*—Mark Twain
    (D) *Children of the Dream*—Bruno Bettelheim
    (E) *History of New York*—Washington Irving

46. Which work above is from the twentieth century?

47. Which author above used the pseudonym of Diedrich Knickerbocker?

48. Which of the following groups is most associated with the philosophy of transcendentalism?

    (A) Wordsworth, Coleridge, Confucius, Bacon
    (B) Schopenhauer, Sidgwick, Chomsky, Muir
    (C) Emerson, Fuller, Thoreau, Alcott
    (D) Dickinson, Frost, Darwin, Dewey
    (E) Confucius, St. Augustine, Kami, Compte

49. John Fowles wrote all of the following works EXCEPT

    (A) *The Magus.*
    (B) *The Collector.*
    (C) *The Sailor Who Fell From Grace With the Sea.*
    (D) *The French Lieutenant's Woman.*
    (E) *Daniel Martin.*

50. Which of the following writers is known as a humorist?

    (A) Theodore Sturgeon
    (B) Erie Stanley Gardner
    (C) John Taine
    (D) Dashiell Hammett
    (E) S.J. Perelman

51. Which of the following poets was a member of the Black Mountain group?

    (A) Countee Cullen
    (B) Charles Olson
    (C) Edgar Lee Masters
    (D) Robert Penn Warren
    (E) Gregory Corso

52. Since it is perhaps the last play written solely by Shakespeare, many commentators have seen the episode where Prospero breaks his staff and buries his book as Shakespeare's renunciation of his life as a London playwright and his return to his "Dukedom of Milan" in Stratford.

    The Shakespearean play referred to in the sentence above is

    (A) *The Taming of the Shrew.*
    (B) *The Merchant of Venice.*
    (C) *The Comedy of Errors.*
    (D) *The Tempest.*
    (E) *The Two Gentlemen of Verona.*

53. *Four Quartets,* a series of four long meditative poems, was written by

    (A) Wallace Stevens.
    (B) Pablo Neruda.
    (C) Federico Garcia Lorca.
    (D) T.S. Eliot.
    (E) Eugenio Montale.

54. Which of the following novels was NOT written by D.H. Lawrence?

    (A) *Sons and Lovers*
    (B) *Lady Chatterley's Lover*
    (C) *Couples*
    (D) *The Plumed Serpent*
    (E) *Women in Love*

55. Lytton Strachey, known for his work *Eminent Victorians,* was a(n)

    (A) poet.
    (B) essayist.
    (C) novelist.
    (D) playwright.
    (E) writer of children's stories.

56. Which of the following plays was NOT written by Tennessee Williams?

    (A) *Cat on a Hot Tin Roof*
    (B) *The Rose Tattoo*
    (C) *A Streetcar Named Desire*
    (D) *The Glass Menagerie*
    (E) *Who's Afraid of Virginia Woolf?*

57. "The best laid schemes o' mice an' men
    Gang aft a–glay.
    An' lea'e us nought but grief an' pain
    For promised joy."
    The author of these lines is

    (A) Emily Dickenson.
    (B) Baudelaire.
    (C) William Blake.
    (D) Robert Burns.
    (E) Sappho.

58. The author of *Sophie's Choice, The Confessions of Nat Turner,* and *Lie Down in Darkness* is

    (A) William Styron.
    (B) John Fowles.
    (C) Alexander Solzhenitsen.
    (D) John O'Hara.
    (E) Ann Beattie.

59. James Boswell is best known as a diarist and as the biographer of

    (A) Dr. Samuel Johnson.
    (B) Alexander Pope.
    (C) Ben Jonson.
    (D) Jonathan Swift.
    (E) Henry Fielding.

60. It is a play about the Salem, Massachusetts witchcraft trials of 1692. Raising the question of freedom of conscience, it provides a parallel to McCarthyism in America during the early 1950s.

    The passage above discusses

    (A) Shaw's *Man and Superman.*
    (B) Miller's *The Crucible.*
    (C) Shafer's *Equus.*
    (D) Jonson's *The Alchemist.*
    (E) O'Neill's *Strange Interlude.*

Questions 61 and 62 refer to the following passage.

"When to the sessions of sweet, silent thought

I summon up remembrance of things past,

I sigh the lack of many a thing I sought,

And with old woes new wail my dear time's waste."

61. In these lines, the poet employs the technique of

    (A) simile.
    (B) alliteration.
    (C) personification.
    (D) metaphor.
    (E) assonance.

62. The author of these lines was

    (A) Shakespeare.
    (B) Virgil.
    (C) Dante.
    (D) Robert Browning.
    (E) Elizabeth Barrett Browning.

63. Which author is out of chronological order?

    (A) Demosthenes
    (B) Cicero
    (C) Hannah Arendt
    (D) John Adams
    (E) Charles Lamb

64. Which of the following plays was NOT written by George Bernard Shaw?

    (A) *The Emperor Jones*
    (B) *Major Barbara*
    (C) *The Devil's Disciple*
    (D) *Pygmalion*
    (E) *Man and Superman*

65. Who is NOT associated with feminist writing?

    (A) Marge Piercy
    (B) Simone de Beauvoir
    (C) Eudora Welty
    (D) Susan Brownmiller
    (E) Gloria Steinem

66. It deals with the effort of Harry Morgan, a native of Key West, to earn a living for himself and his family. He has operated a boat for rental to fishing parties, but, during the depression of the 1930s, he turns to the smuggling of Chinese immigrants and illegal liquor.

    The passage above discusses

    (A) de Beauvoir's *The Mandarins*.
    (B) Dreiser's *An American Tragedy*.
    (C) Sinclair's *The Jungle*.
    (D) Hemingway's *To Have and Have Not*.
    (E) Steinbeck's *The Grapes of Wrath*.

67. "With malice toward none; with charity for all" is a quotation from a speech by

    (A) George Washington.
    (B) Franklin D. Roosevelt.
    (C) Abraham Lincoln.
    (D) Theodore Roosevelt.
    (E) Thomas Jefferson.

68. Which of the following poems was written by T.S. Eliot?

    (A) *The Bridge*
    (B) *The Age of Anxiety*
    (C) "Sailing to Byzantium"
    (D) "The Road Not Taken"
    (E) *The Waste Land*

69. *Tales of the Jazz Age,* a collection of short stories, was written by

    (A) Ernest Hemingway.
    (B) Robert McAlmon.
    (C) Kay Boyle.
    (D) F. Scott Fitzgerald.
    (E) Gertrude Stein.

70. The moral philosopher and economist best known for *An Inquiry into the Nature and Cause of the Wealth of Nations* (1776) is

    (A) Baruch Spinoza.
    (B) John Stuart Mill.
    (C) John Locke.
    (D) Adam Smith.
    (E) John Maynard Keynes.

71. The poem "Trees" was written by

    (A) Joyce Kilmer.
    (B) Lawrence Ferlinghetti.
    (C) Gregory Corso.
    (D) Langston Hughes.
    (E) Ezra Pound.

72. Which of the following short stories was written by Ernest Hemingway?

    (A) "The Snows of Kilimanjaro"
    (B) "The Grey Champion"
    (C) "In the Penal Colony"
    (D) "Babylon Revisited"
    (E) "The Purloined Letter"

73. Prophecy plays an important part in which of the following plays?

    (A) *Death of a Salesman*
    (B) *King Lear*
    (C) *Oedipus Rex*
    (D) *A Raisin in the Sun*
    (E) *Short Eyes*

74. Which of the following was NOT written by Henry James?

    (A) *The Ambassadors*
    (B) *Washington Square*
    (C) *The Europeans*
    (D) *The Portrait of a Lady*
    (E) *Pale Horse, Pale Rider*

75. Which of the following groups is most associated with the philosophy of empiricism?

    (A) Aristotle, Horney, Peirce, Lovejoy
    (B) Schopenhauer, Socrates, Wittenstein, Pascal
    (C) Marx, Engels, Westheimer, Ockham
    (D) Schiller, Dewey, Bergson, Galena
    (E) Locke, Berkeley, Hume, James

Section II: Fine Arts

75 Questions

Time—45 minutes

Directions: For each question, choose the best answer from the five choices offered. Blacken your answer sheet for the letter of the correct answer.

76. "Good Morning Starshine" and "Aquarius" are songs from what Broadway musical about a group of hippies?

    (A) *The Indian Wants the Bronx*
    (B) *Sticks and Bones*
    (C) *The Way We Were*
    (D) *The Effect of Gamma Rays on Man–in–the–Moon Marigolds*
    (E) *Hair*

77. Woody Allen was the major force behind all of the following films EXCEPT

    (A) *Annie Hall*
    (B) *Sleeper*
    (C) *All That Jazz*
    (D) *Bananas*
    (E) *Interiors*

78. Seurat and his circle were known as the

    (A) Vorticists.
    (B) Surrealists.
    (C) Cubists.
    (D) Neo–impressionists.
    (E) Expressionists.

79. Working for the United States government over a period of thirty years, Edward S. Curtis created a monumental photographic survey of

    (A) North American wildlife.
    (B) the North American Plains Indian.
    (C) antebellum architecture in the South.
    (D) the Pacific Northwest fur trade.
    (E) gold mining in the Southwest.

80. Which of the following created massive, heroic sculptures, marked by a quality of repose in action, and figures that look as though they are trying to free themselves from the stone block?

    (A) Michelangelo
    (B) Rodin
    (C) Giacometti
    (D) Donatello
    (E) Callimachus

81. The rock musician long associated with The Rolling Stones is

    (A) Ringo Starr.
    (B) Mick Jagger.
    (C) Janis Joplin.
    (D) Elton John.
    (E) George Harrison.

82. The outstanding tenor of the Metropolitan Opera Company over the past decade has been

    (A) Rise Stevens.
    (B) Joan Sutherland.
    (C) Luciano Pavarotti.
    (D) Beverly Sills.
    (E) Enrico Caruso.

83. He was originally an engineer and his main inventions—stabiles and mobiles—can be regarded as a marriage between engineering and sculpture.

    The sculptor referred to in the sentence above is

    (A) Eduardo Paolozzi.
    (B) Vladimir Tatlin.
    (C) Constantin Brancusi.
    (D) Naum Gabo.
    (E) Alexander Calder.

84. *Mean Streets* and *Taxi Driver* are works of director

    (A) Michelangelo Antonioni.
    (B) Martin Scorcese.
    (C) Peter Bogdanovich.
    (D) John Cassavetes.
    (E) Woody Allen.

85. Which of the following was NOT composed by Gilbert and Sullivan?

    (A) *The Mikado*
    (B) *Ruddigore*
    (C) *Pygmalion*
    (D) *Pirates of Penzance*
    (E) *H.M.S. Pinafore*

86. Which of the following painters is incorrectly paired with the group or movement with which he was associated?

    (A) Vuillard . . . *Les Nabis*
    (B) Sickert . . . Camden Town Group
    (C) Tanguy . . . Surrealism
    (D) Shahn . . . Pop Art
    (E) Matisse . . . Fauvism

87. The early example of Cubism below was created by

    (A) Renoir.
    (B) Braque.
    (C) Picasso.
    (D) Modigliani.
    (E) Nevelson.

88. Which of the following architects designed the Guggenheim Museum in New York City?

    (A) Philip Johnson
    (B) Walter Gropius
    (C) Frank Lloyd Wright
    (D) Raymond Hood
    (E) Louis H. Sullivan

89. Which of the following groups is most associated with performance art?

    (A) Jennifer Bartlett, Walter DeMaria, Gilbert & George, Sam Gilliam
    (B) Claudio Bravo, Cindy Sherman, Bruce Nauman, Sandro Chia
    (C) Jenny Holzer, Anselm Kiefer, Lynda Benglis, Nam June Park
    (D) Joseph Beuys, Chris Burden, Laurie Anderson, Vito Acconci
    (E) Andy Warhol, Lucas Samaras, Robert Rauschenberg, Duane Hanson

90. Whose "veil dances" in the cabarets of Paris at the beginning of the twentieth century were immensely popular and had a profound influence on the development of modern dance?

    (A) Mistinguette
    (B) Sarah Fuller
    (C) Isadora Duncan
    (D) Edith Piaf
    (E) Joan Sutherland

91. In the early twentieth century, he developed a new method of musical composition (which became known as the 12–tone system) that was a substitute for the older practice of fixed harmonic relationships.

    Which of the following composers is described in the sentence above?

    (A) Erik Satie
    (B) John Cage
    (C) Aaron Copland
    (D) Arnold Schoenberg
    (E) Virgil Thomson

92. *Messiah* is an oratorio composed by

    (A) Richard Strauss.
    (B) Gustav Mahler.
    (C) George Handel.
    (D) (Franz) Joseph Haydn.
    (E) Johann Sebastian Bach.

93. Which of the following is a medium consisting of dry powdered color mixed with just enough gum (usually gum arabic) to bind it?

    (A) Tempera
    (B) Acrylic
    (C) Pastel
    (D) Encaustic wax
    (E) Gouache

94. Who is the Polish composer called "the poet of the piano"?

    (A) Glinka
    (B) Rachmaninoff
    (C) Chopin
    (D) Dvoräk
    (E) Smetana

95. The rounded arch was a dominant form of architectural construction in

    (A) Gothic cathedrals.
    (B) Egyptian temples.
    (C) Assyrian temples.
    (D) Roman basilicas.
    (E) Mayan temples.

96. Which of the following is usually defined as the "revival of art and letters under the influence of classical models in the fourteenth to sixteenth centuries"?

    (A) Neoclassicism
    (B) Renaissance
    (C) Gothic
    (D) Baroque
    (E) Mannerism

97. All of the following are James Bond movies EXCEPT

    (A) *The Spy Who Came in From the Cold*
    (B) *Diamonds Are Forever*
    (C) *Moonraker*
    (D) *Goldfinger*
    (E) *Dr. No*

98. A famous requiem was composed by

    (A) Beethoven.
    (B) Schumann.
    (C) Verdi.
    (D) Handel.
    (E) Liszt.

99. Which of the following kinds of scenes is most often associated with Paul Cézanne?

    (A) Still life
    (B) Formal portrait
    (C) Informal portrait
    (D) Action study
    (E) Architectural rendering

Questions 100–102 refer to the pictures on the following page.

100. Which is by Toulouse–Lautrec?

101. Which is an example of Art Nouveau?

102. Which is by Vuillard?

103. In which opera is the heroine not only an Ethiopian princess but also a slave of the Egyptian king's daughter?

    (A) *Aida*
    (B) *Lucia de Lammermoor*
    (C) *Carmen*
    (D) *City of the Pyramid*
    (E) *Madame Butterfly*

104. Which cathedral, famed for its triple portals, rose windows, and the cobalt blue of its glass, is often considered the greatest Gothic cathedral in France?

    (A) Amiens
    (B) Reims
    (C) Strasbourg
    (D) Chartres
    (E) Notre–Dame

105. The monument pictured on page 139 was designed by

    (A) Robert Venturi.
    (B) I. M. Pei.
    (C) Maya Lin.
    (D) Richard Meier.
    (E) Alison Sky.

106. Diane Arbus is well known for her photograph of

    (A) trees.
    (B) Navaho Indians.
    (C) a cabbage leaf.
    (D) Martha Graham.
    (E) identical twins.

(A)

(B)

(C)

(D)

(E)

107. Of the following, the song that was NOT composed by Stephen Foster is

    (A) "Nelly Bly."
    (B) "Jeanie with the Light Brown Hair."
    (C) "Beautiful Dreamer."
    (D) "Over the Rainbow."
    (E) "Swanee."

108. The star of Josef von Sternberg's *The Blue Angel* and *Morocco* was

    (A) Gloria Swanson.
    (B) Mae West.
    (C) Marlene Dietrich.
    (D) Lillian Gish.
    (E) Jeanette MacDonald.

109. It consists of the use, as sources, of artifacts, photographs, advertising, and strip cartoons, often blown up to enormous size, and painted usually in a hard–edged technique and garish color, or of various objects which are assembled in a manner reminiscent of Surrealism.

    Which of the following is referred to in the sentence above?

    (A) Vorticism
    (B) Pop Art
    (C) Futurism
    (D) Cubism
    (E) Fauvism

Questions 110 and 111 refer to the pictures on the following page.

110. Which is by Brueghel?

111. Which is by Giotto?

112. The "King of Ragtime Composers" was

    (A) Ferdinand "Jelly Roll" Morton.
    (B) Edward "Duke" Ellington.
    (C) Scott Joplin.
    (D) William "Count" Basie.
    (E) Charlie Parker.

113. Introduced in Zurich during World War I, it was deliberately anti–art and antisense, intended to outrage and scandalize.

    Which of the following is described in the sentence above?

    (A) Op Art
    (B) Pop Art
    (C) Vorticism
    (D) Fauvism
    (E) Dada

114. The star of *Modern Times, Monsieur Verdoux,* and *A Countess from Hong Kong* is

    (A) Buster Keaton.
    (B) Lionel Barrymore.
    (C) John Wayne.
    (D) Charlie Chaplin.
    (E) Emil Jannings.

(A)

(C)

(D)

(E)

(B)

115. Which of the following composers represent the late Baroque period?

    (A) Haydn and Mozart
    (B) Bach and Handel
    (C) Liszt and Wagner
    (D) Brahms and Bruckner
    (E) Debussy and Ravel

116. What American city is generally considered to be the birthplace of jazz?

    (A) New Orleans
    (B) San Francisco
    (C) Kansas City
    (D) New York
    (E) Chicago

117. In painting, emphasis on inner emotions, sensations, or ideas rather than actual appearances is called

    (A) Impressionism.
    (B) Futurism.
    (C) Expressionism.
    (D) Cubism.
    (E) Realism.

118. The painting pictured below is the work of

    (A) Nancy Holt.
    (B) Lucien Freud.
    (C) Alice Neel.
    (D) Eva Hesse.
    (E) Jean Edouard Vuillard.

119. The white–haired conductor associated for many years with the Boston Symphony Orchestra "Pops" Concerts was

    (A) Leonard Bernstein.
    (B) Seiji Ozawa.
    (C) Zubin Mehta.
    (D) Arthur Fiedler.
    (E) Isaac Stern.

120. Which of the following U.S. presidents had an abiding interest in architecture?

    (A) George Washington
    (B) Thomas Jefferson
    (C) Abraham Lincoln
    (D) Calvin Coolidge
    (E) John F. Kennedy

Questions 121–123 refer to pictures on the following page.

121. Which is by Gaudi?

122. Which was designed by Le Corbusier?

123. Which is related to Gothic style?

124. The name "Tanglewood" is most closely associated with

    (A) a summer theater movement.
    (B) the Empire Music Festival.
    (C) a summer literary workshop.
    (D) the Berkshire music center.
    (E) an American dance movement.

125. Which of the following is a group of Impressionist painters?

    (A) Picasso, Gris, Braque
    (B) Ernst, Schwitters, Tanguy
    (C) Monet, Renoir, Degas
    (D) Millais, Burne–Jones, Rossetti
    (E) Nolde, Kollowitz, Kandinsky

Questions 126 and 127 refer to the following ballets.

    (A) *Dark Elegies*
    (B) *The Nutcracker*
    (C) *Firebird*
    (D) *Coppélia*
    (E) *Moves*

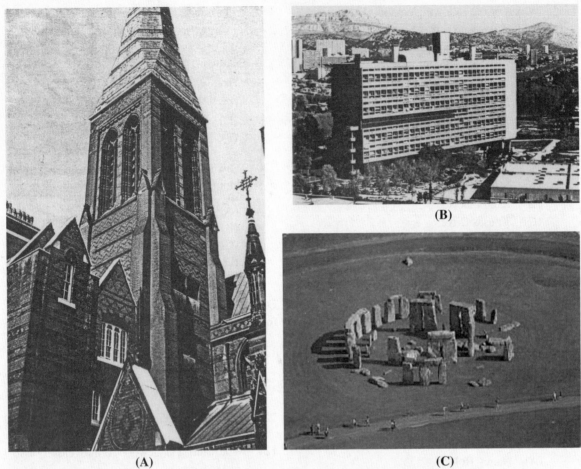

(A)

(B)

(C)

(D)

(E)

126. In which ballet does a girl deceive a toymaker into thinking that she is one of his own dolls come to life?

127. In which ballet does the king of the mice lose a battle on Christmas Eve?

128. The picture writing of the ancient Egyptians is known as

(A) cuneiform.
(B) cursive.
(C) hieroglyphics.
(D) sans serif.
(E) bas relief.

129. The name of Pablo Casals is associated with the

(A) piano.
(B) cello.
(C) organ.
(D) violin.
(E) flute.

130. The words "truss" and "girder" refer to two of the five basic designs utilized in the construction of

(A) bridges.
(B) highways.
(C) ships.
(D) tunnels.
(E) houses

131. The company associated with the Russian expatriate George Balanchine and famed for a choreography that occupies an intermediate position between ballet and modern dance is the

(A) Royal Ballet.
(B) New York City Ballet.
(C) Joffrey Ballet.
(D) Stuttgart Ballet.
(E) Bolshoi Ballet.

132. The ceiling of the Sistine Chapel was painted by

(A) Raphael.
(B) Leonardo.
(C) Rembrandt.
(D) Michelangelo.
(E) Rubens.

133. A vocal arrangement in which the same melody is sung by several voices starting one after the other at regular intervals to produce pleasant harmony and rhythm is called a(n)

(A) art song.
(B) round.
(C) descant.
(D) a cappella.
(E) chant.

Questions 134 and 135 refer to the pictures on the following page.

134. Which is by Paul Cézanne?

135. Which is a famous antiwar painting by Pablo Picasso?

136. Which of the following painters is incorrectly paired with the group or movement with which he was associated?

(A) Derain . . . Fauvism
(B) Kline . . . Abstract Expressionism
(C) Rauschenberg . . . Pop Art
(D) Magritte . . . Art Nouveau
(E) Arp . . . Dada

137. A group that utilized smoke, fire, and makeup in performances and performed in the closing ceremonies of the 2002 Winter Olympics is

(A) Blood, Sweat & Tears.
(B) Kiss.
(C) Bee Gees.
(D) David Bowie.
(E) Jefferson Starship.

138. Which of the following films signaled the start of the German Golden Age of films?

(A) *The Joyless Street*
(B) *Metropolis*
(C) *Nosferatu*
(D) *The Cabinet of Dr. Caligari*
(E) *Triumph of the Will*

139. The incorrectly matched pair is

(A) Beethoven . . . Pastoral Symphony.
(B) Schumann . . . Spring Symphony.
(C) Mozart . . . Eroica Symphony.
(D) Haydn . . . Clock Symphony.
(E) Mahler . . . Resurrection Symphony.

(A)

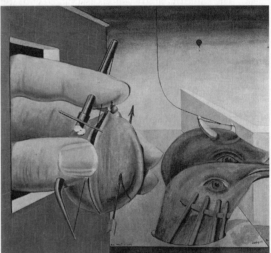

(B)

(C)

140. One of the finest painters of marine pictures is
    - (A) George Bellows.
    - (B) John Steuart Curry.
    - (C) El Greco.
    - (D) Winslow Homer.
    - (E) James McNeil Whistler.

141. Which of the following literary works was the first to be made into a film?
    - (A) *The Tin Drum*
    - (B) *Death in Venice*
    - (C) *A Tree Grows in Brooklyn*
    - (D) *Gone With The Wind*
    - (E) *Portnoy's Complaint*

142. "Gouge," "knife," "roller," "venier," and "relief printing" are all terms associated with
    - (A) etching.
    - (B) linoleum block printing.
    - (C) wood carving.
    - (D) leather work.
    - (E) ceramics.

143. Which French filmmaker has satirized the American consumer mentality and has created *Breathless*, *Weekend*, and *Made in U.S.A.?*
    - (A) Truffaut
    - (B) Bresson
    - (C) Bunuel
    - (D) Bergman
    - (E) Godard

Questions 144–147 refer to pictures on the following page.

144. Which is by Marcel Duchamp?

145. Which is by Constantin Brancusi?

146. Which is by Alberto Giacometti?

147. Which is by Tony Smith?

148. A style of music native to the Caribbean is
    - (A) calypso.
    - (B) rock.
    - (C) new wave.
    - (D) progressive jazz.
    - (E) polka.

149. Bob Dylan wrote all of the following songs EXCEPT
    - (A) "Mr. Tambourine Man."
    - (B) "Blowin' in the Wind."
    - (C) "Masters of War."
    - (D) "Mrs. Robinson."
    - (E) "Forever Young."

150. A painter of decorative, barbaric Tahitian landscape was
    - (A) Edgar Degas.
    - (B) Paul Gauguin.
    - (C) George Inness.
    - (D) Pierre Renoir.
    - (E) Vincent Van Gogh.

End of Practice Examination II

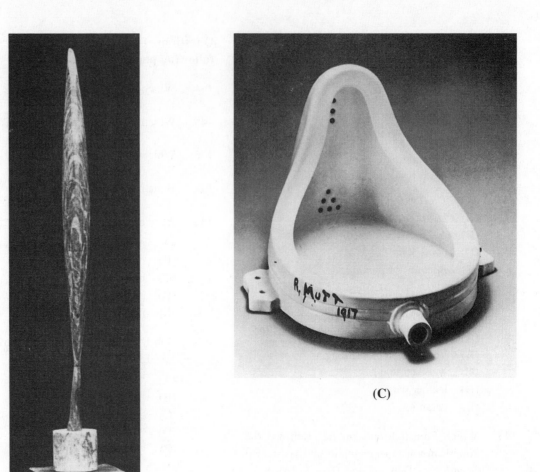

(A)

(C)

(B)

(D)

Answer Key

Section I

1.	B	16.	D	31.	A	46.	D	61.	B
2.	C	17.	A	32.	B	47.	E	62.	A
3.	D	18.	B	33.	C	48.	C	63.	C
4.	E	19.	A	34.	C	49.	C	64.	A
5.	C	20.	E	35.	D	50.	E	65.	C
6.	C	21.	A	36.	A	51.	B	66.	D
7.	D	22.	C	37.	B	52.	D	67.	C
8.	C	23.	D	38.	A	53.	D	68.	E
9.	D	24.	D	39.	D	54.	C	69.	D
10.	B	25.	C	40.	B	55.	B	70.	D
11.	A	26.	D	41.	C	56.	E	71.	A
12.	B	27.	E	42.	C	57.	D	72.	A
13.	D	28.	E	43.	C	58.	A	73.	C
14.	C	29.	D	44.	D	59.	A	74.	E
15.	B	30.	A	45.	C	60.	B	75.	E

Section II

76.	E	91.	D	106.	E	121.	E	136.	D
77.	C	92.	C	107.	D	122.	B	137.	B
78.	D	93.	C	108.	C	123.	A	138.	D
79.	B	94.	C	109.	B	124.	D	139.	C
80.	A	95.	D	110.	B	125.	C	140.	D
81.	B	96.	B	111.	D	126.	D	141.	D
82.	C	97.	A	112.	C	127.	B	142.	B
83.	E	98.	C	113.	E	128.	C	143.	E
84.	B	99.	A	114.	D	129.	B	144.	D
85.	C	100.	B	115.	B	130.	A	145.	B
86.	D	101.	D	116.	A	131.	B	146.	D
87.	C	102.	E	117.	C	132.	D	147.	B
88.	C	103.	A	118.	C	133.	B	148.	A
89.	D	104.	D	119.	D	134.	A	149.	D
90.	C	105.	C	120.	B	135.	C	150.	B

Explanatory Answers

Section I

1. **The correct answer is (B).** Ezra Pound (1885–1972) was a poet, critic, and editor whose major works include *The Cantos, Hugh Selwyn Mauberley* and *Homage to Sextus Propertius.*

2. **The correct answer is (C).** Sir Arthur Conan Doyle (1859–1930) created Sherlock Holmes of Baker Street, London, and his friend Dr. Watson, in such works as *The Sign of the Four* and *The Hound of the Baskervilles.*

3. **The correct answer is (D).** *The Picture of Dorian Gray* was written in 1891 by the Irish writer and dramatist Oscar Wilde (1856–1900), who expounded the philosophy of "art for art's sake."

4. **The correct answer is (E).** "The Vision Concerning Piers Plowman" is an alliterative poem ascribed to William Langland and written in three versions (1360–1399).

5. **The correct answer is (C).** Theodore H. White (1915–1986) began the series in 1960 with a public and private view of John F. Kennedy's campaign and continued these studies of "American politics in action."

6. **The correct answer is (C).** *Don Quixote,* Miguel de Cervantes' (1547–1616) masterpiece, contains the characters Don Quixote, Sancho Panza, and Dulcinea, as well as the broken–down horse, Rocinante.

7. **The correct answer is (D).** In these lines, the poet addresses "Death" directly, as if "Death" were a listening person. This technique, related in a sense to "personification," is called *apostrophe.*

8. **The correct answer is (C).** Stephen Dedalus appears in *A Portrait of the Artist as a Young Man* and in *Ulysses,* both by James Joyce (1882–1941).

9. **The correct answer is (D).** Aristotle (384–322 B.C.E.), the Greek philosopher who was Plato's student and Alexander the Great's tutor, headed the Peripatetic School in Athens and discussed tragedy and epic poetry in *Poetics.*

10. **The correct answer is (B).** *A Doll's House* concludes when Nora "slams the door" on husband and family. Henrik Ibsen (1828–1906) is known for his strong female characters and for such works as *Hedda Gabler, Enemy of the People, The Wild Duck,* and *The Master Builder.*

11. **The correct answer is (A).** Written in Middle English, "The Cuckoo Song" is an anonymous thirteenth–century lyric.

12. **The correct answer is (B).** The early lyrics were short poems meant to be sung to a lyre.

13. **The correct answer is (D).** Robbe–Grillet (1922–) wrote the script and dialogue for the film *Last Year in Marienbad* as well as a critical essay entitled "Pour un nouveau roman." The literary New Wave is also called "nouveau roman" and is associated with French experimenters who rejected conventional novel forms and who were thus termed "antinovelists." Sarraute (1900–1999), an early "antinovelist," wrote *Tropisms* and other experimental works.

14. **The correct answer is (C).** Ray Bradbury (1920–) created *The Martian Chronicles* and *Fahrenheit 451.*

15. **The correct answer is (B).** *Pygmalion,* written in 1912 by George Bernard Shaw (1856–1950), is based on the story of Pygmalion and Galatea, in which a sculptor carves a statue of a maiden and falls in love with it.

16. **The correct answer is (D).** *The Jungle* was written in 1906 by the muckraker writer and politician Upton Sinclair (1878–1968), a socialist much concerned with exposing the horrors faced by working people of his time.

17. **The correct answer is (A).** Friedrich Nietzsche (1844–1900) was a German philosopher and poet who espoused the "morals of masters," the glorification of the superman that is regarded as having influenced German attitudes in World War I and in the 1933 Third Reich.

18. **The correct answer is (B).** Ralph Waldo Emerson (1803–1882), the American essayist and poet, described the beginning of the American Revolution in "Concord Hymn," which was sung at the completion of a monument commemorating the battles of Lexington and Concord (Massachusetts), April 19, 1775.

19. **The correct answer is (A).** *The Divine Comedy* records Dante Alighieri's (1265–1321) imaginary journey through Hell and Purgatory, guided by Vergil, and through Paradise, guided by Beatrice.

20. **The correct answer is (E).** Written in 1924, the play ends when Eben admits his part in the murder and is arrested with Abbie. Eugene O'Neill (1888–1953), the first American playwright to win the Nobel Prize for literature, also created *Beyond the Horizon, The Hairy Ape, Mourning Becomes Electra, The Iceman Cometh,* and *Long Day's Journey Into Night,* among others.

21. **The correct answer is (A).** Metaphor is the comparison of essentially unlike things without the use of "like" or "as." In the stanza cited, "her channeled muscles" are compared with "cluster grapes of sorrow. . . ."

22. **The correct answer is (C).** *Pride and Prejudice* was written at the end of the eighteenth century by Jane Austen (1775–1817), the British author of *Sense and Sensibility, Northanger Abbey, Emma,* and *Persuasion.*

23. **The correct answer is (D).** Samuel Clemens (1835–1910) was the American humorist and author of such works as *The Adventures of Huckleberry Finn, The Adventures of Tom Sawyer,* and *The Prince and the Pauper.* The pseudonym Mark Twain, a Mississippi riverboat worker's term, means "two fathoms deep."

24. **The correct answer is (D).** The Irish writer James Joyce wrote the highly complex masterpiece, as well as *Chamber Music, Finnegans Wake, Dubliners, Exiles, A Portrait of the Artist as a Young Man,* and *Pomes Penyeach.*

25. **The correct answer is (C).** In *Down These Mean Streets,* Piri Thomas (1928–   ) documents the passage of a youngster in New York's Spanish Harlem from childhood to maturity. Thomas is also known for *Savior, Savior, Hold My Hand,* and *Seven Long Times.*

26. **The correct answer is (D).** The Greek dramatists observed the unity of place and, therefore, did not employ changes of scene.

27. **The correct answer is (E).** This is one of the best–known poems of Carl Sandburg (1878–1967), who also wrote *Good Morning, America* and *The People, Yes.* He received a Pulitzer Prize for poetry in 1951 and another for history in 1939 (for *Abraham Lincoln–The War Years*).

28. **The correct answer is (E).** Most of Sandburg's poetry is in free verse, usually unrhymed lines of varied length and unfixed metrical pattern.

29. **The correct answer is (D).** Aldous Huxley (1894–1963) also wrote *Antic Hay, Point Counter Point, Brief Candles,* and *Eyeless in Gaza,* among others.

30. **The correct answer is (A).** The muckraking movement lasted in the United States from 1902 until World War I. Many periodicals and authors were dedicated to exposing unscrupulous methods and motives in private business and in government.

31. **The correct answer is (A).** Augustine of Hippo (354–430) explains his conversion to Christianity in *Confessions.* St. Augustine is also known for *City of God.*

32. **The correct answer is (B).** e.e. cummings' (1894–1962) concern with typography—with how his poem looked on the page—is evident in these lines.

33. **The correct answer is (C).** *Dutchman* was written in 1964 by the Black American writer LeRoi Jones (Imamu Amiri Baraka) (1934–), who is also known for *The System of Dante's Hell, The Slave, The Toilet,* and *Preface to a Twenty Volume Suicide Note.*

34. **The correct answer is (C).** Brett Ashley appears in Ernest Hemingway's *The Sun Also Rises* (1926).

35. **The correct answer is (D).** *The Plough and the Stars* was written in 1926 by the Irish

playwright Sean O'Casey (1880–1964), who is also known for *Juno and the Paycock.*

36. **The correct answer is (A).** *Lolita* was written in 1955 by Vladimir Nabokov (1899–1977), who also wrote *Ada, Pale Fire,* and *Laughter in the Dark.*

37. **The correct answer is (B).** Written in 1945 by George Orwell (1903–1950), this Swiftian animal story is a satiric allegory of Stalinism and of totalitarianism in general.

38. **The correct answer is (A).** The *New York Times* and the U.S. Justice Department argued in June 1971 before the U.S. Supreme Court as to whether the newspaper had the right to print material describing the history of U.S. involvement in Southeast Asia. The information was supplied by Daniel Ellsberg; the court case has been called a "historic clash between a free press and a powerful government."

39. **The correct answer is (D).** Since the ocean is "purposeless," it is not *resolute,* choice (A); since the ocean "comes and goes," it is not *steadfast,* choice (B). A noisy, choice (C), ocean would be contrary to the relaxed mood established in the lines, and recurrent, choice (E), is merely redundant and cannot be deduced from "glad." So *lapping* is correct; it agrees with the soothing atmosphere of the poem and also reminds the reader of a happy animal licking a master's face.

40. **The correct answer is (B).** Cordelia, sister to Goneril and Regan, daughter of Lear, appears in Shakespeare's *King Lear.*

41. **The correct answer is (C).** Rhyme scheme is based on the final sound of each line. In this case, the first and fourth lines rhyme, as do the second and third; thus, the scheme is ABBA.

42. **The correct answer is (C).** A quatrain is a four-line stanza, rhymed or unrhymed.

43. **The correct answer is (C).** Stanley Kowalski appears in *A Streetcar Named Desire,* written in 1947 by Tennessee Williams (1911–1983). Marlon Brando portrayed Stanley in the original production.

44. **The correct answer is (D).** William Blake (1757–1827) was an English artist, poet, and mystic. *Songs of Experience,* written in 1794, contains the poem that begins, "Tyger! Tyger! burning bright."

45. **The correct answer is (C).** In Greek mythology, Sisyphus was a cruel king of Corinth condemned forever to roll a huge stone up a hill in Hades, only to have it roll down again on nearing the top. Albert Camus (1913–1960) used the character as a symbol of the absurd in his 1942 work, *The Myth of Sisyphus.*

46. **The correct answer is (D).** Bruno Bettelheim (1903–1990) was an authority on childhood emotional development; *Children of the Dream* is a study of communal child–rearing on the Israeli kibbutz.

47. **The correct answer is (E).** Washington Irving (1783–1859) wrote the humorous and mildly satirical *History of New York, by Diedrich Knickerbocker,* and also created "The Legend of Sleepy Hollow" and "Rip Van Winkle."

48. **The correct answer is (C).** After meeting Wordsworth, Coleridge, and Carlyle in Europe, Emerson set forth in *Nature* (1836) the basis for his transcendental philosophy, which is explained as the belief that knowledge of reality is attained from intuitive sources rather than from objective experience. Associated with the transcendental movement in New England were Bronson Alcott, Margaret Fuller, and Henry David Thoreau, among others.

49. **The correct answer is (C).** *The Sailor Who Fell from Grace with the Sea* was written in 1965 by Yukio Mishima (1925–1970), the prolific Japanese author who committed suicide in a public display reminiscent of the ancient Japanese tradition.

50. **The correct answer is (E).** The humorist S. J. Perelman (1904–1979) wrote such works as *Strictly from Hunger, Look Who's Talking,* and *The Dream Department.*

51. **The correct answer is (B).** From 1954–1957 at Black Mountain College in North Carolina,

a group of poets and critics (Charles Olson (1910–1970)—who was rector of the college—among them) published *Black Mountain Review,* a little magazine with such contributors as James Purdy, Kenneth Rexroth, and William Carlos Williams.

52. **The correct answer is (D).** *The Tempest* was written in 1611 and is often considered Shakespeare's (1564–1616) farewell to the theater.

53. **The correct answer is (D).** T. S. Eliot (1888–1965) was awarded the Nobel Prize in literature in 1948 for work that includes "The Love Song of J. Alfred Prufrock," "Sweeny Among the Nightingales," *The Sacred Wood, The Waste Land, Murder in the Cathedral,* and *The Cocktail Party.*

54. **The correct answer is (C).** *Couples* was written in 1968 by John Updike (1932–), author of *The Centaur, Rabbit Run, Rabbit Redux,* and other stories and poetry.

55. **The correct answer is (B).** Lytton Strachey (1880–1932) also wrote books concerning *Queen Victoria, Pope,* and *Elizabeth and Essex,* among others.

56. **The correct answer is (E).** *Who's Afraid of Virginia Woolf?* was written in 1962 by Edward Albee (1928–), who is also known for *The Zoo Story, The American Dream, A Delicate Balance,* and *Tiny Alice.*

57. **The correct answer is (D).** The language indicates that the Scottish poet Robert Burns (1759–1796) wrote these lines; lines one and two are especially famous.

58. **The correct answer is (A).** William Styron (1925–) was born and educated in the southern United States but now lives in Connecticut. *Lie Down in Darkness* is set in the South, as is *Nat Turner,* which was highly controversial when it was published; *Sophie's Choice* is set in the North but also utilizes the author's knowledge of Southern history and culture.

59. **The correct answer is (A).** James Boswell (1740–1795) was a Scottish lawyer who met Dr. Johnson in London, visited him often,

travelled with him, recorded his conversations, and created the masterpiece of biography, *Life of Samuel Johnson (1791),* as well as *Account of Corsica* and *Journal of Tour to Hebrides.*

60. **The correct answer is (B).** *The Crucible* was written in 1953 by Arthur Miller (1915–), who is famous also for *Death of a Salesman, View from the Bridge, Incident at Vichy, The Fall, The Price,* and *All My Sons.*

61. **The correct answer is (B).** Alliteration is the repetition of sounds in two or more words; these lines employ quick repetition of "s" and "w" sounds, for instance.

62. **The correct answer is (A).** The lines are from Shakespeare's Sonnet 30.

63. **The correct answer is (C).** John Adams (1735–1826) and Charles Lamb (1775–1834) lived *before* Hannah Arendt (1906–1975), the author, political scientist, and teacher noted for *The Origins of Totalitarianism, The Human Condition,* and *Eichman in Jerusalem.*

64. **The correct answer is (A).** *The Emperor Jones,* by Eugene O'Neill, tells of a man who went "from stowaway to emperor in three years" and who was killed by a silver bullet molded from melted coins.

65. **The correct answer is (C).** Born in Mississippi, Eudora Welty (1909–2001) is concerned with developing concepts related to her native region and not with feminist issues. Her works include *The Robber Bridegroom, Delta Wedding,* and *Losing Battles.*

66. **The correct answer is (D).** Ernest Hemingway (1899–1961) is also known for *The Sun Also Rises, For Whom the Bell Tolls, A Farewell to Arms, The Old Man and the Sea, Across the River and Into the Trees,* and many other stories. As a film, *To Have and Have Not* brought together Humphrey Bogart and Lauren Bacall.

67. **The correct answer is (C).** Abraham Lincoln (1809–1865) included these words in his second inaugural address: "With malice toward none, with charity for all, let us strive on to

finish the work we are in; to bind up the nation's wounds. . . ."

68. **The correct answer is (E).** One of T.S. Eliot's most important poems, *The Waste Land* was edited by Ezra Pound and begins with the well–known line, "April is the cruelest month. . . ."

69. **The correct answer is (D).** F. Scott Fitzgerald (1896–1940) also created *This Side of Paradise, The Great Gatsby,* and *Tender is the Night.*

70. **The correct answer is (D).** Adam Smith (1723–1790) is best known for his economic theory based on an individualistic system of free enterprise. He also contributed to the study of ethics with *The Theory of Moral Sentiments* (1759).

71. **The correct answer is (A).** Joyce Kilmer (1886–1916) was an American poet who contributed verse to various periodicals and was killed in action during World War I.

72. **The correct answer is (A).** In "The Snows of Kilimanjaro," Ernest Hemingway tells of a dying writer's recollections and his dream of a "dried and frozen carcass of a leopard" atop Africa's Mt. Kilimanjaro.

73. **The correct answer is (C).** The story of *Oedipus Rex* is developed by Sophocles from the tale in Greek mythology of the son of Laius and Jocasta who was abandoned at birth and who unwittingly killed his father and married his mother, as the oracle at Delphi had prophesied.

74. **The correct answer is (E).** *Pale Horse, Pale Rider* was written in 1939 by Katherine Anne Porter, who is also known for *Ship of Fools* and *Flowering Judas.*

75. **The correct answer is (E).** Empiricism suggests that our concepts or knowledge are in some way based on experience through the senses and introspection. William James (1842–1910), brother of novelist Henry James, wrote *Essays in Radical Empiricism* and also *The Principles of Psychology, The Varieties of Religious Experience, Pragmatism,* and *The Nature of Truth.* John Locke (1632–1704), the first main "British Empiricist," wrote *Two Treatises of Government* and *An Essay Concerning Human Understanding.* He used the phrase *tabula rasa* (a blank slate, erased tablet) to describe his concept of the mind. George Berkeley (1685–1753) wrote *An Essay Towards a New Theory of Vision* and *A Treatise Concerning the Principles of Human Knowledge.* David Hume (1711–1776), author of *A Treatise of Human Nature*, developed a philosophy based on "impressions."

Section II

76. **The correct answer is (E).** *Hair,* created by Gerome Ragni, James Rado, and Galt MacDermot, also features "I Got Life," "Where Do I Go," and "Easy to be Hard."

77. **The correct answer is (C).** *All That Jazz* is associated with Bob Fosse, as are *Sweet Charity* and *Cabaret.*

78. **The correct answer is (D).** Seurat and his followers converted impressionism into a more severe classical style. Seurat called his technique "divisionism," because he had *divided* his colors into their physical constituents, but the method was also termed "pointillism" or "neo–impressionism."

79. **The correct answer is (B).** Edward S. Curtis (1868–1952) created three important works: *North American Indian, Indian Days of the Long Ago,* and *In the Land of the Head Hunters.*

80. **The correct answer is (A).** Michelangelo Buonarroti (1475–1564) was the great Italian sculptor, painter, and architect of the High Renaissance. Some of his sculptures include "Pieta," "David," "Bacchus," and "Moses."

81. **The correct answer is (B).** Called "the most imitated singer in rock," vocalist–songwriter Mick Jagger is famous for his onstage sensuality and has been lead singer for the Rolling Stones since 1964.

82. **The correct answer is (C).** Luciano Pavarotti (1936–   ) is one of the world's leading lyric tenors. He made his debut with the Metropolitan Opera in 1967, as Rodolfo in *La Bohème.*

83. **The correct answer is (E).** Alexander Calder (1898–1976) is most noted for his abstract compositions and constructions known as "stabiles" ("static abstract sculptures") and "mobiles" ("plastic forms in motion"), which were first executed in 1931.

84. **The correct answer is (B).** Martin Scorcese (1942–), raised in New York City's Little Italy area, was perhaps the most personal filmmaker among the wave of young directors during the late 1960s.

85. **The correct answer is (C).** *Pygmalion* is George Bernard Shaw's story of Henry Higgins and Liza Doolittle. It was the inspiration for the well–known show and film, *My Fair Lady*.

86. **The correct answer is (D).** Ben Shahn (1898–1969) was associated with Social Realism and created strongly expressive images of social criticism, such as *The Passion of Sacco and Vanzetti* and *Miner's Wives*.

87. **The correct answer is (C).** Pablo Picasso: *Man with a Violin* (1912).

88. **The correct answer is (C).** Frank Lloyd Wright (1869–1959) was the architect who also designed "Taliesin," his residence in Wisconsin; Imperial House, Tokyo; and Oak Park Temple, Chicago.

89. **The correct answer is (D).** Beuys (1921–1986)—*Coyote: I Like America and America Likes Me*; Burden (1946–)— *Doorway to Heaven*; Anderson (1947–)—*Duets on Ice, United States*; Acconci (1960–)— *Seedbed*.

90. **The correct answer is (C).** Isadora Duncan (1878–1927) was an American dancer and teacher who developed a style she considered a revival of the Greek dance of ancient times, complete with loosely flowing tunic.

91. **The correct answer is (D).** Arnold Schoenberg (1874–1951) called his system "pantonal" ("inclusive of all tonalities"), but it is more commonly known as "atonal" ("not tonal") music.

92. **The correct answer is (C).** George Frederic Handel (1685–1759) did not compose the work as church music but rather for the concert hall, although *Messiah* has a purely scriptural text. It is a series of contemplations, from the Old Testament through the life of Christ, on the Christian concept of redemption.

93. **The correct answer is (C).** Pastel: powdered pigment molded into sticks, yielding the effects of line, tone, and color simultaneously (see Degas' work, for example).

94. **The correct answer is (C).** Frederic Chopin (1810–1849) composed almost exclusively for piano, and although he lived the second half of his life in France, his native Poland's folk themes and popular music are evident in many of his compositions.

95. **The correct answer is (D).** The Romans were the first to utilize the rounded arch in monumental architecture, although the Egyptians had employed it on a small scale in underground tombs (but not in temples).

96. **The correct answer is (B).** The Renaissance originated in Italy and may be traced back to the work of the poet Petrarch in the 1330s. Then it flourished in the characters of Donatello, Ghiberti, Michelangelo, Bellini, Botticelli, Masaccio, Fra Angelico, Leonardo da Vinci, Raphael, and Cellini. It also spread throughout Europe: Titian, El Greco, Dürer. Later: Brueghel, Rubens, Rembrandt, Bernini, and Velazquez.

97. **The correct answer is (A).** *The Spy Who Came in From the Cold,* from a story by John Le Carré (1931–), is a somber view of the spy network, made as a corrective to Ian Fleming's James Bond variety of tales.

98. **The correct answer is (C).** Giuseppe Verdi (1813–1901) composed his Requiem in 1874 in memory of Alessandro Manzoni, author of a famous nineteenth–century Italian novel (*I promessi sposi*).

99. **The correct answer is (A).** Paul Cézanne's (1839–1906) still lifes (such as *The Basket of Apples*) illustrate his view that space is defined by the relationships of the objects within it.

100. **The correct answer is (B).** Henri Toulouse–Lautrec: *Jane Avril* (1899).

101. **The correct answer is (D).** Aubrey Beardsley: *How Guenever Made Her a Nun* (1893–94)

102. **The correct answer is (E).** Jean Edouard Vuillard: *Madame Arthur Fontaine* (1904–05).

The other works shown are:

(A) Paul Gauguin: *Still Life with Three Puppies* (1888).

(C) Georges Seurat: *La Grande Jatte* (1884–86).

103. **The correct answer is (A).** Giuseppe Verdi's *Aida* was first performed in Cairo in 1871. The plot provides tremendous spectacle and a powerful love story.

104. **The correct answer is (D).** Chartres in its present form was constructed from 1194–1220 and represents High Gothic style.

105. **The correct answer is (C).** While a student at Yale School of Architecture, Maya Lin (1959–) won the design competition for the Vietnam Veterans Memorial, dedicated in 1982 in Washington, D.C.

106. **The correct answer is (E).** Diane Arbus (1923–1971) chose for her subjects extremely unusual people: dwarfs, burlesque dancers, and transvestites. Her work has been described as "akin to an unexpected punch in the stomach."

107. **The correct answer is (D).** "Over the Rainbow," from the film *The Wizard of Oz,* was composed by Harold Arlen (1905–1986).

108. **The correct answer is (C).** German singer-actress Marlene Dietrich starred in both 1930 films, as well as in *Shanghai Express, Blonde Venus, The Devil is a Woman*, and many others.

109. **The correct answer is (B).** The word "Pop" was first used to describe art in 1954 by an English critic who was referring to such images of "popular culture" as advertisements, billboards, and movie posters.

110. **The correct answer is (B).** Pieter Brueghel: *Tower of Babel* (1563).

111. **The correct answer is (D).** Giotto: *Tower of Babel* (c. 1305).

The other works shown are:

(A) Albrecht Dürer: *Self–Portrait* (1500).

(C) Jacques–Louis David: *Madame Récamier* (c. 1793).

(E) El Greco: *Cleansing of the Temple* (c. 1565–1567).

112. **The correct answer is (C).** Scott Joplin (1868–1917), the pianist–songwriter who composed *Maple Leaf Rag, Wall Street Rag,* and *Sugar Cane Rag,* was the major ragtime composer of his time.

113. **The correct answer is (E).** "Dada" (a French term meaning "hobbyhorse") is an infantile-sounding word that conveyed the spirit of a movement whose purpose was to show the public that the catastrophe of World War I had made all values—moral or aesthetic—meaningless.

114. **The correct answer is (D).** The legendary Charlie Chaplin (1889–1977) also starred in *The Gold Rush, The Great Dictator,* and *City Lights.*

115. **The correct answer is (B).** Johann Sebastian Bach (1685–1750) and George Frederic Handel (1685–1759) exemplify the heights of the Baroque period in music, which is said to extend from about the end of the sixteenth century to the middle of the eighteenth.

116. **The correct answer is (A).** Although jazz developed at the same time in other parts of the United States, the New Orleans of Louis Armstrong and King Oliver is generally granted the distinction of being the birthplace of jazz.

117. **The correct answer is (C).** Expressionism stresses the artist's *emotional* attitude toward himself and the world.

118. **The correct answer is (C).** This work by Alice Neel (1900–1984) — *Mother and Child (Nancy and Olivia),* 1967— is an example of Neel's practice of "collecting souls."

119. **The correct answer is (D).** Arthur Fiedler (1894–1979) conducted the Boston Symphony

Orchestra "Pop" concerts from 1930 until his death half a century later. He had been associated with the orchestra since 1915 and also conducted for many other groups.

120. **The correct answer is (B).** Thomas Jefferson (1743–1826), third President of the United States, was also a surveyor and architect who designed Monticello, his home near Charlottesville. He designed many other private homes and planned the Virginia state capitol.

121. **The correct answer is (E).** Antoni Gaudi: Casa Milá Apartment House, Barcelona (1905–07).

122. **The correct answer is (B).** Le Courbusier: L'Unité d' Habitation, Marseilles (1946–1952).

123. **The correct answer is (A).** William Butterfield: All Saints, London (1859).

Other buildings shown are:

(C) Stonehenge: Wiltshire (late Neolithic, between 1900–1700 B.C.E. to Bronze Age c. 1500 B.C.E.).

(D) Eliel Saarinen: Railway Station, Helsinki (1904–14).

124. **The correct answer is (D).** Tanglewood, located in the Berkshires in the town of Lenox, Mass., is the scene of numerous music events every year.

125. **The correct answer is (C).** Claude Monet (1840–1926), Auguste Renoir (1841–1919), and Edgar Degas (1834–1917) are all associated with *impressionism*. The name comes from Monet's painting *Impression: Sunrise* and was coined by a disapproving critic.

126. **The correct answer is (D).** Coppélia (music by Leo Delibes, choreography by Arthur Saint-Leon, book by Charles Nuitter). First presented in 1870, ballet's great comedy combines a story of romance with a story of the doll–maker Coppelius, whose foremost desire is to create a doll with a soul.

127. **The correct answer is (B).** *The Nutcracker* (music by Tchaikovsky, choreography and book by Lev Ivanov). First presented in 1892,

it tells of a girl who is given a large nutcracker, a soldier, by her godfather for Christmas. She falls asleep and dreams that she defends it against the King of the Mice. The nutcracker then changes into a handsome prince who takes her on a magic journey during which she meets the Sugarplum Fairy.

128. **The correct answer is (C).** Hieroglyphics are the form of Egyptian writing in which the characters are for the most part recognizable pictures of objects.

129. **The correct answer is (B).** Pablo Casals (1876–1973): the great Spanish cellist recognized for his supremacy in his art (also a fine pianist and conductor).

130. **The correct answer is (A).** The three other basic bridge types are "arch," "suspension," and "cantilever."

131. **The correct answer is (B).** After 1940, the New York City Ballet became one of the world's foremost troupes, with Lincoln Kirstein as general manager, George Balanchine as artistic director, and Jerome Robbins as artistic codirector.

132. **The correct answer is (D).** Michelangelo spent the years from 1508–1512 decorating the Chapel ceiling. The *Creation of Adam* is one of the most famous of the scenes from Genesis he created; the ceiling is covered with hundreds of figures in a variety of gradations of color.

133. **The correct answer is (B).** "Round" in music means a short, rhythmical work sung in unison, with the several voices entering at equally spaced intervals in time.

134. **The correct answer is (A).** Paul Cézanne: *Bathers* (1890–1891).

135. **The correct answer is (C).** Pablo Picasso: *Guernica* (1937).

The other work shown is choice (B) Max Ernst: *Oedipus Rex* (1922).

136. **The correct answer is (D).** The Belgian painter Rene Magritte (1898–1967) is associated with surrealism.

137. **The correct answer is (B).** Kiss is a "hard rock" group that has been called both "flamboyantly theatrical" and "an outrage." The group has sold millions of records.

138. **The correct answer is (D).** *The Cabinet of Doctor Caligari* (1919) is a classic horror film, interesting for its expressionistic sets, clever story, and definite influence on later German filmmaking.

139. **The correct answer is (C).** *Eroica* ("heroic") is another name for Beethoven's (1770–1827) Third Symphony. It was probably originally entitled Bonaparte but changed as a result of the composer's anger when Napoleon was proclaimed Emperor instead of creating a democratic system of government.

140. **The correct answer is (D).** Winslow Homer (1836–1910), trained as an illustrator, progressed from Civil War sketches to small genre scenes of nature to simple but powerful paintings of life at sea.

141. **The correct answer is (D).** *Gone with the Wind,* a novel by Margaret Mitchell, was made into a film in 1939, with Clark Gable as Rhett Butler and Vivian Leigh as Scarlett O'Hara.

142. **The correct answer is (B).** A block print (linocut) is produced by cutting away with knife or gouge the surface of a linoleum block to produce negative spaces of a design—the areas not intended to print. Printing ink is applied to the remaining surface, paper is put on, and pressure is applied, resulting in a print.

143. **The correct answer is (E).** Jean–Luc Godard (1930–) is a New Wave French director–writer whose work also includes *Pierrot Le Fou* and *Tout va Bien.*

144. **The correct answer is (D).** Marcel Duchamp: *Fountain* (1917).

145. **The correct answer is (B).** Constantin Brancusi: *Bird in Space* (1925).

146. **The correct answer is (D).** Alberto Giacometti: *City Square* (1948).

147. **The correct answer is (B).** Tony Smith: *Spitball* (1961).

148. **The correct answer is (A).** The calypso musical style is of West Indian origin, influenced by jazz, usually with topical, often improvised, lyrics.

149. **The correct answer is (D).** "Mrs. Robinson" (1968) is by Paul Simon and Art Garfunkel and was featured in the film *The Graduate.*

150. **The correct answer is (B).** Paul Gauguin (1848–1903) was a Paris stockbroker and amateur painter when he decided to devote himself entirely to art. He voyaged to Tahiti in search of an unspoiled existence and spent the rest of his life there, returning only once to France.

Answer Sheet for Practice Examination III

Section I

1 Ⓐ Ⓑ Ⓒ Ⓓ Ⓔ	16 Ⓐ Ⓑ Ⓒ Ⓓ Ⓔ	31 Ⓐ Ⓑ Ⓒ Ⓓ Ⓔ	46 Ⓐ Ⓑ Ⓒ Ⓓ Ⓔ	61 Ⓐ Ⓑ Ⓒ Ⓓ Ⓔ
2 Ⓐ Ⓑ Ⓒ Ⓓ Ⓔ	17 Ⓐ Ⓑ Ⓒ Ⓓ Ⓔ	32 Ⓐ Ⓑ Ⓒ Ⓓ Ⓔ	47 Ⓐ Ⓑ Ⓒ Ⓓ Ⓔ	62 Ⓐ Ⓑ Ⓒ Ⓓ Ⓔ
3 Ⓐ Ⓑ Ⓒ Ⓓ Ⓔ	18 Ⓐ Ⓑ Ⓒ Ⓓ Ⓔ	33 Ⓐ Ⓑ Ⓒ Ⓓ Ⓔ	48 Ⓐ Ⓑ Ⓒ Ⓓ Ⓔ	63 Ⓐ Ⓑ Ⓒ Ⓓ Ⓔ
4 Ⓐ Ⓑ Ⓒ Ⓓ Ⓔ	19 Ⓐ Ⓑ Ⓒ Ⓓ Ⓔ	34 Ⓐ Ⓑ Ⓒ Ⓓ Ⓔ	49 Ⓐ Ⓑ Ⓒ Ⓓ Ⓔ	64 Ⓐ Ⓑ Ⓒ Ⓓ Ⓔ
5 Ⓐ Ⓑ Ⓒ Ⓓ Ⓔ	20 Ⓐ Ⓑ Ⓒ Ⓓ Ⓔ	35 Ⓐ Ⓑ Ⓒ Ⓓ Ⓔ	50 Ⓐ Ⓑ Ⓒ Ⓓ Ⓔ	65 Ⓐ Ⓑ Ⓒ Ⓓ Ⓔ
6 Ⓐ Ⓑ Ⓒ Ⓓ Ⓔ	21 Ⓐ Ⓑ Ⓒ Ⓓ Ⓔ	36 Ⓐ Ⓑ Ⓒ Ⓓ Ⓔ	51 Ⓐ Ⓑ Ⓒ Ⓓ Ⓔ	66 Ⓐ Ⓑ Ⓒ Ⓓ Ⓔ
7 Ⓐ Ⓑ Ⓒ Ⓓ Ⓔ	22 Ⓐ Ⓑ Ⓒ Ⓓ Ⓔ	37 Ⓐ Ⓑ Ⓒ Ⓓ Ⓔ	52 Ⓐ Ⓑ Ⓒ Ⓓ Ⓔ	67 Ⓐ Ⓑ Ⓒ Ⓓ Ⓔ
8 Ⓐ Ⓑ Ⓒ Ⓓ Ⓔ	23 Ⓐ Ⓑ Ⓒ Ⓓ Ⓔ	38 Ⓐ Ⓑ Ⓒ Ⓓ Ⓔ	53 Ⓐ Ⓑ Ⓒ Ⓓ Ⓔ	68 Ⓐ Ⓑ Ⓒ Ⓓ Ⓔ
9 Ⓐ Ⓑ Ⓒ Ⓓ Ⓔ	24 Ⓐ Ⓑ Ⓒ Ⓓ Ⓔ	39 Ⓐ Ⓑ Ⓒ Ⓓ Ⓔ	54 Ⓐ Ⓑ Ⓒ Ⓓ Ⓔ	69 Ⓐ Ⓑ Ⓒ Ⓓ Ⓔ
10 Ⓐ Ⓑ Ⓒ Ⓓ Ⓔ	25 Ⓐ Ⓑ Ⓒ Ⓓ Ⓔ	40 Ⓐ Ⓑ Ⓒ Ⓓ Ⓔ	55 Ⓐ Ⓑ Ⓒ Ⓓ Ⓔ	70 Ⓐ Ⓑ Ⓒ Ⓓ Ⓔ
11 Ⓐ Ⓑ Ⓒ Ⓓ Ⓔ	26 Ⓐ Ⓑ Ⓒ Ⓓ Ⓔ	41 Ⓐ Ⓑ Ⓒ Ⓓ Ⓔ	56 Ⓐ Ⓑ Ⓒ Ⓓ Ⓔ	71 Ⓐ Ⓑ Ⓒ Ⓓ Ⓔ
12 Ⓐ Ⓑ Ⓒ Ⓓ Ⓔ	27 Ⓐ Ⓑ Ⓒ Ⓓ Ⓔ	42 Ⓐ Ⓑ Ⓒ Ⓓ Ⓔ	57 Ⓐ Ⓑ Ⓒ Ⓓ Ⓔ	72 Ⓐ Ⓑ Ⓒ Ⓓ Ⓔ
13 Ⓐ Ⓑ Ⓒ Ⓓ Ⓔ	28 Ⓐ Ⓑ Ⓒ Ⓓ Ⓔ	43 Ⓐ Ⓑ Ⓒ Ⓓ Ⓔ	58 Ⓐ Ⓑ Ⓒ Ⓓ Ⓔ	73 Ⓐ Ⓑ Ⓒ Ⓓ Ⓔ
14 Ⓐ Ⓑ Ⓒ Ⓓ Ⓔ	29 Ⓐ Ⓑ Ⓒ Ⓓ Ⓔ	44 Ⓐ Ⓑ Ⓒ Ⓓ Ⓔ	59 Ⓐ Ⓑ Ⓒ Ⓓ Ⓔ	74 Ⓐ Ⓑ Ⓒ Ⓓ Ⓔ
15 Ⓐ Ⓑ Ⓒ Ⓓ Ⓔ	30 Ⓐ Ⓑ Ⓒ Ⓓ Ⓔ	45 Ⓐ Ⓑ Ⓒ Ⓓ Ⓔ	60 Ⓐ Ⓑ Ⓒ Ⓓ Ⓔ	75 Ⓐ Ⓑ Ⓒ Ⓓ Ⓔ

Section II

76 Ⓐ Ⓑ Ⓒ Ⓓ Ⓔ	91 Ⓐ Ⓑ Ⓒ Ⓓ Ⓔ	106 Ⓐ Ⓑ Ⓒ Ⓓ Ⓔ	121 Ⓐ Ⓑ Ⓒ Ⓓ Ⓔ	136 Ⓐ Ⓑ Ⓒ Ⓓ Ⓔ
77 Ⓐ Ⓑ Ⓒ Ⓓ Ⓔ	92 Ⓐ Ⓑ Ⓒ Ⓓ Ⓔ	107 Ⓐ Ⓑ Ⓒ Ⓓ Ⓔ	122 Ⓐ Ⓑ Ⓒ Ⓓ Ⓔ	137 Ⓐ Ⓑ Ⓒ Ⓓ Ⓔ
78 Ⓐ Ⓑ Ⓒ Ⓓ Ⓔ	93 Ⓐ Ⓑ Ⓒ Ⓓ Ⓔ	108 Ⓐ Ⓑ Ⓒ Ⓓ Ⓔ	123 Ⓐ Ⓑ Ⓒ Ⓓ Ⓔ	138 Ⓐ Ⓑ Ⓒ Ⓓ Ⓔ
79 Ⓐ Ⓑ Ⓒ Ⓓ Ⓔ	94 Ⓐ Ⓑ Ⓒ Ⓓ Ⓔ	109 Ⓐ Ⓑ Ⓒ Ⓓ Ⓔ	124 Ⓐ Ⓑ Ⓒ Ⓓ Ⓔ	139 Ⓐ Ⓑ Ⓒ Ⓓ Ⓔ
80 Ⓐ Ⓑ Ⓒ Ⓓ Ⓔ	95 Ⓐ Ⓑ Ⓒ Ⓓ Ⓔ	110 Ⓐ Ⓑ Ⓒ Ⓓ Ⓔ	125 Ⓐ Ⓑ Ⓒ Ⓓ Ⓔ	140 Ⓐ Ⓑ Ⓒ Ⓓ Ⓔ
81 Ⓐ Ⓑ Ⓒ Ⓓ Ⓔ	96 Ⓐ Ⓑ Ⓒ Ⓓ Ⓔ	111 Ⓐ Ⓑ Ⓒ Ⓓ Ⓔ	126 Ⓐ Ⓑ Ⓒ Ⓓ Ⓔ	141 Ⓐ Ⓑ Ⓒ Ⓓ Ⓔ
82 Ⓐ Ⓑ Ⓒ Ⓓ Ⓔ	97 Ⓐ Ⓑ Ⓒ Ⓓ Ⓔ	112 Ⓐ Ⓑ Ⓒ Ⓓ Ⓔ	127 Ⓐ Ⓑ Ⓒ Ⓓ Ⓔ	142 Ⓐ Ⓑ Ⓒ Ⓓ Ⓔ
83 Ⓐ Ⓑ Ⓒ Ⓓ Ⓔ	98 Ⓐ Ⓑ Ⓒ Ⓓ Ⓔ	113 Ⓐ Ⓑ Ⓒ Ⓓ Ⓔ	128 Ⓐ Ⓑ Ⓒ Ⓓ Ⓔ	143 Ⓐ Ⓑ Ⓒ Ⓓ Ⓔ
84 Ⓐ Ⓑ Ⓒ Ⓓ Ⓔ	99 Ⓐ Ⓑ Ⓒ Ⓓ Ⓔ	114 Ⓐ Ⓑ Ⓒ Ⓓ Ⓔ	129 Ⓐ Ⓑ Ⓒ Ⓓ Ⓔ	144 Ⓐ Ⓑ Ⓒ Ⓓ Ⓔ
85 Ⓐ Ⓑ Ⓒ Ⓓ Ⓔ	100 Ⓐ Ⓑ Ⓒ Ⓓ Ⓔ	115 Ⓐ Ⓑ Ⓒ Ⓓ Ⓔ	130 Ⓐ Ⓑ Ⓒ Ⓓ Ⓔ	145 Ⓐ Ⓑ Ⓒ Ⓓ Ⓔ
86 Ⓐ Ⓑ Ⓒ Ⓓ Ⓔ	101 Ⓐ Ⓑ Ⓒ Ⓓ Ⓔ	116 Ⓐ Ⓑ Ⓒ Ⓓ Ⓔ	131 Ⓐ Ⓑ Ⓒ Ⓓ Ⓔ	146 Ⓐ Ⓑ Ⓒ Ⓓ Ⓔ
87 Ⓐ Ⓑ Ⓒ Ⓓ Ⓔ	102 Ⓐ Ⓑ Ⓒ Ⓓ Ⓔ	117 Ⓐ Ⓑ Ⓒ Ⓓ Ⓔ	132 Ⓐ Ⓑ Ⓒ Ⓓ Ⓔ	147 Ⓐ Ⓑ Ⓒ Ⓓ Ⓔ
88 Ⓐ Ⓑ Ⓒ Ⓓ Ⓔ	103 Ⓐ Ⓑ Ⓒ Ⓓ Ⓔ	118 Ⓐ Ⓑ Ⓒ Ⓓ Ⓔ	133 Ⓐ Ⓑ Ⓒ Ⓓ Ⓔ	148 Ⓐ Ⓑ Ⓒ Ⓓ Ⓔ
89 Ⓐ Ⓑ Ⓒ Ⓓ Ⓔ	104 Ⓐ Ⓑ Ⓒ Ⓓ Ⓔ	119 Ⓐ Ⓑ Ⓒ Ⓓ Ⓔ	134 Ⓐ Ⓑ Ⓒ Ⓓ Ⓔ	149 Ⓐ Ⓑ Ⓒ Ⓓ Ⓔ
90 Ⓐ Ⓑ Ⓒ Ⓓ Ⓔ	105 Ⓐ Ⓑ Ⓒ Ⓓ Ⓔ	120 Ⓐ Ⓑ Ⓒ Ⓓ Ⓔ	135 Ⓐ Ⓑ Ⓒ Ⓓ Ⓔ	150 Ⓐ Ⓑ Ⓒ Ⓓ Ⓔ

PRACTICE EXAMINATION III

Section I: Literature

75 Questions

Time—45 minutes

Directions: Each of the questions or incomplete statements below is followed by five suggested answers or completions. Select the one that is best in each case and blacken your answer sheet (A), (B), (C), (D), or (E) accordingly.

1. Though she wrote poetry throughout her life, only seven poems of the almost 2,000 she wrote were published in her lifetime. The poems are uniformly short, consisting usually of four–line stanzas with very weak rhymes. Her diction is taken from the homespun traditions of New England and its Calvinist background.

   The passage above discusses

   (A) Elizabeth Barrett Browning.
   (B) Sylvia Plath.
   (C) H.D. (Hilda Doolittle).
   (D) Emily Dickinson.
   (E) Marianne Moore.

2. Which of the following novels was NOT written by Fyodor Dostoyevski?

   (A) *Crime and Punishment*
   (B) *The Possessed*
   (C) *Fathers and Sons*
   (D) *The Gambler*
   (E) *The Brothers Karamazov*

3. "anyone lived in a pretty how town

   (with up so floating many bells down)

   spring summer autumn winter

   he sang his didn't he danced his did."

   The author of these lines is

   (A) Alexander Pope.
   (B) John Dryden.
   (C) Amy Lowell.
   (D) e.e. cummings.
   (E) Robert Frost.

4. "Ask not what your country can do for you; ask what you can do for your country," is from an inaugural address by

   (A) Abraham Lincoln.
   (B) Harry S. Truman.
   (C) John F. Kennedy.
   (D) George Washington.
   (E) Gerald Ford.

5. Which of the following is a devastating exposé of the inhuman treatment of children in nine-teenth–century England?

   (A) Dickens' *David Copperfield*
   (B) Galsworthy's *The Man of Property*
   (C) Thackeray's *Vanity Fair*
   (D) Fielding's *Tom Jones*
   (E) Austen's *Sense and Sensibility*

6. Which Shakespearean hero is correctly matched with the heroine of the play in which he appears?

   (A) Malvolio—Juliet
   (B) Lear—Desdemona
   (C) Romeo—Olivia
   (D) Othello—Hermia
   (E) Prospero—Miranda

7. The philosophy that pleasure and happiness are the natural end of life was a tenet of the

   (A) Epicurean school.
   (B) Epistemological system.
   (C) Peripatetic and Stoic teachings.
   (D) Rationalists and Cynics.
   (E) Lyceum's aesthetics.

8. "Gather ye rosebuds while ye may,

   Old time is still a–flying;

   And this same flower that smiles today

   Tomorrow will be dying."

   The theme of these lines is related to

   (A) preparing for the future.
   (B) enjoying nature.
   (C) not fearing death.
   (D) enjoying the present.
   (E) benefitting from past mistakes.

9. All of the following novels were written by Bernard Malamud EXCEPT

   (A) *The Fixer.*
   (B) *The Natural.*
   (C) *The Naked and the Dead.*
   (D) *The Assistant.*
   (E) *Dubin's Lives.*

10. Which of the following plays is NOT paired with its correct author?

    (A) *All My Sons* . . . Arthur Miller
    (B) *Murder in the Cathedral* . . . T.S. Eliot
    (C) *Strange Interlude* . . . Eugene O'Neill
    (D) *Lady Windermere's Fan* . . . George Bernard Shaw
    (E) *The Cherry Orchard* . . . Anton Chekhov

11. "Underneath the living flowers.

    Deeper than the sound of showers:

    There we shall not count the hours

    By the shadows as they pass."

    In the context of the lines quoted above, "There" (line 3) means

    (A) old age.
    (B) the night.
    (C) the grave.
    (D) the winter.
    (E) infancy.

12. The novel tells of the hardships of the Joad family. "Okie" farmers forced out of their home in the Oklahoma dust–bowl region by economic desperation, they drive to California in search of work as migrant fruit–pickers.

    The passage above describes

    (A) Steinbeck's *The Grapes of Wrath.*
    (B) Hemingway's *To Have and Have Not.*
    (C) Faulkner's *The Sound and the Fury.*
    (D) Dreiser's *An American Tragedy.*
    (E) Styron's *Lie Down in Darkness.*

13. "The yellow fog that rubs its back upon the windowpanes

    The yellow smoke that rubs its muzzle on the windowpanes

    Licked its tongue into the corners of the evening"

    The main figure of speech employed in these lines is

    (A) personification.
    (B) iambic pentameter.
    (C) simile.
    (D) allusion.
    (E) alliteration.

14. The hero of the novel, a bank assessor named Joseph K., is accused, by a mysterious legal authority whose headquarters are in a run-down tenement, of an unnamed crime of which he knows nothing.

    The sentence above describes

    (A) Conrad's *The Secret Agent.*
    (B) Kafka's *The Trial.*
    (C) Greene's *A Burnt–Out Case.*
    (D) Mailer's *Barbary Shore.*
    (E) Mann's *Confessions of Felix Krull: Confidence Man.*

15. Its principal characters suffer from radical loneliness and a lack of self–knowledge. Through the mediation of an uninvited guest who is ostensibly a psychoanalyst but partly a sort of mysterious father–confessor, three of them attain "salvation."

The passage above describes

(A) Williams' *The Glass Menagerie.*
(B) Eliot's *The Cocktail Party.*
(C) Lawrence and Lee's *Inherit the Wind.*
(D) Ionesco's *The Chairs.*
(E) Albee's *The American Dream.*

16. All of the following wrote studies of history EXCEPT

(A) Toynbee.
(B) Herodotus.
(C) Thucydides.
(D) Mencken.
(E) Gibbon.

Questions 17 and 18 refer to the following stanzas.

"Do not go gentle into that good night,

Old age should burn and rave at close of day;

Rage, rage against the dying of the light.

Though wise men at their end know dark is right,

Because their words had forked no lightning they

Do not go gentle into that good night."

17. The lines above were written by

(A) Dylan Thomas.
(B) T.S. Eliot.
(C) William Carlos Williams.
(D) Robert Frost.
(E) Walt Whitman.

18. The lines above begin a

(A) lyric.
(B) sonnet.
(C) villanelle.
(D) tanka.
(E) haiku.

19. Which of the following novels is NOT paired with its correct author?

(A) *The Old Man and the Sea* . . . Joseph Conrad
(B) *The Collector* . . . John Fowles
(C) *1919* . . . John Dos Passos
(D) *Group Portrait with Lady* . . . Heinrich Boll
(E) *I Know Why the Caged Bird Sings* . . . Maya Angelou

20. "Let us go then, you and I,

when the evening is spread out against the sky

Like a patient etherized upon a table"

These lines are by the author who also wrote

(A) *The Waste Land.*
(B) *Paradise Lost.*
(C) *The Cantos.*
(D) *The Rubaiyat.*
(E) *Tristan and Isolde.*

21. The central figure of the tale is the convict Jean Valjean. One of society's victims, Valjean, originally an honest peasant, stole a single loaf of bread to feed his sister's starving family and was sentenced to five years in prison of hard labor.

The passage above describes

(A) Hugo's *Les Misérables.*
(B) Gide's *Strait Is the Gate.*
(C) Malraux's *Man's Fate.*
(D) Celine's *Death on the Installment Plan.*
(E) Robbe–Grillet's *In the Labyrinth.*

22. All of the following were essayists EXCEPT

(A) Charles Darwin.
(B) Plato.
(C) Francis Bacon.
(D) Mary Shelley.
(E) John Locke.

23. The Scopes "monkey" trial provided the basis for which of the following plays?

(A) Williams' *The Glass Menagerie*
(B) Miller's *The Crucible*
(C) Shaw's *Man and Superman*
(D) Lawrence and Lee's *Inherit the Wind*
(E) O'Neill's *The Iceman Cometh*

Questions 24 and 25 refer to the following lines.

"The apparition of these faces in the crowd: Petals on a wet, black bough."

24. The lines above are a(n)

   (A) metaphysical poem by John Donne.
   (B) symbolist poem by Paul Verlaine.
   (C) surrealist poem by Paul Eluard.
   (D) imagist poem by Ezra Pound.
   (E) limerick by Ogden Nash.

25. Which of the following describes the lines above?

   (A) Blank verse
   (B) A tercet
   (C) A triolet
   (D) A quatrain
   (E) Onomatopoeia

26. The play developed from Ken Kesey's novel about inmates of a mental institution is

   (A) *King of Hearts.*
   (B) *Coconuts.*
   (C) *Sticks and Bones.*
   (D) *One Flew Over the Cuckoo's Nest.*
   (E) *The Turn of the Screw.*

27. Which of the following characters is incorrectly paired with the novel in which he/she appears?

   (A) Darley . . . *Justice*
   (B) Sancho Panza . . . *Don Quixote*
   (C) Holden Caulfield . . . *Lolita*
   (D) Marianne Dashwood . . . *Sense and Sensibility*
   (E) Gino Carelli . . . *Where Angels Fear to Tread*

Questions 28 and 29 refer to the following.

   (A) *Parallel Lives*—Plutarch
   (B) *Seize the Day*—Bellow
   (C) *Ethics*—Spinoza
   (D) *My Life and Hard Times*—Thurber
   (E) *Simple Speaks His Mind*—Hughes

28. Which of the above is set in a Harlem bar?

29. Which of the above is a series of biographical sketches?

30. Set among the derelicts of a sleazy flophouse, its theme is the problem of whether to live on one's own strength without illusions or to shield oneself from the pain of life by accepting a romanticized view of things.

The passage above discusses

   (A) O'Neill's *Beyond the Horizon.*
   (B) Ionesco's *The Chairs.*
   (C) Osborne's *Look Back in Anger.*
   (D) Gorki's *The Lower Depths.*
   (E) Miller's *The Price.*

31. "Minstrel and Genius, to whose songs or sighs

   The round earth modulates her changeful sphere,

   That bend'st in shadow from yon western skies,

   And lean'st, cloud–hid, along the woodlands sere,

   Too deep thy notes—too pure—for mortal ear!"

   In the context of the lines quoted above, "mortal ear" (line 5) means

   (A) human perception.
   (B) the earth.
   (C) the average person.
   (D) human hearing.
   (E) the dead.

32. John Osborne and Kingsley Amis were the leading

   (A) Cambridge critics.
   (B) muckrakers.
   (C) Angry Young Men.
   (D) metaphysical poets.
   (E) members of the Saturday Club.

33. In Greek drama, the group that sings and dances and serves as a character or to comment on the action is the

   (A) ode.
   (B) chorus.
   (C) skene.
   (D) dirge.
   (E) messenger.

34. Which of the following was the name given to a group of English writers, artists, and philosophers who began to meet around 1906?

    (A) Muckrakers
    (B) The New Critics
    (C) The New Wave
    (D) Bloomsbury Group
    (E) Formalists

Questions 35 and 36 refer to the following lines.

"I was born in the congo

I walked to the fertile crescent and built the sphinx

I designed a pyramid so tough that a star
   that only glows every one hundred years falls
   into the center giving divine perfect light

I am bad"

35. The lines above begin a(n)

    (A) sonnet by William Wordsworth.
    (B) villanelle by Dylan Thomas.
    (C) poem by Nikki Giovanni.
    (D) elegy by Elizabeth Bishop.
    (E) poem by Thomas Hardy.

36. Which of the following elements is NOT utilized in the lines above?

    (A) Fixed rhyme scheme
    (B) Tone
    (C) Imagery
    (D) Theme
    (E) Setting

37. The *Communist Manifesto* was written by

    (A) Spinoza.
    (B) Hegel.
    (C) Khruschev.
    (D) Marx and Engels.
    (E) Silone.

38. Which of the following groups is most associated with or most influenced by the proposer of a dialectic of thesis, antithesis, and synthesis?

    (A) Galena, Heisenberg, Wells, Morris
    (B) Jaspers, Kant, Heracleitus, Russell
    (C) Croce, Marx, Bradley, Hegel
    (D) Heidegger, Hobbes, Hume, Erasmus
    (E) Russell, Rand, Camus, Maslow

39. Which of the following Shakespearean plays is a fantasy of folklore and fairies?

    (A) *Twelfth Night*
    (B) *The Taming of the Shrew*
    (C) *Love's Labor's Lost*
    (D) *Much Ado about Nothing*
    (E) *A Midsummer Night's Dream*

40. *Paradise Lost* is a(n)

    (A) epic poem by John Milton.
    (B) Old English (Anglo–Saxon) epic in alliterative verse.
    (C) epic poem attributed to Homer.
    (D) unfinished epic satire by Lord Byron.
    (E) Middle English poem in alliterative verse.

41. A story of whaling as well as a profound symbolic study of good and evil, the novel describes the monomaniacal Captain Ahab's pursuit of the great white whale.

    The sentence above describes

    (A) Melville's *Moby Dick.*
    (B) Faulkner's *Absalom, Absalom!*
    (C) Conrad's *Lord Jim.*
    (D) Porter's *Ship of Fools.*
    (E) London's *The Sea Wolf.*

42. The winner of a Pulitzer Prize for *Armies of the Night,* a book of essays on the theme of protests against U.S. involvement in Vietnam, is

    (A) Norman Mailer.
    (B) Arthur Miller.
    (C) Truman Capote.
    (D) Joan Didion.
    (E) Joyce Carol Oates.

43. Which character and play are incorrectly paired?

    (A) Iago . . . *Othello*
    (B) Tinkerbell . . . *Peter Pan*
    (C) Henry Higgins . . . *A View from the Bridge*
    (D) Tiresias . . . *Oedipus Rex*
    (E) Mack the Knife . . . *Threepenny Opera*

44. *The Flowers of Evil,* a volume of poetry, was written by

    (A) Paul Verlaine.
    (B) Guillaume Apollinaire.
    (C) Tristan Tzara.
    (D) Arthur Rimbaud.
    (E) Charles Baudelaire.

45. Who created the character of Candide?

    (A) Leonard Bernstein
    (B) Voltaire
    (C) Albert Camus
    (D) Neil Simon
    (E) Jean–Jacques Rousseau

46. Which of the following refers to a group of twentieth–century American writers in the South?

    (A) Transcendentalists
    (B) Agrarians
    (C) The New Wave
    (D) Muckrakers
    (E) Formalists

47. "The greatest good for the greatest number" is a phrase associated with the philosophy of

    (A) Albert Schweitzer.
    (B) William James.
    (C) John Dewey.
    (D) Jeremy Bentham.
    (E) Albert Camus.

48. Which of the following poems was written by Robert Frost?

    (A) "Ode to a Nightingale"
    (B) "Ash Wednesday"
    (C) "Starting from Paumanok"
    (D) "The People, Yes"
    (E) "Birches"

49. Many of Oscar Wilde's plays are classified as

    (A) Regional Romances.
    (B) Pseudo–historical Chronicles.
    (C) Comedy of Manners.
    (D) Revenge Tragedy.
    (E) Commedia dell'arte.

50. Which of the following novels is NOT paired with its correct author?

    (A) *Women in Love* . . . T.E. Lawrence
    (B) *Oliver Twist* . . . Charles Dickens
    (C) *Frankenstein* . . . Mary Shelley
    (D) *Death in Venice* . . . Thomas Mann
    (E) *The 42nd Parallel* . . . John Dos Passos

51. "To see a World in a Grain of Sand

    And a Heaven in a Wild Flower

    Hold Infinity in the palm of your hand

    And Eternity in an hour"

    The rhyme scheme employed in these lines is

    (A) ABBA
    (B) AABB
    (C) ABCB
    (D) ABCD
    (E) ABAB

52. All of the following writers are correctly paired with the language in which they wrote EXCEPT

    (A) Voltaire . . . French.
    (B) Plato . . . Greek.
    (C) De Quincey . . . French.
    (D) Darwin . . . English.
    (E) Caesar . . . Latin.

53. The mysterious hero lives in a luxurious mansion on the wealthy Long Island shore, entertaining hundreds of guests at lavish parties that have become a legend on the island.

    The sentence above describes the hero of

    (A) Ellison's *Invisible Man.*
    (B) Hughes' *A Fox in the Attic.*
    (C) Fitzgerald's *The Great Gatsby.*
    (D) Mailer's *Barbary Shore.*
    (E) Faulkner's *Sanctuary.*

54. King Creon decrees that the body of Polynices shall lie unburied, in defiance of the rites due the dead.

    The sentence above describes

    (A) Sophocles' *Antigone.*
    (B) Camus' *Caligula.*
    (C) Aeschylus' *Seven Against Thebes.*
    (D) Marlowe's *Tamburlaine.*
    (E) Aristophanes' *Lysistrata.*

55. The real name of the author of *Alice's Adventures in Wonderland* and *Through the Looking Glass* is
    (A) John Tenniel.
    (B) Lewis Carroll.
    (C) Paul Hamlyn.
    (D) C.L. Dodgson.
    (E) Alice Pleasance Liddell.

56. Which of the following was identified with the Southern Fugitives and Agrarians?
    (A) Robert Penn Warren
    (B) Plato
    (C) Rousseau
    (D) Henry David Thoreau
    (E) E.M. Forster

57. Which of the following plays was NOT written by Eugene O'Neill?
    (A) *Anna Christie*
    (B) *A View from the Bridge*
    (C) *Desire Under the Elms*
    (D) *Beyond the Horizon*
    (E) *The Iceman Cometh*

58. In his novel *Nausea*, Jean–Paul Sartre espouses which of the following literary philosophies?
    (A) Nihilism
    (B) Super–Realism
    (C) Existentialism
    (D) Hedonism
    (E) Neo–Romanticism

Questions 59–61 refer to the following lines.

"Whan that April with his showres soote

The droughte of March hath perced to the roote,

And bathed every veine in swich licour,

Of which vertu engendred is the flowr. . . ."

59. These lines are the opening of
    (A) *The Decameron.*
    (B) *The Faerie Queene.*
    (C) *The Canterbury Tales.*
    (D) *The Rape of the Lock.*
    (E) *The Divine Comedy.*

60. The author of the lines is
    (A) Shakespeare.
    (B) Henryson.
    (C) Boccaccio.
    (D) Spenser.
    (E) Chaucer.

61. The lines are written in
    (A) Middle English.
    (B) Modern English.
    (C) Anglo–Saxon.
    (D) Germanic.
    (E) Indo–European.

62. Which novel was NOT written by Ernest Hemingway?
    (A) *A Farewell to Arms*
    (B) *Bread and Wine*
    (C) *The Sun Also Rises*
    (D) *For Whom the Bell Tolls*
    (E) *To Have and Have Not*

63. The prizewinning play about a boy who blinds several horses in an act of great passion is
    (A) *Destry Rides Again.*
    (B) *The Black Stallion.*
    (C) *Equus.*
    (D) *Horse Feathers.*
    (E) *A Day at the Races.*

64. The theme of exile is one that preoccupied
    (A) Ernest Hemingway.
    (B) D.H. Lawrence.
    (C) Feodor Dostoyevski.
    (D) James Joyce.
    (E) Upton Sinclair.

65. A stage manager is an important character in
    (A) *Our Town.*
    (B) *Carousel.*
    (C) *The Glass Menagerie.*
    (D) *The Boys in the Band.*
    (E) *Hogan's Goat.*

66. "Reverence for life" is a phrase associated with the philosophy of
    (A) Bertrand Russell.
    (B) Albert Schweitzer.
    (C) John Dewey.
    (D) Immanuel Kant.
    (E) Arthur Schopenhauer.

67. *Hiawatha,* a long narrative poem, was written by
    (A) Pablo Neruda.
    (B) Kenneth Patchen.
    (C) Allen Ginsberg.
    (D) Henry Wadsworth Longfellow.
    (E) Robert Penn Warren.

68. Which novel was NOT written by Alexander Solzhenitsyn?
    (A) *The Cancer Ward*
    (B) *The First Circle*
    (C) *Gulag Archipelago*
    (D) *Dr. Zhivago*
    (E) *One Day in the Life of Ivan Denisovich*

69. Which of the following is a series of semi-weekly essays written by Samuel Johnson, dealing with mores and literature?
    (A) *The Spectator*
    (B) *The Liberator*
    (C) *The Criterion*
    (D) *The Rambler*
    (E) *The New York Herald*

70. Which of the following short stories was written by Mark Twain?
    (A) "Babylon Revisited"
    (B) "The Woman Who Rode Away"
    (C) "The Grey Champion"
    (D) "The Devil and Daniel Webster"
    (E) "The Celebrated Jumping Frog of Calaveras County"

71. Within recent years, all the following were made into musical shows EXCEPT
    (A) *Pygmalion.*
    (B) *Tales of the South Pacific.*
    (C) *Men of Iron.*
    (D) *Candide.*
    (E) *The Wizard of Oz.*

Questions 72 and 73 refer to the following lines.

"O my luve's like a red, red rose,

That's newly sprung in June;

O my luve's like the melodie

That's sweetly played in tune."

72. The primary figure of speech employed in these lines is
    (A) simile.
    (B) refrain.
    (C) personification.
    (D) pentameter.
    (E) allusion.

73. The author of the lines often employed
    (A) Latin and Greek terms.
    (B) Scotch dialect.
    (C) French phrases.
    (D) Anglo–Saxon words.
    (E) Italianate phrases.

74. All of the following were Roman writers EXCEPT
    (A) Tacitus.
    (B) Caesar.
    (C) Herodotus.
    (D) Plutarch.
    (E) Horace.

75. The terms "stream of consciousness" and "epiphany" are associated with
    (A) Jack London.
    (B) James Joyce.
    (C) Ernest Hemingway.
    (D) Thomas Wolfe.
    (E) George Orwell.

Section II: Fine Arts

75 Questions

Time—45 minutes

Directions: For each question, choose the best answer from the five choices offered. Blacken your answer sheet for the letter of the correct answer.

76. The group who won recognition for the music in the film *Saturday Night Fever* is

    (A) The Bee Gees.
    (B) Weather Report.
    (C) The Band.
    (D) Electric Light Orchestra.
    (E) Blood, Sweat & Tears.

77. Often using the poor for his models and the Old Testament for his subject, which painter is known for his moving portraits, with startling, brilliant light emerging from a dark canvas?

    (A) Franz Hals
    (B) Caravaggio
    (C) Ingres
    (D) Rembrandt
    (E) Vermeer

78. The flute's airy theme evokes the image of a faun in a descriptive orchestral piece by

    (A) Saint–Saens.
    (B) Ravel.
    (C) Debussy.
    (D) Chopin.
    (E) Stravinsky.

79. Which of the following artists is associated with "drip–painting"?

    (A) de Kooning
    (B) Motherwell
    (C) Pollock
    (D) Rothko
    (E) Johns

80. It was the most important architectural school in the United States during the last two decades of the nineteenth century and sought to furnish utility within handsome, innovative buildings.

    Which of the following is described in the sentence above?

    (A) The Chicago school
    (B) The École des Beaux–Arts
    (C) The Crystal Palace
    (D) The Bauhaus
    (E) The Halles Centrales

81. The choreographer of *Summerspace* has explored dance-by-chance methods, not making designs and sequences deliberately but, instead, duplicating the patterns formed by Chinese sticks that have been tossed into the air and land at random.

    The sentence above describes

    (A) Alwin Nikolais.
    (B) Michel Fokine.
    (C) Mikhail Baryshnikov.
    (D) Merce Cunningham.
    (E) Rudolf Nureyev.

82. In what contemporary Italian film is the emptiness of modern life exemplified in the evidently pointless lives of the members of a segment of Roman high society and their hangers–on?

    (A) Atonioni's *L'Avventura*
    (B) Fellini's *La Dolce Vita*
    (C) Rossellini's *Open City*
    (D) Visconti's *Garden of the Finzi–Continis*
    (E) Scorcese's *Mean Streets*

83. Which film did NOT star Marlon Brando?

    (A) *On the Waterfront*
    (B) *Casablanca*
    (C) *Last Tango in Paris*
    (D) *A Streetcar Named Desire*
    (E) *Viva Zapata!*

84. This painting, *Woman: Sunlight/Moonlight,* is an example of

    (A) Cubism.
    (B) Pop Art.
    (C) Impressionism.
    (D) Op Art.
    (E) Pointillism.

85. Who composed the famous American musical composition entitled "4'33"" that consists of four minutes and thirty-three seconds of silence?

    (A) Cole Porter
    (B) John Cage
    (C) Elliott Carter
    (D) Irving Berlin
    (E) Aaron Copland

86. Which of the following composers wrote the great national hymn, *Finlandia?*

    (A) Hilding Rosenberg
    (B) Edvard Grieg
    (C) Niels Gade
    (D) Jean Sibelius
    (E) Leevi Madetoja

87. Picasso's *Les Demoiselles d'Avignon,* the first Cubist painting, was influenced by

    (A) Japanese netsuke.
    (B) Byzantine enamels.
    (C) Indian temple statuary.
    (D) African masks.
    (E) Inca statuary.

88. All of the following are well known designers of modern furniture EXCEPT

    (A) Willem de Kooning.
    (B) Ludwig Mies van der Rohe.
    (C) Le Corbusier.
    (D) Marcel Breuer.
    (E) Eero Saarinen.

89. An outstanding jazz trumpeter was

    (A) John Coltrane.
    (B) Charlie Parker.
    (C) John "Dizzy" Gillespie.
    (D) Sonny Rollins.
    (E) Thelonious Monk.

90. Which of the following sculptors was a Baroque master?

    (A) Donatello
    (B) Peter Flötner
    (C) Nikolaus Gerhaert
    (D) Gianlorenzo Bernini
    (E) Antonio Pollaiuolo

91. A minimal sculpture, *Tilted Arc* (1981), was installed in Federal Plaza, Foley Square, New York. A few years later, as the result of a court order, the 120–foot–long 12–foot–high slab of rusted steel was removed from the site. Who had created the sculpture?

    (A) Frank Gehry
    (B) Claes Oldenberg
    (C) Richard Serra
    (D) Frank Stella
    (E) Alexander Calder

92. A cofounder of the influential Photo–Secession group, he was one of the first to demonstrate the pictorial possibilities of the hand camera with his straightforward photographs of New York under all weather conditions.

    The photographer referred to in the sentence above is

    (A) Lewis Hine.
    (B) L.J.M. Daguerre.
    (C) Edward Steichen.
    (D) Alfred Stieglitz.
    (E) Andre Kertesz.

93. Waslaw Nijinsky, Jerome Robbins, and Agnes de Mille were/are well-known

    (A) photographers.
    (B) biographers.
    (C) architects.
    (D) choreographers.
    (E) poets.

94. In his films, he has been concerned with the subject of women's roles. One success was a quasi–documentary study of the disintegration of a marriage.

    The statement above describes

    (A) Bergman.
    (B) Fellini.
    (C) Wertmuller.
    (D) Altman.
    (E) Hitchcock.

Questions 95 and 96 refer to the art on the following page.

95. Which is by Renoir?

96. Which is a surrealist painting?

97. The thin, vertical, Etruscan idol–like figures he developed after World War II showed his avoidance of rounded and smooth body surfaces or strong references to the flesh.

    The sculptor described is
    (A) Auguste Rodin.
    (B) Henry Moore.
    (C) Jean Arp.
    (D) Alberto Giacometti.
    (E) Jacques Lipchitz.

98. An outstanding performer in the area of Latin music is
    (A) John Belushi.
    (B) Enrico Caruso.
    (C) Placido Domingo.
    (D) Eddie Palmieri.
    (E) Edith Piaf.

99. What would be the probable type of a musical program devoted solely to the compositions of Mahler, Beethoven, Shostakovitch, and Hindemith?

    (A) Piano recital
    (B) Symphony orchestra concert
    (C) String quartet recital
    (D) Organ recital
    (E) Song recital

Questions 100 and 101 refer to the following operas.
    (A) *Lohengrin*
    (B) *Aida*
    (C) *Madame Butterfly*
    (D) *Carmen*
    (E) *Parsifal*

100. In which opera is the heroine a seductive Spanish gypsy who works in a cigarette factory?

101. In which opera is the Japanese heroine deserted by an American naval lieutenant?

102. Which of the following films openly praised the Ku Klux Klan and implicitly condemned miscegenation?

    (A) Arthur Penn's *Bonnie and Clyde*
    (B) D. W. Griffith's *Intolerance*
    (C) Jean Renoir's *The Rules of the Game*
    (D) D. W. Griffith's *The Birth of a Nation*
    (E) Man Ray's *Return to Reason*

(A)

(C)

(B)

(D)

(E)

103. Which of the following does NOT refer to a column?

    (A) Capital
    (B) Doric
    (C) Cornice
    (D) Necking
    (E) Shaft

104. What style of music was popularized by Donna Summer, Gloria Gaynor, and The Village People?

    (A) Bebop
    (B) Disco
    (C) Punk
    (D) Motown
    (E) Rockabilly

105. Creator of the *Brandenburg Concertos,* he served as Cantor (director of music) at St. Thomas's church in Leipzig, in which post he died shortly after becoming blind.

    Which of the following composers is described in the sentence above?

    (A) Johann Sebastian Bach
    (B) Carl Philipp Emanuel Bach
    (C) Johannes Brahms
    (D) Ludwig van Beethoven
    (E) Wolfgang Amadeus Mozart

106. The symphonic suite *Scheherazade* was composed by

    (A) Shostakovich.
    (B) Rimsky–Korsakov.
    (C) Prokofiev.
    (D) Borodin.
    (E) Moussorgsky.

Questions 107–109 refer to the pictures on the following page.

107. Which is by Michelangelo?

108. Which is a Greek sculpture from around 500 B.C.E.?

109. Which is by Alexander Calder?

110. In his hands, the dashes of pure color turned and twisted, tracing invisible and unstable lines of force. They were woven into rhythmical and convulsive patterns reflecting the mounting intensity of his own feelings.

    The preceding sentences discuss

    (A) Vuillard.
    (B) Whistler.
    (C) Modigliani.
    (D) Gauguin.
    (E) van Gogh.

111. The *Victory of Samothrace* is a famous

    (A) bas–relief.
    (B) cathedral.
    (C) mural.
    (D) statue.
    (E) tapestry.

112. The Beatles introduced all of the following songs EXCEPT

    (A) "I Wanna Hold Your Hand."
    (B) "Yesterday."
    (C) "Eleanor Rigby."
    (D) "Norwegian Wood."
    (E) "Jamaica Farewell."

113. Which of the following painters is incorrectly paired with the group or movement with which he was associated?

    (A) Lichtenstein . . . Pop Art
    (B) Pontormo . . . Mannerism
    (C) Bonnard . . . *Les Nabis*
    (D) Cole . . . Hudson River School
    (E) Léger . . . Impressionism

114. The photographer who is known for black–and–white prints of nature and the American southwest is

    (A) Eugene Smith.
    (B) Ansel Adams.
    (C) Henri Cartier–Bresson.
    (D) Matthew Brady.
    (E) Imogen Cunningham.

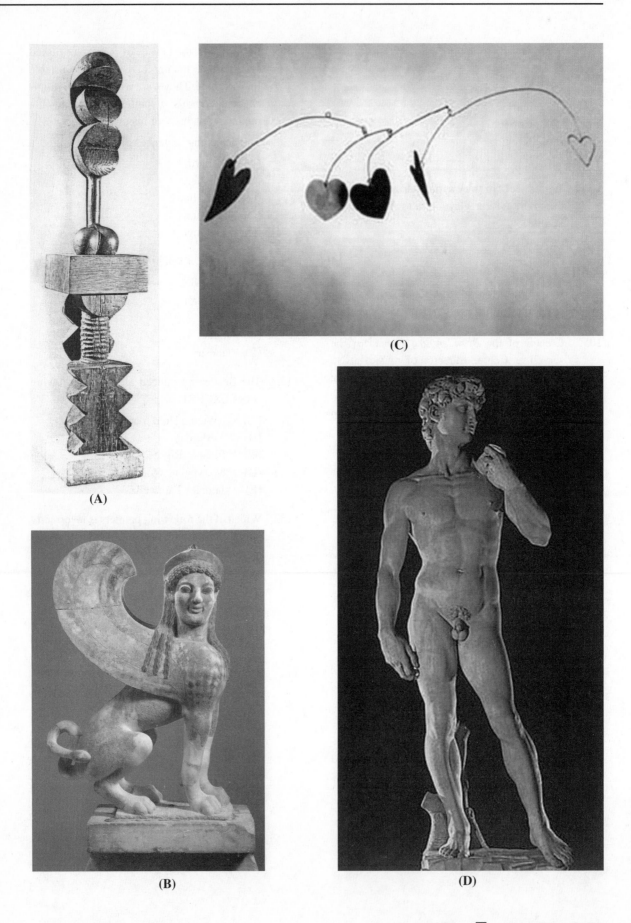

(A)

(B)

(C)

(D)

115. Most of his public commissions were unlucky: His "Thinker" was not erected as he wished and was savaged by a vandal with a chopper; his "Balzac" monument was refused by the commissioning committee in 1893 and only erected much later.

    The sentence above describes

    (A) Clodion.
    (B) Constantin Brancusi.
    (C) Auguste Rodin.
    (D) Gianlorenzo Bernini.
    (E) Umberto Boccioni.

116. Who was NOT one of the early pioneers of rock-and-roll?

    (A) Chuck Berry
    (B) Little Richard
    (C) Mick Jagger
    (D) Jerry Lee Lewis
    (E) Fats Domino

117. All of the following characters are in *Star Wars* EXCEPT

    (A) Mister Spock.
    (B) Darth Vader.
    (C) Luke Skywalker.
    (D) Princess Leia.
    (E) R2–D2.

118. Who created the graffiti–related work *Art in Transit* pictured?

    (A) Eric Fischl
    (B) Keith Haring
    (C) David Salle
    (D) Sandro Chia
    (E) Francesco Clemente

119. Which lead singer and group are incorrectly paired?

    (A) Bill Haley . . . The Comets
    (B) Martha . . . The Vandellas
    (C) Billy Joel . . . The E Street Band
    (D) Smoky Robinson . . . The Miracles
    (E) Gladys Knight . . . The Pips

120. Which of the following artists is best known for combining thought–provoking sayings with computer–animated LED (Light–Emitting Diode) machines?

    (A) Kenny Scharf
    (B) George Segal
    (C) Louise Bourgeois
    (D) Jennifer Bartlett
    (E) Jenny Holzer

Questions 121–123 refer to the pictures on the following page.

121. Which is by Michelangelo?

122. Which is by Mary Cassatt?

123. Which is by Rubens?

124. Of the following, the painter whose work is well known for its rich and exciting color is

    (A) Courbet.
    (B) Chardin.
    (C) Matisse.
    (D) Daumier.
    (E) Rembrandt.

125. Which ballet tells the story of the daughter of Zeus and Demeter who was abducted by Pluto, king of the underworld?

    (A) *Persephone*
    (B) *Dark Elegies*
    (C) *Giselle*
    (D) *Swan Lake*
    (E) *Sylvia*

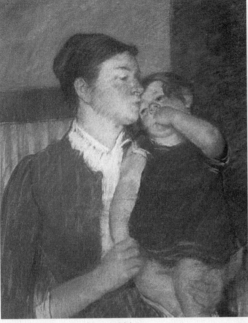

(A)

(C)

(B)

(D)

(E)

126. Its true aim was to achieve ever greater naturalism, by exact analysis of tone and color, and by trying to render the play of light on the surface of objects.

    The sentence above refers to

    (A) Expressionism.
    (B) Impressionism.
    (C) Cubism.
    (D) Surrealism.
    (E) Vorticism.

127. Which architect, striving for geometric purism in his austere glass structures, declared that "less is more"?

    (A) Walter Gropius
    (B) Mies van der Rohe
    (C) Francesco Borromini
    (D) Frank Lloyd Wright
    (E) Jules Hardouin–Mansart

128. The jazz alto saxophonist known as "Bird" was

    (A) Charlie Parker.
    (B) Thelonious Monk.
    (C) Louis Armstrong.
    (D) John Gillespie.
    (E) Scott Joplin.

129. The conductor-composer whose works include classical symphonies and ballets as well as Broadway musicals is

    (A) Arturo Toscanini.
    (B) Leopold Stokowski.
    (C) Fritz Reiner.
    (D) Leonard Bernstein.
    (E) Seiji Ozawa.

130. The flying buttress is a(n)

    (A) ornamental gargoyle.
    (B) element in modern sculpture.
    (C) structural unit in Gothic architecture.
    (D) device introduced by Frank Lloyd Wright.
    (E) Calder sculpture.

131. A contemporary illustrator whose magazine cover designs have become known for their interpretation of American types and scenes is

    (A) Elmore J. Brown.
    (B) Walt Disney.
    (C) R. John Holmgren.
    (D) Rockwell Kent.
    (E) Norman Rockwell.

Questions 132–134 refer to the pictures on the following page.

132. Which was designed by Walter Gropius?

133. Which is in the Neoclassical style?

134. Which was designed by Christopher Wren?

135. In a musical composition, a coda is a(n)

    (A) introduction.
    (B) solo for one instrument.
    (C) concluding passage.
    (D) motive.
    (E) round.

136. Which of the following is wall painting in a medium like watercolor on wet plaster?

    (A) Fresco
    (B) Pastel
    (C) Latex
    (D) Still life
    (E) Acrylic

137. The Emma Lazarus poem containing the words "Give Me Your Tired, Your Poor" was used in a song by the composer who also wrote "White Christmas." He is

    (A) Irving Berlin.
    (B) Stephen Foster.
    (C) Cole Porter.
    (D) Paul McCartney.
    (E) Aaron Copland.

138. The pointed arch was a motif of which of the following architectural styles?

    (A) Roman
    (B) Renaissance
    (C) Neoclassical
    (D) Greek
    (E) Gothic

(A)

(D)

(B)

(C)

(E)

139. Which of the following is the most famous of the surreal films?

    (A) *The Seventh Seal*
    (B) *Grand Illusion*
    (C) *The Magician*
    (D) *Un Chien Andalou*
    (E) *Psycho*

140. A revolutionary music concert of the 1960s was staged near

    (A) Carmel.
    (B) Bennington.
    (C) Chatauqua.
    (D) Woodstock.
    (E) San Francisco.

141. Cubism was founded by

    (A) Degas and Monet.
    (B) Braque and Picasso.
    (C) Magritte and Tanguy.
    (D) Derain and Matisse.
    (E) Balla and Marinetti.

142. A portrait of George Washington that has frequently been reproduced was painted by

    (A) George Innes.
    (B) Gilbert Stuart.
    (C) John Singer Sargent.
    (D) Cass Gilbert.
    (E) Leonardo Da Vinci.

143. Satie, Picasso, and Cocteau collaborated with Massine and Diaghilev on a work called *Parade,* which is a

    (A) cabaret piece.
    (B) mass.
    (C) radio program.
    (D) ballet.
    (E) symphony.

Questions 144–146 refer to pictures on the following page.

144. Which is by Botticelli?

145. Which is by Vermeer?

146. Which is by Delacroix?

147. Lina Wertmuller directed all of the following films EXCEPT

    (A) *Swept Away.*
    (B) *The Wedding.*
    (C) *Seven Beauties.*
    (D) *The Seduction of Mimi.*
    (E) *All Screwed Up.*

148. This instrument has mainly been used informally, but works by Milhaud and Vaughan Williams have been written for Larry Adler, its most notable exponent. Bob Dylan and Paul Butterfield also use it.

    The statement above describes the

    (A) balalaika.
    (B) recorder.
    (C) banjo.
    (D) harmonica.
    (E) kazoo.

149. A picture built up wholly or partly from pieces of paper, cloth, or other material stuck on to the canvas or other ground is called a

    (A) ready–made.
    (B) drypoint.
    (C) stabile.
    (D) still life.
    (E) collage.

150. Which of the following was a group of nineteenth/twentieth–century American "realist" painters and illustrators who were interested in the sordid side of city life (especially in New York)?

    (A) Camden Town Group
    (B) Ashcan School
    (C) *Les Nabis*
    (D) Hudson River School
    (E) Pre–Raphaelite Brotherhood

End of Practice Examination III

(A)

(B)

(D)

(C)

(E)

Answer Key

Section I

1.	D	16.	D	31.	A	46.	B	61.	A
2.	C	17.	A	32.	C	47.	D	62.	B
3.	D	18.	C	33.	B	48.	E	63.	C
4.	C	19.	A	34.	D	49.	C	64.	D
5.	A	20.	A	35.	C	50.	A	65.	A
6.	E	21.	A	36.	A	51.	E	66.	B
7.	A	22.	D	37.	D	52.	C	67.	D
8.	D	23.	D	38.	C	53.	C	68.	D
9.	C	24.	D	39.	E	54.	A	69.	D
10.	D	25.	A	40.	A	55.	D	70.	E
11.	C	26.	D	41.	A	56.	A	71.	C
12.	A	27.	C	42.	A	57.	B	72.	A
13.	A	28.	E	43.	C	58.	C	73.	B
14.	B	29.	A	44.	E	59.	C	74.	C
15.	B	30.	D	45.	B	60.	E	75.	B

Section II

76.	A	91.	C	106.	B	121.	E	136.	A
77.	D	92.	D	107.	D	122.	A	137.	A
78.	C	93.	D	108.	B	123.	D	138.	E
79.	C	94.	A	109.	C	124.	C	139.	D
80.	A	95.	E	110.	E	125.	A	140.	D
81.	D	96.	B	111.	D	126.	B	141.	B
82.	B	97.	D	112.	E	127.	B	142.	B
83.	B	98.	D	113.	E	128.	A	143.	D
84.	B	99.	B	114.	B	129.	D	144.	B
85.	B	100.	D	115.	C	130.	C	145.	C
86.	D	101.	C	116.	C	131.	E	146.	D
87.	D	102.	D	117.	A	132.	A	147.	B
88.	A	103.	C	118.	B	133.	B	148.	D
89.	C	104.	B	119.	C	134.	E	149.	E
90.	D	105.	A	120.	E	135.	C	150.	B

Explanatory Answers

Section I

1. **The correct answer is (D).** The poetry of Emily Dickinson (1830–1886) is concerned with themes of love, death, and immortality. Some of her best known poems are "I taste a liquor never brewed," "Because I could not stop for Death," "I'm Nobody, who are you," "I like to see it lap the Miles," and "I heard a Fly buzz—when I died."

2. **The correct answer is (C).** *Fathers and Sons* was written in 1862 by Ivan Turgenev (1818–1883), the first of the great Russian writers to be read widely in Europe. He also wrote *Virgin Soil, A Sportsman's Sketches,* and *A Month in the Country.*

3. **The correct answer is (D).** In terms of syntax, language, punctuation, and content, e.e. cummings is the only poet listed who would have written these lines.

4. **The correct answer is (C).** John F. Kennedy's (1917–1963) 1961 inaugural address contained this line. His writings include *Why England Slept* and *Profiles in Courage,* winner of the 1956 Pulitzer Prize.

5. **The correct answer is (A).** *David Copperfield* was written by Charles Dickens (1812–1870) in 1849. The story of a young man's growth to maturity, it tells in part of his emotional alliance with the underprivileged and the victimized in his society and involves the characters David Copperfield, Barkis, Uriah Heep, and Mr. Micawber.

6. **The correct answer is (E).** Prospero, the former Duke of Milan who has lived on an island in the distant seas since he was deposed, and his innocent daughter Miranda appear in Shakespeare's *The Tempest.*

7. **The correct answer is (A).** The school founded by Epicurus of Samos (342–270 B.C.E.) advocated hedonism, but only to the extent that it was consistent with intelligence and moderation.

8. **The correct answer is (D).** These lines are taken from Robert Herrick's "To the Virgins, to Make Much of Time" (1648), which expresses the philosophy of *carpe diem,* seize the time.

9. **The correct answer is (C).** *The Naked and the Dead,* a highly recognized novel concerning a group of soldiers who survive the invasion of a Japanese–held island in World War II, was written in 1948 by Norman Mailer.

10. **The correct answer is (D).** *Lady Windermere's Fan* was written by Oscar Wilde (1854–1901) in 1892.

11. **The correct answer is (C).** The "place" mentioned in these lines, "Underneath the living flowers," cues us to think of *the grave,* where ". . . we shall not count the hours. . . ."

12. **The correct answer is (A).** John Steinbeck (1902–1968) won the Pulitzer Prize in 1939 for *The Grapes of Wrath.* The 1962 recipient of the Nobel Prize for Literature, he is also noted for *Of Mice and Men, Tortilla Flat, The Red Pony, The Pearl, East of Eden,* and *Travels with Charley in Search of America.*

13. **The correct answer is (A).** Personification is the technique of attributing human qualities or feelings to inanimate objects, such as when the "yellow fog" "rubs its back" or the "yellow smoke" "Licked its tongue. . . ."

14. **The correct answer is (B).** The Czech writer Franz Kafka (1883–1924) also wrote *The Castle, Amerika, Metamorphosis, In the Penal Colony,* and *The Country Doctor;* his works were assembled after his death by his friend Max Brod and have been termed "obscure allegories. . . set amid dreamlike, surrealist landscapes."

15. **The correct answer is (B).** *The Cocktail Party* was first presented in 1949. T.S. Eliot's (1888–1962) other plays include *The Rock: A Pageant Play, Murder in the Cathedral, The Family Reunion,* and *The Confidential Clerk.*

16. **The correct answer is (D).** H.L. Mencken (1880–1950) was a journalist, critic, and essayist associated with George Jean Nathan on *Smart Set* and *The American Mercury* magazines; he was widely known for his important work of scholarship, *The American Language.*

17. **The correct answer is (A).** Dylan Thomas (1914–1953), who wrote these lines for his father, was one of the great lyric poets of his time, the author of such works as "The Force That Through the Green Fuse Drives the Flower,"

"Fern Hill," "In My Craft or Sullen Art," "And Death Shall Have No Dominion," and also *Adventures in the Skin Trade, Portrait of the Artist as a Young Dog,* and *Under Milk Wood.*

18. **The correct answer is (C).** A villanelle is a poem with five *tercets* (three–line stanzas), all rhyming *aba,* and a concluding quatrain (four–line stanza), rhyming *abaa.* Lines six, twelve, and eighteen repeat line one; lines nine, fifteen, and nineteen repeat line three.

19. **The correct answer is (A).** *The Old Man and the Sea* was written by Ernest Hemingway (1899–1961) in 1952. It tells of the struggle of an old Cuban fisherman named Santiago to land a large fish after nearly three months without a catch.

20. **The correct answer is (A).** These are the famous opening lines of T.S. Eliot's "The Love Song of J. Alfred Prufrock," in which the poet also writes, "I have measured out my life with coffee spoons." *The Waste Land* is another of Eliot's best known poems; it opens by stating, "April is the cruelest month," and is filled with allusions and quotations from much of world literature, anthropology, geography, and other sources.

21. **The correct answer is (A).** Victor Hugo (1802–1885) wrote *Les Misérables* in 1862. He is better known in the United States as the author of *The Hunchback of Notre Dame.*

22. **The correct answer is (D).** Mary Wollstonecraft Godwin Shelley (1797–1851) is best known as the author of *Frankenstein* (1818), a masterpiece of fictional horror that has been dramatized often in the twentieth century.

23. **The correct answer is (D).** Jerome Lawrence and Robert E. Lee wrote *Inherit the Wind* in 1960. They were also highly successful with *Auntie Mame.*

24. **The correct answer is (D).** Ezra Pound (1885–1972) was a leader of the Imagists, a poetic movement (1909–1917) opposed to the romantic conception of poetry that included the use of the language of common speech, precision, the creation of new rhythms, and the presentation of images in hard, clear poetry and concentration.

25. **The correct answer is (A).** Although they resemble *blank verse* (unrhymed iambic pentameter), the lines might more aptly be termed *free verse,* rhythmical lines varying in length, adhering to no fixed metrical pattern, and usually unrhymed.

26. **The correct answer is (D).** Ken Kesey (1935–2001) wrote *One Flew Over the Cuckoo's Nest* in 1962. A satire on bureaucratic attitudes and contemporary society's disregard for the individual, the work has been presented on the screen as well as in the theater.

27. **The correct answer is (C).** Holden Caulfield appears in the novel *The Catcher in the Rye,* written in 1951 by J.D. Salinger (1919–). Holden's sensitivity and disgust with "phoniness" made him a symbol for a generation of high school and college students.

28. **The correct answer is (E).** Langston Hughes (1902–1967) is known for his stories concerning a character named Jess Simple, as well as for many volumes of poetry (such as "A Dream Deferred") and for anthologies of Black poets and storytellers.

29. **The correct answer is (A).** *Parallel Lives* by the biographer Plutarch (c. 45–c. 125) provided Shakespeare (through a 1579 translation by Thomas Nash) with the plots of *Julius Caesar, Antony and Cleopatra,* and *Coriolanus. Parallel Lives* sets important Greek and Roman commanders or statesmen beside each other in pairs and then compares their characters for purposes of moral instruction.

30. **The correct answer is (D).** The Russian writer Maxim Gorki (1868–1936) wrote *The Lower Depths* in 1902. The work created a furor when it was produced and has been called "The proletarian drama of the century."

31. **The correct answer is (A).** The metaphorical reference to the sun as a "Minstrel," a musician or singer of verses, is central to the meaning of these lines. Earth's changing seasons are said to be adjusted to the "songs or sighs" of the Minstrel, or sun. The earth, or nature, reacts to them: The natural laws that regulate the earth's revolution around the sun cause the seasons.

Man only perceives the *effect,* the seasonal changes; he does not directly perceive the sun's influence. The correct answer, therefore, is choice (A), "human perception"; choice (B), "the earth," is contradicted in lines 1–2; choice (C), "the average person," is incorrect, since "mortal" refers to all human beings; choice (D), "human hearing," is too literal a reading, overlooking the "minstrel" metaphor; choice (E), "the dead," mistakes mortal for "post–human" rather than "human being."

32. **The correct answer is (C).** John Osborne (1929–1994) wrote the play *Look Back in Anger* (as well as *Luther* and the films *The Entertainer* and *Tom Jones*). Kingsley Amis (1922–1995) is the author of the comic novel *Lucky Jim.* A new age in British theater began with the production of Osborne's play in 1956; many new voices rose in opposition to the British establishment, and the artists involved were termed "Angry Young Men" after Osborne's "antihero."

33. **The correct answer is (B).** Greek drama developed from the activities of groups of singers and dancers participating in ancient festivals. According to Aristotle, the immediate source of tragedy is the choral hymn in honor of Dionysus.

34. **The correct answer is (D).** The Bloomsbury Group met in a house owned by the novelist Virginia Woolf (1882–1941) in the Bloomsbury district of London, and included the economist John Maynard Keynes, the artist Roger Fry, the biographer Lytton Strachey, and others.

35. **The correct answer is (C).** The imagery and language indicate that of the choices given, only Nikki Giovanni (1943–) would have authored the lines. Writing out of the experience of an African-American woman, she has created such works as *Black Feeling, Black Talk/Black Judgment, Cotton Candy on a Rainy Day, Ego–Tripping and Other Poems for Young People,* and *Spin a Soft Black Song.*

36. **The correct answer is (A).** The stanza is an example of free verse, which usually does not employ rhyme patterns, though it does utilize most of the other familiar poetic conventions.

37. **The correct answer is (D).** Karl Marx (1818–1883) began but Engels finished *Das Kapital* after Marx died. With Friedrich Engels (1820–1895), Marx also wrote the *Communist Manifesto* in 1847.

38. **The correct answer is (C).**) Georg W. F. Hegel (1770–1831), an "objective idealist," developed a system characterized by the dialectic of thesis, antithesis, and synthesis. His views influenced, among others: Benedetto Croce (1866–1952), an idealist best known now for work in aesthetics and literary criticism; Karl Marx (1818–1883), who used Hegel's dialectic in collaboration with Friederich Engels (1820–1895) to expound the doctrine of dialectical materialism; and Francis H. Bradley (1846–1924), another idealist, author of *Ethical Studies* and *Essays on Truth and Reality.*

39. **The correct answer is (E).** Shakespeare's *A Midsummer Night's Dream* involves Titania, Queen of the Fairies; her husband Oberon, King of the Fairies, who plots with Puck, the mischievous elf; Robin Goodfellow of English folk legend; Bottom; Peter Quince; Hermia; and Lysander.

40. **The correct answer is (A).** In *Paradise Lost* (1667), a blank verse religious epic in 12 books, John Milton (1608–1674) sought "to justify the ways of God to men."

41. **The correct answer is (A).** Herman Melville (1819–1891) created in *Moby Dick* the famous characters Ishmael, Queequeg, and Captain Ahab. Melville is also known for *Typee, Omoo, Redburn, Pierre,* and *The Confidence Man.*

42. **The correct answer is (A).** Norman Mailer (1923–) is also known for *Advertisements for Myself, The Deer Park, An American Dream, Marilyn, A Fire on the Moon,* and *The Executioner's Song.*

43. **The correct answer is (C).** Henry Higgins appears in George Bernard Shaw's *Pygmalion.*

44. **The correct answer is (E).** When Charles Baudelaire (1821–1867) published *Les Fleurs du Mal* in 1857, the work became a "synonym for everything decadent and unwholesome." Baudelaire had learned the art of brevity from his reading and translating of Edgar Allan Poe and represents the beginning of modernism in French poetry.

45. **The correct answer is (B).** Voltaire (François Marie Arouet, 1694–1778) created *Candide* in 1759. The hero is an honest and gentle young man who has been taught that "this is the best of all possible worlds," but whose experience teaches him otherwise.

46. **The correct answer is (B).** The Agrarians were Southern writers in the 1920s and 30s (including John Crowe Ransom, John Gould Fletcher, Robert Penn Warren, and Allen Tate) who championed an agrarian economy for the South and in their works emphasized the history, manners, and folkways of their area.

47. **The correct answer is (D).** Jeremy Bentham (1748–1832) espoused the philosophy of utilitarianism, that the morality of actions is determined by whatever conduct and legislation will provide "the greatest happiness of the greatest number."

48. **The correct answer is (E).** In "Birches," Robert Frost (1874–1963) expressed a desire to "get away from earth awhile," and then come back for a new start.

49. **The correct answer is (C).** Oscar Wilde was known for what he termed "trivial comedies for serious people" and used his gift of satire and his clever wit to criticize nineteenth–century English society (*Lady Windermere's Fan, An Ideal Husband, A Woman of No Importance, The Importance of Being Earnest,* and *Salome*).

50. **The correct answer is (A).** D.H. Lawrence (1885–1930) wrote *Women in Love* in 1920. He is also known for *Sons and Lovers, Lady Chatterley's Lover, Aaron's Rod, The Plumed Serpent,* and *Studies in Classic American Literature.*

51. **The correct answer is (E).** Rhyme is determined by the final sounds in lines of poetry. In this case, "Sand" (A) and "hand" (A) rhyme, as do "Flower" (B) and "hour" (B), so the rhyme scheme is said to be *ABAB.*

52. **The correct answer is (C).** Thomas De Quincey (1785–1859), a close associate of Lamb, Hazlitt, Coleridge, and Wordsworth, wrote in English; he is best known for *Confessions of an English Opium Eater* (1822).

53. **The correct answer is (C).** F. Scott Fitzgerald (1896–1940) wrote *The Great Gatsby* in 1925. In addition to the mysterious hero, Jay Gatsby, it involves the characters Nick Carraway, Daisy Buchanan, and Tom Buchanan.

54. **The correct answer is (A).** *Antigone* is part of Sophocles' (c. 496 B.C.E.–c. 405 B.C.E.) trilogy (with *Oedipus Rex* and *Oedipus at Colonus*) concerning the Thebes legend. Antigone refuses to allow the body of her brother to lie unburied, in defiance of King Creon's decree.

55. **The correct answer is (D).** The mathematician C.L. Dodson (1832–1898) assumed the pseudonym Lewis Carroll when he wrote *Alice's Adventures in Wonderland* in 1865. He is also famous for the "Jabberwocky" poem.

56. **The correct answer is (A).** Born in Kentucky, Robert Penn Warren (1905–1989) employed his Southern background in nearly all of his writing. He won a Pulitzer Prize in 1947 for *All the King's Men,* contributed to *The Fugitive* magazine, was a leader of the New Critics school of literary criticism, and also published numerous volumes of poetry and criticism.

57. **The correct answer is (B).** *A View From the Bridge* was written in 1955 by Arthur Miller (1915–   ).

58. **The correct answer is (C).** Jean–Paul Sartre's *Nausea* has been called "a landmark in Existentialist fiction." It is written in the form of the diary of Antoine Roquentin, a French writer who is horrified at his own existence and who attempts to come to terms with life.

59. **The correct answer is (C).** *The Canterbury Tales* was written between 1387 and 1400.

60. **The correct answer is (E).** The medieval English writer Geoffrey Chaucer (1343–1400) is best known for *The Canterbury Tales,* a series of stories told by Pilgrims on their way to Canterbury.

61. **The correct answer is (A).** Chaucer wrote in Middle English, a language that in his day was understood by everyone, not simply by the learned.

62. **The correct answer is (B).** *Bread and Wine* was written in 1936 by Ignazio Silone (1900–

1978), a writer who helped to found the Italian Communist Party.

63. **The correct answer is (C).** Peter Shaffer's *Equus* won many awards during the 1973 theater season. Shaffer is also known for *Five Finger Exercise, The Royal Hunt of the Sun,* and *The Private Ear and the Public Eye.*

64. **The correct answer is (D).** James Joyce wrote a play entitled *Exiles* in 1918. In *A Portrait of the Artist as a Young Man,* the main character is named Stephen Dedalus, after the Greek craftsman who created wings to fly from the labyrinth that imprisoned him.

65. **The correct answer is (A).** Thornton Wilder (1897–1975) won the Pulitzer Prize in 1938 for *Our Town,* an account of life and death in a New England village. Wilder is also known for *The Skin of Our Teeth, The Bridge of San Luis Rey,* and *The Matchmaker* (later made into *Hello, Dolly!*).

66. **The correct answer is (B).** Albert Schweitzer (1875–1965) was a French Protestant clergyman, philosopher, physician, and music scholar who served as a missionary physician in French Equatorial Africa and won the Nobel Peace Prize in 1952.

67. **The correct answer is (D).** Henry Wadsworth Longfellow (1807–1882) wrote *The Song of Hiawatha* in 1855. It tells of the life of the young Indian who is raised by his grandmother. ("By the shores of Gitche Gumee, By the Shining Big–Sea–Water, Stood the wigwam of Nokomis, Daughter of the Moon, Nokomis.")

68. **The correct answer is (D).** *Dr. Zhivago* was written by the Russian author Boris Pasternak (1890–1960) who was awarded the Nobel Prize for literature in 1958 (which his country did not allow him to receive).

69. **The correct answer is (D).** Samuel Johnson (1709–1784) wrote the 200 or so essays entitled *The Rambler* between 1750 and 1752. A famous lexicographer (*Dictionary of the English Language,* 1755), he also wrote *Lives of the Poets, The Vanity of Human Wishes,* and *Rasselas.*

70. **The correct answer is (E).** Mark Twain (1835–1910) wrote "The Celebrated Jumping Frog of Calaveras County" in 1865; it was this tall tale that first brought him fame.

71. **The correct answer is (C).** *Men of Iron* was written in 1891 by Howard Pyle (1853–1911). It is an account of Chivalric adventure in medieval England.

72. **The correct answer is (A).** *Simile* is a comparison between essentially unlike things, with the use of "like" or "as." In this case, "my luve" is compared to "a red, red rose" and to "a melodie/That's sweetly played in tune."

73. **The correct answer is (B).** The Scottish poet Robert Burns (1759–1796) often used Scotch dialect in his poetry; his principal poetic works are collected in two volumes entitled *Poems, Chiefly in the Scottish Dialect.*

74. **The correct answer is (C).** Herodotus (484 B.C.E.–425 B.C.E.) was a Greek historian, called the "Father of History" since his *History of the Persian Wars* is the earliest example of secular narrative of events.

75. **The correct answer is (B).** For James Joyce, *epiphany* was the "sudden revelation of the whatness of a thing," "a sudden spiritual manifestation." In *Ulysses* (1922), he utilizes *stream of consciousness* or "interior monologue" to tell the story of a day in the lives of Stephen Dedalus and Leopold and Molly Bloom.

Section II

76. **The correct answer is (A).** The Bee Gee's soundtrack to the 1977 film marks both the zenith and the nadir of disco.

77. **The correct answer is (D).** Rembrandt van Rijn (1606–1669), the foremost genius of Dutch Art, is known for *The Blinding of Sampson, The Night Watch,* and *The Return of the Prodigal Son,* among others.

78. **The correct answer is (C).** Claude Debussy's (1862–1918) controversial first success was his 1894 *Afternoon of a Faun* (*Prélude à l'Après–midi d'un faune*).

79. **The correct answer is (C).** Jackson Pollock (1912–1956) became known for his immense canvases and methods of dripping liquid paint from a brush or spattering it with a stick or

dribbling it from a can and then scattering sand and pebbles over the wet surface.

80. **The correct answer is (A).** The Chicago School included Louis Sullivan, Daniel H. Burnham, John W. Root, and the young Frank Lloyd Wright.

81. **The correct answer is (D).** Merce Cunningham (1922–) is the dancer–choreographer who broke away from the representational, expressionistic school of dancing. The costumes and set of *Summerspace* were created by Robert Rauschenberg.

82. **The correct answer is (B).** *La Dolce Vita* was made by Frederico Fellini in 1959, with Marcello Mastroianni, Anouk Aimee, and Anita Ekberg.

83. **The correct answer is (B).** *Casablanca*, made in 1943, starred Humphrey Bogart, Ingrid Bergman, Claude Rains, and Peter Lorre.

84. **The correct answer is (B).** Pop Art.

85. **The correct answer is (B).** John Cage (1912–1992) has been musical director of the Merce Cunningham Dance Company. The elements of Cage's music (some critics wonder if his works are indeed "music") are silence, sound, and rhythm.

86. **The correct answer is (D).** Jean Sibelius (1865–1957) is generally regarded as the founder of national Finnish music. *Finlandia* (1899–1900) is a tone–poem for orchestra.

87. **The correct answer is (D).** Said to have been introduced to African sculpture by Henri Matisse, Picasso appreciated its exaggeration of certain head, face, and body features at the expense of others. In *Les Demoiselles,* some figures resemble Egyptian sculpture, others have hollowed faces as in African masks.

88. **The correct answer is (A).** Willem de Kooning (1904–1997) is associated with abstract expressionism.

89. **The correct answer is (C).** John "Dizzy" Gillespie (1917–1993) was a trumpet player, composer, and bandleader who worked with such stars as Cab Calloway, Ella Fitzgerald, Benny Carter, Billy Eckstine, Charlie Parker, and Quincy Jones. He was a primary influence in shaping the Bebop movement in jazz.

90. **The correct answer is (D).** Gianlorenzo Bernini (1598–1680), the greatest sculptor–architect of the seventeenth century, designed the colonnade around St. Peter's Square in Rome and the Throne of St. Peter in St. Peter's Cathedral.

91. **The correct answer is (C).** Although many art critics appreciated Richard Serra's work, many people working in the Foley Square area did not. The massive sculpture was removed in 1989.

92. **The correct answer is (D).** Alfred Stieglitz (1864–1946) was editor of *American Amateur Photography,* founder and editor of *Camera Notes,* editor and publisher of *Camera Work,* and the husband of the artist Georgia O'Keeffe.

93. **The correct answer is (D).** Nijinsky (1890–1960): Russian choreographer associated with Sergei Diaghilev's Ballet Russes. Robbins (1918–1998): Associated with *On The Town, Call Me Madam,* and *The King and I.* de Mille (1905–1993): Associated with *Oklahoma, Brigadoon,* and *Carousel.*

94. **The correct answer is (A).** Ingmar Bergman (1918–), the Swedish filmmaker, created *The Seventh Seal, Wild Strawberries, Shame, Persona, Cries and Whispers, Now About These Women,* and *Scenes From a Marriage.*

95. **The correct answer is (E).** Auguste Renoir: *On the Terrace* (1881)

96. **The correct answer is (B).** Yves Tanguy: *Indefinite Divisibility* (1942).

    The other works shown are:

    (A) Whistler: *Arrangement in Grey* and *Black: Portrait of the Painter's Mother* (1871).

    (C) Claude Monet: *Poplars* (1881).

    (D) Juan Gris: *The Guitar* (1914).

97. **The correct answer is (D).** Alberto Giacometti (1901–1966): The major surrealist sculptor, he found very few forms to express what he termed his "different vision of reality."

98. **The correct answer is (D).** Eddie Palmieri's music often combines African rhythmic patterns, conga drums, timbales, tom–toms, Latin jazz beat (as in Lucumi Macumba Voodoo), and salsa.

99. **The correct answer is (B).** What Gustav Mahler, Ludwig van Beethoven, Dimitri Shostakovitch, and Paul Hindemith have in common is that they are all known for their many important symphonies.

100. **The correct answer is (D).** Georges Bizet's *Carmen* was first produced in Paris in 1875, to the displeasure of the critics; yet Tchaikovsky predicted that the opera, which contains the famous "Toreador's Song," would someday be world popular.

101. **The correct answer is (C).** Giacomo Puccini's *Madame Butterfly,* first performed in Milan in 1904, is set in Nagasaki at the start of the twentieth century. The heroine, Cho–cho–san (Madame Butterfly), is absolutely alone, deserted by husband, abandoned by relatives.

102. **The correct answer is (D).** *The Birth of a Nation,* made in 1915 by D.W. Griffith and assisted by Erich von Stroheim, was a great financial success but denounced by churches and press as inciting racial hatred. Griffith defended himself in a pamphlet, "The Rise and Fall of Free Speech in America."

103. **The correct answer is (C).** "Cornice" is an ornamental horizontal feature; all the other choices are parts of a column, which is vertical.

104. **The correct answer is (B).** The Disco sound may be heard in Summer's "Bad Girls," and "Love To Love You, Baby"; Gaynor's *Stories* album; The Village People's *Cruisin',* "Y.M.C.A.," and "Can't Stop The Music."

105. **The correct answer is (A).** Johann Sebastian Bach (1685–1750), the German composer and instrumentalist noted as one of the foremost musicians of all time, composed six concertos for chamber orchestra at the request of the elector of Brandenburg. Bach suffered serious eye trouble and by 1749 was virtually blind.

106. **The correct answer is (B).** Nikolay Rimsky–Korsakov (1844–1908) was a Russian composer, professor of music, and Inspector of Naval Bands who composed *Scheherazade* in 1888.

107. **The correct answer is (D).** Michelangelo: *David* (1503–1504).

108. **The correct answer is (B).** Greek: *Guardian Sphinx* (530 B.C.E.)

109. **The correct answer is (C).** Alexander Calder: *Heart Mobile* (1947).

The other works shown are:

(A) Constantin Brancusi: *Adam and Eve* (1916–21).

(D) Henry Moore: *Reclining Figure* (1939).

110. **The correct answer is (E).** Vincent van Gogh (1853–1890) felt that Impressionism was a constraint to the expression of his emotions. In a sense he might be termed an expressionist, although that name is usually given to painters of a later period.

111. **The correct answer is (D).** The masterpiece of Hellenistic sculpture, this eight–foot–high monument demonstrates an impressive relationship between itself and the space that envelops it (c. 200–190 B.C.E.).

112. **The correct answer is (E).** "Jamaica Farewell" is a calypso standard popularized by Harry Belafonte.

113. **The correct answer is (E).** Fernand Léger (1881–1955) was a major Cubist, after Braque and Picasso. His inspiration was the modern city and machine–produced forms.

114. **The correct answer is (B).** Ansel Adams (1902–1984), recognized as "virtually without peer" in nature and landscape photography, was associated with the photography departments in New York's Museum of Modern Art and in the California School of Fine Arts.

115. **The correct answer is (C).** It is ironic, then, that with Bernini, Rodin (1840–1917) has been called the greatest sculptor since Michelangelo.

116. **The correct answer is (C).** Mick Jagger has appeared with The Rolling Stones rock music group since 1964. Berry, Richard, Lewis, and Domino were all stars of rock-and-roll in the 1950s.

117. **The correct answer is (A).** Mr. Spock is a character who appeared in *Star Trek.*

118. **The correct answer is (B).** Before his work appeared in galleries, museums, and commercial ventures, Keith Haring (1958–1990) was

known for creating graffiti art on New York City subway system walls.

119. **The correct answer is (C).** It is Bruce Springsteen and the E Street Band.

120. **The correct answer is (E).** Using modern technology, Jenny Holzer (1952–) creates lettered ribbons of light with brightly colored expressions such as "PROTECT ME FROM WHAT I WANT" and "MONEY CREATES TASTE."

121. **The correct answer is (E).** Michelangelo: *Creation of Adam, Sistine Chapel* (1508–1512).

122. **The correct answer is (A).** Mary Cassatt: *Mother and Child* (1888).

123. **The correct answer is (D).** Rubens: *An Allegory of Peace and War* (1629).

    The other works shown are:

    (B) Leonardo Da Vinci: *Mona Lisa* (c. 1503–1505).

    (C) Holman Hunt: *The Light of the World* (1853).

124. **The correct answer is (C).** Henri Matisse (1869–1954) was a member of the Fauves ("wild beasts"), noted for employing violent color and bold distortions.

125. **The correct answer is (A).** *Persephone* (music by Igor Stravinsky, French text by Andre Gide, choreography by Kurt Jooss; first presented in 1934). When Persephone—daughter of Demeter, the goddess of fertility—is taken to the Underworld by Pluto, Spring disappears from the earth. Persephone bites a pomegranate and men learn to till the earth's soil; then Persephone is reborn and the seasons restored. Later, however, Persephone returns to rule with Pluto.

126. **The correct answer is (B).** The impressionists recorded what they observed at the moment and recreated the physical quality of the light they saw as color on the canvas.

127. **The correct answer is (B).** Mies van der Rohe (1886–1969), the German architect, defined the International Style in architecture in the 1920s and 1930s by emphasizing clarity and precision in glass and steel construction.

128. **The correct answer is (A).** Charles Christopher (Charlie) Parker (1920–1955) was known with Dizzy Gillespie as cofounder of the Bebop movement in jazz. He starred with Billy Eckstine's band, with Gillespie, and with Miles Davis. The club Birdland was named after him.

129. **The correct answer is (D).** Leonard Bernstein (1918–1990) had a fabulous career as conductor (of New York City Symphony and New York Philharmonic) and composer (*Fancy Free, On The Town,* and *West Side Story*).

130. **The correct answer is (C).** Buttresses—heavy supports—are not visible from inside churches; when employed within as "flying buttresses," they are arched bridges that reach upward to critical spots between clerestory windows where the outward thrust of the nave vault is concentrated. Later they became esthetically, as well as structurally, important.

131. **The correct answer is (E).** Norman Rockwell (1894–1978) is known especially for paintings of boys, often on covers of *Saturday Evening Post* and *Life* magazines.

132. **The correct answer is (A).** Walter Gropius: Gropius Residence, Mass. (1938).

133. **The correct answer is (B).** John Nash: Carlton House, London (1815).

134. **The correct answer is (E).** Christopher Wren: St. Paul, London (1675–1710).

    The other works shown are:

    (C) Richard Meier: Ackerberg House, California (1984–1986).

    (D) Louis H. Sullivan: Guaranty Building, Buffalo (1895).

135. **The correct answer is (C).** A "coda" is a more or less independent passage at the end of a composition, introduced to bring it to a satisfactory close.

136. **The correct answer is (A).** Fresco: In the art of painting on freshly spread plaster before it dries, the pigments are applied with water, and the lime of the ground, which penetrates the painting, is converted by exposure into carbonate, which acts as a binding material (also called buono fresco).

137. **The correct answer is (A).** Irving Berlin (1888–1989) is also known for "Alexander's

Ragtime Band," "Oh, How I Hate to Get Up in the Morning," and "Russian Lullaby."

138. **The correct answer is (E).** Although the pointed arch design was not new, it was first combined with the pilgrimage choir plan and the ribbed groin vault when the Abby Church of St. Denis (near Paris) was rebuilt between 1137 and 1144. The pointed arch could be built to any height regardless of its base width.

139. **The correct answer is (D).** *Un Chien Andalou,* by Luis Buñuel and Salvador Dali, is a 24–minute masterpiece of surrealism, created in 1928.

140. **The correct answer is (D).** Woodstock, New York, was the proposed site of a concert, which at the time was the largest music gathering ever held; the name refers also to the film of the concert, as well as to the general concept of love, peace, and music that the organizers espoused. The concert was actually held at Bethel, New York.

141. **The correct answer is (B).** Georges Braque and Pablo Picasso were the first to create paintings with sharp edges and angles, called cubist by critics.

142. **The correct answer is (B).** The portrait painter Gilbert Stuart (1755–1828) is best known for his portrayals of Washington. One, the so–called Athenaeum head of Washington with its pendant portrait of Martha Washington, is in the Boston Athenaeum; the so–called Gibbs–Channing portrait is in the New York Metropolitan Museum of Art.

143. **The correct answer is (D).** *Parade* (music by Erik Satie, book by Jean Cocteau, scenery and costumes by Pablo Picasso, choreography by Leonide Massine) was first presented by Diaghilev's Ballets Russes in Paris in 1917 and in the United States in 1973. *Parade* is considered a landmark for its introduction of cubism into the theater. Guillaume Apollinaire called the work "surrealism" in the program; it concerns performers in a travelling circus and their managers or impresarios who must persuade the public to attend their shows.

144. **The correct answer is (B).** Botticelli: *Birth of Venus* (c. 1480)

145. **The correct answer is (C).** Jan Vermeer: *The Artist's Studio* (1665)

146. **The correct answer is (D).** Eugene Delacroix: *Liberty on the Barricades* (c. 1831).

Other works shown are:

(A) Hieronymus Bosch: *Hell* (c. 1500).

(E) Francisco De Goya: *The Third of May, 1808* (1814–1815).

147. **The correct answer is (B).** *The Wedding* was directed by Robert Altman, who is also known for *Brewster McCloud, McCabe and Mrs. Miller,* and *Nashville.*

148. **The correct answer is (D).** The mouth harmonica is also called the mouth organ, with tones produced by free–beating metal reeds set vibrating by the air from the mouth.

149. **The correct answer is (E).** See, for examples, the Cubist collages (from coller, to paste or glue) of Braque and Picasso, and the Dada constructions of Arp, Ernst, and Kurt Schwitters.

150. **The correct answer is (B).** The Ashcan School: a group of American painters led by Robert Henri (1865–1929) in protest against the turn-of-the-twentieth-century art establishment. Named by critics appalled by its down–to–earth, socially conscious subject matter, the Ashcan School also included Maurice Prendergast and Edward Hopper, among others.

Chapter

Mathematics

ABOUT THE GENERAL EXAMINATION IN COLLEGE MATHEMATICS

The CLEP General Examination in College Mathematics covers the mathematics taught in a college course for nonmathematics majors who do not require a knowledge of advanced mathematics. The exam is equally divided between straightforward routine problems and nonroutine problems designed to test your understanding of mathematical concepts.

The College Mathematics exam contains a total of approximately 65 questions presented in two separately timed 45–minute sections. All of the questions are multiple–choice questions with four choices labeled (A), (B), (C), and (D). The exam draws its material from the following basic subject areas in the approximate percentages indicated:

- Sets 10%
- Rules of Logic 10%
- Real Number Systems 20%
- Functions and Graphs 20%
- Probability and Statistics 25%
- Algebra Topics 15%

The exam does not require the use of a calculator; however, a calculator is allowed. You may use a nonprogrammable, nongraphing scientific calculator during the test.

Scoring the Test

Your raw score is determined by counting the number of questions you answer correctly (+1 raw score point for each correct answer) and subtracting from this number a percentage of the number of incorrect answers ($-\frac{1}{3}$ raw score point for each incorrect answer). This figure is then converted to a scaled score between 200 and 800 according to a specially constructed conversion table.

ROAD MAP

- *About the General Examination in College Mathematics*
- *Mini-Exam in College Mathematics*
- *Practice Examination I*
- *Practice Examination II*
- *Practice Examination III*

Symbology

The CLEP exam in College Mathematics assumes familiarity with basic mathematics symbols. Here are some of the symbols you should know.

General

$=$	Equal to
$\neq$	Not equal to
$\approx$	Approximately equal to
$>$	Greater than
$\geq$	Greater than or equal to
$<$	Less than
$\leq$	Less than or equal to
$0.\overline{11}$	The repeating decimal 0.11111...
$a < x < b$	x is greater than a and less than b
$\lvert x \rvert$	Absolute value of x
b^n	b to the nth power
$\sqrt[n]{a}$	The nth root of a
$\sqrt{a}$	The square root of a
i	The imaginary unit, $\sqrt{-1}$
$a + bi$	A complex number
$\pm$	Plus or minus
(a, b)	An ordered pair (a is the first component, b is the second component)
f, g, h, etc.	Function names
$f(x)$	A function expressed in terms of x
$(f \circ g)(x)$	A composite function, same as $f(g(x))$
$f(g(x))$	A composite function, same as $(f \circ g)(x)$
f^{-1}	The inverse of function f
$\log_b x$	The logarithm of x in the base b
$\log x$	The logarithm of x in the base 10 (common or Napier logarithm)
$\therefore$	Therefore
$:$	Ratio

Geometry

$\sim$	Similar
$\cong$	Congruent
Δ	Triangle
$\angle$ or $\measuredangle$	Angle
$\parallel$	Parallel
$\perp$	Perpendicular
$\llcorner$	Right angle
π	Pi
$\square$	Parallelogram
$\overline{AB}$	Line segment AB
$\overparen{AB}$	Arc AB

Logic

∧	And (conjunction)
∨	Or (disjunction)
→	Implies (If…, then…)
↔	Iff (If and only if)
~	Negation

Sets

$\{a, b\}$	A set with 2 elements, a and b
$\{x \mid x \geq 2\}$	The set of all x such that x is greater than or equal to 2
$\emptyset$ or $\{\ \}$	The null or empty set
$a \in B$	a is an element of B
$a \notin B$	a is not an element of B
$A \subseteq B$	Set A is a subset of set B
$A \not\subseteq B$	Set A is not a subset of set B
$A \cap B$	The intersection of sets A and B
$A \cup B$	The union of sets A and B

Probability, Statistics, and Counting

a^n	The value of the nth term of a sequence
S^N	The sum of n consecutive terms of a sequence
$\displaystyle\sum_{i=1}^{n} f(i)$	The summation of $f(i)$ from $i = 1$ to $i = n$
$n!$	n factorial, $n(n-1)(n-2)(n-3)\ldots(1)$
$\left.\begin{array}{l} {}_nP_r \\ P(n,r) \\ P_{n,r} \end{array}\right.$	The permutations of n things taken r at a time
$\left.\begin{array}{l} {}_nC_r \\ C(n,r) \\ \binom{n}{r} \\ C_{n,r} \end{array}\right]$	The combinations of n things taken r at a time
$P(E)$	The probability of event E
$\bar{x}$	The arithmetic mean, average

Preparing for the College Math Exam

Start your preparation for the CLEP exam in College Mathematics by taking the mini–exam that follows. These ten questions will give you a good idea of the scope of the exam and the level of difficulty of the questions. Next, move on to the first practice examination. This exam is like the actual CLEP exam in topics covered, numbers of questions devoted to each topic, and level of difficulty of the questions. Take this exam under actual test conditions. Allow yourself 45 minutes for each part. When you have completed the exam, compare your answers to the solutions provided. Following each exam is a Diagnostic Chart to help you pinpoint your strengths and weaknesses. Refer to the selected bibliography for a sampling of math texts to which you may refer for additional study in the areas that proved most difficult for you.

Then move on to the second and third practice exams. Take each one as if it were the real thing. Check your answers with the answer key and study the solutions provided at the end of each exam.

MINI–EXAM IN COLLEGE MATHEMATICS

Directions: Choose the best answer for each of the following questions.

1. Which of the following is an imaginary number?
   (A) $3 - \sqrt{7}$
   (B) π
   (C) $\sqrt{17}$
   (D) $\sqrt{-3}$

2. Which set contains all values of x for which the fraction $\dfrac{x+2}{x^2-49}$ is undefined?
   (A) $\{0\}$
   (B) $\{-2\}$
   (C) $\{7\}$
   (D) $\{-7, 7\}$

3. Joshua asserts that $m \geq \dfrac{1}{m}$ for all real numbers. Which of the following values of m serves as a counterexample to Joshua's claim?
   (A) -1
   (B) $\dfrac{1}{2}$
   (C) 1
   (D) 2

4. What are the factors of $3y^2 + 4y - 4$?
   (A) $(3y - 2)(y + 2)$
   (B) $(3y - 4)(y + 1)$
   (C) $(3y + 2)(y - 2)$
   (D) $(3y + 1)(y - 4)$

5. Which of the following is a graph of a function?

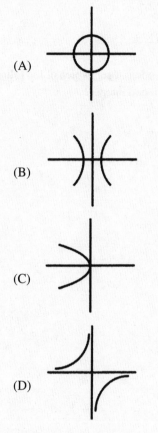

   (A)

   (B)

   (C)

   (D)

6. If $f(x) = 3[g(x + 1)]$ and $g(x) = 3x - 7$, what is the value of $f(-1)$?
   (A) -21
   (B) -6
   (C) 0
   (D) 4

7. What are the roots of the equation $2x^2 - 6x + 3 = 0$?

   (A) $\dfrac{-3 \pm \sqrt{3}}{2}$

   (B) $\dfrac{-3 \pm \sqrt{15}}{2}$

   (C) $\dfrac{3 \pm \sqrt{3}}{2}$

   (D) $\dfrac{3 \pm \sqrt{15}}{2}$

8. If Q is an odd integer, which of the following is NOT an odd integer?

   (A) $Q - 2$
   (B) $2Q - 3$
   (C) $Q^2 - 1$
   (D) $5Q - 4Q$

9. A number p equals $\dfrac{3}{2}$ the average of 10, 12, and q. What is q in terms of p?

   (A) $\dfrac{2}{3}p - 22$

   (B) $\dfrac{1}{2}p + 11$

   (C) $2p - 22$

   (D) $\dfrac{4}{3}p - 22$

10. If $\log_x a = 3$ and $\log_x b = 5$, then $\log_x a^2 \sqrt{b} =$

    (A) $9 + \sqrt{5}$

    (B) $9\sqrt{5}$

    (C) $8\dfrac{1}{2}$

    (D) $13\dfrac{1}{2}$

Answer Key

1. D	3. B	5. D	7. C	9. C
2. D	4. A	6. A	8. C	10. C

Explanatory Answers

1. **The correct answer is (D).** Imaginary numbers occur from the square root of a negative number. Imaginary numbers are usually written in terms of the letter "i", which is defined as: $i = \sqrt{-1}$.

    $\sqrt{-3} = \sqrt{-1}\sqrt{3} = i\sqrt{3}$

2. **The correct answer is (D).** The fraction is undefined when the denominator $= 0$.

    $x^2 - 49 = 0$

    $x^2 = 49$

    $x = \pm 7$

    $\{-7, 7\}$

3. **The correct answer is (B).**

    $-1 = \dfrac{1}{-1}, \ 1 = \dfrac{1}{1}, \ 2 > \dfrac{1}{2}$

    However, when $m = \dfrac{1}{2} \to \dfrac{1}{2}$ is not greater than or equal to $\dfrac{1}{\frac{1}{2}}$

    $\dfrac{1}{2} < \dfrac{1}{\frac{1}{2}}$

    $\dfrac{1}{2} < 2$

4. **The correct answer is (A).** $3y^2 + 4y - 4$

    $(3y - 2)(y + 2)$

5. **The correct answer is (D).** Only graph (D) passes the vertical line test.

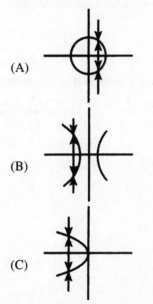

    (A)

    (B)

    (C)

6. **The correct answer is (A).**

    $f(-1) = 3[g(-1+1)]$

    $= 3[g(0)]$

    $g(0) = 3(0) - 7 = -7$

    $\therefore f(-1) = 3[-7] = -21$

7. **The correct answer is (C).**

$$x = \frac{-b \pm \sqrt{b^2 - 4ac}}{2a} \qquad a = 2$$

$$x = \frac{-(-6) \pm \sqrt{(-6)^2 - (4)(2)(3)}}{(2)(2)} \qquad b = -6$$

$$c = 3$$

$$x = \frac{6 \pm \sqrt{36 - 24}}{4}$$

$$x = \frac{6 \pm \sqrt{12}}{4}$$

$$x = \frac{6 \pm 2\sqrt{3}}{4}$$

$$x = \frac{3 \pm \sqrt{3}}{2}$$

8. **The correct answer is (C).** Try numbers:

let Q	= 1		let Q	= 7	
$Q - 2$	$= -1$	odd	$Q - 2$	$= 5$	
$2Q - 3$	$= -1$	odd	$2Q - 3$	$= 11$	
$Q^2 - 1$	$= 0$	even	$Q^2 - 1$	$= 48$	
$5Q - 4Q$	$= 1$	odd	$5Q - 4Q$	$= 7$	

9. **The correct answer is (C).**

$$\text{Average} = \frac{\text{Sum of the numbers}}{\text{Quantity of numbers}}$$

$$p = \frac{3}{2}\left[\frac{10 + 12 + q}{3}\right]$$

$$p = \frac{10 + 12 + q}{2}$$

$$p = \frac{22 + q}{2}$$

$$2p = 22 + q$$

$$q = 2p - 22$$

10. **The correct answer is (C).**

$$\log_x a^2 \sqrt{b} = \log_x a^2 + \log_x \sqrt{b}$$

$$= 2\log_x a + \frac{1}{2}\log_x b$$

$$= 2(3) + \frac{1}{2}(5)$$

$$= 6 + 2\frac{1}{2} = 8\frac{1}{2}$$

Answer Sheet for Practice Examination I

Section I

1 Ⓐ Ⓑ Ⓒ Ⓓ   8 Ⓐ Ⓑ Ⓒ Ⓓ   15 Ⓐ Ⓑ Ⓒ Ⓓ   22 Ⓐ Ⓑ Ⓒ Ⓓ   29 Ⓐ Ⓑ Ⓒ Ⓓ

2 Ⓐ Ⓑ Ⓒ Ⓓ   9 Ⓐ Ⓑ Ⓒ Ⓓ   16 Ⓐ Ⓑ Ⓒ Ⓓ   23 Ⓐ Ⓑ Ⓒ Ⓓ   30 Ⓐ Ⓑ Ⓒ Ⓓ

3 Ⓐ Ⓑ Ⓒ Ⓓ   10 Ⓐ Ⓑ Ⓒ Ⓓ   17 Ⓐ Ⓑ Ⓒ Ⓓ   24 Ⓐ Ⓑ Ⓒ Ⓓ   31 Ⓐ Ⓑ Ⓒ Ⓓ

4 Ⓐ Ⓑ Ⓒ Ⓓ   11 Ⓐ Ⓑ Ⓒ Ⓓ   18 Ⓐ Ⓑ Ⓒ Ⓓ   25 Ⓐ Ⓑ Ⓒ Ⓓ   32 Ⓐ Ⓑ Ⓒ Ⓓ

5 Ⓐ Ⓑ Ⓒ Ⓓ   12 Ⓐ Ⓑ Ⓒ Ⓓ   19 Ⓐ Ⓑ Ⓒ Ⓓ   26 Ⓐ Ⓑ Ⓒ Ⓓ   33 Ⓐ Ⓑ Ⓒ Ⓓ

6 Ⓐ Ⓑ Ⓒ Ⓓ   13 Ⓐ Ⓑ Ⓒ Ⓓ   20 Ⓐ Ⓑ Ⓒ Ⓓ   27 Ⓐ Ⓑ Ⓒ Ⓓ

7 Ⓐ Ⓑ Ⓒ Ⓓ   14 Ⓐ Ⓑ Ⓒ Ⓓ   21 Ⓐ Ⓑ Ⓒ Ⓓ   28 Ⓐ Ⓑ Ⓒ Ⓓ

Section II

34 Ⓐ Ⓑ Ⓒ Ⓓ   41 Ⓐ Ⓑ Ⓒ Ⓓ   48 Ⓐ Ⓑ Ⓒ Ⓓ   55 Ⓐ Ⓑ Ⓒ Ⓓ   62 Ⓐ Ⓑ Ⓒ Ⓓ

35 Ⓐ Ⓑ Ⓒ Ⓓ   42 Ⓐ Ⓑ Ⓒ Ⓓ   49 Ⓐ Ⓑ Ⓒ Ⓓ   56 Ⓐ Ⓑ Ⓒ Ⓓ   63 Ⓐ Ⓑ Ⓒ Ⓓ

36 Ⓐ Ⓑ Ⓒ Ⓓ   43 Ⓐ Ⓑ Ⓒ Ⓓ   50 Ⓐ Ⓑ Ⓒ Ⓓ   57 Ⓐ Ⓑ Ⓒ Ⓓ   64 Ⓐ Ⓑ Ⓒ Ⓓ

37 Ⓐ Ⓑ Ⓒ Ⓓ   44 Ⓐ Ⓑ Ⓒ Ⓓ   51 Ⓐ Ⓑ Ⓒ Ⓓ   58 Ⓐ Ⓑ Ⓒ Ⓓ   65 Ⓐ Ⓑ Ⓒ Ⓓ

38 Ⓐ Ⓑ Ⓒ Ⓓ   45 Ⓐ Ⓑ Ⓒ Ⓓ   52 Ⓐ Ⓑ Ⓒ Ⓓ   59 Ⓐ Ⓑ Ⓒ Ⓓ

39 Ⓐ Ⓑ Ⓒ Ⓓ   46 Ⓐ Ⓑ Ⓒ Ⓓ   53 Ⓐ Ⓑ Ⓒ Ⓓ   60 Ⓐ Ⓑ Ⓒ Ⓓ

40 Ⓐ Ⓑ Ⓒ Ⓓ   47 Ⓐ Ⓑ Ⓒ Ⓓ   54 Ⓐ Ⓑ Ⓒ Ⓓ   61 Ⓐ Ⓑ Ⓒ Ⓓ

PRACTICE EXAMINATION I

Section I

33 Questions

Time—45 minutes

Directions: For each question that follows, choose the best answer choice (A), (B), (C), or (D) and darken the corresponding oval on the answer sheet.

Time: 45 minutes for Part 1, 45 minutes for Part 2

Notes:
(1) i represents $\sqrt{-1}$.
(2) Figures that accompany a problem are designed to provide information and are drawn as accurately as possible UNLESS the wording "Figure not drawn to scale" is indicated.
(3) All figures lie in a plane unless otherwise indicated.
(4) The domain of a function is assumed to be the set of all real numbers unless otherwise indicated.

1. Which of the following is the greatest in value?

$$|-9|,-\frac{1}{2},-\frac{1}{4},7,0$$

(A) $|-9|$
(B) $-\frac{1}{4}$
(C) 7
(D) 0

2. All of the following numbers are real EXCEPT

(A) .13131
(B) $\frac{1}{127}$
(C) $\sqrt{59}$
(D) $\sqrt{-11}$

3. If n is an odd integer, which of the following must be odd?

(A) $n + 1$
(B) $(n + 1)^2$
(C) n^2
(D) $n^2 + 1$

4. Which of the following sets contains only the prime factor(s) of 18?

(A) {3}
(B) {2, 3}
(C) {2, 3, 6}
(D) {2, 3, 6, 9}

5. If $a = \{x \mid 5 > x > 2\}$ and $b = \{x \mid 9 > x > 7\}$, how many integers are in $a \bigcup b$?

(A) Seven
(B) Five
(C) Three
(D) One

6. If $m(r) = (1)r - (r)^0 - r$, then $m(-7) =$

(A) 1
(B) 5
(C) 7
(D) 9

7. Which of the following tables expresses a relation that is NOT a function?

(A)

x	y
1	7
2	7
3	7
4	7

(B)

x	y
7	1
7	2
7	3
7	4

(C)

x	y
1	1
2	2
3	3
4	4

(D)

x	y
1	2
2	1
3	4
4	3

8. Which of the following does $(A \cap C) \cup B$ represent?

    (A)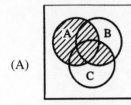

    (B)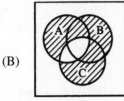

    (C)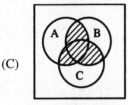

    (D)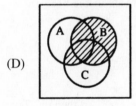

9. If $f(x) = x^2$, then $f(x-1) =$

    (A) $x^2(x-1)$
    (B) $(x-1)^2$
    (C) $x^2 - 1$
    (D) $(x-1)^2 - 1$

10. If $f(x) = (x-3)(x+3)(x-1)$, what is the product of the roots?

    (A) -9
    (B) -1
    (C) 1
    (D) 9

11. What is the slope of the line whose equation is $\frac{x}{3} + \frac{y}{2} = 1$?

    (A) -3
    (B) -2
    (C) $\frac{-3}{2}$
    (D) $\frac{-2}{3}$

12. Dawn asserts that $x^3 \geq x^2$ for all real values of x. Of the following, which is a value of x that provides a counterexample to Dawn's claim?

    (A) -7
    (B) 0
    (C) 1
    (D) 7

13. The binary number preceding the binary number 101010 is

    (A) 101110
    (B) 100011
    (C) 101001
    (D) 101011

14. If set $A = \{$quadrilaterals$\}$ and set $B = \{$square, pentagon, trapezoid, rhombus, diamond$\}$,

    what is $A \text{ I } B$?

    (A) {square, trapezoid, rhombus, diamond}
    (B) {square, trapezoid, diamond}
    (C) {square, pentagon, trapezoid, rhombus}
    (D) {square, trapezoid, rhombus}

15. If the mode of the following numbers is 8, what is the value of x?

    $1, 2, 3, 4, 4, 5, 6, 7, 8, 8, x$

    (A) 4
    (B) 8
    (C) 9
    (D) 10

16. Which set contains the number π?

    (A) Integers
    (B) Rational numbers
    (C) Natural numbers
    (D) Irrational numbers

17. There are seven boys and three girls on the school tennis team. The coach must select four people from this group to participate in a match. In how many ways can two boys and two girls be chosen for the team?

    (A) 21
    (B) 42
    (C) 54
    (D) 63

18. What is the negation of "I am blue OR I am tall"?

    (A) I am not blue OR I am not tall
    (B) I am not tall OR I am not blue
    (C) I am not blue AND I am not tall
    (D) I am not tall AND I am blue

19. What is the value of $d * (a * n)$ in the system defined in the accompanying table?

*	d	a	w	n
d	w	n	d	a
a	n	w	a	d
w	d	a	w	n
n	a	d	n	w

    (A) d
    (B) a
    (C) w
    (D) n

20. What is the average (arithmetic mean) of $\frac{a+b}{3}$ and $\frac{a-b}{2}$?

    (A) $\frac{2a-3b}{5}$
    (B) $\frac{5a-b}{12}$
    (C) $\frac{-a-b}{6}$
    (D) $\frac{5a-2b}{12}$

21. In the accompanying figure, the degree measure of central angle NJL is 70. What is the degree measure of angle NBL?

    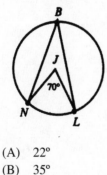

    (A) 22°
    (B) 35°
    (C) 50°
    (D) 70°

22. If a club has 12 members, how many different two–person committees can be formed?

    (A) 6
    (B) 22
    (C) 33
    (D) 66

23. Which of the following functions is represented in the accompanying graph?

    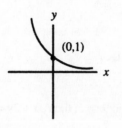

    (A) $y = f(x) = 3x$
    (B) $y = f(x) = 3^{-x}$
    (C) $y = f(x) = \log_3 x$
    (D) $y = f(x) = -3x$

24. For which one of the following values of c are the roots of the given equation imaginary? $y = 2x^2 - 3x + c$

    (A) -1
    (B) 0
    (C) 1
    (D) 2

25. $(x - 1)(x - 2)(x - 3)$ is equal to all of the following EXCEPT

    (A) $-(1 - x)(2 - x)(3 - x)$
    (B) $(1 - x)(2 - x)(x - 3)$
    (C) $(x - 1)(2 - x)(3 - x)$
    (D) $-(x - 1)(2 - x)(3 - x)$

26. If the diagonal of square $ABCD$ is 3, what is the length of one of its sides?

    (A) $\frac{\sqrt{6}}{2}$
    (B) $\frac{2\sqrt{2}}{3}$
    (C) $\frac{9\sqrt{2}}{2}$
    (D) $\frac{3\sqrt{2}}{2}$

27. The accompanying graph could represent which one of the following equations?

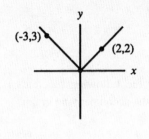

(A) $y = -x$
(B) $y = |x|$
(C) $x = |y|$
(D) $y = x^2$

28. If $3x = 12$ and $9y = 5$, then $3x + 2y =$

(A) 30
(B) 60
(C) 90
(D) 120

29. If $8^{1.3741} = a$, then $\log_8 8a =$

(A) $(8)(1.3741)$
(B) $(1.3741) + 8$
(C) $(1.3741) + 1$
(D) $.3741$

30. In the accompanying figure of quadrilateral $ABCD$, the degree measure of $\angle A = 120°$, the degree measure of $\angle B = 82°$, and the degree measure of $\angle D = 93°$. What is the degree measure of $\angle C$?

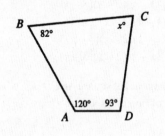

(A) 60°
(B) 65°
(C) 78°
(D) 103°

31. If $\dfrac{x}{y} = \dfrac{1}{3}$, which of the following must be true?

(A) $x = 1$
(B) $x \geq 1$
(C) $y > x$
(D) $y^2 > x^2$

32. If $\log_7 2 = w$ and $\log_7 3 = r$, then in terms of w and r, $\log_7 42 =$

(A) $r + w$
(B) $1 + r + w$
(C) $7rw$
(D) $7 + r + w$

33. If n represents the term number, then in terms of n, which of the following represents the sum of the first n terms of the series:

$$1^3 + 2^3 + 3^3 + 4^3 + \dots n^3$$

(A) $\dfrac{n}{n+1}$

(B) $\dfrac{n(n+1)}{2}$

(C) $\dfrac{n^2(n+1)^2}{4}$

(D) $\dfrac{n^3 + 3}{n}$

Section II

32 Questions
Time—45 minutes

34. Which of the following is a rational number?
    (A) -3
    (B) $\sqrt{3}$
    (C) $\sqrt{-3}$
    (D) π

35. $\dfrac{(-1)(2)(-3)(4)(-5)}{(5)(-4)(3)(-2)(1)} =$
    (A) 1
    (B) -1
    (C) 2
    (D) -2

36. Which of the following is a factor of $3x^3 - x^2 - 2x$?
    (A) $x + 1$
    (B) $x - 2$
    (C) $3x + 2$
    (D) $3x - 2$

37. If x and y are negative integers, which of the following must be a negative integer?
    (A) $x + y$
    (B) $x - y$
    (C) xy
    (D) $\dfrac{x}{y}$

38. In the accompanying figure, line l_1 is parallel to line l_2. Transversals t_1 and t_2 are drawn. What is the value of $a + b + c + d$?

    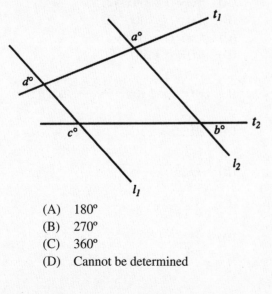

    (A) 180°
    (B) 270°
    (C) 360°
    (D) Cannot be determined

39. Which of the following is NOT the graph of a function?

    (A)

    (B)

    (C)

    (D)

    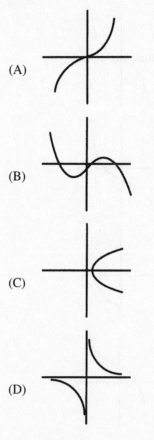

40. If the x-intercept of a line is 3 and the y-intercept is 5, which one of the following represents the equation of the line?
    (A) $\dfrac{x}{3} + \dfrac{y}{5} = 1$
    (B) $\dfrac{x}{5} + \dfrac{y}{3} = 1$
    (C) $\dfrac{x}{3} - \dfrac{y}{5} = 1$
    (D) $\dfrac{x}{5} - \dfrac{y}{3} = 1$

41. A cafeteria offers a choice of five sandwiches, three salads, and three beverages. How many different meals can be chosen if each meal consists of one sandwich, one salad, and one beverage?
    (A) 1
    (B) 5
    (C) 11
    (D) 45

42. Which of the following represents a graph of $y = x^3 - 2$?

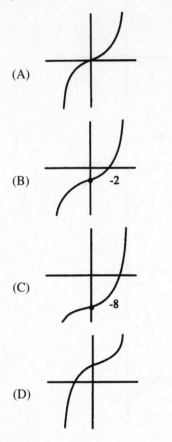

(A)

(B)   -2

(C)

    -8

(D)

43. If $i = \sqrt{-1}$, then $i^{4,097} =$
    (A) 1
    (B) i
    (C) −1
    (D) −i

44. In the figure shown, A is the midpoint of $\overline{NJ}$ and B is the midpoint of $\overline{NL}$. What is the area ratio of $\triangle NAB$ to $\triangle NJL$?

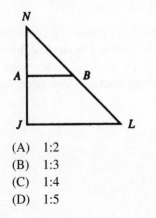

    (A) 1:2
    (B) 1:3
    (C) 1:4
    (D) 1:5

45. If the point (2, 3) is on the graph of $f(x) = 2x^2 + 2x + K$, what is the value of K?
    (A) −17
    (B) −12
    (C) −9
    (D) 9

46. For what value of x is $\dfrac{(x-7)(x+4)}{x^2 - 2x + 1}$ undefined?
    (A) 7
    (B) 4
    (C) 2
    (D) 1

47. For which one of the following values of a are the roots of the given equation equal? $y = ax^2 - 3x + 4$
    (A) $\dfrac{9}{16}$
    (B) $\dfrac{3}{4}$
    (C) 1
    (D) $\dfrac{15}{8}$

48. The accompanying graph could represent which of the following functions?

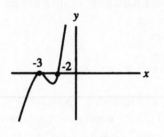

    (A) $f(x) = (x - 3)^2(x - 2)$
    (B) $f(x) = (x - 3)(x - 2)^2$
    (C) $f(x) = (x + 3)^2(x + 2)$
    (D) $f(x) = (x + 3)(x + 2)^2$

49. If $g(f(x)) = x$ and $g(x) = \dfrac{3x - 2}{4}$, then $f(x) =$
    (A) $\dfrac{3x + 2}{4}$
    (B) $\dfrac{2x - 3}{4}$
    (C) $\dfrac{4x + 2}{3}$
    (D) $\dfrac{3x - 2}{4}$

50. What is the solution set of the equation $|x - 1| = 2x$?

    (A) { }

    (B) $\left\{ \dfrac{1}{3} \right\}$

    (C) $\left\{ \dfrac{1}{3}, -1 \right\}$

    (D) $\{-1\}$

51. Leighna picked a letter from the word "WIN" at random and then picked a letter from the word "GAME" at random. Find the probability that one of the letters chosen was an "N" and the other was an "M".

    (A) $\dfrac{1}{12}$

    (B) $\dfrac{1}{7}$

    (C) $\dfrac{2}{12}$

    (D) $\dfrac{2}{7}$

52. If 1 twig = 2 branches, 1 branch = 3 limbs, and 1 limb = 4 stems, then 4 twigs are equal to how many stems?

    (A) 12

    (B) 24

    (C) 48

    (D) 96

53. If $x \odot y$ is a binary operation defined as $x + \dfrac{1}{y}$, evaluate $\dfrac{1}{2} \odot \dfrac{1}{4}$.

    (A) $\dfrac{2}{9}$

    (B) $\dfrac{3}{4}$

    (C) $\dfrac{9}{2}$

    (D) 6

54. If $i = \sqrt{-1}$, what is the value of $(1 + 2i)^2$?

    (A) $2 + 4i$

    (B) $1 + 4i$

    (C) $-1 + 4i$

    (D) $-3 + 4i$

55. Which of the following is NOT equal to $x^2 - 1$?

    (A) $(x - 1)(x + 1)$

    (B) $(x - 1)^2 - 2$

    (C) $(x + 1)^2 - 2x - 2$

    (D) $(x + 2)(x - 2) + 3$

56. The average of four items is 10. The average of 6 other items is 12. What is the average of all ten items?

    (A) 10.8

    (B) 10.9

    (C) 11

    (D) 11.2

57. Which statement would be a correct heading for the last column of the accompanying table?

p	q	NOT q ($\sim q$)	?
T	T	F	F
T	F	T	T
F	T	F	T
F	F	T	F

    (A) q implies not q $(q \rightarrow \sim q)$

    (B) p and not q $(p \wedge \sim q)$

    (C) p iff not q $(p \leftrightarrow \sim q)$

    (D) p or not q $(p \vee \sim q)$

58. In a standard deck of 52 cards, what is the probability of picking a red card or a 5?

    (A) $\dfrac{24}{52}$

    (B) $\dfrac{26}{52}$

    (C) $\dfrac{28}{52}$

    (D) $\dfrac{30}{52}$

59. In the accompanying figure, l_1 is parallel to l_2, the degree measure of angle x is 70, and the degree measure of angle y is 105. What is the degree measure of angle z?

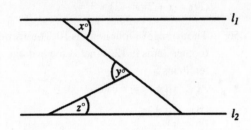

Figure not drawn to scale.

(A) 15°
(B) 35°
(C) 75°
(D) 110°

60. What is the remainder when $2x^3 - 3x^2 + 4x - 1$ is divided by $x - 1$?

(A) 2
(B) 3
(C) 4
(D) 5

61. In a box, there are five balls. Three are red and two are white. Two balls are drawn without replacement. What is the probability that both are red?

(A) $\dfrac{3}{5}$

(B) $\dfrac{6}{25}$

(C) $\dfrac{3}{10}$

(D) $\dfrac{1}{2}$

62. Which of the following is a root of $3x^2 + 2x + 1 = 0$?

(A) $\dfrac{-1 + i\sqrt{2}}{3}$

(B) $\dfrac{-2 + 3i\sqrt{2}}{5}$

(C) $-1 - i\sqrt{2}$

(D) $\dfrac{-2 + 5i\sqrt{2}}{6}$

63. If $6x = 18$ and $6y = 24$, then $6^{(x + y)} =$

(A) 432
(B) 252
(C) 42
(D) 7

64. If $\log ab = 7$, then $\log a\dfrac{1}{b} =$

(A) –7
(B) 7
(C) $\dfrac{1}{7}$
(D) $\dfrac{-1}{7}$

65. $2^{400} + 2^{400} =$

(A) 2^{401}
(B) 2^{800}
(C) 2^{160000}
(D) 4^{800}

End of Practice Examination I

Answer Key

Section I

1.	A	8.	D	15.	B	22.	D	29.	C
2.	D	9.	B	16.	D	23.	B	30.	B
3.	C	10.	A	17.	D	24.	D	31.	D
4.	B	11.	D	18.	C	25.	D	32.	B
5.	C	12.	A	19.	C	26.	D	33.	C
6.	C	13.	C	20.	B	27.	B		
7.	B	14.	A	21.	B	28.	B		

Section II

34.	A	41.	D	48.	C	55.	B	62.	A
35.	B	42.	B	49.	C	56.	D	63.	A
36.	C	43.	B	50.	B	57.	C	64.	A
37.	A	44.	C	51.	A	58.	C	65.	A
38.	C	45.	C	52.	D	59.	B		
39.	C	46.	D	53.	C	60.	A		
40.	A	47.	A	54.	D	61.	C		

Explanatory Answers

Section I

1. **The correct answer is (A).** $|-9| = 9$, which is the greatest of the five values.

2. **The correct answer is (D).** .13131 is real and rational, $\frac{1}{127}$ is real and rational, $\sqrt{59}$ is real and irrational, and $\sqrt{-11}$ is imaginary.

   Imaginary numbers are NOT real numbers. Real numbers can be either rational or irrational.

3. **The correct answer is (C).** Try using a numerical value.

   Let $n = 3$ $\quad n + 1 = 4$
   $$(n+1)^2 = 16$$
   $$n^2 = 9$$
   $$n^2 + 1 = 10$$

4. **The correct answer is (B).** $18 = 2 \cdot 3^2$

   Two and three are the prime factors of 18.

5. **The correct answer is (C).** In set a, the integers are $\{4,3\}$. The only integer in set b is $\{8\}$. a , b is the union of both sets $\{3,4,8\}$.

6. **The correct answer is (C).**

   $$m(r) = (1)^r - (r)^0 - r$$
   $$m(-7) = (1)^{-7} - (-7)^0 - (-7)$$
   $$= 1 - (1) + 7$$
   $$= 7$$

7. **The correct answer is (B).** Simply stated, to be a function the same value of x cannot give two or more different y–values. If it does, it is not a function. Choice (B) maps $x = 7$ into $y = 1, 2, 3, 4$; therefore choice (B) is NOT a function.

8. **The correct answer is (D).** First find $(A \cap C)$. This is the intersection of the sets that consists of the common elements.

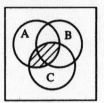

Then, locate B.

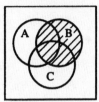

Finally, construct $(A \cap C) \cup B$, which is the union of all the elements in $(A \cap C)$ and B.

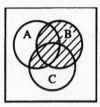

9. **The correct answer is (B).**

   $$f(x) = x^2$$
   $$f(x-1) = (x-1)^2$$

10. **The correct answer is (A).**

    $$f(x) = (x - 3)(x + 3)(x - 1)$$
    $$(x - 3)(x + 3)(x - 1) = 0$$
    $$x = 3 \quad x = -3 \quad x = 1$$

    Sum = 1, Product = –9

11. **The correct answer is (D).** Rearrange the equation into $y = mx + b$ form. First, multiply each side of the equation by 6:

$$(6)\left(\frac{x}{3}\right)+\left(\frac{y}{2}\right)(6)=(1)(6)$$

$$2x+3y=6$$

Next, solve for y: $3y = -2x+6$

$$y = -\frac{2}{3}x+2$$

$$\text{Slope} = -\frac{2}{3}$$

12. **The correct answer is (A).**

$(-7)^3$ is less than $(-7)^2$ while $(0)^3 = (0)^2$

$$(1)^3 = (1)^2$$

$$(7)^3 > (7)^2$$

13. **The correct answer is (C).** 1 0 1 0 1 0 is preceded by 1 0 1 0 0 1 and followed by 1 0 1 0 1 1.

14. **The correct answer is (A).** Quadrilaterals are four–sided polygons. A square, a trapezoid, a rhombus, and a diamond are all four–sided polygons.

A pentagon has five sides.

The intersection (overlap) includes the square, trapezoid, rhombus, and diamond.

15. **The correct answer is (B).** The mode is the most frequently occurring number. Since there are two 4s, and the mode is 8, there are more 8s than 4s. Hence $x = 8$.

16. **The correct answer is (D).** π is a never-ending, nonrepeating decimal number. It is real and irrational.

17. **The correct answer is (D).**

7	3
Boys	Girls

2 boys are chosen: $_7C_2$ ways = 21

2 girls are chosen: $_3C_2$ ways = 3

A 2 boy, 2 girl team can be chosen in $21(3) = 63$ ways.

18. **The correct answer is (C).**

Symbolically $\sim (P \lor Q) = \sim P \land \sim Q$

The negation of "I am blue OR I am tall" is

"I am not blue AND I am not tall."

This is DeMorgan's Law.

19. **The correct answer is (C).**

$$(a*n)=d$$
$$d*(a*n)=d*d=w$$

20. **The correct answer is (B).**

$$\text{Average} = \frac{\text{Sum of the items}}{\text{Quantity of items}}$$

$$=\frac{\left(\frac{a+b}{3}\right)+\left(\frac{a-b}{2}\right)}{2}$$

$$=\frac{\frac{2(a+b)+3(a-b)}{6}}{2}$$

$$=\frac{2a+2b+3a-3b}{12}$$

$$=\frac{5a-b}{12}$$

21. **The correct answer is (B).** Angle NJL is a central angle. Arc $\overset{\frown}{NL} = 70°$ because a central angle is equal in measure to its intercepted arc. Angle NBL is an inscribed angle, whose intercepted arc is $\overset{\frown}{NL} = 70°$. The measure of an inscribed angle is half of the measure of its intercepted arc.

Angle $NBL = \frac{1}{2}(70°) = 35°$.

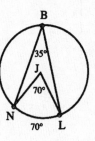

22. **The correct answer is (D).** $_{12}C_2 = \frac{12(11)}{2(1)} = 66$

23. **The correct answer is (B).** This is the graph of $y = 3-x$ or $y = \left(\frac{1}{3}\right)^x$.

24. **The correct answer is (D).** $y = ax^2 + bx + c$.

    The roots are imaginary when $b^2 - 4ac < 0$

    $a = 2$, $b = -3$, $c = c$

    $b^2 - 4ac = (-3)^2 - 4(2)(c)$

    $b^2 - 4ac = 9 - 8c$

    if $c = -1$ $9 - 8c = 17$

    if $c = 0$ $9 - 8c = 9$

    if $c = 1$ $9 - 8c = 1$

    if $c = 2$ $9 - 8c = -7 \leftarrow$ imaginary roots

25. **The correct answer is (D).**

    (A) $(x-1)(x-2)(x-3)$

    $=$ $[-(1-x)][-(2-x)][-(3-x)]$

    $=$ $-(1-x)(2-x)(3-x)$

    (B) $(x-1)(x-2)(x-3)$

    $=$ $[-(1-x)][-(2-x)][(x-3)]$

    $=$ $(1-x)(2-x)(x-3)$

    (C) $(x-1)(x-2)(x-3)$

    $=$ $[(x-1)][-(2-x)][-(3-x)]$

    $=$ $(x-1)(2-x)(3-x)$

    (D) $(x-1)(x-2)(x-3)$

    $=$ $[(x-1)][-(2-x)][-(3-x)]$

    $=$ $(x-1)(2-x)(3-x)$

    $\neq$ $-(x-1)(2-x)(3-x)$

26. **The correct answer is (D).**

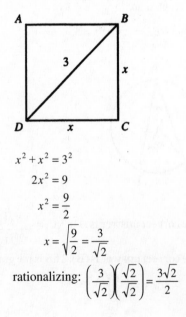

$x^2 + x^2 = 3^2$

$2x^2 = 9$

$x^2 = \dfrac{9}{2}$

$x = \sqrt{\dfrac{9}{2}} = \dfrac{3}{\sqrt{2}}$

rationalizing: $\left(\dfrac{3}{\sqrt{2}}\right)\left(\dfrac{\sqrt{2}}{\sqrt{2}}\right) = \dfrac{3\sqrt{2}}{2}$

27. **The correct answer is (B).** A V–shaped graph is usually indicative of an absolute value function.

    By substituting the given coordinates $(2, 2)$, $(0, 0)$, and $(-3, 3)$ into the answer choices, only $y = |x|$ satisfies all the ordered pairs.

28. **The correct answer is (B).**

    $3x + {}^2y = 3x \cdot 3^2 y = 12(5) = 60$

    because: $3^x = 12$

    $9^y = \left(3^2\right)^y = 3^{2y} = 5$

29. **The correct answer is (C).**

    $\log_8 8a = \log_8 8 + \log_8 a$

    $\log_8 8 = 1$ $8^{1.3741} = a$

    $\Downarrow$

    $\log_8 a = 1.3741$

    $\therefore \log_8 8a = 1 + 1.3741 = 2.3741$

30. **The correct answer is (B).** The sum of the measures of the four angles of a quadrilateral is 360°.

    $m\angle A + m\angle B + m\angle C + m\angle D = 360°$

    $120° + 82° + x + 93° = 360°$

    $295° + x = 360°$

    $x = 65°$

31. **The correct answer is (D).** Examine each choice.

    (A) If $x = 2$ and $y = 6$

    $\dfrac{x}{y} = \dfrac{2}{6} = \dfrac{1}{3}$

    $\therefore x$ must equal one is NOT TRUE.

    (B) If $x = \dfrac{1}{2}$ and $y = \dfrac{3}{2}$

    $\dfrac{x}{y} = \dfrac{\left(\dfrac{1}{2}\right)}{\left(\dfrac{3}{2}\right)} =$

    $\therefore x$ must be greater than or equal to one is NOT TRUE.

    (C) If $x = -1$ and $y = -3$

    $\dfrac{x}{y} = \dfrac{-1}{-3} = \dfrac{1}{3}$

    y is NOT greater than x.

32. **The correct answer is (B).**

$$log_7 42 = log_7(7)(3)(2)$$
$$= log_7 7 + log_7 3 + log_7 2$$
$$= 1 + r + w$$

33. **The correct answer is (C).** By trial and error

i.e., let $n = 4$

$$1^3 + 2^3 + 3^3 + 4^3 =$$
$$\frac{n^2(n+1)^2}{4} = \frac{4^2(4+1)^2}{4} = \frac{16(25)}{4} = 100$$
$$1 + 8 + 27 + 64 = 100$$

Section II

34. **The correct answer is (A).** -3 is rational, $\sqrt{3}$ is irrational, $\sqrt{-3}$ is imaginary, and π is irrational.

A rational number can be expressed in the form $\frac{p}{q}$, where p and q are integers ($q \neq 0$).

Irrational numbers include:

•Never-ending, nonrepeating decimals

•The square root of numbers that are not perfect squares

35. **The correct answer is (B).**

$$\frac{(-1)(2)(-3)(4)(-5)}{(1)(-2)(3)(-4)(5)} = \frac{-120}{+120} = -1$$

or by rearranging the denominator

$$\frac{(-1)(2)(-3)(4)(-5)}{(1)(-2)(3)(-4)(5)} = (-1)(-1)(-1)(-1)(-1) = -1$$

36. **The correct answer is (C).**

$$3x^3 - x^2 - 2x$$
$$= x(3x^2 - x - 2)$$
$$= x(3x + 2)(x - 1)$$

37. **The correct answer is (A).** Using a numerical example, we can demonstrate that choices (B), (C), and (D) can be made positive.

Let $x = -3$, $y = -4$.

(A) $x - y = -3 - (-4) = 1$

(B) $xy = (-3)(-4) = 12$

(C) $\frac{x}{y} = \frac{-3}{-4} = \frac{3}{4}$ and is also not an integer.

38. **The correct answer is (C).**

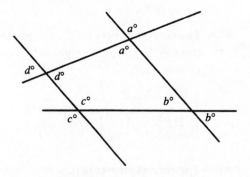

The sum of the interior angles of a quadrilateral is $360°$
$$\therefore a° + b° + c° + d° = 360$$

39. **The correct answer is (C).** Graph (C) fails the vertical line test.

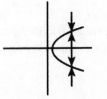

40. **The correct answer is (A).** x–intercept is 3 $\therefore$ (3, 0) is on the line.

y–intercept is 5 $\therefore$ (0, 5) is on the line.

slope $= \frac{\Delta y}{\Delta x} = \frac{5}{-3}$

$y = mx + b$

$y = -\frac{5}{3}x + 5$

$\Downarrow$

$y + \frac{5}{3}x = 5$

divide by 5

$$\frac{y}{5} + \frac{\left(\frac{5}{3}\right)x}{5} = \frac{(5)}{5}$$

$$\frac{y}{5} + \frac{x}{3} = 1$$

$\Downarrow$

$$\frac{x}{3} + \frac{y}{5} = 1$$

41. **The correct answer is (D).**

$$\underset{\text{(Sandwiches)}}{5} \times \underset{\text{(Salads)}}{3} \times \underset{\text{(Beverages)}}{3} = 45$$

42. **The correct answer is (B).**

(A) $y = x^3$

(B) $y = x^3 - 2$

(C) $y = (x-2)^3$

(D) $y = x^3 + 2$ or $y = (x+2)^3$

43. **The correct answer is (B).** $4\overline{)4097}$ with 1024 on top

$\therefore i4{,}097 = i^1 = i$

44. **The correct answer is (C).** The area ratio of two similar triangles is equal to the square of the line ratio.

$\Delta NAB \sim \Delta NJL$

$\dfrac{\text{Area } \Delta NAB}{\text{Area } \Delta NJL} = \left(\dfrac{NB}{NL}\right)^2 = \left(\dfrac{1}{2}\right)^2 = \dfrac{1}{4}$

45. **The correct answer is (C).**

$y = 2x^2 + 2x + K$

$3 = 2(2)^2 + 2(2) + K$

$3 = 2(4) + (4) + K$

$3 = 12 + K$

$K = -9$

46. **The correct answer is (D).** An expression is undefined when the denominator equals zero.

$x^2 - 2x + 1 = 0$

$(x-1)(x-1) = 0$

$x = 1$

47. **The correct answer is (A).** $y = ax^2 + bx + c$

The roots are real and equal when $b^2 - 4ac = 0$

$a = a, b = -3, c = 4$

$b^2 - 4ac = (-3)^2 - 4(a)(4)$

$= 9 - 16a = 0$

$16a = 9$

$a = \dfrac{9}{16}$

48. **The correct answer is (C).** There is a double root at $x = -3$ and a single root at $x = -2$.

The factors are: $(x + 3)$, $(x + 3)$, and $(x + 2)$

$\therefore f(x) = (x + 3)^2(x + 2)$

49. **The correct answer is (C).** If $g(f(x)) = x$, then $f(x)$ and $g(x)$ are inverse functions. To find the inverse of $\dfrac{3x-2}{4}$:

1) Replace $g(x)$ with y $\qquad y = \dfrac{3x-2}{4}$

2) Swap x and y $\qquad x = \dfrac{3y-2}{4}$

3) Solve for y $\qquad y = \dfrac{4x+2}{3}$

50. **The correct answer is (B).**

$|x - 1| = 2x$

$x - 1 = -2x \qquad\qquad x - 1 = 2x$

$-1 = -3x \qquad\qquad\quad x = -1$

$x = \dfrac{1}{3}$

check

$\left|\dfrac{1}{3} - 1\right| \overset{?}{=} 2\left(\dfrac{1}{3}\right) \qquad |-1 - 1| = 2(-1)$

$\left|-\dfrac{2}{3}\right| \overset{?}{=} \dfrac{2}{3} \qquad\qquad |-2| = -2$

$\checkmark \dfrac{2}{3} = \dfrac{2}{3} \qquad\qquad 2 \neq -2$

$\qquad\qquad\qquad\qquad$ Reject

51. **The correct answer is (A).** $P(N) = \frac{1}{3}$

$P(M) = \frac{1}{4}$

Probability $P(N \text{ and } M) = \left(\frac{1}{3}\right)\left(\frac{1}{4}\right) = \frac{1}{12}$

52. **The correct answer is (D).** $1T = 2B$

$1B = 3L$

$1L = 4S$

$1T = 2B = 2(3L) = 6L = 6(4S) = 24S$

$1T = 24S$

$\therefore 4T = 96S$

53. **The correct answer is (C).**

$x \odot y = x + \dfrac{1}{y}$

$\dfrac{1}{2} \odot \dfrac{1}{4} = \left(\dfrac{1}{2}\right) + \dfrac{1}{\left(\dfrac{1}{4}\right)} = \left(\dfrac{1}{2}\right) + (4) = \dfrac{9}{2}$

54. **The correct answer is (D).**

$(1 + 2i)^2 = (1 + 2i)(1 + 2i)$

$= 1 + 4i + 4i^2$

$= 1 + 4i + 4(-1)$

$= -3 + 4i$

55. **The correct answer is (B).**

(A) $(x - 1)(x + 1) = \boxed{x^2 - 1}$

(B) $(x - 1)^2 - 2 = (x - 1)(x - 1) - 2$

$= x^2 - 2x + 1 - 2 = \boxed{x^2 - 2x - 1}$

(C) $(x + 1)^2 - 2x - 2 = (x + 1)(x + 1) - 2x - 2$

$= x^2 + 2x + 1 - 2x - 2$

$= \boxed{x^2 - 1}$

(D) $(x + 2)(x - 2) + 3 = x^2 - 4 + 3 = \boxed{x^2 - 1}$

56. **The correct answer is (D).**

$$\text{Average} = \frac{\text{Sum of the items}}{\text{Quantity of items}}$$

$$\text{Average} = \frac{(4)(10)+(6)(12)}{10} = \frac{112}{10} = 11.2$$

57. **The correct answer is (C).** $p \leftrightarrow q$ is a biconditional. It is an "if and only if" statement, usually abbreviated as "iff." A biconditional is only true if both p and q have the same truth values. Otherwise, it is false. In the given table, $p \leftrightarrow \sim q$ is shown.

58. **The correct answer is (C).**

$$P(A \text{ or } B) = P(A) + P(B) - P(A \text{ and } B)$$
$$P(A) = P(\text{red card}) = \frac{26}{52}$$
$$P(B) = P(5) = \frac{4}{52}$$
$$P(A \text{ and } B) = P(\text{red } 5) = \frac{2}{52}$$
$$P(A \text{ or } B) = \frac{26}{52} + \frac{4}{52} - \frac{2}{52} = \frac{28}{52}$$

59. **The correct answer is (B).**

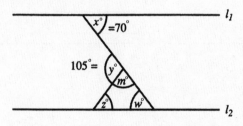

$m = 180° - 105° = 75°$ (Supplementary angles)

$w = x = 70°$ (Alternate interior angles)

$m + z + w = 180°$
$75° + z + 70° = 180°$
$z = 35°$

60. **The correct answer is (A).**

Method 1:

$$\begin{array}{r} 2x^2 - x + 3 \\ x-1\overline{)2x^3 - 3x^2 + 4x - 1} \\ \underline{2x^3 - 2x^2} \\ -x^2 + 4x - 1 \\ \underline{-x^2 + x} \\ 3x - 1 \\ \underline{3x - 3} \\ 2 \end{array}$$

Method 2:

$$\begin{array}{r|rrrr} \underline{1}| & 2 & -3 & 4 & -1 \\ & & 2 & -1 & 3 \\ \hline & 2 & -1 & 3 & \underline{|2} \end{array}$$

Method 3: $f(x) = 2x^3 - 3x^2 + 4x - 1$

$$f(1) = 2(1)^3 - 3(1)^2 + 4(1) - 1 = 2$$

61. **The correct answer is (C).** $P(\text{first is red}) = \frac{3}{5}$

There are now four balls to consider, with two reds left.

$P(\text{2nd ball is red, given that the first was red})$ $= \frac{2}{4}$

$P(\text{both red}) = P(\text{first red}) \cdot P(\text{2nd is red given that the first was red})$

$$= \left(\frac{3}{5}\right)\left(\frac{2}{4}\right) = \left(\frac{6}{20}\right) = \left(\frac{3}{10}\right)$$

62. **The correct answer is (A).**

$$x = \frac{-b \pm \sqrt{b^2 - 4ac}}{2a} \qquad a = 3$$
$$\qquad\qquad\qquad\qquad b = 2$$
$$= \frac{(-2) \pm \sqrt{4 - 4(3)(1)}}{2(3)} \qquad c = 1$$
$$= \frac{-2 \pm \sqrt{4 - 12}}{6}$$
$$= \frac{-2 \pm \sqrt{-8}}{6}$$
$$= \frac{-2 \pm 2i\sqrt{2}}{6} = \frac{-1 \pm i\sqrt{2}}{3}$$

63. **The correct answer is (A).**

$$6^{(x+y)} = 6^x \cdot 6^y$$
$$= 18 \cdot 24 = 432$$

64. **The correct answer is (A).**

$$\log a \frac{1}{b} = \log a 1 - \log ab$$
$$\log a 1 = 0$$
$$\log ab = 7$$
$$\therefore \log a \frac{1}{b} = 0 - 7 = -7$$

65. **The correct answer is (A).** $2^{400} + 2^{400}$

$$= (2)(2^{400})$$
$$= 2^1 \cdot 2^{400}$$
$$= 2^{401}$$

Practice Examination I Diagnostic Chart

Subject Area*	Question Numbers	Number Wrong
Logic and Sets	Part 1: 5, 8, 12, 14	_____
	Part 2: 57	_____
Number System and Systems	Part 1: 1, 2, 3, 4, 13, 16, 19, 31	_____
	Part 2: 34, 35, 37, 46, 53	_____
Functions and Graphs (Basic Algebra)	Part 1: 7, 11, 23, 27	_____
	Part 2: 39, 40, 42, 45, 48	_____
Probability, Statistics, and Counting	Part 1: 15, 17, 18, 20, 22, 33	_____
	Part 2: 41, 51, 56, 58, 61	_____
Algebra (Beyond Basics)	Part 1: 6, 9, 10, 24, 25, 28, 29, 32	_____
	Part 2: 36, 43, 47, 49, 50, 52, 54, 55, 60, 62, 63, 64, 65	_____
Geometry	Part 1: 21, 26, 30	_____
	Part 2: 38, 44, 59	_____

*Many questions overlap more than one subject area.

Answer Sheet for Practice Examination II

Section I

1 Ⓐ Ⓑ Ⓒ Ⓓ   8 Ⓐ Ⓑ Ⓒ Ⓓ   15 Ⓐ Ⓑ Ⓒ Ⓓ   22 Ⓐ Ⓑ Ⓒ Ⓓ   29 Ⓐ Ⓑ Ⓒ Ⓓ

2 Ⓐ Ⓑ Ⓒ Ⓓ   9 Ⓐ Ⓑ Ⓒ Ⓓ   16 Ⓐ Ⓑ Ⓒ Ⓓ   23 Ⓐ Ⓑ Ⓒ Ⓓ   30 Ⓐ Ⓑ Ⓒ Ⓓ

3 Ⓐ Ⓑ Ⓒ Ⓓ   10 Ⓐ Ⓑ Ⓒ Ⓓ   17 Ⓐ Ⓑ Ⓒ Ⓓ   24 Ⓐ Ⓑ Ⓒ Ⓓ   31 Ⓐ Ⓑ Ⓒ Ⓓ

4 Ⓐ Ⓑ Ⓒ Ⓓ   11 Ⓐ Ⓑ Ⓒ Ⓓ   18 Ⓐ Ⓑ Ⓒ Ⓓ   25 Ⓐ Ⓑ Ⓒ Ⓓ   32 Ⓐ Ⓑ Ⓒ Ⓓ

5 Ⓐ Ⓑ Ⓒ Ⓓ   12 Ⓐ Ⓑ Ⓒ Ⓓ   19 Ⓐ Ⓑ Ⓒ Ⓓ   26 Ⓐ Ⓑ Ⓒ Ⓓ   33 Ⓐ Ⓑ Ⓒ Ⓓ

6 Ⓐ Ⓑ Ⓒ Ⓓ   13 Ⓐ Ⓑ Ⓒ Ⓓ   20 Ⓐ Ⓑ Ⓒ Ⓓ   27 Ⓐ Ⓑ Ⓒ Ⓓ

7 Ⓐ Ⓑ Ⓒ Ⓓ   14 Ⓐ Ⓑ Ⓒ Ⓓ   21 Ⓐ Ⓑ Ⓒ Ⓓ   28 Ⓐ Ⓑ Ⓒ Ⓓ

Section II

34 Ⓐ Ⓑ Ⓒ Ⓓ   41 Ⓐ Ⓑ Ⓒ Ⓓ   48 Ⓐ Ⓑ Ⓒ Ⓓ   55 Ⓐ Ⓑ Ⓒ Ⓓ   62 Ⓐ Ⓑ Ⓒ Ⓓ

35 Ⓐ Ⓑ Ⓒ Ⓓ   42 Ⓐ Ⓑ Ⓒ Ⓓ   49 Ⓐ Ⓑ Ⓒ Ⓓ   56 Ⓐ Ⓑ Ⓒ Ⓓ   63 Ⓐ Ⓑ Ⓒ Ⓓ

36 Ⓐ Ⓑ Ⓒ Ⓓ   43 Ⓐ Ⓑ Ⓒ Ⓓ   50 Ⓐ Ⓑ Ⓒ Ⓓ   57 Ⓐ Ⓑ Ⓒ Ⓓ   64 Ⓐ Ⓑ Ⓒ Ⓓ

37 Ⓐ Ⓑ Ⓒ Ⓓ   44 Ⓐ Ⓑ Ⓒ Ⓓ   51 Ⓐ Ⓑ Ⓒ Ⓓ   58 Ⓐ Ⓑ Ⓒ Ⓓ   65 Ⓐ Ⓑ Ⓒ Ⓓ

38 Ⓐ Ⓑ Ⓒ Ⓓ   45 Ⓐ Ⓑ Ⓒ Ⓓ   52 Ⓐ Ⓑ Ⓒ Ⓓ   59 Ⓐ Ⓑ Ⓒ Ⓓ

39 Ⓐ Ⓑ Ⓒ Ⓓ   46 Ⓐ Ⓑ Ⓒ Ⓓ   53 Ⓐ Ⓑ Ⓒ Ⓓ   60 Ⓐ Ⓑ Ⓒ Ⓓ

40 Ⓐ Ⓑ Ⓒ Ⓓ   47 Ⓐ Ⓑ Ⓒ Ⓓ   54 Ⓐ Ⓑ Ⓒ Ⓓ   61 Ⓐ Ⓑ Ⓒ Ⓓ

PRACTICE EXAMINATION II

Section I

33 Questions

Time—45 minutes

Directions: For each question that follows, choose the best answer choice (A), (B), (C), or (D) and darken the corresponding oval on the answer sheet.

Time: 45 minutes for Part 1, 45 minutes for Part 2

Notes: (1) i represents $\sqrt{-1}$.

(2) Figures that accompany a problem are designed to provide information and are drawn as accurately as possible UNLESS the wording "figure not drawn to scale" is indicated.

(3) All figures lie in a plane unless otherwise indicated.

(4) The domain of a function is assumed to be the set of all real numbers unless otherwise indicated.

1. Evaluate $-3(2 + (-3) + 3(-1))$.
    (A) -9
    (B) 9
    (C) 12
    (D) 27

2. Which of the following is the greatest in value?
    $$-\frac{1}{9}, -\frac{1}{11}, -|-3|, -|3|$$
    (A) $-\dfrac{1}{9}$

    (B) $-\dfrac{1}{11}$

    (C) $-|-3|$
    (D) $-|3|$

3. Which of the following represents the domain of $y = \dfrac{1}{\sqrt{x-1}}$?

    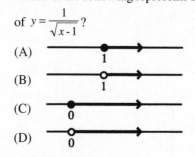

    (A)
    (B)
    (C)
    (D)

4. Given the numbers 1, 5, 1, 5, which of the following is NOT true?
    (A) mean = median
    (B) mean > median
    (C) median = 3
    (D) mean = 3

5. Which of the following is an irrational number?
    (A) $\sqrt{121}$

    (B) $\sqrt{\dfrac{4}{9}}$

    (C) $\sqrt{5}$

    (D) $\sqrt[3]{-27}$

6. If $x^2 > y^2$, which of the following must be true?
    (A) $x > y$
    (B) $x > 0$
    (C) $x + 3 > y$
    (D) $|x| > |y|$

7. If x and y are negative integers, which of the following must be a positive integer?
    (A) $x + y$
    (B) $\dfrac{x+y}{x}$

    (C) $\dfrac{x^2 + y^2}{x}$

    (D) $x^2 + y^2$

8. Which of the following is a prime number?
    (A) 7
    (B) 14
    (C) 21
    (D) 25

9. If x represents the largest of three consecutive odd integers, then the smallest of these numbers would be represented by
   - (A) $x + 3$
   - (B) $x - 3$
   - (C) $x + 4$
   - (D) $x - 4$

10. In triangle NJL, the measure of angle J is twice the measure of angle N and an exterior angle at vertex L measures $120°$. What is the degree measure of angle N?
    - (A) $40°$
    - (B) $45°$
    - (C) $50°$
    - (D) $55°$

11. $(x - 1)(x + 2)(x - 3)$ is equal to each of the following EXCEPT
    - (A) $-(1 - x)(x + 2)(x - 3)$
    - (B) $(x - 1)(2 + x)(x - 3)$
    - (C) $-(x - 1)(x + 2)(3 - x)$
    - (D) $-(1 - x)(2 + x)(3 - x)$

12. Which one of the following graphs has origin symmetry?

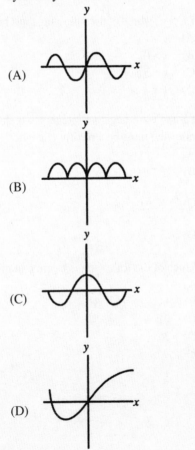

    (A)

    (B)

    (C)

    (D)

13. What is the remainder when $5x^2 - 7x - 10$ is divided by $x - 3$?
    - (A) 7
    - (B) 14
    - (C) 21
    - (D) 28

14. The accompanying graph could represent which of the following functions?

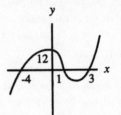

Figure not drawn to scale.

    - (A) $f(x) = (x - 4)(x + 1)(x + 3)$
    - (B) $f(x) = (x + 4)(x - 1)(x - 3)$
    - (C) $f(x) = (x - 4)(x + 1)(x + 3)(x + 12)$
    - (D) $f(x) = (x + 4)(x - 1)(x - 3)(x + 12)$

15. Solve the equation $a * y = b$ for y within the following system.

*	e	a	b	c
e	e	a	b	c
a	a	b	c	e
b	b	c	e	a
c	c	e	a	b

    - (A) e
    - (B) a
    - (C) b
    - (D) c

16. If $\frac{1}{2}$ fup = 3 glicks, 2 glicks = 3 homs, and 2 homs = 1 gat, then 18 gats are how many fups?
    - (A) 1
    - (B) 2
    - (C) 3
    - (D) 4

17. What is a solution of $x^2 + 2x + 3 = 0$?
    - (A) $-1 + i\sqrt{2}$
    - (B) $1 + i\sqrt{2}$
    - (C) $2 + 2i$
    - (D) $-1 - i\sqrt{3}$

18. If $i = \sqrt{-1}$, what is the reciprocal of $2i$?
    (A) $-2i$
    (B) $\dfrac{i}{2}$
    (C) $\dfrac{-i}{2}$
    (D) i

19. What is the negation of the statement, "Some groups are not commutative"?
    (A) Some groups are commutative.
    (B) All groups are not commutative.
    (C) All groups are commutative.
    (D) Some groups are associative.

20. If $h(x) = -x^2 - 3x$, then $h(-3) =$
    (A) 0
    (B) 3
    (C) 9
    (D) 18

21. Which of the following functions is represented in the accompanying graph?

    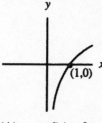

    (A) $y = f(x) = 2^{-x}$
    (B) $y = f(x) = \log_2 x$
    (C) $y = 2x$
    (D) $y = \left(\dfrac{1}{2}\right)^x$

22. The average of two numbers is xy. If the first number is y, what is the other number?
    (A) $2xy - y$
    (B) $xy - 2y$
    (C) x
    (D) $xy + 2y$

23. If the probability of hitting a target is $\dfrac{1}{3}$, what is the probability of 2 target hits in 3 tries?
    (A) $\dfrac{1}{3}$
    (B) $\dfrac{2}{3}$
    (C) $\dfrac{2}{9}$
    (D) $\dfrac{5}{9}$

24. If $w = \{y \mid -2 < y < 1\}$ and $x = \{y \mid 3 < y < 7\}$, how many integers are in $w \cup x$?
    (A) Five
    (B) Four
    (C) Three
    (D) Zero (Empty)

25. Which of the following is NOT true for the parabola in the accompanying diagram?

    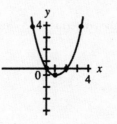

    (A) The equation of the axis of symmetry is $x = 1$.
    (B) The x–intercepts are at 0 and at 2.
    (C) The equation of the parabola is $y = -x^2 + 2x$.
    (D) The coordinates of the turning point are $(1, -1)$.

26. If $w = 3m$, then the value of $3w^2$ is which of the following?
    (A) $9^2 m$
    (B) $9m^{+2}$
    (C) $3^2 m$
    (D) $3^2 m^{+1}$

27. If $\dfrac{1}{8} + \dfrac{x}{y} + \dfrac{5}{8} = \dfrac{7}{8}$, which of the following must be true?
    (A) $y = 8$
    (B) $x = 1$
    (C) $y = 8x$
    (D) $y > x$

28. If the angles of a triangle are in the ratio of 3:5:7, what is the degree measure of the smallest angle?
    (A) 6
    (B) 18
    (C) 36
    (D) 54

29. For all values for which the fractions are defined, $\dfrac{a-b}{b-a}$ is equal to which of the following?

    (A) $\dfrac{c-d}{c+d}$

    (B) $\dfrac{e-f}{f-e}$

    (C) $\dfrac{g+h}{h+g}$

    (D) None of the above

30. If $10a = 45.2$, then in terms of "a" log $4.52 =$

    (A) a^{-1}

    (B) a^{+1}

    (C) $10a$

    (D) $a - 10$

31. Joan picked a letter from the word "WIN" at random and then picked a letter from the word "GAME" at random. Find the probability that neither letter chosen was a vowel.

    (A) $\dfrac{1}{3}$

    (B) $\dfrac{1}{4}$

    (C) $\dfrac{1}{6}$

    (D) $\dfrac{1}{8}$

32. $3^{100} + 3^{100} + 3^{100} =$

    (A) 3^{101}

    (B) 3^{300}

    (C) 27^{100}

    (D) 9^{100}

33. How many distinct four–digit numbers can be formed from the digits in 1996?

    (A) 6

    (B) 12

    (C) 18

    (D) 24

Section II

32 Questions

Time—45 minutes

34. For which ordered pair (x, y) is the fraction $\dfrac{5}{x-y}$ undefined?

    (A) $(1, -1)$
    (B) $(3, 3)$
    (C) $(-3, 3)$
    (D) $(5, 0)$

35. How many different values of x satisfy the equation $2(x-3) = 3(x+1) - (x+9)$?

    (A) None
    (B) One
    (C) Two
    (D) Three or more

36. If $y = -a^2b^3$, evaluate y when $a = -3$ and $b = -2$.

    (A) 72
    (B) 48
    (C) -48
    (D) -72

37. Which one of the following is NOT a function?

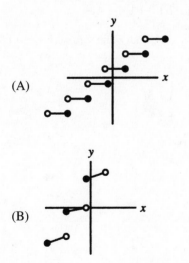

(A)

(B)

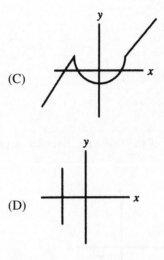

(C)

(D)

38. What is the product of $3x^3$ and $4x^4$?

    (A) $7x^7$
    (B) $12x^7$
    (C) $7x^{12}$
    (D) $12x^{12}$

39. If k is an odd integer, which of the following must be odd?

    (A) $8k - 4$
    (B) $8k + 4$
    (C) $8k^2 - 8k$
    (D) $4k^2 - 4k + 1$

40. Which of the following sets contains only the prime factor(s) of 16?

    (A) $\{2\}$
    (B) $\{1, 16\}$
    (C) $\{1, 2\}$
    (D) $\{2, 4, 8, 16\}$

41. The degree measures of two consecutive angles of a parallelogram are represented by $2x - 40$ and $3x + 10$. What is the value of x?

    (A) 57
    (B) 52
    (C) 50
    (D) 42

42. Which of the following is a factor of $2x^2 + 5x - 12$?

    (A) $x - 4$
    (B) $x + 4$
    (C) $2x + 3$
    (D) $2x - 1$

43. What is the additive inverse of $2 + \sqrt{5}$?

    (A) $2 - \sqrt{5}$
    (B) $-2 + \sqrt{5}$
    (C) $-2 - \sqrt{5}$
    (D) $\dfrac{1}{2 + \sqrt{5}}$

44. Which of the following lines has a positive slope?

    (A)

    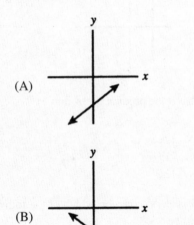

    (B)

    (C)

    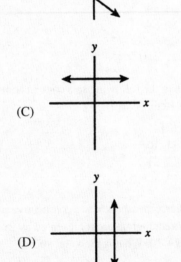

    (D)

45. $(3x - 1)^2 - (2x - 1)^2 =$

    (A) $5x^2 - 2x$
    (B) $5x^2 - 10x + 2$
    (C) $5x^2 - 2x + 2$
    (D) $5x^2$

46. If $f(x)$ is a linear function, find the value of $f(-1)$ if $f(2) = 6$ and $f(-2) = 8$.

    (A) $6\dfrac{1}{2}$

    (B) 7

    (C) $7\dfrac{1}{2}$

    (D) $7\dfrac{3}{4}$

47. If $a \,\square\, b$ is a binary operation defined as $ab - b$, evaluate $-1 \,\square\, x$ in terms of x.

    (A) $-2x$
    (B) 0
    (C) x
    (D) $2x$

48. Which of the following expresses the base 10 number 21 in binary?

    (A) $1\,0\,1\,0\,1$
    (B) $1\,0\,0\,1\,0$
    (C) $1\,1\,0\,0\,1$
    (D) $1\,1\,0\,1\,1$

49. If $i = \sqrt{-1}$, what is the sum of $i^{27} + i^{28} + i^{29} + i^{30}$?

    (A) 4
    (B) 0
    (C) $1 + 3i$
    (D) $2 + 2i$

50. Which of the following is a Venn diagram of A $\cup$ (B $\cup$ C)?

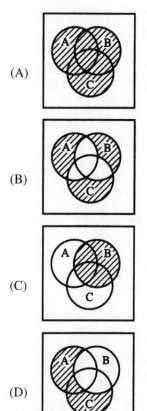

(A)

(B)

(C)

(D)

51. Which statement would be a correct heading for the last column in the accompanying table?

p	q	?
T	T	T
T	F	F
F	T	F
F	F	F

(A) p implies q ($p \rightarrow q$)
(B) p or q ($p \lor q$)
(C) p and q ($p \land q$)
(D) p if q ($p \leftrightarrow q$)

52. Which statement has the same truth value as "If it is not raining, then it is blue"?

(A) It is not raining or it is blue.
(B) If it is not raining, then it is not blue.
(C) If it is not blue, then it is not raining.
(D) If it is not blue, then it is raining.

53. If the domain for $f(x) = x^2 - 3$ is $-1 \le x \le 4$, the smallest value in the range of $f(x)$ is

(A) 0
(B) −1
(C) −2
(D) −3

54. If $f(x) = 3x$ and $g(x) = x^2$, then $g(f(-1)) =$

(A) $\dfrac{1}{9}$

(B) $\dfrac{1}{3}$

(C) 3

(D) 9

55. If x is a positive integer, which of the following represents the median of the integers $2x + 1$, $3x + 1$, $4x + 1$, and $5x + 1$?

(A) $\dfrac{3x+1}{2}$

(B) $\dfrac{4x+1}{2}$

(C) $\dfrac{7x+1}{2}$

(D) $\dfrac{7x+2}{2}$

56. The NJL basketball team consists of 15 players. The accompanying table shows the number of players who scored within specified point ranges during one season. Which interval contains the median of the data?

Interval	Frequency
101–120	1
81–100	4
61–80	2
41–60	3
21–40	3
0–20	2

(A) 61–80
(B) 41–60
(C) 21–40
(D) 0–20

57. From a deck of 52 cards, two cards are randomly drawn without replacement. What is the probability of drawing two hearts?

    (A) $\dfrac{2}{52}$

    (B) $\dfrac{13}{52} \cdot \dfrac{13}{51}$

    (C) $\dfrac{13}{52} \cdot \dfrac{12}{51}$

    (D) $\dfrac{13}{52} \cdot \dfrac{12}{52}$

58. Given the graph of $f(x)$, which of the following best describes the graph of $f(x + 3)$ as compared to the graph of $f(x)$?

    (A) 3 units up
    (B) 3 units down
    (C) 3 units to the right
    (D) 3 units to the left

59. At what value of x does the line $\dfrac{x}{3} - \dfrac{y}{4} = 7$ intercept the x–axis?

    (A) –28
    (B) –21
    (C) 21
    (D) 28

60. The expression $\log a + \dfrac{1}{2}\log b$ is equivalent to which of the following?

    (A) $\log \sqrt{ab}$

    (B) $\log a\sqrt{b}$

    (C) $\log\left(a + \sqrt{b}\right)$

    (D) $(\log a)\left(\dfrac{1}{2}\log b\right)$

61. What is the area bounded by the four lines: $x = 2$, $x = 8$, $y = 1$, and $y = -4$?

    (A) 12
    (B) 18
    (C) 24
    (D) 30

62. If n represents the term number, then in terms of n, which of the following represents the sum of the first n terms of the following series?
$$\frac{1}{1\cdot 2} + \frac{1}{2\cdot 3} + \frac{1}{3\cdot 4} + \cdots + \frac{1}{n(n+1)}$$

    (A) $\dfrac{n}{n+1}$

    (B) $\dfrac{n(n+1)}{2}$

    (C) $\dfrac{n(n+1)^2}{3}$

    (D) $\dfrac{n^3 + 5}{2}$

63. If $\log_x 5 = 2$, then $\dfrac{x^2}{10} =$

    (A) $-\dfrac{1}{2}$

    (B) $\dfrac{1}{2}$

    (C) 1

    (D) 2

64. If $2x = w$ and $8y = m$, in terms of w and m, what is the value of $2^2 x^{+3} y$?

    (A) $2wm$
    (B) w^2m
    (C) wm^2
    (D) w^2m^3

65. Using the letters in the word "SQUARE," what is the probability that in a 6–letter arrangement the first 2 letters are vowels?

    (A) $\dfrac{3}{7}$

    (B) $\dfrac{1}{4}$

    (C) $\dfrac{1}{5}$

    (D) $\dfrac{1}{6}$

End of Practice Examination II

Answer Key

Section I

1. C	8. A	15. B	22. A	29. B
2. B	9. D	16. D	23. C	30. A
3. B	10. A	17. A	24. A	31. A
4. B	11. D	18. C	25. C	32. A
5. C	12. A	19. C	26. D	33. B
6. D	13. B	20. A	27. C	
7. D	14. B	21. B	28. C	

Section II

34. B	41. D	48. A	55. D	62. A
35. D	42. B	49. B	56. B	63. B
36. A	43. C	50. A	57. C	64. B
37. D	44. A	51. C	58. D	65. C
38. B	45. A	52. D	59. C	
39. D	46. C	53. D	60. B	
40. A	47. A	54. A	61. D	

Explanatory Answers

Section I

1. **The correct answer is (C).**

    $-3\big(2+(-3)+3(-1)\big)$

    $= -3(2-3-3)$

    $= -3(-4)$

    $= 12$

2. **The correct answer is (B).**

    $-\dfrac{1}{9} = -.\overline{11}$

    $-\dfrac{1}{11} = -.\overline{09}$

    $-|-3| = -3$

    $-|3| = -3$

3. **The correct answer is (B).** The domain of $y = \dfrac{1}{\sqrt{x-1}}$ is the value of x for which y is both real and defined.

    $x \neq 1$ or we would have division by 0

    $x > 1$ or we would have imaginary numbers

    D: $\{x \mid x > 1\}$

4. **The correct answer is (B).**

    The (arithmetic) mean = average

    $= \dfrac{\text{sum of the items}}{\text{quantity of items}}$

    $= 1 + 5 + 1 + 5$

    $= \dfrac{12}{4} = 3$

    The median is the middle number when the given numbers are placed in ascending order. For an even number of terms, average the two "middle values."

    1, 1, 5, 5

    $\dfrac{1+5}{2} = 3$

    median = 3, mean = 3

5. **The correct answer is (C).**

    $\sqrt{121} = 11, \quad \sqrt{\dfrac{4}{9}} = \dfrac{2}{3}, \quad \sqrt[3]{-27} = -3$

    A rational number can be expressed in the form $\dfrac{p}{q}$, where p and q are integers ($q \neq 0$).

    Irrational numbers include:

    • Never–ending, nonrepeating decimals.

    • The square roots of numbers that are not perfect squares.

6. **The correct answer is (D).** If $x^2 > y^2$, this does not mean $x > y$. For example, if $y = 2$, x could equal -10 or $+10$. However, $|-10|$ or $|10|$ is greater than $|2|$ or $|-2|$.

7. **The correct answer is (D).** Using a numerical counterexample, we can show that choices (A), (B), and (C) do not meet the "must" requirement.

    Let $x = -3$ and $y = -5$

    $x + y = (-3) + (-5) = -8$

    $\dfrac{x+y}{x} = \dfrac{(-3)+(-5)}{(-3)} = \dfrac{(-8)}{(-3)} = \dfrac{8}{3}$

    (This is not an integer.)

    $\dfrac{x^2 + y^2}{x} = \dfrac{(-3)^2 + (-5)^2}{(-3)} = \dfrac{9+25}{-3} = \dfrac{34}{-3}$

    (This is not positive and not an integer.)

8. **The correct answer is (A).** A prime number is an integer greater than 1 that is divisible only by itself and one.

9. **The correct answer is (D).** If x represents the largest of the three consecutive odd integers, then $x - 2$ represents the previous one and $x - 4$ the one before that.

10. **The correct answer is (A).**

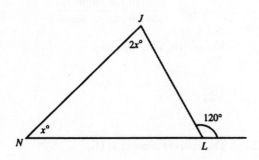

An exterior angle of a triangle is equal to the sum of the two remote interior angles.

$$x° + 2x° = 120°$$
$$3x° = 120°$$
$$x° = 40°$$

11. **The correct answer is (D).**

(A)　　$(x - 1)(x + 2)(x - 3)$

　　　$= [-(1 - x)][(x + 2)][(x - 3)]$

　　　$= (1 - x)(x + 2)(x - 3)$　　✔

(B)　　$(x - 1)(x + 2)(x - 3)$

　　　$= [(x - 1)][(2 + x)][(x - 3)]$

　　　$= (x - 1)(2 + x)(x - 3)$　　✔

(C)　　$(x - 1)(x + 2)(x - 3)$

　　　$= [(x - 1)][(x + 2)][-(3 - x)]$

　　　$= -(x - 1)(x + 2)(3 - x)$　　✔

(D)　　$(x - 1)(x + 2)(x - 3)$

　　　$= [-(1 - x)][(2 + x)][-(3 - x)]$

　　　$= +(1 - x)(2 + x)(3 - x)$　　✘

12. **The correct answer is (A).** Origin symmetry means that if any point on the graph is reflected through the origin, the reflection is also a point on the graph.

13. **The correct answer is (B).**

Method 1:

$$\begin{array}{r} 5x + 8 \\ x - 3 \overline{\smash{\big)}\ 5x^2 - 7x - 10} \\ \underline{5x^2 - 15x} \\ 8x - 10 \\ \underline{8x - 24} \\ 14 \end{array}$$

Method 2:

3		5	−7	−10
			15	24
		5	8	⌊14

Method 3:

$$f(x) = 5x^2 - 7x - 10$$

$$f(3) = 5(3)^2 - 7(3) - 10 = 14$$

14. **The correct answer is (B).** Since the roots are $x = -4$, $x = 1$, and $x = 3$, the factors are $(x + 4)$, $(x - 1)$, and $(x - 3)$

$$f(x) = (x + 4)(x - 1)(x - 3)$$

Note: The y–intercept of 12 does not affect the factors. It does affect the coefficient of the function such that

$$= K(x + 4)(x - 1)(x - 3)$$

$$f(0) = 12$$

15. **The correct answer is (B).** $a * y$ is evaluated by entering the * table in the row labeled a.

Then locate the column title whose intersection with the row labeled a is b.

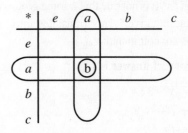

Therefore, $y = a$.

16. **The correct answer is (D).**

$$\frac{1}{2}\text{fup} = 3 \text{ glick} \rightarrow \text{glick} = \frac{1}{6}\text{fup}$$

$$2 \text{ glicks} = 3 \text{ homs} \rightarrow 1\text{hom} = \frac{2}{3} \text{ glick}$$

$$2 \text{ homs} = 1 \text{ gat} \rightarrow 1 \text{ gat} = 2 \text{ homs}$$

$$1 \text{ gat} = 2 \text{ homs}$$

$$= 2[\frac{2}{3} \text{ glick}]$$

$$= \frac{4}{3} \text{ glick}$$

$$= \frac{4}{3}[\frac{1}{6}\text{fup}]$$

$$= \frac{2}{9} \text{ fup}$$

Therefore, 18 gats = $18\left(\frac{2}{9}\text{fup}\right) = 4$ fups

17. **The correct answer is (A).**

$$x = \frac{-b \pm \sqrt{b^2 - 4ac}}{2a} \qquad a = 1$$

$$= \frac{-2 \pm \sqrt{(2)^2 - 4(1)(3)}}{2(1)} \qquad b = 2$$

$$c = 3$$

$$= \frac{-2 \pm \sqrt{4 - 12}}{2}$$

$$= \frac{-2 \pm \sqrt{-8}}{2}$$

$$= \frac{-2 \pm 2i\sqrt{2}}{2} = -1 \pm i\sqrt{2}$$

18. **The correct answer is (C).**

$$\frac{1}{2i} \cdot \frac{i}{i} = \frac{i}{2i^2} = \frac{i}{2(-1)} = \frac{-i}{2}$$

19. **The correct answer is (C).** The negation can be read as "It is not true that .. some groups are not commutative." This translates into "All groups are commutative."

20. **The correct answer is (A).**

$$h(x) = -x^2 - 3x$$

$$= -(-3)^2 - 3(-3)$$

$$= -(9) + 9$$

$$= 0$$

21. **The correct answer is (B).** This is the graph of $y = \log_2 x$.

22. **The correct answer is (A).**

$$\text{Average} = \frac{\text{Sum of the numbers}}{\text{Quantity of numbers}}$$

Let w = the other number

$$xy = \frac{y + w}{2}$$

$$2xy = y + w$$

$$w = 2xy - y$$

23. **The correct answer is (C).**

$$_nC_r \, p^r q^{n-r}$$

n = number of tries (attempts) = 3

r = number of successes = 2

p = probability of a success = $\left(\frac{1}{3}\right)$

q = probability of a failure = $\left(\frac{2}{3}\right)$

$$_3C_2\left(\frac{1}{3}\right)^2\left(\frac{2}{3}\right)^1$$

$$= 3\left(\frac{1}{9}\right)\left(\frac{2}{3}\right) = \frac{2}{9}$$

24. **The correct answer is (A).** Looking only at integers

Set $w = \{-1, 0\}$ and Set $x = \{4, 5, 6\}$. The union of w and x is $\{-1, 0, 4, 5, 6\}$.

25. **The correct answer is (C).** (A) The vertical line that divides the graph into 2 symmetrical pieces is the axis of symmetry.

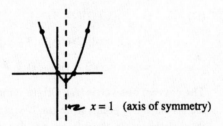

(B) The x–intercepts (or roots) are where the graph intersects the x–axis, in this case at $x = 0$ and $x = 2$.

(C) The roots are $x = 0$ and $x = 2$, the factors are (x) and $(x - 2)$. The equation is $y = (x)(x - 2) = x^2 - 2x$.

Choice (C) is NOT true.

(D) The turning point is the minimum point of this graph. This occurs at $(1, -1)$.

26. **The correct answer is (D).**
$$3w^2 = 3(3^m)^2$$
$$= 3(3^{2m})$$
$$= (3^1)(3^{2m})$$
$$= 3^{2m+1}$$

27. **The correct answer is (C).**

If $\frac{1}{8} + \frac{x}{y} + \frac{5}{8} = \frac{7}{8}$, then $\frac{x}{y} = \frac{1}{8}$ is a must.

If $\frac{x}{y} = \frac{1}{8}$ then $y = 8x$ is a must.

$\frac{x}{y}$ must equal $\frac{1}{8}$, but it could have been that $x = 2$ and $y = 16$ because $\frac{2}{16} = \frac{1}{8}$, or $x = -2$ and $y = -16$ because $\frac{-2}{-16} = \frac{1}{8}$

28. **The correct answer is (C).**
$$3x + 5x + 7x = 180$$
$$15x = 180$$
$$x = 12$$
$$3x = 36$$

29. **The correct answer is (B).** $\frac{a-b}{b-a} = -1 = \frac{e-f}{f-e}$

30. **The correct answer is (A).** If $10^a = 45.2$ then dividing each side by 10
$$\frac{10^a}{10} = \frac{45.2}{10}$$
$$10^{a-1} = 4.52$$
$$\log_{10} 4.52 = a - 1$$

31. **The correct answer is (A).**
$$P \ (W \ or \ N) = \frac{2}{3}$$
$$P \ (G \ or \ M) = \frac{2}{4}$$
$$P \ (NO \ VOWEL) = \left(\frac{2}{3}\right)\left(\frac{2}{4}\right) = \frac{4}{12} = \frac{1}{3}$$

32. **The correct answer is (A).**
$$3^{100} + 3^{100} + 3^{100}$$
$$= (3)(3^{100})$$
$$= 3^1 \cdot 3^{100}$$
$$= 3^{101}$$

33. **The correct answer is (B).**

4 digits available

$$\frac{4!}{2!} = \frac{(4)(3)(2)(1)}{(2)(1)} = 12$$

repeating 9s

Section II

34. **The correct answer is (B).** A fraction is undefined when the denominator equals zero.
$$x - y = 0$$
$$x = y$$
Only choice (B) has x equal to y.

35. **The correct answer is (D).**
$$2(x-3) = 3(x+1) - (x+9)$$
$$2x - 6 = 3x + 3 - x - 9$$
$$2x - 6 = 2x - 6$$
There are an infinite number of solutions.

36. **The correct answer is (A).**
$$y = a^2 b^3$$
$$= -(3)^2(-2)^3$$
$$= -(9)(-8)$$
$$= 72$$

37. **The correct answer is (D).** Choices (A), (B), and (C) pass the vertical line test. Choice (D) does NOT.

38. **The correct answer is (B).**
$$ax^n \cdot bx^m = (ab)x^{(n+m)}$$
$$3x^3 \cdot 4x^4 = 12x^7$$

39. **The correct answer is (D).** Try substituting an odd integer into the answer choices.

If $k = 1$, $8k - 4 = 4$	even
$8k + 4 = 12$	even
$8k^2 - 8k = 0$	even
$4k^2 - 4k + 1 = 1$	odd
If $k = -5$, $8k = -40$	even
$8k + 4 = -36$	even
$8k^2 - 8k = 240$	even
$4k^2 - 4k + 1 = 121$	odd

40. **The correct answer is (A).** $16 = 2 \cdot 2 \cdot 2 \cdot 2 = 2^4$

    Two is the only prime factor of 16.

    Note: A prime factor is greater than 1. One is not a prime number.

41. **The correct answer is (D).**

    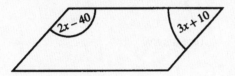

    Any two consecutive angles of a parallelogram are supplementary.

    $$(2x - 40) + (3x + 10) = 180$$
    $$5x - 30 = 180$$
    $$5x = 210$$
    $$x = 42$$

42. **The correct answer is (B).**

    $2x^2 + 5x - 12$

    $= (2x - 3)(x + 4)$

43. **The correct answer is (C).** Two numbers are additive inverses if their sum is zero. Additive inverses are also called opposites. The opposite (additive inverse) of $2 + \sqrt{5}$ is $-2 - \sqrt{5}$.

44. **The correct answer is (A).**

    Let m = slope

    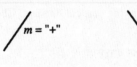

45. **The correct answer is (A).**

    $$(3x - 1)^2 - (2x - 1)^2$$
    $$= [(3x - 1)(3x - 1)] - [(2x - 1)(2x - 1)]$$
    $$= [9x^2 - 6x + 1] - [4x^2 - 4x + 1]$$
    $$= 9x^2 - 6x + 1 - 4x^2 + 4x - 1$$
    $$= 5x^2 - 2x$$

46. **The correct answer is (C).**

    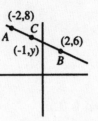

    A linear function has a constant slope.

    $$m_{AB} = \frac{8 - 6}{-2 - 2} = \frac{2}{-4} = -\frac{1}{2}$$

    $$m_{AC} = \frac{8 - y}{-2 - (-1)} = \frac{8 - y}{-1}$$

    $$-\frac{1}{2} = \frac{8 - y}{-1}$$

    $$2(8 - y) = 1$$

    $$8 - y = \frac{1}{2}$$

    $$y = 7\frac{1}{2}$$

47. **The correct answer is (A).**

    $$a \, \square \, b = ab - b$$

    $$-1 \, \square \, x = (-1)\,x - x = -x - x = -2x$$

48. **The correct answer is (A).**

    $$
    \begin{array}{l}
    \underline{2\,\lfloor}\ 21 \\
    \underline{2\,\lfloor}\ 10\ \text{r}\ 1 \\
    \underline{2\,\lfloor}\ 5\ \text{r}\ 0 \\
    \underline{2\,\lfloor}\ 2\ \text{r}\ 1 \\
    \underline{2\,\lfloor}\ 1\ \text{r}\ 0 \\
    \phantom{\underline{2\,\lfloor}\ }0\ \text{r}\ 1 \\
    \phantom{\underline{2\,\lfloor}\ }1\ 0\ 1\ 0\ 1
    \end{array}
    $$

49. **The correct answer is (B).**

    $i^{27} = i^3 = -i$

    $i^{28} = i^0 = 1$

    $i^{29} = i^1 = i$

    $i^{30} = i^2 = -1$

    $i^{27} + i^{28} + i^{29} + i^{30} = -i + 1 + i + (-1) = 0$

50. **The correct answer is (A).** First find what region (B ∪ C) represents:

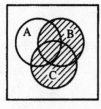

Then, find the region A occupies:

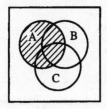

Therefore, A ∪ (B ∪ C) is their union (All Elements in both):

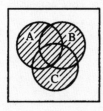

51. **The correct answer is (C).** An "and" statement, $p \wedge q$, is true only if both p is true and q is true. Otherwise it is false.

52. **The correct answer is (D).** The contrapositive of a statement maintains the same truth value as the original statement. Symbolically the contrapositive of $p \rightarrow q$ is $\sim q \rightarrow \sim p$. The contrapositive of "If it is not raining then it is blue" is "If it is not blue, then it is raining."

53. **The correct answer is (D).** For a parabola, to find the minimum or maximum value in a specific domain you must evaluate the function at three values of x.

$$f\left(\begin{smallmatrix}\text{lowest}\\x\,\text{value}\end{smallmatrix}\right) = f(-1) = (-1)^2 - 3 = -3$$

$$f\left(\begin{smallmatrix}\text{greatest}\\x\,\text{value}\end{smallmatrix}\right) = (4)^2 - 3 = 13$$

$$f\left(\begin{smallmatrix}\text{turning}\\\text{point}\end{smallmatrix}\right)* = f\left(\frac{-b}{2a}\right) = f(0) = -3$$

The smallest value of $f(x)$ within the domain is –3.

Note: If $ax^2 + bx + c = 0$, the x–value of the turning point is $x = \frac{-b}{2a}$

If $f(x) = x^2 + 0x - 3$, $x = \frac{-b}{2a}$

$$= \frac{0}{2(1)} = 0$$

To qualify, the x–value of the turning point must be in the domain. In this example, $x = 0$ is in the domain.

54. **The correct answer is (A).**

$$f(-1) = 3^{-1} = \frac{1}{3}$$

$$g\left(\frac{1}{3}\right) = \left(\frac{1}{3}\right)^2 = \frac{1}{9}$$

55. **The correct answer is (D).** The median is the middle number when listed in ascending order. If there are an even number of integers, the median is the mean (average) of the "middle" two integers when listed in ascending order.

$$\text{median} = \frac{(3x+1)+(4x+1)}{2} = \frac{7x+2}{2}$$

56. **The correct answer is (B).** The median is the middle number when listed in ascending order. It is the 50th percentile number. There are 15 scores. The 8th score is in the 41–60 interval.

57. **The correct answer is (C).** Probability of first heart $= \frac{13}{52}$

Having chosen a heart, there are 12 hearts left and 51 cards left.

Probability of second heart $= \frac{12}{51}$

$$\frac{13}{52} \cdot \frac{12}{51}$$

58. **The correct answer is (D).** The graph of $f(x + 3)$ is a horizontal shift of $f(x)$ 3 units to the left.

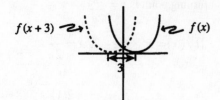

59. **The correct answer is (C).** At the x–intercept, $y = 0$.

$$\frac{x}{3} - \frac{(0)}{4} = 7$$
$$x = 21$$

60. **The correct answer is (B).**

$$\log xy = \log x + \log y$$
$$\log x^a = a \log x$$
$$\log a + \frac{1}{2}\log b = \log a + \log \sqrt{b}$$
$$= \log\left(a\sqrt{b}\right)$$

61. **The correct answer is (D).**

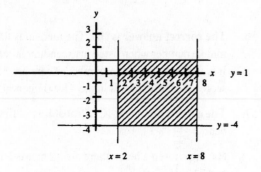

Area of a rectangle is base × height

$A = bh$

$A = 6(5) = 30$

62. **The correct answer is (A).** By trial and error i.e., let $n = 3$

$$\frac{1}{1 \cdot 2} + \frac{1}{2 \cdot 3} + \frac{1}{3 \cdot 4} = \frac{?}{} \frac{n}{n+1} = \frac{3}{4}$$
$$\frac{1}{2} + \frac{1}{6} + \frac{1}{12} = \frac{?}{} \frac{3}{4}$$
$$\frac{3}{4} = \frac{3}{4}$$

63. **The correct answer is (B).**

$$\log x\, 5 = 2 \rightarrow x^2 = 5$$
$$\therefore \frac{x^2}{10} = \frac{5}{10} = \frac{1}{2}$$

64. **The correct answer is (B).**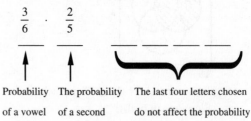

$2x$	$=$	w		$8y$	$=$	m
$(2x)2$	$=$	w^2		$(2^3)y$	$=$	m
$2^2 x$	$=$	w^2		$2^3 y$	$=$	m

$$\therefore 2^2 x \cdot 3^3 y = w^2 \cdot m = w^2 m$$

65. **The correct answer is (C).**

$$\frac{3}{6} \cdot \frac{2}{5}$$

Probability of a vowel $= \dfrac{3}{6}$

The probability of a second vowel having already chosen a vowel $= \dfrac{2}{5}$

The last four letters chosen do not affect the probability associated with the first two letters.

$$\frac{3}{6} \cdot \frac{2}{5} = \frac{1}{5}$$

Practice Examination II Diagnostic Chart

Subject Area*	Question Numbers	Number Wrong
Logic and Sets	Part 1: 19, 24	_____
	Part 2: 50, 51, 52	_____
Number System and Systems	Part 1: 1, 2, 5, 6, 7, 8, 9, 15, 27	_____
	Part 2: 34, 35, 39, 40, 47, 48	_____
Functions and Graphs (Basic Algebra)	Part 1: 3, 12, 14, 20, 21, 25	_____
	Part 2: 36, 37, 44, 46, 53, 54, 58, 59	_____
Probability, Statistics, and Counting	Part 1: 4, 22, 23, 31, 33	_____
	Part 2: 55, 56, 57, 62, 65	_____
Algebra (Beyond Basics)	Part 1: 11, 13, 16, 17, 18, 26, 29, 30, 32	_____
	Part 2: 38, 42, 43, 45, 49, 60, 63, 64	_____
Geometry	Part 1: 10, 28	_____
	Part 2: 41, 61	_____

*Many questions overlap more than one subject area.

Answer Sheet for Practice Examination III

Section I

1 Ⓐ Ⓑ Ⓒ Ⓓ   8 Ⓐ Ⓑ Ⓒ Ⓓ   15 Ⓐ Ⓑ Ⓒ Ⓓ   22 Ⓐ Ⓑ Ⓒ Ⓓ   29 Ⓐ Ⓑ Ⓒ Ⓓ

2 Ⓐ Ⓑ Ⓒ Ⓓ   9 Ⓐ Ⓑ Ⓒ Ⓓ   16 Ⓐ Ⓑ Ⓒ Ⓓ   23 Ⓐ Ⓑ Ⓒ Ⓓ   30 Ⓐ Ⓑ Ⓒ Ⓓ

3 Ⓐ Ⓑ Ⓒ Ⓓ   10 Ⓐ Ⓑ Ⓒ Ⓓ   17 Ⓐ Ⓑ Ⓒ Ⓓ   24 Ⓐ Ⓑ Ⓒ Ⓓ   31 Ⓐ Ⓑ Ⓒ Ⓓ

4 Ⓐ Ⓑ Ⓒ Ⓓ   11 Ⓐ Ⓑ Ⓒ Ⓓ   18 Ⓐ Ⓑ Ⓒ Ⓓ   25 Ⓐ Ⓑ Ⓒ Ⓓ   32 Ⓐ Ⓑ Ⓒ Ⓓ

5 Ⓐ Ⓑ Ⓒ Ⓓ   12 Ⓐ Ⓑ Ⓒ Ⓓ   19 Ⓐ Ⓑ Ⓒ Ⓓ   26 Ⓐ Ⓑ Ⓒ Ⓓ   33 Ⓐ Ⓑ Ⓒ Ⓓ

6 Ⓐ Ⓑ Ⓒ Ⓓ   13 Ⓐ Ⓑ Ⓒ Ⓓ   20 Ⓐ Ⓑ Ⓒ Ⓓ   27 Ⓐ Ⓑ Ⓒ Ⓓ

7 Ⓐ Ⓑ Ⓒ Ⓓ   14 Ⓐ Ⓑ Ⓒ Ⓓ   21 Ⓐ Ⓑ Ⓒ Ⓓ   28 Ⓐ Ⓑ Ⓒ Ⓓ

Section II

34 Ⓐ Ⓑ Ⓒ Ⓓ   41 Ⓐ Ⓑ Ⓒ Ⓓ   48 Ⓐ Ⓑ Ⓒ Ⓓ   55 Ⓐ Ⓑ Ⓒ Ⓓ   62 Ⓐ Ⓑ Ⓒ Ⓓ

35 Ⓐ Ⓑ Ⓒ Ⓓ   42 Ⓐ Ⓑ Ⓒ Ⓓ   49 Ⓐ Ⓑ Ⓒ Ⓓ   56 Ⓐ Ⓑ Ⓒ Ⓓ   63 Ⓐ Ⓑ Ⓒ Ⓓ

36 Ⓐ Ⓑ Ⓒ Ⓓ   43 Ⓐ Ⓑ Ⓒ Ⓓ   50 Ⓐ Ⓑ Ⓒ Ⓓ   57 Ⓐ Ⓑ Ⓒ Ⓓ   64 Ⓐ Ⓑ Ⓒ Ⓓ

37 Ⓐ Ⓑ Ⓒ Ⓓ   44 Ⓐ Ⓑ Ⓒ Ⓓ   51 Ⓐ Ⓑ Ⓒ Ⓓ   58 Ⓐ Ⓑ Ⓒ Ⓓ   65 Ⓐ Ⓑ Ⓒ Ⓓ

38 Ⓐ Ⓑ Ⓒ Ⓓ   45 Ⓐ Ⓑ Ⓒ Ⓓ   52 Ⓐ Ⓑ Ⓒ Ⓓ   59 Ⓐ Ⓑ Ⓒ Ⓓ

39 Ⓐ Ⓑ Ⓒ Ⓓ   46 Ⓐ Ⓑ Ⓒ Ⓓ   53 Ⓐ Ⓑ Ⓒ Ⓓ   60 Ⓐ Ⓑ Ⓒ Ⓓ

40 Ⓐ Ⓑ Ⓒ Ⓓ   47 Ⓐ Ⓑ Ⓒ Ⓓ   54 Ⓐ Ⓑ Ⓒ Ⓓ   61 Ⓐ Ⓑ Ⓒ Ⓓ

PRACTICE EXAMINATION III

Section I

33 Questions
Time—45 minutes

Directions: For each question that follows, choose the best answer choice (A), (B), (C), or (D) and darken the corresponding oval on the answer sheet.

Time: 45 minutes for Part 1, 45 minutes for Part 2

Notes: (1)   i represents $\sqrt{-1}$.

(2)   Figures that accompany a problem are designed to provide information and are drawn as accurately as possible UNLESS the wording "figure not drawn to scale" is indicated.

(3)   All figures lie in a plane unless otherwise indicated.

(4)   The domain of a function is assumed to be the set of all real numbers unless otherwise indicated.

1.   Which of the following is a prime number?

(A)   39
(B)   49
(C)   51
(D)   53

2.   Joan asserts that $x + y \geq xy$ for all positive real numbers. Which ordered pair (x, y) serves as a counterexample to Joan's claim?

(A)   (1, 1)
(B)   (1, 2)
(C)   (2, 2)
(D)   (2, 3)

3.   If $M = \{x \mid x > 2\}$ and $N = \{x \mid x < 9\}$, how many integers are in $M \cap N$?

(A)   Eight
(B)   Six
(C)   Four
(D)   Two

4.   If x and y are nonzero integers, and y does not equal x, which of the following must be a positive integer?

(A) $x - y$
(B) $\dfrac{x + y}{x - y}$
(C) $\dfrac{x - y}{y - x}$
(D) $-\dfrac{(x - y)}{(y - x)}$

5.   If $f(x) = kx_2$ and $f(2) = 12$, what is the value of k?

(A)   1
(B)   2
(C)   3
(D)   4

6.   What is the average (arithmetic mean) of the numbers represented by $3n + 1, n + 7,$ and $2n - 2$?

(A) $2n + 2$
(B) $3n + 3$
(C) $5n + 5$
(D) $6n + 6$

7.   For what values of x will the function $f(x) = \sqrt{x - 9}$ be real?

(A) $\{x \mid x > 0\}$
(B) $\{x \mid x \geq 9\}$
(C) $\{x \mid x < 0\}$
(D) $\{x \mid x \leq 9\}$

8. $-3(-3 + (-3)(-4) -2) - 1 =$

(A) -22
(B) -7
(C) 5
(D) 26

9. Which of the following is a root of $2x^2 + x + 1 = 0$?

   (A) $\dfrac{-1+3i}{4}$

   (B) $\dfrac{-1-i\sqrt{7}}{2}$

   (C) $-1-i\sqrt{7}$

   (D) $\dfrac{-1+i\sqrt{7}}{4}$

10. What is the binary representation of 62 (in base 10)?

    (A) 1 1 1 1 1 0
    (B) 1 1 1 1 0 0
    (C) 1 0 1 1 1 0
    (D) 1 1 0 1 1 0

11. Which of the following graphs represents the function $y = f(x) = \left(\dfrac{1}{4}\right)^x$?

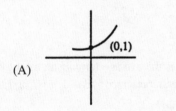

    (A)

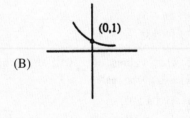

    (B)

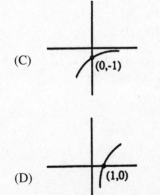

    (C)

    (D)

12. If the legs of a right triangle are $\sqrt{7}$ and $\sqrt{11}$, what is the length of the hypotenuse?

    (A) $\sqrt{2}$
    (B) $2\sqrt{2}$
    (C) $3\sqrt{2}$
    (D) $4\sqrt{2}$

13. What is the y–intercept of $\dfrac{x^2}{4} - \dfrac{x}{3} + \dfrac{y}{2} = 1$?

    (A) 2
    (B) 1
    (C) 0
    (D) −1

14. If the pattern shown is continued, what is the sum of the 113th line?

$$1$$
$$1+3$$
$$1+3+5$$
$$1+3+5+7$$
$$\vdots$$

    (A) 226
    (B) 12,321
    (C) 12,769
    (D) 13,749

15. If $f(x) = 3x - 7$ and $g(x) = 1$, then $g(f(4)) =$

    (A) −4
    (B) 1
    (C) 4
    (D) 5

16. If set A = {letters with horizontal line symmetry} and set B = {H, I, M, W, E} then which of the following is A ∩ B?

    (A) {H,I,M,W}
    (B) {H,I,W,E}
    (C) {H,I,M,W,E}
    (D) {H,I,E}

17. If $i = \sqrt{-1}$, what is the multiplicative inverse of $2 - 2i$?

    (A) $-2 - 2i$
    (B) $-2 + 2i$
    (C) $2 + 2i$
    (D) $\dfrac{1+i}{4}$

18. If the quantity of bacteria "q" present after time "t" (expressed in hours) is given by the equation $q = q_0 (3^{-2t})$, where q_0 is the initial number of the bacteria, then how many bacteria are present after 1 hour if the initial number of bacteria is 9,000?
    (A) −6,000
    (B) 1,000
    (C) 3,000
    (D) 6,000

19. Jessica Dawn received marks of 88, 92, and 86 on three successive tests. What grade must she receive on a fourth test in order to have an average of 90?
    (A) 91
    (B) 92
    (C) 93
    (D) 94

20. Which of the following is the prime factorization of 24?
    (A) $2 \cdot 12$
    (B) $2 \cdot 3 \cdot 4$
    (C) $2 \cdot 2 \cdot 6$
    (D) $2 \cdot 2 \cdot 2 \cdot 3$

21. There are 3 roads from Williston Park to Albertson, 3 roads from Albertson to Roslyn, and 4 roads from Roslyn to NJL College Preparation. How many different paths are there to go from Williston Park to NJL College Preparation passing through Albertson and Roslyn?
    (A) 10
    (B) 13
    (C) 36
    (D) 40

22. Which of the following is represented by the accompanying Venn diagram?

    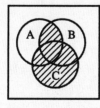

    (A) $(B \cap A) \cap C$
    (B) $C \cup (A \cap B)$
    (C) $A \cup (B \cap C)$
    (D) $(C \cup A) \cap B$

23. If $x \odot y$ is a binary operation defined as $x^y + y^x$, evaluate $4 \odot \dfrac{1}{2}$.

    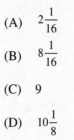

    (A) $2\dfrac{1}{16}$
    (B) $8\dfrac{1}{16}$
    (C) 9
    (D) $10\dfrac{1}{8}$

24. Which of the following tables expresses a relation that is NOT a function?

    (A)
x	y
1	1
2	2
3	1
4	2

    (B)
x	y
2	1
1	2
2	3
1	4

    (C)
x	y
1	5
2	6
3	7
4	8

    (D)
x	y
1	1
0	0
2	2
0	0

25. If $x^2 + y^2 = 16$ and $x = 5$, what is the value of y?
    (A) $\pm\sqrt{11}$
    (B) $\pm i\sqrt{11}$
    (C) ± 3
    (D) $\pm 3i$

26. Two women, Joan and Dawn, and three men, Norm, Joshua, and Howard, prepare examinations. A committee of three is to be randomly chosen from these examination writers to make up a test. How many different 3–person committees can be formed?
    (A) 5
    (B) 6
    (C) 10
    (D) 60

27. $(x − 1)(x + 1)(x − 2)$ is equal to all of the following EXCEPT
    (A) $(x^2 − 1)(x − 2)$
    (B) $(x^2 − x − 2)(x − 1)$
    (C) $(x^2 − 3x + 2)(x + 1)$
    (D) $(x^2 − 3x − 2)(x − 1)$

28. The expression $\frac{x-2}{x-3}$ is undefined when x is equal to

    (A) 3
    (B) 2
    (C) $-\frac{2}{3}$
    (D) -3

29. What is the converse of "not p implies q"?

    (A) p implies not q $(p \rightarrow \sim q)$
    (B) not q implies p $(\sim q \rightarrow p)$
    (C) q implies not p $(q \rightarrow \sim p)$
    (D) not p implies not q $(\sim p \rightarrow \sim q)$

30. A fair die and a fair coin are tossed. Find the probability of a number greater than 5 and a tail.

    (A) $\frac{1}{12}$
    (B) $\frac{1}{6}$
    (C) $\frac{3}{8}$
    (D) $\frac{2}{5}$

31. If 2 *Zits* = 3 *Zats*, 1 *Zat* = 5 *Zims*, and 3 *Zims* = 2 *Zags*, then 5 *Zags* are equal to how many *Zits*?

    (A) $\frac{1}{2}$
    (B) 1
    (C) $1\frac{1}{2}$
    (D) 2

32. If $\log_5 2 + \log_5 x = \log_5 20$, solve for x.

    (A) 5
    (B) 10
    (C) 15
    (D) 20

33. What is the sum of the roots of $f(x) = (x-3)(x-2)(x^2-1)$?

    (A) 6
    (B) 5
    (C) -5
    (D) -6

Section II

32 Questions
Time—45 minutes

34. Which of the following is a rational number?
    (A) $\sqrt{13}$
    (B) π
    (C) $\sqrt{3}$
    (D) $\sqrt{.16}$

35. Which of the following represents a graph of $y = |x - 3|$?

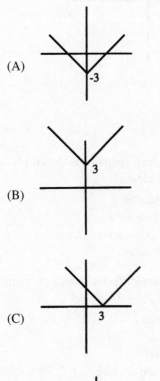

    (A)

    (B)

    (C)

    (D)

36. If $x > y$, which of the following must be true?
    (A) $x^2 > y^2$
    (B) $xy > 0$
    (C) $x + y > 0$
    (D) $x > y - 3$

37. If set $A = \{2, 3, 4, 5, 6\}$ and set $B = \{\text{prime numbers}\}$, then $A \cap B$ is which of the following?
    (A) $\{3, 5\}$
    (B) $\{2, 4, 6\}$
    (C) $\{2, 3, 5\}$
    (D) $\{2, 3, 4, 5\}$

38. Jessica asserts that $x^3 \geq x$ for all real numbers. Which of the following serves as a counterexample to Jessica's claim?
    (A) -10
    (B) -1
    (C) 0
    (D) 10

39. What is the solution set of the equation $|x - 1| = -9$?
    (A) $\{\ \}$
    (B) $\{-8\}$
    (C) $\{10\}$
    (D) $\{-8, 10\}$

40. What is the remainder when $x^3 - 2x^2 + 3x - 4$ is divided by $x + 2$?
    (A) -13
    (B) -26
    (C) -39
    (D) -52

41. Which statement is the inverse of the statement: "If Norm is not injured, he will win the race"?
    (A) If Norm wins the race, he is not injured.
    (B) If Norm is injured, he will win the race.
    (C) If Norm is injured, he will not win the race.
    (D) If Norm does not win the race, he is injured.

42. If m is an integer, which of the following must be odd?

    (A) $2m$
    (B) $m + 3$
    (C) $2m - 5$
    (D) $m^2 + 2m + 1$

43. If $f(x) = 2x + x^2$, then $f(-1) =$

    (A) -1
    (B) 1
    (C) $\dfrac{1}{2}$
    (D) $\dfrac{3}{2}$

44. Which of the following represents the domain of $y = \dfrac{1}{\sqrt{1-x}}$?

    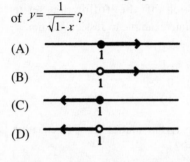

    (A)
    (B)
    (C)
    (D)

45. What is the difference between the mode and the median of the numbers 13, 14, 14, 14, 15, 18?

    (A) 0
    (B) 1
    (C) 3
    (D) 5

46. If $f(x)$ is a linear function, find the value of $f(-1)$ if $f(2) = 8$ and $f(-2) = 0$.

    (A) $\dfrac{5}{2}$
    (B) 2
    (C) $\dfrac{3}{2}$
    (D) 1

47. Which of the following equations has irrational roots?

    (A) $x^2 - 4 = 0$
    (B) $x^2 - 2 = 0$
    (C) $x^2 - 2x + 1 = 0$
    (D) $x^2 - 2x = 0$

48. How many different nine-letter arrangements can be formed from the letters in the word "TENNESSEE"?

    (A) $\dfrac{9!}{3!}$
    (B) $\dfrac{9!}{2!2!4!}$
    (C) $\dfrac{9!}{4 \cdot 2 \cdot 2}$
    (D) $\dfrac{9!}{4!} \cdot \dfrac{9!}{2!} \cdot \dfrac{9!}{2!}$

49. Based on the accompanying table, what is the inverse of N?

☺	N	J	L
N	J	L	N
J	L	N	J
L	N	J	L

    (A) N
    (B) J
    (C) L
    (D) L ☺ L

50. Under which operation is the set {1, 3, 9, 27, 81, . . . } closed?

    (A) Addition
    (B) Subtraction
    (C) Multiplication
    (D) Division

51. How many different values of x satisfy the equation $2(x - 3) - 2x = 5$?

    (A) None
    (B) One
    (C) Two
    (D) Three or more

52. Which of the following is a factor of $6x^2 + 5x - 4$?

    (A) $2x - 1$
    (B) $3x - 4$
    (C) $6x + 1$
    (D) $3x + 1$

53. A vase contains 6 yellow, 4 red, and 2 pink roses. How many random selections of 4 roses will have 2 yellow, 1 red, and 1 pink rose?

    (A) 12
    (B) 15
    (C) 120
    (D) 240

54. What is the base 10 equivalent of the binary number 1010?

    (A) 8
    (B) 10
    (C) 12
    (D) 14

55. Which of the following sets of numbers could be the lengths of the sides of a right triangle?

    (A) $\{2, 6, \sqrt{40}\}$
    (B) $\{2, 18, 20\}$
    (C) $\{4, 6, \sqrt{40}\}$
    (D) $\{4, 36, 40\}$

56. Which of the following sets consists only of prime numbers?

    (A) $\{2, 3, 5\}$
    (B) $\{3, 5, 7, 9\}$
    (C) $\{1, 2, 3, 4\}$
    (D) $\{3, 5, 51\}$

57. Which of the following graphs represents a quadratic function with imaginary roots?

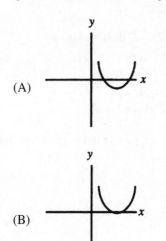

    (A)

    (B)

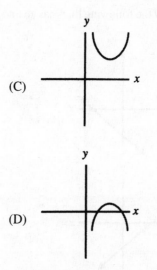

    (C)

    (D)

58. Without looking, Jessica chooses one chip from a box containing four chips numbered 1 through 4. Next she chooses one chip from a second box containing four chips lettered N, O, R, and M. Find the probability that Jessica chooses a number less than 4 OR the letter R.

    (A) $\dfrac{3}{16}$
    (B) $\dfrac{3}{8}$
    (C) $\dfrac{3}{4}$
    (D) $\dfrac{13}{16}$

59. If the median of five numbers is 10, which of the following must be true?

    (A) Two of the numbers are more than 10.
    (B) The average (arithmetic mean) is 10.
    (C) There is only one value of 10.
    (D) At least one of the numbers is a 10.

60. Which of the following lines has an undefined slope?

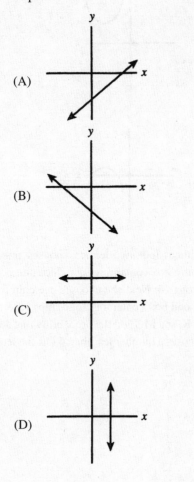

(A)

(B)

(C)

(D)

61. The accompanying graph shows the distribution of the number of children in the families of the students in a science class. What is the mode of the set of data?

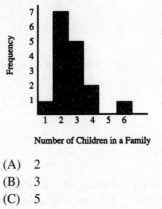

Number of Children in a Family

(A) 2
(B) 3
(C) 5
(D) 7

62. If $i = \sqrt{-1}$, which expression is NOT equal to the other three?

(A) $i^{17} + i^{18} + i^{19} + i^{20}$
(B) $i^3 + i^5 + i^7 + i^9$
(C) $i^2 + i^4 + i^6 + i^8$
(D) $i^4 + i^8 + i^{12} + i^{16}$

63. If $x = 5a$, then the value of $25x$ is which of the following?

(A) $30a$
(B) 5^{a+1}
(C) 5^{a+2}
(D) $125a$

64. If $f(x) = 2x - 1$, then $f(x + h) =$

(A) $x + h - 1$
(B) $2x + h - 1$
(C) $2x + 2h - 1$
(D) $x + 2h - 1$

65. If $\log_6 2 = m$, then in terms of m, $\log_6 3 =$

(A) $\dfrac{3}{2} m$
(B) $1 - m$
(C) $1 + m$
(D) $m - 1$

End of Practice Examination III

Answer Key

Section I

1.	D	8.	A	15.	B	22.	B	29.	C
2.	D	9.	D	16.	D	23.	A	30.	A
3.	B	10.	A	17.	D	24.	B	31.	B
4.	D	11.	B	18.	B	25.	D	32.	B
5.	C	12.	C	19.	D	26.	C	33.	B
6.	A	13.	A	20.	D	27.	D		
7.	B	14.	C	21.	C	28.	A		

Section II

34.	D	41.	C	48.	B	55.	A	62.	D
35.	C	42.	C	49.	B	56.	A	63.	C
36.	D	43.	D	50.	C	57.	C	64.	C
37.	C	44.	D	51.	A	58.	D	65.	B
38.	A	45.	A	52.	A	59.	D		
39.	A	46.	B	53.	C	60.	D		
40.	B	47.	B	54.	B	61.	A		

Explanatory Answers

Section I

1. **The correct answer is (D).** A prime number is a number greater than 1 that is divisible only by itself and one.

   53 is a prime number

   39 is divisible by 3

   49 is divisible by 7

   51 is divisible by 3

2. **The correct answer is (D).** $(2 + 3)$ is less than $(2)(3)$, while $(1+1) > (1)(1)$

   $$(1+2) > (1)(2)$$
   $$(2+2) = (2)(2)$$

3. **The correct answer is (B).** $M = \{$all integers greater than $2\}$.

   $N = \{$all integers less than $9\}$

   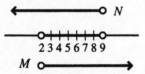

   $M + N$ is the overlap $= \{3, 4, 5, 6, 7, 8\}$

4. **The correct answer is (D).** $x - y$ is the opposite of $y - x$, $\Rightarrow \dfrac{x-y}{y-x} = -1$ and $-\dfrac{(x-y)}{(y-x)} = +1$

5. **The correct answer is (C).**

   $$f(x) = kx^2$$
   $$f(2) = k(2)^2 = 12$$
   $$= 4k = 12$$
   $$k = 3$$

6. **The correct answer is (A).**

   $$\text{Average} = \frac{\text{Sum of the items}}{\text{Quantity of items}}$$
   $$\text{Average} = \frac{(3n+1)+(n+7)+(2n-2)}{3}$$
   $$= \frac{6n+6}{3} = 2n+2$$

7. **The correct answer is (B).** To be real, the value under the radical must be ≥ 0.

   $$x - 9 \geq 0$$
   $$x \geq 0$$

8. **The correct answer is (A).**

   $$-3\big(-3+(-3)(-4)-2\big)-1$$
   $$=-3\big(-3+(12)-2\quad\big)-1$$
   $$=-3(7\qquad\quad)-1$$
   $$=-21-1$$
   $$=-22$$

9. **The correct answer is (D).**

   $$x = \frac{-b \pm \sqrt{b^2 - 4ac}}{2a} \qquad \begin{aligned} a &= 2 \\ b &= 1 \\ c &= 1 \end{aligned}$$

   $$x = \frac{-(1) \pm \sqrt{(1)^2 - 4(2)(1)}}{2(2)}$$

   $$x = \frac{-1 \pm \sqrt{1 - 8}}{4}$$

   $$x = \frac{-1 \pm \sqrt{-7}}{4}$$

   $$x = \frac{-1 \pm i\sqrt{7}}{4}$$

10. **The correct answer is (A).**

    ```
    2 | 62
    2 | 31 r 0
    2 | 15 r 1
    2 | 7  r 1
    2 | 3  r 1
    2 | 1  r 1
        0 r 1
    ```

    1 1 1 1 1 0

11. **The correct answer is (B).**

    (A) is $y = 4x$

    (B) is $y = 4^{-x}$ or $y = \left(\dfrac{1}{4}\right)^x$

    (C) is $y = -4^{-x}$ or $y = \left(\dfrac{1}{4}\right)^x$

    (D) is $y = \log_4 x$

12.   **The correct answer is (C).**

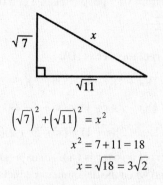

$$\left(\sqrt{7}\right)^2 + \left(\sqrt{11}\right)^2 = x^2$$
$$x^2 = 7 + 11 = 18$$
$$x = \sqrt{18} = 3\sqrt{2}$$

13.   **The correct answer is (A).**

At the y–intercept, $x = 0$

$$\frac{(0)^2}{4} - \frac{(0)}{3} + \frac{y}{2} = 1$$
$$\frac{y}{2} = 1$$
$$y = 2$$

14.   **The correct answer is (C).**

1st line: $1 = 1 = 1^2$

2nd line: $1 + 3 = 4 = 2^2$

3rd line: $1 + 3 + 5 = 9 = 3^2$

4th line: $1 + 3 + 5 + 7 = 16 = 4^2$

113th line: $(113)^2 = 12{,}769$

15.   **The correct answer is (B).**

$$f(x) = 3x - 7$$
$$f(4) = 3(4) - 7 = 5$$
$$g(x) = 1$$
$$g(5) = 1$$

Note: $g(x)$ is always 1. It does not depend on the value of x or $f(x)$.

16.   **The correct answer is (D).** H has horizontal line symmetry H.

I has horizontal line symmetry I.

M and W do not have horizontal line symmetry.

E has horizontal line symmetry E.

17.   **The correct answer is (D).** The multiplicative inverse is the reciprocal.

$$\frac{1}{(2-2i)} \cdot \frac{(2+2i)}{(2+2i)} = \frac{2+2i}{4-4i^2} = \frac{2+2i}{4+4}$$
$$= \frac{2+2i}{8} = \frac{1+i}{4}$$

18.   **The correct answer is (B).**

$$q = q_0 3^{-2t}$$
$$q = 9{,}000 \cdot 3^{-2(1)}$$
$$q = 9{,}000\left(3^{-2}\right)$$
$$q = 9{,}000\left(\frac{1}{9}\right) = 1{,}000$$

19.   **The correct answer is (D).**

$$\text{Average} = \frac{\text{Sum of the items}}{\text{Quantity of items}}$$
$$\text{Average} = \frac{88 + 92 + 86 + x}{4} = 90$$
$$\frac{266 + x}{4} = 90$$
$$266 + x = 360$$
$$x = 94$$

20.   **The correct answer is (D).**

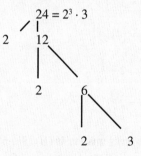

21.   **The correct answer is (C).**

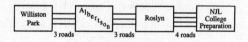

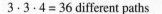

$3 \cdot 3 \cdot 4 = 36$ different paths

22. **The correct answer is (B).**

$(A \cap B) =$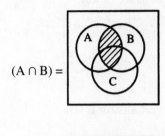

$C =$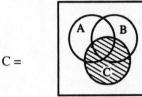

$C \cup (A \cap B) =$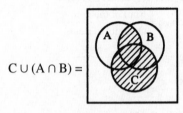

23. **The correct answer is (A).**

$$x \odot y = x^y + y^x$$
$$4 \odot \frac{1}{2} = (4)^{\frac{1}{2}} + \left(\frac{1}{2}\right)^4$$
$$= 2 + \frac{1}{16}$$
$$= 2\frac{1}{16}$$

24. **The correct answer is (B).** Simply stated, to be a function the same value of x cannot give two or more different values of y. If it does, it is not a function. Choice (B) shows $x = 2$ as $y = 1, 3$; therefore choice (B) is not a function.

25. **The correct answer is (D).**

$$x^2 + y^2 = 16$$
$$(5)^2 + y^2 = 16$$
$$25 + y^2 = 16$$
$$y^2 = -9$$
$$y = \pm\sqrt{-9} = \pm 3i$$

26. **The correct answer is (C).** The number of combinations of 5 people taken 3 at a time is $_5C_3 = \frac{5 \cdot 4 \cdot 3}{3 \cdot 2 \cdot 1} = 10.$

27. **The correct answer is (D).**

(A) $(x-1)(x+1)(x-2) = (x^2-1)(x-2)$

(B) $(x+1)(x-2)(x-1) = (x^2-x-2)(x-1)$

(C) $(x-1)(x-2)(x+1) = (x^2-3x+2)(x+1)$

28. **The correct answer is (A).** An expression is undefined when the denominator equals zero.

$x - 3 = 0$ when $x = 3$

29. **The correct answer is (C).** The converse of an implication reverses the hypothesis and conclusion.

30. **The correct answer is (A).**

$P(\text{number} > 5) = \frac{1}{6}$

$P(\text{tail}) = \frac{1}{2}$

$P(\text{number} > 5 \text{ AND tail}) = \frac{1}{6}\left(\frac{1}{2}\right) = \frac{1}{12}$

31. **The correct answer is (B).**

$$2 \text{ Zits } = 3 \text{ Zats}$$
$$= 3[5 \text{ Zims}]$$
$$= 15 \text{ Zims}$$
$$= 15\left[\frac{2}{3} \text{ Zags}\right]$$
$$= 10 \text{ Zags}$$
$$\therefore 5 \text{ Zags } = 1 \text{ Zit}$$

32. **The correct answer is (B).**

$$\log_5 2 + \log_5 x = \log_5 20$$
$$\log_5 2x = \log_5 20$$
$$2x = 20$$
$$x = 10$$

33. **The correct answer is (B).**

The roots of $(x-3)(x-2)(x+1)(x-1)$ are:

$3, 2, -1, 1$

$3 + 2 - 1 + 1 = 5$

Section II

34. **The correct answer is (D).**

    $\sqrt{13}$ is irrational

    π is irrational

    $\sqrt{3}$ is irrational

    $\sqrt{.16} = .4$ is rational

    Irrational numbers include:

    • Never–ending, nonrepeating decimals

    • The square roots of numbers that are not perfect squares

35. **The correct answer is (C).**

    (A) $y = |x| - 3$

    (B) $y = |x| + 3$

    (C) $y = |x - 3|$

    (D) $y = |x + 3|$

36. **The correct answer is (D).** Using a numerical counterexample can show that choices (A), (B), and (C) do not meet the "must" requirement.

    • If $x = 2$ and $y = -4$, then $x > y$

    However, $x^2 = (2)^2$, which is not greater than $y^2 = (-4)^2 = 16$.

    • If $x = 2$ and $y = -4$, then $x > y$

    However, $xy = (2)(-4) = -8$, which is not greater than zero.

    • If $x = -2$ and $y = -4$, then $x > y$

    However, $x + y = (-2) + (-4) = -6$, which is not greater than zero.

    Note: $x > y - 3$ for all values of x and y for which $x > y$.

37. **The correct answer is (C).** Prime numbers are integers greater than one that are divisible only by themselves and one.

    The intersection of set A and set B is $\{2, 3, 5\}$.

38. **The correct answer is (A).** $(-10)^3 = -1,000$ is less than (-10) while $(-1)^3 = -1$

    $$(0)^3 = 0$$

    $$(10)^3 > 10$$

39. **The correct answer is (A).**

    $$|x - 1| = -9$$

    $$\downarrow$$

$x - 1 = +9$	$x - 1 = -9$
$x = 10$	$x = -8$

    check

$|10 - 1| \stackrel{?}{=} -9$	$|-8 - 1| \stackrel{?}{=} -9$
$|9| \stackrel{?}{=} -9$	$|-9| \stackrel{?}{=} -9$
$9 \neq -9$	$9 \neq -9$
Reject	Reject

    The answer is the empty or null set.

40. **The correct answer is (B).**

    Method 1:

    $$\begin{array}{r} x^2 - 4x + 11 \\ x+2\overline{)x^3 - 2x^2 + 3x - 4} \\ \underline{x^3 + 2x^2} \\ -4x^2 + 3x - 4 \\ \underline{-4x^2 - 8x} \\ 11x - 4 \\ \underline{11x + 22} \\ -26 \end{array}$$

    Method 2:

-2	1	-2	3	-4
		-2	8	-22
	1	-4	11	$\underline{|-26}$

    Method 3:

    $$f(x) = x^3 - 2x^2 + 3x - 4$$

    $$f(-2) = (-2)^3 - 2(-2)^2 + 3(-2) - 4 = -26$$

41. **The correct answer is (C).** The inverse of a statement negates both the hypothesis and the conclusion. In symbolic form, the inverse of $p \rightarrow q$ is $\sim p \rightarrow \sim q$.

42. **The correct answer is (C).** If m is an integer, then $2m$ must be even and $2m-5$ must be odd.

    By counterexample, choices (A), (B), and (D) can be shown to violate the "must" requirement.

    If $m = 4 \rightarrow 2m = (2)(4) = 8$

    If $m = 5 \quad m + 3 = (5) + (3) = 8$

    If $m = 1 \quad m^2 + 2m + 1 = (1)^2 + 2(1) + 1 = 4$

43. **The correct answer is (D).**

    $$f(x) = 2^x + x^2$$
    $$f(-1) = 2^{-1} + (-1)^2$$
    $$= \frac{1}{2} + 1 = \frac{3}{2}$$

44. **The correct answer is (D).** The domain of $y = \dfrac{1}{\sqrt{1-x}}$ is values of x for which y is real and defined.

    $x \neq 1$ because y would be undefined (division by 0)

    $x < 1$ otherwise y would be imaginary

45. **The correct answer is (A).** The mode is the most frequent value = 14.

    The median is the middle value when listed in ascending order. If there is no single middle number, average the two middle numbers.

    $$\text{median} = \frac{14 + 14}{2} = 14$$
    $$14 - 14 = 0$$

46. **The correct answer is (B).** A linear function has a constant slope.

    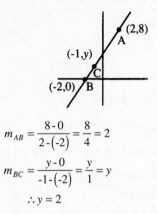

    $$m_{AB} = \frac{8-0}{2-(-2)} = \frac{8}{4} = 2$$
    $$m_{BC} = \frac{y-0}{-1-(-2)} = \frac{y}{1} = y$$
    $$\therefore y = 2$$

47. **The correct answer is (B).** Radicals that do not simplify to integers, fractions, terminating decimals, or infinite repeating decimals are irrational.

    If $x^2 - 4 = 0 \qquad x = \pm 2$ rational

    If $x^2 - 2 = 0 \qquad x = \pm\sqrt{2}$ irrational

    If $x^2 - 2x + 1 = 0$

    $(x-1)(x-1) = 0 \quad x = 1$ rational

    If $x^2 - 2x = 0$

    $x(x-2) = 0 \qquad x = 0, 2$ rational

48. **The correct answer is (B).** TENNESSEE

    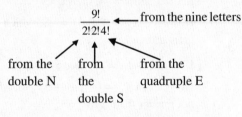

    $$\frac{9!}{2!2!4!} = \frac{9 \cdot 8 \cdot 7 \cdot 6 \cdot 5 \cdot 4 \cdot 3 \cdot 2 \cdot 1}{(2 \cdot 1)(2 \cdot 1)(4 \cdot 3 \cdot 2 \cdot 1)} = 3,780$$

49. **The correct answer is (B).** To find the inverse of N, first identify the "identity element." The identity element is "L." Next, read the chart under the letter "N" to see which element yields the identity element "L." Under "N" the element "J" yields the identity element. Therefore, "J" is the inverse of "N."

50. **The correct answer is (C).** A set is closed under a particular operation if after performing that operation on two set members the result is also contained within the set.

    (+) $1 + 3 = 4$, which is NOT in the set

    (−) $1 - 3 = -2$, which is NOT in the set

    (÷) $\frac{1}{3}$ is NOT in the set

    The set consists of whole number powers of 3

    $\{3^0, 3^1, 3^2, 3^3, 3^4 ...\}$

    By the laws (rules) of exponents: $3a \cdot 3b = 3^{a+b}$.

    Therefore, the product of two set members yields another set member.

51. **The correct answer is (A).**

    $2(x - 3) - 2x = 5$

    $2x - 6 - 2x = 5$

    $-6 \neq 5$

    There are no values of x that satisfy the equation.

52. **The correct answer is (A).**

    $6x^2 + 5x - 4$

    $= (2x - 1)(3x + 4)$

53. **The correct answer is (C).** To select 2 yellows from 6 yellows $= {}_6C_2 = \frac{6 \cdot 5}{2 \cdot 1} = 15$ ways.

    To select 1 red from 4 reds $= {}_4C_1 = 4$ ways.

    To select 1 pink from 2 pinks $= {}_2C_1 = 2$ ways.

    Using the counting principle, which states that if one activity can be performed in "a" ways and a second (independent) activity can be performed in "b" ways, then there are $a \cdot b$ possible ways in which both activities can be performed.

    $15 \cdot 4 \cdot 2 = 120$

54. **The correct answer is (B).**

    $$
    \begin{array}{llll}
    1 & 0 & 1 & 0 \\
    \end{array}
    $$

    $0 \times 2^0 = 0 \cdot 1 = 0$

    $1 \times 2^1 = 1 \cdot 2 = 2$

    $0 \times 2^2 = 0 \cdot 4 = 0$

    $1 \times 2^3 = 1 \cdot 8 = \underline{8}$

    10

55. **The correct answer is (A).**

    To be a right triangle:

    $$\left(\text{leg 1}\right)^2 + \left(\text{leg 2}\right)^2 = \left(\text{hypotenuse}\right)^2$$

    $$2^2 + 6^2 = \left(\sqrt{40}\right)^2$$

    $$4 + 36 = 40$$

    $$40 = 40$$

    Choice (B) $2^2 + 18^2 \neq 20^2$

    Choice (C) $4^2 + 6^2 \neq (\sqrt{40})^2$

    Choice (D) $4^2 + 36^2 \neq 40^2$

56. **The correct answer is (A).** A prime number is a number greater than 1 that is divisible only by itself and one. Fifty–one is divisible by 3.

57. **The correct answer is (C).** The roots of a quadratic are where the graph intersects the x–axis. If the roots are imaginary, then the graph is either entirely above or entirely below the x–axis.

58. **The correct answer is (D).**

    $P(\text{a number less than 4}) = \frac{3}{4}$

    $P(R) = \frac{1}{4}$

    $P(\text{both}) = \left(\frac{3}{4}\right)\left(\frac{1}{4}\right) = \frac{3}{16}$ this is "and"

    $P(\text{or}) = P(\text{a number less than 4}) + P(R) - P(\text{both})$

    $= \frac{3}{4} + \frac{1}{4} - \frac{3}{16} = \frac{13}{16}$

59. **The correct answer is (D).** Counterexamples to choices:

    (A) 3, 3, 10, 10, 10

    (B) 3, 3, 10, 10, 10

    (C) 3, 3, 10, 10, 10

60. **The correct answer is (D).** Let m = slope

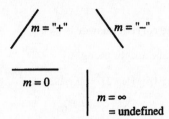

61. **The correct answer is (A).** The mode is the value with the greatest frequency. The mode of the data set is 2.

62. **The correct answer is (D).**

$$i^{17} + i^{18} + i^{19} + i^{20} = (i) + (-1) + (-i) + (1) = 0$$

$$i^3 + i^5 + i^7 + i^9 = (-i) + (i) + (-i) + (i) = 0$$

$$i^2 + i^4 + i^6 + i^8 = (-1) + (1) + (-1) + (1) = 0$$

$$i^4 + i^8 + i^{12} + i^6 = (1) + (1) + (1) + (1) = 4$$

63. **The correct answer is (C).**

$$25x = (25)(5^a)$$
$$= (5^2)(5^a) = 5^{a+2}$$

64. **The correct answer is (C).**

$$f(x+h) = 2(x+h) - 1$$
$$= 2x + 2h - 1$$

65. **The correct answer is (B).**

$$\log_6 3 = \log_6 \left(\frac{6}{2}\right)$$
$$= \log_6 6 - \log_6 2$$
$$= 1 - m$$

Practice Examination III Diagnostic Chart

Subject Area*	Question Numbers	Number Wrong
Logic and Sets	Part 1: 2, 3, 16, 22, 29	_____
	Part 2: 37, 38, 41	_____
Number System and Systems	Part 1: 1, 7, 8, 10, 20, 23, 28	_____
	Part 2: 34, 36, 42, 49, 50, 51, 54, 56	_____
Functions and Graphs (Basic Algebra)	Part 1: 5, 11, 13, 15, 24	_____
	Part 2: 35, 43, 44, 46, 52, 57, 60, 64	_____
Probability, Statistics, and Counting	Part 1: 6, 14, 19, 21, 26, 30	_____
	Part 2: 45, 48, 53,58, 59, 61	_____
Algebra (Beyond Basics)	Part 1: 4, 9, 17, 18, 25, 27, 31, 32, 33	_____
	Part 2: 39, 40, 47, 62, 63, 65	_____
Geometry	Part 1: 12	_____
	Part 2: 55	_____

*Many questions overlap more than one subject area.

Natural Sciences

ABOUT THE GENERAL EXAMINATION IN NATURAL SCIENCES

The CLEP General Examination in Natural Sciences is a 90-minute, 120-question examination intended to measure the knowledge and understanding of scientific concepts that are expected of a well-educated adult. Most questions are general enough so that they can be answered by all whose interests in science have prompted them to keep up with scientific advances through articles in newspapers and magazines, even though they may not have attended formal science classes for some time. Many questions are related to the role of science in today's world, to the understanding and application of fundamental scientific concepts and principles, and to the understanding of scientific thought processes. The skills measured by the General Exam in Natural Sciences are broken down as follows:

1. Knowledge of fundamental facts, concepts, and principles—approximately 40%.

2. Interpretation and comprehension of graphs, diagrams, tables, equations, or written passages—approximately 25%.

3. Qualitative and quantitative application of scientific principles (greater emphasis on qualitative applications)—approximately 35%.

The three Practice Exams that follow have been designed to conform as closely as possible to the actual examination. The approximate percentages for topic areas have been translated into a specific number of questions. The topics covered and the number of questions in each exam area are detailed below.

SECTION I: THE LIFE SCIENCES (60 QUESTIONS TO BE ANSWERED IN 45 MINUTES)

1. Origin and evolution of life; classification of organisms—12 questions.

2. Cell organization; cell division; chemical nature of the gene; bioenergetics and biosynthesis—12 questions.

3. Structure, function, and development of organisms; pattern of heredity—24 questions.

4. Concepts of population biology with an emphasis on ecology—12 questions.

ROAD MAP

- *About the General Examination in Natural Sciences*
- *Mini-Exam in Natural Sciences*
- *Practice Examination I*
- *Practice Examination II*
- *Practice Examination III*

SECTION II: THE PHYSICAL SCIENCES (60 QUESTIONS TO BE ANSWERED IN 45 MINUTES)

1. Atom structure and properties; elementary particles; nuclear reactions—8 questions.

2. Chemical elements, compounds, and reactions; molecular structure and bonding—12 questions.

3. Heat, thermodynamics, and states of matter; classical mechanics and relativity—14 questions.

4. Electricity and magnetism; waves, light, and sound—6 questions.

5. The universe: galaxies, stars, the solar system—8 questions.

6. The earth: atmosphere, hydrosphere, structure, properties, surface features, geological processes, history—12 questions.

It should be clearly understood that these distributions may vary slightly from examination to examination and that a few questions may be interdisciplinary and are, therefore, difficult to classify.

Study Plan

Preparation for the General Examination in the Natural Sciences can be accomplished in a number of different ways, depending on the background and skills of the person doing the preparing. The following plan of study is one that has proved successful for many candidates for the CLEP Examination.

1. From a library, a friend, or a bookstore obtain a few of the books suggested in the reference list. Make sure to select one book from each of the five subject areas.

2. Read through the materials in the topic areas in which you feel you are weak. Take notes to reinforce your study, but keep them brief, avoiding esoteric detail while focusing on the general concepts and principles.

3. When you feel that you are prepared, take the first Practice Exam under actual timed conditions, recording your answers on the answer sheet provided at the beginning of the exam.

4. Score the exam by checking your answers against the answer key at the end of the exam. Fill in the Diagnostic Chart in order to determine your areas of strength and your areas of weakness.

5. Check the explanations to the answers provided at the end of the exam, not only to see why your incorrect answers were wrong but also to make sure that you employed the correct reasoning in selecting the correct answer.

6. Return to the references to review those areas of weakness identified by the Practice Exam.

7. Take the second Practice Exam under actual timed conditions.

8. Repeat steps 4–6 and then take the third Practice Exam.

9. Repeat steps 4–6. By this time, you should be well prepared to take the actual CLEP exam.

Finally, it should be noted that for purposes of evaluation, the questions on each Practice Exam are grouped together by topic area. This may or may not be the case for the actual CLEP exam.

MINI-EXAM IN NATURAL SCIENCES

Section I: Life Sciences

10 Questions

Directions: Choose the best answer for each of the following questions.

1. The "use and disuse" theory of evolution was proposed by
    (A) Mendel.
    (B) Wallace.
    (C) Aristotle.
    (D) Lamarck.

2. Cell reproduction specifically involves
    (A) vacuoles.
    (B) mitochondria.
    (C) centrosomes.
    (D) lysosomes.

3. During the embryonic development of animals, the ectodermal germ layer eventually gives rise to the
    (A) nervous system, muscles, lining of the digestive tract.
    (B) supportive tissues, muscles, lining of the body cavity.
    (C) external body covering, nervous system, sense organs.
    (D) muscles, external body covering, nervous system.

4. Unstable populations are most associated with
    (A) J-shaped growth forms.
    (B) sigmoid growth forms.
    (C) S-shaped growth forms.
    (D) cyclic growth forms.

Section II: Physical Sciences

5. Calcium has an atomic weight of 40. Which of the following arrangements represents the correct number of protons, electrons, and neutrons for this element?

    (A) 19, 21, 19
    (B) 22, 14, 14
    (C) 13, 14, 13
    (D) 20, 20, 20

6. Polar molecules

    (A) are cryogenic.
    (B) have different charges at either end.
    (C) are chlorogenic.
    (D) have an excess of electrons.

7. The Second Law of Thermodynamics is best summarized as follows:

    (A) Energy transformations are not 100% efficient.
    (B) The ultimate energy source in the biosphere is our sun.
    (C) Energy cannot be created or destroyed.
    (D) For each action there exists an equal and opposite reaction.

8. Sound waves are best described as

    (A) electromechanical.
    (B) transverse.
    (C) longitudinal.
    (D) polarized.

9. Two commonly used methods of determining the distance from Earth to various stars are

    (A) interplanetary distances, angle bisection.
    (B) apparent vs. absolute magnitude of brightness, triangulation.
    (C) solar flares, planetary rotation.
    (D) comparison to absolute zero, satellite speed.

10. A negative temperature gradient would be expected as one moves from the earth's surface through the

    (A) stratosphere.
    (B) thermosphere.
    (C) exosphere.
    (D) troposphere.

Answer Key

Section I

1. D   2. C   3. C   4. A

Section II

5. D   6. B   7. A   8. C   9. B   10. D

Explanatory Answers

Section I

1. **The correct answer is (D).** Jean Baptiste de Lamarck proposed the first general theory of evolution in 1809. It addressed the inheritance of acquired characteristics and is frequently referred to as the theory of "use and disuse." Briefly summarized, it states that the shape and organization of animals are directly affected by their environment. Continual use results in enlargement of an organ, while disuse results in eventual disappearance. These results, according to the theory, are preserved by reproduction. There is no reliable evidence to support this theory.

2. **The correct answer is (C).** During cell reproduction the centrosome divides into two centrioles. Each centriole migrates toward a pole of the cell and eventually serves as an attachment site for the chromosomes.

3. **The correct answer is (C).** At the completion of gastrulation three distinct germ layers are evident: ectoderm, mesoderm, and endoderm. The ectodermal layer is eventually responsible for the development of the external covering of the body, the nervous system, and the sense organs. The mesoderm gives rise to various supportive tissues, muscles, the lining of the body cavity, and several internal organs. The endoderm is responsible for the lining of the digestive tract, its glands, and several associated structures.

4. **The correct answer is (A).** J-shaped growth forms are characterized by rapid population increase over a short period of time. A subsequent population crash usually results since the organisms have exceeded the carrying capacity of their environment.

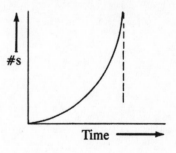

Section II

5. **The correct answer is (D).** The atomic weight of an element is calculated by adding the number of protons and neutrons. The electrons, because of their small size and insignificant weight, are not generally factored in the atomic weight.

6. **The correct answer is (B).** A polar molecule has a positive charge at one end and a negative charge at the opposite end.

7. **The correct answer is (A).** According to the First Law of Thermodynamics, energy is neither created nor destroyed but is transformed from one type to another. When energy changes form, according to the Second Law of Thermodynamics, some energy is always dispersed or lost. Thus, the transformation is not 100% efficient.

8. **The correct answer is (C).** During sound production, the vibratory motion of the molecules of the transmitting medium is in the same direction as the traveling wave front. The waves are therefore longitudinal.

9. **The correct answer is (B).** The apparent vs. absolute magnitude of brightness method utilizes the light spectrum of known-distance stars (brightness) and compares this with the light spectrum of unknown-distance stars to calculate approximate distance from Earth. Triangulation is based upon the geometric calculation of the earth, our sun (known distance from Earth), and the unknown-distance star.

10. **The correct answer is (D).** Because of the radiation of heat from the earth's surface, the troposphere is warmer close to the earth and cooler as one moves through the troposphere toward the stratosphere.

Answer Sheet for Practice Examination I

Section I

1 Ⓐ Ⓑ Ⓒ Ⓓ Ⓔ	13 Ⓐ Ⓑ Ⓒ Ⓓ Ⓔ	25 Ⓐ Ⓑ Ⓒ Ⓓ Ⓔ	37 Ⓐ Ⓑ Ⓒ Ⓓ Ⓔ	49 Ⓐ Ⓑ Ⓒ Ⓓ Ⓔ
2 Ⓐ Ⓑ Ⓒ Ⓓ Ⓔ	14 Ⓐ Ⓑ Ⓒ Ⓓ Ⓔ	26 Ⓐ Ⓑ Ⓒ Ⓓ Ⓔ	38 Ⓐ Ⓑ Ⓒ Ⓓ Ⓔ	50 Ⓐ Ⓑ Ⓒ Ⓓ Ⓔ
3 Ⓐ Ⓑ Ⓒ Ⓓ Ⓔ	15 Ⓐ Ⓑ Ⓒ Ⓓ Ⓔ	27 Ⓐ Ⓑ Ⓒ Ⓓ Ⓔ	39 Ⓐ Ⓑ Ⓒ Ⓓ Ⓔ	51 Ⓐ Ⓑ Ⓒ Ⓓ Ⓔ
4 Ⓐ Ⓑ Ⓒ Ⓓ Ⓔ	16 Ⓐ Ⓑ Ⓒ Ⓓ Ⓔ	28 Ⓐ Ⓑ Ⓒ Ⓓ Ⓔ	40 Ⓐ Ⓑ Ⓒ Ⓓ Ⓔ	52 Ⓐ Ⓑ Ⓒ Ⓓ Ⓔ
5 Ⓐ Ⓑ Ⓒ Ⓓ Ⓔ	17 Ⓐ Ⓑ Ⓒ Ⓓ Ⓔ	29 Ⓐ Ⓑ Ⓒ Ⓓ Ⓔ	41 Ⓐ Ⓑ Ⓒ Ⓓ Ⓔ	53 Ⓐ Ⓑ Ⓒ Ⓓ Ⓔ
6 Ⓐ Ⓑ Ⓒ Ⓓ Ⓔ	18 Ⓐ Ⓑ Ⓒ Ⓓ Ⓔ	30 Ⓐ Ⓑ Ⓒ Ⓓ Ⓔ	42 Ⓐ Ⓑ Ⓒ Ⓓ Ⓔ	54 Ⓐ Ⓑ Ⓒ Ⓓ Ⓔ
7 Ⓐ Ⓑ Ⓒ Ⓓ Ⓔ	19 Ⓐ Ⓑ Ⓒ Ⓓ Ⓔ	31 Ⓐ Ⓑ Ⓒ Ⓓ Ⓔ	43 Ⓐ Ⓑ Ⓒ Ⓓ Ⓔ	55 Ⓐ Ⓑ Ⓒ Ⓓ Ⓔ
8 Ⓐ Ⓑ Ⓒ Ⓓ Ⓔ	20 Ⓐ Ⓑ Ⓒ Ⓓ Ⓔ	32 Ⓐ Ⓑ Ⓒ Ⓓ Ⓔ	44 Ⓐ Ⓑ Ⓒ Ⓓ Ⓔ	56 Ⓐ Ⓑ Ⓒ Ⓓ Ⓔ
9 Ⓐ Ⓑ Ⓒ Ⓓ Ⓔ	21 Ⓐ Ⓑ Ⓒ Ⓓ Ⓔ	33 Ⓐ Ⓑ Ⓒ Ⓓ Ⓔ	45 Ⓐ Ⓑ Ⓒ Ⓓ Ⓔ	57 Ⓐ Ⓑ Ⓒ Ⓓ Ⓔ
10 Ⓐ Ⓑ Ⓒ Ⓓ Ⓔ	22 Ⓐ Ⓑ Ⓒ Ⓓ Ⓔ	34 Ⓐ Ⓑ Ⓒ Ⓓ Ⓔ	46 Ⓐ Ⓑ Ⓒ Ⓓ Ⓔ	58 Ⓐ Ⓑ Ⓒ Ⓓ Ⓔ
11 Ⓐ Ⓑ Ⓒ Ⓓ Ⓔ	23 Ⓐ Ⓑ Ⓒ Ⓓ Ⓔ	35 Ⓐ Ⓑ Ⓒ Ⓓ Ⓔ	47 Ⓐ Ⓑ Ⓒ Ⓓ Ⓔ	59 Ⓐ Ⓑ Ⓒ Ⓓ Ⓔ
12 Ⓐ Ⓑ Ⓒ Ⓓ Ⓔ	24 Ⓐ Ⓑ Ⓒ Ⓓ Ⓔ	36 Ⓐ Ⓑ Ⓒ Ⓓ Ⓔ	48 Ⓐ Ⓑ Ⓒ Ⓓ Ⓔ	60 Ⓐ Ⓑ Ⓒ Ⓓ Ⓔ

Section II

61 Ⓐ Ⓑ Ⓒ Ⓓ Ⓔ	73 Ⓐ Ⓑ Ⓒ Ⓓ Ⓔ	85 Ⓐ Ⓑ Ⓒ Ⓓ Ⓔ	97 Ⓐ Ⓑ Ⓒ Ⓓ Ⓔ	109 Ⓐ Ⓑ Ⓒ Ⓓ Ⓔ
62 Ⓐ Ⓑ Ⓒ Ⓓ Ⓔ	74 Ⓐ Ⓑ Ⓒ Ⓓ Ⓔ	86 Ⓐ Ⓑ Ⓒ Ⓓ Ⓔ	98 Ⓐ Ⓑ Ⓒ Ⓓ Ⓔ	110 Ⓐ Ⓑ Ⓒ Ⓓ Ⓔ
63 Ⓐ Ⓑ Ⓒ Ⓓ Ⓔ	75 Ⓐ Ⓑ Ⓒ Ⓓ Ⓔ	87 Ⓐ Ⓑ Ⓒ Ⓓ Ⓔ	99 Ⓐ Ⓑ Ⓒ Ⓓ Ⓔ	111 Ⓐ Ⓑ Ⓒ Ⓓ Ⓔ
64 Ⓐ Ⓑ Ⓒ Ⓓ Ⓔ	76 Ⓐ Ⓑ Ⓒ Ⓓ Ⓔ	88 Ⓐ Ⓑ Ⓒ Ⓓ Ⓔ	100 Ⓐ Ⓑ Ⓒ Ⓓ Ⓔ	112 Ⓐ Ⓑ Ⓒ Ⓓ Ⓔ
65 Ⓐ Ⓑ Ⓒ Ⓓ Ⓔ	77 Ⓐ Ⓑ Ⓒ Ⓓ Ⓔ	89 Ⓐ Ⓑ Ⓒ Ⓓ Ⓔ	101 Ⓐ Ⓑ Ⓒ Ⓓ Ⓔ	113 Ⓐ Ⓑ Ⓒ Ⓓ Ⓔ
66 Ⓐ Ⓑ Ⓒ Ⓓ Ⓔ	78 Ⓐ Ⓑ Ⓒ Ⓓ Ⓔ	90 Ⓐ Ⓑ Ⓒ Ⓓ Ⓔ	102 Ⓐ Ⓑ Ⓒ Ⓓ Ⓔ	114 Ⓐ Ⓑ Ⓒ Ⓓ Ⓔ
67 Ⓐ Ⓑ Ⓒ Ⓓ Ⓔ	79 Ⓐ Ⓑ Ⓒ Ⓓ Ⓔ	91 Ⓐ Ⓑ Ⓒ Ⓓ Ⓔ	103 Ⓐ Ⓑ Ⓒ Ⓓ Ⓔ	115 Ⓐ Ⓑ Ⓒ Ⓓ Ⓔ
68 Ⓐ Ⓑ Ⓒ Ⓓ Ⓔ	80 Ⓐ Ⓑ Ⓒ Ⓓ Ⓔ	92 Ⓐ Ⓑ Ⓒ Ⓓ Ⓔ	104 Ⓐ Ⓑ Ⓒ Ⓓ Ⓔ	116 Ⓐ Ⓑ Ⓒ Ⓓ Ⓔ
69 Ⓐ Ⓑ Ⓒ Ⓓ Ⓔ	81 Ⓐ Ⓑ Ⓒ Ⓓ Ⓔ	93 Ⓐ Ⓑ Ⓒ Ⓓ Ⓔ	105 Ⓐ Ⓑ Ⓒ Ⓓ Ⓔ	117 Ⓐ Ⓑ Ⓒ Ⓓ Ⓔ
70 Ⓐ Ⓑ Ⓒ Ⓓ Ⓔ	82 Ⓐ Ⓑ Ⓒ Ⓓ Ⓔ	94 Ⓐ Ⓑ Ⓒ Ⓓ Ⓔ	106 Ⓐ Ⓑ Ⓒ Ⓓ Ⓔ	118 Ⓐ Ⓑ Ⓒ Ⓓ Ⓔ
71 Ⓐ Ⓑ Ⓒ Ⓓ Ⓔ	83 Ⓐ Ⓑ Ⓒ Ⓓ Ⓔ	95 Ⓐ Ⓑ Ⓒ Ⓓ Ⓔ	107 Ⓐ Ⓑ Ⓒ Ⓓ Ⓔ	119 Ⓐ Ⓑ Ⓒ Ⓓ Ⓔ
72 Ⓐ Ⓑ Ⓒ Ⓓ Ⓔ	84 Ⓐ Ⓑ Ⓒ Ⓓ Ⓔ	96 Ⓐ Ⓑ Ⓒ Ⓓ Ⓔ	108 Ⓐ Ⓑ Ⓒ Ⓓ Ⓔ	120 Ⓐ Ⓑ Ⓒ Ⓓ Ⓔ

PRACTICE EXAMINATION I

Section I: Life Sciences

60 Questions

Time—45 minutes

Directions: Choose the response that best completes the statement or answers the question.

Answer questions 1 and 2 on the basis of this square:

	0.7B	0.3b
0.7B	0.49	0.21
0.3b	0.21	0.16

1. As indicated, the homozygous dominant individuals constitute what proportion of the population?

   (A) 0.6%
   (B) 42%
   (C) 16%
   (D) 49%
   (E) 65%

2. The proportion of offspring that contain the gene b is

   (A) 40%
   (B) 58%
   (C) 52%
   (D) 16%
   (E) 0.09%

3. Gulls can identify their own species by the distinguishing ring pattern around the eye. This is an example of

   (A) geographic isolation.
   (B) ecological isolation.
   (C) natural selection.
   (D) behavioral isolation.
   (E) physiological isolation.

4. The common factor in mutation, gene flow, and genetic drift is that

   (A) they all affect the individual.
   (B) they can all contribute to gene pool change.
   (C) they can all contribute to evolution.
   (D) All of the above
   (E) (B) and (C)

5. List the following in order to show the origin of life; i.e., simple to complex.

   I.   proteins
   II. CH_4 and NH_3
   III. amino acids
   IV.   C, H, O, N

   (A) I, II, III, IV
   (B) II, IV, I, III
   (C) IV, I, II, III
   (D) IV, II, III, I
   (E) (A) and (B)

6. The classic work of Stanley Miller showed that

   (A) it is possible to filter cells.
   (B) primitive gases can react together to produce small organic molecules.
   (C) bacteria can grow on gold and silver media.
   (D) the first cell was probably made of nucleic acids.
   (E) atmospheric pressure is required for life to begin.

7. In the origin of life, the heterotrophic hypothesis states that

    (A) plants at one time produced nitrogen gas.
    (B) the primitive atmosphere was similar to today's atmosphere.
    (C) preformed organic compounds served as a source of energy and growth for the first cells.
    (D) organic compounds were formed before inorganic compounds.
    (E) oxygen respiration came before fermentation.

8. A characteristic of all chordates is the presence of a

    (A) chorda tympanum.
    (B) chorda tendonae.
    (C) mammary gland.
    (D) vertebral column.
    (E) notochord.

9. Of the following organisms, the one that has an incomplete, but functional, digestive system is

    (A) lumbricus.
    (B) lobster.
    (C) clam.
    (D) grasshopper.
    (E) planaria.

10. Pollination characteristically occurs among which one of the following pairs?

    (A) Angiosperms and psilopsids
    (B) Angiosperms and gymnosperms
    (C) Pteridophytes and bryophytes
    (D) Bryophytes and angiosperms
    (E) Angiosperms and fungi

11. Ferns, conifers, and flowering plants are classified as

    (A) bryophyta.
    (B) spermatophyta.
    (C) psilophyta.
    (D) chlorophyta.
    (E) tracheophyta.

12. The best explanation for placing the echinoderms near the top of the evolutionary tree is that

    (A) the larval form of echinoderms shows close relationships to the vertebrates.
    (B) echinoderms have rudimentary hair and feathers.
    (C) echinoderms are advanced as adults.
    (D) the larval form of the echinoderms indicates that they are closely related to the coelenterates.
    (E) (C) and (D)

13. Which of the following properties make water indispensable to life as we know it?

    (A) Water expands at temperatures below 4°C.
    (B) Water has an extremely high surface tension.
    (C) Water has a very high heat capacity, heat of vaporization, and heat of fusion.
    (D) Water has a high dielectric constant.
    (E) All of the above

14. The cell seems to be the basic unit of life for the following reason(s).

    I. All cells are self-reproductive without a host.
    II. All cells have the same general size and shape.
    III. All cells are self-regulating.

    (A) I
    (B) II
    (C) III
    (D) (A) and (B)
    (E) (A) and (C)

15. Of the following, the pairs that are examples of complex organic compounds with high energy bonds are

    (A) DNA, ATP.
    (B) DDT, 2, 4-D.
    (C) RNA, DNA.
    (D) 2, 4-D, DNA.
    (E) ATP, ADP

16. It is probable that a mammal smaller than a shrew could not exist because it would

    (A) not get sufficient oxygen.
    (B) reproduce too rapidly.
    (C) have to eat at too tremendous a rate.
    (D) not be able to defend itself.
    (E) be unable to bear live young.

17. Which of the following is true of enzyme catalysis but is not true of inorganic catalysis?

    (A) The catalyst speeds up the reaction.
    (B) The catalyst itself undergoes no change in the reaction.
    (C) The catalyst is subject to cellular controls.
    (D) Only a small amount of the catalyst is necessary.
    (E) The effect of the catalyst is similar to an increase in temperature, pressure, or concentration.

18. A leaf from a green and white variegated coleus that was placed in the sun for several hours was treated in the following manner: 1) placed in hot alcohol until colorless, 2) placed in a clean Petri dish and flooded with Lugol's iodine, 3) washed in distilled water, and 4) spread out on clean white paper. The same procedure was followed with the leaf from a green and white variegated plant that was stored without light for 12 hours. The following chart shows the results.

TREAT-MENT	WHITE AREA OF LEAF		GREEN AREA OF LEAF	
	without light	with light	without light	with light
alcohol	white	white	white	white
Lugol's	brown	brown	brown	blue-black
water	no change	no change	no change	no change

Which of the following statements best explains the observed results of the experiment?

    (A) In green plants, light plus the green pigment chlorophyll result in the presence of starch.
    (B) Plants must have chlorophyll in order to synthesize organic nutrients.
    (C) Plants cannot grow without light.
    (D) The green chlorophyll molecule uses light energy to split one molecule of water.
    (E) Enzymes convert the sugar produced during photosynthesis into starch.

19. The second meiotic division is essentially a mitosis except for the product that is

    (A) haploid.
    (B) diploid.
    (C) triploid.
    (D) heterozygous.
    (E) achromatic.

20. The theory of endosymbiosis states that

    (A) animal cells were plant cells that lost their mitochondria.
    (B) organelles were originally independent cells.
    (C) all cells are parasitic.
    (D) organelles arose through a partitioning off of cell membrane.
    (E) All of the above

For questions 21–24, match the smaller structures listed below with the larger structures named in each question.

    (A) cristae
    (B) ribosomes
    (C) grana
    (D) vacuoles
    (E) microtubules

21. Chloroplast

22. Mitochondria

23. Endoplasmic reticulum

24. Cilia

25. A typical vegetative plant organ is the

    (A) cone.
    (B) flower.
    (C) pistil.
    (D) stem.
    (E) seed.

26. The type of muscle tissue found within the walls of blood vessels and of other internal organs is

    (A) smooth muscle.
    (B) skeletal muscle.
    (C) cardiac muscle.
    (D) voluntary muscle.
    (E) striated muscle.

27. The plant tissue responsible for an increase in the width of plants is

    (A) cork.
    (B) epidermis.
    (C) lateral meristem.
    (D) apical meristem.
    (E) cortex.

28. The blood-clotting mechanism is dependent upon the formed element of blood known as the

    (A) erythrocyte.
    (B) leucocyte.
    (C) thrombocyte.
    (D) plasma.
    (E) heme group.

29. If motor neurons are cut, the individual

    (A) cannot hear or see.
    (B) cannot feel or sense anything.
    (C) loses all sense of balance.
    (D) is incapable of making voluntary motions.
    (E) Both (A) and (C)

30. Hemophilia and color blindness are diseases that are

    (A) sex-linked.
    (B) sex-limited.
    (C) viral.
    (D) bacterial.
    (E) triploid.

31. Organisms in temperate zones are able to time their activities by cues given by the photoperiod, since

    (A) all organisms need time to rest.
    (B) light is a limiting factor.
    (C) all organisms have a biological clock.
    (D) day length is always constant for a specific locality and season.
    (E) some plants need long days in order to bloom.

For questions 32–34, select the one of the five lettered graphs below that best depicts the situation described in each question.

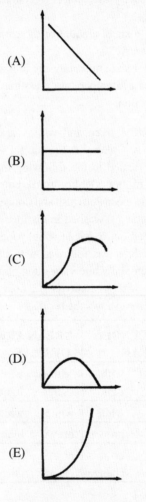

32. Growth of a colony of bacteria under ideal conditions.

    Vertical axis: number of organisms
    Horizontal axis: time

33. Growth of a colony of bacteria in a limited environment.

    Vertical axis: number of organisms
    Horizontal axis: time

34. Human body temperature during moderate exercise.

    Vertical axis: temperature (°C)
    Horizontal axis: time

35. The results of some of the early experiments on plant hormones can be easily reproduced by the following experiment. The tips of four oat seedlings are cut off. One tip is placed on a small block of agar for 2 hours and is then discarded. The four plants are then treated in the following manner: 1) the first plant is left without a tip, 2) the tip is replaced on the second plant, 3) the agar cube that was in contact with a cut tip is placed on the third plant, and 4) an agar cube that has not been in contact with a tip is placed on the fourth plant. The plants are then observed for one or two days.

PLANT	GROWTH
#1	no
#2	yes
#3	yes
#4	no

    From the data obtained from all four plants, it is apparent that

    (A) there is a chemical substance present in agar that causes oat seedlings to grow.
    (B) negative geotropism causes oat seedlings to grow.
    (C) it is possible to stop growth in oat seedlings because the tissues are not differentiated.
    (D) the growth inducing element in oat seedlings is probably a chemical that can diffuse into agar from the tip of the seedling.
    (E) the substance produced in the tips of oat seedlings acts as an inhibitor to root growth.

36. Final cellular differentiation within a developing embryo is
    (A) determined by the physical and chemical environment surrounding the cell.
    (B) entirely dependent upon the germ layer from which the cell is derived.
    (C) dependent upon the specific chromosomes the cell receives.
    (D) controlled by the cytoplasm of the unfertilized egg.
    (E) determined before gastrulation of the embryo.

37. Much of the phenomenon of phototropism in plants was first observed by which one of the following?
    (A) Charles Darwin
    (B) Hugo De Vries
    (C) Ivan Pavlov
    (D) Lloyd Morgan
    (E) Jacques Loeb

38. Sodium citrate is added to bottles of donor blood to prevent clotting because it removes the
    (A) serum.
    (B) plasma.
    (C) calcium.
    (D) prothrombin.
    (E) fibrinogen.

39. Of the following, which one best describes phenylketonuria?
    (A) A vitamin deficiency resulting in abnormal metabolism of proteins
    (B) An inherited metabolic disorder resulting in a lack of an enzyme
    (C) A mineral deficiency resulting in abnormal bone formation
    (D) An abnormal shape in red blood cells
    (E) A chronic disease of unknown causes

40. The center for temperature regulation in the human is the
    (A) skin.
    (B) lungs.
    (C) thalamus.
    (D) medulla.
    (E) cerebellum.

41. Select the cross in which all offspring will be hybrids.

    (A) RRYY × RRYY
    (B) RRYY × rryy
    (C) RrYy × RrYy
    (D) RrYy × rryy
    (E) rryy × rryy

42. If one parent belongs to blood group B and the other belongs to blood group AB, the children could belong to

    (A) A, B, or AB only.
    (B) A or B only.
    (C) A, B, O, or AB.
    (D) B or O only.
    (E) A or O only.

43. Biochemists have found that, though the amount of any given base found in DNA varies considerably from one species to another, the amount of thymine is always equal to the amount of

    (A) cytosine.
    (B) guanine.
    (C) uracil.
    (D) adenine.
    (E) ATP.

44. The function of DNA prior to protein synthesis is to

    (A) attract transfer RNA with appropriate amino acids.
    (B) destroy anticodons.
    (C) serve as a template for the production of messenger RNA.
    (D) adhere to the ribosomes waiting for transfer RNA.
    (E) All of the above

For questions 45–48, choose the lettered term that is most closely related to the numbered statement:

    (A) Morula
    (B) Blastula
    (C) Gastrula
    (D) Mesoderm formation
    (E) Neurulation

45. Shows the presence of the blastocoele.

46. Is the end result of cleavage.

47. In amphibians, this stage results from the process of gastrulation.

48. The next structure to develop directly from the zygote, in humans.

49. Given the Hardy-Weinberg Law, $p^2 + 2pq + q^2 = 1.0$, the p represents the

    (A) rate of mutation.
    (B) frequency of the dominant gene.
    (C) percentage of people showing the recessive trait.
    (D) frequency of the recessive gene.
    (E) hybrid and homozygous dominant ratio.

50. Life scientists now agree that

    (A) life on Earth is impossible.
    (B) $E = mc^2$ is the best explanation for photosynthesis.
    (C) it is possible to use all of the energy in glucose for biological work.
    (D) usable energy is constantly being lost when chemical reactions occur.
    (E) all life started in Earth's atmosphere.

51. The best illustration of a food chain is

    (A) algae→larval insect→fish→man.
    (B) fish→larval insect→algae→man.
    (C) larval insect→algae→fish→man.
    (D) algae→fish→larval insect→man.
    (E) algae→fish→man→larval insect.

52. The greenhouse effect of CO_2 is best opposed by

    (A) deep respirations.
    (B) water pollution.
    (C) X rays.
    (D) smog particles.
    (E) All of the above

53. In order to maintain a balanced ecosystem,

    (A) decay through bacterial and fungal action is required.
    (B) an outside source of energy is necessary.
    (C) matter itself must cycle.
    (D) a proportionality must be maintained among consumer and producer populations.
    (E) All of the above

54. Producers in an ecosystem are most often

    (A) saprophytes.
    (B) carnivores.
    (C) heterotrophs.
    (D) omnivores.
    (E) autotrophs.

55. Under conditions of stability in food chains,

    (A) limitations on food, space, and disease relationships usually keep populations in check.
    (B) destruction of one particular species will have no ill effects on the chain.
    (C) relative sizes of populations are important to maintenance of the food chain.
    (D) (A) and (B)
    (E) (A) and (C)

56. The biosphere is composed of

    (A) lithospheres.
    (B) hydrospheres.
    (C) atmospheres.
    (D) ecosystems.
    (E) tropospheres.

57. When DDT or PCB are introduced into the base of a food pyramid, they will

    (A) decompose rapidly.
    (B) become incorporated into nucleic acids.
    (C) show a biomagnification up the pyramid.
    (D) dilute themselves out as they move up the pyramid.
    (E) become less toxic substances.

58. As carbon cycles on Earth, it returns to the atmosphere by

    (A) water evaporation.
    (B) animal and plant external respiration.
    (C) increased Calvin Cycle activity.
    (D) photosynthesis.
    (E) (A) and (D)

59. Algae growth is directly related to phosphates. The dumping of phosphate detergents into a pond will

    (A) increase algal growth.
    (B) decrease algal growth.
    (C) destroy the algae but leave the fish.
    (D) result in no change in the pond.
    (E) make the water sudsy when the algae swim through it.

60. The organism that nourishes a parasite is known as a

    (A) mutualist.
    (B) host.
    (C) saprophyte.
    (D) autotroph.
    (E) barrier.

Section II: Physical Sciences

60 Questions

Time—45 minutes

Directions: Choose the response that best completes the statement or answers the question.

61. The isotope $_6C^{14}$ has
    (A) 6 electrons.
    (B) 8 protons.
    (C) 20 atoms.
    (D) 6 carbons.
    (E) (A) and (B)

62. Isotopes of any given element have
    (A) the same molecular structures but different charges.
    (B) the same atomic number but different atomic weights.
    (C) the same number of neutrons but different numbers of electrons.
    (D) the same number of protons and electrons.
    (E) different atomic numbers but the same atomic weights.

63. The chemical properties of an atom are directly related to the
    (A) protons in the nucleus.
    (B) electrons in the outer orbital.
    (C) temperature of nitrogen gas.
    (D) number of neutrons in the k, 1, and m orbitals.
    (E) atomic weight of the atom.

64. In order for an atom to become an anion, it must
    (A) gain protons.
    (B) lose electrons.
    (C) not change at all.
    (D) gain electrons.
    (E) lose protons.

Questions 65–67 are to be answered on the basis of the electronic configuration for chlorine shown below:

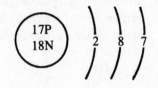

65. The chlorine anion is charged because
    (A) it has equal numbers of protons and electrons.
    (B) the outer orbit picks up an additional electron.
    (C) the outer orbit loses one electron.
    (D) it loses one neutron.
    (E) (A) and (C)

66. The atomic number of chlorine is
    (A) 17 + 18 = 35
    (B) 18 – 17 = 1
    (C) 17 + 18 + 17 = 52
    (D) 18 + 18 = 36
    (E) 17

67. The atom chlorine has
    (A) 2 electrons.
    (B) 7 electrons.
    (C) 17 electrons.
    (D) 18 protons.
    (E) (C) and (D)

68. Many physicists now believe that the elementary particles of the atom are themselves composed of still more elementary particles known as
    (A) photons.
    (B) quarks.
    (C) granuellas.
    (D) (A) and (C)
    (E) (A), (B), and (C)

Answer questions 69–72 on the basis of the experiment that follows. For each statement, mark your answer sheet

(A) if the experiment proves the statement is *true.*

(B) if the experiment shows that the statement is *probably true.*

(C) if the experiment *does not show* whether the statement is true or false.

(D) if the experiment shows that the statement is *probably false.*

(E) if the experiment proves that the statement is *false.*

In a chemistry experiment, five solutions were tested to determine whether they were acids or bases. The indicator used was litmus paper. The data given in the table shows the findings. Strips of litmus paper were dipped into a half liter of each solution for 10 seconds.

SOLUTION	COLOR
1	red
2	red
3	blue
4	no change
5	red

69. At least one of the solutions had a pH greater than 7.

70. Solution 1 would show a higher pH than solution 4.

71. If solutions 2 and 4 were added together and tested with litmus paper, the color would show no change.

72. Solution 2 would show a lower pH than solution 5.

73. If water is electrolyzed, which of the following best describes the products obtained?

(A) H^+ and OH^-

(B) H_2 and OH

(C) H_2 and O_2

(D) H_2O_2 and H_2

(E) H_2O_2

74. Which of the following statements best describes the action of catalysts?

(A) They alter the ratio of products.

(B) They change the rate of reactions.

(C) They change the ratio of products and the rate of reaction.

(D) They change the products.

(E) They change neither the products nor the rate of reaction.

75. When a beam of light is passed through a beaker filled with a clear liquid, the beam can be seen in the solution. This describes a characteristic of what type of system?

(A) A true solution

(B) A colloidal system

(C) A thermally unstable system

(D) A mixture

(E) A system in the process of being heated.

76. Which of the following statements best distinguishes electrolytes from nonelectrolytes?

(A) Electrolytes are always ionic compounds, while nonelectrolytes are always covalent compounds.

(B) Electrolytes are usually covalent compounds, while nonelectrolytes are usually ionic compounds.

(C) Electrolytes and nonelectrolytes are really both covalent compounds.

(D) Nonelectrolytes are usually insoluble in water, while electrolytes are usually soluble.

(E) Electrolytes can be covalent or ionic compounds but must be ionic in solution.

77. When small particles are added to a liquid, they can often be seen to be undergoing very rapid motion on the surface of the liquid. The explanation for this motion is best described by which of the following?

    (A) The electrical interactions between the liquid and the suspended particles
    (B) The molecular vibrations of the liquid causing collisions with the suspended particles
    (C) The low density of the particles causing them to try to rise above the surface of the liquid
    (D) Air currents above the liquid moving the particles
    (E) The heat rising, causing the particles to move

78. Consider the following chemical formula: CH_4, CCl_4, $CHCl_3$. These formulae show that

    (A) the carbon atom has four combining sites.
    (B) many compounds contain carbon.
    (C) carbon is important to living things.
    (D) ionic bonds have been formed.
    (E) carbon is a very complex element.

79. Which of the following is a balanced chemical equation?

    (A) $H_2 + Br_2 \rightarrow HBr$
    (B) $P_4 + O_2 \rightarrow P_4O_{10}$
    (C) $C_3H_8 + 5O_2 \rightarrow 3CO_2 + 4H_2O$
    (D) $H_2 + O_2 \rightarrow 2H_2O$
    (E) $H_2O + CO_3 \rightarrow H_2CO_3 + 2OH$

80. The formula for an alcohol is

    (A) $CH_3 \cdot CH_2 \cdot NH_2$
    (B) CH_4
    (C) $C_6H_{12}O_6$
    (D) $CH_3 \cdot CH_2 \cdot OH$
    (E) $NH_2 \cdot CH_2 CH_3$

81. Young's modulus of a material is equal to

    (A) tensile stress/compressive stress.
    (B) compressive strain/tensile strain.
    (C) tensile stress/tensile strain.
    (D) compressive stress/tensile stress.
    (E) shear stress/shear strain.

82. A 100 g piece of lead is heated to a temperature of 100°C and then dropped into a cavity in a large block of ice at 0°C. In calculating how much ice will melt, one can assume that

    (A) the ice will not melt because no heat is transferred between the lead and the ice.
    (B) the heat lost by the lead will be used to melt the ice.
    (C) the kinetic equation for gravity can be used.
    (D) ice cools lead ten times faster than water.
    (E) (A) and (C)

For questions 83–88, select the one of the five lettered graphs below that best depicts the situation described in each question.

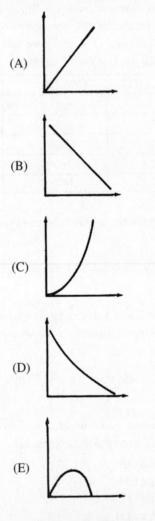

83. A sample of gas kept at constant pressure.

    Vertical axis: average velocity of molecules
    Horizontal axis: absolute temperature

84. An automobile traveling along the highway.

    Vertical axis: fluid friction of the air
    Horizontal axis: speed of the automobile

85. A body is under constant acceleration.

    Vertical axis: speed
    Horizontal axis: time

86. Force is applied to stretch a helical spring below its elastic limit.

    Vertical axis: applied force
    Horizontal axis: elongation

87. Variation of force during a collision.

    Vertical axis: force
    Horizontal axis: time

88. A bowling ball is dropped from the Leaning Tower of Pisa.

    Vertical axis: distance traveled from point of release
    Horizontal axis: time

89. Suppose a man in a sealed boxcar drops a steel ball as the car moves horizontally at a constant velocity. We can assume that the man will

    (A) see the ball drop straight down to the floor.
    (B) see the ball move backward in an arc as it falls to the floor.
    (C) see the ball move horizontally briefly.
    (D) be able to see the ball rise briefly before falling.
    (E) None of the above

90. Albert Einstein's special theory of relativity utilizes

    (A) the basic laws of nature, which are the same in all inertial reference frames.
    (B) the fact that the measured speed of light in a vacuum is the same for observers in all inertial reference frames.
    (C) the fact that force is equal to mass times acceleration.
    (D) angular momentum and Torricelli's theorem.
    (E) (A) and (B)

Answer questions 91–94 on the basis of the following data.

A cylinder of weight W is shown in the following diagram. The coefficient of static friction for all surface is $\frac{1}{3}$. The applied force: $P = 2W$.

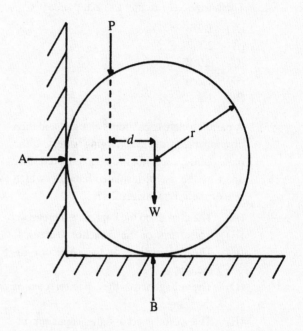

91. Find the distance d for which counterclockwise motion is initiated by P.

    (A) $d = \frac{1}{3}r$

    (B) $d = \frac{1}{2}d$

    (C) $d = \frac{1}{4}r$

    (D) $d = \frac{2}{5}d$

    (E) $d = \frac{3}{5}r$

92. The vertical reaction force at point A is
    (A) 0.3 W
    (B) 0.5 W
    (C) 0.8 W
    (D) 0.9 W
    (E) 1.5 W

93. The vertical reaction force at point *B* is

    (A) 3 *W*
    (B) 2.7 *W*
    (C) 1.5 *W*
    (D) 2.1 *W*
    (E) 2.5 *W*

94. The horizontal reaction force at point *A* is

    (A) 1.5 *W*
    (B) 2.1 *W*
    (C) 0.9 *W*
    (D) 1.2 *W*
    (E) 1.8 *W*

95. A parallel-plate capacitor is charged and then disconnected from the charging battery. If the plates of the capacitor are then moved farther apart by the use of insulated handles, which one of the following results?

    (A) The charge on the capacitor increases.
    (B) The charge on the capacitor decreases.
    (C) The capacitance of the capacitor increases.
    (D) The voltage across the capacitor remains the same.
    (E) The voltage across the capacitor increases.

96. If it requires two joules of work to move 20 coulombs from point *A* to point *B*, a distance of 0.2 meter, the potential difference between points *A* and *B*, in volts, is

    (A) 2×10^{-2}
    (B) 4×10^{-2}
    (C) 4×10^{-1}
    (D) 8
    (E) 1×10^{-1}

97. A parallel plate capacitor with 0.3 cm thickness of air between its two plates has a capacitance of 15 μμf. When the air is replaced by mica (dielectric constant = 6) the capacitance, in μμf, becomes

    (A) 5
    (B) 15
    (C) 90
    (D) 300
    (E) 2.5

98. Opposition to the flow of electric current through a conductor is known as

    (A) voltage.
    (B) amperage.
    (C) resistance.
    (D) magnetism.
    (E) wattage.

For questions 99 and 100, select the one of the five lettered graphs below that best depicts the situation described in each question.

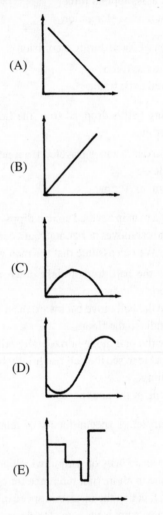

(A)

(B)

(C)

(D)

(E)

99. A vibrating string at its fundamental frequency.

    Vertical axis: frequency of vibration
    Horizontal axis: length of the string

100. The relationship of two properties of light.

    Vertical axis: energy
    Horizontal axis: increasing wave length

101. In the solar system, the correct sequence for five of the planets is

    (A) Venus, Neptune, Jupiter, Mars, Earth.
    (B) Venus, Uranus, Saturn, Mercury, Earth.
    (C) Earth, Mars, Jupiter, Saturn, Uranus.
    (D) Pluto, Mercury, Earth, Venus, Mars.
    (E) Jupiter, Saturn, Uranus, Neptune, Earth.

102. During a lunar eclipse, the

    (A) sun casts a shadow on the earth.
    (B) earth casts a shadow on the sun.
    (C) moon casts a shadow on the earth.
    (D) earth casts a shadow on the moon.
    (E) None of the above

103. The seasons on Earth are the result of

    (A) the distance of the sun from the earth.
    (B) gravitational forces between the earth and the moon.
    (C) the tilted axis of the earth.
    (D) pulsations from the surface of the sun.
    (E) forces that have not yet been explained by scientists.

104. In order to detect the presence of a black hole, it probably

    (A) has to give off high-intensity light of shorter wavelengths than the light that enters the black hole.
    (B) should be part of a binary system.
    (C) must move at a speed faster than the speed of light.
    (D) (A) and (C)
    (E) None of the above

105. Radio astronomers

    (A) can only make their observations at night when most radio stations are silent.
    (B) make observations in a pattern similar to optical astronomers.
    (C) can make their measurements day or night.
    (D) make observations only on clear, cloudless days.
    (E) require visual energy to make their readings.

106. The Viking lander carried out three biological experiments on the planet Mars. These were

    (A) gas-exchange, labeled release, and pyrolytic release experiments.
    (B) photosynthesis, mitosis, and evolution experiments.
    (C) photolysis, dehydration synthesis, and auxin secretion experiments.
    (D) nuclear bombardment, nuclear retraction, and electromagnetic resonance experiments.
    (E) None of the above

107. Spectral lines consist of a series of

    (A) lines that are arranged horizontally and vertically.
    (B) emission lines if the element is vaporized and heated.
    (C) absorption lines if a continuous spectrum radiated by a source of energy at a high temperature passes through cooler vapor of an element.
    (D) (A) and (B)
    (E) (B) and (C)

108. In the spectrum of light emitted by the galaxies, there is a shift toward the red end of the spectrum that increases in proportion to the galaxies' distance from the earth. Most astronomers interpret this phenomenon to mean that

    (A) galaxies get larger as they get farther away.
    (B) matter is being produced at a constant rate.
    (C) the galaxies are moving radially away from each other.
    (D) the most distant galaxies are made up of hotter stars.
    (E) some radiant energy is absorbed over great distances.

109. With reference to the illustration below, which statement shows the correct age relationship?

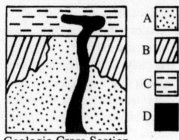

Geologic Cross Section

(A) D is older than B.
(B) C is the oldest rock unit.
(C) A and B are older than C and D.
(D) C and B are older than A and D.
(E) A and D are older than C.

110. The location of earthquakes and volcanoes can best be described by which of the following statements?

(A) They are basically random in location.
(B) They usually occur where the inner core is leaking into the crust.
(C) They usually occur at the junction of lithospheric plates.
(D) They usually occur away from regions with water.
(E) They usually occur where the earth's mantle is weak.

111. Which of the following statements best characterizes the earth's continents?

(A) The continents are evenly distributed on the surface of the earth.
(B) The continents are now believed to have been immobile since their formation.
(C) The continents cover most of the earth's surface.
(D) The movements of the continents coincide with the tidal changes.
(E) The continents are now believed to be moving very slowly.

112. Which of the following is the second most abundant element in the earth's crust?

(A) Oxygen
(B) Aluminum
(C) Potassium
(D) Silicon
(E) Iron

113. Many of the most common minerals may be identified in hand specimens by their physical properties. Which of the following is NOT useful for this purpose?

(A) Luster
(B) Hardness
(C) Cleavage
(D) Weight
(E) Streak

114. According to plate tectonics, the reason that California has so many earthquakes is that

(A) California is sinking into the ocean.
(B) Mexico is pulling California southward.
(C) Mexico is pushing California northward.
(D) the Rocky Mountains are still rising.
(E) the whole North American continent is moving westward.

115. Crude oil and natural gas are often found together because

(A) the same plants that produced oil as a natural by-product also produced gas.
(B) the same plants that were decomposed to produce oil were decomposed to produce gas.
(C) gas gets trapped by oil-bearing rock and is unable to escape.
(D) the building pressure of the gas squeezes the oil out of the rock and into pools.
(E) gas and oil are basically slightly different compounds of the same chemicals; and both are produced at the same time in the chemical process that makes them.

116. The low rolling surface of an old mountain region is

(A) a geosyncline.
(B) an isostasy.
(C) a peneplane.
(D) a laccolith.
(E) caldera.

117. Deflation is the geological term for the

    (A) deposition of a white porous substance around the opening of geysers.
    (B) removal of loose particles by the wind.
    (C) formation of stalactites and stalagmites in caves.
    (D) removal of topsoil from land by rain.
    (E) slow, invisible, downslope movement of the soil.

118. Considering the following evidence, which hypothesis—(A), (B), (C), (D), or (E)—is the most probable?

    I. Identical fossil species of terrestrial plants and animals, older than Carboniferous, are found in Africa, South America, India, and Australia.
    II. The Cape Mountains of South Africa are the same type of folded mountain, made up of the same type rocks as the mountains south of Buenos Aires in South America.
    III. The rock on the crests of the mid-oceanic ridges is younger than the rock on either side of the crest.

    (A) The earth has been formed by the shrinking and cooling of an originally molten mass; this process ended prior to the Carboniferous.
    (B) Radioactive heat has caused thermal convection currents in the mantle of the earth.
    (C) Since its creation, the earth's surface has changed little.
    (D) Prior to the Carboniferous, all the land on the surface of the earth was one great continent, which subsequently began to split apart.
    (E) All life on Earth originally began in one small geographic area.

119. Theories about the interior structure of the earth are largely based on

    (A) actual explorations into the mantle and the core.
    (B) the analysis of how earthquake (seismic) waves travel.
    (C) actual core samples that have reached through the mantle into the outer core.
    (D) our knowledge of the moon and the sun.
    (E) evidence from Einstein's theory of special relativity.

120. The four main divisions of Earth's atmosphere are

    (A) troposphere, stratosphere, mesosphere, and thermosphere.
    (B) troposphere, hydrosphere, lithosphere, and mesosphere.
    (C) thermocline, mesosphere, lithosphere, and troposphere.
    (D) lithosphere, thermosphere, thermocline, and hydrosphere.
    (E) hydrosphere, lithosphere, hemisphere, and hyposphere.

End of Practice Examination I

Answer Key

Section I

1.	D	13.	E	25.	D	37.	E	49.	B
2.	B	14.	E	26.	A	38.	E	50.	D
3.	D	15.	E	27.	C	39.	B	51.	A
4.	E	16.	C	28.	C	40.	C	52.	D
5.	D	17.	C	29.	D	41.	B	53.	E
6.	B	18.	A	30.	A	42.	A	54.	E
7.	C	19.	A	31.	D	43.	D	55.	E
8.	E	20.	B	32.	E	44.	C	56.	D
9.	E	21.	C	33.	C	45.	B	57.	C
10.	B	22.	A	34.	C	46.	A	58.	B
11.	E	23.	B	35.	D	47.	C	59.	A
12.	A	24.	E	36.	A	48.	A	60.	B

Section II

61.	A	73.	C	85.	A	97.	C	109.	C
62.	D	74.	B	86.	A	98.	C	110.	C
63.	D	75.	B	87.	E	99.	A	111.	E
64.	D	76.	E	88.	C	100.	A	112.	D
65.	B	77.	B	89.	A	101.	C	113.	D
66.	E	78.	A	90.	E	102.	D	114.	C
67.	C	79.	C	91.	E	103.	C	115.	E
68.	B	80.	D	92.	A	104.	B	116.	C
69.	A	81.	C	93.	B	105.	C	117.	B
70.	E	82.	B	94.	C	106.	A	118.	D
71.	D	83.	C	95.	E	107.	E	119.	B
72.	C	84.	C	96.	E	108.	C	120.	A

Explanatory Answers

Section I

1. **The correct answer is (D).** In a monohybrid cross, only one of the four boxes represents the homozygous dominant when the parents are heterozygous. In this case, BB is the box representing 0.49 or 49%.

2. **The correct answer is (B).** Three out of four offspring will contain the b gene: the two heterozygotes and the homozygous recessive. $0.21 + 0.21 + 0.16 = 58\%$.

3. **The correct answer is (D).** Visual identification of a species leads to some sort of behavioral change; therefore, the correct answer is behavioral isolation.

4. **The correct answer is (E).** Mutation may affect the individual, but gene flow and genetic drift are factors that only affect an entire species. However, mutation, gene flow, and genetic drift all contribute to gene pool change and, therefore, ultimately to evolution.

5. **The correct answer is (D).** Proteins are composed of amino acids, amino acids can be formed from such molecules as CH_4 and NH_3, and these in turn are composed of C, H, N, or O; therefore, the correct sequence is IV, II, III, I.

6. **The correct answer is (B).** The classic work of Stanley Miller showed that heating mixtures of methane, ammonia, nitrogen, etc. and exposing the vapors to electrical discharges could produce such things as amino acids in a cell-free environment.

7. **The correct answer is (C).** The heterotrophic hypothesis presupposes that the oceans were a type of "organic soup" in which heterotrophic cells appeared and nourished themselves on preformed foods. Later autotrophs appeared, changing a reducing atmosphere to the oxidizing type that is familiar to us today.

8. **The correct answer is (E).** All chordates possess a notochord at some time during their life span.

9. **The correct answer is (E).** The planaria do not have complete digestive systems—that is, a separate mouth and anal opening. However, the digestive system does secrete enzymes that digest food sucked in through the proboscis. There are no specialized digestive organs like stomach, liver, esophagus, etc., but rather a diverse, branching intestine.

10. **The correct answer is (B).** Pollination occurs only in plants that produce seeds. In order for seed formation to take place, pollen grains must come into effective contact with ovules. Pollination transfers the pollen from the anther to the stigma of a plant. Among the choices listed, only angiosperms and gymnosperms produce seeds and as such exhibit the vital process of pollination.

11. **The correct answer is (E).** Ferns, gymnosperms, and angiosperms possess conducting tubes for transporting vital materials to all parts of the plant. This characteristic distinguishes a member of the tracheophyta.

12. **The correct answer is (A).** Many taxonomic relationships are based on embryologic similarities. The embryonic echinoderm bears a close resemblance to very primitive chordates and, therefore, is placed near the top of the evolutionary tree.

13. **The correct answer is (E).** Water just below the freezing point, choice (A), is denser than ice; therefore, it sinks, protecting bottom-dwelling organisms from freezing. High surface tension, choice (B), causes water to rise unusually high in capillary tubes, which is very important in plant physiology. High heat capacity, choice (C), causes water to act as a thermal buffer. High heats of vaporization and fusion also help in keeping environmental temperatures stable. A high dielectric constant, choice (D), makes water a solvent for a large variety of molecules that are necessary for the chemical functioning of organisms. Since all the properties mentioned are indispensable to life, the correct answer is (E).

14. **The correct answer is (E).** There are many one-celled organisms that are self-regulating and self-reproductive but one need only compare the yolk of a chicken egg and a rod-shaped bacteria to realize that cells come in many sizes and shapes. The correct answer, (E), includes only the first two possibilities.

15. **The correct answer is (E).** Adenosine triphosphate and adenosine diphosphate possess high-energy bonds among their phosphate groups. They are vital to all cells, providing the needed energy for cellular reactions.

16. **The correct answer is (C).** The shrew is the smallest mammal in the world. Each day it must consume several times its own body weight in order to survive, insects supplying most of these demands. The great frequency of hunting, killing, and feeding would make it almost impossible for any smaller mammal to exist.

17. **The correct answer is (C).** Enzyme catalysis takes place in living systems and therefore is subject to cellular controls. This is not true of inorganic catalysis, which is a laboratory procedure. Therefore, (C) is the correct choice.

18. **The correct answer is (A).** This question requires knowledge of the process of photosynthesis in which sugar is produced from $CO_2 + H_2O$ and of the fact that the sugar is then changed into starch. One also must be familiar with an elementary chemical test for starch. This experiment has a double purpose: testing the effects of both the presence and absence of light and the presence and absence of chlorophyll. Only choice (A) relates all these factors, and it is the correct answer.

19. **The correct answer is (A).** The second meiotic division occurs with no chromosome replication and, therefore, results in the formation of haploid cells.

20. **The correct answer is (B).** The theory of endosymbiosis supports the idea that many cell organelles were originally independent units that invaded simple cells and established symbiotic relationships that have evolved into the complex integration recognized today as the cell ultrastructure.

21. **The correct answer is (C).** Chloroplasts are membranous cell organelles with stacked membranes called grana. The grana contain the chlorophyll responsible for the initiation of photosynthetic chemistry.

22. **The correct answer is (A).** Mitochondria are double-membrane cell organelles with the in-ner membrane being thrown into folds for increased surface area activity related to oxidative phosphorylation. The folds are called cristae.

23. **The correct answer is (B).** Endoplasmic reticulum is a complex membrane structure in cell cytoplasm, which when associated with ribosomes is called rough endoplasmic reticulum. The ribosomes are the sites of protein synthesis.

24. **The correct answer is (E).** Cilia are cell organelles responsible for locomotion in some cells. Cilia are found to contain groups of microtubules in a typical 9 + 2 arrangement.

25. **The correct answer is (D).** The cone, flower, pistil, and seed are all reproductive structures or parts of reproductive structures; therefore, choice (D) is the correct answer.

26. **The correct answer is (A).** Skeletal, voluntary, and striated muscle are three different names for the same type of muscle. Cardiac muscle is found only in the heart; therefore, the only correct answer is smooth muscle.

27. **The correct answer is (C).** Growth in plants is the result of meristem activity. Primary meristems are responsible for growth up or down at the apical ends of roots and shoots. Secondary meristems, lateral types, are responsible for growth in width. Cork is a protective tissue in older stems and roots; cortex is a storage tissue under the cork or epidermis; and epidermis is the protective layer on young stems and roots.

28. **The correct answer is (C).** Erythrocytes transport oxygen and, to a small extent, carbon dioxide. Leucocytes are involved in body defense. Plasma is the watery part of blood and not a formed element. The heme group is part of hemoglobin. The correct answer is thrombocyte, also known as platelet.

29. **The correct answer is (D).** Motor neurons conduct impulses away from the central nervous system to a muscle or gland and, therefore, are involved in voluntary responses.

30. **The correct answer is (A).** Hemophilia and color blindness are due to defective genes on the x-chromosomes and although they are of-

ten observed in heterozygotes, in this case XY, they can still express themselves in females from time to time under the correct conditions.

31. **The correct answer is (D).** Only choices (D) and (E) are directly related to cues that are given by the photoperiod. However, choice (E) is too limited, while choice (D) encompasses all activities in all plants. Thus, choice (D) is the correct answer.

32. **The correct answer is (E).** Under ideal conditions, bacteria divide about every 20 minutes. (If this rate were maintained for three days, their volume would be greater than that of the earth!) The rate of growth is a geometrical progression with a common multiple of two. Graphs (A) and (E) show both properties increasing; however, graph (A) shows a proportional increase. Graph (E) shows one property increasing faster than the other, which is the situation in this instance; therefore, (E) is the correct answer.

33. **The correct answer is (C).** In a limited environment, bacteria still start out dividing about every 20 minutes after a short "lag period." Geometric growth occurs for a period until there is a buildup of toxic wastes and a depletion of food and growth levels off. The only graph that depicts this is choice (C).

34. **The correct answer is (C).** During moderate exercise, body temperature may rise as much as one or two degrees. After this initial rise, regulatory mechanisms go into effect that keep the temperature stable. Since temperature is plotted on the vertical axis, only graph (C) illustrates an initial rise up to the point at which a constant temperature is maintained.

35. **The correct answer is (D).** No growth was observed in Plant 4; therefore, choice (A) can be eliminated. There is no evidence given that would support choices (B), (C), or (E). However, when the agar, which was in contact with a cut tip, is placed on a seedling, the seedling grows as if the tip itself had been replaced. Something within the tip must have diffused into the agar, and this can occur only if the substance is a chemical.

36. **The correct answer is (A).** Final cell differentiation occurs well after gastrulation and is controlled by the physical and chemical environment interacting with specific genes. Every cell, in theory at least, inherits the same sets of chromosomes. Therefore, the only correct choice is (A).

37. **The correct answer is (E).** Jacques Loeb compared the tropistic movements of plants to light with a behavioral pattern similar to that of the pill bug.

38. **The correct answer is (E).** Fibrinogen, a plasma protein, is vital for the clotting of blood. When acted upon by thrombin, fibrinogen causes threads of fibrin to be formed. It is this interlocking network of fibrin that traps red blood corpuscles, etc. and prevents the blood from flowing out of the wound.

39. **The correct answer is (B).** Phenylketonuria is caused by a lack of a single gene responsible for initiating the production of an enzyme that normally converts phenylalanine to tyrosine.

40. **The correct answer is (C).** The body temperature is controlled and regulated by the thalamus of the brain. It is not understood how this region functions.

41. **The correct answer is (B).** In any cross, in order for *all* offspring to be hybrids, it is necessary for one parent to be homozygous dominant and the other parent homozygous recessive for the same characteristic. Only choice (B) meets this requirement.

42. **The correct answer is (A).** A, B, and O blood genes are alleles, with A and B being codominant and O being recessive; therefore, the two possible crosses indicated by the wording of the problem are BB × AB or BO × AB. Working out a Punnett's square for the crosses shows that the correct answer is (A).

43. **The correct answer is (D).** It is now an accepted fact that base pairing is quite specific in DNA molecules. Cytosine always pairs with guanine, and thymine always pairs with adenine. Uracil is found only in RNA molecules.

44. **The correct answer is (C).** As it is now known that DNA molecules in the nucleus are restricted to the nucleus and carry the code for protein synthesis, which occurs in the cytoplasm, it is clear that there is some intermediate compound for which DNA serves as a

template. This compound is messenger RNA. The production of messenger RNA by DNA is known as transcription.

45. **The correct answer is (B).** The blastula is an embryonic stage of development that contains a hollow space (coele-cavity).

46. **The correct answer is (A).** The morula is a solid ball of cells formed by a number of mitotic divisions of the zygote. These divisions are referred to as cleavages.

47. **The correct answer is (C).** Gastrulation is a complex process as of germ layer formation leading to a three-layered gastrula.

48. **The correct answer is (A).** See explanation 46.

49. **The correct answer is (B).** According to the Hardy-Weinberg Law, under certain conditions of stability, both gene frequencies and genotype ratios remain constant from generation to generation in sexually reproducing populations. In the equation, p represents the dominant gene frequency, while q represents the recessive gene frequency.

50. **The correct answer is (D).** The second law of thermodynamics tells us that usable energy is lost each time energy is transformed. Choices (A), (B), (C), and (E) are incorrect as there is no evidence to support any of them.

51. **The correct answer is (A).** Food chains start with producers (algae) and move to primary consumers (insect larvae), secondary consumers (fish), and tertiary consumers (man).

52. **The correct answer is (D).** Heat radiated from the earth is absorbed by atmospheric CO_2 and reradiated back to the surface, tending to warm the surface (the "greenhouse effect"). Atmospheric particulate matter influences the temperature balance of the earth; therefore, the correct answer is (D).

53. **The correct answer is (E).** Bacterial and fungal decay are necessary to return organic material to the pool required for new growth, a cycling of matter. Because of the second law of thermodynamics, usable energy is continually being lost, and a constant source of energy is therefore required. Producers' numbers determine the numbers of consumers and therefore must be proportional. For these reasons, all answers contribute to the maintenance of a balanced ecosystem.

54. **The correct answer is (E).** Producers are the foundation of a food chain and do not feed on other organisms. They produce complex organic materials from simple inorganic compounds such as carbon dioxide and water. Therefore, they must be self-feeders, autotrophs.

55. **The correct answer is (E).** Stable food chains keep populations in check through complex interrelationships, including relative population sizes. Any change in the population size of one species will have a definite ill effect on the food chain. Therefore, choice (E) is correct.

56. **The correct answer is (D).** The lithosphere is the solid crust of the earth; the hydrosphere includes the oceans, lakes, and rivers; the atmosphere includes the gasses and water vapor of the earth; and the troposphere is a segment of the atmosphere. Ecosystems are segments of the biosphere that are composed of interacting organisms plus the associated environmental factors.

57. **The correct answer is (C).** DDT and PCB are lipid soluble compounds and are therefore found in lipid tissues. As their half-lives are quite long, DDT = 10 years, there is a magnification of these compounds in food chains; e.g., DDT has been found in high concentrations in the fatty tissues of Antarctic penguins.

58. **The correct answer is (B).** In order for carbon to exist in the atmosphere, it must be in the form of a gas, primarily carbon dioxide. Photosynthesis fixes carbon dioxide through the activity of the Calvin cycle. The evaporation of water produces non-carbon-bearing water vapor. Carbon dioxide, the end product of cellular respiration, is released into the atmosphere by almost all living things. Therefore, choice (B) is the correct answer.

59. **The correct answer is (A).** Phosphates promote algal growth with significant increases in toxins produced by algae. Algal "blooms" cause fish to die in ponds.

60. **The correct answer is (B).** All parasites, ectoparasites, or endoparasites require a host. Some endoparasite lifecycles may have one or two intermediate hosts as well as a final host.

Section II

61. **The correct answer is (A).** Isotopes are forms of the same element that differ only in neutron number. The atomic number represents the number of protons in the atom. Since atoms are electrically neutral, the number of electrons equals the number of protons in the atom. The atomic weight of an atom is equal to the sum of protons and neutrons. Therefore, the correct answer is (A).

62. **The correct answer is (D).** See explanation 61.

63. **The correct answer is (D).** The chemical properties of an atom are determined by the status of the electrons in the outer orbit. Atoms with electrically stable outer orbits do not usually react with other atoms. Atoms with electrical instability in the outer orbit react with other unstable atoms.

64. **The correct answer is (D).** Anions are negatively charged atoms, while cations are positively charged atoms.

65. **The correct answer is (B).** Atoms become ions because they have a tendency to achieve orbital stability by either gaining or losing electrons. In the case of chlorine, stability in the outer orbit is achieved by the addition of an electron.

66. **The correct answer is (E).** See explanation 61.

67. **The correct answer is (C).** See explanation 61.

68. **The correct answer is (B).** Many physicists believe that protons and neutrons are composed of quarks. There are believed to be four kinds of quarks: *up*, *down*, *charm*, and *strange*. Apparently, it takes three of the four types of quarks to make a proton or a neutron.

69. **The correct answer is (A).** Knowledge that an acid turns litmus paper red, a base turns it blue, and a neutral solution shows no change is necessary to solve this problem. From the data given, each solution can be determined to be an acid, a base, or neutral. A base has a pH greater than seven.

70. **The correct answer is (E).** In the experiment, solution one is an acid. Solution four is neutral. An acid does not show a higher pH than a neutral solution.

71. **The correct answer is (D).** Unless the acid is extremely weak so that the concentration of hydrogen ions when placed in a neutral solution is no longer sufficient to react with the indicator, the indicator will probably turn red.

72. **The correct answer is (C).** Litmus paper will not show relative acidity.

73. **The correct answer is (C).** When a sample of water is placed in an electrical circuit, the water is said to be *electrolyzed*. The action of the electricity converts water to hydrogen (H_2) and oxygen (O_2). These two molecules can then be reconverted to water.

74. **The correct answer is (B).** The action of a catalyst is *only to change the rate of a reaction*. Catalysts do not affect the products or the distribution of products at all.

75. **The correct answer is (B).** This question concerns a type of behavior characteristic of *colloidal solutions*. These are not true solutions but dispersions of very fine particles in a liquid so that the liquid appears clear but in actuality contains solid material. The effect described in the question is called the *Tyndall* effect.

76. **The correct answer is (E).** An electrolyte is a substance that when added to water will conduct an electric current (very pure water will not do this). In order to conduct the current, it must 1) dissolve and 2) carry an electrical charge (i.e., be ionic). Therefore, the prime characteristic for an electrolyte is that it be ionic in solution.

77. **The correct answer is (B).** This question can be answered when one pictures the actions of molecules on a molecular level. They are continually vibrating and colliding. The addition of very fine particles will cause collisions between these particles and the molecules of the liquid resulting in the movement of the particles. This behavior is called *Brownian motion*.

78. **The correct answer is (A).** All the formulae show four other atoms bound to the carbon atom. One can only deduce from this information that carbon has four combining sites.

79. **The correct answer is (C).** A balanced chemical equation must have the same amount of each element on both sides. In choice (C),

there are 3C, 8H, and 10O on both sides of the equation.

80. **The correct answer is (D).** Alcohols are characterized by the presence of a carbinol group (C · OH).

81. **The correct answer is (C).** By Hooke's Law (supplied in terms of Young's modulus), $F = -EA\dfrac{\Delta l}{l_0}$ where E is Young's modulus. Therefore, Young's modulus must have units equal to tensile strength divided by tensile strain.

82. **The correct answer is (B).** A large number of situations involving heat interchange can be elucidated by the application of the following equation: heat lost = heat gained. It is an application of the First Law of Thermodynamics.

83. **The correct answer is (C).** Both graphs (A) and (C) continually increase with time, but only graph (A) rises in a direct proportional relationship of the vertical and horizontal axes. As temperature rises in a sample of gas kept at constant pressure, so will the average velocity of molecules, but not in a direct proportional relationship.

84. **The correct answer is (C).** The faster an automobile moves, the greater the fluid friction of the air.

85. **The correct answer is (A).** In a body under constant acceleration, speed increases in direct proportion to time. Only in graph (A) does one property increase in direct proportion to the other.

86. **The correct answer is (A).** Question 4 is based on Hooke's law, which states that elastic deformation is proportional to the force producing it. Graph (A) is the only one that illustrates a direct proportionality.

87. **The correct answer is (E).** During a collision, force reaches a peak at the time of closest, approach. It is zero before the first contact and after the objects have separated. Since the magnitude of the force does not decrease more rapidly than it increases, the correct choice is the simple bell-shaped curve, graph (E).

88. **The correct answer is (C).** Over time, acceleration is constant: Velocity increases in direct proportion to the time, and distance increases as the square of the time. The only graph that shows this dramatic increase is choice (C).

89. **The correct answer is (A).** Since the horizontal velocities of the man, the ball, and the car were the same, the man could not detect the horizontal motion of the ball with respect to the earth's surface. An observer outside of the boxcar would see the ball fall along a typical trajectory.

90. **The correct answer is (E).** These two postulates were important in proving that no object can move faster than the speed of light. Repeated tests of Einstein's theory have yielded results that confirm the theory.

91. **The correct answer is (E).** The net torque and the net force must be zero if there is to be no motion.

Horizontal force: $NA - FB = 0$

Vertical force: $P + W - NB - FA = 0$

Torque: $Pd - r(FA + FB) = 0$

$FA = \mu NA$

$FB = \mu NB$

$NA = \mu NB$

$NB + \mu NA = P + W$

$\mu r(NA + NB) = Pd$

$NB(1 + \mu^2) = P + W$

$\mu rNB(1 + \mu) = Pd$

$NB = Pd/\mu r(1 + \mu)$

$Pd/\mu r(1 + \mu) = (P + W)(1 + \mu^2)$

$d = (P + W)\mu r(1 + \mu)/P(1 + \mu^2)$

$P = 2W, \mu = 1/3$

$d = 3r/5.$

92. **The correct answer is (A).**

$NB = PD/\mu r(1 + \mu)$

$NB = 2.7\ W$

$NA = NB/3$

$NA = 0.9\ W$

$FA = NA/3$

$FA = 0.3\ W$

93. **The correct answer is (B).** From the explanation to question 92, we see that $NB = 2.7W$.

94. **The correct answer is (C).** From the explanation to question 92, we see that $NA = 0.9W$.

95. **The correct answer is (E).** Since the plates are moved apart by the use of insulated handles, the charge on the capacitor must remain constant. For a parallel plate, capacitor C is proportional to A/l, where A is the area of the plate and l is the distance between the plates. Therefore, C must decrease. By definition, $C = Q/V$. Therefore, the voltage must increase.

96. **The correct answer is (E).** The potential difference is the work required to move a test charge from point A to B divided by the magnitude of the test charge.

V = 2 joules/20 coulomb
V = 0.1 joule/coulomb
one volt = one joule/coulomb
$V = 1 \times 10^{-1}$ volt.

97. **The correct answer is (C).** For a parallel plate, capacitor C = ŒŒ$_0$A/l, where Œ is the relative dielectric constant.

Œ = 1 for air. Thus,

$$C_{air} = \varepsilon_0 A / l$$
$$C_{mica} = \varepsilon_{mica}\varepsilon_0 A / l = \varepsilon_{mica} C_{air}$$
$$= 6(15\mu\mu f)$$
$$C_{mica} = 90\mu\mu f.$$

98. **The correct answer is (C).** Resistance is the term for opposition to the flow of electric current through a conductor and is measured in ohms.

99. **The correct answer is (A).** As the length of the string grows longer, the frequency of vibration decreases.

100. **The correct answer is (A).** There is an inverse relationship between energy of light and the wavelength of light. As wavelengths shorten, energy increases.

101. **The correct answer is (C).** The sequence of the nine planets around the sun is Mercury, Venus, Earth, Mars, Jupiter, Saturn, Uranus, Neptune, and Pluto.

102. **The correct answer is (D).** Lunar eclipses occur when the earth positions itself between the sun and the moon, thereby causing the earth's shadow to fall on the moon.

103. **The correct answer is (C).** The changing angle at which the sun's rays hit the earth as the earth moves around the sun causes the seasonal changes experienced in both the Northern and Southern Hemispheres.

104. **The correct answer is (B).** X-rays might be given off from surrounding gas, but in the absence of a companion star to allow for the measurement of its mass, scientists would be hard pressed to demonstrate the presence of a black hole.

105. **The correct answer is (C).** The atmosphere scatters optical energy, restricting optical astronomers, but it does not affect radio energy.

106. **The correct answer is (A).** The gas-exchange experiment sought to detect atmospheric changes due to any metabolism of things in the soil. The pyrolytic-release experiment used a furnace to cause chemical changes by means of heat.

107. **The correct answer is (E).** Various elements have spectral patterns that are to each element as fingerprints are to each human.

108. **The correct answer is (C).** This question requires a knowledge of the various theories of the origin of the universe. The discovery of the red shift led to the evolutionary theory that requires an initial point in time at which all matter exploded radially outward from a concentrated mass. Choice (C) is the only choice that mentions this radial expansion and is the correct answer.

109. **The correct answer is (C).** The rock units in order of formation are A,B,C,D.

110. **The correct answer is (C).** Earthquakes do not occur randomly, but only where the lithospheric plates (which cover the earth) meet. This can occur on land or underwater.

111. **The correct answer is (E).** This is a question from the field of geology. The continents make up less than half of the earth's surface. Oceans, seas, and lakes take up most of this planet's surface area. Therefore, choice (C) is wrong. Recent evidence suggests that the continents are slowly drifting apart (Africa and South America were once close neighbors).

112. **The correct answer is (D).** The second most abundant element in the earth's crust is silicon.

113. **The correct answer is (D).** Hardness, cleavage, luster, and streak are all physical properties of minerals useful in their identification. Weight is not of primary importance except in the calculation of the specific gravity of a mineral sample, which is another physical property used to identify minerals.

114. **The correct answer is (C).** Although the whole continent is moving westward, this is not the cause of California's woes.

115. **The correct answer is (E).** Gas and oil are both hydrocarbons and differ only in the number of carbon atoms that are linked together. Natural gas (methane) has only one carbon, while crude oil has many.

116. **The correct answer is (C).** A peneplane is a land surface of considerable area and slight relief shaped by erosion.

117. **The correct answer is (B).** Deflation is defined as a wearing away of land by the action of wind.

118. **The correct answer is (D).** From the evidence given, it is most probable that all the land on the surface of the earth was once connected.

119. **The correct answer is (B).** Seismic evidence suggests that the earth is composed of a crust (barely 40 miles thick), a mantle (about 1,800 miles thick), a liquid outer core (about 1,300 miles thick), and a solid inner core (about 800 miles thick).

120. **The correct answer is (A).** Closest to Earth's surface is a 6-mile layer called the troposphere. Above this layer are the stratosphere (about 24 miles thick), the mesosphere (about 20 miles thick) and the thermosphere (the remainder of the atmosphere).

Practice Examination I Diagnostic Chart

Question Type	Question Numbers	Number of Questions	Number Wrong
Section I: Life Sciences			
Origin and evolution of life; classification of organisms	1–12	12	_____
Cell organization and division; genes, bioenergetics, and biosynthesis	13–24	12	_____
Structure, function, and development of organisms; hereditary patterns	25–48	24	_____
Population biology and ecology	49–60	12	_____
Section II: Physical Sciences			
Atomic structure; particles and nuclear reactions	61–68	8	_____
Elements, compounds, and reactions; molecular structure and bonding	69–80	12	_____
Thermodynamics, mechanics, and relativity	81–94	14	_____
Electricity and magnetism, light, and sound	95–100	6	_____
The universe	101–108	8	_____
The earth	109–120	12	_____

Answer Sheet for Practice Examination II

Section I

1 Ⓐ Ⓑ Ⓒ Ⓓ Ⓔ	13 Ⓐ Ⓑ Ⓒ Ⓓ Ⓔ	25 Ⓐ Ⓑ Ⓒ Ⓓ Ⓔ	37 Ⓐ Ⓑ Ⓒ Ⓓ Ⓔ	49 Ⓐ Ⓑ Ⓒ Ⓓ Ⓔ
2 Ⓐ Ⓑ Ⓒ Ⓓ Ⓔ	14 Ⓐ Ⓑ Ⓒ Ⓓ Ⓔ	26 Ⓐ Ⓑ Ⓒ Ⓓ Ⓔ	38 Ⓐ Ⓑ Ⓒ Ⓓ Ⓔ	50 Ⓐ Ⓑ Ⓒ Ⓓ Ⓔ
3 Ⓐ Ⓑ Ⓒ Ⓓ Ⓔ	15 Ⓐ Ⓑ Ⓒ Ⓓ Ⓔ	27 Ⓐ Ⓑ Ⓒ Ⓓ Ⓔ	39 Ⓐ Ⓑ Ⓒ Ⓓ Ⓔ	51 Ⓐ Ⓑ Ⓒ Ⓓ Ⓔ
4 Ⓐ Ⓑ Ⓒ Ⓓ Ⓔ	16 Ⓐ Ⓑ Ⓒ Ⓓ Ⓔ	28 Ⓐ Ⓑ Ⓒ Ⓓ Ⓔ	40 Ⓐ Ⓑ Ⓒ Ⓓ Ⓔ	52 Ⓐ Ⓑ Ⓒ Ⓓ Ⓔ
5 Ⓐ Ⓑ Ⓒ Ⓓ Ⓔ	17 Ⓐ Ⓑ Ⓒ Ⓓ Ⓔ	29 Ⓐ Ⓑ Ⓒ Ⓓ Ⓔ	41 Ⓐ Ⓑ Ⓒ Ⓓ Ⓔ	53 Ⓐ Ⓑ Ⓒ Ⓓ Ⓔ
6 Ⓐ Ⓑ Ⓒ Ⓓ Ⓔ	18 Ⓐ Ⓑ Ⓒ Ⓓ Ⓔ	30 Ⓐ Ⓑ Ⓒ Ⓓ Ⓔ	42 Ⓐ Ⓑ Ⓒ Ⓓ Ⓔ	54 Ⓐ Ⓑ Ⓒ Ⓓ Ⓔ
7 Ⓐ Ⓑ Ⓒ Ⓓ Ⓔ	19 Ⓐ Ⓑ Ⓒ Ⓓ Ⓔ	31 Ⓐ Ⓑ Ⓒ Ⓓ Ⓔ	43 Ⓐ Ⓑ Ⓒ Ⓓ Ⓔ	55 Ⓐ Ⓑ Ⓒ Ⓓ Ⓔ
8 Ⓐ Ⓑ Ⓒ Ⓓ Ⓔ	20 Ⓐ Ⓑ Ⓒ Ⓓ Ⓔ	32 Ⓐ Ⓑ Ⓒ Ⓓ Ⓔ	44 Ⓐ Ⓑ Ⓒ Ⓓ Ⓔ	56 Ⓐ Ⓑ Ⓒ Ⓓ Ⓔ
9 Ⓐ Ⓑ Ⓒ Ⓓ Ⓔ	21 Ⓐ Ⓑ Ⓒ Ⓓ Ⓔ	33 Ⓐ Ⓑ Ⓒ Ⓓ Ⓔ	45 Ⓐ Ⓑ Ⓒ Ⓓ Ⓔ	57 Ⓐ Ⓑ Ⓒ Ⓓ Ⓔ
10 Ⓐ Ⓑ Ⓒ Ⓓ Ⓔ	22 Ⓐ Ⓑ Ⓒ Ⓓ Ⓔ	34 Ⓐ Ⓑ Ⓒ Ⓓ Ⓔ	46 Ⓐ Ⓑ Ⓒ Ⓓ Ⓔ	58 Ⓐ Ⓑ Ⓒ Ⓓ Ⓔ
11 Ⓐ Ⓑ Ⓒ Ⓓ Ⓔ	23 Ⓐ Ⓑ Ⓒ Ⓓ Ⓔ	35 Ⓐ Ⓑ Ⓒ Ⓓ Ⓔ	47 Ⓐ Ⓑ Ⓒ Ⓓ Ⓔ	59 Ⓐ Ⓑ Ⓒ Ⓓ Ⓔ
12 Ⓐ Ⓑ Ⓒ Ⓓ Ⓔ	24 Ⓐ Ⓑ Ⓒ Ⓓ Ⓔ	36 Ⓐ Ⓑ Ⓒ Ⓓ Ⓔ	48 Ⓐ Ⓑ Ⓒ Ⓓ Ⓔ	60 Ⓐ Ⓑ Ⓒ Ⓓ Ⓔ

Section II

61 Ⓐ Ⓑ Ⓒ Ⓓ Ⓔ   73 Ⓐ Ⓑ Ⓒ Ⓓ Ⓔ   85 Ⓐ Ⓑ Ⓒ Ⓓ Ⓔ   97 Ⓐ Ⓑ Ⓒ Ⓓ Ⓔ   109 Ⓐ Ⓑ Ⓒ Ⓓ Ⓔ

62 Ⓐ Ⓑ Ⓒ Ⓓ Ⓔ   74 Ⓐ Ⓑ Ⓒ Ⓓ Ⓔ   86 Ⓐ Ⓑ Ⓒ Ⓓ Ⓔ   98 Ⓐ Ⓑ Ⓒ Ⓓ Ⓔ   110 Ⓐ Ⓑ Ⓒ Ⓓ Ⓔ

63 Ⓐ Ⓑ Ⓒ Ⓓ Ⓔ   75 Ⓐ Ⓑ Ⓒ Ⓓ Ⓔ   87 Ⓐ Ⓑ Ⓒ Ⓓ Ⓔ   99 Ⓐ Ⓑ Ⓒ Ⓓ Ⓔ   111 Ⓐ Ⓑ Ⓒ Ⓓ Ⓔ

64 Ⓐ Ⓑ Ⓒ Ⓓ Ⓔ   76 Ⓐ Ⓑ Ⓒ Ⓓ Ⓔ   88 Ⓐ Ⓑ Ⓒ Ⓓ Ⓔ   100 Ⓐ Ⓑ Ⓒ Ⓓ Ⓔ   112 Ⓐ Ⓑ Ⓒ Ⓓ Ⓔ

65 Ⓐ Ⓑ Ⓒ Ⓓ Ⓔ   77 Ⓐ Ⓑ Ⓒ Ⓓ Ⓔ   89 Ⓐ Ⓑ Ⓒ Ⓓ Ⓔ   101 Ⓐ Ⓑ Ⓒ Ⓓ Ⓔ   113 Ⓐ Ⓑ Ⓒ Ⓓ Ⓔ

66 Ⓐ Ⓑ Ⓒ Ⓓ Ⓔ   78 Ⓐ Ⓑ Ⓒ Ⓓ Ⓔ   90 Ⓐ Ⓑ Ⓒ Ⓓ Ⓔ   102 Ⓐ Ⓑ Ⓒ Ⓓ Ⓔ   114 Ⓐ Ⓑ Ⓒ Ⓓ Ⓔ

67 Ⓐ Ⓑ Ⓒ Ⓓ Ⓔ   79 Ⓐ Ⓑ Ⓒ Ⓓ Ⓔ   91 Ⓐ Ⓑ Ⓒ Ⓓ Ⓔ   103 Ⓐ Ⓑ Ⓒ Ⓓ Ⓔ   115 Ⓐ Ⓑ Ⓒ Ⓓ Ⓔ

68 Ⓐ Ⓑ Ⓒ Ⓓ Ⓔ   80 Ⓐ Ⓑ Ⓒ Ⓓ Ⓔ   92 Ⓐ Ⓑ Ⓒ Ⓓ Ⓔ   104 Ⓐ Ⓑ Ⓒ Ⓓ Ⓔ   116 Ⓐ Ⓑ Ⓒ Ⓓ Ⓔ

69 Ⓐ Ⓑ Ⓒ Ⓓ Ⓔ   81 Ⓐ Ⓑ Ⓒ Ⓓ Ⓔ   93 Ⓐ Ⓑ Ⓒ Ⓓ Ⓔ   105 Ⓐ Ⓑ Ⓒ Ⓓ Ⓔ   117 Ⓐ Ⓑ Ⓒ Ⓓ Ⓔ

70 Ⓐ Ⓑ Ⓒ Ⓓ Ⓔ   82 Ⓐ Ⓑ Ⓒ Ⓓ Ⓔ   94 Ⓐ Ⓑ Ⓒ Ⓓ Ⓔ   106 Ⓐ Ⓑ Ⓒ Ⓓ Ⓔ   118 Ⓐ Ⓑ Ⓒ Ⓓ Ⓔ

71 Ⓐ Ⓑ Ⓒ Ⓓ Ⓔ   83 Ⓐ Ⓑ Ⓒ Ⓓ Ⓔ   95 Ⓐ Ⓑ Ⓒ Ⓓ Ⓔ   107 Ⓐ Ⓑ Ⓒ Ⓓ Ⓔ   119 Ⓐ Ⓑ Ⓒ Ⓓ Ⓔ

72 Ⓐ Ⓑ Ⓒ Ⓓ Ⓔ   84 Ⓐ Ⓑ Ⓒ Ⓓ Ⓔ   96 Ⓐ Ⓑ Ⓒ Ⓓ Ⓔ   108 Ⓐ Ⓑ Ⓒ Ⓓ Ⓔ   120 Ⓐ Ⓑ Ⓒ Ⓓ Ⓔ

PRACTICE EXAMINATION II

Section I: Life Sciences

60 Questions
Time—45 minutes

Directions: Choose the response that best completes the statement or answers the question.

1. An organism having characteristics of both plants and animals is the

    (A) amoeba.
    (B) paramecium.
    (C) sponge.
    (D) euglena.
    (E) planaria.

2. Under the Linnaean system of classification, each kingdom is divided into related

    (A) phyla.
    (B) classes.
    (C) families.
    (D) genera.
    (E) species.

3. The term homo sapiens is an example of

    (A) phylum-class.
    (B) phylum-order.
    (C) a complete classification.
    (D) individual identification.
    (E) binomial nomenclature.

4. The Linnaean system of taxonomy classifies all plants and animals on the basis of their

    (A) similarities in structure.
    (B) place of origin.
    (C) value to man.
    (D) relationship to the environment.
    (E) physical chemistry.

5. Bacteria are usually classified as

    (A) animals.
    (B) minerals.
    (C) viruses.
    (D) plants.
    (E) bryophytes.

6. It is currently believed that the origin of life on Earth

    (A) occurred in a reducing atmosphere.
    (B) began with heterotrophic nutrition, which was followed by autotrophic nutrition.
    (C) began with autotrophic nutrition, which was followed by heterotrophic nutrition.
    (D) (A) and (B)
    (E) (A) and (C)

7. The "organic soup" thought to have given rise to the first cells probably contained

    (A) glucose and amino acids.
    (B) water and bubbling hot gases only.
    (C) numerous green plants, which supported the first cells.
    (D) (A) and (C)
    (E) None of the above

8. During the evolution of man, it is believed by scientists that

    (A) Neanderthal man was replaced by Cro-Magnon man.
    (B) Neanderthal man was replaced by Homo erectus.
    (C) Homo erectus replaced Homo sapiens.
    (D) All of the above
    (E) None of the above

9. Bullfrogs and grass frogs cannot mate with one another because
    (A) they are the product of a divergent type of evolution.
    (B) hybridization mechanisms do not exist.
    (C) they are different species.
    (D) (A) and (C)
    (E) (A), (B), and (C)

10. Although Charles Darwin is credited with the theory of evolution, credit must also go to
    (A) Charles Lyell.
    (B) Thomas Malthus.
    (C) Alfred Wallace.
    (D) Gregor Mendel.
    (E) All of the above

11. Related species develop a great external diversity of form, although basic similarities in the fundamental structural plan can be traced, in the process of
    (A) divergent evolution.
    (B) convergent evolution.
    (C) special creation.
    (D) geographic isolation.
    (E) synapsis during mitosis.

12. The earliest human belonged to
    (A) Homo erectus.
    (B) Brachydanio rerio.
    (C) Rana pipiens.
    (D) Notropus hudsonius.
    (E) None of the above

Answer questions 13–16 on the basis of the experiment described below. Analyze each statement solely on the basis of the experiment and mark your answer sheet:
    (A) if the experiment proves the statement is *true*.
    (B) if the experiment shows that the statement is *probably true*.
    (C) if the experiment *does not show* whether the statement is true or false.
    (D) if the experiment shows that the statement is *probably false*.
    (E) if the experiment proves that the statement is *false*.

In the following biochemical experiment, paper chromatography was used to effect the separation of a mixture of seven amino acids (A, B, C, D, E, F, and G). A sample of the mixture was placed in the lower left-hand corner of a sheet of filter paper. The paper was placed vertically in a solution of water (stationary phase) and solvent #1 (mobile phase) in such a manner that the sample was not immersed in the solution. After sufficient time lapsed to allow the solvent to approach the upper edge of the paper by capillary action, the paper was removed. The paper was rotated 90° and the same procedure was followed with solvent #2. The paper was then dried and sprayed with a developing solution.

The illustration below depicts the results of the separation.

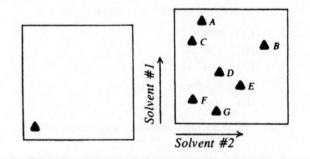

Before separation   After separation

13. The principle behind paper chromatography is that substances move up the paper with varying needs, depending upon their solubility in the solvent being used.

14. Paper chromatography is the easiest method to use in separating amino acids.

15. Amino acid A moved the farthest in solvent #1.

16. If the paper had been developed after the treatment with solvent #1 only, acids B and C would not have been separated.

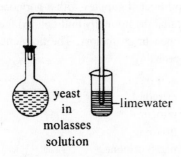

yeast in molasses solution —limewater

17. If the apparatus shown above is placed in a moderately warm location, within a few hours the

    (A) molasses solution will flow into the beaker.
    (B) molasses solution will turn brown.
    (C) limewater will turn milky.
    (D) limewater will flow into the flask.
    (E) None of the above

Side A   Side B

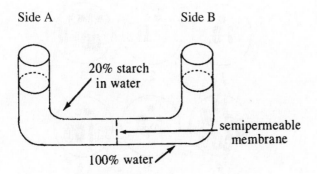

20% starch in water

semipermeable membrane

100% water

18. The starch solution on side A will become

    (A) less concentrated since starch moves from A to B.
    (B) less concentrated since water moves from B to A.
    (C) colder as side B becomes warmer.
    (D) more concentrated since water moves from A to B.
    (E) more concentrated since water moves from B to A.

Questions 19–21 are concerned with the following experiment:

Ocean water is isotonic to sea urchin eggs. Three sea urchin eggs are placed into three different solutions lettered (A), (B), and (C). For each statement below, select the one of the five lettered options that best corresponds to the situation described.

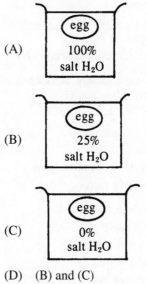

(A)   egg   100% salt H_2O

(B)   egg   25% salt H_2O

(C)   egg   0% salt H_2O

    (D) (B) and (C)
    (E) None of the above

19. Causes the sea urchin egg to swell.

20. Solution with the greatest solute concentration.

21. Causes the sea urchin egg to divide immediately.

22. During mitosis, daughter nuclei are formed in the

    (A) interphase.
    (B) prophase.
    (C) metaphase.
    (D) anaphase.
    (E) telophase.

23. The structure that does not include nucleic acid is the

    (A) gene.
    (B) chromosome.
    (C) centriole.
    (D) ribosome.
    (E) chromatin.

24. A cell concerned with synthesizing and secreting large quantities of protein hormone would be expected to have
    (A) very few mitochondria and ribosomes and a poorly developed Golgi apparatus.
    (B) many more chromosomes than the average human cell.
    (C) large numbers of mitochondria and ribosomes and a well-developed Golgi apparatus.
    (D) only an endoplasmic reticulum in the cytoplasm.
    (E) a division rate of once per hour.

25. Which is most closely associated with the process of transpiration?
    (A) Root of a geranium
    (B) Leaf of a geranium
    (C) Gills of a fish
    (D) Spiracles of a grasshopper
    (E) Lungs of a man

26. During inspiration, the ribs
    (A) do not move.
    (B) move downward.
    (C) move inward.
    (D) move outward.
    (E) contract.

27. As blood flows in the capillaries of the walls of the small intestine, it gains mainly
    (A) oxygen.
    (B) digested nutrients.
    (C) urea.
    (D) waste matter.
    (E) momentum.

28. A white-cell count is helpful in determining whether a patient has
    (A) an infection.
    (B) antitoxins.
    (C) diabetes.
    (D) heart disease.
    (E) the Rh factor.

29. Radioactive iron could best be used to measure the life span of
    (A) an enzyme.
    (B) a nerve cell.
    (C) erythrocyte.
    (D) an antibody.
    (E) a hormone.

30. A pupil treated guppies with a hormone and found that the normally dull-colored females developed bright colors. The hormone was most probably
    (A) androgen.
    (B) estradiol.
    (C) pitocin.
    (D) thyroxin.
    (E) parathormone.

Answer questions 31–35 with the following graph.

Diagram *X* represents the nucleus of a somatic cell of a mature spermatocyte. The following questions relate to the six *numbered* diagrams immediately below Diagram *X*.

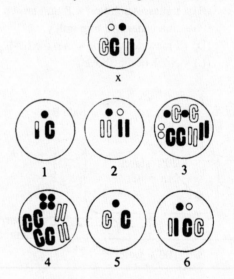

31. A cutting was made from this plant. The nucleus of a cell of a plant grown from this cutting would most likely resemble
    (A) 1
    (B) 6
    (C) 3
    (D) 4
    (E) 5

32. A functional sperm nucleus from a pollen grain produced by this plant could resemble
    (A) 1
    (B) 2
    (C) 5
    (D) 4
    (E) 6

33. The nucleus of a cell from a cotyledon that had nourished this plant would most likely resemble
    (A) 6
    (B) 2
    (C) 3
    (D) 1
    (E) 5

34. If meiotic division had *not* accompanied the formation of both gametes, a nucleus of the zygote formed would most likely have resembled
    (A) 1
    (B) 2
    (C) 3
    (D) 4
    (E) 5

35. If, during meiosis, crossing over occurred between a single pair of homologous chromosomes, the nucleus of the resulting gamete would most likely resemble
    (A) 2
    (B) 3
    (C) 4
    (D) 6
    (E) 1

Answer questions 36–40 on the basis of the following information and graph.

Base your answers on the pedigree chart below, where individual B is a hemophiliac male who is heterozygous for brown eyes. Individual A is his blue-eyed wife who does NOT carry any genes for hemophilia.

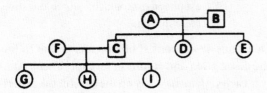

36. What is the probability that individual D is a hemophiliac?
    (A) 0
    (B) $\frac{1}{1}$
    (C) $\frac{1}{2}$
    (D) $\frac{1}{3}$
    (E) $\frac{1}{4}$

37. What is the probability that individual D is a carrier for hemophilia and has blue eyes?
    (A) 0
    (B) $\frac{1}{1}$
    (C) $\frac{1}{2}$
    (D) $\frac{1}{3}$
    (E) $\frac{1}{4}$

38. What is the probability that individual E is blue-eyed?
    (A) $\frac{1}{2}$
    (B) $\frac{1}{4}$
    (C) $\frac{1}{8}$
    (D) $\frac{1}{3}$
    (E) It cannot be determined from the information given.

39. Which best represents the genetic makeup for eye color of individual H?
    (A) Homozygous brown
    (B) Homozygous blue
    (C) Heterozygous brown
    (D) Heterozygous blue
    (E) It cannot be determined from the information given.

40. If individual E marries a male who is a hemophiliac, which statement is true?
    (A) All of her sons must be hemophiliacs.
    (B) All of her daughters must carry at least one gene for hemophilia.
    (C) All of her daughters must be hemophiliacs.
    (D) 50% of her sons can be hemophiliacs, but none of her daughters can be hemophiliacs.
    (E) 50% of her daughters can be hemophiliacs, but none of her sons can be hemophiliacs.

41. A form of binary fission, in which one of the two offspring is smaller than the other, is
    (A) spermatogenesis.
    (B) budding.
    (C) mitosis.
    (D) parthenogenesis.
    (E) cogenesis.

42. Species that practice internal fertilization are characterized by a
    (A) fetus that develops entirely in the oceans.
    (B) wide degree of care for their young.
    (C) parental non-interest once the eggs have been laid.
    (D) diminished potency as they reach maturity.
    (E) need for continual feeding because of the excessive energy needs during internal fertilization.

43. The layer of tissue immediately adjacent to the gastrocoele is the
    (A) zygoderm.
    (B) ectoderm.
    (C) mesoderm.
    (D) endoderm.
    (E) cortoderm.

44. Human embryos float in an isotonic fluid that serves the important function of
    (A) food supply.
    (B) mutagen enhancer.
    (C) shock absorber.
    (D) cardiac arrester.
    (E) All of the above

45. A complex plant tissue composed of parenchyma, sclerenchyma, specialized conducting cells known as sieve-tubes, and companion cells is called
    (A) cambium.
    (B) stem.
    (C) xylem.
    (D) phloem.
    (E) collenchyma.

46. The fluid mosaic model of the cell membrane suggests that
    (A) cell membranes are three-layered sandwiches of lipid/protein/lipid.
    (B) cell membranes are a sea of double layers of lipid molecules in which protein molecules are floating.
    (C) cell membranes are rigid structures composed of cellulose and pectin.
    (D) cell membranes are trilaminar and contain only primary and secondary proteins.
    (E) mitosis and binary fission are prerequisites to divergent evolution.

47. Neurons that conduct impulses from the central nervous system to a muscle or a gland are known as
    (A) apolar neurons.
    (B) sensory neurons.
    (C) motor neurons.
    (D) afferent neurons.
    (E) rods and cones.

48. The correct sequence of digestive structures is
    (A) esophagus, liver, large intestine, small intestine.
    (B) small intestine, esophagus, stomach, large intestine.
    (C) stomach, spleen, liver, large intestine.
    (D) esophagus, stomach, large intestine, small intestine.
    (E) esophagus, stomach, small intestine, large intestine.

Questions 49–55 consist of statements that follow the description and results of an experiment. Analyze each statement solely on the basis of the experiment. Mark your answer sheet:
    (A) if the experiment proves the statement *true.*
    (B) if the experiment shows that the statement is *probably true.*
    (C) if the experiment *does not show* whether the statement is true or false.
    (D) if the experiment shows that the statement is *probably false.*
    (E) if the experiment shows that the statement is *false.*

Questions 49–52 refer to the following data.

An experiment was designed to test the tolerance of marine fiddler crabs, *Uca pugilator*, to varying concentrations of weed killer. A commercially available preparation was used that contained 26.2% active ingredients and 73.8% inert ingredients—oil based. Six aquaria were used and ten organisms, six female and four male, were placed in each aquarium. The following data were obtained:

GROUP	1	2	3	4	5	6
Concentration of active ingredients (ppm)	0	131	262	524	1048	2096

ELAPSED TIME	NUMBER OF DEAD ORGANISMS					
24 hours	0	0	1♂	0	0	1♂
48 hours	0	0	0	0	1♂	5♂ 4♀
72 hours	0	0	0	0	3♂ 1♀	
96 hours	0	0	0	0	5♀	
120 hours	0	0	1♂	1♂		
144 hours	0	0	1♀	1♀		
168 hours	0	0	1♀	0		

49. Male fiddler crabs are less able to tolerate weed killer than are females.

50. At the end of four days, concentrations of weed killer over 524 ppm were fatal to all crabs tested.

51. The inert ingredients had an effect on the experiment.

52. An animal that survived a given concentration would have survived any lower one.

Questions 53–55 refer to the following data.

A laboratory culture is inoculated with equal amounts of paramecium and yeast cells. At equal time intervals, the numbers of each organism in the culture are determined. The results are summarized below.

TIME INTERVALS	% OF ORIGINAL NUMBER OF ORGANISMS	
	Paramecia	*Saccharomyces sp.*
0	100	100
1	200	50
2	100	25
3	50	10
4	10	50
5	25	100
6	100	75
7	75	10
8	10	50
9	50	100

53. Both organisms follow a cyclical pattern of population growth.

54. The rate of reproduction is constant for both organisms.

55. A predator-prey relationship exists between paramecia and yeast.

For questions 56–58, select the one of the five lettered graphs below that best depicts the situation described.

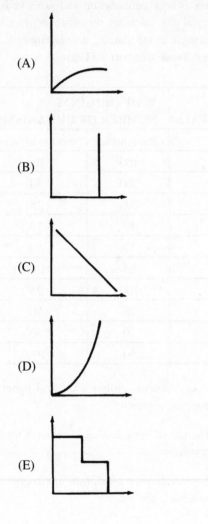

(A)

(B)

(C)

(D)

(E)

56. Growth occurring in a bacterial colony under ideal conditions.

    Vertical axis: number of organisms
    Horizontal axis: time

57. A population in which the environmental resistance becomes greater than the biotic potential.

    Vertical axis: population size
    Horizontal axis: time

58. The growth of an organism.

    Vertical axis: age of the organism
    Horizontal axis: number of chromosomes in the cells

59. Grizzly bears, moose, wolves, squirrels, spruce, hemlock, fir, and pine trees are characteristic of

    (A) tropical rain forests.
    (B) grasslands.
    (C) deserts.
    (D) taigas.
    (E) veldts.

60. The basic pattern or organism interaction in which one species benefits from the association while the other is essentially unaffected is known as

    (A) commensalism.
    (B) mutualism.
    (C) parasitism.
    (D) competition.
    (E) autotrophism.

Section II: Physical Sciences

60 Questions

Time—45 minutes

Directions: Choose the response that best completes the statement or answers the question.

61. If the atomic numbers of five different elements total 163, we can assume that
    (A) all of these elements will react with one another.
    (B) two of these elements contain 69 and 14 protons each.
    (C) there are a total of 163 electrons.
    (D) there are a total of 163 neutrons.
    (E) three of the elements are members of the heavy metals family.

For questions 62 and 63, select the one of the five lettered graphs that best depicts the situation described.

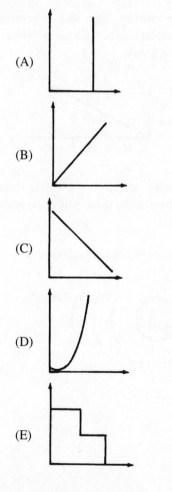

(A)

(B)

(C)

(D)

(E)

62. A nuclear chain reaction occurs in a large group of atoms.

    Vertical axis: number of atoms reacting
    Horizontal axis: time

63. Increasing numbers of different types of atoms are mixed together.

    Vertical axis: number of electrons in total
    Horizontal axis: number of protons in total

Answer questions 64–66 on the basis of the following data.

In the studies following the discovery of radioactivity, quite a number of substances were found to show activity. This kind of activity was finally described as the half-life of an element. The chart below lists radioactive elements, their atomic numbers, and half-lives.

ATOMIC NUMBER	ELEMENT	HALF-LIFE
92	Uranium	4.5×10^9 years
88	Radium	1,612 years
86	Radon	3.82 days
83	Bismuth	19.7 minutes
90	Thorium	24.5 days
91	Protactinium	68 seconds

64. According to the table, if a quantity X of radium was measured again in 1,612 years, the quantity remaining would be
    (A) X
    (B) 2X
    (C) $\frac{1}{2}X$
    (D) $\frac{1}{4}X$
    (E) 0

65. The activity of a radioactive sample

    (A) increases with time.
    (B) decreases with time.
    (C) doubles with time.
    (D) always remains the same.
    (E) increases and decreases with time.

66. The rate of decay of a radioactive material is known as its

    (A) half-life.
    (B) isotope.
    (C) radioactivity.
    (D) disintegration constant.
    (E) curie.

67. In order to predict the path of an electron, we must know both its position and velocity at the same time. One factor that influences this prediction is the

    (A) Heisenberg Uncertainty Principle.
    (B) Trouton's Rule.
    (C) Avogadro's Principle.
    (D) First Law of Thermodynamics.
    (E) Law of Hess.

68. What minimum energy in eV must the electron in a spark discharge have to be to strip a sodium $(Z = 11)$ atom of its last electron, assuming that the other ten have already been removed?

    (A) 1.00 keV
    (B) 3.17 ergs
    (C) 37 eV
    (D) 1.64 keV
    (E) None of the above

Questions 69–72 consist of statements about an experiment and its results. Analyze each statement solely on the basis of the experiment. From the information given about the experiment, select:

    (A) if the experiment proves the statement *true.*
    (B) if the experiment shows that the statement is *probably true.*
    (C) if the experiment *does not show* whether the statement is true or false.
    (D) if the experiment shows that the statement is *probably false.*
    (E) if the experiment proves that the statement is *false.*

An experiment is designed that permits the determination of the rates of diffusion of gases. The rate of diffusion of a gas is measured by determining the distance it travels down a tube in a specified period of time. The following table shows the results of the experiment with several gases.

GAS	MOLECULAR WEIGHT	DISTANCE TRAVELED (CM)
CO^2	44	0.20
O^2	32	0.25
H^2	2	1.00

69. An unknown gas travels 0.23 cm in the tube in a specified period of time. On the basis of the data presented, the molecular weight of the gas is approximately 34.

70. The distance traveled in the tube is directly proportional to the temperature.

71. The rate of diffusion of a gas is proportional to the molecular weight of the gas as shown in the following graph:

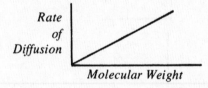

72. The rate of diffusion of a gas is inversely proportional to the number of atoms in the gas molecule.

73. The Lewis symbol for aluminum is

    (A) Al^{+++}

    (B)

    (C) $\cdot Al \cdot$
    (D) $A - 1$
    (E) $_{27}Al^{13}$

74. An example of a double covalent bond is

    (A) $Na^+:\ddot{\underset{..}{Cl}}:^-$

    (B) $(K^+)_2:\ddot{\underset{..}{S}}:^{2-}$

    (C) $H:\overset{\displaystyle H}{\underset{\displaystyle H}{\ddot{C}}}:H$

    (D) $H:N:::N:H$

    (E) $:\ddot{O}::\ddot{O}:$

75. The only common metal that is a liquid at room temperature is

    (A) aluminum.
    (B) iron.
    (C) platinum.
    (D) mercury.
    (E) silver.

76. The present picture of the atomic structure is the

    (A) Rutherford model.
    (B) Bohr model.
    (C) Thomson model.
    (D) quantum mechanical model.
    (E) fluid mosaic model.

77. The periodic table depicts the law that states

    (A) the properties of the elements are periodic functions of their atomic numbers.
    (B) fifteen family groupings are periodically divided into elementary particles.
    (C) neutrons follow a periodicity in the 92 elements.
    (D) no two electrons in the same atom may have the same four quantum numbers.
    (E) None of the above

Answer questions 78–80 on the basis of the following data.

The table shows some radioactive isotopes, the kind of radiation emitted, and their half-life. (Half-life is the time required for the disintegration of half of the atoms in a sample of some specific radioactive substance.)

ISOTOPE	RADIATION EMITTED	HALF-LIFE
Nitrogen-16	beta and gamma	7.4 seconds
Sulfur-37	beta and gamma	5 minutes
Sodium-24	beta and gamma	15 hours
Gold-108	beta and gamma	2.7 days
Iodine-131	beta and gamma	8 days
Iron-59	beta and gamma	45 days
Cobalt-60	beta and gamma	5.2 years
Strontium-90	beta	28 years
Radium-226	alpha and gamma	1,620 years
Carbon-14	beta	5,600 years
Chlorine-36	beta	310,005 years
Uranium-235	alpha, beta, gamma, and neutrons	710 million years

78. Which one of the following statements is most nearly correct?

    (A) The greater the number of kinds of radiation emitted, the longer the half-life of the isotope.
    (B) Filtering out the beta radiation and leaving the gamma rays will decrease the half-life of sulfur-37.
    (C) Carbon-14 cannot be used for dating archeological artifacts more than 5,600 years old.
    (D) There appears to be some relationship between kind of radiation emitted and the length of half-life.
    (E) None of the above

79. Which one of the isotopes listed below has a half-life nearest the time required for iodine-131 to have expended 63/64 of its radiation?

    (A) Sodium-24
    (B) Gold-108
    (C) Iron-59
    (D) Cobalt-60
    (E) Strontium-90

80. How long does it take a radioactive isotope to lose at least 99% of its radioactivity?

    (A) Two half-lives
    (B) Four half-lives
    (C) Seven half-lives
    (D) Fifteen half-lives
    (E) Twenty half-lives

81. As an object sinks in water, the pressure on the object

    (A) decreases.
    (B) increases.
    (C) remains the same.
    (D) first increases then decreases.
    (E) first decreases then increases.

For questions 82–86, select the one of the five lettered graphs below that best depicts the situation described.

(A)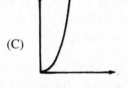

(B)

(C)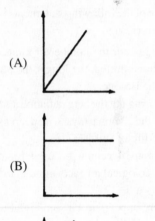

(D)

(E)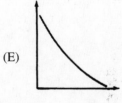

82. Pleural changes during lung inspiration.

    Vertical axis: intrapleural pressure.
    Horizontal axis: intrapleural volume.

83. A capillary tube in a beaker of water.

    Vertical axis: height of water in capillary tube.
    Horizontal axis: diameter of capillary tube.

84. An alternating current.

    Vertical axis: increasing current.
    Horizontal axis: time.

85. The speed of light in a uniform piece of glass.

    Vertical axis: speed.
    Horizontal axis: distance.

86. Energy invisible light.

    Vertical axis: energy.
    Horizontal axis: red light to violet light.

87. Planck's constant may be expressed in which one of the following units?

    (A) Watt-seconds
    (B) Joules per cycle
    (C) Joule-seconds
    (D) Ergs per second
    (E) Quarks per second

88. The image formed by a convex mirror compared to the object is usually

    (A) inverted and imaginary.
    (B) erect and smaller.
    (C) real and inverted.
    (D) erect and imaginary.
    (E) inverted and larger.

89. A correct expression for the conversion of mass into energy is

    (A) $E = mc$

    (B) $m = c^2/E$

    (C) $c = \sqrt{E/m}$

    (D) $E = m/c^2$

    (E) $PV = K$

90. The apparent pitch of a stationary sound source heard by a moving observer depends only on the

    (A) velocity of sound in air.
    (B) direction of motion of the observer.
    (C) speed of the observer.
    (D) direction of the observer's motion relative to the source and the observer's speed.
    (E) crosscurrents from windows.

91. Two skaters, A and B, of equal mass go around a circular ring at the same time. Skater A is twice as far from the center of the rink as skater B. Which one of the following is true?

    (A) The velocities of both A and B are the same.
    (B) The centripetal force on A is greater than that on B.
    (C) The centripetal force on B is greater than that on A.
    (D) The centripetal force on both is the same.
    (E) Skater A is the only one to accelerate.

92. The Heisenberg principle postulates that

    (A) the momentum and position of an electron cannot be known simultaneously.
    (B) two electrons may not occupy the same orbital.
    (C) for every proton, there must exist an antiproton.
    (D) every radioactive decay results in the production of isotopic lead.
    (E) gravity is a special case of electrical attraction.

93. Given the following thermochemical equations:

    $Zn + \frac{1}{2} O_2 + ZnO + 84,000$ cals

    $Hg + \frac{1}{2} O_2 = HgO + 21,700$ cals

    Accordingly, the heat of reaction for the following reaction

    $Zn + HgO = ZnO + Hg + heat$ is

    (A) 105,700 cals
    (B) 61,000 cals
    (C) 105,000 cals
    (D) 62,300 cals
    (E) 106,000 cals

94. The phenomenon of interference is accepted as evidence to show that light is (a)

    (A) wave.
    (B) transverse.
    (C) longitudinal.
    (D) quantized.
    (E) photoelectric discharge.

95. A charge Q is located at the center of a cube of edge length l. The electric flux through any one face is

    (A) $4\pi Q$

    (B) $\dfrac{Q}{4\pi}$

    (C) $\dfrac{Q}{3}$

    (D) $\dfrac{Q}{4}$

    (E) $\dfrac{Q}{6}$

96. Four charges, each with charges $+q$, are placed at the four corners of a square of edge length l. The force on any one charge arising from the other three is

    (A) $\dfrac{q^2}{l^2}$

    (B) $\dfrac{0.5q^2}{l^2}$

    (C) $\dfrac{0.75q^2}{l^2}$

    (D) $\dfrac{1.50q^2}{l^2}$

    (E) $\dfrac{1.91q^2}{l^2}$

97. An electric generator dissipates energy internally at the rate of 20W when it establishes a potential difference across its output terminals of 120V and when, at the same time, a current of 2 amps flows through it. The generator's emf is

    (A) 110 volts.
    (B) 140 volts.
    (C) 130 volts.
    (D) 125 volts.
    (E) 120 volts.

98. In order for a 30-volt, 90-watt lamp to work properly when inserted in a 120-volt *d-c* line, it should have in series with it a resistor whose resistance in ohms is

    (A) 10
    (B) 20
    (C) 30
    (D) 40
    (E) 50

99. A galvanometer, having an armature coil with a resistance of 10 ohms, requires .01 amperes for a full-scale deflection. To convert this galvanometer to a voltmeter, which will give a full-scale deflection when the voltage is 120 volts, a coil in series must be added that will have a resistance in ohms of

    (A) 40
    (B) 120
    (C) 1,200
    (D) 1,210
    (E) 11,990

100. The work required to transfer a charge of 6 coulombs against a difference of potential of 110 volts is in joules

    (A) 18.2
    (B) 6.6×10^2
    (C) 6.6×10^7
    (D) 6.6×10^5
    (E) 6.6×10^9

Answer questions 101–103 on the basis of the following data.

From observation and reference tables, a student compiles the following values for some of the physical properties of 5 stars.

	Apparent Magnitude	Absolute Magnitude	(Sun = 1) Luminosity
1. Sirius	1.58	+1.3	30
2. Canopus	0.86	-3.2	1,900
3. Alpha Centauri	+0.06	+4.7	1.3
4. Vega	+0.41	+0.5	60
5. Capella	+0.21	0.4	150

101. The brightest star of the group is

    (A) Capella.
    (B) Vega.
    (C) Alpha Centauri.
    (D) Canopus.
    (E) Sirius.

102. The distance from the earth to one of these stars could be determined from the given information, the correct formula, and which additional piece of information?

    (A) Temperature
    (B) Density
    (C) Mass
    (D) Diameter
    (E) No further information is necessary.

103. The latitude of an observatory is 47° North. How far south can stars be observed?

    (A) 43° S
    (B) 2° S
    (C) 0° Equator
    (D) 47° N
    (E) 47° S

104. A star that is so dense that its gravitational field traps almost all of the electromagnetic radiation it gives off is called a

    (A) quasar.
    (B) nebula.
    (C) black hole.
    (D) nova.
    (E) galactic cluster.

105. The Doppler Effect (Redshift) observed in the spectrum of light from a star is an effect caused by the

    (A) elements of which the star is composed.
    (B) temperature of the star.
    (C) rotation of the star.
    (D) magnitude of the star.
    (E) movement of the star toward or away from Earth.

106. Quasars appear to be strange objects because they

    (A) appear to be receding from Earth at fantastic speeds.
    (B) appear, in some cases, to be dwelling far beyond the realm of the remote galaxies.
    (C) appear, in many cases, to vary in both light and radio output.
    (D) All of the above
    (E) None of the above

107. The Milky Way is approximately

    (A) 100,000 eons in diameter.
    (B) 100,000 light-years in diameter.
    (C) 1,000,000 light-years in diameter.
    (D) 100,000 angstroms in diameter.
    (E) None of the above

108. Presently, astronomers recognize

    (A) 52 constellations.
    (B) 88 constellations.
    (C) 93 constellations.
    (D) 154 constellations.
    (E) 391 constellations.

109. Four factors produce and direct the winds. Which of the following is NOT one of these factors?

    (A) The differential heating or cooling of air masses
    (B) The earth's gravitational field
    (C) The earth's rotation
    (D) Air friction with the ground
    (E) Air motion in a curved path

110. A hygrometer is used to measure

    (A) barometric pressure.
    (B) relative humidity.
    (C) wind speed.
    (D) temperature.
    (E) altitude.

111. Which of the following statements best describes the reason that coastal regions have milder climates than inland regions?

    (A) Coastal climates have more rain.
    (B) Inland regions lack salt in the soil.
    (C) A moderating effect on the temperature is exerted on coastal climates by the oceans.
    (D) Coastal climates are usually in the paths of storms that keep a high humidity in these regions.
    (E) Coastal climates have many underground water sources.

Questions 112 and 113 relate to the five figures below.

(A)

(B)

(C)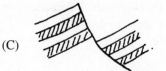

(D)

(E)

112. The mountain type known as a dome mountain

113. The mountain type known as a fault-block mountain

114. Two major forms of igneous rock are
     (A) granite and sandstone.
     (B) basalt and shale.
     (C) shale and sandstone.
     (D) granite and basalt.
     (E) conglomerate and siltstone.

115. Sedimentary rock forms as a result of
     (A) mechanical and chemical weathering.
     (B) melting of bedrock.
     (C) rock being exposed to heat and pressure.
     (D) volcanic activity.
     (E) fault blocks moving in horizontal directions.

116. The correct sequence for the geological time scale is
     (A) Precambrian, Mesozoic, Paleozoic, Cenozoic eras.
     (B) Mesozoic, Precambrian, Paleozoic, Cenozoic eras.
     (C) Precambrian, Mesozoic, Cenozoic, Paleozoic eras.
     (D) Mesozoic, Precambrian, Cenozoic, Paleozoic eras.
     (E) Precambrian, Paleozoic, Mesozoic, Cenozoic eras.

117. The era of the Reptiles is the
     (A) Paleozoic.
     (B) Cenozoic.
     (C) Mesozoic.
     (D) Precambrian.
     (E) Devonian.

118. The best explanation for the Coriolis effect is the
     (A) tilt of the earth's axis.
     (B) north-south lines of magnetic force.
     (C) earth's rotation around its axis.
     (D) granite-basalt ratio.
     (E) None of the above

119. Ninety-nine percent of the earth's crust is made up of
     (A) 92 different elements.
     (B) 9 different elements.
     (C) 103 different elements.
     (D) 54 different elements.
     (E) 76 different elements.

120. The three main types of waves or vibrations that move out from the site of an earthquake are
     (A) QRS, T, and P waves.
     (B) A, B, and C waves.
     (C) surface, P, and S waves.
     (D) surface, low, and tectonic waves.
     (E) surface, QRS, and T waves.

End of Practice Examination II

Answer Key

Section I

1.	D	13.	B	25.	B	37.	C	49. B
2.	A	14.	C	26.	D	38.	A	50. A
3.	E	15.	A	27.	B	39.	E	51. C
4.	A	16.	A	28.	A	40.	B	52. A
5.	D	17.	C	29.	C	41.	B	53. A
6.	D	18.	B	30.	A	42.	B	54. E
7.	A	19.	D	31.	B	43.	D	55. B
8.	A	20.	A	32.	A	44.	C	56. D
9.	E	21.	E	33.	A	45.	D	57. A
10.	C	22.	E	34.	C	46.	B	58. B
11.	A	23.	C	35.	E	47.	C	59. D
12.	E	24.	C	36.	A	48.	E	60. A

Section II

61.	C	73.	C	85.	B	97.	C	109. B
62.	D	74.	E	86.	C	98.	C	110. B
63.	B	75.	D	87.	C	99.	E	111. C
64.	C	76.	D	88.	B	100.	B	112. A
65.	B	77.	A	89.	C	101.	E	113. C
66.	A	78.	D	90.	D	102.	E	114. D
67.	A	79.	C	91.	B	103.	A	115. A
68.	D	80.	C	92.	A	104.	C	116. E
69.	B	81.	B	93.	D	105.	E	117. C
70.	C	82.	E	94.	A	106.	D	118. C
71.	E	83.	E	95.	E	107.	B	119. B
72.	E	84.	D	96.	E	108.	B	120. C

Explanatory Answers

Section I

1. **The correct answer is (D).** The euglena has chloroplast, a characteristic of plant cells, but it has no cell wall, a characteristic of animal cells.

2. **The correct answer is (A).** Under the Linnaean system, the next major division under kingdom is phylum, followed by class, order, family, genus, and species.

4. **The correct answer is (E).** Binomial nomenclature means a two-term system of names. Homo sapiens as a term is an example of this system. Under the system, it designates the genus and species of man.

4. **The correct answer is (A).** Organisms are grouped into phyla, etc., because they resemble each other structurally.

5. **The correct answer is (D).** Bacteria are unicellular plants.

6. **The correct answer is (D).** The presently accepted view is that the first life forms were heterotrophs and that they formed at a time when the earth had a reducing atmosphere.

7. **The correct answer is (A).** Experiments by Stanley Miller and later by Sidney Fox support the hypothesis that life on Earth began with the formation of protein in the primitive oceans. Sugars like glucose supplied energy requirements for the earliest cells. Choices (B) and (C) do not relate in any way to the question.

8. **The correct answer is (A).** The first true manlike humanoids are believed to be members of the genus *Australopithecus*. A later stage of development is *Homo erectus*. Cro-Magnon man is the earliest representative of *Homo sapiens*, whose origins are still uncertain. Neanderthal man was well established by the time Cro-Magnon man came along. Cro-Magnon man eventually replaced Neanderthal man (*Homo neanderthalensis*).

9. **The correct answer is (E).** Members of different species are ordinarily incapable of interbreeding. There are no fewer than ten factors that can change one ancestral species into two or more divergent species. These factors are geographic isolation, habitat isolation, seasonal isolation, behavioral isolation, mechanical isolation, gamete isolation, developmental isolation, hybrid inviability, hybrid sterility, and selective hybrid elimination.

10. **The correct answer is (C).** Alfred Russel Wallace was a young naturalist who had, independent of Darwin, constructed the theory of natural selection while lying ill with malaria on a Malaysian island. Wallace even claimed inspiration from Malthus' essay on population.

11. **The correct answer is (A).** See explanation for number 9.

12. **The correct answer is (E).** See explanation for number 8.

13. **The correct answer is (B).** Although no direct information is given in support of this statement, it is a logical deduction from the information provided. However, since direct evidence is not given, choice (B) is correct.

14. **The correct answer is (C).** No information is given about the relative ease of separating amino acids by paper chromatography.

15. **The correct answer is (A).** Reference to the illustration will demonstrate the accuracy of this statement. All the other acids fall below A, so this statement is true.

16. **The correct answer is (A).** The illustration shows B and C on the same horizontal plane. This means that they would have occupied the same area after the first separation.

17. **The correct answer is (C).** Yeast will ferment molasses and other sugars under anaerobic conditions, producing alcohol and carbon dioxide. As this gas bubbles through colorless limewater, it turns the solution cloudy or milky white, as a precipitate of calcium carbonate is formed.

18. **The correct answer is (B).** The situation depicted is one in which osmosis will take place; therefore, there will be a net movement of water from side B to side A, thereby diluting the original 20% starch solution.

19. **The correct answer is (D).** Solution (A) is isotonic to the sea urchin egg, while both solutions (B) and (C) are hypotonic; therefore, water enters the cell in (B) as well as the cell in (C).

20. **The correct answer is (A).** In this series of beakers, the pure seawater has the greatest amount of dissolved material, while the others have proportionally less as indicated by the percentages.

21. **The correct answer is (E).** The division of a sea urchin egg would not depend on the salt concentration of the environment.

22. **The correct answer is (E).** Mitosis, a form of cell division, can be described in four stages: prophase, metaphase, anaphase, and telophase. After paired chromosomes separate (anaphase) and cytokinesis begins (early telophase), the two daughter nuclei form.

23. **The correct answer is (C).** Genes are believed to be long chains of DNA. Chromatin is a long thread composed of genes and associated proteins. Chromosomes are coiled chromatin threads. Ribosomes are composed of protein, structural RNA, and, during protein synthesis, messenger RNA. Of the cell organelles listed, only centrioles appear to lack any form of nucleic acid.

24. **The correct answer is (C).** Cells involved with synthesizing and secreting large quantities of protein hormone would be expected to have all of the machinery necessary to accomplish these jobs. Mitochondria supply energy for work, ribosomes are the sites for protein synthesis, and the Golgi apparatus packages cell materials to be secreted.

25. **The correct answer is (B).** Transpiration is the evaporation of water from the leaf of a plant.

26. **The correct answer is (D).** Inspiration is the act of inhaling. When air is taken into the lungs, the chest expands, and the ribs move upward and outward.

27. **The correct answer is (B).** Absorption of nutrients takes place in the small intestine. For the nutrients to be transported, they must enter the bloodstream.

28. **The correct answer is (A).** The function of white cells is to remove unwanted organisms from the bloodstream and surrounding tissue. Of the choices given, only an infection indicates the presence of unwanted organisms. The white cell count in this case would go up.

29. **The correct answer is (C).** The only choice that has iron as a major permanent constituent is the erythrocyte.

30. **The correct answer is (A).** The male guppy is very brightly colored, while the female is dull and drab. This is known as a secondary sex characteristic directly controlled by the male sex hormone androgen. If injected into the female, it will make these normally suppressed traits pronounced.

31. **The correct answer is (B).** All somatic cells contain the same chromosomal configuration. Diagram 6 contains the same six chromosomes as cell X.

32. **The correct answer is (A).** All sex cells receive the haploid number of chromosomes. One member from each chromosome pair in cell X, through reduction division, was passed on to the sperm nucleus of the pollen grain.

33. **The correct answer is (A).** Again, all somatic cells contain the same number and type of chromosomes. Diagram 6 and cell X are virtually identical.

34. **The correct answer is (C).** If reduction division had not accompanied gametogenesis, the pollen grain and ovule would both have contained the diploid number of chromosomes as shown in cell X. If the two gametes unite, the resulting zygote would contain 12 chromosomes, or double the normal amount, as shown in diagram 3.

35. **The correct answer is (E).** The rod chromosome in diagram 1 is half black and half white, a fine example of crossing-over.

36. **The correct answer is (A).** Individual A is a female possessing only normal genes for blood clotting. Individual B is a male possessing a gene for hemophilia inherited from his mother. It is impossible for individual D to be a hemo-

philiac female, as shown by the following genetic problem:

h = hemophiliac gene

	X^h	Y
X	X^{h}X	XY
X	X^{h}X	XY

Only carrier females are produced. These females have normal blood clotting but can transmit this gene to their male offspring.

37. **The correct answer is (C).** As explained before, individual D must be a hemophiliac carrier. Her mother (individual A) possesses only genes for blue eyes (recessive trait). Her father (individual B) is heterozygous for eye color, possessing one gene for blue eyes and one gene for dark eyes. If Aa times aa are then crossed, there is a 50-50 chance of having a blue-eyed or dark-eyed child.

38. **The correct answer is (A).** Individual E is the sister of the aforementioned individual D. Obviously they have the same parents, so that the same reasoning employed for question 37 (above) holds true here.

39. **The correct answer is (E).** We definitely do not know the eye color of individual F and are not sure of individual C's eye color, so that it is quite impossible even to predict individual H's eye color.

40. **The correct answer is (B).** Individual E is a carrier female, possessing a normal blood clotting gene and a hemophilia gene. If she marries a hemophiliac male, the following genetic problem is noted:

h = hemophiliac gene

	X^h	Y
X^h	X^h X^h	X^{h}Y
X	X^{h}X	XY

Results: 25% (1) normal male
25% (1) hemophiliac male
25% (1) carrier female
25% (1) hemophiliac female

Therefore, all of the daughters possess at least one gene for hemophilia.

41. **The correct answer is (B).** Budding is a modified mitotic cell division in which one daughter cell is larger than the other at the time of separation. Budding occurs in yeasts.

42. **The correct answer is (B).** Internal fertilization is important in terrestrial forms, many of which provide no care for their young, while others provide extensive care for their young.

43. **The correct answer is (D).** The gastrocoele is the cavity in the embryonic structure known as the gastrula. The gastrula is composed of three layers: ectoderm, mesoderm, and the innermost layer, the endoderm.

44. **The correct answer is (C).** The isotonic fluid, known as amniotic fluid, surrounds the human embryo and acts as an effective shock absorber.

45. **The correct answer is (D).** There are only two complex plant tissues, xylem and phloem. Xylem differs from phloem tissue in that xylem contains specialized cells called vessels and tracheids, while phloem contains specialized cells called sieve-tubes and companion cells.

46. **The correct answer is (B).** Several models for cell membrane structure have been proposed since the original model described by Darson and Danielli in 1941. Currently, the model receiving the most support is the fluid mosaic model. It suggests that cell membranes are seas of lipid in which large globular proteins float about.

47. **The correct answer is (C).** Sensory neurons convey information from sense receptors to the central nervous system, while motor neurons convey information from the central nervous system to effector structures such as muscles and glands.

48. **The correct answer is (E).** The mouth-to-anus digestive tube is specialized along its length into a number of structures, including the esophagus, stomach, small intestine, and large intestine.

49. **The correct answer is (B).** In every case, males were the first to die. A greater percentage of males died in aquaria three and four. These facts suggest that males might be less able to tolerate the toxin than are females. However, no definitive statement can be made from this one experiment. The number of organisms was not sufficiently large to prevent chance occurrences from influencing the data.

50. **The correct answer is (A).** One can see that this is a true statement by referring to the table. In the aquarium with the highest concentration of toxin (2,096 ppm), all organisms were dead at the end of two days. In the aquarium with the next highest concentration (1,048 ppm), all organisms were dead at the end of 96 hours or four days.

51. **The correct answer is (C).** The inert ingredients were inert in terms of their effect on weeds. It is very possible that they could have a detrimental effect on animals. It is not possible to determine the accuracy of this statement without knowing the nature of these ingredients and this information was not provided in the experiment.

52. **The correct answer is (A).** This statement is a necessary presumption in tolerance tests. If it were not true, the death of any one organism would be strictly a matter of chance. Therefore, choice (A) is correct.

53. **The correct answer is (A).** Cycles have alternate peaks and depressions and this pattern is apparent in both populations.

54. **The correct answer is (E).** A constant growth rate for either organism would appear as a continual increase in the population. This is obviously not the case.

55. **The correct answer is (B).** During the first time period, the population of paramecia has doubled while that of the yeast has been halved. Subsequent peaks in the population *follow* the peaks in the population of yeast. This suggests that yeast is a food source for paramecia; an increase in the population of yeast supports a larger population of paramecia. The larger population of paramecia then decreases the food supply to such an extent that there are some organisms who cannot obtain enough food to survive. As the population of paramecia decreases, more yeast survive to reproduce, increasing the population. The repetition of this pattern gives rise to the observed cycles. However, this evidence is *indirect*. Direct evidence—the observation of paramecia consuming yeast—would be needed for absolute proof that a predator-prey relationship exists.

56. **The correct answer is (D).** Under ideal conditions, bacteria reproduce quickly following a geometric progression. The only graph that illustrates this increase is choice (D).

57. **The correct answer is (A).** If environmental resistance becomes greater than the biotic potential of a population, the population will decrease.

58. **The correct answer is (B).** The number of chromosomes an organism has does not change over a lifetime. Therefore, the proper graph will depict a situation where one property does not change as the other increases. The only possible answer is (B).

59. **The correct answer is (D).** Taiga is a region dotted by countless lakes, ponds, and bogs. Both conifers and deciduous trees are present. Many large and small mammals are permanent residents, while many birds are only present in the summer.

60. **The correct answer is (A).** There are three symbiotic relationships: parasitism is a relationship in which one species is often harmed, mutualism is a relationship in which neither species is harmed but both actually benefit, and commensalism is a relationship in which one species benefits while the other receives neither benefit nor harm.

Section II

61. **The correct answer is (C).** The atomic number of an element represents the number of protons in the atomic nucleus. Since atoms are electrically balanced, this number also represents the number of electrons in the atom. The proton

number of the five atoms in the problem is 163 and, therefore, there are 163 electrons in total.

62. **The correct answer is (D).** A chain reaction can be pictured as an event where one atom causes its neighbors to react, in turn causing increasing numbers of atoms to react. The only graph to indicate this type of geometric progression of events is (D).

63. **The correct answer is (B).** See explanation 61.

64. **The correct answer is (C).** The table shows that the half-life of radium is 1,612 years. Half-life means the time required for a given amount to decay to $\frac{1}{2}$ the amount.

65. **The correct answer is (B).** The activity of a radioactive sample means the number of disintegrations per second. As the sample disintegrates, the activity must decrease with time.

66. **The correct answer is (A).** Half-life is the rate of decay of a radioactive element.

67. **The correct answer is (A).** The Heisenberg Uncertainty Principle states that it is impossible to determine simultaneously the exact position and exact momentum of a body as small as an electron. The more precisely one tries to determine one of these values, the more uncertain one is of the other value.

68. **The correct answer is (D).** Using the Bohr model, we see that the energy of the last electron left is

$$En = - (2\pi^2 \, \mu e^4/h^2) \, (Z^2/n^2)$$

and in this case $n = 1$, $Z = 11$, and m is the mass of the electron. Therefore, the minimum energy needed would be

$$(2\pi^2 \, \mu e^4/h^2) \, (121)$$

Remembering that the binding energy of the electron to the proton in hydrogen is 13.6 eV, we find the minimum energy is

$$(13.6 \text{eV}) \, (121) = 1.64 \text{ keV}.$$

69. **The correct answer is (B).** We observe that as the molecular weight of the gas *decreases,* the distance traveled *increases.* Therefore, a gas that

travels 0.23 cm should have a molecular weight slightly greater than 32. However, this statement is not definitely proved but only probably true. Therefore, the correct answer is (B).

70. **The correct answer is (C).** Since the temperature of the gases was not specified, the correct answer is (C).

71. **The correct answer is (E).** The data presented indicates that the rate of diffusion *decreases* with increasing molecular weight. The graph shows the opposite situation and is therefore false. The correct answer is (E).

72. **The correct answer is (E).** The data presented shows that although H^2 and O^2 have the same number of atoms, their rates of diffusion are quite different. Therefore, this statement is also false, and the correct answer is (E).

73. **The correct answer is (C).** Since only valence electrons are important in describing how bonding occurs, it is convenient to use the Lewis symbol for the element. The Lewis symbol lists the symbol of the element and the number of dots that represent only the valence electrons.

74. **The correct answer is (E).** When two or three pairs of electrons are shared between two atoms in a molecule, the resulting bonds are called multiple bonds. A double covalent bond involves two pairs of shared electrons.

75. **The correct answer is (D).** Metals are elements that conduct heat and electricity, generally melt at very high temperatures, possess relatively high densities, are usually malleable and ductile, and display a brilliant luster. With the exception of mercury, metals are solids at room temperature.

76. **The correct answer is (D).** Erwin Schrödinger, Louis de Broglie, P. A. M. Dirac, and Werner Heisenberg contributed to the modern quantum mechanical model of the atom, which presents a view of energy levels as groupings of sublevels with different quantum numbers.

77. **The correct answer is (A).** When the relatively stable elements are written out in order of their atomic numbers, there are properties that repeat in regular intervals, forming a peri-

odic table of elements. Elements are arranged in rows and columns by increasing atomic number in such a way as to form families of elements.

78. **The correct answer is (D).** The chart shows an array of different radiations that are emitted from radioactive elements. Some half-lives are very short; others are very long. There seems to be some correlation between the kind of radiation emitted and the duration of half-life.

79. **The correct answer is (C).** It is an established fact that seven half-lives are necessary for a radioactive element to lose approximately 99 percent of its total radioactivity (see next answer). 63/64 is 95 percent of an atom's total emissions. If, at the end of seven half-lives, 56 days have elapsed ($8 \times 7 = 56$), we can easily calculate that 95 percent of this is 53.2 days. Iron-59 on the chart is the closest isotope to this figure, having a half-life of 45 days.

80. **The correct answer is (C).** If we start with a 100-gram sample of uranium, at the end of the first half-life, 50 grams will be left; at the end of the second half-life, 25 grams will remain; third, 12.5; fourth, 6; fifth, 3; sixth, 1.5; and finally seventh, 0.75 (less than 1 percent will remain).

81. **The correct answer is (B).** Water pressure increases with depth. For every foot of depth in fresh water, the pressure increases 62.5 pounds, while in salt water it increases 64 pounds for each foot of depth.

82. **The correct answer is (E).** As the pleural cavity is a closed system, pressure and volume are inversely related. An inspiration requires a decrease in intrapleural pressure that can be accomplished only by increasing intrapleural volume.

83. **The correct answer is (E).** As the diameter of the capillary tube increases, the height of water in the tube decreases.

84. **The correct answer is (D).** Alternating current is positive as much as it is negative. Choice (D) is the only curve that suggests an alternating sign function.

85. **The correct answer is (B).** The speed of light is constant in a particular medium and only changes when light passes from one medium into another.

86. **The correct answer is (C).** The energy in the electromagnetic spectrum is inversely proportional to wavelength. Red light has the longest wavelengths of visible light, while violet light has the shortest wavelengths of visible light.

87. **The correct answer is (C).** We may arrive at the units of Planck's constant by considering that hv is equal to the energy of a photon. This gives it the units of joule-seconds.

88. **The correct answer is (B).** Convex lenses are shaped like the lens of the eye. They are prescribed in spectacles for the treatment of farsightedness, where they shorten the focal length, creating an erect and much smaller image.

89. **The correct answer is (C).** The familiar form of the expression is

$E = mc^2$, which is equivalent to $c = \sqrt{E/m}$.

90. **The correct answer is (D).** Sound waves travel at a speed of 34,400 cm. per second at normal conditions of temperature and pressure. An observer moving faster than this speed will not hear the sound, proving that the listener's rate of speed is critical to the proper perception of sound waves. Also the direction (toward or away from) of movement is equally important in ascertaining the pitch of a sound.

91. **The correct answer is (B).**

Centripetal force $F_A = \frac{mv^2}{r}$, where r is the radius of the object's path and v is its linear velocity. If $r_A = 2r_B$, V_A must be 4 times V_B. Thus, F_A must be greater than F_B.

92. **The correct answer is (A).** The Heisenberg principle states quantitatively that, for any object, the product of the uncertainties in position (along a path) and velocity of the object must be unpredictable since it is not possible to measure both simultaneously.

93. **The correct answer is (D).**

    (1) $Zn + \frac{1}{2}0_1 = ZnO + 84{,}000$ cal

    (2) $HgO = Hg + \frac{1}{2}O_2 - 21{,}700$ cal

    Adding (1) and (2) and dropping the term $\frac{1}{2}O_2$, which appears on both sides of the chemical equation, results in

    $Zn + HgO = ZnO + Hg + 62{,}300$

94. **The correct answer is (A).** The concept of light as a particle cannot explain interference; only the wave concept can.

95. **The correct answer is (E).** By Gauss's Law, the electric flux through a closed surface must equal the enclosed charge, Q. The flux through each face is equal, so the flux through a face must be one sixth of the total flux, or $\frac{Q}{6}$.

96. **The correct answer is (E).**

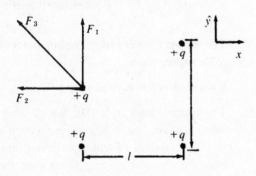

$$F_1 = \left(q^2 / l^2\right)\hat{y} \qquad F_1 = -\left(q^2 / l^2\right)\hat{x}$$

$$F_3 = \frac{p^2}{2l^2}\left(-\frac{1}{\sqrt{2}}\hat{x} + \frac{1}{\sqrt{2}}\hat{y}\right)$$

$$F = F_1 + F_2 + F_3$$

$$|F| = \frac{q^2}{l^2}\left[2\left(1 + \frac{1}{2\sqrt{2}}\right)^2\right]^{\frac{1}{2}}$$

$$|F| = 1.91\frac{q^2}{l^2}$$

97. **The correct answer is (C).**

    120 volts $1 = V - IR$

    $P = I^2R$

    $R = P/I^2$

    $V = 120$ volts $+ P/I$

    $V = 120$ volts $+ (20\ W/2A)$

    $V = 130$ volts

98. **The correct answer is (C).**

    I^2R_1 = 90 watts; R_1 = resistance of lamp

    IR_1 = 30 volts

    I = 3 amps

    120 volts = $(R + R_1)I$

    Thus, IR = 90 volts

    R = 30W.

99. **The correct answer is (E).** We must have, at full scale, a voltage drop of 120 volts across the resistor and galvanometer while having a current of .01 amp flowing through the galvanometer. Therefore, the resistor and galvanometer must be in series.

    (.01 amp) $(R + 10W) = 120$ volt

    $R + 10W = 12{,}000W$

    $R = 11{,}990W$

100. **The correct answer is (B).**

    $W = qV$

    V = 110 volts = 100 joules/coulomb

    q = 6 coulombs

    W = 660 joules

101. **The correct answer is (E).** The brightness of a star refers to its apparent magnitude. In actuality, the star may be brighter or dimmer, in relation to other stars, than it appears to us on Earth. The brightest stars have apparent magnitudes under 1.0 continuing into the negative numbers. The higher a positive number, the dimmer the star. Sirius appears brightest although Canopus is actually much brighter, because of their relative distances from the earth.

102. **The correct answer is (E).** The distance can be determined knowing only apparent and absolute magnitudes using the proper formula. The other physical parameters are useful, but no other information is needed to determine distance.

103. **The correct answer is (A).** An observer can see stars as far beyond the equator as 90° minus his latitude. At this observatory, stars are visible that are (90° – 47°) or 43° south of the equator.

104. **The correct answer is (C).** The term "black hole" is given to a body that is so dense that it traps most of the radiation that passes nearby.

105. **The correct answer is (E).** The Doppler Effect enables astronomers to tell at what speed a star is moving toward or away from the earth.

106. **The correct answer is (D).** The high-speed recession of quasars is evidenced by the red shift of their spectra. The high speeds suggest that quasars must be very distant celestial bodies.

107. **The correct answer is (B).** Galactic distances are measured in light-years. Eons are time measurements, while angstroms are microscopic distance measurements.

108. **The correct answer is (B).** Ancient stargazers divided the sky into a number of constellations. Many were named after characters or objects in ancient mythology. Present day astronomers recognize 88.

109. **The correct answer is (B).** Choice (A) is the main cause of air movement. Choices (C), (D), and (E) are forces that determine the direction this movement will take. Only choice (B) neither produces nor directs the winds.

110. **The correct answer is (B).** A hygrometer can be any of several instruments for measuring the humidity of the atmosphere.

111. **The correct answer is (C).** Coastal regions have milder climates due to the fact that nearby oceans exert a temperature moderating effect. This means that as a general rule, coastal climates will have cooler summers and warmer winters when compared with an inland region. The correct answer is (C). The amount of rain, salt in the soil, underground water sources, and storms have no important effects with respect to the severity of the climate.

112. **The correct answer is (A).** The dome mountain is the result of rock being pushed up by forces within the crust. They are not folded or faulted.

113. **The correct answer is (C).** The fault-block mountain is the result of movements along faults.

114. **The correct answer is (D).** There are more than 600 kinds of igneous rock. Of these, 95% of all igneous rocks are granite and basalt. The continents are granite masses floating in a sea of basalt.

115. **The correct answer is (A).** The weathering process produces the particles that make the sediments necessary in the formation of sedimentary rocks.

116. **The correct answer is (E).** The geological time scale was worked out by grouping rocks according to relative age. The Precambrian era began some 4,500 million years ago, the Paleozoic era began some 600 million years ago, the Mesozoic era some 225 million years ago, and the Cenozoic era some 65 million years ago.

117. **The correct answer is (C).** In the Mesozoic era, the reptiles completely dominated the land. Some even went back to the watery home of their remote ancestors. Some became the largest land animals of all time—the dinosaurs.

118. **The correct answer is (C).** The transfer of energy from the atmosphere to the ocean by winds directly affects surface currents and frequently affects deep water movements. This movement of water or wind resulting from the earth's rotation is called the Coriolis Effect.

119. **The correct answer is (B).** Although there are 92 naturally occurring elements, most of the minerals in the earth's crust are made up of only nine of them—oxygen, silicon, aluminum, iron, calcium, sodium, potassium, magnesium, and titanium.

120. **The correct answer is (C).** A "P" wave (push-pull wave) is similar to a sound wave with condensations and rarifications; an "S" wave (shake wave) is a wave whose particles vibrate at right angles to the direction of wave travel, and a surface wave is a slow, complex wave only capable of moving through solids.

Practice Examination II Diagnostic Chart

Question Type	Question Numbers	Number of Questions	Number Wrong
Section I: Life Sciences			
Origin and evolution of life; classification of organisms	1–12	12	_____
Cell organization and division; genes, bioenergetics, and biosynthesis	13–24	12	_____
Structure, function, and development of organisms; hereditary patterns	25–48	24	_____
Population biology and ecology	49–60	12	_____
Section II: Physical Sciences			
Atomic structure; particles and nuclear reactions	61–68	8	_____
Elements, compounds, and reactions; molecular structure and bonding	69–80	12	_____
Thermodynamics, mechanics, and relativity	81–94	14	_____
Electricity and magnetism, light, and sound	95–100	6	_____
The universe	101–108	8	_____
The earth	109–120	12	_____

Answer Sheet for Practice Examination III

Section I

1 Ⓐ Ⓑ Ⓒ Ⓓ Ⓔ   13 Ⓐ Ⓑ Ⓒ Ⓓ Ⓔ   25 Ⓐ Ⓑ Ⓒ Ⓓ Ⓔ   37 Ⓐ Ⓑ Ⓒ Ⓓ Ⓔ   49 Ⓐ Ⓑ Ⓒ Ⓓ Ⓔ

2 Ⓐ Ⓑ Ⓒ Ⓓ Ⓔ   14 Ⓐ Ⓑ Ⓒ Ⓓ Ⓔ   26 Ⓐ Ⓑ Ⓒ Ⓓ Ⓔ   38 Ⓐ Ⓑ Ⓒ Ⓓ Ⓔ   50 Ⓐ Ⓑ Ⓒ Ⓓ Ⓔ

3 Ⓐ Ⓑ Ⓒ Ⓓ Ⓔ   15 Ⓐ Ⓑ Ⓒ Ⓓ Ⓔ   27 Ⓐ Ⓑ Ⓒ Ⓓ Ⓔ   39 Ⓐ Ⓑ Ⓒ Ⓓ Ⓔ   51 Ⓐ Ⓑ Ⓒ Ⓓ Ⓔ

4 Ⓐ Ⓑ Ⓒ Ⓓ Ⓔ   16 Ⓐ Ⓑ Ⓒ Ⓓ Ⓔ   28 Ⓐ Ⓑ Ⓒ Ⓓ Ⓔ   40 Ⓐ Ⓑ Ⓒ Ⓓ Ⓔ   52 Ⓐ Ⓑ Ⓒ Ⓓ Ⓔ

5 Ⓐ Ⓑ Ⓒ Ⓓ Ⓔ   17 Ⓐ Ⓑ Ⓒ Ⓓ Ⓔ   29 Ⓐ Ⓑ Ⓒ Ⓓ Ⓔ   41 Ⓐ Ⓑ Ⓒ Ⓓ Ⓔ   53 Ⓐ Ⓑ Ⓒ Ⓓ Ⓔ

6 Ⓐ Ⓑ Ⓒ Ⓓ Ⓔ   18 Ⓐ Ⓑ Ⓒ Ⓓ Ⓔ   30 Ⓐ Ⓑ Ⓒ Ⓓ Ⓔ   42 Ⓐ Ⓑ Ⓒ Ⓓ Ⓔ   54 Ⓐ Ⓑ Ⓒ Ⓓ Ⓔ

7 Ⓐ Ⓑ Ⓒ Ⓓ Ⓔ   19 Ⓐ Ⓑ Ⓒ Ⓓ Ⓔ   31 Ⓐ Ⓑ Ⓒ Ⓓ Ⓔ   43 Ⓐ Ⓑ Ⓒ Ⓓ Ⓔ   55 Ⓐ Ⓑ Ⓒ Ⓓ Ⓔ

8 Ⓐ Ⓑ Ⓒ Ⓓ Ⓔ   20 Ⓐ Ⓑ Ⓒ Ⓓ Ⓔ   32 Ⓐ Ⓑ Ⓒ Ⓓ Ⓔ   44 Ⓐ Ⓑ Ⓒ Ⓓ Ⓔ   56 Ⓐ Ⓑ Ⓒ Ⓓ Ⓔ

9 Ⓐ Ⓑ Ⓒ Ⓓ Ⓔ   21 Ⓐ Ⓑ Ⓒ Ⓓ Ⓔ   33 Ⓐ Ⓑ Ⓒ Ⓓ Ⓔ   45 Ⓐ Ⓑ Ⓒ Ⓓ Ⓔ   57 Ⓐ Ⓑ Ⓒ Ⓓ Ⓔ

10 Ⓐ Ⓑ Ⓒ Ⓓ Ⓔ   22 Ⓐ Ⓑ Ⓒ Ⓓ Ⓔ   34 Ⓐ Ⓑ Ⓒ Ⓓ Ⓔ   46 Ⓐ Ⓑ Ⓒ Ⓓ Ⓔ   58 Ⓐ Ⓑ Ⓒ Ⓓ Ⓔ

11 Ⓐ Ⓑ Ⓒ Ⓓ Ⓔ   23 Ⓐ Ⓑ Ⓒ Ⓓ Ⓔ   35 Ⓐ Ⓑ Ⓒ Ⓓ Ⓔ   47 Ⓐ Ⓑ Ⓒ Ⓓ Ⓔ   59 Ⓐ Ⓑ Ⓒ Ⓓ Ⓔ

12 Ⓐ Ⓑ Ⓒ Ⓓ Ⓔ   24 Ⓐ Ⓑ Ⓒ Ⓓ Ⓔ   36 Ⓐ Ⓑ Ⓒ Ⓓ Ⓔ   48 Ⓐ Ⓑ Ⓒ Ⓓ Ⓔ   60 Ⓐ Ⓑ Ⓒ Ⓓ Ⓔ

Section II

61 Ⓐ Ⓑ Ⓒ Ⓓ Ⓔ	73 Ⓐ Ⓑ Ⓒ Ⓓ Ⓔ	85 Ⓐ Ⓑ Ⓒ Ⓓ Ⓔ	97 Ⓐ Ⓑ Ⓒ Ⓓ Ⓔ	109 Ⓐ Ⓑ Ⓒ Ⓓ Ⓔ
62 Ⓐ Ⓑ Ⓒ Ⓓ Ⓔ	74 Ⓐ Ⓑ Ⓒ Ⓓ Ⓔ	86 Ⓐ Ⓑ Ⓒ Ⓓ Ⓔ	98 Ⓐ Ⓑ Ⓒ Ⓓ Ⓔ	110 Ⓐ Ⓑ Ⓒ Ⓓ Ⓔ
63 Ⓐ Ⓑ Ⓒ Ⓓ Ⓔ	75 Ⓐ Ⓑ Ⓒ Ⓓ Ⓔ	87 Ⓐ Ⓑ Ⓒ Ⓓ Ⓔ	99 Ⓐ Ⓑ Ⓒ Ⓓ Ⓔ	111 Ⓐ Ⓑ Ⓒ Ⓓ Ⓔ
64 Ⓐ Ⓑ Ⓒ Ⓓ Ⓔ	76 Ⓐ Ⓑ Ⓒ Ⓓ Ⓔ	88 Ⓐ Ⓑ Ⓒ Ⓓ Ⓔ	100 Ⓐ Ⓑ Ⓒ Ⓓ Ⓔ	112 Ⓐ Ⓑ Ⓒ Ⓓ Ⓔ
65 Ⓐ Ⓑ Ⓒ Ⓓ Ⓔ	77 Ⓐ Ⓑ Ⓒ Ⓓ Ⓔ	89 Ⓐ Ⓑ Ⓒ Ⓓ Ⓔ	101 Ⓐ Ⓑ Ⓒ Ⓓ Ⓔ	113 Ⓐ Ⓑ Ⓒ Ⓓ Ⓔ
66 Ⓐ Ⓑ Ⓒ Ⓓ Ⓔ	78 Ⓐ Ⓑ Ⓒ Ⓓ Ⓔ	90 Ⓐ Ⓑ Ⓒ Ⓓ Ⓔ	102 Ⓐ Ⓑ Ⓒ Ⓓ Ⓔ	114 Ⓐ Ⓑ Ⓒ Ⓓ Ⓔ
67 Ⓐ Ⓑ Ⓒ Ⓓ Ⓔ	79 Ⓐ Ⓑ Ⓒ Ⓓ Ⓔ	91 Ⓐ Ⓑ Ⓒ Ⓓ Ⓔ	103 Ⓐ Ⓑ Ⓒ Ⓓ Ⓔ	115 Ⓐ Ⓑ Ⓒ Ⓓ Ⓔ
68 Ⓐ Ⓑ Ⓒ Ⓓ Ⓔ	80 Ⓐ Ⓑ Ⓒ Ⓓ Ⓔ	92 Ⓐ Ⓑ Ⓒ Ⓓ Ⓔ	104 Ⓐ Ⓑ Ⓒ Ⓓ Ⓔ	116 Ⓐ Ⓑ Ⓒ Ⓓ Ⓔ
69 Ⓐ Ⓑ Ⓒ Ⓓ Ⓔ	81 Ⓐ Ⓑ Ⓒ Ⓓ Ⓔ	93 Ⓐ Ⓑ Ⓒ Ⓓ Ⓔ	105 Ⓐ Ⓑ Ⓒ Ⓓ Ⓔ	117 Ⓐ Ⓑ Ⓒ Ⓓ Ⓔ
70 Ⓐ Ⓑ Ⓒ Ⓓ Ⓔ	82 Ⓐ Ⓑ Ⓒ Ⓓ Ⓔ	94 Ⓐ Ⓑ Ⓒ Ⓓ Ⓔ	106 Ⓐ Ⓑ Ⓒ Ⓓ Ⓔ	118 Ⓐ Ⓑ Ⓒ Ⓓ Ⓔ
71 Ⓐ Ⓑ Ⓒ Ⓓ Ⓔ	83 Ⓐ Ⓑ Ⓒ Ⓓ Ⓔ	95 Ⓐ Ⓑ Ⓒ Ⓓ Ⓔ	107 Ⓐ Ⓑ Ⓒ Ⓓ Ⓔ	119 Ⓐ Ⓑ Ⓒ Ⓓ Ⓔ
72 Ⓐ Ⓑ Ⓒ Ⓓ Ⓔ	84 Ⓐ Ⓑ Ⓒ Ⓓ Ⓔ	96 Ⓐ Ⓑ Ⓒ Ⓓ Ⓔ	108 Ⓐ Ⓑ Ⓒ Ⓓ Ⓔ	120 Ⓐ Ⓑ Ⓒ Ⓓ Ⓔ

PRACTICE EXAMINATION III

Section I: Life Sciences

60 Questions
Time—45 minutes

Directions: Choose the response that best completes the statement or answers the question.

1. Charles Darwin, in his *The Origin of Species*, formulated the theory of

   (A) mutations producing new species.
   (B) natural selection producing new species.
   (C) radiation producing mutations.
   (D) use and disuse in forming new species.
   (E) spontaneous generation.

2. Darwin discovered and formulated the theory of evolution, popularized as: "The survival of the fittest." Which of the following traits would Darwin regard as the most important for survival in the long run?

   (A) Strength
   (B) Intelligence
   (C) Agility
   (D) Economy
   (E) Adaptability

3. What is the probable order of evolution among the following animal phyla?

1. protozoa	4. birds	7. fish
2. sponges	5. arthropod	8. amphibians
3. mammals	6. worms	9. reptiles

   (A) 1, 5, 3, 4, 7, 6
   (B) 5, 3, 2, 6, 4, 8
   (C) 1, 2, 7, 9, 8, 3
   (D) 2, 9, 7, 8, 3, 4
   (E) 1, 2, 8, 9, 4, 3

4. Serological tests of phylogenetic relationships have strengthened the view that the vertebrates are most closely associated with which one of the following?

   (A) Peripatus
   (B) King crabs
   (C) Echinoderms
   (D) Mollusks
   (E) Insects

5. In both taxonomic and evolutionary studies, homologous structures are significant because they may indicate

   (A) structural diversity.
   (B) functional similarity.
   (C) genetic relationship.
   (D) genetic diversity.
   (E) functional diversity.

6. Of the following, which one probably gives the correct succession of early man?

   (A) Neanderthal, Piltdown, Sinanthropus
   (B) Sinanthropus, Pithecanthropus
   (C) Cro-Magnon, Neanderthal
   (D) Pithecanthropus, Neanderthal, Cro-Magnon
   (E) Cro-Magnon, Piltdown

7. Which one of the following pairs is composed of the two least related members?

   (A) Sea cucumber—sea lily
   (B) Horseshoe crab—octopus
   (C) Nautilus—garden slug
   (D) Scallop—squid
   (E) Hydra—sea anemone

8. In general, biogeographical evidence of evolution has shown that
   (A) centers of dispersion of animals usually have the most advanced forms predominating.
   (B) the farther one gets from the center of dispersion, the more variation is found in the species and genera.
   (C) geographic barriers usually result in the extinction of genera.
   (D) fossils rarely form in river valleys.
   (E) None of the above

9. In the evolution of life, the photocell most probably
   (A) carried on photophosphorylation.
   (B) took in organic molecules as food and gave off carbon dioxide.
   (C) carried on only meiosis at all times during reproduction.
   (D) took in organic molecules and gave off molecular oxygen.
   (E) consumed small multicellular photosynthetic algae.

10. In the laboratory, proteinoids were actually observed to
    (A) explode after a period of osmosis.
    (B) carry on oxidative phosphorylation.
    (C) produce offspring.
    (D) change to sugars.
    (E) (A) and (B)

11. Just as the theory of evolution predicts, biochemical similarities can be demonstrated by means of
    (A) genetic drift.
    (B) isolation.
    (C) serological techniques.
    (D) Wallace's Second Law.
    (E) reverse ionization.

12. Diverse structures such as a dolphin's flipper, a bat's wing, a horse's foreleg, or a man's arm and hand all have similar embryological and anatomical relationships and are therefore
    (A) genetic isolates.
    (B) analogous structures.
    (C) homologous structures.
    (D) evolved from one common ancestor.
    (E) vestigial structures.

Answer questions 13–15 on the basis of the experiment that follows.

Cellophane membranes permeable to water molecules and impermeable to sugar molecules are filled according to the table below. They are then suspended in beakers filled with water or sugar and water according to the table. Assume that temperatures are constant and all sugar/water solutions were obtained from the same source.

BEAKER	MEMBRANE CONTENTS	BEAKER CONTENTS
1	water	water
2	sugar water	water
3	water	sugar water

13. Which of the following will occur in beaker two?
    (A) The bag will shrink.
    (B) Water molecules will diffuse out of the bag.
    (C) Sugar molecules will diffuse out of the bag.
    (D) Water molecules will diffuse into the bag.
    (E) There is no movement of molecules.

14. Which of the following will occur in beaker three?
    (A) The bag will swell.
    (B) Water molecules will diffuse into the bag.
    (C) Sugar draws water out of the bag.
    (D) The bag will shrink.
    (E) There is no movement of molecules.

15. Which of the following will occur in beaker one?
    (A) Water will diffuse out of the bag.
    (B) Water will diffuse into the bag.
    (C) The water molecules are in equilibrium.
    (D) The addition of sugar to the bag will cause it to shrink.
    (E) The addition of sugar to the beaker will cause the bag to swell.

16. Cells are broadly divided into eukaryotes and prokaryotes according to whether
    - (A) they have genes.
    - (B) their genes are enclosed by a nuclear membrane.
    - (C) the nuclear membrane is permeable.
    - (D) they have ribosomes.
    - (E) they are plant or animal.

17. Of the following, the type of enzyme most closely associated with cellular respiration is
    - (A) chlorophyll.
    - (B) lipase.
    - (C) sucrase.
    - (D) transaminase.
    - (E) dehydrogenase.

18. An albino corn plant lacks chlorophyll and therefore cannot carry on photosynthesis. Continuation of this genetic trait in corn plants occurs because
    - (A) albino plants become green in the sunlight.
    - (B) self-pollination occurs in albino plants.
    - (C) green plants may carry the albino gene.
    - (D) albino plants mutate to green plants.
    - (E) mutations occur once a month.

19. Which environmental change is most likely to increase the rate of photosynthesis in a bean plant?
    - (A) A drop in temperature to 15°C
    - (B) An increase in the intensity of green light
    - (C) A rise in the oxygen concentration in the air
    - (D) A rise in the carbon dioxide concentration in the air
    - (E) An increase in plant fertilization

20. Unicellular organisms ingest large molecules into their cytoplasm from the external environment without previously digesting them. This process is called
    - (A) pinocytosis.
    - (B) peristalsis.
    - (C) plasmolysis.
    - (D) osmosis.
    - (E) transpiration.

21. Which one of the following compounds stores energy that is immediately available for active muscle cells?
    - (A) Creatine phosphate
    - (B) Glycogen
    - (C) Glucose
    - (D) Glycine
    - (E) Messenger RNA

22. The ciliary muscle is used for the process of
    - (A) locomotion.
    - (B) food transportation.
    - (C) blinking.
    - (D) accommodation.
    - (E) respiration.

23. According to recent studies, a bacteriophage consists essentially of an internal metabolic mechanism that contains nucleic acid and an external coat of
    - (A) keratin.
    - (B) phosphide.
    - (C) polysaccharide.
    - (D) protein.
    - (E) hyaluronidase.

24. An organism that can successfully reproduce without utilizing the process of meiosis is the
    - (A) fruit fly.
    - (B) dog.
    - (C) ameba.
    - (D) grasshopper.
    - (E) mammal.

Questions 25–33 consist of the description of an experiment followed by statements about the experiment. Analyze each statement on the basis of the data provided and mark your answer sheet:

(A) if the data proves that the statement is *true.*

(B) if the data shows that the statement is *probably true.*

(C) if the data *does not show* whether the statement is true or false.

(D) if the data shows that the statement is *probably false.*

(E) if the data proves that the statement is *false.*

Questions 25–27 refer to the following data.

Six members of a biology class were tested as to blood type. The table lists the results of the tests:

SUBJECT	BLOOD TYPE
1	O
2	A
3	A
4	O
5	AB
6	B

25. Subject six could be transfused with blood from subject one if they are both Rh positive.

26. Subject two is female. Subject six is male. If the two were to have children, the second child is likely to suffer from erythroblastosis fetalis.

27. Subject five could donate blood to all of the other subjects if their Rh factors match.

Questions 28–33 refer to the following data.

Two plants were crossed. The traits to be noted were stem length and seed shape. Both of these traits are controlled by allelic pairs according to Table 1. Table 2 shows the phenotypes of the F1 generation as determined by successive crosses. The alleles are defined and given representing letters in Table 1. The term heterozygous means the trait has one dominant and one recessive allele. The term homozygous means both alleles are dominant or both alleles are recessive.

Table 1	Table 2
L—dominant long	LLSS
l—recessive short	LlSS
S—dominant smooth	Llss
s—recessive wrinkled	LLSS
	LlSs

28. Both parents were heterozygous long-stemmed.

29. Both parents were homozygous long-stemmed.

30. At least one parent was homozygous for wrinkled seeds.

31. At least one parent was heterozygous for smooth seeds.

32. Both parents are doubly heterozygous.

33. A cross between plants LLSS and LlSs in Table 2 would produce all long-stemmed, smooth seed offspring.

34. Of the following senses, the one most seriously affected by weightlessness during space flight would be the

(A) auditory.
(B) visual.
(C) tactile.
(D) kinesthetic.
(E) olfactory.

35. The stage in embryology at which the primitive gut is well-formed is called the

(A) blastula.
(B) gastrula.
(C) hollow ball stage.
(D) morula.
(E) zygote.

36. The transport of which one of the following is a function of human blood but not a function of grasshopper blood?

(A) Oxygen
(B) Antibodies
(C) Hormones
(D) Wastes
(E) Foods

37. The incidence of type A blood increases with increase of latitude in North America. Which of the following statements is in best agreement with our understanding of this problem?

(A) The incidence of persons of North European descent increases with latitude in North America.

(B) The incidence of type A blood is influenced by temperature during pregnancy.

(C) The incidence is related to the percentage of Indian blood in the population.

(D) At present there is no explanation for the observation.

(E) None of the above

38. Among normal members of homo sapiens, the size of the brain

(A) is directly related to body type.

(B) is unrelated to intelligence.

(C) varies consistently from one race to another.

(D) varies directly with intelligence.

(E) All of the above

39. Bile is used in digesting

(A) sugars.

(B) proteins.

(C) vitamins.

(D) amino acids.

(E) fats.

40. The human nervous system is very complex. Let us consider one of the simplest examples: the knee-jerk reflex. The pathway of this reflex's causeway is through

(A) 3 neurons: 1 from knee to spinal cord; 1 from 1st to 3rd within spinal cord; 1 from spinal cord to leg muscle.

(B) 4 neurons: the three from choice (A); 1 along the leg muscle.

(C) 5 neurons: 1 from knee to spinal cord; 1 from spinal cord to brain; 1 within brain (affected by other stimuli); 1 from brain to spinal cord; 1 from spinal cord to muscle.

(D) 6 neurons: same as choice (C) plus 1 along the leg muscle.

(E) 7 neurons: same as choice (D) except that there are two nerves within the brain.

41. The human embryo goes through various stages resembling lower forms of animals. Which of the following structures has a similar structure appearing sometime during the development of the human embryo?

I. Gills
II. Tail
III. Spiracles

(A) I

(B) II

(C) III

(D) I and II

(E) I, II, and III

42. Which organ is associated with the largest gland in the body?

(A) Mouth

(B) Stomach

(C) Liver

(D) Intestine

(E) Pancreas

43. Which of the following is a ductless gland?

(A) Thyroid

(B) Liver

(C) Spleen

(D) Salivary gland

(E) Gastric gland

44. The secretion given off by the liver is

(A) ptyalin.

(B) pepsin.

(C) bile.

(D) renin.

(E) amylase.

45. Blood is carried to the heart by the

(A) auricles.

(B) ventricles.

(C) veins.

(D) arteries.

(E) capillaries.

46. The number of chromosomes found in the body cells of every member of a species is known as the

    (A) haploid number.
    (B) diploid number.
    (C) reduced number.
    (D) gamete number.
    (E) triploid number.

47. Of the following hormones, the one that is most directly associated with the maintenance of pregnancy is

    (A) insulin.
    (B) progestin.
    (C) secretin.
    (D) somatotrophin.
    (E) cortisone.

48. The normal body temperature for man, in degrees Celsius, is closest to which one of the following?

    (A) 20
    (B) 27
    (C) 37
    (D) 98.6
    (E) 102.8

49. Disease-producing agents include which of the following?

    I. Bacteria
    II. Protozoa
    III. Fungi

    (A) I
    (B) II
    (C) I and II
    (D) II and III
    (E) I, II, and III

50. Which one of the following would NOT likely be captured from a pond by means of a net?

    (A) Larvae of dragon flies
    (B) Flatworms
    (C) Fucus
    (D) Elodea
    (E) Water spiders

51. Which one of the following gives the varieties of trees present normally in a climax forest common to much of the northeastern United States?

    (A) Ponderosa pine
    (B) Beech and maple forest
    (C) Pine and oak
    (D) Oak and tulip trees
    (E) Liverworts and giant fern trees

52. Fossils are most likely to be discovered in which one of the following?

    (A) Lava
    (B) Granite
    (C) Basalt
    (D) Volcanic deposits
    (E) River valley deposits

53. The catastrophic red tides that kill many fish are most directly caused by

    (A) depletion of the supply of oxygen.
    (B) increase in the mean temperature of the water.
    (C) the bloom of a certain dinoflagellate.
    (D) interference with metabolite equilibrium.
    (E) hurricanes and tornados.

54. Examination of soils in some areas has shown that what is now maple and basswood forest-land was once occupied by lakes. The lake first choked up with water plants, and swamp vegetation appeared. Then spruce and pine grew. Finally basswood and maple became the dominant forms. The above process is best known as

    (A) ecological succession.
    (B) geological evidence.
    (C) natural selection.
    (D) survival of the fittest.
    (E) artificial selection.

55. An example of a plant that has its seeds dispersed chiefly by animals is

    (A) ash.
    (B) burdock.
    (C) maple.
    (D) thistle.
    (E) oleander.

56. A population exhibiting a birth rate of 26 per 1,000 and a death rate of 6 per 1,000 is exhibiting

(A) a growth rate of 26 percent.
(B) a population rate decrease of 30,000 per year.
(C) a growth rate of 2 percent.
(D) the serious effect of disease on the Antarctic penguin.
(E) (A) and (B)

57. In nature, biotic potential is opposed by

(A) hybrid vigor.
(B) behavioral resistance.
(C) birth control in sheep and horses.
(D) environmental resistance.
(E) (A) and (C)

Questions 58–60 are to be answered on the basis of the population curve for a hypothetical population as presented below. For each question, select the numbered part of the curve that is called for and mark your answer sheet as follows:

(A) Point 1
(B) Point 2
(C) Point 3
(D) Point 4
(E) Not shown here

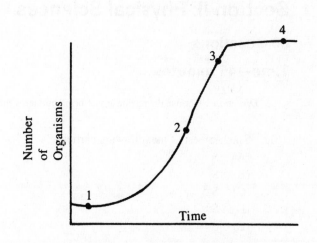

58. The part of the curve that represents the exponential growth of the population.

59. The part of the curve that best represents the biotic potential.

60. The part of the curve that represents the carrying capacity of the environment.

Section II: Physical Sciences

60 Questions

Time—45 minutes

Directions: Choose the response that best completes the statement or answers the question.

61. The heaviest of the following particles is
    (A) S^{-2}
    (B) S^0
    (C) S^{+4}
    (D) S^{-4}
    (E) S^{-1}

62. An atom of chlorine, atomic number 17 and atomic weight 35, contains in its nucleus
    (A) 35 protons.
    (B) 17 neutrons.
    (C) 35 neutrons.
    (D) 18 neutrons.
    (E) 18 electrons.

For questions 63 and 64, select the one of the five lettered graphs below that best depicts the situation described in each question.

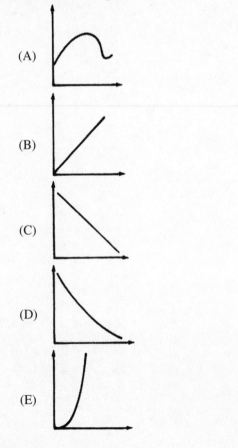

(A)

(B)

(C)

(D)

(E)

63. Radioactive decay occurs in a sample of radium.

    Vertical axis: percentage of original radioactivity remaining

    Horizontal axis: time

64. A sample of Nitrogen gas in a glass container.

    Vertical axis: the number of molecules at a specific kinetic energy

    Horizontal axis: the specific kinetic energy for those molecules

65. Element 102, with a mass number of 253, was synthesized by bombarding $_{96}Cm^{240}$ with a single nuclear particle, which it captured. The particle used was
    (A) $_{12}X^{13}$
    (B) $_6X^{13}$
    (C) $_{13}X^6$
    (D) $_6X^{12}$
    (E) $_9X^{17}$

66. The emission of an alpha particle from the nucleus of $_{88}Ra^{226}$ will produce
    (A) $_{88}Ra^{222}$
    (B) $_{87}Fr^{222}$
    (C) $_{86}Rn^{223}$
    (D) $_{86}Rn^{222}$
    (E) $_{80}Rn^{222}$

67. U^{235} may be separated from natural uranium by a process called
    (A) ionization.
    (B) electrolysis.
    (C) precipitation.
    (D) gaseous diffusion.
    (E) active transport.

68. The atomic bomb is an example of which of the following principles?

    (A) The conversion of matter into energy
    (B) The conversion of energy into an explosion
    (C) The conversion of energy into nuclear material
    (D) The conversion of energy into more energy
    (E) The conversion of matter into more matter

69. The Markovnikoff rule is used in connection with

    (A) stereochemistry of elimination reactions.
    (B) electrophilic aromatic substitution.
    (C) activity of enzymes.
    (D) addition of acids to double bonds.
    (E) reduction of oxidative phosphorylase.

Questions 70–72 are based on the description and results of the experiment given below. Analyze each statement solely on the basis of the experiment and mark your answer sheet:

    (A) if the experiment proves the statement is *true.*
    (B) if the experiment shows that the statement is probably true.
    (C) if the experiment *does not show* whether the statement is true or false.
    (D) if the experiment shows that the statement is *probably false.*
    (E) if the experiment proves that the statement is *false.*

An experiment is done to test the activity of a particular enzyme in media of varying pH. The result of the experiment is graphed thus:

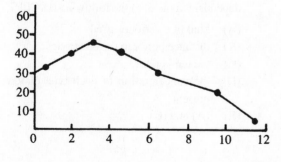

70. The enzyme graphed will be most active in an acid medium.

71. The enzyme graphed will be most active at a temperature of 50°C.

72. Enzymes are more active in alkaline media than in neutral media.

73. Naphthalene, $C_{10}H_8$, is most soluble in

    (A) water.
    (B) alcohol.
    (C) benzene.
    (D) acetic acid.
    (E) benzoic acid.

74. Which one of the following is an illustration of a reversible reaction?

    (A) $Pb(NO_3)_2 + 2NaI \rightarrow PbI_2 + 2NaNO_3$
    (B) $KNO_3 + NaCl \rightarrow KCl + NaNO_3$
    (C) $2Na + 2HOH \rightarrow 2\ NaOH + H_2$
    (D) $AgNO_3 + HBr \rightarrow AgBr + HNO_3$
    (E) $2K + 2HOH \rightarrow 2KOH + H_2$

75. Of the following, the compound possessing optical isomerism is

    (A) $CH_3 \cdot CH_2OH$
    (B) $CH_2OH \cdot CHOH \cdot CH_2OH$
    (C) $CH_3 \cdot CHOH \cdot C_2H_5$
    (D) CCl_2BrF_2
    (E) CH_4

76. The process, $_1H^2 + _1H^3 \rightarrow _2He^4 + _0n^1$, represents the type of reaction known as

    (A) fission.
    (B) thermal reaction.
    (C) autocatalysis.
    (D) fusion.
    (E) autolysis.

77. If the dissociation constant of NH_4OH is 1.8×10^{-5}, the concentration of OH ions, in moles per liter, of a 0.1 molar NH_4OH solution, is

    (A) 1.80×10^{-6}
    (B) 1.34×10^{-3}
    (C) 4.20×10^{-3}
    (D) 5.00×10^{-2}
    (E) 7.93×10^{-4}

78. Chemical analysis of a gas shows that it contains one atom of carbon for each two atoms of hydrogen. If its density is 1.25 g per liter at standard temperature and pressure, its formula is

    (A) CH_2
    (B) C_2H_4
    (C) C_4H_8
    (D) C_3H_6
    (E) CH_4

79. The volume of 0.25 molar H_3PO_4 necessary to neutralize 25 ml. of 0.30 molar $Ca(OH)_2$ is

    (A) 8.3 ml.
    (B) 20 ml.
    (C) 50 ml.
    (D) 40 ml.
    (E) 130 ml.

80. Accepting the definition that an acid is a proton donor, the acid in the reaction $NH_3 + H_2O \rightarrow NH^+_4 + OH^-$, is

    (A) NH_3
    (B) H^+
    (C) H_2O
    (D) OH
    (E) NH_2^-

81. Two lamps of 20 and 125 candles, respectively, equally illuminate the opposite sides of a photometer screen placed between them. If the 20 candle lamp is 2 ft. from the screen, the distance of the 125 candle lamp from the screen is

    (A) 5 ft.
    (B) 10 ft.
    (C) 12.5 ft.
    (D) 20 ft.
    (E) 145 ft.

82. When light beams travel through an interface separating two media with different indices of refraction,

    (A) the reflected wave suffers no phase change when reflected from the interface beyond which the medium has a higher index of refraction.
    (B) the reflected wave suffers a phase change of $\frac{\pi}{2}$ when reflected from the interface beyond which the medium has a higher index of refraction.
    (C) the reflected wave suffers a phase change of π when reflected from the interface beyond which the medium has a lower index of refraction.
    (D) the transmitted wave suffers a phase change of $\frac{\pi}{4}$ when going from the lower index medium into the higher index medium.
    (E) the reflected waves are only from those wavelengths that are longer than 550 angstroms.

83. A small object is 10 cm. in front of a plane mirror. If you stand behind the object, 30 cm. from the mirror, and look at its image, for what distance must you focus your eyes?

    (A) 25 cm.
    (B) 35 cm.
    (C) 45 cm.
    (D) 40 cm.
    (E) 80 cm.

84. In the conductometric method of analysis, the electrical resistance between two electrodes is dependent upon all of the following EXCEPT

    (A) kind of electrodes used.
    (B) distance between the electrodes.
    (C) the temperature.
    (D) the concentration of each type of ion present.
    (E) (A) and (C)

85. Two light rays from separate incandescent sources each illuminates a surface with an intensity of illumination 1. If the two light rays are combined, they will illuminate the surface with an intensity of illumination

    (A) 1
    (B) $\sqrt{21}$
    (C) 21
    (D) 41
    (E) $\sqrt{\pi}$

86. A ball is thrown vertically into the air. When it reaches its zenith, which of the following statements is most correct?

    (A) The potential energy is at a minimum, and the kinetic energy is at a maximum.
    (B) The potential energy is at a maximum, and the kinetic energy is at a minimum.
    (C) The potential energy and the kinetic energy are both at a maximum.
    (D) The potential energy and the kinetic energy are both at a minimum.
    (E) The potential energy is equal to the kinetic energy.

87. A spring is attached to a wall at one end and to a block on the other. The block rests on a horizontal surface and moves back and forth on a frictionless surface. This type of motion is best described by which of the following terms?

    (A) Brownian motion
    (B) Centripetal motion
    (C) Centrifugal motion
    (D) Harmonic motion
    (E) Gravitational motion

88. When an object enters the earth's atmosphere and falls to the surface, it is heated. Which of the following statements best describes the reason for this process?

    (A) The air resistance heats the object.
    (B) Gravitational attraction heats the object.
    (C) The sun's rays heat the object.
    (D) The rotation of the earth around its axis causes the object to heat up.
    (E) The heat in the earth's atmosphere heats the object.

For questions 89–91, select the one lettered graph below that best matches the statement.

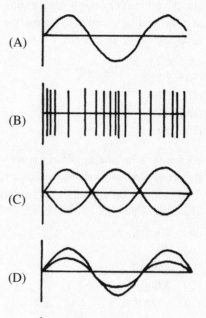

89. A longitudinal wave.

90. Silence will result.

91. Beats rather than a clear tone will result.

92. Which of the following is true of quantum mechanics but is not true of Newtonian mechanics?

    (A) It is strictly a causal "if—then" theory.
    (B) Known particles, subject to various forces, are believed to act in a predictable manner.
    (C) When dealing with large numbers of molecules or particles, calculations are made on the basis of the behavior of an average particle or molecule.
    (D) Gravitational phenomena on Earth are predicted consistently.
    (E) Radioactive phenomena are explained by using calculations based on probability.

93. A string that can sustain a tension of 25 newtons is fastened to a mass of 2kg lying on a smooth table. The largest acceleration in m/sec^2 that can be imparted to the mass without breaking the string will be

    (A) 6.25
    (B) 12.25
    (C) 27
    (D) 36
    (E) 50

94. Assume that on coming out of a power-drive, the net acceleration on a pilot of 70 kg. mass is 7g. The force exerted on the pilot in newtons is closest to which one of the following?

    (A) 10
    (B) 70
    (C) 490
    (D) 4,800
    (E) 48,000

95. In the unmagnetized state, the magnetic domains of a magnetic substance are oriented at

    (A) 45°
    (B) 30°
    (C) random
    (D) 120°
    (E) 90°

96. The mass of material deposited on the cathode of an electrolytic cell, other things being equal, is proportional to the

    (A) area of the cathode surface.
    (B) quantity of charge passing through the cell.
    (C) concentration of electrolyte in solution.
    (D) temperature of the cell.
    (E) altitude at which the cell is operated.

97. A capacitor C and inductor L are connected in series across an A.C. source. As the value of C is increased, the current in the circuit

    (A) increases.
    (B) decreases.
    (C) remains constant.
    (D) may increase or decrease.
    (E) None of the above

98. The term *solar energy* is most closely described by which of the following statements?

    (A) The conversion of the sun's energy into useful electrical or thermal energy on earth
    (B) The way the sun generates its own power
    (C) The conversion of heat into light
    (D) The conversion of electricity into solar power
    (E) The high wavelength rays emitted by the sun

99. Assume that two capacitors, one of 3 microfarads and the other of 6 microfarads, are connected in series and charged to a difference of potential of 120 volts. The potential difference, in volts, across the 3 microfarad capacitor is

    (A) 40
    (B) 50
    (C) 80
    (D) 180
    (E) 360

100. In an experiment simulating the Millikan oil drop experiment, a plastic sphere (weight = 2.8×10^{-14} newtons) moves downward at a speed $\frac{3}{2}$ of that under gravity alone. The electric force, in newtons, acting on the sphere is

    (A) 1.4×10^{-14}
    (B) 2.8×10^{-14}
    (C) 3.5×10^{-14}
    (D) 4.2×10^{-14}
    (E) 1.4×10^{-10}

101. Which theory best accounts for the fact that when stars are viewed at night in the field of the sun, they shift their positions away from the sun, relative to their own positions?

   (A) The light from the stars, passing close to the sun, has been deflected by the curvature of space, which creates the sun's gravitational field.

   (B) This shift, referred to as the red shift, is caused by the lengthened wavelengths of light as the stars escape the gravitational field of the sun.

   (C) The light from the stars is refracted upon passing through the dense gases making up the sun's outer atmosphere.

   (D) The light rays from the stars are deflected by the solar wind, which travels in a curved path.

   (E) The sun continually emits charged particles, which impinge upon the light rays from the stars, thus deflecting them.

102. Which of the following has NOT been detected in more than trace amounts in the atmospheres of the four great planets?

   (A) Free oxygen—O_2
   (B) Water vapor—H_2O
   (C) Methane—CH_4
   (D) Ammonia—NH_2
   (E) Free hydrogen—H_2

103. Which of the following statements concerning a total solar eclipse is most correct?

   (A) The event is a very general one for all planets in the solar system.

   (B) The event is specific for planets with more than one moon.

   (C) The event is unusual since a moon must be of the proper size and the proper distance between the planet and the sun.

   (D) The event occurs at regular intervals for all planets with moons.

   (E) The event will not occur unless a planet has a tilted axis of rotation and has at least one moon.

104. The basic mechanism for the generation of energy by the sun can best be described by which of the following processes?

   (A) Thermoelectric
   (B) Hydrostatic
   (C) Atomic fusion
   (D) Light generation
   (E) Atomic fission

105. In order to calculate the distance of a star, the astronomer requires

   (A) observations made 100 miles apart.

   (B) as large a base as possible for observations to determine the star's parallax.

   (C) one supergiant star within the field of vision.

   (D) (A) and (C)

   (E) None of the above

106. Supernova explosions produce

   (A) dwarf stars of fantastically high densities.

   (B) rapidly expanding gas clouds called nebulae.

   (C) the heavy elements in the universe.

   (D) All of the above

   (E) None of the above

107. The Milky Way is a(n)

   (A) spiral galaxy.
   (B) elliptical galaxy.
   (C) irregular galaxy.
   (D) split level galaxy.
   (E) nebula.

108. Spectral lines of a star that is in relative motion away from the earth are seen to be

   (A) in the same position as those of a stationary star.

   (B) shifted toward the violet end of the spectrum.

   (C) shifted toward the red end of the spectrum.

   (D) shifted toward the red end of the spectrum but dependent on the relative velocity as v^3.

   (E) None of the above

109. Which type of cloud might be an indicator of a high-altitude jet stream?

    (A) Cirrus
    (B) Cumulus
    (C) Stratocumulus
    (D) Altostratus
    (E) Nimbostratus

110. Recent evidence points to the destruction of which portion of the earth's atmosphere by the freons released from aerosol cans?

    (A) Nitrogen
    (B) Carbon dioxide
    (C) Hydrogen
    (D) Water
    (E) Ozone

111. Which of the following statements concerning clouds is false?

    (A) They are all basically composed of water.
    (B) They are all at the same altitude.
    (C) They are quite rarified.
    (D) Their dissolution is called rain.
    (E) There are several types of clouds.

112. It is least likely to rain when the clouds in our sky are

    (A) nimbostratus.
    (B) nimbus.
    (C) cirrus.
    (D) altocumulus.
    (E) cumulonimbus.

113. Earthquakes are caused by

    (A) magma movements.
    (B) volcanic explosions.
    (C) the release of pressure along a fault.
    (D) All of the above
    (E) None of the above

114. The type of rock depicted in the diagram is

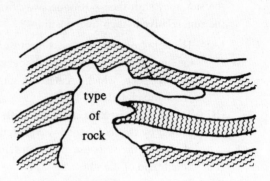

    (A) sedimentary rock.
    (B) igneous rock.
    (C) metamorphic rock.
    (D) condensation rock.
    (E) None of the above

115. One example of mass wasting is

    (A) gradation.
    (B) fold influence relief.
    (C) slumping.
    (D) All of the above
    (E) None of the above

116. All of the following listed are folding patterns EXCEPT

    (A) warps.
    (B) synclines.
    (C) monoclines.
    (D) fumaroles.
    (E) recumbent folds.

117. Depressions in glacial rock waste (drift) due to the melting of buried ice blocks are known as

    (A) kettles.
    (B) kames.
    (C) eskers.
    (D) lateral moraine.
    (E) terminal moraine.

118. The Moho Discontinuity is between the

    (A) solid inner core and liquid outer core.
    (B) solid outer core and liquid inner core.
    (C) solid mantle and solid crust.
    (D) solid crust and liquid crust.
    (E) None of the above

119. The major portion of ultraviolet radiation that reaches the earth is absorbed in the
    (A) troposphere.
    (B) stratosphere.
    (C) mesosphere.
    (D) thermosphere.
    (E) hydrosphere.

120. The Coriolis Effect is responsible for
    (A) the complex movements of the winds.
    (B) the complex movements of the oceans.
    (C) movements along vertical and horizontal fault lines.
    (D) (A) and (B)
    (E) (A) and (C)

End of Practice Examination III

Answer Key

Section I

1.	B	13.	D	25.	A	37.	D	49.	E
2.	E	14.	D	26.	D	38.	B	50.	C
3.	E	15.	C	27.	E	39.	E	51.	B
4.	C	16.	B	28.	C	40.	A	52.	E
5.	E	17.	E	29.	E	41.	D	53.	C
6.	D	18.	C	30.	E	42.	C	54.	A
7.	B	19.	D	31.	A	43.	A	55.	B
8.	B	20.	A	32.	B	44.	C	56.	C
9.	B	21.	A	33.	A	45.	C	57.	D
10.	C	22.	D	34.	D	46.	B	58.	B
11.	C	23.	D	35.	B	47.	B	59.	B
12.	C	24.	C	36.	A	48.	C	60.	D

Section II

61.	D	73.	C	85.	C	97.	D	109.	A
62.	D	74.	B	86.	B	98.	A	110.	E
63.	D	75.	C	87.	D	99.	C	111.	B
64.	A	76.	D	88.	A	100.	A	112.	C
65.	B	77.	B	89.	B	101.	A	113.	D
66.	D	78.	B	90.	C	102.	A	114.	B
67.	D	79.	B	91.	B	103.	C	115.	C
68.	A	80.	C	92.	C	104.	C	116.	D
69.	D	81.	A	93.	B	105.	B	117.	A
70.	A	82.	C	94.	D	106.	D	118.	C
71.	C	83.	D	95.	C	107.	A	119.	B
72.	D	84.	A	96.	B	108.	C	120.	D

Explanatory Answers

Section I

1. **The correct answer is (B).** Charles Darwin, in 1858, published his theory of natural selection advanced to explain the evolution of living things. Its four fundamental concepts are overproduction, struggle for existence, variation, and survival of the fittest.

2. **The correct answer is (E).** The most adaptable animal is the one that will tend to be "fittest" in *any* environment. The other points mentioned help, but this is the most beneficial.

3. **The correct answer is (E).** One-celled animals, followed by simple multicelled animals, followed by amphibians (living in water and on land), followed by reptiles (living on land only), followed by birds, followed by mammals, perhaps the newest comer of all.

4. **The correct answer is (C).** Many enzymes and other chemicals involved in metabolic activities have been discovered in organisms otherwise entirely different. Serologic analysis of body fluids of echinoderms and vertebrates show a marked similarity even though these animals appear so unrelated. This is evidence for common ancestry.

5. **The correct answer is (E).** Homologous structures exhibit very strong evidence for common ancestry. Homologous organs are very similar in structure but adapted for widely different functions. Example: wing of bat, foreleg of cat, flipper of whale, and arm of man are very similar in bone structure but widely adapted for different uses (wing of bat for flying, foreleg of cat for running, flipper of whale for swimming, and arm of man for manipulating).

6. **The correct answer is (D).** The Java man (*Pithecanthropus erectus*) dates back to the Pleistocene period and is considered to be one of the most primitive ape-men. The Neanderthal man (*Homo neanderthalensis*) dates back to approximately 150,000 years and became extinct only about 25,000 years ago. The Cro-Magnon man (*Homo sapiens*) is modern man, whose first fossils date back 15,000 to 60,000 years.

7. **The correct answer is (B).** The horseshoe crab is an arthropod, belonging to the Arachnida class, which possess the underlying similarity of having eight jointed legs. The octopus is a mollusk, having no exoskeleton and no jointed legs. Its arms contain suction discs (suckers) for locomotion and defense.

8. **The correct answer is (B).** As living things migrate and travel from the center of a given geographical point, the more diverse forms are encountered. As long as mating can successfully be accomplished between certain distant forms, eventually new species and new varieties become established.

9. **The correct answer is (B).** There are two major hypotheses for the origin of life. The *autotroph hypothesis* states that the first living things must have been autotrophs. The *heterotroph hypothesis* states that the first living things must have been heterotrophs. Most of the experimental evidence today supports the latter.

10. **The correct answer is (C).** Stanley Fox and his coworkers successfully formed proteinoids from amino acids. In water the proteinoids cluster together, forming large numbers of microspheres, which produce offspring microspheres in a process that appears to resemble cells when they divide.

11. **The correct answer is (C).** The evolution theory proposed by Darwin predicts many forms of animal are more or less related to one another. Serological studies and utilization of antibodies have now confirmed these relationships.

12. **The correct answer is (C).** Homologous structures are inherited from a common ancestor, while analogous structures are similar in function and often in superficial structure but have different evolutionary origins. All of the animals mentioned in this question are mammals and are fairly closely related, having a common ancestry.

13. **The correct answer is (D).** Diffusion of molecules from an area of high concentration to an area of low concentration is a fundamental concept in cell biology. Since the cellophane bags in this experiment are not permeable to sugar, only water molecules can diffuse. In beaker two, there is a higher concentration of water in the container than in the bag. Water molecules will diffuse into the area of lower concentration in the bag.

14. **The correct answer is (D).** In beaker three, there is a higher concentration of water in the bag. Movement of the water from the bag into the container will cause the bag to shrink.

15. **The correct answer is (C).** In beaker one, the water is in the same concentration on both sides of the membrane. Therefore, the water molecules are in equilibrium.

16. **The correct answer is (B).** This question is elementary to cell biology. Cells are divided into eukaryotes and prokaryotes according to whether their genes are enclosed by a nuclear membrane. The only cytoplasmic inclusions always found in prokaryotes are the ribosomes and a nuclear body, whereas eukaryotes have all the features of prokaryotes and more.

17. **The correct answer is (E).** Dehydrogenase mediates the removal of electrons from a substrate to a primary or intermediate acceptor. This is exemplified by the oxidation of succinic acid, a vital part of cellular respiration.

18. **The correct answer is (C).** Albinism is a recessive trait and can manifest itself only when two such genes meet. However, "normal" photosynthetic plants can transmit this gene via their heterozygous genetic makeup. The plants possessing this hybrid condition are completely normal as far as ability to manufacture food is concerned.

19. **The correct answer is (D).** An increase in the number of carbon dioxide molecules will cause more of these to accept hydrogen atoms stored in the plant. Powered by ATP, the excess hydrogen atoms being transported by molecules of carbon dioxide will form a highly reactive compound, PGA (phosphoglyceric acid). These molecules combine to form sugar. The more PGA molecules, the more sugar produced. All of these sequences stem from an original increase in carbon dioxide availability.

20. **The correct answer is (A).** Large molecules adhere to the surface of the cell membrane, which then infolds or invaginates. Eventually, the sides of the pocket meet, trapping the large molecules within the cytoplasm. Special digestive structures within the cytoplasm convert these large insoluble molecules into a soluble form.

21. **The correct answer is (A).** Creatine phosphate participates in muscle metabolism by virtue of the freely reversible reaction with ATP:

$$creatine + ATP \rightarrow ADP + creatine \ phosphate$$

The phosphoamide structure of this compound is highly reactive with respect to phosphate group transfer.

22. **The correct answer is (D).** Accommodation is the automatic adjustment of the eye to focus light from a distant object onto the retina. This is brought about by a contraction of the ciliary muscle, by which the choroid coat is pulled forward and the tension on the suspensory ligaments of the lens is lessened.

23. **The correct answer is (D).** The head of a typical bacteriophage virus consists of DNA surrounded by a protein coat. Using the tail portion as an inoculation needle, the phage penetrates the bacteria by injecting its DNA. The viral-protein coat remains outside the bacterial cell.

24. **The correct answer is (C).** The ameba reproduces by binary fission, an asexual method of reproduction. No sex cells are necessary, so reduction division (meiosis) does not take place. Each daughter cell is an exact duplicate of the original parent cell, as there is only one set of genes.

25. **The correct answer is (A).** Blood group O is the universal donor and can donate blood to someone of any other group assuming that the Rh factor matches.

26. **The correct answer is (D).** The child who might suffer from erythroblastosis fetalis would have a mother who is Rh negative and a father who is Rh positive. The Rh factor is not given; therefore, it cannot be determined whether the statement is true or false.

27. **The correct answer is (E).** A person with blood group AB is a universal receiver and not a universal donor.

28. **The correct answer is (C).** The presence of heterozygous long-stemmed offspring and homozygous long-stemmed offspring means that at least one parent was heterozygous long-stemmed. Whether or not this is true of both parents is not possible to tell from the given information.

29. **The correct answer is (E).** Both parents could not have been homozygous long-stemmed because of the presence of the recessive allele for the trait in at least two of the offspring.

30. **The correct answer is (E).** Neither parent could be homozygous for the recessive trait of wrinkled seeds. The reason is that more than one of the offspring is homozygous for the dominant trait.

31. **The correct answer is (A).** Finding offspring that are homozygous dominant, homozygous recessive, and heterozygous for a trait means that both parents were heterozygous for the trait.

32. **The correct answer is (B).** It is known that both parents were heterozygous for one trait. It is not known whether there are any offspring that are homozygous recessive for the long-stemmed trait. However, the ratio of heterozygous to homozygous dominant offspring for the trait indicates that it is probably true.

33. **The correct answer is (A).** If one parent is doubly homozygous dominant, all offspring will show the dominant traits regardless of the other parent's traits.

34. **The correct answer is (D).** Kinesthetic refers to detecting movement—i.e., sense organs of muscles, tendons, joints, etc. In a state of weightlessness during space flight, there is no way of detecting or perceiving muscular movement because of the absence of gravitational pull.

35. **The correct answer is (B).** The primitive gut differentiates into the alimentary canal during the gastrula stage of embryology. In the human, this process starts on the twentieth day. It is during gastrulation that the cells of the primary germ layers start differentiating into the various organs and organ systems of the embryo.

36. **The correct answer is (A).** Hemoglobin, in red blood corpuscles, combines with oxygen to transport oxyhemoglobin to the cells of humans. Grasshoppers obtain their oxygen by simply having the gas enter through openings in the body called spiracles. The gas then comes into contact with the cells directly, eliminating the need for a complex respiratory system in this respect.

37. **The correct answer is (D).** No acceptable reason for this occurrence has been presented. The link, if any, between latitude and blood type cannot be explained according to any of our present genetic concepts.

38. **The correct answer is (B).** The size of the brain is no measure of intelligence—however, the number of convolutions per surface area is. Albert Einstein, for example, was rated a genius yet had a brain smaller in size than the average man.

39. **The correct answer is (E).** The primary use of bile is to reduce the surface tension of the fat and produce a colloidal suspension of the fat in our digestive tract, so that our enzymes can get at more of it. Otherwise, our enzymes would have to work on large fat globules and be unable to reach most of the fat before it passes out of the system.

40. **The correct answer is (A).** Three neurons are involved—the sensory neuron, the association neuron, and the motor neuron. This is a simple reflex arc.

41. **The correct answer is (D).** Gill-like and tail-like structures appear during the development of the human embryo.

42. **The correct answer is (C).** The liver is the largest gland.

43. **The correct answer is (A).** The thyroid is a ductless gland. Ductless glands produce endocrine secretions and therefore are endocrine glands.

44. **The correct answer is (C).** Bile is secreted by the liver.

45. **The correct answer is (C).** The veins carry blood toward the heart.

46. **The correct answer is (B).** Gametes, which unite in sexual reproduction, each carry n chromosomes, a haploid number. When the gametes are fertilized, that number becomes 2n, a diploid number. Those cells make up the body tissue of a species.

47. **The correct answer is (B).** Progestin (progesterone) is produced by the corpus luteum and is vital to the establishment and development of pregnancy. It makes possible implantation of the zygote in the uterine wall and causes development of the mammary glands during late pregnancy.

48. **The correct answer is (C).** To convert Fahrenheit degrees to Celsius, use the formula $\frac{5}{9}$ (F – 32), where F = 98.6. When calculated, body temperature is equal to 37 degrees Celsius.

49. **The correct answer is (E).** All three forms—the Bacteria, Protozoa, and Fungi—contain species that are disease producing to numerous forms of life.

50. **The correct answer is (C).** Fucus is a brown alga (seaweed) found only in marine water. No fresh water (pond) species exist, and therefore fucus cannot be obtained from this habitat by any means.

51. **The correct answer is (B).** The final stage of succession in most northeastern United States regions is the beech-maple forest. It will exist indefinitely until a forest fire, flood, or other catastrophe occurs.

52. **The correct answer is (E).** River valley deposits contain many fossils. They are composed of sedimentary rock that has been deposited, layer upon layer, over millions of years. By subjecting a fossil or layer to radiocarbon dating and other similar techniques, it is possible to ascertain its approximate age.

53. **The correct answer is (C).** Dinoflagellates are classified as pyrrophytes, or algae possessing interlocking cell walls. When they become too greatly concentrated in a certain area, they impart a red color to the water and choke off the supply of air from the submerged animal life.

54. **The correct answer is (A).** Succession is the gradual change in composition of plant life (population) from initial appearance to attainment of climax form.

55. **The correct answer is (B).** Burdock seeds contain sharp, spiny projections radiating from a hard, dry seed coat. As fur-bearing animals brush against these seeds, the sharp spines catch onto and adhere to their bodies. It may be several miles before the animal realizes that one is attached and then proceeds to shake or scratch it free, thereby serving to disperse the new generation over a wide area.

56. **The correct answer is (C).** A population exhibiting a gain of 26 and a loss of 6 per 1,000 is showing a net gain of 20 per 1,000, which is 2 percent.

57. **The correct answer is (D).** Birth control has nothing to do with this question. Behavioral resistance and hybrid vigor are both components of biotic potential. Biotic potential and environmental resistance work against one another in forming a stable population in a particular environment. A change in either biotic potential or environmental resistance can alter population size.

58. **The correct answer is (B).** In the hypothetical growth curve depicted, 1 represents a lag period typically thought to be a time of adjustment to the new environment; 2 represents exponential growth; 3 represents a leveling off as the population reaches a maximum size for a restricted environment; and 4 represents the stable population size for that restricted environment.

59. **The correct answer is (B).** See explanation 58.

60. **The correct answer is (D).** See explanation 58.

Section II

61. **The correct answer is (D).** The sulfur nucleus is identical in each of the particles and only the number of electrons differs. S^{-4} has the most electrons and hence is the heaviest.

62. **The correct answer is (D).** The atomic number is equal to the number of protons in the nucleus. The atomic weight is equal to the sum of the number of protons and neutrons in the nucleus. Hence, the nucleus of chlorine contains 18 neutrons.

63. **The correct answer is (D).** As time increases, the amount of radioactivity decreases. It decreases in half-lives, from 100 percent at time = 0 to 50 percent at time = 1 to 25 percent at time = 2, etc. As time increases, its rate of fall decreases, but nears 0 percent, and eventually will reach it. Graph (D) illustrates this.

64. **The correct answer is (A).** The huge majority of molecules of the gas will have a kinetic energy dictated by the temperature of the sample. This kinetic energy is an average of all the individual kinetic energies, and the actual shape is somewhat of a skewed bell curve, most often extending further into the high energy regions than the low. Hence, graph (A) is the proper choice.

65. **The correct answer is (B).** Upon the capture of a particle of atomic number 6 and mass number 13, the $_{96}Cm^{240}$ nucleus is converted into $_{102}No^{253}$ (No = Nobelium). The nuclear reaction may be represented as

    $$_{96}Cm^{240} + {}_{6}X^{13} \rightarrow {}_{102}No^{253}$$

66. **The correct answer is (D).** An alpha particle is a helium nucleus and, therefore, has atomic number 2 and mass number 4. The nuclear reaction is

    $$_{88}Ra^{226} \rightarrow {}_{2}He^{4} + {}_{86}Rn^{222}$$

67. **The correct answer is (D).** Graham's Law states that the rate of diffusion is inversely proportional to the square root of the molecular weight. U^{235} is separated from natural uranium (U^{238}) by a diffusion method involving the fluoride compounds $^{238}UF_6$ and $^{235}UF_6$.

68. **The correct answer is (A).** The atomic bomb concerns the conversion of certain atoms (uranium) to other atoms with the evolution of energy in the process. The energy is obtained from the conversion of a certain mass of the starting atoms into energy. Choice (A) is therefore the correct answer.

69. **The correct answer is (D).** It has been found that the heterolytic addition of hydrogen halides to double bonds proceeds in such a way as to lead to an alkyl halide with the halogen at the more substituted end of the double bond. This observation has been formalized as the Markovnikoff Rule.

70. **The correct answer is (A).** On the basis of the experiment, at the temperature given, the enzyme graphed was most active in an acid medium.

71. **The correct answer is (C).** The experiment was conducted using only one temperature. At which temperature the enzyme would show the most activity cannot be determined from the experiment.

72. **The correct answer is (D).** Based on the experiment with one enzyme, the statement is false. It is probably false in regard to enzymes in general.

73. **The correct answer is (C).** Naphthalene is a nonpolar molecule of relatively low molecular weight. Using the general rule of thumb, "Like dissolves like," it is seen that benzene is the only solvent that has the proper characteristics.

74. **The correct answer is (B).** In an aqueous solution, the two products remain in solution in ionized form and the reaction is reversible. In reactions (A) and (D), precipitates are formed and the reactions proceed to completion. Reactions (C) and (E) proceed to completion as H_2 gas is given off.

75. **The correct answer is (C).** The central carbon atom of $CH_3 \cdot CHOH \cdot C_2H_5$ is asymmetric, being bonded to four differing groups. Hence, the mirror images of this compound are not superimposable and optical isomerism exists.

76. **The correct answer is (D).** Fusion is a process in which two or more nuclei join together to form a heavier nucleus.

77. **The correct answer is (B).** Consider the dissociation of NH_4OH

    $$NH_4OH \rightleftharpoons NH_4^+ + OH^-$$

    If x is the number of moles of NH_4OH that dissociates, then for a 0.1M solution, the following equation holds

    $$\frac{(x)(x)}{(0.1-x)} = 1.8 \cdot 10^{-5}$$

    where $0.1 - x$ is the concentration of NH_4OH after dissociation and x is equal to the concentrations of NH_4^+ and OH^- ions. Neglecting x compared to 0.1 and solving gives $x = 1.34 \cdot 10^{-3}M$.

78. **The correct answer is (B).** Recalling that one mole of an ideal gas occupies 22.4 liters at standard temperature and pressure, the molecular weight of the gas is found from

    $$M.W. = (1.25 g/1)(22.4 \ 1/mole)$$
    $$= 28 g/mole$$

    A molecular weight of 28 is consistent with compound (B).

79. **The correct answer is (B).** There are three equivalents of H_3PO_4 per mole and two equivalents of $Ca(OH)_2$ per mole so that the normalities of the two solutions are

    $N(H_3PO_4) = 3(0.25) = 0.75 = N_1$
    and $N(CA(OH)_2)$
    $= 2(0.30) = 0.60 = N_2$. Using the equation $N_1 V_1 = N_2 V_2$ with $V_2 = 25$ ml. then yields $V_1 = 20$ ml.

80. **The correct answer is (C).** The water molecule donates one of its hydrogen atoms to the ammonia molecule and becomes a hydroxide ion.

81. **The correct answer is (A).** The illumination is related to the distance by

    $$\frac{I_1}{R_1^2} = \frac{I_2}{R_2^2}$$
    $$\frac{20}{2^2} = \frac{125}{x^2}$$
    $$x^2 = 25$$
    $$x = 5$$

82. **The correct answer is (C).** Because of the continuity of the tangential component of the electric field, $E_T^I + E_T^{refl} = E_T^{refr}$. Since in going from a medium of low index to one of higher index, $E_T^{refr} < E_T^I$, E_T^{refl} has to be in the opposite direction of E_T^I—that is, it has suffered a phase change of 180°.

83. **The correct answer is (D).** For a plane mirror, the image appears to be as far behind the mirror as is the object in front of the mirror. Therefore, you must focus your eyes for a distance of 40 cm.

84. **The correct answer is (A).** The electrical resistance of a solution is not dependent on the type of electrode used but only on the distance between them, the temperature, the type of ions present in solution, and the concentration of these ions.

85. **The correct answer is (C).** Since these light sources are completely incoherent, the amplitude will average out—that is, the intensities will simply add.

86. **The correct answer is (B).** When the ball is at its zenith, it is momentarily motionless. As such, it has no *kinetic* energy (since this energy is related to movement) but has a great deal of *potential* energy (since it is in an unstable situation—i.e., it is about to fall). The only choice that correctly describes this situation is choice (B).

87. **The correct answer is (D).** The spring moving back and forth is similar in its type of motion to the pendulum on a grandfather clock. This is called *harmonic* motion. Choice (A) concerns the movement of small suspended particles in liquids, while choices (B) and (C) concern motion involved in rotational movement. Choice (E) concerns the attraction of one mass for another mass. Therefore, the correct answer is (D).

88. **The correct answer is (A).** When two objects are rubbed together for any length of time, heat is generated. This is due to friction. The object entering the earth's atmosphere hits the air, which offers it resistance and causes the buildup of heat. Choice (B) is wrong since no heat is

involved in gravitational attraction. The sun's rays or the heat of the earth's atmosphere have only a negligible effect on the object's temperature. Choice (D) is irrelevant. Thus, the correct answer is (A).

89. **The correct answer is (B).** Longitudinal waves are those in which the vibrations of the particles are along straight lines, parallel to the direction of propagation.

90. **The correct answer is (C).** Complete extinction of sound or silence occurs if two sound waves of equal intensity meet in opposite phase.

91. **The correct answer is (B).** Beats result if two sound waves of slightly different frequency travel together.

92. **The correct answer is (C).** Newton's law of gravitation states that every body *attracts* every other body with a force directly proportional to the product of their masses and inversely proportional to the square of the distance between their centers. Thus, there are no repulsive forces in gravitational fields, while repulsive forces do occur between like charges in electrical and magnetic fields.

93. **The correct answer is (B).**
$$F \quad = \quad ma \leq 25 \text{ nt}$$
$$25 \text{ nt} = \quad (2\text{kg})a$$
$$a \quad = \quad 12.5 \text{ m/sec}^2$$

94. **The correct answer is (D).**

$$F = ma$$
$$a = 7g = \left(9.8\text{m}/\text{sec}^2\right)\left(7\right)$$
$$F = \left(70\text{kg}\right)\left(7\right)\left(9.8\text{m}/\text{sec}^2\right)$$
$$F = 4,800 \text{ nt}.$$

95. **The correct answer is (C).** The magnetic domains are oriented at random so that the net magnetism is essentially zero.

96. **The correct answer is (B).** Regardless of the physical characteristics of the cell, the flow of charge proceeds only insofar as the anode and cathode reactions proceed. The amount of charge that has flowed is therefore a direct measure of the mass of material deposited on the cathode.

97. **The correct answer is (D).** As C is increased, the impedance may increase or decrease depending on the value of the inductor L. This could shift impedance away from the resonant value so that the current may increase or decrease.

98. **The correct answer is (A).** Solar energy is a possible solution to our energy crisis and involves the conversion of the sun's rays into either electrical energy and/or thermal energy. It refers to neither the means of the sun's power nor the conversion of heat into light or electricity to solar power. Therefore, the correct answer is (A).

99. **The correct answer is (C).** Since the capacitors are connected in series, they must have the same charge, Q.

$$120 \text{ V} = V_1 + V_2$$
$$C_1 = \frac{Q}{V_1} \qquad C_2 = \frac{Q}{V_2}$$
$$Q = C_1 V_1$$
$$V_2 = \frac{C_1 V_1}{C_2}$$
$$120 \text{ V} = V_1 \left(1 + \frac{C_1}{C_2}\right)$$
$$120 \text{ V} = \frac{3V_1}{2}$$
$$V_1 = 80 \text{ volts}$$

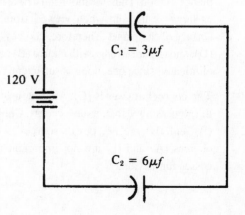

100. **The correct answer is (A).** In the Millikan oil drop experiment, a charged particle is placed in an electric field and by measurement of its rise or fall time with the field on as compared to its fall time with no field, one may find its charge to mass ratio. But we are concerned here only with finding the electric field needed.

$$ma = mg + F$$
$$a = 3g/2$$
$$\tfrac{1}{2}mg = F$$
$$\tfrac{1}{2}\left(2.8 \times 10^{-14}\,\text{nt}\right) = F$$
$$F = 1.4 \times 10^{-14}\,\text{nt}$$

101. **The correct answer is (A).** According to Einstein's general theory of relativity, the curvature of space accounts for gravitation. In 1916, Einstein predicted that light from distant stars would be deflected on passing through the sun's field of gravity. Photographs made during the total eclipse of 1919 confirmed Einstein's prediction and helped make him famous. Some knowledge of the general theory of relativity is necessary to determine that choice (A) is correct.

102. **The correct answer is (A).** Spectroscopic analysis of the light from the four great planets has not detected any free oxygen. Apparently all the oxygen is bound up in the water molecule. Choice (A) is correct.

103. **The correct answer is (C).** A total eclipse involves the blockage of the entire sun by a planet's moon. Thus, the moon must be at least as large as the sun when viewed from the surface of the planet. Therefore, choices (A), (D), and (E) are wrong, with choice (B) being eliminated since one moon is sufficient.

104. **The correct answer is (C).** Atomic fusion is the power source for the sun's energy. Choices (B) and (D) are not power sources, while choices (A) and (E) are not important processes for the sun.

105. **The correct answer is (B).** Small bases are not sufficient to determine a star's parallax. The German scientist Friedrich Bessel used the diameter of the earth's orbit, making observations six months apart to compute the distance of stars.

106. **The correct answer is (D).** A star undergoing a supernova explosion ends up as a fantastically high-density dwarf surrounded by a rapidly expanding gas cloud. Atoms in the highly compressed and hot interior form into nickel, platinum, gold, lead, and other heavy metals.

107. **The correct answer is (A).** Despite the great numbers, galaxies are divisible into three basic types: spiral galaxies like the Milky Way system, elliptical galaxies, and irregular galaxies. The irregular galaxies represent about 3 percent of the observable galaxies. They appear to be communities of stars in chaotic arrangements.

108. **The correct answer is (C).** The radiation we see from the star will undergo a Doppler shift and, since it is moving away from us, it will be shifted toward the red end of the spectrum. $v' = v(1 - v/c)$, where v is the relative velocity. Therefore, it is not dependent on v^3.

109. **The correct answer is (A).** All the clouds but Cirrus, which is a high altitude formation, are middle or low altitude formations and could not indicate a high altitude air stream.

110. **The correct answer is (E).** Aerosol cans contain propellants known as freons, which are mainly fluorocarbons. These materials have been accused of slowly destroying the ozone layer of the earth.

111. **The correct answer is (B).** Clouds are basically composed of water that will precipitate to Earth's surface in the form of rain. There are quite a few types of clouds one notices when looking at the sky on a mild day as opposed to a stormy day. Choices (A), (D), and (E) are true statements and therefore incorrect. Choice (C) is also true, thus leaving choice (B) as the correct answer.

112. **The correct answer is (C).** These are the highest and lightest clouds.

113. **The correct answer is (D).** Although all of these cause earthquakes, most are the result of fault blocks moving against one another along a fault line.

114. **The correct answer is (B).** Magma that forces its way into or intrudes into existing rock and cools is one type of igneous rock.

115. **The correct answer is (C).** Rock material loosened by weathering and moving from gravity alone is called mass wasting. Slumping is one example of mass wasting in which earth slides or slips along curved surfaces.

116. **The correct answer is (D).** Warps are minor distortions due to bending and twisting; synclines are trough-shaped down folds; monoclines are local steepenings of dip into layered rock; and recumbent folds are axial planes and limbs nearly horizontal, lying on their sides. Fumaroles are fissures producing volcanic steam.

117. **The correct answer is (A).** All of the choices are forms of drift. Lateral moraines are long, low ridges of mass-wasted rock carried along the glacier's sides. Terminal moraines are till accumulations pushed up when glacial fronts are almost stationary. Eskers are winding ridges of stratified sediments deposited by streams that run on, in, and beneath a glacier. Kames are irregular, rounded hillocks of stratified drift deposited by meltwater running off the sides of a glacier.

118. **The correct answer is (C).** Based on all of the available evidence supporting the present model of the earth, the Moho discontinuity is the boundary between the crust and the mantle.

119. **The correct answer is (B).** The ozone layer in the stratosphere is very important in filtering out harmful ultraviolet radiations that would "fry" all land life on Earth if those rays were allowed to reach the surface.

120. **The correct answer is (D).** The rotation of the earth around its axis causes a number of movements, including those of winds and also some movements in water. These movements are called the Coriolis Effect.

Practice Examination III Diagnostic Chart

Question Type	Question Numbers	Number of Questions	Number Wrong
Section I: Life Sciences			
Origin and evolution of life; classification of organisms	1–12	12	_____
Cell organization and division; genes, bioenergetics, and biosynthesis	13–24	12	_____
Structure, function, and development of organisms; hereditary patterns	25–48	24	_____
Population biology and ecology	49–60	12	_____
Section II: Physical Sciences			
Atomic structure; particles and nuclear reactions	61–68	8	_____
Elements, compounds, and reactions; molecular structure and bonding	69–80	12	_____
Thermodynamics, mechanics, and relativity	81–94	14	_____
Electricity and magnetism, light, and sound	95–100	6	_____
The universe	101–108	8	_____
The earth	109–120	12	_____

Chapter

Social Sciences and History

ABOUT THE GENERAL EXAMINATION IN SOCIAL SCIENCES AND HISTORY

The CLEP General Examination in Social Sciences and History covers a wide range of topics from the fields of social science and history. The test contains approximately 125 questions and is delivered in two separately timed 45-minute sessions. Approximately 60 percent of the questions deal with the social sciences and 40 percent with history. The topics covered by this exam and the proportion of questions devoted to each are approximately as follows:

History (40 percent of the exam)

1. U.S. History: 17 percent of the exam, covering the events and issues of the major periods in U.S. history, including the colonial, Revolutionary, late-eighteenth/early-nineteenth centuries, Civil War and Reconstruction, recent, and present eras.

2. Western Civilization: 15 percent of the exam, covering the major events and issues of the ancient, medieval, and modern periods.

3. World History: 8 percent of the exam, covering important topics in the following periods:

   Prehistory
   Ancient history to 500 B.C.E.
   500 B.C.E. to 500 C.E.
   500 C.E. to 1500 C.E.
   1500 C.E. to 1900 C.E.
   Twentieth-century Africa, Asia, Europe, and Latin America

Social Sciences (60 percent of the exam)

1. Sociology: 10 percent of the exam, covering methodology, statistics, demography and ecology, social stratification and organization, as well as concepts such as social change and social interaction.

2. Economics: 10 percent of the exam, covering consumer theory, production theory, fiscal policy, monetary policy, international trade, money and banking, and business cycles.

ROAD MAP

- *About the General Examination in Social Sciences and History*
- *Mini-Exam in Social Sciences and History*
- *Practice Examination I*
- *Practice Examination II*
- *Practice Examination III*

3. Government and Political Science: 13 percent of the exam, covering constitutional government, voting and political behavior, comparative government, and international relations.

4. Psychology: 10 percent of the exam, covering socialization, conformity, methodology, aggression, abnormal psychology, and performance.

5. Geography: 10 percent of the exam, covering cultural and physical geography, weather and climate, and ecology.

6. Anthropology: 6 percent of the exam, covering cultural and physical anthropology, demography, family structure and formation, and anthropological methodology.

Since the range of subjects covered in the General Examination in Social Sciences and History is extremely broad, you will not be expected to answer every question correctly. You will probably find that you are able to answer some of the questions from general knowledge, newspaper and magazine reading, and familiarity with current affairs. But the examination also seeks to measure your preparation in social sciences, and many questions require more specific knowledge of the various subjects, as well as of their methodologies. You should have a background in each of these fields similar to what would be acquired in a college course on the introductory level. A closer look at the subjects covered in the examination and the types of questions that are asked may suggest the amount of preparation you will need.

Types of Questions

The examination not only covers a broad range of subjects, but it also tests a broad range of skills and therefore includes a wide variety of multiple-choice questions. Some will measure your memory for facts. You might be asked to select the correct definition of a term or the correct information about a topic from among the answer choices. Other questions measure your comprehension. You might be asked to interpret written or graphic material, including excerpts from documents, narratives, tables, charts, graphs, maps, or cartoons. Finally, some of the questions will ask you to apply your understanding of a concept or theory to a specific problem or set of data. You might be asked to identify the most likely author of a quotation or to draw conclusions from the information you are given on a table or chart.

MINI-EXAM IN SOCIAL SCIENCES AND HISTORY

Directions: For each question, choose the lettered alternative that best completes the statement or answers the question.

1. Laissez-faire is a policy associated with
   - (A) Cardinal Richelieu.
   - (B) Charles de Montesquieu.
   - (C) J. M. Keynes.
   - (D) Adam Smith.
   - (E) Robert Owen.

2. The Supreme Court decided that separate facilities for blacks were legally equal to those provided for whites in
   - (A) *Brown v. Board of Education.*
   - (B) *Muller v. Oregon.*
   - (C) *Plessy v. Ferguson.*
   - (D) *Gibbons v. Ogden.*
   - (E) *Dartmouth v. Woodward.*

3. "The refusal of the native American to work with his hands when he can hire or import serfs to do manual labor for him is the prelude to his extinction and the immigrant laborers are now breeding out their masters and killing by filth and by crowding as effectively as by the sword. . . . Our jails, insane asylums, and almshouses are filled with this human flotsam and the whole tone of American life, social, moral, and political, has been lowered and vulgarized by them." This statement was probably made by
   - (A) Upton Sinclair, *The Jungle.*
   - (B) Henry George, *Progress and Poverty.*
   - (C) Madison Grant, *The Passing of the Great Race.*
   - (D) Jacob Riis, *How the Other Half Lives.*
   - (E) Theodore Dreiser, *An American Tragedy.*

4. The Treaty of Versailles was rejected by the
   - (A) League of Nations.
   - (B) World Court.
   - (C) U.S. Senate.
   - (D) Supreme Court.
   - (E) British Parliament.

5. Which of the following was a Portuguese colony in the eighteenth century?
   - (A) Jamaica
   - (B) Angola
   - (C) Cuba
   - (D) Antigua
   - (E) Curaçao

6. In which of the following African countries is the population predominantly Muslim?
   - (A) Burundi
   - (B) Namibia
   - (C) Zambia
   - (D) Tunisia
   - (E) South Africa

7. *Real income* is best defined as
   - (A) the consumer's ability to save part of his or her income.
   - (B) the consumer's ability to buy actual goods and services.
   - (C) the wage earner's income before taxes.
   - (D) the proportion of income spent on luxuries.
   - (E) income from earned wages as opposed to income from investments.

8. Which statement concerning India is incorrect?

 (A) Punjab is one of India's most prosperous states.

 (B) Indira Gandhi served as India's prime minister.

 (C) The Sikhs have been associated with a demand for constitutional changes.

 (D) Both the Sikhs and the Hindus have always supported the central government in India.

 (E) India is divided into a number of member states.

9. "This system will provide pensions as well as widows' and orphans' benefits. It will help the states provide public health services and care for the crippled and blind. It will relieve economic distress, boost the economy, and give old-age insurance to most employees."

 The system described in the statement is

 (A) the Medicare system.
 (B) the Social Security system.
 (C) the free enterprise system.
 (D) the Negative Income Tax.
 (E) National Socialism.

Question 10 is based on the following graph.

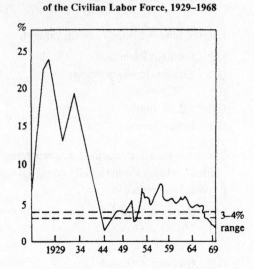

Unemployment Rates as a Percentage of the Civilian Labor Force, 1929–1968

10. All of the following conclusions can be drawn from the graph below EXCEPT

 (A) in 1933, almost a quarter of the civilian labor force was unemployed.

 (B) civilian employment increases in time of war.

 (C) employment dropped precipitously between 1938 and 1942.

 (D) in 1959, about 5 percent of the civilian population was unemployed.

 (E) unemployment rose sharply immediately after the Korean War.

Answer Key

1.	D	3.	C	5.	B	7.	B	9.	B
2.	C	4.	C	6.	D	8.	D	10.	C

Explanatory Answers

1. **The correct answer is (D).** In The Wealth of Nations (1776), Scottish political economist Adam Smith propounded the economic policy of laissez-faire. Smith attacked mercantilism, advocated a free market, and contended that pursuit of individual self-interest would foster economic progress.

2. **The correct answer is (C).** The *Plessy* v. *Ferguson* decision of 1896 upheld a Louisiana statute to enforce racial segregation in railroad cars. The decision supported the "separate but equal" doctrine and encouraged further legislation to enforce segregation of blacks in public facilities. The court contended that the Fourteenth Amendment was intended to enforce equality but not to abolish social distinctions.

3. **The correct answer is (C).** Grant's work, published in 1916, was a prominent defense of Anglo-Saxon superiority. Even if you are not familiar with this work or have never heard of it, you can determine the correct answer by eliminating the others. In his novel *The Jungle*, Upton Sinclair decried conditions in Chicago meat-packing plants and expressed sympathy for the plight of immigrant laborers who worked there. In *Progress and Poverty*, Henry George proposed the "single tax" to remedy economic inequality. Muckraker Jacob Riis described conditions in immigrant ghettos in 1890 with sympathy for the plight of the immigrants. Dreiser's novel, about a young midwesterner who commits murder and is sentenced to death, would be unlikely to contain such a polemical passage as the one presented here.

4. **The correct answer is (C).** The Treaty of Versailles, supported by President Wilson, was defeated in the U.S. Senate in 1920. Choice (A) could not be the answer because the League of Nations was created by the treaty. The United Nations and the World Court were not established until after World War II. Britain approved the treaty and joined the League of Nations, so choice (E) is incorrect as well.

5. **The correct answer is (B).** Angola was discovered by a Portuguese explorer in 1482 while he was seeking a sea route to the Indies. It remained a Portuguese possession until the 1970s when it became independent, a result of revolution in Portugal. If you have never heard of Angola, you might still be able to select the correct answer by eliminating the others. Jamaica and Antigua were English colonies, Cuba was Spanish, and Curaçao, or the Netherlands Antilles, was Dutch.

6. **The correct answer is (D).** Tunisia is a nation of North Africa with a mainly Muslim population.

7. **The correct answer is (B).** Real income is the consumer's purchasing power or his ability to buy goods and services. Although a person's earnings may be higher in 1985 than in 1965, for instance, that person's real income, or what he can buy with his earnings, might be the same or even less. Even if earnings increase, real income can decrease.

8. **The correct answer is (D).** During the 1980s, the Sikhs were very much opposed to India's central government.

9. **The correct answer is (B).** The Social Security Act, passed in 1935, created a national system of old-age insurance, in which most employees were compelled to participate. It also created a federal-state system of unemployment insurance and helped states provide

public health services and care for the disabled. Medicare supports health care for those over 65. The Negative Income Tax plan, proposed by the Nixon administration in 1969 and rejected by Congress, was intended to provide income supplements to the working poor as well as payments to those who were unemployed. National Socialism is another label for Nazism.

10. **The correct answer is (C).** Unemployment dropped precipitously between 1938 and 1942; employment rose. The other answers are illustrated by the graph. As it shows, unemployment increased to almost 25 percent, at its peak, during the Great Depression of the 1930s. It dropped during World War II (1941–45) and during the Korean War (1950–53).

Answer Sheet for Practice Examination I

Section I

1 Ⓐ Ⓑ Ⓒ Ⓓ Ⓔ	14 Ⓐ Ⓑ Ⓒ Ⓓ Ⓔ	27 Ⓐ Ⓑ Ⓒ Ⓓ Ⓔ	40 Ⓐ Ⓑ Ⓒ Ⓓ Ⓔ	52 Ⓐ Ⓑ Ⓒ Ⓓ Ⓔ
2 Ⓐ Ⓑ Ⓒ Ⓓ Ⓔ	15 Ⓐ Ⓑ Ⓒ Ⓓ Ⓔ	28 Ⓐ Ⓑ Ⓒ Ⓓ Ⓔ	41 Ⓐ Ⓑ Ⓒ Ⓓ Ⓔ	53 Ⓐ Ⓑ Ⓒ Ⓓ Ⓔ
3 Ⓐ Ⓑ Ⓒ Ⓓ Ⓔ	16 Ⓐ Ⓑ Ⓒ Ⓓ Ⓔ	29 Ⓐ Ⓑ Ⓒ Ⓓ Ⓔ	42 Ⓐ Ⓑ Ⓒ Ⓓ Ⓔ	54 Ⓐ Ⓑ Ⓒ Ⓓ Ⓔ
4 Ⓐ Ⓑ Ⓒ Ⓓ Ⓔ	17 Ⓐ Ⓑ Ⓒ Ⓓ Ⓔ	30 Ⓐ Ⓑ Ⓒ Ⓓ Ⓔ	43 Ⓐ Ⓑ Ⓒ Ⓓ Ⓔ	55 Ⓐ Ⓑ Ⓒ Ⓓ Ⓔ
5 Ⓐ Ⓑ Ⓒ Ⓓ Ⓔ	18 Ⓐ Ⓑ Ⓒ Ⓓ Ⓔ	31 Ⓐ Ⓑ Ⓒ Ⓓ Ⓔ	44 Ⓐ Ⓑ Ⓒ Ⓓ Ⓔ	56 Ⓐ Ⓑ Ⓒ Ⓓ Ⓔ
6 Ⓐ Ⓑ Ⓒ Ⓓ Ⓔ	19 Ⓐ Ⓑ Ⓒ Ⓓ Ⓔ	32 Ⓐ Ⓑ Ⓒ Ⓓ Ⓔ	45 Ⓐ Ⓑ Ⓒ Ⓓ Ⓔ	57 Ⓐ Ⓑ Ⓒ Ⓓ Ⓔ
7 Ⓐ Ⓑ Ⓒ Ⓓ Ⓔ	20 Ⓐ Ⓑ Ⓒ Ⓓ Ⓔ	33 Ⓐ Ⓑ Ⓒ Ⓓ Ⓔ	46 Ⓐ Ⓑ Ⓒ Ⓓ Ⓔ	58 Ⓐ Ⓑ Ⓒ Ⓓ Ⓔ
8 Ⓐ Ⓑ Ⓒ Ⓓ Ⓔ	21 Ⓐ Ⓑ Ⓒ Ⓓ Ⓔ	34 Ⓐ Ⓑ Ⓒ Ⓓ Ⓔ	47 Ⓐ Ⓑ Ⓒ Ⓓ Ⓔ	59 Ⓐ Ⓑ Ⓒ Ⓓ Ⓔ
9 Ⓐ Ⓑ Ⓒ Ⓓ Ⓔ	22 Ⓐ Ⓑ Ⓒ Ⓓ Ⓔ	35 Ⓐ Ⓑ Ⓒ Ⓓ Ⓔ	48 Ⓐ Ⓑ Ⓒ Ⓓ Ⓔ	60 Ⓐ Ⓑ Ⓒ Ⓓ Ⓔ
10 Ⓐ Ⓑ Ⓒ Ⓓ Ⓔ	23 Ⓐ Ⓑ Ⓒ Ⓓ Ⓔ	36 Ⓐ Ⓑ Ⓒ Ⓓ Ⓔ	49 Ⓐ Ⓑ Ⓒ Ⓓ Ⓔ	61 Ⓐ Ⓑ Ⓒ Ⓓ Ⓔ
11 Ⓐ Ⓑ Ⓒ Ⓓ Ⓔ	24 Ⓐ Ⓑ Ⓒ Ⓓ Ⓔ	37 Ⓐ Ⓑ Ⓒ Ⓓ Ⓔ	50 Ⓐ Ⓑ Ⓒ Ⓓ Ⓔ	62 Ⓐ Ⓑ Ⓒ Ⓓ Ⓔ
12 Ⓐ Ⓑ Ⓒ Ⓓ Ⓔ	25 Ⓐ Ⓑ Ⓒ Ⓓ Ⓔ	38 Ⓐ Ⓑ Ⓒ Ⓓ Ⓔ	51 Ⓐ Ⓑ Ⓒ Ⓓ Ⓔ	63 Ⓐ Ⓑ Ⓒ Ⓓ Ⓔ
13 Ⓐ Ⓑ Ⓒ Ⓓ Ⓔ	26 Ⓐ Ⓑ Ⓒ Ⓓ Ⓔ	39 Ⓐ Ⓑ Ⓒ Ⓓ Ⓔ		

Section II

64 Ⓐ Ⓑ Ⓒ Ⓓ Ⓔ   77 Ⓐ Ⓑ Ⓒ Ⓓ Ⓔ   90 Ⓐ Ⓑ Ⓒ Ⓓ Ⓔ   102 Ⓐ Ⓑ Ⓒ Ⓓ Ⓔ   114 Ⓐ Ⓑ Ⓒ Ⓓ Ⓔ

65 Ⓐ Ⓑ Ⓒ Ⓓ Ⓔ   78 Ⓐ Ⓑ Ⓒ Ⓓ Ⓔ   91 Ⓐ Ⓑ Ⓒ Ⓓ Ⓔ   103 Ⓐ Ⓑ Ⓒ Ⓓ Ⓔ   115 Ⓐ Ⓑ Ⓒ Ⓓ Ⓔ

66 Ⓐ Ⓑ Ⓒ Ⓓ Ⓔ   79 Ⓐ Ⓑ Ⓒ Ⓓ Ⓔ   92 Ⓐ Ⓑ Ⓒ Ⓓ Ⓔ   104 Ⓐ Ⓑ Ⓒ Ⓓ Ⓔ   116 Ⓐ Ⓑ Ⓒ Ⓓ Ⓔ

67 Ⓐ Ⓑ Ⓒ Ⓓ Ⓔ   80 Ⓐ Ⓑ Ⓒ Ⓓ Ⓔ   93 Ⓐ Ⓑ Ⓒ Ⓓ Ⓔ   105 Ⓐ Ⓑ Ⓒ Ⓓ Ⓔ   117 Ⓐ Ⓑ Ⓒ Ⓓ Ⓔ

68 Ⓐ Ⓑ Ⓒ Ⓓ Ⓔ   81 Ⓐ Ⓑ Ⓒ Ⓓ Ⓔ   94 Ⓐ Ⓑ Ⓒ Ⓓ Ⓔ   106 Ⓐ Ⓑ Ⓒ Ⓓ Ⓔ   118 Ⓐ Ⓑ Ⓒ Ⓓ Ⓔ

69 Ⓐ Ⓑ Ⓒ Ⓓ Ⓔ   82 Ⓐ Ⓑ Ⓒ Ⓓ Ⓔ   95 Ⓐ Ⓑ Ⓒ Ⓓ Ⓔ   107 Ⓐ Ⓑ Ⓒ Ⓓ Ⓔ   119 Ⓐ Ⓑ Ⓒ Ⓓ Ⓔ

70 Ⓐ Ⓑ Ⓒ Ⓓ Ⓔ   83 Ⓐ Ⓑ Ⓒ Ⓓ Ⓔ   96 Ⓐ Ⓑ Ⓒ Ⓓ Ⓔ   108 Ⓐ Ⓑ Ⓒ Ⓓ Ⓔ   120 Ⓐ Ⓑ Ⓒ Ⓓ Ⓔ

71 Ⓐ Ⓑ Ⓒ Ⓓ Ⓔ   84 Ⓐ Ⓑ Ⓒ Ⓓ Ⓔ   97 Ⓐ Ⓑ Ⓒ Ⓓ Ⓔ   109 Ⓐ Ⓑ Ⓒ Ⓓ Ⓔ   121 Ⓐ Ⓑ Ⓒ Ⓓ Ⓔ

72 Ⓐ Ⓑ Ⓒ Ⓓ Ⓔ   85 Ⓐ Ⓑ Ⓒ Ⓓ Ⓔ   98 Ⓐ Ⓑ Ⓒ Ⓓ Ⓔ   110 Ⓐ Ⓑ Ⓒ Ⓓ Ⓔ   122 Ⓐ Ⓑ Ⓒ Ⓓ Ⓔ

73 Ⓐ Ⓑ Ⓒ Ⓓ Ⓔ   86 Ⓐ Ⓑ Ⓒ Ⓓ Ⓔ   99 Ⓐ Ⓑ Ⓒ Ⓓ Ⓔ   111 Ⓐ Ⓑ Ⓒ Ⓓ Ⓔ   123 Ⓐ Ⓑ Ⓒ Ⓓ Ⓔ

74 Ⓐ Ⓑ Ⓒ Ⓓ Ⓔ   87 Ⓐ Ⓑ Ⓒ Ⓓ Ⓔ   100 Ⓐ Ⓑ Ⓒ Ⓓ Ⓔ   112 Ⓐ Ⓑ Ⓒ Ⓓ Ⓔ   124 Ⓐ Ⓑ Ⓒ Ⓓ Ⓔ

75 Ⓐ Ⓑ Ⓒ Ⓓ Ⓔ   88 Ⓐ Ⓑ Ⓒ Ⓓ Ⓔ   101 Ⓐ Ⓑ Ⓒ Ⓓ Ⓔ   113 Ⓐ Ⓑ Ⓒ Ⓓ Ⓔ   125 Ⓐ Ⓑ Ⓒ Ⓓ Ⓔ

76 Ⓐ Ⓑ Ⓒ Ⓓ Ⓔ   89 Ⓐ Ⓑ Ⓒ Ⓓ Ⓔ

PRACTICE EXAMINATION I

Section I

63 Questions

Time—45 Minutes

Directions: For each question, choose the lettered answer that best completes the statement or answers the question. Mark the letter of your choice on the answer sheet provided. When you have completed the examination, check your answers with the answer key and explanations that follow the exam.

1. The Pendleton Act of 1883 was an attempt to eliminate the abuses of

   (A) the Specie Circular.
   (B) the Crédit Mobilier.
   (C) the railroads.
   (D) the spoils system.
   (E) combinations in restraint of trade.

2. Lincoln justified the Emancipation Proclamation on the basis of which of the following presidential powers?

   (A) The duty to take care that the laws be faithfully executed
   (B) The "necessary and proper" clause
   (C) The duty to promote the general welfare
   (D) Military authority as commander in chief
   (E) Executive privilege

3. Alexander Hamilton's economic program included proposals for all of the following EXCEPT the

   (A) promotion of commerce and industry.
   (B) investment of capital in American industry.
   (C) establishment of a national bank.
   (D) assumption of state debts.
   (E) removal of protective tariffs.

Question 4 refers to the following chart.

Civil War Casualties

	Union	Confederacy
Total serving in armed forces	1,556,678	1,082,119
Killed in battle or died from wounds	110,070	94,000
Died from illness	249,458	164,000
Wounded	275,175	100,000

4. Based on the above chart, select the statement that is incorrect about Civil War soldiers.

   (A) The number who died from illness, in both the Union and Confederate armies, exceeded the number who were killed in battle or died from wounds.
   (B) The number of deaths, in both the Union and Confederate armies, exceeded the number of wounded.
   (C) The total number of deaths in the Union Army exceeded the total number of deaths in the Confederate Army.
   (D) The total number of dead and wounded in the Union Army was more than double the total number of dead and wounded in the Confederate Army.
   (E) Almost a sixth of the Union Army died from illness.

5. In the election of 1912, the central campaign issue of both Theodore Roosevelt's New Nationalism and Woodrow Wilson's New Freedom was in the area of

(A) the regulation of business.
(B) foreign policy.
(C) morals in politics.
(D) conservation.
(E) civil liberties.

6. A historian analyzing the causes of the American Revolution might legitimately point to all of the following EXCEPT the

(A) breakdown of the British mercantile system.
(B) colonial anger at the loss of political powers.
(C) influence of political propaganda.
(D) influence of enlightenment ideology.
(E) influence of the French Revolution.

7. The U.S. armed forces were racially integrated during the administration of

(A) Woodrow Wilson.
(B) Franklin D. Roosevelt.
(C) Harry Truman.
(D) Dwight D. Eisenhower.
(E) Lyndon B. Johnson.

8. Which of the following statements describes most accurately the gist of Roger B. Taney's majority decision in the Dred Scott case of 1857?

(A) An African American was not entitled to the rights of federal citizenship, and the Missouri Compromise was unconstitutional.
(B) An African American was not entitled to the rights of federal citizenship, and the Missouri Compromise was constitutional.
(C) An African American was entitled to the rights of federal citizenship, and the Missouri Compromise was constitutional.
(D) An African American was entitled to the rights of federal citizenship, and the Missouri Compromise was unconstitutional.
(E) Congress had the right to prohibit slavery in the territories.

9. Which is the correct chronological order for the following immigration acts?

I. Literacy Test Act
II. National Origins Act
III. Chinese Exclusion Act
IV. McCarran Walter Act
(A) III, I, II, and IV
(B) III, II, I, and IV
(C) I, II, IV, and III
(D) II, I, IV, and III
(E) I, II, III, and IV

Question 10 refers to the following graph.

Slave Population as Percentage of Total African-American Population, 1790–1860

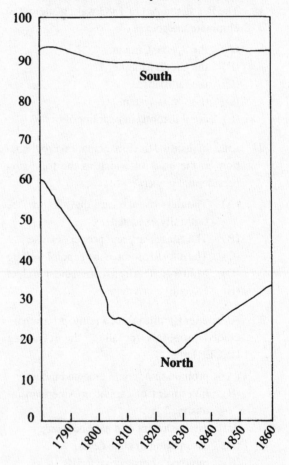

10. The graph supports all of the following conclusions EXCEPT

(A) from 1790 to 1860, free African Americans remained a small percentage of the total African-American population in the South.

(B) from 1790 to 1860, the number of slaves in the South remained the same.

(C) the percentage of slaves in the Northern African-American population decreased until 1830 and then began to rise.

(D) the slave population of the North, 1790 to 1860, never diminished to under 10 percent of the total Northern African-American population.

(E) the number of slaves in the North at the beginning of the Civil War cannot be determined from this graph.

11. The Wool Act of 1699, the Hat Act of 1732, and the Iron Act of 1750 were British attempts to

(A) tax ships entering American ports.

(B) punish Bostonian merchants.

(C) increase American manufacturing.

(D) limit American manufacturing.

(E) provide colonial manufacturers with European markets.

12. Which of the following novels deals with World War I?

(A) *The Naked and the Dead*

(B) *The Red Badge of Courage*

(C) *All Quiet on the Western Front*

(D) *From Here to Eternity*

(E) *The Caine Mutiny*

13. Which of the following statements best describes the political status of Southern African Americans during the Reconstruction?

(A) African Americans dominated Southern state legislatures by great majorities.

(B) African Americans were deprived of suffrage during the Reconstruction.

(C) Although African Americans voted, none was elected to public office.

(D) Two African-American senators were elected but no African-American governors.

(E) For two years, the majority of senators and governors in the Southern states were African American.

14. The major cause of Anne Hutchinson's banishment from Massachusetts in 1638 was

(A) adultery.

(B) idolatry.

(C) heresy.

(D) blasphemy.

(E) covetousness.

15. Before ratifying the Articles of Confederation, which of the following did Maryland demand?

(A) That individual states maintain funds derived from taxes they levy

(B) That individual states have the right to issue their own currency

(C) That all states cede to the Union all claims to western lands

(D) That the right of Congress to levy taxes be restricted

(E) That Congress assume both legislative and executive functions

16. The elections of 1800 and 1824 were alike in that

(A) former presidents were reelected.

(B) Northern presidents were elected.

(C) the House of Representatives chose the president.

(D) vice presidents succeeded to the presidency.

(E) the losing candidate received a popular plurality.

17. The Manhattan Project was a

(A) secret committee investigating security clearances during the early 1950s.

(B) pressure group seeking support for urban renewal projects.

(C) group of physicists working at Los Alamos under J. Robert Oppenheimer.

(D) presidential advisory commission concerned with rehabilitation of the victims of Hiroshima and Nagasaki.

(E) committee of intelligence agents assigned to break the German code during World War II.

18. Women became the major source of employees at New England textile mills at approximately the same time that women

    (A) won the vote.
    (B) formed temperance and antislavery societies.
    (C) were victims of the Triangle Fire.
    (D) began to work in munitions factories.
    (E) became secretaries and typists, replacing male clerks.

19. Which of the following best reflects the economic hardships of the Critical Period?

    (A) The Stamp Act Congress
    (B) Tom Paine's *Common Sense*
    (C) The Northwest Ordinance
    (D) Shays' Rebellion
    (E) The Boston Tea Party

20. "Resolved, that whoever shall be aiding, or assisting, in the landing, or carting of such tea, from any ship, or vessel, or shall hire any house . . . whatsoever, to deposit the tea, subject to a duty as aforesaid, he shall be deemed an enemy to the liberties of America. . . . Whoever shall transgress any of these resolutions, we will not deal with, or employ, or have any connection with him."

    The statement above is most likely to have been made by

    (A) Parliament in the Tea Act.
    (B) Joseph Galloway in the "Plan of Union."
    (C) The Sons of Liberty in a resolution.
    (D) Lord North in the "Intolerable Acts."
    (E) Tom Paine in *Common Sense*.

21. Which of the following was the primary issue that led James Bacon to march on Jamestown in 1676 in what became known as Bacon's Rebellion?

    (A) Dissatisfaction over high taxes
    (B) Falling tobacco prices
    (C) Rumors of rampant political corruption
    (D) Debate over how the Indians and their raids should be dealt with
    (E) Dissatisfaction with Quaker land grants

22. The Calvinist doctrine of predestination is the belief

    (A) that those who work hard will win God's favor.
    (B) in universal salvation.
    (C) that good actions toward others insure heavenly rewards.
    (D) that damnation or salvation is preordained by God.
    (E) that each man controls his own fate.

23. Dante Alighieri's *Divine Comedy* can be best described as a(n)

    (A) allegory.
    (B) farce.
    (C) satire.
    (D) opera.
    (E) political tract.

24. The Sophists of ancient Athens were best known as

    (A) dramatists.
    (B) philosophy teachers.
    (C) politicians.
    (D) criminals.
    (E) merchants.

25. Diocletian's significant contribution to the Roman Empire was the

    (A) development of roads and bridges.
    (B) development of a legal code.
    (C) creation of a powerful army.
    (D) introduction of religious freedom.
    (E) administrative reorganization of the Empire.

26. The right to a trial by a jury of one's peers was guaranteed by

    (A) Parliamentary law.
    (B) the Magna Carta.
    (C) the Domesday Book.
    (D) the Curia Regis.
    (E) the Revolution of 1688.

27. All of the following contributed to the rise of fascism in Germany EXCEPT the

    (A) inflation of the 1920s followed by depression and unemployment.
    (B) inability of the Weimar government to subordinate the army to civilian authority.
    (C) reaction to the humiliation of German defeat in 1918.
    (D) inability of Germans to accept or tolerate National Socialism.
    (E) lack of popular enthusiasm for the Weimar Republic.

28. Toussaint L'Ouverture was best known for

    (A) the revolt of Quebec against France.
    (B) establishing the Republic of Haiti.
    (C) the exploration of New France.
    (D) the defense of Fort Duquesne.
    (E) devising military strategy against the English.

29. All of the following powers were represented at the Congress of Vienna in 1814 EXCEPT

    (A) Austria.
    (B) Great Britain.
    (C) Russia.
    (D) France.
    (E) Spain.

30. The *phalanx* in ancient Athens was a

    (A) military formation.
    (B) family dwelling.
    (C) suit of armor.
    (D) type of ship.
    (E) political party.

31. The Domesday Book of the eleventh century was a

    (A) religious relic.
    (B) land survey.
    (C) legal code.
    (D) bill of rights.
    (E) mortality table.

32. Arrange the following events of World War II in chronological order.

    I.   Battle of the Bulge
    II. Battle of Britain
    III. Nazi invasion of Poland
    IV. Munich Pact

    (A) I, II, III, and IV
    (B) II, III, I, and IV
    (C) III, II, I, and IV
    (D) IV, II, III, and I
    (E) IV, III, II, and I

33. The main purpose of the Congress of Vienna was to

    (A) end the seven-year war between England and France.
    (B) promote "enlightened despotism" in Europe.
    (C) restore stability to Europe.
    (D) end the Revolutions of 1848.
    (E) end the Franco-Prussian War.

34. Eighteenth-century mercantilists believed all of the following EXCEPT that

    (A) a favorable balance of trade is good for the nation.
    (B) the state treasury should accumulate bullion.
    (C) exports should exceed imports.
    (D) a weak central government fosters trade and profit.
    (E) a state needs colonies for markets and raw materials.

35. Which of the following resulted from the Revolutions of 1848?

    I.   Abolition of serfdom in the Hapsburg Dominions
    II. Creation of a short-lived French Republic
    III. A return to absolute monarchy throughout Europe
    IV. Extension of universal manhood suffrage throughout Europe

    (A) I and II
    (B) I, II, and III
    (C) II and III
    (D) II and IV
    (E) I and IV

36. The connection between Protestantism and the rise of capitalism was drawn by
    (A) Max Weber.
    (B) Karl Marx.
    (C) Arnold Toynbee.
    (D) Robert Owen.
    (E) Bertrand Russell.

37. Which of the following statements most accurately describes the impact of Stalin's death on U.S.-Soviet relations?
    (A) Soviet foreign policy became more belligerent when the new leader Khrushchev claimed he would "bury" capitalism.
    (B) The new Soviet leaders were more inclined to accept peaceful competition between social systems.
    (C) The new Soviet leaders adopted a "hard line" policy and expelled American reporters and diplomats.
    (D) The new Soviet leader Khrushchev vowed to maintain all Stalinist policies, especially those hostile to American interests.
    (E) The new Soviet leaders sought a confrontation with the United States and shipped missiles to Cuba.

38. The first European explorers of the African coast were the
    (A) Portuguese.
    (B) British.
    (C) Spanish.
    (D) French.
    (E) Scandinavians.

39. The Ostrogoth King Theodoric, who ruled over the Goths and Romans during the fifth century, established his capital in which of the following regions?
    (A) Bavaria
    (B) Lombardy
    (C) Scandinavia
    (D) Italy
    (E) Spain

40. All of the following fell under the rule of the Emperor Charlemagne EXCEPT
    (A) the British Isles.
    (B) Bavaria.
    (C) Lombardy.
    (D) Saxony.
    (E) the Frankish Kingdom.

41. *Haiku* is the Japanese term for a
    (A) short verse form.
    (B) popular beverage.
    (C) means of suicide.
    (D) martial art.
    (E) type of drama.

42. Put the following events in Japanese history into chronological order.
    I.   Beginning of Sino-Japanese War
    II.   Introduction of Christianity
    III. Introduction of Buddhism
    IV.   End of Russo-Japanese War

    (A) III, II, IV, and I
    (B) II, III, I, and IV
    (C) II, III, IV, and I
    (D) III, I, IV, and II
    (E) III, IV, I, and II

43. China was declared a republic in
    (A) 1900.
    (B) 1912.
    (C) 1941.
    (D) 1949.
    (E) 1960.

Questions 44–46 are based on the following map.

44. The Cape of Good Hope, reached by Portuguese explorer Bartholomeu Diaz in 1488, is best represented by letters

   (A) E and G.
   (B) F and H.
   (C) H and C.
   (D) C and J.
   (E) E and K.

45. During the seventeenth century, Dutch settlers arrived in the region represented by letter(s)

   (A) A.
   (B) B.
   (C) D.
   (D) K.
   (E) D and K.

46. The Democratic Republic of Congo is located in the region represented by letter(s)

   (A) A.
   (B) B.
   (C) D.
   (D) K.
   (E) D and K.

47. During the struggle for control of Africa in the nineteenth century, all of the following nations took over territory EXCEPT

   (A) Belgium.
   (B) France.
   (C) Germany.
   (D) Great Britain.
   (E) the United States.

48. Which of the following Muslim leaders reconquered Jerusalem from the Crusaders?

   (A) Sulieman the Magnificent
   (B) Saladin
   (C) Ataturk
   (D) Mohammed
   (E) Tamarlane

49. In which of the following *pairs* of nations did revolutions occur during the 1970s?

   (A) Iran and Thailand
   (B) Portugal and Nicaragua
   (C) Haiti and Cuba
   (D) Egypt and Pakistan
   (E) Mexico and Cambodia

50. In the mid-second century B.C.E. the city-states of ancient Greece lost their independence and came under the control of the

   (A) Celts.
   (B) Germans.
   (C) Teutons.
   (D) Romans.
   (E) Bretons.

51. "This act gave employees the fight to organize, form, or become members of labor organizations. It gave these organizations the right to bargain collectively. It also established the National Labor Relations Board."

   The act of Congress described above is the

   (A) Clayton Antitrust Act.
   (B) Norris-LaGuardia Act.
   (C) Taft-Hartley Act.
   (D) Employment Act of 1946.
   (E) Wagner Act.

52. Which of the following most accurately describes a constitutional monarchy?
    (A) The constitution is written by the monarch.
    (B) Democracy is prohibited.
    (C) A lawmaking body limits the monarch.
    (D) The monarch serves as a member of the legislature.
    (E) There is never a king or queen.

53. An oligarchy is a state
    (A) without a hereditary ruler.
    (B) with a mixture of political systems.
    (C) ruled by a small group of nobles.
    (D) without a written constitution.
    (E) administered by priests.

54. The International Court of Justice meets at
    (A) Geneva.
    (B) New York.
    (C) Paris.
    (D) Rome.
    (E) the Hague.

55. When Fidel Castro gained control of Cuba in 1959, he overthrew the
    (A) Trujillo regime.
    (B) Perón regime.
    (C) Batista regime.
    (D) Allende regime.
    (E) Somoza regime.

56. Which of the following best describes the distinction between the office of President of the United States and the office of Prime Minister of Great Britain?
    (A) The president is responsible to the people of the nation, while the prime minister is responsible to the majority party in Parliament.
    (B) The president is elected, while the prime minister is appointed by the monarch.
    (C) The president has a cabinet, but the prime minister does not.
    (D) The president is considered the leader of his political party, while the prime minister is not.
    (E) There is no particular distinction since both the president and the prime minister can veto legislation.

57. The United States and its United Nations allies fought the Gulf War of 1991 in order to regain the independence of which Middle Eastern country?
    (A) Bahrain
    (B) Iraq
    (C) Afghanistan
    (D) Kuwait
    (E) Yemen

58. The Good Neighbor policy was originally intended to apply to
    (A) Canada.
    (B) Latin America.
    (C) China.
    (D) Mexico.
    (E) Western Europe.

59. The Truman Plan was intended to
    (A) help Greece and Turkey resist Communist aggression.
    (B) defeat Japan by 1945.
    (C) spur European economic recovery after World War II.
    (D) aid the unemployed and disadvantaged after World War II.
    (E) rid the State Department of Communists.

60. The redrawing of legislative districts for partisan purposes is commonly called
    (A) logrolling.
    (B) gerrymandering.
    (C) quartering.
    (D) court packing.
    (E) obstructing justice.

61. The party whip is a member of Congress who is expected to
    (A) raise funds for congressional campaigns and other partisan purposes.
    (B) preside over the House of Representatives.
    (C) insure that party members are on the floor for important debates and votes.
    (D) confer with the cabinet.
    (E) supervise the drafting of legislation.

62. Which *pair* of the following presidents first served as vice presidents?

    (A) Theodore Roosevelt and William McKinley
    (B) Woodrow Wilson and F. D. Roosevelt
    (C) James Madison and James Monroe
    (D) John Adams and John Quincy Adams
    (E) Andrew Johnson and Lyndon Johnson

63. A legislative rider can be best described as

    (A) an attempt to prevent debate from continuing.
    (B) an extraneous provision attached to a bill, usually an appropriations bill.
    (C) an exchange of favors among legislators.
    (D) a bill passed by Congress for the primary purpose of incurring presidential wrath.
    (E) any suggestion made by a lobbyist to a legislator.

Section II

62 Questions

Time—45 minutes

Directions: For each question, choose the lettered answer that best completes the statement or answers the question. Mark the letter of your choice on the answer sheet provided. When you have completed the examination, check your answers with the answer key and explanations that follow the exam.

64. The federal principle of government has been put into practice in which of the following nations?

    I.   United States
    II. Canada
    III. Switzerland
    IV. France

    (A) I, II, III, and IV
    (B) I, II, and III
    (C) I and II
    (D) I and IV
    (E) Only I

65. The citizen's constitutional right to protection from unwarranted arrest is provided by the

    (A) right of eminent domain.
    (B) writ of assistance.
    (C) writ of habeas corpus.
    (D) bill of attainder.
    (E) elastic clause.

66. The first assembly in the English colonies in North America was the

    (A) House of Burgesses.
    (B) Mayflower Compact.
    (C) Continental Congress.
    (D) General Court.
    (E) town meeting.

67. A pattern of behavior associated with a distinctive social position is called a(n)

    (A) role.
    (B) status.
    (C) caste.
    (D) identity.
    (E) complex.

Question 68 is based on the following table.

Life Expectancy in the United States in 1970

Classification	Life Expectancy in Years
All classes	70.9
White	71.7
Male	68.0
Female	75.6
Nonwhite	65.3
Male	61.3
Female	69.4

68. On the basis of the above table, it is possible to conclude all of the following EXCEPT

    (A) in 1970, the average life expectancy of whites was about six years longer than that of nonwhites.
    (B) in 1970, female life expectancies exceeded male life expectancies in both white and nonwhite groups.
    (C) in 1970, white males could expect to live longer than nonwhite males.
    (D) in 1970, socioeconomic factors had an impact on life expectancy.
    (E) in 1970, biological factors had an impact on life expectancy.

69. If the median age of a nation is 30.2, this means that
    (A) half the people in the population are under this age and half are over this age.
    (B) the population as a whole is becoming older.
    (C) more people in the population are under 30 than over 30.
    (D) the group of people who are 30 years old in this population is larger than the group of people who are any other age, such as 25 or 35.
    (E) the population as a whole is becoming younger.

70. All of the following statements about the U.S. Census are true EXCEPT
    (A) the U.S. Census is mentioned in the U.S. Constitution.
    (B) some of the data collected by the Census Bureau is based on a sample of the population rather than on the whole population.
    (C) the U.S. Census asks the race or color of each household member.
    (D) the U.S. Census is taken every other year.
    (E) the expense of taking the U.S. Census is assumed by the federal government.

71. A sex ratio of 120 tells us that
    (A) there are more males than females in the population.
    (B) there are 20 more males than females in the sample.
    (C) there are 20 more females than males in the sample.
    (D) there are more females than males in the sample.
    (E) the sample population is sexually active.

72. Which of the following statements about the sex ratio in the United States is correct?
    (A) The sex ratio declines with increasing age.
    (B) The sex ratio increases with increasing age.
    (C) The sex ratio is always higher among nonwhites than whites.
    (D) The sex ratio does not vary according to age.
    (E) The sex ratio of the U.S. population cannot be determined.

73. All of the following are examples of social sanctions EXCEPT
    (A) taxes.
    (B) a prison sentence.
    (C) an honorary degree.
    (D) ostracism.
    (E) "blackball."

Question 74 is based on the following diagram.

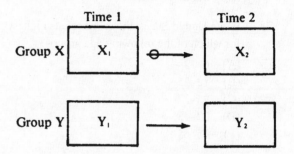

In the above diagram, X_1 and X_2 represent the members of Group X at times 1 and 2. Y_1 and Y_2 represent members of Group Y at times 1 and 2.

74. In an experiment, people are randomly assigned to Groups X and Y. Some experimental variation (0) is introduced between X_1 and X_2. Under these conditions, Group Y would be called a(n)
    (A) experimental group.
    (B) primary group.
    (C) control group.
    (D) in-group.
    (E) out-group.

75. The theory that population increases by geometrical ratio while the means of subsistence increase by arithmetical ratio can be attributed to
    (A) Plato.
    (B) Aristotle.
    (C) Marx.
    (D) Malthus.
    (E) Durkheim.

76. Since 1650, the population of the world has
    (A) decreased only slightly.
    (B) approximately doubled.
    (C) approximately tripled.
    (D) increased more than tenfold.
    (E) decreased by about one quarter.

77. Which of the following functions, performed by the family, has most markedly decreased in relative importance for the American family since colonial times?

    (A) Affectional
    (B) Protective
    (C) Sexual regulation
    (D) Socialization
    (E) Status-giving

78. In the United States, the crime rate is highest for which of the following age groups?

    (A) 6–12
    (B) 12–25
    (C) 25–37
    (D) 37–45
    (E) 45–65

79. A primary group is characterized by

    (A) close kinship ties among the members.
    (B) small group size and face-to-face relationships.
    (C) members with the same sex and similar ages.
    (D) frequent conflict and competition among members.
    (E) members with the same place of residence.

80. Ethology can be best described as the study of

    (A) ethical systems.
    (B) animal behavior.
    (C) racial relations.
    (D) primitive societies.
    (E) subcultures.

Question 81 is based on the following diagram.

New Young Workers in 1980

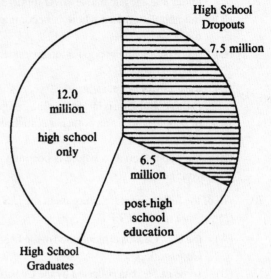

81. Approximately what percentage of the new young workers in 1980 were high school dropouts according to the diagram?

    (A) 24 percent
    (B) 27 percent
    (C) 29 percent
    (D) 32 percent
    (E) 34 percent

82. A study of microeconomics would include which of the following?

    I. How prices are set
    II. How national monetary policy is established
    III. The nature of fiscal policy
    IV. How buyers and sellers behave

    (A) I and II
    (B) II and III
    (C) II and IV
    (D) III and IV
    (E) I and IV

83. The policy of government activism in the economy to promote high employment and business activity is associated with

    (A) J. M. Keynes.
    (B) David Ricardo.
    (C) T. R. Malthus.
    (D) Adam Smith.
    (E) Thomas Jefferson.

84. Personal disposable income is

    (A) personal income minus personal income taxes.
    (B) the amount of personal income that can be saved after basic expenses have been paid.
    (C) the gross national product divided by the total population.
    (D) income from investments as opposed to take-home pay.
    (E) the proportion of personal income devoted to charitable contributions.

85. In constructing the consumer price index, the Department of Labor takes into consideration all of the following EXCEPT the cost of

    (A) food.
    (B) clothing.
    (C) transportation.
    (D) recreation.
    (E) education.

86. When the economy is healthy, the percentage of unemployed can be expected to be

    (A) 0 percent.
    (B) 3–4 percent.
    (C) 8–12 percent.
    (D) about 15 percent.
    (E) about 20 percent.

87. "This agency supervises the way in which the lending activities of the banking system change the size of the money supply. It also regulates banking activities in order to serve the economic needs of the nation."

    The agency described above is probably the

    (A) Federal Deposit Insurance Corporation.
    (B) Federal Reserve Board.
    (C) Securities and Exchange Commission.
    (D) Bureau of the Budget.
    (E) Office of Economic Opportunity.

88. An "easy money" policy is intended to

    (A) reduce total spending.
    (B) increase interest rates.
    (C) reduce the reserves of the banking system.
    (D) increase the money supply.
    (E) cut back borrowing.

89. Which one of the following types of tax is most regressive?

    (A) Excise and sales taxes
    (B) Property taxes
    (C) Payroll taxes
    (D) Personal income taxes
    (E) Corporate income and profit taxes

90. The primary purpose of these institutions is to make mortgage loans to their members. Which of the following best fits this description?

    (A) Mutual savings banks
    (B) Savings and loan associations
    (C) Credit unions
    (D) Life insurance companies
    (E) Fire and casualty insurance companies

Question 91 is based on the following diagram.

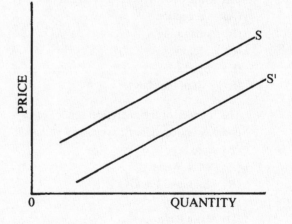

91. If the supply curve moves from S to S¹, which of the following has occurred?

    (A) An increase in supply
    (B) A decrease in supply
    (C) A decrease in quantity supplied
    (D) An increase in quantity supplied
    (E) A decrease in product quality

92. A firm remains in business as long as it can cover which one of the following types of costs?
    (A) Solid
    (B) Fixed
    (C) Variable
    (D) Constant
    (E) Invisible

93. The branch of psychology that emphasizes the study of direct, observable response to stimuli in a controlled environment is
    (A) Associational Psychology.
    (B) Freudian Psychology.
    (C) Behavioral Psychology.
    (D) Clinical Psychology.
    (E) Social Psychology.

94. Which of the psychologists listed below is most famous for his or her work in child psychology?
    (A) Jean Piaget
    (B) August Strinburn
    (C) John Watson
    (D) Penny Patterson
    (E) None of the above

95. What processes or activities are considered part of the overall process of cognition?
    (A) Perception
    (B) Imagining
    (C) Memory
    (D) Speech
    (E) All of the above

96. The founder of the analytical school of psychology and author of *Psychology of the Unconscious* was
    (A) Max Weber.
    (B) Sigmund Freud.
    (C) Carl Jung.
    (D) Ivan Pavlov.
    (E) Alexander Bain.

97. The method of experimentation most closely associated with B.F. Skinner is
    (A) classical conditioning.
    (B) stimulus-response.
    (C) associationism.
    (D) functionalism.
    (E) operant conditioning.

98. Which of the following philosophers developed the idea that human bodies are like clockwork machines, but that human minds and souls are separate and unique, and that each person is born with unique ideas that shape the way he or she experiences the world?
    (A) John Locke
    (B) Sigmund Freud
    (C) René Descartes
    (D) John Watson
    (E) Wilhelm Wundt

99. Which of the following functions, performed by the family, has increased in relative importance for the American family since colonial times?
    (A) Affectional
    (B) Economic
    (C) Reproductive
    (D) Protective
    (E) Socialization

100. Which of the following is NOT a psychological defense mechanism?
    (A) Rationalization
    (B) Repression
    (C) Reaction formation
    (D) Regression
    (E) Assimilation

101. A man who has just been fired from his job comes home and kicks his dog. Which of the following defense mechanisms is he displaying?
    (A) Projection
    (B) Displacement
    (C) Identification
    (D) Sublimation
    (E) Reaction formation

102. Which of the following would NOT be considered a behavioral deviant?
    (A) A presidential assassin
    (B) An armed robber
    (C) A mentally challenged person
    (D) A rapist
    (E) A traitor

103. According to the biological interpretation of deviance advanced by psychologist William H. Sheldon in the 1950s, the *mesomorph* is a

    (A) lean, agile, strong individual.
    (B) stout, round person.
    (C) frail, delicate person.
    (D) lazy, stupid person of middle size.
    (E) nervous, impulsive person of middle size.

104. According to Robert K. Merton's explanation of deviance, a drug addict would be classified as a(n)

    (A) retreatist.
    (B) conformist.
    (C) rebel.
    (D) innovator.
    (E) hereditary deviant.

105. John Doe left his wife and family in Detroit, quit his job with an insurance company, and moved to southern California. He now supports himself by carving small wooden animals, associates with people half his age, and spends most of his time on the beach. He rejects his old way of life entirely because it is incompatible with the new values and attitudes he has acquired. The process described above could most accurately be called

    (A) assimilation.
    (B) accommodation.
    (C) impulsive socialization.
    (D) repressive socialization.
    (E) resocialization.

106. Which of the following countries currently governs Antarctica?

    (A) France
    (B) Great Britain
    (C) The United States
    (D) Argentina
    (E) None of the above

107. What part of Antarctica makes up its northernmost tip?

    (A) The Antarctic Peninsula
    (B) Gondwanaland
    (C) Queen Maud Land
    (D) The Transantarctic Mountains
    (E) Vostok

108. Which country, located on the tectonically active Mid-Atlantic Ridge, has more hot springs than any other country on earth?

    (A) Russia
    (B) The United States
    (C) Brazil
    (D) Iceland
    (E) Canada

109. The two fundamental branches of geography are

    (A) cultural and physical geography.
    (B) geomorphology and oceanography.
    (C) regional and systematic geography.
    (D) microgeology and macrogeology.
    (E) None of the above

110. Which of the following describes the Russian *taiga*?

    (A) Russia's politically and economically crucial waterway system of dams and canals, constructed in the 1950s
    (B) The black-earth belt that forms Russia's most important area of crop and livestock production
    (C) The area covered by glaciers and ice caps along Russia's Arctic coast
    (D) Russia's northern coniferous forest, which is the largest continuous area of forest on Earth
    (E) The agricultural settlement method developed by the Soviets after World War II

111. Which of the following climates can be found in the area of the former Soviet Union?

    (A) Desert
    (B) Tundra
    (C) Humid continental
    (D) Mediterranean
    (E) All of the above

112. Which order represents the geologic time scale, from the oldest geologic era to the most recent?

    (A) Paleozoic, Mesozoic, Precambrian, Cambrian
    (B) Cambrian, Paleozoic, Mesozoic, Cenozoic
    (C) Precambrian, Paleozoic, Mesozoic, Cenozoic
    (D) Mesozoic, Cenozoic, Precambrian, Paleozoic
    (E) Cenozoic, Precambrian, Paleozoic, Mesozoic

113. The field of geography that deals with the distribution of plants and animal life is

    (A) geomorphology.
    (B) systems geography.
    (C) hydrography.
    (D) biogeography.
    (E) ecology.

114. Which of the following lists accurately names the four main islands in the Japanese archipelago?

    (A) Sendai, Kanto, Honshu, Shikoku
    (B) Shikoku, Hokkaido, Honshu, Sapporo
    (C) Hokkaido, Kyushu, Shikoku, Honshu
    (D) Fukuoka, Matsuyama, Honshu, Kanto
    (E) Fukuoka, Matsuyama, Sendai, Kanto

115. All of the following are African nations EXCEPT

    (A) Gabon.
    (B) Uganda.
    (C) Zambia.
    (D) Liberia.
    (E) Bangladesh.

116. On a Mercator projection map,

    (A) east-west dimensions of geographic areas are accurate.
    (B) north-south dimensions of geographic areas are accurate.
    (C) mathematical locations are accurate.
    (D) mathematical locations are inaccurate.
    (E) lines of longitude converge at the poles.

117. As customarily used by geographers, the term *region* is defined as a(n)

    (A) areal category.
    (B) land-mass category.
    (C) cultural category.
    (D) economic category.
    (E) population category.

118. By definition, in *kinship-based societies*, the members of a lineage, clan, or other kin group are usually

    (A) dominated by males.
    (B) dominated by females.
    (C) descendants of a common ancestor.
    (D) descendants of a dominant male.
    (E) descendants of a dominant female.

119. All of the following cultural groups are examples of hunter-gatherer societies EXCEPT

    (A) Australian aborigines.
    (B) Congo pygmies.
    (C) Inuits.
    (D) Pueblos.
    (E) Neanderthals.

120. The term *matrilocal* is most likely to refer to

    (A) a mother's authority over her children.
    (B) control over child's choice of spouse.
    (C) an individual's female descendents.
    (D) an individual's female ancestors.
    (E) a family's place of residence.

121. Which primate group is physically and genetically most closely related to humans?

    (A) Orangutan
    (B) Baboons
    (C) Gorillas
    (D) Old World monkeys
    (E) Chimpanzees

122. Which of the following Native American cultures participated in ceremonies known as *potlatch*?

    (A) Menominee
    (B) Mandan
    (C) Kwakiutl
    (D) Seminole
    (E) Iroquois

123. The beginning of the Archaic period in North America coincided with the end of the Ice Age, which is dated to approximately

(A) 25000 B.C.E.
(B) 12000 B.C.E.
(C) 8000 B.C.E.
(D) 1000 B.C.E.
(E) 300 B.C.E.

124. Based on the discoveries of the anthropologist Richard Leakey, modern humans are believed to have originated in

(A) Asia.
(B) Africa.
(C) Europe.
(D) North America.
(E) South America.

125. Which of the following best defines *internal migration?*

(A) The movement of any large group of people, as in the Mongol invasion of Europe
(B) Migration necessitated by natural disaster, such as the movement of residents of a flooded area to a safe area
(C) The movement of people within a specific country, such as the move of a family from Chicago to New York
(D) The involuntary movement of a large group of people, such as the movement of captured slaves from Africa to the Americas
(E) The voluntary movement of any group of people, such as the emigration of English colonists to New England in the seventeenth century

End of Practice Examination I

Answer Key

Section I

1.	D	14.	C	27.	D	40.	A	52.	C
2.	D	15.	C	28.	B	41.	A	53.	C
3.	E	16.	C	29.	E	42.	A	54.	E
4.	D	17.	C	30.	A	43.	B	55.	C
5.	A	18.	B	31.	B	44.	B	56.	A
6.	E	19.	D	32.	E	45.	B	57.	D
7.	C	20.	C	33.	C	46.	A	58.	B
8.	A	21.	D	34.	D	47.	E	59.	A
9.	A	22.	D	35.	A	48.	B	60.	B
10.	B	23.	A	36.	A	49.	B	61.	C
11.	D	24.	B	37.	B	50.	D	62.	E
12.	C	25.	E	38.	A	51.	E	63.	B
13.	D	26.	B	39.	D				

Section II

64.	B	77.	B	90.	B	102.	C	114.	C
65.	C	78.	B	91.	A	103.	A	115.	E
66.	A	79.	B	92.	C	104.	A	116.	C
67.	A	80.	B	93.	C	105.	E	117.	A
68.	D	81.	C	94.	A	106.	E	118.	C
69.	A	82.	E	95.	E	107.	A	119.	D
70.	D	83.	A	96.	C	108.	D	120.	E
71.	A	84.	A	97.	E	109.	C	121.	E
72.	A	85.	E	98.	C	110.	D	122.	C
73.	A	86.	B	99.	A	111.	E	123.	C
74.	C	87.	B	100.	E	112.	C	124.	B
75.	D	88.	D	101.	B	113.	D	125.	C
76.	D	89.	A						

Explanatory Answers

Section I

1. **The correct answer is (D).** The Pendleton Act of 1883, establishing the Civil Service Commission, sought to end the abuses of the spoils system or patronage in politics.

2. **The correct answer is (D).** The Emancipation Proclamation, which freed all slaves in areas controlled by the rebels as of January 1, 1863, was issued as a war measure on the grounds of Lincoln's military authority as commander in chief.

3. **The correct answer is (E).** Hamilton proposed protective tariffs in his *Report on Manufactures* in 1791; he did not oppose them or propose their removal. Hamilton favored the development and protection of home industry.

4. **The correct answer is (D).** The total number of dead and wounded in the Union Army was not over double the total number of dead and wounded in the Confederate Army; it was somewhat less than double.

5. **The correct answer is (A).** The issue of business regulation was the focus of this campaign. Roosevelt in the New Nationalism advocated the expansion of federal power in business regulation and welfare legislation. Wilson in the New Freedom called for the enforcement of antitrust laws to restore competition.

6. **The correct answer is (E).** Since the French Revolution did not occur until 1789, it cannot be considered a cause of the American Revolution.

7. **The correct answer is (C).** During the Truman administration, major steps were taken to integrate the armed forces. A committee appointed by President Truman in 1948 proposed steps for integration. In 1949, the Army opened all jobs to qualified personnel without regard to race and abolished racial quotas. The Navy and Air Force adopted similar policies.

8. **The correct answer is (A).** According to Taney's majority opinion, an African American could not be entitled to the rights of federal citizenship; the Missouri Compromise was unconstitutional because Congress had no power to prohibit slavery in the territories; slaves were property and no citizen could be deprived of property without due process of law.

9. **The correct answer is (A).** The dates of the acts are Chinese Exclusion Act, 1882; Literacy Test Act, 1917; National Origins Act, 1924; and McCarran Walter Act, 1952.

10. **The correct answer is (B).** The graph does *not* indicate that the *number* of slaves in the South remained approximately the same from 1790 to 1860. It does not indicate the *number* of slaves or of free African Americans in the South at all. The graph gives only percentages. It *does* show that the free African-American population remained approximately the same percentage of the total African-American population in the South during this period.

11. **The correct answer is (D).** The Wool Act, Hat Act, and Iron Act were British attempts to curtail or prohibit American manufacturing in order to prevent colonial manufacturers from competing with British manufacturers of these items.

12. **The correct answer is (C).** *All Quiet on the Western Front* (1929) by Erich Maria Remarque expresses a prevalent attitude of disillusionment with war following World War I.

13. **The correct answer is (D).** African-American people never dominated Reconstruction governments in the South. No state legislature had an African-American majority except for South Carolina. Two African-American senators were elected from Mississippi and African-American people also served in lesser offices. No African-American governors were elected.

14. **The correct answer is (C).** Anne Hutchinson's admission before the General Court in 1637 that she had received direct revelations from God was considered heresy. She was excommunicated and banished from Massachusetts Bay in 1638.

15. **The correct answer is (C).** Maryland refused to ratify the Articles of Confederation until all

states agreed to cede to the Union their claims to all lands in the western territories.

16. **The correct answer is (C).** In both 1800 and 1824, no candidate received a majority in the Electoral College. Thus, both elections were determined by the House of Representatives. Jefferson won in 1800 and John Quincy Adams in 1824.

17. **The correct answer is (C).** The Manhattan Project, a secret effort to develop a transportable atomic bomb, was initiated in 1942. The bomb was constructed at Los Alamos.

18. **The correct answer is (B).** The first workers in the New England textile mills of the antebellum era were women. During the 1830s, women also formed temperance and antislavery societies.

19. **The correct answer is (D).** In Shays' Rebellion of 1787, farmers in western Massachusetts protested against the refusal of the Massachusetts legislature to issue paper money. Paper money would have eased the plight of debtors whose mortgages on homes and farms were being foreclosed.

20. **The correct answer is (C).** The statement is from a colonial resolution of opposition to the Tea Act of 1773 and is more likely to have been made by the Sons of Liberty than by Parliament, a British official, Galloway, or Paine.

21. **The correct answer is (D).** James Bacon marched on Jamestown to insist that he be made commander in chief over forces he would organize to quell the Indian uprising in Virginia.

22. **The correct answer is (D).** The Calvinist doctrine of predestination is the belief that God determines, before an individual is born, whether his soul will go to heaven or hell when he dies. The doctrines of John Calvin, Protestant reformer, were introduced to Europe in the sixteenth century.

23. **The correct answer is (A).** *The Divine Comedy,* written around 1300, presents a symbolic system or allegory. It describes a visionary journey through hell, heaven, and purgatory and the progress of a soul from sin to purification.

24. **The correct answer is (B).** The Sophists were a class of philosophy teachers in ancient Athens. Known for their ingenuity in argument, they taught the relativity of good and evil.

25. **The correct answer is (E).** Diocletian divided the Roman Empire into two sections, each of which was administered separately.

26. **The correct answer is (B).** The Magna Carta, or Great Charter, of English liberties was forced from King John in 1215. This fundamental constitution guarantees basic rights, including that of trial by jury.

27. **The correct answer is (D).** National Socialism was the policy of the Nazi Party. The Nazis' rise to power marked the end of the Weimar Republic and the beginning of fascist rule.

28. **The correct answer is (B).** Toussaint L'Ouverture led the Haitian revolt against France in 1798. Haiti became an independent republic. The French name for the colony had been Saint Domingue.

29. **The correct answer is (E).** The major powers represented at the Congress of Vienna were Austria, Great Britain, Russia, Prussia, and France.

30. **The correct answer is (A).** The *phalanx* was a military formation of heavily armed infantry in close rank and file. Warriors with shields marched in parallel lines.

31. **The correct answer is (B).** The Domesday Book, ordered by William the Conqueror in 1085, was a land survey of the kingdom of England to determine how much tax could be assessed.

32. **The correct answer is (E).** The Munich Pact was signed in 1938; the invasion of Poland was in 1939; the Battle of Britain was in 1940–41; the Battle of the Bulge was in 1944.

33. **The correct answer is (C).** The purpose of the Congress of Vienna in 1814 was to establish a balance of power in Europe and restore stability. The hope of the Congress was that monarchical regimes would cooperate to preserve peace and domestic order and prevent change.

The leading spirit of the Congress was Prince Von Metternich of Austria.

34. **The correct answer is (D).** An important mercantilist belief was that a strong government is needed to regulate commerce and production and to promote trade. A strong state can also provide a navy to protect the merchant fleet.

35. **The correct answer is (A).** The Revolutions of 1848 liberated the serfs in eastern Prussia and the Austrian empire. The Second French Republic lasted from 1848 until 1852.

36. **The correct answer is (A).** Pioneer sociologist Max Weber's work, *The Protestant Ethic and the Spirit of Capitalism,* is the source of this idea.

37. **The correct answer is (B).** Khrushchev's rise to power several years after Stalin's death in 1952 led to improved U.S.-Soviet relations.

38. **The correct answer is (A).** Bartholomeu Diaz and Vasco da Gama explored the African coast in 1488 and 1499. Soon after, Portugal established coastal settlements.

39. **The correct answer is (D).** Theodoric the Great was founder of the Ostrogothic kingdom in Italy; his capital was Ravenna.

40. **The correct answer is (A).** The British Isles maintained independence from the Frankish rule of Charlemagne, who in addition to reigning as king of the Franks from 768–814 was Emperor of the Romans from 800 until 814. He was the most influential of all European rulers of the Middle Ages.

41. **The correct answer is (A).** A *haiku* is a verse form of three lines with a total of 17 syllables in a 5–7–5 arrangement. One of the shortest verse forms in world literature, it is noted for its imagery.

42. **The correct answer is (A).** The dates of the events are introduction of Buddhism, 552; introduction of Christianity, 1549; end of the Russo-Japanese War, 1905; and beginning of the Sino-Janapese War, 1937. Christianity was introduced to Japan by Francis Xavier, a Spanish Jesuit missionary.

43. **The correct answer is (B).** The last Chinese dynasty was brought to an end after revolution broke out in 1911. China was declared a republic in 1912 by Sun Yat-sen.

44. **The correct answer is (B).** The Cape of Good Hope is at the southernmost tip of Africa

45. **The correct answer is (B).** The Dutch settlers, called Boers, arrived in South Africa in the seventeenth century.

46. **The correct answer is (A).** The nation of the Democratic Republic of Congo (formerly Zaire) is located in the center of Africa.

47. **The correct answer is (E).** The United States did not participate in the nineteenth-century struggle for control of Africa.

48. **The correct answer is (B).** Saladin (1138–1193) was the Muslim leader who recaptured Jerusalem from the Crusaders in 1187, precipitating the Third Crusade.

49. **The correct answer is (B).** In 1974, the government of Portugal was taken over by a military junta led by General Antonio de Spinola. Revolution in Nicaragua took place in 1979 when the dictator, General Somoza, fled into exile. Other major revolutions of the 1970s occurred in Iran in 1978–9, when Shah Mohammed Reza Pahlevi went into exile and Ayatollah Ruhollah Khomeini returned from exile to take control, and in Cambodia in 1975, when the Khmer Rouge gained control. Only choice (B) names a *pair* of revolutions.

50. **The correct answer is (D).** The city-states of ancient Greece submitted to Roman rule following a series of wars in the mid–second century B.C.E.

51. **The correct answer is (E).** The Wagner Act of 1935 gave employees the right to organize, to form and join unions, and to bargain collectively. It ordered employers not to resist unionization. The National Labor Relations Board was established to administer the act.

52. **The correct answer is (C).** A constitutional monarchy is a form of government in which the ruler is checked in the exercise of his power by a parliamentary or lawmaking body and written guarantees.

53. **The correct answer is (C).** An oligarchy is a state in which power is held by a small group of people.

54. **The correct answer is (E).** The International Court of Justice, a branch of the United Nations, is composed of fifteen judges from member nations. Meeting in the Hague, its purpose is to render decisions in legal disputes between nations.

55. **The correct answer is (C).** Castro overthrew the regime of Fulgencia Batista, who had headed a military dictatorship in Cuba since 1952. Although the United States immediately recognized the new regime, Castro's Marxism and the arrival of thousands of Cubans who fled into exile soon caused the United States to regard Cuba, under Castro, as a threat to the security of the nation and the western hemisphere.

56. **The correct answer is (A).** A major distinction between the British and American forms of government is the nature of the relationship between the legislative and executive functions. The prime minister assumes office when his party wins a majority of seats in the House of Commons in a general election. His responsibility is to his party, the current majority party, which has put him in office. The president is of course responsible to the entire electorate. Both officials have cabinets, both are regarded as party leaders, and both are put into office through electoral procedures. The prime minister, unlike the president, cannot veto legislation.

57. **The correct answer is (D).** The United States and its United Nations allies fought the Gulf War of 1991 in order to regain independence for Kuwait, a small Middle Eastern country that had been invaded by forces from the neighboring country of Iraq.

58. **The correct answer is (B).** The Good Neighbor policy toward Latin America, or an American reluctance to use armed intervention in Latin American affairs, is associated with the New Deal era. In his first inaugural address, President Roosevelt referred to the need to establish friendly relations with Latin American nations and used the phrase "good neighbor."

59. **The correct answer is (A).** In March 1947, President Truman urged Congress to appropriate funds to help Greece and Turkey preserve their independence and resist Communist expansion. The plan was intended to insure that Communist expansionism would not threaten the security of the United States or its friends and allies.

60. **The correct answer is (B).** Gerrymandering is the attempt to redraw congressional districts so that the nominees from one's own political party will be successful in the next election in as many districts as possible.

61. **The correct answer is (C).** The major function of the party whip is to advise members of Congress when bills will be considered and to insure their attendance at congressional sessions when important measures will be considered and votes taken.

62. **The correct answer is (E).** Andrew Johnson was vice president under Lincoln, and Lyndon Johnson was vice president under John F. Kennedy. Presidential assassinations brought both of the Johnsons into office. John Adams and Theodore Roosevelt also served as vice president, Adams under Washington, and Roosevelt under McKinley.

63. **The correct answer is (B).** A good example of a rider was provided by Congress in 1867 when the Republican-dominated legislature was at odds with President Johnson. Congress attached an extraneous provision to an Army appropriations bill. The rider deprived the president of control over the U.S. Army. Johnson vetoed the bill, and Congress overrode his veto.

Section II

64. **The correct answer is (B).** France has a centralized administration, not a federal one. The French state forms a single unit, and the *départements* exist only for administrative purposes. When the federal principle is followed, a nation is made up of distinctive political subdivisions. In the United States, the subdivisions are states; in Switzerland, cantons; and in Canada, provinces.

65. **The correct answer is (C).** The privilege of the writ of habeas corpus is a part of the English common law tradition that was incorporated in the U.S. Constitution. Its function is to provide a safeguard against unwarranted arrest. A writ of habeas corpus orders a law enforcement official to produce the person of a prisoner in court so a judge can determine whether or not that individual should be detained. During the Civil War, President Lincoln suspended the writ by executive order and subsequently, in 1863, Congress endorsed the suspension.

66. **The correct answer is (A).** The first assembly in the English colonies was the Virginia House of Burgesses, formed in 1619. By the eighteenth century, all the colonies had assemblies.

67. **The correct answer is (A).** Each society has many social categories or roles; for instance, father, child, student, teacher, doctor, and patient. Each role is associated with a particular behavior pattern. Individuals perform numerous roles.

68. **The correct answer is (D).** According to the table, sex differences (biological factors) affect life expectancy, as does race. Socioeconomic factors may well affect life expectancy also, but they are not mentioned in the table.

69. **The correct answer is (A).** The median age is the point at which the population divides in half, half falling below the median age and half above it.

70. **The correct answer is (D).** The U.S. Census is taken every ten years. It is mentioned in the Constitution, it is financed by the federal government, it inquires into race or color, and some of its conclusions are based on sample surveys.

71. **The correct answer is (A).** The sex ratio is the number of males per 100 females in a given population. A sex ratio of 120 means there are 120 men for every 100 women in the population, therefore, more males than females.

72. **The correct answer is (A).** As people age in American society, the proportion of females rises. Slightly more males are born than females, but once people reach adulthood, the sex ratio starts to fall. In 1970, for instance, the sex ratio in the United States was 95 for ages 35–39 and 56 for ages 85 and over.

73. **The correct answer is (A).** A sanction is a punishment or reward aimed at inducing conformity with a social norm. The purpose of taxation is not to punish or reward but to raise revenue. Tax regulations may influence behavior, but that is not their main purpose.

74. **The correct answer is (C).** Group Y is not subject to experimental variation. If the changes between X_1 and X_2 are compared with changes between Y_1 and Y_2, any differences that emerge can be presumed to be the result of the experimental variation that was introduced. Group Y is therefore the control group. X can be checked against Y at time 2.

75. **The correct answer is (D).** This famous theory was put forth by Thomas Malthus in his *Essay on the Principle of Population* (1798). Malthus contended that poverty, hunger, and distress were unavoidable since population would exceed means of subsistence.

76. **The correct answer is (D).** The world population in 1650 was 470 million, approximately. It reached 3.8 billion in the mid 1970s and was estimated at about 5,321,000,000 in *The World Almanac* for 1990.

77. **The correct answer is (B).** The protective functions of the family have, to a great degree, been transferred to social groups and agencies outside the family, such as the police or the armed forces.

78. **The correct answer is (B).** Young adults have the highest crime rate. The official arrest rate for males peaks at age 20 in the United States and then declines. The arrest rate for women peaks at age 23 and then declines.

79. **The correct answer is (B).** A primary group, defined by American sociologist Charles Horton Cooley in 1909, is characterized by face-to-face relationships, which means that the group is small. It is also characterized by a high degree of intimacy, cooperation, and permanence.

80. **The correct answer is (B).** In the early twentieth century, scientists such as Lorenz and Tinbergen began to investigate and describe animal behavior with an integrated conceptual and methodological approach. This scientific study of animals on their own terms is known as ethology.

81. **The correct answer is (C).** The total number of new young workers is 26 million (12.0 + 7.5 + 6.5). Divide the number of high school dropouts by 26: 7.5 divided by 26 is .2884 or 29 percent.

82. **The correct answer is (E).** Microeconomics is the study of the *parts* of a market economy, including, for instance, how the price system works or how buyers respond to shortages. Macroeconomics deals with the economic system as a whole.

83. **The correct answer is (A).** In 1936, John Maynard Keynes created a new theory that was used to bolster the case for an active government policy to end the Depression. The government would have to increase public expenditures and make money and credit available. This would increase production and employment. "Deficit financing" is one name for the economic policy introduced during the Depression.

84. **The correct answer is (A).** Disposable personal income is personal income minus personal taxes. Consumers can spend *more* than their personal disposable income by borrowing or by using up their savings.

85. **The correct answer is (E).** The consumer price index, as set forth by the Department of Labor, contains the typical expenditures for an urban family of four on such items as food, clothing, transportation, medical care, and recreation. Educational costs for family members are not part of the index.

86. **The correct answer is (B).** An unemployment rate of 0 percent, or full employment, never exists because there are always some workers changing jobs, being fired, or entering or leaving the labor market. Others are affected by cutbacks or seasonal unemployment. A healthy economy can expect an unemployment rate of 3–4 percent.

87. **The correct answer is (B).** The Federal Reserve system was established by Congress in 1913. A seven-man board of governors, appointed by the President for staggered fourteen-year terms, controls the Federal Reserve. The purpose of the agency is to supervise the nation's monetary and banking affairs, to regulate its money supply, and to promote economic stability.

88. **The correct answer is (D).** An easy money policy on the part of the Federal Reserve is intended to promote employment and price stability. An increase of reserves in the banking system will push down interest rates, encourage borrowing and spending, increase the money supply, and stimulate the economy.

89. **The correct answer is (A).** Excise taxes tend to be the most regressive because a large portion of the commodities taxed, such as liquor, telephone service, and appliances, are commodities for which consumption does not increase in proportion to income.

90. **The correct answer is (B).** Savings and loan associations issue shares to savers, making them owners. The funds collected by the associations are usually spent to grant home mortgages.

91. **The correct answer is (A).** The diagram shows that at a given price, the quantity supplied at S^1 is greater than that supplied at S. An increase in supply has occurred.

92. **The correct answer is (C).** Variable costs are those that increase or decrease in the short run, relative to the level of production, as opposed to fixed costs, which remain constant regardless of the level of production. In the short run, the firm will continue to produce as long as it can meet its variable costs. In the long run, all costs are variable.

93. **The correct answer is (C).** Behavioral psychology emphasizes the study of observable responses to stimuli within a controlled environment, rather than on interpretation of inner experiences and remembered events.

94. **The correct answer is (A).** The Swiss psychologist Jean Piaget (1896–1980) is most famous for his work on the development of intelligence in children.

95. **The correct answer is (E).** These processes, along with reasoning, thinking, attention, and judgment, make up the cognitive process.

96. **The correct answer is (C).** Carl Jung is considered to be the father of the analytical school of psychology and introduced the personality types 'introvert' and 'extrovert' in his 1912 publication, *Psychology of the Unconscious.*

97. **The correct answer is (E).** B.F. Skinner (1904–1990) named his method of experimentation, which involved controlling and shaping a subject's behavior, *operant conditioning.*

98. **The correct answer is (C).** René Descartes was the first modern philosopher to promote the idea that people are born with ideas that shape their experience of the world. Locke believed that experience shapes ideas.

99. **The correct answer is (A).** The family has become a more markedly important source of affectionate support since colonial times and fulfills a relatively larger affectional function in modern times than it did in colonial times.

100. **The correct answer is (E).** A defense mechanism is an unconscious process that opposes the acting out of unacceptable or painful impulses. Assimilation is a process in which the beliefs, customs, and behavior patterns of one group are merged with those of another group. This does not fall into the category of psychological defense mechanisms.

101. **The correct answer is (B).** *Displacement* refers to the release of dangerous, unpleasant, or hostile impulses in a substitute situation or in a disguised activity. In this instance, the man has displaced his hostility toward his office or his employer onto the dog.

102. **The correct answer is (C).** Behavioral deviance is believed to be harmful to society or to individuals within it. The mentally challenged person, who is not harmful to others, is an example of concrete deviance—that is, any characteristic that is statistically unusual. The mentally challenged person is not a behavioral deviant.

103. **The correct answer is (A).** In *Varieties of Delinquent Youth* (1949), Sheldon suggested a connection between body type, or somatotype, and deviant behavior. He contended that each of the body types he defined (endomorph, mesomorph, and ectomorph) was linked to a particular behavioral mode.

104. **The correct answer is (A).** The retreatist, according to Merton, rejects societal means and goals. The conformist, rebel, and innovator have different approaches to means and goals, or different adaptations. The conformist, for instance, totally accepts societal goals and the means of achieving them.

105. **The correct answer is (E).** Resocialization is a process of basic change in an adult. It usually means the abandonment of one way of life and the adoption of a new way of life incompatible with the old.

106. **The correct answer is (E).** Though seven different nations have laid territorial claim to Antarctica, those claims were put aside in 1962 to enable cooperative research in the area.

107. **The correct answer is (A).** The Antarctic Peninsula is the northernmost tip of Antarctica, and it reaches toward the southern tip of South America.

108. **The correct answer is (D).** Iceland has more hot springs than any other country on Earth; Iceland uses the thermal energy from these springs to heat homes and power businesses.

109. **The correct answer is (C).** Regional and systematic geography are the two fundamental branches of this science. Cultural and physical geography are classifications of Systematic geography.

110. **The correct answer is (D).** Russia's *taiga* is the largest continuous area of forest on Earth, and it is also one of the world's major lumbering areas.

111. **The correct answer is (E).** The post-Soviet region is one of the largest and most geographically diverse areas on Earth. All of the listed climates (and more) exist in the post-Soviet region.

112. **The correct answer is (C).** From the oldest geologic era to the most recent, the geologic time scale unfolds in this order: Precambrian, Paleozoic, Mesozoic, and Cenozoic.

113. **The correct answer is (D).** Biogeography deals with the geographical distribution of plants and animals.

114. **The correct answer is (C).** The four main islands are Hokkaido, Honshu, Shikoku, and Kyushu.

115. **The correct answer is (E).** Bangladesh, formerly East Pakistan, is on the Indian subcontinent.

116. **The correct answer is (C).** Lines of latitude and longitude are parallel on a Mercator map; thus, mathematical locations are accurate, but dimensions of areas are distorted.

117. **The correct answer is (A).** A region is a classification or categorization of an area, usually of considerable size, that is largely homogenous and differs substantially from adjoining areas. Economy, land-mass, population, and culture are factors in regionalization, but none is used individually to classify a region.

118. **The correct answer is (C).** A kinship-based society can be either matrilineal (dominated by females) or patrilineal (dominated by males), but members of a kinship-based society are all descendants of a common ancestor.

119. **The correct answer is (D).** The Pueblo culture built permanent settlements and is thus a culture founded upon agriculture and herding/grazing, not hunting and gathering.

120. **The correct answer is (E).** A matrilocal family lives in the residence of the wife's family or with the wife's tribe.

121. **The correct answer is (E).** Chimpanzees differ from humans by less than 1 percent of their total genetic material, making them the primate group most closely linked—physically and biologically—to humans.

122. **The correct answer is (C).** Potlatch is a ceremony associated with Native American tribes of the Pacific Northwest; the Kwakiutl are the only people of this region appearing in the list.

123. **The correct answer is (C).** The Ice Age ended around 8000 B.C.E. in North America; the Archaic period in most of North America ran from 8000 B.C.E. to 300 B.C.E.

124. **The correct answer is (B).** Modern humans are believed to have originated in Africa and to have migrated from there throughout the world.

125. **The correct answer is (C).** Internal migration is population movement within the confines of a country.

Practice Examination I Diagnostic Chart

Subject Area	Approx. % of Exam	Question Numbers	Number of Questions	Number Wrong
U.S. History	17 %	1–21	21	_____
Western Civilization	15 %	22–40	19	_____
World Civilization	8 %	41–50	10	_____
Government/Political Science	13 %	51–66	16	_____
Sociology	11 %	67–80	14	_____
Economics	10 %	81–92	12	_____
Psychology	10 %	93–105	13	_____
Geography	10 %	106–117	12	_____
Anthropology	6 %	118–125	8	_____
TOTAL	100 %		125	_____

Answer Sheet for Practice Examination II

Section I

1 Ⓐ Ⓑ Ⓒ Ⓓ Ⓔ   14 Ⓐ Ⓑ Ⓒ Ⓓ Ⓔ   27 Ⓐ Ⓑ Ⓒ Ⓓ Ⓔ   40 Ⓐ Ⓑ Ⓒ Ⓓ Ⓔ   52 Ⓐ Ⓑ Ⓒ Ⓓ Ⓔ

2 Ⓐ Ⓑ Ⓒ Ⓓ Ⓔ   15 Ⓐ Ⓑ Ⓒ Ⓓ Ⓔ   28 Ⓐ Ⓑ Ⓒ Ⓓ Ⓔ   41 Ⓐ Ⓑ Ⓒ Ⓓ Ⓔ   53 Ⓐ Ⓑ Ⓒ Ⓓ Ⓔ

3 Ⓐ Ⓑ Ⓒ Ⓓ Ⓔ   16 Ⓐ Ⓑ Ⓒ Ⓓ Ⓔ   29 Ⓐ Ⓑ Ⓒ Ⓓ Ⓔ   42 Ⓐ Ⓑ Ⓒ Ⓓ Ⓔ   54 Ⓐ Ⓑ Ⓒ Ⓓ Ⓔ

4 Ⓐ Ⓑ Ⓒ Ⓓ Ⓔ   17 Ⓐ Ⓑ Ⓒ Ⓓ Ⓔ   30 Ⓐ Ⓑ Ⓒ Ⓓ Ⓔ   43 Ⓐ Ⓑ Ⓒ Ⓓ Ⓔ   55 Ⓐ Ⓑ Ⓒ Ⓓ Ⓔ

5 Ⓐ Ⓑ Ⓒ Ⓓ Ⓔ   18 Ⓐ Ⓑ Ⓒ Ⓓ Ⓔ   31 Ⓐ Ⓑ Ⓒ Ⓓ Ⓔ   44 Ⓐ Ⓑ Ⓒ Ⓓ Ⓔ   56 Ⓐ Ⓑ Ⓒ Ⓓ Ⓔ

6 Ⓐ Ⓑ Ⓒ Ⓓ Ⓔ   19 Ⓐ Ⓑ Ⓒ Ⓓ Ⓔ   32 Ⓐ Ⓑ Ⓒ Ⓓ Ⓔ   45 Ⓐ Ⓑ Ⓒ Ⓓ Ⓔ   57 Ⓐ Ⓑ Ⓒ Ⓓ Ⓔ

7 Ⓐ Ⓑ Ⓒ Ⓓ Ⓔ   20 Ⓐ Ⓑ Ⓒ Ⓓ Ⓔ   33 Ⓐ Ⓑ Ⓒ Ⓓ Ⓔ   46 Ⓐ Ⓑ Ⓒ Ⓓ Ⓔ   58 Ⓐ Ⓑ Ⓒ Ⓓ Ⓔ

8 Ⓐ Ⓑ Ⓒ Ⓓ Ⓔ   21 Ⓐ Ⓑ Ⓒ Ⓓ Ⓔ   34 Ⓐ Ⓑ Ⓒ Ⓓ Ⓔ   47 Ⓐ Ⓑ Ⓒ Ⓓ Ⓔ   59 Ⓐ Ⓑ Ⓒ Ⓓ Ⓔ

9 Ⓐ Ⓑ Ⓒ Ⓓ Ⓔ   22 Ⓐ Ⓑ Ⓒ Ⓓ Ⓔ   35 Ⓐ Ⓑ Ⓒ Ⓓ Ⓔ   48 Ⓐ Ⓑ Ⓒ Ⓓ Ⓔ   60 Ⓐ Ⓑ Ⓒ Ⓓ Ⓔ

10 Ⓐ Ⓑ Ⓒ Ⓓ Ⓔ   23 Ⓐ Ⓑ Ⓒ Ⓓ Ⓔ   36 Ⓐ Ⓑ Ⓒ Ⓓ Ⓔ   49 Ⓐ Ⓑ Ⓒ Ⓓ Ⓔ   61 Ⓐ Ⓑ Ⓒ Ⓓ Ⓔ

11 Ⓐ Ⓑ Ⓒ Ⓓ Ⓔ   24 Ⓐ Ⓑ Ⓒ Ⓓ Ⓔ   37 Ⓐ Ⓑ Ⓒ Ⓓ Ⓔ   50 Ⓐ Ⓑ Ⓒ Ⓓ Ⓔ   62 Ⓐ Ⓑ Ⓒ Ⓓ Ⓔ

12 Ⓐ Ⓑ Ⓒ Ⓓ Ⓔ   25 Ⓐ Ⓑ Ⓒ Ⓓ Ⓔ   38 Ⓐ Ⓑ Ⓒ Ⓓ Ⓔ   51 Ⓐ Ⓑ Ⓒ Ⓓ Ⓔ   63 Ⓐ Ⓑ Ⓒ Ⓓ Ⓔ

13 Ⓐ Ⓑ Ⓒ Ⓓ Ⓔ   26 Ⓐ Ⓑ Ⓒ Ⓓ Ⓔ   39 Ⓐ Ⓑ Ⓒ Ⓓ Ⓔ

Section II

64 Ⓐ Ⓑ Ⓒ Ⓓ Ⓔ   77 Ⓐ Ⓑ Ⓒ Ⓓ Ⓔ   90 Ⓐ Ⓑ Ⓒ Ⓓ Ⓔ   102 Ⓐ Ⓑ Ⓒ Ⓓ Ⓔ   114 Ⓐ Ⓑ Ⓒ Ⓓ Ⓔ

65 Ⓐ Ⓑ Ⓒ Ⓓ Ⓔ   78 Ⓐ Ⓑ Ⓒ Ⓓ Ⓔ   91 Ⓐ Ⓑ Ⓒ Ⓓ Ⓔ   103 Ⓐ Ⓑ Ⓒ Ⓓ Ⓔ   115 Ⓐ Ⓑ Ⓒ Ⓓ Ⓔ

66 Ⓐ Ⓑ Ⓒ Ⓓ Ⓔ   79 Ⓐ Ⓑ Ⓒ Ⓓ Ⓔ   92 Ⓐ Ⓑ Ⓒ Ⓓ Ⓔ   104 Ⓐ Ⓑ Ⓒ Ⓓ Ⓔ   116 Ⓐ Ⓑ Ⓒ Ⓓ Ⓔ

67 Ⓐ Ⓑ Ⓒ Ⓓ Ⓔ   80 Ⓐ Ⓑ Ⓒ Ⓓ Ⓔ   93 Ⓐ Ⓑ Ⓒ Ⓓ Ⓔ   105 Ⓐ Ⓑ Ⓒ Ⓓ Ⓔ   117 Ⓐ Ⓑ Ⓒ Ⓓ Ⓔ

68 Ⓐ Ⓑ Ⓒ Ⓓ Ⓔ   81 Ⓐ Ⓑ Ⓒ Ⓓ Ⓔ   94 Ⓐ Ⓑ Ⓒ Ⓓ Ⓔ   106 Ⓐ Ⓑ Ⓒ Ⓓ Ⓔ   118 Ⓐ Ⓑ Ⓒ Ⓓ Ⓔ

69 Ⓐ Ⓑ Ⓒ Ⓓ Ⓔ   82 Ⓐ Ⓑ Ⓒ Ⓓ Ⓔ   95 Ⓐ Ⓑ Ⓒ Ⓓ Ⓔ   107 Ⓐ Ⓑ Ⓒ Ⓓ Ⓔ   119 Ⓐ Ⓑ Ⓒ Ⓓ Ⓔ

70 Ⓐ Ⓑ Ⓒ Ⓓ Ⓔ   83 Ⓐ Ⓑ Ⓒ Ⓓ Ⓔ   96 Ⓐ Ⓑ Ⓒ Ⓓ Ⓔ   108 Ⓐ Ⓑ Ⓒ Ⓓ Ⓔ   120 Ⓐ Ⓑ Ⓒ Ⓓ Ⓔ

71 Ⓐ Ⓑ Ⓒ Ⓓ Ⓔ   84 Ⓐ Ⓑ Ⓒ Ⓓ Ⓔ   97 Ⓐ Ⓑ Ⓒ Ⓓ Ⓔ   109 Ⓐ Ⓑ Ⓒ Ⓓ Ⓔ   121 Ⓐ Ⓑ Ⓒ Ⓓ Ⓔ

72 Ⓐ Ⓑ Ⓒ Ⓓ Ⓔ   85 Ⓐ Ⓑ Ⓒ Ⓓ Ⓔ   98 Ⓐ Ⓑ Ⓒ Ⓓ Ⓔ   110 Ⓐ Ⓑ Ⓒ Ⓓ Ⓔ   122 Ⓐ Ⓑ Ⓒ Ⓓ Ⓔ

73 Ⓐ Ⓑ Ⓒ Ⓓ Ⓔ   86 Ⓐ Ⓑ Ⓒ Ⓓ Ⓔ   99 Ⓐ Ⓑ Ⓒ Ⓓ Ⓔ   111 Ⓐ Ⓑ Ⓒ Ⓓ Ⓔ   123 Ⓐ Ⓑ Ⓒ Ⓓ Ⓔ

74 Ⓐ Ⓑ Ⓒ Ⓓ Ⓔ   87 Ⓐ Ⓑ Ⓒ Ⓓ Ⓔ   100 Ⓐ Ⓑ Ⓒ Ⓓ Ⓔ   112 Ⓐ Ⓑ Ⓒ Ⓓ Ⓔ   124 Ⓐ Ⓑ Ⓒ Ⓓ Ⓔ

75 Ⓐ Ⓑ Ⓒ Ⓓ Ⓔ   88 Ⓐ Ⓑ Ⓒ Ⓓ Ⓔ   101 Ⓐ Ⓑ Ⓒ Ⓓ Ⓔ   113 Ⓐ Ⓑ Ⓒ Ⓓ Ⓔ   125 Ⓐ Ⓑ Ⓒ Ⓓ Ⓔ

76 Ⓐ Ⓑ Ⓒ Ⓓ Ⓔ   89 Ⓐ Ⓑ Ⓒ Ⓓ Ⓔ

PRACTICE EXAMINATION II

Section I

63 Questions

Time—45 minutes

Directions: For each question, choose the lettered response that best completes the statement or answers the question. Mark the letter of your choice on the answer sheet provided. When you have completed the examination, check your answers with the answer key and explanations that follow the exam.

1. Writs of Assistance were

   (A) orders given to colonists to quarter British troops.
   (B) summonses to court.
   (C) documents presented by colonial agents to Parliament.
   (D) the equivalent of cease and desist orders.
   (E) general search warrants used by customs officials.

2. The most significant provision of the Proclamation of 1763 is the one that

   (A) forbade further migration into the Ohio country.
   (B) gave England control of all areas east of the Mississippi.
   (C) provided for settlement of the Great Lakes region.
   (D) added Quebec to the British empire.
   (E) prohibited intercolonial migration.

3. The number of justices on the Supreme Court was originally determined by

   (A) *Marbury* v. *Madison.*
   (B) the Judiciary Act of 1789.
   (C) Article III of the Constitution.
   (D) executive order.
   (E) constitutional amendment.

4. A political party that arose as a result of a wave of racial and religious intolerance was the

   (A) Prohibition Party.
   (B) Anti-Masonic Party.
   (C) Liberty Party.
   (D) Know-Nothing Party.
   (E) Communist Party.

5. The Progressive movement in the United States in the early twentieth century

   (A) believed that social and economic problems could be solved without government intervention.
   (B) favored the intervention of a strong government to reach progressive goals.
   (C) believed in the theory of economic determinism to explain the abuses of industrialism.
   (D) believed in a return to the agrarian liberal theories of Thomas Jefferson.
   (E) opposed regulatory agencies to supervise business practices.

6. "But armed neutrality, it now appears, is impractical. Because submarines are in effect outlaws when used as the German submarines have been used against merchant shipping, it is impossible to defend ships against their attacks. . . . There is one choice we cannot make, we are incapable of making: we will not choose the path of submission and suffer the sacred right of our nation and our people to be ignored and violated."

The statement above is most characteristic of which of the following?

(A) The Atlantic Charter
(B) A fireside chat
(C) Woodrow Wilson's war message to Congress
(D) The "Four Freedoms" speech
(E) The Treaty of Versailles

7. The settlers at Plymouth in 1620 were

(A) Calvinists who wished to purify the Church of England.
(B) separatists who wished to leave the Church of England.
(C) Calvinists who wished to purify the Church of Rome.
(D) English Protestants in favor of religious toleration.
(E) adventurers who were looking for Virginia.

8. A list of presidents elected by a minority of the popular vote would include

(A) Theodore Roosevelt in 1900 and Taft in 1908.
(B) Harding in 1920 and Hoover in 1928.
(C) Franklin D. Roosevelt in 1944 and Eisenhower in 1952.
(D) Cleveland in 1892 and Wilson in 1912.
(E) Eisenhower in 1952 and Kennedy in 1960.

9. What aspect of constitutional law did Hamilton and Jefferson interpret differently when arguing over the constitutionality of the First National Bank?

(A) The extent of executive powers in Article II
(B) The elastic clause in Article I
(C) The system of checks and balances
(D) The guarantee of rights in the First Amendment
(E) The residual powers of the states in the Eleventh Amendment

10. "We maintain that no compensation should be given to the planters emancipating their slaves—because it would be a surrender of the great fundamental principle that man cannot hold property in man; because slavery is a crime, and therefore it is not an article to be sold . . . freeing the slave is not depriving [the owner] of property, but restoring it to the right owner; it is not wronging the master, but righting the slave—restoring him to himself."

The statement above expressed the views on emancipation held by

(A) colonization societies in the 1820s.
(B) the Democratic Party in 1860.
(C) an antislavery society in the 1830s.
(D) Jefferson in 1800.
(E) the Supreme Court majority in the Dred Scott decision of 1857.

Questions 11 and 12 are based on the following graph.

**Growth of Population
in the United States, 1870–1910**

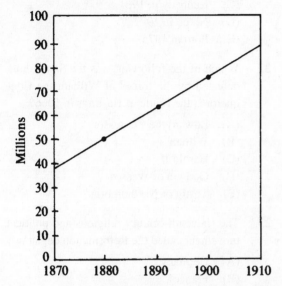

11. Between 1870 and 1910, it would be most accurate to say that the population of the United States.

    (A) more than doubled.
    (B) almost doubled.
    (C) was increased by 40 percent.
    (D) was increased by 50 percent.
    (E) was increased by 150 percent.

12. According to the information given above, which of the following statements is true?

    (A) The rate of population increase between 1870 and 1880 was approximately the same as the rate of population increase between 1890 and 1900.
    (B) The percentage of foreign-born Americans in the United States between 1900 and 1910 was greater than the percentage of foreign-born Americans in the United States from 1870 to 1880.
    (C) Between 1880 and 1890, immigration accounted for approximately 10 percent of the population.
    (D) The rate of population increase grew steadily from 1870 to 1910.
    (E) The percentage of immigrants in the United States population was greater in the 1900–10 period than in any of the decades from 1870 to 1900.

13. Americans in the post-Civil War decades who "waved the bloody shirt" were

    (A) Republicans denouncing corruption in office.
    (B) southern Democrats reviving the sectional spirit of the confederacy.
    (C) Union Army veterans claiming their pensions.
    (D) labor supporters protesting the Haymarket riot.
    (E) Republicans reviving the memory of southern Democratic disloyalty during the Civil War.

14. Which of the following groups of items are associated with corruption in government?

    (A) Dollar diplomacy—the Mann Act
    (B) Hatch Act—Comstock law
    (C) Crédit Mobilier—Teapot Dome
    (D) *Muller* v. *Oregon*—Taft-Hartley Act
    (E) Fair Labor Standards Act—granger laws

15. A common demand of labor organizations during the Jacksonian era was

    (A) the 10-hour day.
    (B) imprisonment for debt.
    (C) unemployment insurance.
    (D) literacy testing.
    (E) the open shop.

16. Which of the following restored the *status quo ante bellum?*

    (A) Treaty of Paris, 1783
    (B) Treaty of Ghent
    (C) Treaty of Guadalupe Hidalgo
    (D) Thirteenth Amendment
    (E) Reconstruction

17. The Alliance for Progress, proposed by President Kennedy in 1961, can be most accurately called an added dimension of

    (A) the Truman Doctrine.
    (B) the League of Nations.
    (C) Point Four.
    (D) the Good Neighbor policy.
    (E) Lend-Lease.

18. A symbol of the "red scare" of the 1920s was the

    (A) Scopes trial.
    (B) Hiss case.
    (C) Smith Act.
    (D) Bonus March.
    (E) Sacco-Vanzetti trial.

19. A historian studying the evolution of American conservative thought would be most interested in examining which of these periodicals?

    (A) *New Republic*
    (B) *Daedalus*
    (C) *Sewanee Review*
    (D) *National Review*
    (E) *Atlantic Monthly*

20. The $\frac{3}{5}$ Compromise of the Constitutional Convention of 1787 provided that

    (A) for purposes of representation and taxation, the votes of three free men were equal to those of five slaves.
    (B) for purposes of representation and taxation, five slaves would be counted as three free people.
    (C) the votes of $\frac{3}{5}$ of the southern states would be needed to pass any federal legislation affecting slavery.
    (D) the votes of $\frac{3}{5}$ of the southern states would be needed to pass any federal legislation affecting representation or taxation.
    (E) for purposes of taxation, the numbers of slaves in a state would not be counted once they had exceeded $\frac{3}{5}$ of the free population.

21. The first U.S. President to visit the People's Republic of China was

    (A) Truman in 1950.
    (B) Eisenhower in 1954.
    (C) Kennedy in 1961.
    (D) Nixon in 1972.
    (E) Ford in 1975.

22. Which of the following was the Saxon king defeated by the forces of William the Conqueror at the Battle of Hastings in 1066?

    (A) Edward the Confessor
    (B) William I
    (C) Harold II
    (D) Godwin of Wessex
    (E) Tostig of Northumbria

23. The sixteenth-century religious and political movement called the Reformation began in

    (A) Germany.
    (B) France.
    (C) England.
    (D) Scotland.
    (E) Spain.

24. Which of the following empires was defunct by 1700?

    (A) Ottoman
    (B) Manchu
    (C) Mogul
    (D) Byzantine
    (E) Holy Roman

25. Which of the following was a major confrontation between Rome and Carthage?

    (A) The Peloponnesian Wars
    (B) The Persian Wars
    (C) The Punic Wars
    (D) The Macedonian Invasion
    (E) The conquest of Alexander the Great

26. The term *helot* refers to a(n)

    (A) Spartan slave.
    (B) Athenian ruler.
    (C) Roman legislator.
    (D) Phoenician workman.
    (E) Babylonian priest.

27. Place the following events in the correct chronological order.

   I.   Weimar Republic
   II. Fourth Republic of France
   III. Spanish Civil War
   IV. Treaty of Versailles

   (A) I, IV, III, and II
   (B) I, IV, II, and III
   (C) IV, I, III, and II
   (D) IV, III, I, and II
   (E) III, I, IV, and II

28. Scholasticism in the Middle Ages was closely connected to the works of

   (A) Archimedes.
   (B) Plato.
   (C) Aristotle.
   (D) Horace.
   (E) Galileo.

29. The revocation of the Edict of Nantes by Louis XIV

   (A) extended religious toleration to all residents of France.
   (B) confiscated the land of the Catholic Church.
   (C) distributed land among the peasants.
   (D) ended freedom of the press.
   (E) denied religious toleration to Huguenots.

30. The French government that lasted from 1871 to 1940 was called the

   (A) Third Republic.
   (B) Fourth Republic.
   (C) First Empire.
   (D) Second Empire.
   (E) Second Republic.

31. At the Congress of Vienna in 1814, all of the following statesmen were present EXCEPT

   (A) Lord Castlereagh.
   (B) James Monroe.
   (C) Metternich.
   (D) Talleyrand.
   (E) Tsar Alexander I.

32. The Napoleonic Code was a(n)

   (A) military strategy.
   (B) style of politics.
   (C) style of etiquette.
   (D) educational policy.
   (E) legal system.

33. The medieval philosopher who fused the ideas of Aristotle with the teachings of the Christian Church was

   (A) Peter Abelard.
   (B) Thomas Aquinas.
   (C) Saint Germain.
   (D) Thomas Becket.
   (E) Thomas More.

34. The Glorious Revolution of 1688 was

   (A) a revolution without bloodshed.
   (B) a brief coup d'état characterized by widespread violence.
   (C) the beginning of the reign of the Hanoverians.
   (D) the beginning of the reign of the Stuarts.
   (E) the beginning of the English Civil Wars.

35. The American reformer William Lloyd Garrison had most in common with which of the following?

   (A) William Pitt
   (B) William Wilberforce
   (C) George Fox
   (D) Benjamin Disraeli
   (E) Lord North

36. The Jacobin Clubs of 1793 were

   (A) advocates of nationalization of private property.
   (B) executioners of priests and nobles.
   (C) auxiliaries of the Revolutionary government in Paris.
   (D) groups of French revolutionaries who emigrated to England.
   (E) politicians who wanted to make Robespierre dictator of France.

37. The preconditions for industrialization included all of the following EXCEPT

    (A) a large and mobile population with skilled, productive workers.

    (B) substantial resources and uncommitted capital.

    (C) transportation facilities to get raw materials to factories.

    (D) a social milieu favorable to innovation.

    (E) a small elite with control over most of a nation's disposable income.

38. Which of the following statements most accurately describes the Bolsheviks and the Mensheviks?

    (A) The Bolsheviks fought in World War I, while the Mensheviks went into exile.

    (B) The Bolsheviks lived in Petrograd, while the Mensheviks lived in Moscow.

    (C) The Bolsheviks and Mensheviks were two groups of Russian army officers.

    (D) The Bolsheviks and Mensheviks were two groups of Russian Marxists.

    (E) The Bolsheviks opposed the Czar, while the Mensheviks supported him.

39. Which of the following was the basic tenet of the seventeenth- and eighteenth-century religious/philosophical movement known as *Deism*?

    (A) Nature is God.

    (B) The mystical nature of God makes faith more important than reason.

    (C) Religious knowledge is accessible through the powers of reason.

    (D) True belief requires an abandonment of reason.

    (E) Strict adherence to Christian doctrine is essential for true salvation.

40. Cubism, which emerged in Paris in 1908, marked the beginning of what major art movement?

    (A) Abstract Art

    (B) Dadaism

    (C) Bauhaus

    (D) Art Deco

    (E) Surrealism

41. The major religions of Japan are

    (A) Shinto, Buddhism, and Christianity.

    (B) Buddhism, Islam, and Taoism.

    (C) Confucianism, Taoism, and Buddhism.

    (D) Confucianism, Taoism, and Shinto.

    (E) Confucianism, Taoism, and Christianity.

42. All of the following were at issue in the Seven Years' War EXCEPT whether

    (A) France or Great Britain would control the American Colonies.

    (B) France or Great Britain would control colonies in India.

    (C) Austria or Prussia would control the province of Silesia.

    (D) Great Britain or Spain would control the southern coast of North America.

    (E) Russia or Turkey would control the Dardanelles.

43. The Communists gained control of China in

    (A) 1900.

    (B) 1912.

    (C) 1939.

    (D) 1949.

    (E) 1960.

44. The purpose of the Marshall Plan was to

    (A) aid European allies during World War II.

    (B) spur European recovery after World War II.

    (C) defeat the Axis powers in the Pacific.

    (D) defeat the Communist Chinese in North Korea.

    (E) enhance the power of organized labor.

45. "In traditional times, many different forms of the language were spoken. Even if people from different regions used the same words, they might pronounce them differently or use different tones, which gave the words different meanings. A man from one city might be unable to understand the language spoken by a man of another city."

    The language described above is most likely to be

    (A) Arabic.

    (B) Japanese.

    (C) Chinese.

    (D) Russian.

    (E) Latin.

46. *Afrikaans* is the

(A) African name for European settlers.
(B) Dutch name for natives of South Africa.
(C) English name for Dutch settlers in South Africa.
(D) European name for tribal language in South Africa.
(E) language spoken by Dutch settlers in South Africa.

47. Neanderthal remains have been found in

I.   Europe.
II.   Africa.
III. Australia.

(A) II
(B) I and II
(C) I and III
(D) II and III
(E) I, II, and III

48. In which of the following countries do Muslims predominate?

(A) Korea
(B) Burma
(C) Pakistan
(D) India
(E) Thailand

49. The Boers were

(A) English settlers in South Africa.
(B) European settlers in Africa.
(C) German explorers of Africa.
(D) Dutch settlers in South Africa.
(E) Africans who immigrated to Europe.

50. The "middle passage" was the

(A) trek made by slaves from interior Africa to the coast.
(B) part of English ships reserved for captured slaves.
(C) route followed by slave trading ships between the Caribbean and North America.
(D) Atlantic crossing made by slaves from Africa to the Americas.
(E) route followed by European ships along the African coast.

51. "Going along with" the behavior, attitude, and belief of a group is

(A) integration.
(B) assimilation.
(C) conformity.
(D) transference.
(E) repression.

52. Which of the following sought to identify "the potentially fascistic individual, one whose personality structure is such as to render him particularly susceptible to anti-democratic propaganda"?

(A) Erik Erikson
(B) Theodor Adorno
(C) Karl Marx
(D) Frederick Nietzche
(E) C. Wright Mills

53. "He feels extremely hostile to others, although he contends that he is friendly and affable. He also insists that all whom he encounters are hostile and unpleasant to him."

The person described above displays the defense mechanism called

(A) projection.
(B) displacement.
(C) rationalization.
(D) identification.
(E) sublimation.

54. Which of the following characterizes a successful experiment?

(A) The experimental and control groups show the same results.
(B) The researcher manipulates all the variables.
(C) The evidence must be reproducible by others.
(D) The experiment must involve random samples.
(E) There must be at least two control groups.

55. A person experiences role conflict when
    (A) the role he learned in one status is no longer appropriate in another.
    (B) he aspires to a higher status than that which he is able to attain.
    (C) he is unable to exert influence over others.
    (D) he is unable to function day to day in a normal manner.
    (E) he dislikes his function within the family or primary group.

56. Social psychology is a field of study concerned with
    (A) the effect of group membership on the individual.
    (B) human behavior in crowds or mobs.
    (C) changes in values and attitudes over the individual's life span.
    (D) the process of learning the traditions of one's culture.
    (E) the development of personality from infancy to maturity.

57. The best example of a behavioral deviant is a(n)
    (A) person with many tattoos.
    (B) murderer.
    (C) spinster.
    (D) person with one leg.
    (E) imbecile.

58. The typology of deviance introduced by Robert K. Merton includes
    (A) mesomorph, ectomorph, endomorph.
    (B) crank, conventionalist, authoritarian.
    (C) retreatist, rebel, innovator.
    (D) neurotic, psychotic, schizophrenic.
    (E) traditional, classic, modern.

59. In a well-known experiment, psychologists frustrated young children by placing a wire fence between the children and a pile of toys. When finally allowed to play with the toys, the children smashed and destroyed them. The above reaction is an example of
    (A) displaced aggression.
    (B) absence of aggression.
    (C) dormant aggression.
    (D) rational aggression.
    (E) sustained aggression.

60. Role-playing can be most accurately described as
    (A) actual behavior while enacting a role.
    (B) pretending to be someone else.
    (C) imitating the behavior of a parent or role model.
    (D) aspiring to a higher status.
    (E) a form of deviance.

61. Reaction formation can be best described as a(n)
    (A) part of socialization.
    (B) defense mechanism.
    (C) prerequisite to accommodation.
    (D) form of behavioral deviance.
    (E) experimental procedure.

62. A social psychologist would be most likely to define *egocentrism* as
    (A) a form of aggression such as boastfulness.
    (B) inability to assume multiple roles or behavior patterns.
    (C) inability to make a clear distinction between the self and others.
    (D) lack of superego or conscience.
    (E) a state of mental health.

63. According to Ferdinand Toennies, the German sociologist, traditional society was based on a *Gemeinschaft*, or
    (A) hierarchical authority system.
    (B) large organization with many rules and regulations.
    (C) system of impersonal human relationships.
    (D) complex legal system.
    (E) community of personal relationships.

Section II

62 Questions

Time—45 minutes

Directions: For each question, choose the lettered response that best completes the statement or answers the question. Mark the letter of your choice on the answer sheet provided. When you have completed the examination, check your answers with the answer key and explanations that follow the exam.

64. Pioneer sociologist Auguste Comte called his philosophy

    (A) positivism.
    (B) capitalism.
    (C) relativism.
    (D) empiricism.
    (E) idealism.

65. Descriptive statistics can be most accurately defined as statistics

    (A) that summarize population data.
    (B) used to make generalizations based on sample data.
    (C) gathered with the intent of changing society.
    (D) that can be expected to contain large sampling errors.
    (E) that will tell us about individuals rather than groups.

66. Having an outsider mediate between two rival groups can best be called

    (A) accommodation.
    (B) reaction formation.
    (C) arbitration.
    (D) social interaction.
    (E) capitulation.

67. The average age at death prevailing in a given population is called the

    (A) average death rate.
    (B) crude death rate.
    (C) average life expectancy.
    (D) mortality curve.
    (E) fecundity rate.

68. The sex ratio of a given population is the

    (A) number of men per one hundred women.
    (B) number of women per one hundred men.
    (C) number of children born per every one hundred women.
    (D) biological maximum number of births.
    (E) same as the fertility rate.

69. Which of the following data would one be likely to learn from a population pyramid?

    (A) Rural/urban ratio of the population
    (B) Racial composition of the population
    (C) Crude birth and death rates of the population
    (D) Age and sex distribution of the population
    (E) Social stratification of the population

70. The term *demographic transition* refers to the

    (A) migration of a large number of people from a rural area to an urban area.
    (B) migration of a large number of people from an urban area to a suburban area.
    (C) movement of a large number of people into or out of a given area.
    (D) shift from a stage of great population growth to a leveling-off stage.
    (E) transformation of a middle-class urban area into a slum.

71. The social scientist examining social stratification would be LEAST interested in which of the following?

    (A) The impact of education on upward mobility
    (B) The distribution of property in a given society
    (C) Which occupations are thought to be most prestigious
    (D) The impact of race on mortality and fertility
    (E) The proportion of the national income earned by the most prosperous tenth of the society

72. The caste system of social stratification connotes all of the following EXCEPT that

    (A) caste membership is hereditary.
    (B) caste membership is permanent.
    (C) marriage within one's caste is required.
    (D) caste membership is acquired by ascription.
    (E) an individual can change caste by gaining wealth.

73. The system of social stratification most likely to be found in a modern, industrialized society is the

    (A) caste system.
    (B) class system.
    (C) slave system.
    (D) estate system.
    (E) ascribed system.

74. Karl Marx formulated his critique of capitalist society while observing conditions in

    (A) nineteenth-century England.
    (B) nineteenth-century Russia.
    (C) twentieth-century Russia.
    (D) twentieth-century Germany.
    (E) nineteenth-century Germany.

75. The term *primary group* was first used by

    (A) Charles Darwin.
    (B) Charles Horton Cooley.
    (C) Auguste Comte.
    (D) Max Weber.
    (E) Stanley G. Hall.

Questions 76 and 77 are based on the following partial table.

	MEN	WOMEN	
Upper Class	(I)	210	300
Middle Class	(II)	615	(VI)
Lower Class	(III)	(IV)	640
	970	(V)	1,925

76. Given the partial table above, what is the total number of women (V)?

    (A) 330
    (B) 970
    (C) 955
    (D) 1,000
    (E) 1,925

77. Given the partial table above, what is the total number of middle-class respondents (VI)?

    (A) 955
    (B) 970
    (C) 615
    (D) 1,000
    (E) 1,285

78. All of the following are consistent with the notion of perfect competition EXCEPT

    (A) a large number of firms.
    (B) homogeneous products.
    (C) free entry.
    (D) very few buyers.
    (E) complete mobility.

79. The theory that "bad money drives out good money" is known as

    (A) Say's Law.
    (B) Gresham's Law.
    (C) Pareto's Law.
    (D) Parkinson's Law.
    (E) the Law of Diminishing Returns.

80. Which of the following made monopolistic restraints of trade illegal and was often used to curb union practices?

    (A) Sherman Antitrust Act
    (B) Clayton Antitrust Act
    (C) Norris-LaGuardia Act
    (D) Taft-Hartley Act
    (E) Interstate Commerce Act

81. The tactic of purchasing the securities of several companies in order to gain control of the companies was *first* a policy of

   (A) holding companies.
   (B) partnerships.
   (C) unions.
   (D) mergers.
   (E) the federal government.

Questions 82–84 are based on the following table.

U.S. FAMILIES BY INCOME LEVEL (FICTITIOUS)

INCOME LEVEL	MILLIONS OF FAMILIES	% OF FAMILIES
Under $15,000	7.0	14.3
Between $15,000 and $20,000	6.8	13.9
Between $20,000 and $25,000	8.7	17.8
Between $25,000 and $30,000	11.9	24.4
Between $30,000 and $35,000	10.0	20.4
$35,000 or over	4.5	9.2
	48.9	100 %

82. Most American families are in the broad middle class, earning annual incomes between $20,000 and $35,000. According to the table, the percentage of American families in this group is about

   (A) 51 percent.
   (B) 56 percent.
   (C) 63 percent.
   (D) 72 percent.
   (E) 76 percent.

83. According to the table, about what percentage of American families earn $20,000 a year or less?

   (A) 6.8 percent
   (B) 13.8 percent
   (C) 14.3 percent
   (D) 20 percent
   (E) 28.2 percent

84. The table illustrates

   (A) disposable personal income.
   (B) real income.
   (C) functional distribution of wages.
   (D) the consumer index.
   (E) personal income distribution.

85. An economic conservative would be likely to advocate

   (A) increased government protection of the elderly.
   (B) the abolition of private property.
   (C) government control over natural resources.
   (D) decreased government intervention in the economy.
   (E) government leadership in economic development.

Questions 86–88 are based on the following diagram.

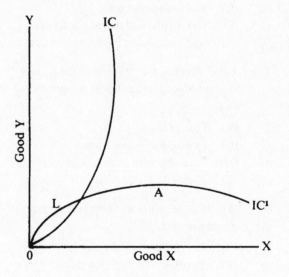

86. If curve IC represents the income consumption curve, then we can conclude that

   (A) only X is an inferior good.
   (B) only Y is an inferior good.
   (C) both X and Y are inferior goods.
   (D) X is a superior good.
   (E) no conclusions are possible.

87. If we assume that curve IC^1 is the income consumption curve, it can be concluded that

    (A) only Y is an inferior good.
    (B) neither X nor Y is an inferior good.
    (C) only X is an inferior good.
    (D) X is inferior but Y is a superior good.
    (E) both X and Y are inferior goods.

88. On curve IC^1, there is a negative income effect

    (A) beyond point L.
    (B) between points O and L.
    (C) beyond point A.
    (D) between L and A only.
    (E) at all points from O to A.

89. In his veto message against rechartering the Second Bank of the United States, Andrew Jackson gave all of the following objections to the bank EXCEPT that it

    (A) was a monopoly.
    (B) encouraged speculation.
    (C) was unconstitutional.
    (D) was involved in partisan politics.
    (E) was undesirable for the government.

90. The concept of the "tyranny of the majority" was introduced into political thought by

    (A) James Bryce.
    (B) James Otis.
    (C) James MacGregor Burns.
    (D) James Monroe.
    (E) Alexis de Tocqueville.

91. Which of the following is the best example of *direct* democracy?

    (A) The UN General Assembly
    (B) The House of Representatives
    (C) The House of Commons
    (D) The town meeting
    (E) The state legislature

92. A coup d'état may be best described as

    (A) a form of guerrilla war.
    (B) a sudden overthrow of a regime.
    (C) any measure that starts a war, such as a blockade.
    (D) a legislative act that starts a war.
    (E) the execution of a former ruler.

93. During the early twentieth century, *Dollar Diplomacy* referred specifically to

    (A) American policy toward Western Europe.
    (B) American policy toward Latin America.
    (C) American policy toward China.
    (D) the appointment of businessmen to high positions in the diplomatic corps.
    (E) the efforts of multinational corporations to affect the nature of American foreign policy.

94. Although only Congress can declare war, the president, as commander in chief, can order the armed forces to protect American interests. On which of the following occasions did such a presidential action lead to war?

    I. When President Polk ordered the occupation of the territory between the Nueces River and the Rio Grande
    II. When President McKinley dispatched the battleship *Maine* to the Caribbean
    III. When President Wilson sent General Pershing into Mexico
    IV. When President Wilson ordered the occupation of Vera Cruz

    (A) I, II, III, and IV
    (B) I and II
    (C) I, II, and IV
    (D) II and IV
    (E) I only

95. A device that makes it possible for voters to approve or reject a measure that has been passed by the legislature is called a(n)

    (A) direct initiative.
    (B) indirect initiative.
    (C) referendum.
    (D) recall.
    (E) short ballot.

96. In which of the following presidential elections did the victor win the electoral college vote without winning the popular vote?

    I.   Lincoln versus Douglas
    II.   Hayes versus Tilden
    III. Harrison versus Cleveland
    IV. Nixon versus Humphrey

    (A) I, II, III, and IV
    (B) II, III, and IV
    (C) II and IV
    (D) II and III
    (E) I and II

97. According to the U.S. Constitution, revenue bills must originate with

    (A) the House of Representatives.
    (B) the Senate.
    (C) either house of Congress.
    (D) the administration.
    (E) the House Ways and Means Committee.

98. Article I of the U.S. Constitution includes which of the following provisions for the election of Senators?

    I.   Each state shall have only two senators.
    II.   Senators shall be directly elected by the people of the states.
    III. Senators shall be elected every six years in a staggered system so that only a minority of senators will be newly elected.
    IV. Senators must live in the states they are chosen to represent at the time the election is held.

    (A) I only
    (B) I, II, and III
    (C) I, II, III, and IV
    (D) I, III, and IV
    (E) I and IV

99. Which of the following statements most accurately describes the function of the "elastic clause" of the Constitution?

    (A) It gives Congress greater powers than those explicitly delegated to it.
    (B) It gives the president authority to affect the course of Congressional legislation.
    (C) It prevents Congress from enacting bills of attainder or *ex post facto* laws.
    (D) It gives the Senate the power to approve or reject treaties negotiated by the president.
    (E) It reserves certain powers to the states.

100. The Constitution prohibits the states from all of the following EXCEPT

    (A) entering into treaties or alliances with other nations.
    (B) coining money or printing paper money.
    (C) levying import taxes.
    (D) granting titles of nobility.
    (E) organizing militia.

101. If, after ten days, the president either fails to approve a bill or to return it to the house of origin with his objections, which of the following occurs?

    (A) The bill automatically becomes law, under the ten-day rule.
    (B) The bill is automatically rejected, under the ten-day rule.
    (C) The bill is automatically rejected, under the pocket veto.
    (D) Congress must assume the bill has been vetoed and act accordingly.
    (E) The bill is returned to the conference committee for revision.

102. Which of the following departments of the executive branch has been most recently established?

    (A) State Department
    (B) Department of the Interior
    (C) Department of Education
    (D) Department of Housing and Urban Development
    (E) Department of Labor

103. A major significance of the *Marbury* v. *Madison* decision of 1803 was that it

    (A) reduced the power of the Supreme Court.
    (B) established a federal judiciary system.
    (C) declared an act of Congress to be unconstitutional.
    (D) enabled Madison to become secretary of state.
    (E) legalized the use of a writ of mandamus.

104. The "Court packing" bill was a(n)

    (A) attempt by President Jefferson to insult John Marshall.
    (B) attempt by President Jackson to limit the power of the Supreme Court.
    (C) attempt by President Roosevelt to enlarge the Supreme Court.
    (D) attempt by President Nixon to make appointments to the Supreme Court.
    (E) proposal of the Warren Court for judicial reform.

105. The fundamental processes by which the earth's climate is formed are radiation and absorption of heat energy. Which of the following statements is NOT true of solar energy?

    (A) The sun's rays strike the earth more nearly vertically at lower latitudes.
    (B) A given amount of solar energy is concentrated on smaller surface areas at lower latitudes than at higher latitudes.
    (C) Abundant cloud cover near many areas of the equator reduces the amount of solar radiation reaching the earth's surface.
    (D) Solar rays pass through a smaller thickness of absorbing and reflecting atmosphere before reaching the surface in lower latitudes than in higher latitudes.
    (E) If we omit the effects of cloud cover, we can say that the higher the latitude of a region, the more solar energy it receives annually.

106. Air heated by intense surface radiation can rise rapidly, cool rapidly, then produce a heavy downpour of rain. This type of precipitation is called

    (A) orographic precipitation.
    (B) cyclonic precipitation.
    (C) frontal precipitation.
    (D) convectional precipitation.
    (E) equatorial precipitation.

107. A *steppe* climate is characterized by

    (A) a long, dramatically cold winter.
    (B) arid or semiarid conditions.
    (C) a short or absent dry season.
    (D) mild to hot summers and mild to cold winters.
    (E) a rainy climate with a pronounced dry season.

108. Which of the following is a human geographic process?

    (A) Inertia
    (B) Innovation
    (C) Natural-resource exploitation
    (D) Migration
    (E) All of the above

109. The total area of the earth's surface is approximately (in square miles)

    (A) 197 million square miles.
    (B) 100 million square miles.
    (C) 57 million square miles.
    (D) 11 million square miles.
    (E) 8 million square miles.

110. Geographical areas of low or absent population make up what portion of the earth's land surface?

    (A) Approximately 10 percent
    (B) Approximately 25 percent
    (C) Approximately 50 percent
    (D) Approximately 75 percent
    (E) Approximately 90 percent

111. In economic terms, the most important internal waterway in Russia is the

    (A) Don River.
    (B) Ural River.
    (C) Volga River.
    (D) Ob River.
    (E) Dnieper River.

112. The interior of Australia is largely comprised of

    (A) steppes and desert.
    (B) savannah and highlands.
    (C) humid tropics and lowlands.
    (D) isolated mountain ranges and grasslands.
    (E) taiga and salt flats.

113. In which of the following countries do the pastoral industries play an important role in the economy?

    (A) France
    (B) Germany
    (C) New Zealand
    (D) Canada
    (E) Russia

114. The ancient rock mass underlying most of eastern and central Canada is called the

    (A) St. Lawrence Formation.
    (B) Newfoundland Outcrop.
    (C) Mesabi Range.
    (D) Canadian Shield.
    (E) Ontario Massif.

115. Which of the following best describes the economic geography of Java?

    (A) Heavily populated and agriculturalized
    (B) Rural with scattered mining settlements
    (C) Prairie devoted to large-scale farming
    (D) Forest wilderness inhabited by hunter-gatherers
    (E) Too mountainous for agriculture

116. Greenland is politically part of which of the following nations?

    (A) Great Britain
    (B) Finland
    (C) Norway
    (D) Denmark
    (E) Holland

117. What is a *toponym*?

    (A) A value used to substitute for a population figure in a census formula
    (B) A place name
    (C) A geologic formation resulting from wind erosion
    (D) An indicator of longitude
    (E) An indicator of latitude

118. A patrilineal society is one in which

    (A) the family resides in the home of the father's relatives.
    (B) descent and inheritance is determined through the male line.
    (C) there is a ruling class of high social rank, usually a hereditary aristocracy.
    (D) the father of a family has total authority over its members.
    (E) church and state are united.

119. The family formed by a polygamous marriage is called a(n)

    (A) extended conjugal family.
    (B) restricted conjugal family.
    (C) extended consanguineal family.
    (D) restricted consanguineal family.
    (E) matrilocal family.

120. Which of the following factors of social evolution lead most directly to the development of political centralization within a culture?

    (A) The ability to craft metal
    (B) The development of the loom
    (C) The shift to an agrarian/settlement-based economy
    (D) A shift to a matrilineal kinship system
    (E) The introduction of writing

121. The term *relocation diffusion* describes what cultural phenomenon?

    (A) The disappearance of customs/traditions/characteristics following a people's migration
    (B) The spread of customs/traditions/characteristics that takes place via a people's migration
    (C) The acceptance of an immigrant population by the native population
    (D) The rejection of an immigrant population by the native population
    (E) An end to migration/immigration in a given region

122. Of the following, which is considered by social anthropologists an *ethnic* rather than a *universalizing* religion?

    (A) Christianity
    (B) Buddhism
    (C) Islam
    (D) Hinduism
    (E) None of the above

123. The centralization of social systems rarely entails which of the following societal changes?

    (A) Social stratification
    (B) The development of ecclesiastical religious systems
    (C) The prohibition of shamanism or family-centered religious observances
    (D) The rise of military fortification
    (E) An increase in moral and political rule-making

124. The pioneering anthropologist who studied the culture of Samoa and wrote *Coming of Age in Samoa* was

    (A) Franz Boas.
    (B) Margaret Mead.
    (C) Alfred Kroeber.
    (D) Margaret Bourke-White.
    (E) Ruth Benedict.

125. The noted anthropologist who studied the myths of primitive societies and wrote *Tristes Tropiques* was

    (A) Franz Boas.
    (B) Mary Leakey.
    (C) Michel Foucault.
    (D) Claude Levi-Strauss.
    (E) Regis Debray.

End of Practice Examination II

Answer Key

Section I

1.	E	14.	C	27.	C	40.	A	52.	B
2.	A	15.	A	28.	C	41.	A	53.	A
3.	B	16.	B	29.	E	42.	E	54.	C
4.	D	17.	D	30.	A	43.	D	55.	A
5.	B	18.	E	31.	B	44.	B	56.	A
6.	C	19.	D	32.	E	45.	C	57.	B
7.	B	20.	B	33.	B	46.	E	58.	C
8.	D	21.	D	34.	A	47.	B	59.	A
9.	B	22.	C	35.	B	48.	C	60.	A
10.	C	23.	A	36.	C	49.	D	61.	B
11.	A	24.	D	37.	E	50.	D	62.	C
12.	A	25.	C	38.	D	51.	C	63.	E
13.	E	26.	A	39.	C				

Section II

64.	A	77.	A	90.	E	102.	C	114.	D
65.	A	78.	D	91.	D	103.	C	115.	A
66.	C	79.	B	92.	B	104.	C	116.	D
67.	C	80.	A	93.	B	105.	E	117.	B
68.	A	81.	A	94.	B	106.	D	118.	B
69.	D	82.	C	95.	C	107.	B	119.	A
70.	D	83.	E	96.	D	108.	E	120.	C
71.	D	84.	E	97.	A	109.	A	121.	B
72.	E	85.	D	98.	D	110.	D	122.	D
73.	B	86.	A	99.	A	111.	C	123.	C
74.	A	87.	A	100.	E	112.	A	124.	B
75.	B	88.	C	101.	A	113.	C	125.	D
76.	C	89.	B						

Explanatory Answers

Section I

1. **The correct answer is (E).** The Writ of Assistance was a search warrant giving English officials extensive powers of entry, search, and seizure. Customs officers were granted Writs of Assistance under the Navigation Acts to prevent smuggling. The colonists considered them illegal.

2. **The correct answer is (A).** The Proclamation of 1763 prohibited settlement of the land recently acquired from France that lay west of the Allegheny mountains.

3. **The correct answer is (B).** The Judiciary Act of 1789 established a Supreme Court of six justices. It also established a federal court system of three circuit courts and thirteen district courts.

4. **The correct answer is (D).** The Know-Nothing Party of the 1850s was an antiforeign, anti-Catholic response to the massive immigration of that era. Initially a secret nativist fraternity, the Know-Nothings entered politics as the American Party in 1855 and 1856.

5. **The correct answer is (B).** The Progressives believed that only government and the courts could enforce their reforms. They supported regulatory agencies to supervise business practices.

6. **The correct answer is (C).** The quotation is from President Wilson's war message to Congress in April 1917. After American ships had been torpedoed by German U-boats, Wilson reversed his neutral position and urged Congress to declare war on Germany.

7. **The correct answer is (B).** The Pilgrims who landed at Plymouth in 1620 were separatists who considered the Church of England beyond redemption and wanted to leave it. The Puritans, who arrived at Massachusetts Bay in 1630, wished to purify the Church of England. Religious toleration was not a goal of either group, nor was the purification of the Church of Rome. The settlers at Plymouth cannot be considered adventurers. It is true, however, that the Mayflower was originally bound for land held by the Virginia Company.

8. **The correct answer is (D).** In 1892, Cleveland won a plurality of the popular vote, defeating the Republican candidate, Harrison, and the Populist candidate, Weaver. In 1912, there were also three major candidates—Taft for the Republicans, Wilson for the Democrats, and Theodore Roosevelt for the Progressives. Wilson won a plurality of the popular vote.

9. **The correct answer is (B).** The elastic clause in Article I, section 8, gives the national government the power to "make all laws which shall be necessary and proper for carrying into execution the foregoing powers." Hamilton, favoring a broad interpretation of this clause, claimed that the establishment of a national bank was "necessary and proper," but Jefferson, favoring a strict interpretation, argued that it was not and that the enumerated powers could be executed without a national bank.

10. **The correct answer is (C).** The quotation is from an antislavery convention declaration of 1833, written by William Lloyd Garrison. Such a strong statement against slavery and in favor of uncompensated emancipation is not likely to have been made by any of the other answer choices.

11. **The correct answer is (A).** Between 1870 and 1910, the population of the United States rose from almost 40 million to approximately 90 million, or more than doubled.

12. **The correct answer is (A).** From 1870 to 1880, the population rose from about 40 million to about 50 million, for about a 25 percent rate of population increase. From 1890 to 1900, the population rose from about 60 million to about 75 million, with again approximately a 25 percent rate of population increase. The rate of population increase did not grow steadily, as suggested in choice (D). Choices (B), (C), and (E) cannot be supported by the information provided in the graph.

13. **The correct answer is (E).** "Bloody shirt" tactics were used by Republican politicians in

the post-Civil War decades to mobilize patriotic sentiment for their party's advantage by pointing to southern Democratic support for slavery and by blaming the Civil War on the Democratic Party.

14. **The correct answer is (C).** The Crédit Mobilier was a construction company involved in a major scandal over the building of the Union Pacific Railroad during the Grant administration. During Harding's administration, a scandal arose over the leases of naval oil reserves at Teapot Dome, Wyoming.

15. **The correct answer is (A).** Among the demands of workingmen during the Jacksonian era were the 10-hour day, education for their children, and an end to imprisonment for debt.

16. **The correct answer is (B).** The Treaty of Ghent in 1814 ended the war of 1812 without providing for any changes of territory, thus returning the situation to what it had been before the war began.

17. **The correct answer is (D).** The Alliance for Progress, a program of economic assistance to Latin America, can be most accurately called an added dimension of President Franklin D. Roosevelt's Good Neighbor policy toward Latin America, which renounced the right of U.S. intervention and sought to promote economic ties.

18. **The correct answer is (E).** Sacco and Vanzetti, Italian immigrants known for their anarchist views, were tried and convicted for murder and robbery in a celebrated trial of 1921 and were executed in 1927. Their trial raised doubts as to their guilt and as to whether they were being tried for their unpopular political views. To many, the trial symbolized the nativism, conservatism, and hostility to leftists that characterized public life in the 1920s.

19. **The correct answer is (D).** The *National Review,* edited by William F. Buckley, is the only one of the answer choices that can be considered a repository of conservative thought.

20. **The correct answer is (B).** The $\frac{3}{5}$ Compromise provided that five slaves would be con-

sidered as three free people in determining the representation of the states in the House of Representatives and also for apportioning taxes. This compromise was a concession to the southern states.

21. **The correct answer is (D).** In 1972, President Nixon made a much-publicized trip to mainland China, initiating the opening of diplomatic relations with Communist China. Since the Communists gained control of China in 1949, the United States had maintained relations only with the Nationalist Chinese who had fled the mainland. Formal diplomatic relations were finally established between the United States and the People's Republic of China on January 1, 1979.

22. **The correct answer is (C).** Harold II, son of Edward the Confessor, was the last of the Saxon kings.

23. **The correct answer is (A).** The Reformation began in Germany in 1517 when Martin Luther protested the sale of indulgences by the Roman Catholic Church.

24. **The correct answer is (D).** The Ottoman Turks conquered Constantinople and ended the Byzantine empire in 1453. The other empires still existed in 1700.

25. **The correct answer is (C).** Rome waged three wars against Carthage, 264–41, 218–01, and 149–46 B.C.E. Carthage was defeated and annexed at the end of the Third Punic War.

26. **The correct answer is (A).** The Spartans had a society of three classes. Slaves were called *helots.*

27. **The correct answer is (C).** The Treaty of Versailles was signed in 1919; the Weimar Republic lasted from 1919–1933; the Spanish Civil War was fought from 1936–1939; and the Fourth Republic of France existed from 1947–1958.

28. **The correct answer is (C).** The works of Aristotle were available in Europe by the beginning of the thirteenth century. A new edition of Aristotle's works, edited by Thomas Aquinas, made the Greek scholar's ideas the basis of scholastic philosophy.

29. **The correct answer is (E).** The Edict of Nantes in 1598 extended religious toleration to the Huguenots, who were French Protestants. The revocation of the Edict in 1685 forced about one million French Protestants either to leave France or to convert to Catholicism. About four fifths of the Huguenots left France.

30. **The correct answer is (A).** The Third Republic was established after the German defeat of France in the Franco-Prussian War. It lasted longer than any French regime since 1789. The Fourth Republic, similar in form to the Third, was not established until after World War II.

31. **The correct answer is (B).** The United States was not a participant in the Congress of Vienna, organized to restore stability to Europe. The leading powers were Austria, Great Britain, Russia, Prussia, and France.

32. **The correct answer is (E).** The Napoleonic Code, derived from Roman law, went into effect in 1805 and remained a lasting monument to Napoleonic rule. Its five sections covered all areas of civil law, from domestic relations to property rights and commercial life.

33. **The correct answer is (B).** An edition of Aristotle's works, edited by Aquinas, made the Greek philosopher's ideas the foundation of scholasticism. Aquinas harmonized the teachings of Aristotle with those of Christianity.

34. **The correct answer is (A).** In 1688, William and Mary, of the Dutch House of Orange, ascended the English throne upon invitation of the gentry who were opposed to the king. Their predecessor, James II, who had encouraged Catholicism, fled to exile in France. The Revolution occurred without violence or war and assured England of Protestant monarchs.

35. **The correct answer is (B).** Wilberforce was a prominent British reformer who agitated for the abolition of the slave trade and of slavery.

36. **The correct answer is (C).** The Jacobin Clubs of 1793 supported the National Convention in Paris. Although the clubs endorsed Robespierre, they rejected the idea of dictatorship by any one person.

37. **The correct answer is (E).** One of the preconditions for industrialization is widespread demand for mass-produced goods. If only a small portion of the population has purchasing power, the economy will produce only a small quantity of expensive goods.

38. **The correct answer is (D).** The Social Democratic Party, formed by Russian Marxists in 1898, broke into two groups at the party's Second Congress. The Bolsheviks (the majority) and the Mensheviks (the minority) were contending factions of Russian Marxists.

39. **The correct answer is (C).** Deism was a rationalist religious movement that supported the idea that each individual inherently holds religious knowledge or can acquire it through reasoning; the movement rejected the strict adherence to the supernatural elements of major religions.

40. **The correct answer is (A).** Cubism, though a short-lived artistic movement, was the first revolt against sentimentalism and naturalism in art and marked the way for the later emergence of abstract art.

41. **The correct answer is (A).** Shinto is the chief religion of Japan. Buddhism was introduced in 552 and Christianity in 1549. The other options cannot be considered major Japanese religions. Taoism is distinctively Chinese, as are the beliefs of Confucius, although these are not considered a religion. Islam is not significant in Japan.

42. **The correct answer is (E).** Neither Russia nor Turkey was involved in the Seven Years' War.

43. **The correct answer is (D).** War between Chinese Nationalists and Communists ended in 1949 when Communist armies took over Peking and made it the capital of the People's Republic of China. The Chinese Nationalists established their capital in Taipei, on the island of Taiwan.

44. **The correct answer is (B).** Congress approved the Marshall Plan in 1948 to spur European recovery. The four-year plan provided extensive financial aid to European countries through loans and grants and helped them

to surmount the economic devastation of World War II.

45. **The correct answer is (C).** In traditional China, words were spoken in different manners in different regions. Since the written language was graphic, or made up of symbols, rather than phonetic, it could be understood by literate people all over China. But the spoken language varied according to region because of differences in pronunciation and intonation.

46. **The correct answer is (E).** Those of Dutch background in South Africa speak Afrikaans, a Germanic language derived from seventeenth-century Dutch.

47. **The correct answer is (B).** Remains of the hominids called Neanderthals have been found in Europe, Africa, and Asia.

48. **The correct answer is (C).** Pakistan was partitioned from India in 1947 and became an independent Muslim nation. The principal religion of India is Hinduism.

49. **The correct answer is (D).** *Boers* refers to Dutch settlers who began to come to South Africa in the seventeenth century. Conflict between British and Dutch settlers in South Africa resulted in the Boer War of 1899–1902.

50. **The correct answer is (D).** The "middle passage," a part of the African's journey from freedom to slavery, was the long, traumatic, and often deadly transatlantic sea voyage. After being captured and taken to the west coast of Africa, new slaves spent several months crammed together in the hold of a ship en route to the Americas. A high proportion of slaves died during the crossing.

51. **The correct answer is (C).** Transference and repression are psychological defense mechanisms. Choices (A) and (B) are inappropriate.

52. **The correct answer is (B).** Adorno, in *The Authoritarian Personality* (1950), described and labeled personality types susceptible to participation in fascist movements. His categories included the stereotyper, the conventionalist, the authoritarian, the rebel-psychopath, the crank, and the manipulator.

53. **The correct answer is (A).** Projection is the assignment to others of urges and wishes that are repudiated by the ego. In projection, the person attributes his own feelings to others. In this case, a hostile person attributes his feelings of hostility to others.

54. **The correct answer is (C).** If the evidence cannot be reproduced by other researchers, the experiment has little validity.

55. **The correct answer is (A).** Role conflict occurs when a person must adjust to a new role, for instance, when a professional woman must suddenly adjust to a subservient role of wife, cook, and homemaker. A popular high school senior or "big shot" might experience role conflict when he becomes an obscure and unimportant freshman at college. These examples are suggested by Denisoff and Wahrman, *An Introduction to Sociology* (1975).

56. **The correct answer is (A).** Choice (D) describes the process of socialization; choice (E) describes developmental psychology. The other answers are inappropriate.

57. **The correct answer is (B).** A *behavioral* deviant is believed to be harmful to the society or to individuals within it. The other answer options illustrate *concrete* deviance, or statistically unusual characteristics.

58. **The correct answer is (C).** Merton's categories of deviance are retreatist, rebel, ritualist, conformist, and innovator.

59. **The correct answer is (A).** The children did not attack the psychologists who caused their frustration but "displaced" their aggression to the toys, a "substitute target."

60. **The correct answer is (A).** Role-playing is the actual behavior an individual engages in while enacting a role, such as mother, teacher, or salesman.

61. **The correct answer is (B).** The defense mechanism of reaction formation is the development of a behavioral tendency that is in direct opposition to a repressed impulse.

62. **The correct answer is (C).** Egocentrism, an inability to make a clear distinction between the self and others, is characteristic of a very young child. Adolescent egocentrism takes the form of a preoccupation with the self. In common usage, *egocentric* means self-centered.

63. **The correct answer is (E).** Toennies described two types of relationships and the societies based upon them. *Gemeinschaft* ("community") means that people are bound to each other by personal ties, kinship, and custom. Industrialization tended to bring about a different condition, *Gesellschaft* ("society"), wherein people deal with each other impersonally.

Section II

64. **The correct answer is (A).** Comte used the term *positivism* to describe his philosophy because the system he presented, he contended, was based on "positive" facts or phenomena rather than on speculation.

65. **The correct answer is (A).** Choice (B) describes inferential statistics.

66. **The correct answer is (C).** Arbitration is the practice of having an outsider negotiate a solution for two groups or individuals who are in dispute.

67. **The correct answer is (C).** The average life expectancy is the number of years lived, on the average, by each member of a given population.

68. **The correct answer is (A).** The sex ratio is the number of males per one hundred females.

69. **The correct answer is (D).** A population pyramid displays the age and sex distribution of the population.

70. **The correct answer is (D).** *Demographic transition* refers to the shift from a stage of great population growth, characterized by high mortality and fertility, to a leveling-off period, characterized by falling mortality, and subsequently to a period in which fertility falls as well. The transition describes population development from premodern to modern times.

71. **The correct answer is (D).** The researcher examining social stratification is interested in the distribution of power, property, and prestige within a society. These factors are mentioned in all answer options except choice (D).

72. **The correct answer is (E).** A caste system is a hierarchy of endogamous divisions, which means that people are required to choose marriage partners from the same division or caste. Caste membership is hereditary and permanent. It is "ascribed" in that it is determined by forces that an individual is unable to change.

73. **The correct answer is (B).** The class system of social stratification characterizes industrial society.

74. **The correct answer is (A).** Marx (1818–1883) went into exile from Germany in 1845 and lived in France and then England, where *Das Kapital* was written. This massive work became the foundation of international socialism.

75. **The correct answer is (B).** Charles Horton Cooley, one of the first American sociologists, introduced the concept of the primary group in his study of *Social Organization* in 1909.

76. **The correct answer is (C).** The figures in the column on the far right may be presumed to represent totals. The total number of respondents (1,925) minus the total number of men (970) equals 955, the total number of women (V).

77. **The correct answer is (A).** $1,925 - (330 + 640) = 955$. Total respondents – (total upper-class respondents + total lower-class respondents) = total middle-class respondents.

78. **The correct answer is (D).** The market condition of perfect competition refers to one in which many sellers compete against each other, many buyers contend with each other, and no single buyer or seller can significantly affect market price. Under the market condition of perfect competition, products are "homogeneous" because it is impossible to distinguish the goods of one producer from those of another. All producers have perfect mobility, and everyone can enter the field of production.

79. **The correct answer is (B).** Gresham's law applies under a monetary system of bimetallism, in which two metals are coined in fixed ration to each other and circulate side by side. Gresham's law is that cheap (or bad) money drives good (or dear) money out of circulation. The result is that the more expensive metal disappears from circulation.

80. **The correct answer is (A).** The Sherman Act of 1890 made monopolistic restraint of trade illegal. In 1908 the Supreme Court, in the Danbury Hatters' case, ruled a union boycott in violation of the law. The Sherman Act was subsequently used against union activities.

81. **The correct answer is (A).** A holding company is a corporation that owns the stock of other companies. This form of organization rose to prominence in the 1890s.

82. **The correct answer is (C).** $17.8 + 24.4 + 20.4 = 62.6$ percent or about 63 percent.

83. **The correct answer is (E).** $14.3 + 13.9 = 28.2$ percent of families with earnings of $20,000 a year or under.

84. **The correct answer is (E).** Disposable personal income is personal income minus personal income tax. Real income refers to the consumer's ability to buy goods and services. The table is not a consumer index, and it refers to income, not wages.

85. **The correct answer is (D).** An economic conservative would be more likely to advocate a reduction of government's role in the economy than any increase of government activism or leadership. It is even less likely that a conservative would advocate abolition of private property.

86. **The correct answer is (A).** If when a consumer's income increases beyond a certain level, the consumer purchases less of a certain good, that good is an inferior good.

87. **The correct answer is (A).** As income increases beyond a certain level, less and less of Good Y is purchased.

88. **The correct answer is (C).** Point A is the income level at which purchases of Good Y begin to decrease.

89. **The correct answer is (B).** Jackson attacked the bank mainly as a monopoly and asserted that it was unconstitutional. He did not accuse the bank of encouraging speculation in the bank veto message to Congress. On the contrary, Jacksonians tended to object to the bank because it restricted credit and speculation.

90. **The correct answer is (E).** In *Democracy in America* (1835), Tocqueville, a young French jurist, contended that the "tyranny of the majority" was a potentially dangerous aspect of democratic government. He feared that under a political system in which "majority rules," there would be inadequate safeguards for minority rights. Tocqueville's observations were based on a tour of the United States in 1831–32.

91. **The correct answer is (D).** Under direct democracy, citizens represent themselves. The New England town meeting, where all who attend can speak and vote, is a prime example. The other answer options all describe some form of representative government.

92. **The correct answer is (B).** *Coup d' état* (or "stroke of state") refers to the sudden overthrow of a government or regime, often by military means, and its replacement with another. Napoleon provided a good example of a coup d' état when he overthrew the French Directory in 1799 and established himself as the head of the French government.

93. **The correct answer is (B).** Dollar Diplomacy was the U.S. policy, in the first quarter of the twentieth century, of active intervention in the affairs of Latin America. The goal of the policy was to promote and protect American trade and investments. During the 1930s, it was replaced by the Good Neighbor policy, which was amicable and noninterventionist.

94. **The correct answer is (B).** General Taylor's occupation of the disputed territory between the Nueces River and the Rio Grande in 1846 led to the Mexican War. McKinley's dispatching of the *Maine* to the Caribbean in 1898 led to the Spanish-American War, which started after the *Maine* was blown up and sunk.

95. **The correct answer is (C).** The referendum is in use in almost all states. Propositions for amendments to state constitutions are often approved in this manner.

96. **The correct answer is (D).** Republican candidate Hayes defeated Democrat Tilden in 1876 by one electoral vote. The popular vote gave Tilden a majority. Republican Harrison defeated Democrat Cleveland in 1888 by an electoral college vote of 233 to 168. Cleveland won the popular vote by about 90,000. He defeated Harrison in the next election.

97. **The correct answer is (A).** Article I, section 7, provides that revenue bills must originate with the House of Representatives. The placing of this power with the lower house was a British tradition. The Senate, of course, may virtually rewrite revenue bills by adding amendments to them.

98. **The correct answer is (D).** The Seventeenth Amendment to the Constitution, adopted in 1913, provides for the direct election of senators. The framers of the Constitution who wrote Article I expected that senators would be chosen by state legislatures.

99. **The correct answer is (A).** The elastic clause of Article I, section 8, states that Congress has the power "to make all laws which shall be necessary and proper for carrying into execution the foregoing powers." The clause, interpreted broadly, can be used to stretch the powers of Congress.

100. **The correct answer is (E).** Article I, section 10, of the Constitution prohibits the states from entering into treaties or alliances, coining or printing money, levying import taxes, or granting titles of nobility. Section 7 of Article I reserves to the states the authority to train the militia.

101. **The correct answer is (A).** If, however, Congress adjourns during the ten-day period, then the bill is automatically killed. This is called a pocket veto.

102. **The correct answer is (C).** The Department of Education was established in 1980. Its functions were formerly performed by the Department of Health, Education, and Welfare. When the new department was established, the old one was renamed the Department of Health and Human Services. The Department of Housing and Urban Development, the next youngest of the answer choices, was established in 1965.

103. **The correct answer is (C).** The 1803 decision, a major accomplishment of the Marshall court, established the Supreme Court's power of judicial review—that is, the authority to determine the constitutionality of legislation and to invalidate laws that are unconstitutional. The decision greatly enhanced the Supreme Court's powers.

104. **The correct answer is (C).** The "Court packing" bill of 1936, initiated by President Roosevelt, proposed the appointment of another Supreme Court justice for each justice then on the Court who reached the age of 70. The maximum number of justices would be fifteen. The bill, if enacted, would have given the president the power to pack the Court with loyal Democrats and prevent it from rejecting New Deal legislation. The measure was defeated in Congress.

105. **The correct answer is (E).** Lower latitudes receive more direct and more concentrated levels of solar energy than do higher latitudes.

106. **The correct answer is (D).** The question describes convectional precipitation. Orographic precipitation is mountain-associated; cyclonic or frontal precipitation is produced when different air masses come into contact via traveling low-pressure cells.

107. **The correct answer is (B).** Steppe climates are arid or semiarid, treeless, and often desert-like climates and are typical of what is known as the "Dry World."

108. **The correct answer is (E).** All of the listed items are processes of human geography.

109. **The correct answer is (A).** The earth's surface occupies a total of 197 million square miles; of that, land surface occupies 57.4 million square miles.

110. **The correct answer is (D).** Approximately $\frac{3}{4}$ of the world's land surface is unpopulated or sparsely populated.

111. **The correct answer is (C).** The Volga is Russia's most important waterway.

112. **The correct answer is (A).** Australia's interior is a large desert surrounded by a wide band of grassland steppes.

113. **The correct answer is (C).** Pastoral industries, such as dairy and sheep farming, are major contributors to the national economy of New Zealand.

114. **The correct answer is (D).** The Canadian Shield is a mass of very ancient granite, gneiss, marble, and other rocks that underlies most of eastern and central Canada.

115. **The correct answer is (A).** Java, one of the most densely populated regions in the world, contains numerous cities and areas of small farms.

116. **The correct answer is (D).** Greenland is politically part of Denmark, but its culture is made up of both Danish and Inuit influences.

117. **The correct answer is (B).** A *toponym* is a place name; geographers study toponyms to judge—among other things—the religious affiliations or geographic profile of an area.

118. **The correct answer is (B).** *Patrilineal* refers to the determination of descent and inheritance through the male line.

119. **The correct answer is (A).** An extended conjugal family may be formed by the addition of new spouses through polygamous marriage. A restricted conjugal family is made up of a husband, wife, and their offspring.

120. **The correct answer is (C).** Only with stabilized settlements and the growing population they could support does true centralized political organization become possible. Nomadic hunting and gathering bands infrequently organize central governing systems.

121. **The correct answer is (B).** *Relocation diffusion* describes the process by which customs, traditions, and other characteristics are spread through migration. The spread of Appalachian folk music to the north, for example, is attributed to relocation diffusion, rather than mechanical processes such as electronic broadcast.

122. **The correct answer is (D).** Although Hinduism is the world's third-largest religion, more than 99 percent of its followers are concentrated in India, thus placing it within the category of *ethnic* religions—those whose followers are typically clustered in a single geographic region.

123. **The correct answer is (C).** Even with the rise of organized religion resulting from centralized systems within a society, centralization rarely eliminates shamanism or family-centered religious practices that evoke kinship ties.

124. **The correct answer is (B).** Margaret Mead was the author of *Coming of Age in Samoa*. Ruth Benedict, another cultural anthropologist and a contemporary of Margaret Mead, focussed her work on Native American and Japanese cultures.

125. **The correct answer is (D).** Claude Levi-Strauss (1908–1990), a French anthropologist, compared the myths of primitive people in *Tristes Tropiques* (1955).

Practice Examination II Diagnostic Chart

Subject Area	Approx. percent of Exam	Question Numbers	Number of Questions	Number Wrong
U.S. History	17 percent	1–21	21	_____
Western Civilization	15 percent	22–40	19	_____
World Civilization	8 percent	41–50	10	_____
Psychology	10 percent	51–62	12	_____
Sociology	11 percent	63–75	13	_____
Economics	10 percent	76–88	13	_____
Government/Political Science	13 percent	89–104	17	_____
Geography	10 percent	105–117	13	_____
Anthropology	6 percent	118–125	8	_____
TOTAL	100 percent		125	_____

Answer Sheet for Practice Examination III

Section I

1 Ⓐ Ⓑ Ⓒ Ⓓ Ⓔ	14 Ⓐ Ⓑ Ⓒ Ⓓ Ⓔ	27 Ⓐ Ⓑ Ⓒ Ⓓ Ⓔ	40 Ⓐ Ⓑ Ⓒ Ⓓ Ⓔ	52 Ⓐ Ⓑ Ⓒ Ⓓ Ⓔ
2 Ⓐ Ⓑ Ⓒ Ⓓ Ⓔ	15 Ⓐ Ⓑ Ⓒ Ⓓ Ⓔ	28 Ⓐ Ⓑ Ⓒ Ⓓ Ⓔ	41 Ⓐ Ⓑ Ⓒ Ⓓ Ⓔ	53 Ⓐ Ⓑ Ⓒ Ⓓ Ⓔ
3 Ⓐ Ⓑ Ⓒ Ⓓ Ⓔ	16 Ⓐ Ⓑ Ⓒ Ⓓ Ⓔ	29 Ⓐ Ⓑ Ⓒ Ⓓ Ⓔ	42 Ⓐ Ⓑ Ⓒ Ⓓ Ⓔ	54 Ⓐ Ⓑ Ⓒ Ⓓ Ⓔ
4 Ⓐ Ⓑ Ⓒ Ⓓ Ⓔ	17 Ⓐ Ⓑ Ⓒ Ⓓ Ⓔ	30 Ⓐ Ⓑ Ⓒ Ⓓ Ⓔ	43 Ⓐ Ⓑ Ⓒ Ⓓ Ⓔ	55 Ⓐ Ⓑ Ⓒ Ⓓ Ⓔ
5 Ⓐ Ⓑ Ⓒ Ⓓ Ⓔ	18 Ⓐ Ⓑ Ⓒ Ⓓ Ⓔ	31 Ⓐ Ⓑ Ⓒ Ⓓ Ⓔ	44 Ⓐ Ⓑ Ⓒ Ⓓ Ⓔ	56 Ⓐ Ⓑ Ⓒ Ⓓ Ⓔ
6 Ⓐ Ⓑ Ⓒ Ⓓ Ⓔ	19 Ⓐ Ⓑ Ⓒ Ⓓ Ⓔ	32 Ⓐ Ⓑ Ⓒ Ⓓ Ⓔ	45 Ⓐ Ⓑ Ⓒ Ⓓ Ⓔ	57 Ⓐ Ⓑ Ⓒ Ⓓ Ⓔ
7 Ⓐ Ⓑ Ⓒ Ⓓ Ⓔ	20 Ⓐ Ⓑ Ⓒ Ⓓ Ⓔ	33 Ⓐ Ⓑ Ⓒ Ⓓ Ⓔ	46 Ⓐ Ⓑ Ⓒ Ⓓ Ⓔ	58 Ⓐ Ⓑ Ⓒ Ⓓ Ⓔ
8 Ⓐ Ⓑ Ⓒ Ⓓ Ⓔ	21 Ⓐ Ⓑ Ⓒ Ⓓ Ⓔ	34 Ⓐ Ⓑ Ⓒ Ⓓ Ⓔ	47 Ⓐ Ⓑ Ⓒ Ⓓ Ⓔ	59 Ⓐ Ⓑ Ⓒ Ⓓ Ⓔ
9 Ⓐ Ⓑ Ⓒ Ⓓ Ⓔ	22 Ⓐ Ⓑ Ⓒ Ⓓ Ⓔ	35 Ⓐ Ⓑ Ⓒ Ⓓ Ⓔ	48 Ⓐ Ⓑ Ⓒ Ⓓ Ⓔ	60 Ⓐ Ⓑ Ⓒ Ⓓ Ⓔ
10 Ⓐ Ⓑ Ⓒ Ⓓ Ⓔ	23 Ⓐ Ⓑ Ⓒ Ⓓ Ⓔ	36 Ⓐ Ⓑ Ⓒ Ⓓ Ⓔ	49 Ⓐ Ⓑ Ⓒ Ⓓ Ⓔ	61 Ⓐ Ⓑ Ⓒ Ⓓ Ⓔ
11 Ⓐ Ⓑ Ⓒ Ⓓ Ⓔ	24 Ⓐ Ⓑ Ⓒ Ⓓ Ⓔ	37 Ⓐ Ⓑ Ⓒ Ⓓ Ⓔ	50 Ⓐ Ⓑ Ⓒ Ⓓ Ⓔ	62 Ⓐ Ⓑ Ⓒ Ⓓ Ⓔ
12 Ⓐ Ⓑ Ⓒ Ⓓ Ⓔ	25 Ⓐ Ⓑ Ⓒ Ⓓ Ⓔ	38 Ⓐ Ⓑ Ⓒ Ⓓ Ⓔ	51 Ⓐ Ⓑ Ⓒ Ⓓ Ⓔ	63 Ⓐ Ⓑ Ⓒ Ⓓ Ⓔ
13 Ⓐ Ⓑ Ⓒ Ⓓ Ⓔ	26 Ⓐ Ⓑ Ⓒ Ⓓ Ⓔ	39 Ⓐ Ⓑ Ⓒ Ⓓ Ⓔ		

Section II

64 Ⓐ Ⓑ Ⓒ Ⓓ Ⓔ	77 Ⓐ Ⓑ Ⓒ Ⓓ Ⓔ	90 Ⓐ Ⓑ Ⓒ Ⓓ Ⓔ	102 Ⓐ Ⓑ Ⓒ Ⓓ Ⓔ	114 Ⓐ Ⓑ Ⓒ Ⓓ Ⓔ
65 Ⓐ Ⓑ Ⓒ Ⓓ Ⓔ	78 Ⓐ Ⓑ Ⓒ Ⓓ Ⓔ	91 Ⓐ Ⓑ Ⓒ Ⓓ Ⓔ	103 Ⓐ Ⓑ Ⓒ Ⓓ Ⓔ	115 Ⓐ Ⓑ Ⓒ Ⓓ Ⓔ
66 Ⓐ Ⓑ Ⓒ Ⓓ Ⓔ	79 Ⓐ Ⓑ Ⓒ Ⓓ Ⓔ	92 Ⓐ Ⓑ Ⓒ Ⓓ Ⓔ	104 Ⓐ Ⓑ Ⓒ Ⓓ Ⓔ	116 Ⓐ Ⓑ Ⓒ Ⓓ Ⓔ
67 Ⓐ Ⓑ Ⓒ Ⓓ Ⓔ	80 Ⓐ Ⓑ Ⓒ Ⓓ Ⓔ	93 Ⓐ Ⓑ Ⓒ Ⓓ Ⓔ	105 Ⓐ Ⓑ Ⓒ Ⓓ Ⓔ	117 Ⓐ Ⓑ Ⓒ Ⓓ Ⓔ
68 Ⓐ Ⓑ Ⓒ Ⓓ Ⓔ	81 Ⓐ Ⓑ Ⓒ Ⓓ Ⓔ	94 Ⓐ Ⓑ Ⓒ Ⓓ Ⓔ	106 Ⓐ Ⓑ Ⓒ Ⓓ Ⓔ	118 Ⓐ Ⓑ Ⓒ Ⓓ Ⓔ
69 Ⓐ Ⓑ Ⓒ Ⓓ Ⓔ	82 Ⓐ Ⓑ Ⓒ Ⓓ Ⓔ	95 Ⓐ Ⓑ Ⓒ Ⓓ Ⓔ	107 Ⓐ Ⓑ Ⓒ Ⓓ Ⓔ	119 Ⓐ Ⓑ Ⓒ Ⓓ Ⓔ
70 Ⓐ Ⓑ Ⓒ Ⓓ Ⓔ	83 Ⓐ Ⓑ Ⓒ Ⓓ Ⓔ	96 Ⓐ Ⓑ Ⓒ Ⓓ Ⓔ	108 Ⓐ Ⓑ Ⓒ Ⓓ Ⓔ	120 Ⓐ Ⓑ Ⓒ Ⓓ Ⓔ
71 Ⓐ Ⓑ Ⓒ Ⓓ Ⓔ	84 Ⓐ Ⓑ Ⓒ Ⓓ Ⓔ	97 Ⓐ Ⓑ Ⓒ Ⓓ Ⓔ	109 Ⓐ Ⓑ Ⓒ Ⓓ Ⓔ	121 Ⓐ Ⓑ Ⓒ Ⓓ Ⓔ
72 Ⓐ Ⓑ Ⓒ Ⓓ Ⓔ	85 Ⓐ Ⓑ Ⓒ Ⓓ Ⓔ	98 Ⓐ Ⓑ Ⓒ Ⓓ Ⓔ	110 Ⓐ Ⓑ Ⓒ Ⓓ Ⓔ	122 Ⓐ Ⓑ Ⓒ Ⓓ Ⓔ
73 Ⓐ Ⓑ Ⓒ Ⓓ Ⓔ	86 Ⓐ Ⓑ Ⓒ Ⓓ Ⓔ	99 Ⓐ Ⓑ Ⓒ Ⓓ Ⓔ	111 Ⓐ Ⓑ Ⓒ Ⓓ Ⓔ	123 Ⓐ Ⓑ Ⓒ Ⓓ Ⓔ
74 Ⓐ Ⓑ Ⓒ Ⓓ Ⓔ	87 Ⓐ Ⓑ Ⓒ Ⓓ Ⓔ	100 Ⓐ Ⓑ Ⓒ Ⓓ Ⓔ	112 Ⓐ Ⓑ Ⓒ Ⓓ Ⓔ	124 Ⓐ Ⓑ Ⓒ Ⓓ Ⓔ
75 Ⓐ Ⓑ Ⓒ Ⓓ Ⓔ	88 Ⓐ Ⓑ Ⓒ Ⓓ Ⓔ	101 Ⓐ Ⓑ Ⓒ Ⓓ Ⓔ	113 Ⓐ Ⓑ Ⓒ Ⓓ Ⓔ	125 Ⓐ Ⓑ Ⓒ Ⓓ Ⓔ
76 Ⓐ Ⓑ Ⓒ Ⓓ Ⓔ	89 Ⓐ Ⓑ Ⓒ Ⓓ Ⓔ			

PRACTICE EXAMINATION III

Section I

63 Questions

Time—45 minutes

Directions: For each question, choose the lettered response that best completes the statement or answers the question. Mark the letter of your choice on the answer sheet provided. When you have completed the examination, check your answers with the answer key and explanations that follow the exam.

1. The Force Acts of 1870 and 1871 were intended by Congress to
   (A) enforce the Fourteenth and Fifteenth Amendments.
   (B) force former Confederate states to rejoin the Union.
   (C) force former Confederate officers to sign a pledge of allegiance.
   (D) force former Confederate soldiers to lay down arms.
   (E) force former Confederate states to write new constitutions.

2. The "gospel of wealth," or the idea that rich men should use their money for public benefit, was advocated by
   (A) Benjamin Franklin.
   (B) Henry Ford.
   (C) Andrew Carnegie.
   (D) John D. Rockefeller.
   (E) Franklin D. Roosevelt.

3. In 1947, President Truman told Congress that the United States could not realize its postwar objectives "unless we are willing to help free peoples to maintain their free institutions and their national integrity against aggressive movements that seek to impose upon them totalitarian regimes."
   This policy was first implemented in
   (A) Greece and Turkey.
   (B) Berlin.
   (C) Hungary.
   (D) Korea.
   (E) China.

4. "We are engaged today in a class war. . . . [Because of] the evolution of the capitalist system in which we live, society has been mainly divided into two economic classes. . . . Between these two classes, there is an irrepressible economic conflict. The unity of labor, economic and political, upon the basis of the class struggle, is at the time the supreme need of the working classes."
   The statement above, from 1905, most likely would have been made by a
   (A) Republican.
   (B) Socialist.
   (C) muckraker.
   (D) social Darwinist.
   (E) capitalist.

5. In the *Open Door Notes* of 1899, John Hay served notice to the other powers that the United States favored a Chinese policy that would provide for the
   (A) abolition of all foreign concessions.
   (B) discontinuance of the Chinese tariff system.
   (C) equal treatment of the ships and goods of all nations.
   (D) repeal of all extraterritorial rights previously granted.
   (E) limitation of Chinese sovereignty over foreign settlements.

6. Both the Grange movement and the Knights of Labor

    (A) began as secret societies.
    (B) engaged in partisan politics.
    (C) were nativist movements.
    (D) urged monetary reform.
    (E) supported the 10-hour day.

7. Which is the correct chronological order of the following events?

    I. Franklin D. Roosevelt's second inauguration as president
    II. Congress rejects the "Court packing" bill
    III. Passage of the National Industrial Recovery Act
    IV. Establishment of the Reconstruction Finance Corporation

    (A) IV, III, I, and II
    (B) I, III, IV, and II
    (C) I, IV, III, and II
    (D) III, IV, I, and II
    (E) IV, III, II, and I

8. The economic changes of the New Deal era can be best described as

    (A) large-scale government spending to stimulate the economy.
    (B) slow introduction of minor changes so as not to upset the economy.
    (C) the use of private relief agencies.
    (D) a system replacing capitalism with socialism.
    (E) involving all of the above elements.

9. All of the following events occurred during the 1920s EXCEPT the

    (A) revival of the Ku Klux Klan.
    (B) Scopes Trial.
    (C) execution of Sacco and Vanzetti.
    (D) Bonus March.
    (E) Great Crash.

10. The term *new immigration* refers to which of the following groups?

    (A) English settlers who arrived in America after the Glorious Revolution
    (B) European immigrants who arrived in the United States after the Revolution of 1848
    (C) Immigrants from southern and eastern Europe who arrived in the United States after 1880
    (D) Southern African Americans who migrated to northern urban areas after 1900
    (E) Immigrants who arrived in the United States after the National Origins Act of 1924

11. "For we must consider that we shall be a City upon a Hill; the eyes of all people are upon us; so that if we shall deal falsely with our God in this work we have undertaken and so cause him to withdraw his present help from us, we shall be made a story and a byword through the world."

    The quotation above is most characteristic of

    (A) John Smith.
    (B) William Penn.
    (C) Lord Baltimore.
    (D) John Winthrop.
    (E) Samuel Adams.

12. The Great Awakening in the 1740s was a(n)

    (A) campaign for religious toleration.
    (B) awakening to the scientific advances of the Enlightenment.
    (C) massive religious revival.
    (D) literary and cultural renaissance.
    (E) political consequence of the Glorious Revolution.

13. Which of the following statements most accurately describes the impact of the National Origins Act of 1924 on American immigration policy?

    (A) It ended immigration to the United States.

    (B) It provided immigration quotas favoring northern and western Europeans.

    (C) It introduced immigration quotas favoring southern and eastern Europeans.

    (D) It limited immigration to the United States by introducing literacy testing.

    (E) It deported a majority of recent immigrants to the countries from which they had come.

14. The *Liberator* was a periodical published and edited by

    (A) Tom Paine.

    (B) Frederick Douglass.

    (C) W. E. B. DuBois.

    (D) William Lloyd Garrison.

    (E) James Otis.

15. William Marbury, a party to the *Marbury* v. *Madison* case of 1803, was

    (A) a Supreme Court justice.

    (B) a federal judicial appointee.

    (C) secretary of state.

    (D) a bank director.

    (E) an impeached federalist judge.

16. In the election of 1860, the Republican Party advocated

    (A) the abolition of slavery throughout the United States.

    (B) the colonization of free African Americans.

    (C) the prevention of the extension of slavery to the territories.

    (D) popular sovereignty.

    (E) compensated emancipation.

17. The Anaconda Plan was

    (A) Lincoln's strategy for preventing the expansion of slavery.

    (B) General Lee's strategy for capturing Washington, D.C.

    (C) General McClellan's plot to become general in chief of the Union Army.

    (D) General Scott's strategy for blockade and containment of the Confederacy.

    (E) Jefferson Davis's strategy for defending Richmond.

18. Sandra Day O'Connor, the first woman justice of the Supreme Court, was appointed by

    (A) President George Bush.

    (B) Chief Justice Warren Burger.

    (C) President Ronald Reagan.

    (D) Chief Justice William Rehnquist.

    (E) President Jimmy Carter.

19. *Nativist* is a term used to describe

    (A) immigrants who did not adapt to American culture.

    (B) immigrants who returned from the U.S. to their native lands.

    (C) Americans who supported an imperialist foreign policy.

    (D) Americans who opposed non-Anglo-Saxon immigration.

    (E) Americans who supported fair treatment for Native Americans.

20. The Sherman Antitrust Act of 1890

    (A) was repealed by the passage of the Interstate Commerce Act.

    (B) was not vigorously enforced by the courts in the 1890s.

    (C) effectively ended combinations in restraint of trade.

    (D) was declared unconstitutional by the Supreme Court in 1896.

    (E) was used to destroy the Standard Oil Company.

21. Which of the following presidents was elected in the *first* election in which women were allowed to vote?

    (A) Woodrow Wilson
    (B) Warren G. Harding
    (C) Calvin Coolidge
    (D) Herbert Hoover
    (E) Franklin D. Roosevelt

22. The Roman Emperor Caesar Augustus was finally succeeded by

    (A) Tiberius.
    (B) Nero.
    (C) Caligula.
    (D) Claudius.
    (E) Diocletian.

23. The Humanists are associated with

    (A) ancient Greece.
    (B) the Roman empire.
    (C) fifteenth-century Florence.
    (D) eighteenth-century France.
    (E) nineteenth-century England.

24. The Black Death of the fourteenth century can be best described as

    (A) a plague affecting sailors at sea.
    (B) a plague affecting European cattle.
    (C) a plague that struck all of Europe.
    (D) a plague affecting European crops.
    (E) another name for famine, malnutrition, and starvation.

25. Which of the following ancient peoples believed that their ruler was divine?

    (A) Spartans
    (B) Israelites
    (C) Egyptians
    (D) Athenians
    (E) Macedonians

26. Clovis was a

    (A) Frankish king.
    (B) Saxon peasant.
    (C) Roman general.
    (D) Spanish martyr.
    (E) Visigoth.

27. The Spanish explorer Cortez is best known as the conqueror of

    (A) Portugal.
    (B) India.
    (C) California.
    (D) Mexico.
    (E) Saint Domingue.

28. The term *agora* in ancient Athens referred to

    (A) the theater.
    (B) the main marketplace.
    (C) the main place of worship.
    (D) the legislature.
    (E) a school open to all citizens.

29. An important function of the Roman state priesthood was to

    (A) serve as state officials.
    (B) supervise education.
    (C) advise the army on tactics.
    (D) draw maps and conduct land surveys.
    (E) predict the future through augery.

30. The Greek philosopher Zeno is best known as the founder of the

    (A) Stoics.
    (B) Cynics.
    (C) Epicureans.
    (D) Sophists.
    (E) Scholastics.

31. The pointed arch, rib vault, and flying buttress are most characteristic of

    (A) Roman architecture.
    (B) Greek architecture.
    (C) Gothic architecture.
    (D) Romanesque architecture.
    (E) Baroque architecture.

32. Italian fascism was characterized by all of the following EXCEPT

    (A) an authoritarian party completely subordinate to Mussolini.
    (B) a perpetual propaganda campaign centered around the *Duce*.
    (C) fascist organizations for teachers, workers, and students.
    (D) replacement of the handshake by the fascist salute.
    (E) idealization of the Italian character as friendly, affectionate, and artistic.

33. "Although these eighteenth-century monarchs enjoyed great reputations as 'enlightened' or 'benevolent' rulers, they modified only certain aspects of absolute monarchy and suffered little real loss of power."

The statement above best describes

(A) Catherine the Great and Frederick the Great.
(B) George II and George III.
(C) Queen Anne and Nicholas I.
(D) Philip II and Louis XV.
(E) Frederick I and George II.

34. The English politician Edmund Burke was best known for his

(A) opposition to the French Revolution.
(B) support for the French Revolution.
(C) participation in the Revolutions of 1848.
(D) opposition to the Revolutions of 1848.
(E) virulent hatred of the American colonies.

35. The Russian Revolution occurred in the middle of

(A) the Napoleonic Wars.
(B) the French Revolution.
(C) the Spanish Civil War.
(D) World War I.
(E) World War II.

36. The purpose of the European Common Market is to

(A) foster trade with the United States.
(B) foster trade with Communist bloc nations.
(C) pool resources of energy and manpower.
(D) eliminate trade barriers among member nations.
(E) end migration of workers within Europe.

37. The French poet and critic André Breton is associated with what social movement?

(A) Intellectualism
(B) Surrealism
(C) Socialism
(D) Marxism
(E) Communism

38. The English language belongs to which language group?

(A) Germanic
(B) Slavic
(C) Romance
(D) Greek
(E) Latin

39. The early medieval kingdom of Mercia was located in which present-day European country?

(A) Denmark
(B) England
(C) France
(D) Spain
(E) Sweden

40. What was the purpose of the Potsdam Conference of 1945?

(A) To determine penalties to be meted out during the military crimes trials at Nuremberg
(B) To draw up a treaty agreement to end the conflict between the USSR and Japan
(C) To implement decisions previously reached by the Allies at the Yalta Conference
(D) To come to agreement among the Allies about the use of nuclear arms against Japan
(E) None of the above

41. In any region, the Neolithic Age is characterized by all EXCEPT which of the following cultural and social practices?

(A) Reliance on stone, bone, and wooden tools and weapons
(B) An economy based on farming
(C) The settlement of villages
(D) The development of pottery, spinning, weaving, and other crafts
(E) An end to "cultural borrowing" brought about by contact with other cultural groups

42. Traditional Chinese society was characterized by all of the following EXCEPT

    (A) civil service examinations.
    (B) patrilineal families.
    (C) irrigation projects.
    (D) the beliefs of Confucius.
    (E) the practice of Shinto.

43. All of the following are Chinese dynasties EXCEPT

    (A) Mongol.
    (B) Ming.
    (C) Manchu.
    (D) T'ang.
    (E) Sinkiang.

44. Most African nations achieved independence during which of the following periods?

    (A) The two decades after the Boer War
    (B) The two decades after World War I
    (C) The two decades after World War II
    (D) The eighteenth century
    (E) The nineteenth century

45. The last Muslim rulers were expelled from Spain in

    (A) 722.
    (B) 1492.
    (C) 1545.
    (D) 1603.
    (E) 1648.

46. During which of the following eras was Japan closed to foreigners?

    (A) 1900–39
    (B) 1867–1900
    (C) 1850–67
    (D) 1939–49
    (E) The seventeenth and eighteenth centuries

47. In 1991, the Soviet Union dissolved into separate states. Eleven of those states joined in a loose political and economic organization known as the

    (A) Russian Federation of States.
    (B) Congress of the People's Deputies.
    (C) Federated Socialist States.
    (D) Commonwealth of Independent States.
    (E) Union Republics.

48. Bantu and Swahili are

    (A) African customs.
    (B) African dwellings.
    (C) African nations.
    (D) African languages.
    (E) kingdoms of ancient Africa.

49. The African nations Mali, Mauritania, Nigeria, and Senegal all gained their independence during the

    (A) 1870s.
    (B) 1890s.
    (C) 1920s.
    (D) 1940s.
    (E) 1960s.

50. Joseph Campbell, the noted author, editor, and teacher, asserted which of the following theories about world mythologies?

    (A) All cultures share the same essential pattern of journey in their various heroic myths.
    (B) Myth exists independent of cultural experience and thus rarely reflects the individuality of a given culture.
    (C) The future development of any culture can be devined by a study of its goddess mythology.
    (D) All mythology is based on three simple premises: love, honor, and devotion.
    (E) Modern religions are devoid of mythology.

Question 51 is based on the following graph.

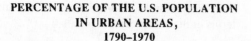

PERCENTAGE OF THE U.S. POPULATION
IN URBAN AREAS,
1790–1970

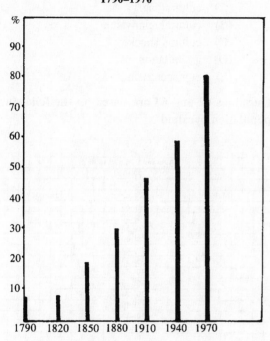

51. Using the information presented on the graph, it is possible to conclude all of the following EXCEPT

(A) during the 1920s, the U.S. population was approximately half urban and half nonurban.

(B) the population of urban areas tripled between 1790 and 1850.

(C) the proportion of the population in nonurban areas has been decreasing ever since 1790.

(D) the proportion of the population in urban areas approximately doubled between 1880 and 1940.

(E) during World War II, the majority of Americans lived in cities.

52. *Social interaction* can be best described as

(A) the ability to confront aggression in others.

(B) interpersonal relations in an institutional setting.

(C) the capacity to learn new norms and values.

(D) acting in relation to others and attuning responses to their responses.

(E) the ability to join groups easily and mingle with peers.

53. All of the following can be considered modes of social interaction EXCEPT

(A) conflict.

(B) accommodation.

(C) assimilation.

(D) projection.

(E) competition.

54. A *norm* is a

(A) specific guide to conduct.

(B) rite or ritual in a given society.

(C) moderate response approved by others.

(D) median, mean, or average.

(E) value-free assertion.

55. *Conjugal family* refers to a

(A) family without children.

(B) family in which the parents are unmarried.

(C) polygamous family.

(D) group formed by marriage.

(E) one-parent family.

56. An *ascribed* position in society is one acquired by

(A) heredity and race.

(B) marriage.

(C) education.

(D) vocational choice.

(E) the judgment of peers.

Questions 57 and 58 refer to the following passage.

"One's position in society is always inherited from one's parents and cannot be altered. Shared beliefs, such as the belief in the purity of the Brahmins and the impurity of the untouchables, necessitate an elaborate system of rules. Many people fear pollution from even the breath or the shadow of an untouchable."

57. The quotation above is from a passage describing the system of social stratification in

   (A) China.
   (B) Japan.
   (C) India.
   (D) any East Asian society.
   (E) any Arab society.

58. The system of social stratification described above illustrates

   (A) the class system.
   (B) the caste system.
   (C) the slave system.
   (D) the estate system.
   (E) social interaction.

59. Sociologists often describe their field as a(n)

   (A) scientific study of human society and social behavior.
   (B) humanistic branch of statistical mathematics.
   (C) comparative study of primitive and modern societies.
   (D) study of human evolution.
   (E) informed attempt to predict the future.

60. Inferential statistics can best be described as

   (A) statistics used to make generalizations about a population based on sample data.
   (B) statistics that summarize information about a population.
   (C) statistics that have been found to contain sampling errors.
   (D) incomplete statistics.
   (E) educated guesses.

61. The concept that different cultural patterns constitute different solutions to problems and that these patterns should be interpreted in terms of their total context is called

   (A) cultural lag.
   (B) cultural relativism.
   (C) cultural shock.
   (D) assimilation.
   (E) ethnocentrism.

Questions 62 and 63 are based on the following population pyramid.

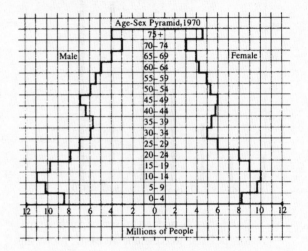

62. The data presented in the population pyramid support the assertion that

   (A) fertility rose in the 1960s.
   (B) fertility fell in the 1960s.
   (C) average life expectancy rose in the 1960s.
   (D) average life expectancy fell in the 1960s.
   (E) None of the above

63. If the base of a population pyramid narrows, we may expect

   (A) an increase in the number of orphans.
   (B) higher taxes.
   (C) a decrease in the potential school-age population.
   (D) a rise in juvenile arrests.
   (E) an increase in the potential college-age population.

Section II

62 Questions

Time—45 minutes

Directions: For each question, choose the lettered response that best completes the statement or answers the question. Mark the letter of your choice on the answer sheet provided. When you have completed the examination, check your answers with the answer key and explanations that follow the exam.

64. According to David Riesman, inner-directed people are those who

    (A) are alienated from society.
    (B) are socialized by their peer groups.
    (C) are susceptible to the influence of anti-democratic propaganda.
    (D) acquire early in life an internalized set of goals.
    (E) are responsive to the feelings and emotions of others.

65. Psychologist B. F. Skinner is best known as an exponent of

    (A) Freudianism.
    (B) hypnotism.
    (C) behaviorism.
    (D) egoism.
    (E) cultural relativism.

66. Let us assume that a society is characterized by social-class conflict. During a period of national crisis, brought about by war, class conflict diminishes. What process is at work?

    (A) Cooperation
    (B) Competition
    (C) Conflict
    (D) Accommodation
    (E) Assimilation

67. Which of the following is NOT a psychological defense mechanism?

    (A) Regression
    (B) Sublimation
    (C) Introspection
    (D) Projection
    (E) Transference

68. A state university serves as a marriage market as well as a regional center of higher learning. This is an example of

    (A) dysfunction.
    (B) primary function.
    (C) latent function.
    (D) dialectic.
    (E) synthesis.

69. W. Lloyd Warner's study of "Yankee City" in the 1930s was primarily a(n)

    (A) demographic analysis of migration patterns during the Depression.
    (B) empirical study of social stratification.
    (C) survey of race relations in the North.
    (D) study of immigrant experiences in an urban area.
    (E) psychological analysis of the impact of technology on individuals.

70. In the 1950s, psychologist William H. Sheldon categorized somatotypes, or body types, in a study of

    (A) sexual attraction.
    (B) social revolution.
    (C) authoritarianism.
    (D) politics.
    (E) deviance.

71. According to the distinction between the aberrant and the nonconformist drawn by sociologist Robert K. Merton,
    (A) the aberrant publicly flouts social rules, while the nonconformist hides his deviance.
    (B) the nonconformist challenges the validity of society's rules, while the aberrant ignores them.
    (C) the nonconformist thinks of himself as a criminal, while the aberrant thinks of himself as a law-abiding citizen.
    (D) the aberrant will claim that society is wrong, while the nonconformist sees himself as wrong.
    (E) the distinction between the aberrant and the nonconformist is minor because the two terms are virtually synonymous.

72. In the late nineteenth century, Gustav Fechner pioneered the field of study known as
    (A) operant conditioning.
    (B) psycholinguistics.
    (C) psychotherapy.
    (D) experimental psychology.
    (E) cognitive psychology.

73. On which of the following premises about human perception is gestalt psychology based?
    (A) Human perception is most strongly influenced by individual events rather than the collective experiences of an individual's life.
    (B) Human perception is shaped by the context within which an observable image or event occurs.
    (C) The events and experiences of childhood have more impact on an individual's perception than do the events and experiences of the present.
    (D) Context plays a minor role in the perception of experience.
    (E) None of the above

74. Which of the following is classed as a *pervasive development disorder*?
    (A) Infantile autism
    (B) Anorexia nervosa
    (C) Enuresis
    (D) Manic-depression
    (E) Attention-Deficit Hyperactivity

75. Which of the following developed the first standardized intelligence test?
    (A) Hermann Rorschach
    (B) Alfred Binet
    (C) Lewis Terman
    (D) William James
    (E) John Dewey

76. When a corporation is granted a state charter, it becomes (a)
    (A) state-financed.
    (B) state bondholder.
    (C) legal cartel.
    (D) legal person.
    (E) legal trust.

77. The Taft-Hartley Act of 1947 provided for all of the following EXCEPT
    (A) permitting employers to sue unions.
    (B) requiring a sixty-day cooling off period before strikes.
    (C) permitting union contributions to political campaigns.
    (D) requiring union leaders to take oaths that they were not Communist party members.
    (E) requiring unions to make public financial statements.

78. Which of the following steps would the federal government take when it wants to "prime the pump"?
    (A) Lower taxes
    (B) Limit exports
    (C) Reduce government spending
    (D) Curtail welfare payments
    (E) Ask the Federal Reserve to raise interest rates

79. The Norris LaGuardia Act and the Wagner Act were both concerned with
    (A) providing a minimum wage for all American workers.
    (B) providing workers with the right to collective bargaining.
    (C) outlawing the union shop.
    (D) establishing protective tariffs.
    (E) prohibiting false and misleading advertising.

80. According to the economic theories of T. R. Malthus, which of the following increases in a geometric ratio?

(A) Means of subsistence
(B) Investments
(C) Land taxes
(D) Population
(E) Misery

81. Which of the following purposes would be best served by a confiscatory tax?

(A) Making home mortgages more difficult to obtain
(B) Increasing consumption of a particular product
(C) Discouraging the exports of raw materials
(D) Limiting imports of foreign products that compete with American-made products
(E) Implicitly cutting off consumption of a particular product

82. There has been a great increase in airplane sales this year. The production of airplanes requires numerous components, such as aluminum and rubber. The increase in airplane sales results in an effect upon these primary materials that can best be described as a(n)

(A) increased effective demand.
(B) decreased effective demand.
(C) increased variable demand.
(D) increased derived demand.
(E) inelastic demand.

83. When drivers are charged a toll for the use of a road, the method of taxation employed is

(A) progressive.
(B) regressive.
(C) exclusionary.
(D) benefit.
(E) proportional.

84. Local authorities are most likely to receive the greatest part of their revenues from

(A) sales taxes.
(B) property taxes.
(C) payroll taxes.
(D) personal income taxes.
(E) corporate income taxes.

85. The U.S. Constitution gave the power to coin money and regulate its value to

(A) Congress.
(B) the president.
(C) the secretary of the treasury.
(D) the First National Bank.
(E) state banks.

86. Marx believed that once the communist society was established,

(A) social classes would engage in a struggle for survival.
(B) social classes would disappear.
(C) the state would increase in size and power.
(D) shortages of manufactured goods would occur.
(E) the oppressed proletariat would overthrow capitalism.

87. Which of the following is characteristic of monopolistic competition?

(A) Paucity of firms
(B) Standardized product
(C) Feeling of mutual interdependence
(D) Comparatively easy entry
(E) No competition among sellers

88. Which of the following is responsible for investigating fraudulent advertising and the sale of harmful products?

(A) Federal Trade Commission
(B) Securities and Exchange Commission
(C) Department of Labor
(A) Interstate Commerce Commission
(E) Department of Human Services

89. A primary goal of the North Atlantic Treaty Organization, at the time of its founding in 1949, was to

(A) strengthen trade relations between the United States and Western Europe.
(B) provide economic aid to postwar Europe.
(C) provide a deterrent to Communist aggression.
(D) foster international collaboration on the development of nuclear weapons.
(E) ban any further development of nuclear weapons.

90. Which of the following statements about Congress is incorrect?

    (A) Members of the House of Representatives are elected every two years.
    (B) The chairmen of congressional committees are determined by the seniority system.
    (C) No congressional officers are mentioned in the Constitution.
    (D) Congress has authority to declare war.
    (E) Revenue bills must originate in the House of Representatives.

91. The Judiciary Act of 1789

    (A) provided for the election of federal judges.
    (B) established a system of lower federal courts.
    (C) provided for the establishment of state courts.
    (D) provided for the impeachment of federal officials.
    (E) was violated by William Marbury.

92. Which of the following statements about amending the Constitution is correct?

    (A) Only the president can propose an amendment to the Constitution.
    (B) An amendment may be proposed by Congress or by a national convention called by Congress.
    (C) All amendments to the Constitution require the president's signature.
    (D) All of the states must ratify a proposed amendment before it is adopted.
    (E) An amendment can be adopted when ratified by a minority of the states.

93. According to the Constitution, the president's powers include all of the following EXCEPT

    (A) to serve as commander in chief of the armed forces.
    (B) to grant reprieves for federal crimes.
    (C) to make treaties with the advice and consent of two thirds of the Senate.
    (D) to admit new states to the Union.
    (E) to nominate ambassadors for approval by the Senate.

94. The importation of slaves into the United States was ended by

    (A) the ratification of the Constitution.
    (B) an amendment to the Constitution.
    (C) an act of Congress.
    (D) a Supreme Court decision.
    (E) the Emancipation Proclamation.

95. The Bill of Rights insures to the people of the United States all of the following EXCEPT

    (A) freedom from the quartering of troops.
    (B) protection against unreasonable search and seizure.
    (C) the right to bear arms.
    (D) the right to vote.
    (E) the right to a speedy and public trial.

96. All of the following can be considered part of the "unwritten Constitution" EXCEPT

    (A) the two-party system.
    (B) the President's Cabinet.
    (C) the party caucus.
    (D) the Congressional committee system.
    (E) the process of impeachment.

Questions 97–99 are based on the following Supreme Court decisions.

    I.   *Marbury* v. *Madison*
    II. *McCulloch* v. *Maryland*
    III. *Dred Scott* v. *Sanford*
    IV. *Plessy* v. *Ferguson*
    V.   *Brown* v. *Board of Education*
    VI. *Dartmouth College* v. *Woodward*

97. In which of the cases did Chief Justice Marshall uphold the doctrine of "implied powers"?

    (A) I
    (B) II
    (C) III
    (D) IV
    (E) VI

98. Which of the Supreme Court decisions repealed a major congressional "Compromise"?

    (A) I
    (B) II
    (C) III
    (D) IV
    (E) V

99. Which of the decisions upheld the doctrine of "separate but equal"?

(A) II
(B) III
(C) IV
(D) V
(E) VI

100. Which of the following statements about the British Parliament is incorrect?

(A) An act of Parliament cannot be overruled by the courts.
(B) An act of Parliament cannot be vetoed by the prime minister.
(C) The upper house of Parliament has more members than the lower house.
(D) Bishops are members of the House of Lords.
(E) A member of Parliament must live in the district he stands for.

101. A major goal of *The Federalist Papers* was to

(A) evoke support for the Hamiltonian faction in Congress.
(B) insure ratification of the Constitution.
(C) explain the American system of government to Europeans.
(D) define the virtues of the Articles of Confederation.
(E) publish the debates of the Constitutional Convention of 1787.

102. Under the American judicial system, the major function of a federal appellate court is to

(A) retry difficult cases decided by trial judges in the lower courts.
(B) decide whether a trial judge applied the law correctly.
(C) determine whether judges of the lower courts are fit to hold office.
(D) select judges for the lower courts.
(E) review cases decided by the U.S. Supreme Court.

103. The function of a congressional conference committee is to

(A) judge the moral conduct of members of Congress.
(B) determine the rules for congressional procedures.
(C) iron out differences between House and Senate versions of bills.
(D) present to the president bills that have been passed by both houses of Congress.
(E) investigate a subject of interest to Congress by holding hearings and calling witnesses.

104. Naturalization is the process of

(A) applying for a visa.
(B) applying for citizenship papers.
(C) becoming a citizen.
(D) returning an alien to his country of origin.
(E) demobilization from military service.

105. All of the following are major Japanese cities EXCEPT

(A) Yokohama.
(B) Kyoto.
(C) Kabuki.
(D) Osaka.
(E) Hiroshima.

106. Which of the following statements best characterizes a *post-industrial* society, as defined and applied in human geography?

(A) The industrial labor force rises to meet increased demand for industrial production.
(B) Employment in trades and services decreases as demand for productivity in those sectors diminishes.
(C) Industrial production decreases as demand for industrial production wanes.
(D) Trades and services incomes and productivity have a greater impact on the welfare of the society.
(E) None of the above

107. All of the following share a border with Israel EXCEPT

    (A) Syria.
    (B) Lebanon.
    (C) Saudi Arabia.
    (D) Jordan.
    (E) Egypt.

108. The plain of the Tigris and Euphrates rivers is located in which of the following countries?

    (A) Jordan
    (B) Egypt
    (C) Saudi Arabia
    (D) Iraq
    (E) Lebanon

109. Which of the following countries is NOT considered to be part of the Indian subcontinent?

    (A) Afghanistan
    (B) Pakistan
    (C) Nepal
    (D) Bangladesh
    (E) Bhutan

110. The sultanate of Brunei is located on which of the following islands?

    (A) Sumatra
    (B) Borneo
    (C) Sulawesi
    (D) New Guinea
    (E) Java

111. Mount Pinatubo, a volcano that erupted violently in 1991, is located in which of the following Pacific Rim countries?

    (A) Indonesia
    (B) South Korea
    (C) Malaysia
    (D) Philippines
    (E) Japan

112. Which of the following is the name of the region that borders Russia between the Black and Caspian seas?

    (A) Gobi Desert
    (B) Asia Minor
    (C) Middle Volga
    (D) Urals
    (E) Caucasus

113. All of the following countries are part of Southeast Asia EXCEPT

    (A) Laos.
    (B) Sri Lanka.
    (C) Myanmar.
    (D) Thailand.
    (E) Cambodia.

114. Guadalcanal is part of which of the following Pacific Island groups?

    (A) Solomon Islands
    (B) Fiji Islands
    (C) Caroline Islands
    (D) Marshall Islands
    (E) Cook Islands

115. Australia and New Zealand are separated by which of the following bodies of water?

    (A) Indian Ocean
    (B) Coral Sea
    (C) Tasman Sea
    (D) Arafura Sea
    (E) Gulf of Carpentaria

116. The cities of Bogota, Medellin, and Cali are located in which of the following South American countries?

    (A) Brazil
    (B) Colombia
    (C) Peru
    (D) Venezuela
    (E) Bolivia

117. Which of the following statements regarding the diffusion of popular and folk customs is NOT true?

    (A) Folk customs tend to have a lesser negative environmental impact than do popular customs.

    (B) The diffusion of popular customs across the world tends to produce more uniform landscapes.

    (C) Popular customs can generate a relatively high amount of residual pollutants, and their diffusion can thus strain the environment.

    (D) Differences in popular customs are less likely to be observed in one place at different points in time than at one point in time in a single place.

    (E) Folk customs in Central America have been linked to very high rates of soil erosion in that area.

118. Which of the following areas of study is NOT an area of specialization within the broader field of anthropology?

    (A) Ethnology
    (B) Sociobiology
    (C) Homeomorphology
    (D) Ethnography
    (E) None of the above

119. Which of the following tools and techniques is NOT employed by archaeological anthropologists in the dating of sites and artifacts?

    (A) The potassium-argon method
    (B) Radioactive carbon
    (C) Stratigraphy
    (D) Provenance
    (E) None of the above

120. The term *acculturation* is defined as the

    (A) abandonment of a social custom, behavior pattern, or belief that has long been a part of a culture.

    (B) cultural exchange that occurs when unlike cultures experience contact over an extended period of time.

    (C) ethnocentric grouping of traditions among diverse cultures.

    (D) erection of artificial boundaries by isolated cultures.

    (E) occurrence of similarities between cultures that have had neither contact nor history of "cultural borrowing."

121. Kingdoms arising from the development of nation-states inevitably result in which of the following sociocultural shifts?

    (A) The de-emphasis of religious systems
    (B) A push toward social egalitarianism
    (C) Social stratification
    (D) The destruction of the military elite
    (E) The rise to power of the peasant majority

122. Which of the following best describes the practice of polyandry?

    (A) A woman has two or more husbands.
    (B) A family has two or more children.
    (C) Two cousins are married to each other.
    (D) Two or more siblings live together.
    (E) A household is composed of a group of unmarried persons or "singles."

123. Alienation is a

    (A) part of acculturation.
    (B) part of socialization.
    (C) part of assimilation.
    (D) response to a pluralistic society.
    (E) response to a technological society.

124. The purpose of rites of passage is to
    (A) celebrate national holidays and foster patriotism.
    (B) mark changes in an individual's status.
    (C) increase awareness of religious traditions.
    (D) encourage obedience of rules and regulations.
    (E) minimize culture shock.

125. Which of the following developments marked the Neolithic Transition, which took place in the Middle East and East Asia approximately 12,000 years ago?
    (A) Domestication of food resources
    (B) Greater concentrations of population in specific areas
    (C) Exchange of cultural practices among a wider group of people
    (D) Centralization of political systems
    (E) All of the above

End of Practice Examination III

Answer Key

Section I

1.	A	14.	D	27.	D	40.	C	52.	D
2.	C	15.	B	28.	B	41.	E	53.	D
3.	A	16.	C	29.	E	42.	E	54.	A
4.	B	17.	D	30.	A	43.	E	55.	D
5.	C	18.	C	31.	C	44.	C	56.	A
6.	A	19.	D	32.	E	45.	B	57.	C
7.	A	20.	B	33.	A	46.	E	58.	B
8.	A	21.	B	34.	A	47.	D	59.	A
9.	D	22.	A	35.	D	48.	D	60.	A
10.	C	23.	C	36.	D	49.	E	61.	B
11.	D	24.	C	37.	B	50.	A	62.	B
12.	C	25.	C	38.	A	51.	B	63.	C
13.	B	26.	A	39.	B				

Section II

64.	D	77.	C	90.	C	102.	B	114.	A
65.	C	78.	A	91.	B	103.	C	115.	C
66.	D	79.	B	92.	B	104.	C	116.	B
67.	C	80.	D	93.	D	105.	C	117.	D
68.	C	81.	E	94.	C	106.	D	118.	C
69.	B	82.	D	95.	D	107.	C	119.	E
70.	E	83.	D	96.	E	108.	D	120.	B
71.	B	84.	B	97.	B	109.	A	121.	C
72.	D	85.	A	98.	C	110.	B	122.	A
73.	B	86.	B	99.	C	111.	D	123.	E
74.	A	87.	D	100.	E	112.	E	124.	B
75.	B	88.	A	101.	B	113.	E	125.	E
76.	D	89.	C						

Explanatory Answers

Section I

1. **The correct answer is (A).** The three Force Acts or Enforcement Acts were passed in 1870 and 1871 to enforce the Fourteenth and Fifteenth Amendments. The acts were intended to insure that eligible voters would not be deprived of the franchise, to provide federal supervision for congressional elections, and to suppress the terrorist activities of the Ku Klux Klan.

2. **The correct answer is (C).** Andrew Carnegie advocated the "gospel of wealth" in a famous essay with that title. Carnegie (1835–1919) put his own policy into practice by contributing his wealth to a multitude of causes, notably the establishing of public libraries.

3. **The correct answer is (A).** The policy described in the quotation, the Truman Doctrine, was first implemented in Greece and Turkey. President Truman asked Congress for funds to provide economic and military assistance to the pro-American governments of Greece and Turkey in order to protect them from Communist subversion.

4. **The correct answer is (B).** The statement was made by Eugene Debs, who helped found the Socialist Party in 1900 and ran for president five times on the Socialist ticket.

5. **The correct answer is (C).** Secretary of State John Hay's *Open Door Notes* of 1899–1900 demanded that China open its doors equally to all the powers and that China's territorial integrity be safeguarded against a takeover by any one power. Britain, Russia, France, and Japan all had spheres of influence in China.

6. **The correct answer is (A).** Both the Grange movement and the Knights of Labor began as secret societies. The Grange, or Patrons of Husbandry, began in 1867 and the Knights of Labor in 1869. Both organizations were theoretically nonpartisan.

7. **The correct answer is (A).** The Reconstruction Finance Corporation, a Hoover measure, came into existence in 1932; the National Industrial Recovery Act, a New Deal measure, in 1933; FDR's second inauguration was in 1937; and after beginning his second term, President Roosevelt introduced his "Court-packing" bill, which Congress rejected.

8. **The correct answer is (A).** New Deal economic policies were introduced rapidly, did not involve private relief agencies, and did not replace capitalism with socialism. They were intended to get the economy in motion and relieve the impact of the Depression.

9. **The correct answer is (D).** In 1932, during the last summer of the Hoover administration, 15,000 unemployed veterans marched on Washington, D.C., to demand congressional passage of the Bonus Bill. After the bill failed in Congress, the "Bonus Army" camped out in Washington until dispersed by federal troops under the direction of General MacArthur.

10. **The correct answer is (C).** The *New Immigration* (from 1880 until massive immigration came to an end in the 1920s) refers to immigrants from southern and eastern Europe— Russians, Slavs, Italians, and Jews.

11. **The correct answer is (D).** John Winthrop, in 1637, described the Puritan community in Massachusetts Bay as a "City upon a Hill" because he viewed the Puritan settlement as an example for the rest of the world.

12. **The correct answer is (C).** The Great Awakening of the 1740s was a massive religious revival that spread throughout the colonies. The best-known revivalist was Jonathan Edwards. Other important ministers were George Whitefield, William and Gilbert Tennent, and Theodore Frelinghuysen.

13. **The correct answer is (B).** The National Origins Act of 1924 established stringent quotas favoring northern and western Europeans and discriminating against southern and eastern Europeans. The quota system, introduced in 1921, remained the basis of American immigration policy until the 1950s.

14. **The correct answer is (D).** The *Liberator* was a militant abolitionist journal, founded in 1831

by William Lloyd Garrison, who founded the New England Antislavery Society the following year.

15. **The correct answer is (B).** William Marbury was appointed a federal justice of the peace by John Adams during his last days as president in 1801. Such last-minute appointees were called "midnight judges." Marbury never received his commission (appointment papers), since Secretary of State Madison refused to deliver it. Marbury's case against Madison, which reached the Supreme Court in 1803, resulted in the famous decision that established the Supreme Court's power of judicial review.

16. **The correct answer is (C).** In the 1860 election, the Republican Party supported prohibition of slavery in the western territories. The Democrats nominated Stephen A. Douglas, who advocated popular sovereignty. Southern Democrats, who wanted to protect slavery in the territories, nominated John C. Breckinridge. A fourth candidate, John Bell, was nominated by the Constitutional Union Party, which advocated preservation of the Union. The Republicans did not urge during the 1860 campaign that slavery be abolished, only that its expansion be prohibited.

17. **The correct answer is (D).** The Anaconda Plan was a long-range scheme for Union victory proposed by General Winfield Scott. The plan called for a blockade of the Confederate coast and containment of the Confederacy along its inland frontier. Thus surrounded, the Confederacy could be squeezed and fragmented.

18. **The correct answer is (C).** President Ronald Reagan appointed Sandra Day O'Connor to the Supreme Court in 1981.

19. **The correct answer is (D).** Nativists opposed non-Anglo-Saxon immigration. The nativist spirit emerged in such organizations as the Know-Nothing Party of 1850 and the American Protective Association of 1887.

20. **The correct answer is (B).** The Sherman Antitrust Act was intended "to protect trade and commerce against unlawful restraint and

monopolies." The courts, however, did not invoke the act against trusts. It was invoked instead against labor on the occasion of the Pullman strike in 1894.

21. **The correct answer is (B).** The Nineteenth Amendment to the Constitution, providing for female suffrage, was adopted in August 1920. In the presidential election that fall, Republican Warren G. Harding defeated Democrat James M. Cox.

22. **The correct answer is (A).** Caesar Augustus had much trouble arranging for his successor. He hoped to insure a dynasty by inheritance, but several possible candidates died before he did. Tiberius was not a blood relative but the son of the emperor's wife, Livia, by her first husband.

23. **The correct answer is (C).** Humanists, scholars and writers in fifteenth-century Florence, were leading figures of the Italian Renaissance.

24. **The correct answer is (C).** The Black Death was an epidemic, or pandemic, of bubonic plague that struck Europe repeatedly during the fourteenth century. It started in 1347 when a merchant ship arrived in Sicily with infected rats.

25. **The correct answer is (C).** The Egyptian ruler was regarded as the human personification of the sun god.

26. **The correct answer is (A).** Clovis was a king of the Franks (481–511) who became a Christian.

27. **The correct answer is (D).** The Spanish explorer Hernando Cortez arrived with an expedition in Mexico in 1519 and crushed resistance, including that of the Aztecs under Montezuma, by 1521.

28. **The correct answer is (B).** The *agora* in ancient Greece was the marketplace or public square. Popular assemblies sometimes met there.

29. **The correct answer is (E).** Roman priests were believed to have insight into the future, or the power of prediction, through their ability to interpret omens.

30. **The correct answer is (A).** Zeno founded the Stoic school of Greek philosophy around 308 B.C.E. Stoics taught that virtue was the highest good and that appetites should be subdued.

31. **The correct answer is (C).** The Gothic style originated in the twelfth century. The pointed arch, rib vault, and flying buttress, features of many famous churches, are the outstanding characteristics of Gothic architecture.

32. **The correct answer is (E).** Italian fascists under Mussolini sought to promote an obedient, tough, and efficient national character.

33. **The correct answer is (A).** Catherine the Great and Frederick the Great were the only rulers of the choices given who were known as "enlightened." Both supported the work of major figures of the French Enlightenment, such as Voltaire and Diderot. Both instituted some domestic reforms. Catherine made moves toward representative government. Frederick advocated religious toleration and judicial reforms. Neither, however, relinquished much power during their reigns.

34. **The correct answer is (A).** Burke's *Reflections on the Revolution in France* (1790) was a critique of the French Revolution.

35. **The correct answer is (D).** The Russian Revolution occurred in 1917, in the middle of World War I.

36. **The correct answer is (D).** The Common Market, or European Economic Community, went into effect in 1958. It provided a system of lower tariffs among member nations and elimination of trade barriers.

37. **The correct answer is (B).** André Breton was a leader of the surrealistic movement in art and literature in both Europe and the U.S..

38. **The correct answer is (A).** Though it encompasses terms and expressions from Greek, French, Latin, and other languages, English is basically a Germanic language, evolved from the language of the Angles and Saxons.

39. **The correct answer is (B).** Mercia was an Anglo-Saxon kingdom located in what is now southern England.

40. **The correct answer is (C).** The Potsdam Conference was held in order for the Allies to implement decisions they had previously agreed upon at the Yalta Conference of 1945.

41. **The correct answer is (E).** As Neolithic groups moved in search of better farming and grazing lands, they encountered other culture groups, with different traditions and practices. Through interaction between the groups, the spread of cultural practices through "cultural borrowing" flourished.

42. **The correct answer is (E).** Shinto is a distinctively Japanese religion. All the other characteristics of traditional Chinese society are correct. Civil service examinations, for instance, were very important in traditional China. Since there was no hereditary nobility, the elite were recruited through these exams.

43. **The correct answer is (E).** Sinkiang is a northwest borderland of China, mostly desert. The other answer choices are all major Chinese dynasties. The Mongol (or Yuan) dynasty lasted 1260–1368; the Ming dynasty, 1368–1644; the Manchu or Ch'ing dynasty, 1644–1912; and the T'ang dynasty, 618–906.

44. **The correct answer is (C).** Africa's "March Toward Independence" took place mainly in the 1950s and 1960s.

45. **The correct answer is (B).** The last Muslim rulers were expelled from Spain when Grenada was conquered in 1492.

46. **The correct answer is (E).** In the 1630s, all foreigners were banned from Japan and Christians were persecuted. Very few links were maintained with the outside world until Japan's doors were finally opened in the 1850s.

47. **The correct answer is (D).** The Commonwealth of Independent States (CIS) was formed in 1991 by eleven of the former Soviet bloc countries.

48. **The correct answer is (D).** As many as a thousand languages are spoken in Africa. Bantu languages are spoken in central and eastern Africa and are dominant in South Africa. Swahili, a Bantu language, is often used as a lingua franca or trading language.

49. **The correct answer is (E).** The African movement toward independence occurred mainly in the 1950s and 1960s. The nations mentioned became independent in 1960.

50. **The correct answer is (A).** Campbell's work on the myth of the hero is among his most famous. In numerous books and essays, Campbell expanded upon the similarity of the hero's journey as it is described in mythologies across multiple cultures around the world; for example, his analysis of the parallels between the journey of Odysseus in Homer's *Odyssey* and that of Luke Skywalker in George Lucas's *Star Wars* trilogy.

51. **The correct answer is (B).** The percentage of the population in urban areas tripled between 1790 and 1850. The graph does not tell us the size of the population in urban areas at either time.

52. **The correct answer is (D).** *Social interaction* refers to reciprocal influences exerted by two or more people upon one another's behavior.

53. **The correct answer is (D).** Projection is a psychological defense mechanism.

54. **The correct answer is (A).** Norms reflect a society's values. They are the rules or standards of a society, the ideas that most people take for granted about what is right or wrong, proper or improper.

55. **The correct answer is (D).** *Conjugal* refers to marriage. Choices (A) and (C) also could describe certain types of conjugal families, but they are misleading as definitions.

56. **The correct answer is (A).** An ascribed position is one forced upon an individual by factors that he or she cannot change or control, such as heredity, race, or sex.

57. **The correct answer is (C).** The references to Brahmins and untouchables clearly suggest that India is under discussion.

58. **The correct answer is (B).** A caste system is a hierarchy of endogamous divisions in which membership is hereditary and permanent. According to the caste system for which India is famous, one is born into one of the castes—Brahmin, Kshatriya, Vaisya, or Sudra. The "untouchables," in effect the lowest caste, are considered beneath the caste system.

59. **The correct answer is (A).** Sociologists view their specialty as a scientific description of human society and social behavior.

60. **The correct answer is (A).** Inferential statistics extrapolates data based on samples and attributes the findings to the population from which the samples were drawn. Choice (B) refers to descriptive statistics.

61. **The correct answer is (B).** Cultural relativism means understanding other people's customs, traditions, behavior, and attitudes in terms of the total context of their own culture. Ethnocentrism is the opposite.

62. **The correct answer is (B).** Choice (B) is the only answer choice supported by the data. The number of youngsters born during the 1960s, as represented in the two bottom lines of the pyramid, is less than the number of children born in the 1950s, as represented in the next two lines. Therefore, we can assume that fertility fell during the 1960s. Of course, millions of children could have been born and wiped out by an epidemic, but it is common knowledge that this did not happen.

63. **The correct answer is (C).** If the base (the bottom line) of a population pyramid narrows, this means that there are fewer children of very young age and that the school-age population can be expected to decrease. The other answer options are either irrelevant or illogical.

Section II

64. **The correct answer is (D).** Riesman described the inner-directed and other-directed persons in *The Lonely Crowd* (1953). The inner-directed person follows his own path through life, while the other-directed person takes his cues from the environment. The nineteenth-century "captain of industry" is an example of the inner-directed person, while the "organization man" of the twentieth century exemplifies the outer-directed person.

65. **The correct answer is (C).** Behaviorism is the school of psychology that explains human behavior in terms of physiological responses to external stimuli. These responses, or behavior patterns, are observable and measurable. Behaviorism was introduced by the American psychologist J. B. Watson in 1913. In *The Behavior of Organisms* (1938) and subsequent books, Skinner emphasizes the relationship of observable behavior patterns to rewards.

66. **The correct answer is (D).** Conflict in society is reduced or avoided during the period of crisis but not resolved. This situation is best described as accommodation.

67. **The correct answer is (C).** All the other choices are psychological defense mechanisms.

68. **The correct answer is (C).** A latent function is one that is not intended or recognized. The intended function of the state university is obviously to serve as a center of learning and not as a marriage market. The latent function is unlikely to be mentioned in university brochures or formally endorsed by the state legislature.

69. **The correct answer is (B).** Warner identified a six-class system in "Yankee City." The classes were primarily hereditary groups, with different income levels, educational levels, occupations, lifestyles, speech styles, and kinship arrangements.

70. **The correct answer is (E).** Sheldon presented a biological interpretation of deviance.

71. **The correct answer is (B).** According to the distinctions drawn by Merton, the nonconformist defies society, announces his dissent, and challenges the rules. The aberrant, however, ignores the rules, hides his deviance, and attempts to evade the law rather than challenge its validity.

72. **The correct answer is (D).** Experimental psychology was pioneered by German physicist Gustav Theodor Fechner (1801–1887).

73. **The correct answer is (B).** Gestalt psychology is founded on the premise that humans perceive images and events as patterns, made up of many components within a given context, rather than as individual elements, separate from the whole.

74. **The correct answer is (A).** Child psychologists class Infantile Autism as a pervasive development disorder.

75. **The correct answer is (B).** The first intelligence test was developed in 1905 by the French psychologist Alfred Binet (1857–1911).

76. **The correct answer is (D).** When a corporation is chartered by a state, it becomes a legal person. This means that it can sue and be sued as if it were a person. It has perpetual existence, as long as its charter remains in effect, no matter who runs it, or how many times its shares of stock are sold, or how many people own shares in the corporation.

77. **The correct answer is (C).** The Taft-Hartley Act, passed by Congress over President Truman's veto, forbade union contributions to political campaigns. In addition to the provisions mentioned in the other answer choices, it banned the closed shop.

78. **The correct answer is (A).** "Priming the pump" means increasing consumer purchasing power and spurring the economy into activity by such measures as tax reductions and increased federal spending.

79. **The correct answer is (B).** The Norris LaGuardia Act of 1932 curbed the use of injunctions against labor unions and asserted the right of labor to organize and bargain collectively. The Wagner Act of 1935 gave workers the right to organize in the union of their choice and to bargain collectively.

80. **The correct answer is (D).** According to Malthus, population increases in a geometric ratio while means of subsistence increase only in an arithmetic ratio. The tendency for population to exceed food supply may be limited by what Malthus called positive checks, such as famines, disease, war, and by preventative checks, such as "moral restraint," by which he meant some means to limit births, such as late marriage.

81. **The correct answer is (E).** A confiscatory tax makes the price of a product so high that there will be no demand for it.

82. **The correct answer is (D).** The demand for a factor of production, in this case aluminum and rubber, is ultimately derived from the consumer's demand for the final product. This derived demand would be increased by the rise in sales of airplanes.

83. **The correct answer is (D).** Under the benefit principle of taxation, taxes are distributed in accordance with the benefits derived from the services on which the taxes are spent. The driver who pays a toll when using a road is being taxed for the use of the road, a service supported by his tax.

84. **The correct answer is (B).** Local governments receive more than 80 percent of their revenues from property taxes.

85. **The correct answer is (A).** The Constitution provides that Congress has the power to coin money and regulate its value. Congress can delegate this power, which has been done under the Federal Reserve system.

86. **The correct answer is (B).** Marx believed that once private property was abolished, as it would be in the communist state, class divisions would have no function and social classes would disappear. In Marxist theory, the overthrow of capitalism by the proletariat occurs *before* the communist state is formed.

87. **The correct answer is (D).** Under monopolistic competition, there are many firms, each producing and selling differentiated products. This means there is relatively easy entry into the market. Under monopoly, however, only one seller exists.

88. **The correct answer is (A).** The Federal Trade Commission, under the Wheeler-Lea Act of 1939, is empowered to investigate false and misleading advertising in the food, drug, and cosmetic industries.

89. **The correct answer is (C).** The primary goal of NATO was to provide security for Western Europe, the region in the greatest danger of Soviet aggression. The original signers of the North Atlantic Defense Pact agreed that an attack on any member nation would be considered an attack on all.

90. **The correct answer is (C).** The vice president, the Speaker of the House, and the President Pro Tempore of the Senate are all mentioned in Article I, section 2, of the Constitution.

91. **The correct answer is (B).** The Judiciary Act of 1789 established a system of federal courts made up of three circuit courts and thirteen district courts. The Act also provided that five associate justices and one chief justice would sit on the Supreme Court.

92. **The correct answer is (B).** Amendments may be proposed either by a two-thirds vote of both houses of Congress or by a national convention called by Congress when demanded by two thirds of the legislatures of the states. An amendment must be ratified either by the legislatures or by special conventions in three quarters of the states. The usual method is proposal by Congress and ratification by state legislatures.

93. **The correct answer is (D).** Only Congress can admit new states to the Union, as provided in Article IV, section 3.

94. **The correct answer is (C).** Article I, section 9, of the Constitution provides that Congress could not prohibit the importation of slaves until 1808. In 1807, Congress passed a law prohibiting the foreign slave trade, to take effect in 1808.

95. **The correct answer is (D).** Suffrage is not guaranteed in the Bill of Rights. According to the Constitution, voting qualifications may be determined by the states. During the 1820s, states began to discard property qualifications for suffrage. Constitutional amendments were needed to insure the vote to blacks and to women.

96. **The correct answer is (E).** The process of impeachment is described in the Constitution, Article I, section 3, and Article II, section 4.

97. **The correct answer is (B).** In *McCulloch* v. *Maryland* (1819), the Supreme Court asserted

the superiority of the federal government over the states and upheld the Hamiltonian doctrine of implied powers. In this case, the Court stated that Congress had the right to establish a national bank and that the states had no right to tax the bank.

98. **The correct answer is (C).** The Dred Scott decision of 1857 declared the Missouri Compromise of 1820 unconstitutional.

99. **The correct answer is (C).** In *Plessy* v. *Ferguson* (1896), the Supreme Court upheld a Louisiana law that provided for segregated railroad facilities. The Court declared that segregation did not constitute discrimination as long as equality of accommodation existed.

100. **The correct answer is (E).** A member of Parliament may live anywhere in the United Kingdom. In general elections for members of Parliament, each constituency chooses among parties rather than among candidates. Members of Parliament are those whose parties won in the constituencies for which they stand.

101. **The correct answer is (B).** *The Federalist Papers,* written by Hamilton, Madison, and Jay and published in 1787 and 1788, were intended to evoke support for ratification of the Constitution in New York. The debates of the Constitutional Convention of 1787 were secret.

102. **The correct answer is (B).** A federal appellate court, such as the U.S. Circuit Court, which hears appeals from the federal district courts, decides whether or not there was an error in the application of the law. The appellate court can reverse a lower-court decision. It can also send a case back to a lower court for retrial. Federal court decisions can also be reviewed by the Supreme Court, the final court of appeal.

103. **The correct answer is (C).** When a bill passed by one house of Congress is amended by the other or when the House and Senate pass different versions of the same bill, a conference committee attempts to smooth out the differences between the bills. The committee is made up of several members from each house.

104. **The correct answer is (C).** Naturalization is the process by which an alien becomes an American citizen.

105. **The correct answer is (C).** Kabuki is a popular form of Japanese drama.

106. **The correct answer is (D).** In a post-industrial society, the industrial labor force shrinks, though industrial production usually rises. The demand for trades and services rises, and the income and productivity of these sectors has a greater impact on the welfare of the society.

107. **The correct answer is (C).** Saudi Arabia is separated from Israel by the Gulf of Aqaba.

108. **The correct answer is (D).** The plain of the Tigris and Euphrates rivers is in Iraq; this plain forms part of the Fertile Crescent.

109. **The correct answer is (A).** The Indian subcontinent includes the following five countries: India, Nepal, Bhutan, Pakistan, and Bangladesh. Afghanistan is on the northern border of Pakistan.

110. **The correct answer is (B).** Brunei is located on the island of Borneo.

111. **The correct answer is (D).** Mount Pinatubo is in the Philippines.

112. **The correct answer is (E).** The Caucasus region borders Russia between the Black and Caspian Seas.

113. **The correct answer is (E).** All of the listed countries are part of Southeast Asia.

114. **The correct answer is (A).** Guadalcanal is part of the Solomon Islands group, in the realm of Melanesia.

115. **The correct answer is (C).** The Tasman Sea separates Australia from New Zealand. The Indian Ocean lies to the northwest of Australia. The Arafura Sea and Gulf of Carpentaria lie to the north of Australia; the Coral Sea lies to the northeast of Australia.

116. **The correct answer is (B).** Bogota, Medellin, and Cali are the three largest cities in Colombia.

117. **The correct answer is (D).** Popular customs spread rapidly through television and other media and can be adopted across a wide global landscape; thus, differences in popular customs are more likely to be observed *across time* in a single place, rather than at the same time in a single place.

118. **The correct answer is (C).** Homeomorphology is the study of close similarities of crystalline forms between substances of different chemical composition and is thus not considered to be directly linked to the broader field of anthropology.

119. **The correct answer is (E).** Archaeological anthropologists use all of the listed tools and techniques to date sites and artifacts.

120. **The correct answer is (B).** *Acculturation* is the cultural exchange that occurs when two dissimilar cultures are in contact over a long period of time.

121. **The correct answer is (C).** Though kingdoms develop in different ways across time and cultures, the formation of nation-states inevitably results in the rise of a small religious and military elite, which is supported by a large peasant population.

122. **The correct answer is (A).** When a man has two or more wives, the practice is called polygamy. When a woman has two or more husbands, the practice is called polyandry.

123. **The correct answer is (E).** The powerlessness, meaninglessness, normalcy, and feeling of isolation that characterize the state of alienation are induced by the impersonality and complexity of technological society.

124. **The correct answer is (B).** Rites of passage are ceremonies that mark an important change in a person's life, such as puberty or marriage, or the passage of an individual from one social status to another.

125. **The correct answer is (E).** All of the listed developments marked the period known as the Neolithic Transition.

Practice Examination III Diagnostic Chart

Subject Area	Approx. % of Exam	Question Numbers	Number of Questions	Number Wrong
U.S. History	17 %	1–21	21	_____
Western Civilization	15 %	22–40	19	_____
World Civilization	8 %	41–50	10	_____
Sociology	11 %	51–63	13	_____
Psychology	10 %	64–75	12	_____
Economics	10 %	76–88	12	_____
Government/Political Science	13 %	89–104	16	_____
Geography	10 %	105–116	12	_____
Anthropology	8 %	116–125	9	_____
TOTAL	100 %		125	_____

The CLEP Subject Exams

The CLEP Subject Exams offer the highly motivated, well-qualified student an opportunity to get greater value from each education dollar by starting right in at an advanced level, thereby learning more. If the college grants actual college credits, the student with a qualifying score can save both time and money as well. Actual college credits substitute for actual college courses; they can shorten the time you must spend in college and reduce the number of terms for which you must pay tuition.

Even at colleges that accept CLEP scores but that do not grant credits, a qualifying CLEP score can help get distribution requirements out of the way or may fulfill introductory course prerequisites. By bypassing the introductory prerequisite, you can start right in with advanced courses in the subject area and progress farther during your undergraduate career.

Overview of the CLEP Subject Exams

Some CLEP Subject Exams presuppose that you have received formal training, even if not in a degree-granting program, in the area being tested. Other CLEP Subject Exams allow for the possibility that you are self-taught through a combination of work experience, life experience, and self-directed reading. Still other such exams lend themselves to individuals with a native background and generally good work and test-taking habits.

The college-level Foreign Language exams fall into this last category. The most popular of all the CLEP Subject Exams is the College Spanish, Levels 1 and 2 exam. This is strictly an exam of language competency; it is in no way based upon familiarity with literature and makes no reference to authors or to their works. While native speakers of Spanish tend to have a rich cultural background related to their country of origin or that of their parents, the Spanish exam presupposes neither any knowledge of the variety of Spanish-speaking cultures nor any outside reading in that language. What all three foreign-language exams do require are reading ability, listening comprehension, and an understanding of the structure of the language.

Obviously, success with a Foreign Language CLEP Exam requires true familiarity with the language—its vocabulary, idioms, grammar, and structure. This familiarity may have been gained through study, through experience living in a foreign country, or through use of the language at home. The source of the knowledge, as with all CLEP Subject Exams, is irrelevant; the sole requirement is that you demonstrate competence.

More than 2,300 colleges accept CLEP scores in some subjects for credit or placement or both. Since the Spanish exam is taken by so many test takers, it obviously has a high acceptance rate. It gives a leg up to the many native Spanish speakers in this country. Even so, we must reiterate the advice given to you earlier in this book: Unless you are taking a CLEP exam just to satisfy yourself that your mastery of the subject matter is of college quality, ask questions before you register. This advice holds especially true for the Foreign Language exams. Many colleges prepare their own internal exams for exemption from language requirements or for placement in upper-level language or foreign-language literature courses. Usually the internal exams are free. If there is an internal exam, be sure that you can gain a real advantage—that you can earn actual college credits with a qualifying CLEP score.

Areas of Difference among CLEP Exams

Most of the CLEP Subject Exams are decidedly verbal, but in the subject groups of Science, Mathematics, and Business, there is a mathematical component as well. In general, the test taker must "do" the math. On multiple-choice exams, you need not show your work, but you must arrive at and choose the correct answer. The use of a non-graphing, non-programmable calculator is permitted but not required during the Calculus, College Algebra, General Chemistry, and Introductory Accounting exams. Being allowed to use a calculator may be a plus or a minus depending on your personal computational skills. The calculator is a factor to consider in choosing to take a particular CLEP subject exam in the realms of Science, Mathematics, and Business.

The optional free-response or essay exam comprises another area of variation among CLEP Subject Exams. Optional 90-minute free-response sections are available for the four Subject Exams in Composition and Literature. These sections are required by some—but not all—institutions. It is up to you to find out whether your college requires the essay section and to register for it if necessary.

THE EXAMS—ONE BY ONE
History and Social Sciences

The catch-all category of Social Sciences and History includes eleven exams and covers a broad range of subject matter. All of the exams in this category presuppose extensive reading, though not necessarily of specific works, and factual knowledge. These exams call for an understanding of cause and effect, of the interrelationships among events. In addition, they require logical reasoning and plain common sense. Some of the exams include questions that require you to recall names of personalities and theories; others are less narrowly focused.

On each of the exams, the bulk of the questions are based upon a statement or on a short quoted excerpt. Nearly all of the exams include some questions based on charts, graphs, tables, photos, cartoons, diagrams, or maps.

Most of the questions follow the familiar (A)-to-(E) format. Some of the questions, however, are of a two-step construction. These offer three, four, or five statements and five combinations of these statements from which to choose your answer. An example of this question style is as follows:

During the late nineteenth century, Congress enacted laws to regulate

    I.   railroad practices.

    II.   the creation of trusts.

    III.   child labor in mines and factories.

    IV.   women's wages and work hours.

(A)   I and II

(B)   II and IV

(C)   I, II, and III

(D)   II, III, and IV

(E)   I, II, III, and IV

The correct answer is (A). ICC regulations of the railroads were enacted in 1887; the Sherman Antitrust Act dates to 1890. Labor, if regulated at all, was regulated only by the states in the nineteenth century.

All of the Social Sciences and History exams are divided into two separately timed 45-minute sections. The number of questions varies from exam to exam.

AMERICAN GOVERNMENT—100 multiple-choice questions based upon subject matter typically covered in a one-semester course.

Topics covered by this exam include, but are by no means limited to, the historical development and current operation of the Constitution and our government institutions; patterns and workings of the political process; the courts; parties and pressure groups; and elections and voting behaviors. Questions may refer to court cases, departments and agencies in the Executive Branch, and published expositions of philosophy of government. Some questions ask the test taker to speculate as to the outcome of certain governmental manipulations. This speculation requires not only understanding of relationships but also careful reasoning based upon pragmatic observations of human behavior.

HISTORY OF THE UNITED STATES I: EARLY COLONIZATIONS TO 1877—120 multiple-choice questions based upon material covered in the first semester of a year course.

This examination asks questions beginning with the French, Spanish, and English colonies, moving through the forces and pressures that led to the formation of the nation, and on through the dynamics of the Civil War and reconstruction. The greatest proportion of the questions concern the period from 1790 to 1877. Exam questions are not sequential through time, but rather are mingled in no particular order.

By virtue of the period covered, there is overlap between this exam and that of American Government. The History of the United States I exam does hinge on specifics, such as names of people, legislative actions, literary works, philosophies, and movements. With reference to these specifics, the exam requires identification, chronology, and understanding of interplay. Success with this exam involves ability to analyze, interpret, explain, and evaluate.

HISTORY OF THE UNITED STATES II: 1865 TO THE PRESENT—120 multiple-choice questions based on material covered in the second semester of a year course.

Aside from the period covered, this exam mirrors the History of the United States I exam. Again the questions are mingled through time, and again emphasis is on the second half of the time period, from 1915 to the present.

HUMAN GROWTH AND DEVELOPMENT (Infancy, Childhood, Adolescence, Adulthood, and Aging)—90 multiple-choice questions based on material taught in a typical one-semester introductory course in child psychology, child development, or developmental psychology.

This exam does presuppose sufficient reading to make the test-taker thoroughly conversant with psychologists and their theories, with terminology, and with design and results of experiments. However, it also relies much more heavily than most CLEP Subject Exams on plain common sense. The Human Growth and Development exam is close behind the two most popular CLEP Subject Exams, College Spanish and College Composition. Its popularity probably stems from the possibility of scoring well simply by drawing on experience and reasoning applied to some reading.

INTRODUCTION TO EDUCATIONAL PSYCHOLOGY—95 multiple-choice questions based on material taught in a one-semester course.

As is the case with the other psychology-related exams, the Educational Psychology exam requires familiarity with psychologists and their theories, with terminology, with specific methods, and with statistics. It also includes many questions that draw upon common sense in applying theories to situations and to speculating on results.

PRINCIPLES OF MACROECONOMICS—80 multiple-choice questions based upon material taught in a one-semester course.

This exam does not require recall of the names of economists, but it does require familiarity with theories and terminology. About 20 percent of the exam covers general economics—that is, concepts familiar to both macroeconomics and microeconomics. Within the realm of macroeconomics—money and banking, taxation, business fluctuations, income distribution, etc.—questions require understanding concepts, interpreting diagrams, evaluating data, and understanding interactions and workings of monetary systems.

PRINCIPLES OF MICROECONOMICS—80 multiple-choice questions based on material taught in a one-semester course.

This exam is similar to that of macroeconomics except that 80 percent of the exam is based on microeconomics. The exam requires test takers to interpret diagrams and to reason on the basis of understanding the interrelationships and true workings of systems, markets, etc.

INTRODUCTORY PSYCHOLOGY—95 multiple-choice questions based on the material presented in a one-semester survey course.

This exam touches upon a little bit of everything. The areas covered include physiological psychology, learning theories, development, behavior, personality models and disorders, social psychology, statistics, and others. Questions require knowledge and understanding of terminology, psychologists' names, and specific theories.

INTRODUCTORY SOCIOLOGY—100 multiple-choice questions based on material taught in a one-semester introductory course.

Questions on the Sociology exam rely heavily on knowledge of terminology and the names of theorists and their beliefs. The questions test understanding of statistics, institutions, processes and patterns, and the interpretation of data. Answering the questions calls for application of common sense to a thorough grasp of meanings in the "language" of the discipline.

WESTERN CIVILIZATION I: ANCIENT NEAR EAST TO 1649—120 multiple-choice questions based on material taught in the first semester of a full-year course on western civilization.

The Western Civilization I exam is an extremely comprehensive exam beginning in Ancient Greece and following through into the mid-seventeenth century. It requires knowledge of facts and events and of the causes and effects of events, as well as an understanding of graphs and maps. The exam requires familiarity with civilizations by name, with people, and with places, and it requires placement of events in time.

WESTERN CIVILIZATION II: 1649 TO THE PRESENT—120 multiple-choice questions based on material taught in the second semester of a full-year course on western civilization.

This exam closely resembles the one given in the first semester. It requires a strong background in names, events, causes and effects, and interrelationships. Test questions involve interpreting ideas and include maps, pictures, and other graphic materials.

Composition and Literature

Four separate examinations fall into the broad category of Composition and Literature. These, in turn, may be divided into two groups: those based heavily upon the reading of specific works and those based upon a more global understanding of works written in the English language, their interpretation, and their structure.

All four exams present excerpts from poetry, drama, fiction, and critical essays. The American and English Literature exams require interpretation of these excerpts in relation to specific authors, their styles, and their works. The other two exams require interpretation based upon overall knowledge of literature and literary analysis without specific reference to known works. The composition-related exam tests both writing skill and analytical ability.

The American Literature and English Literature exams cover ground that is very familiar to most well-educated people. However, since they are predicated on one's having read specific works on an unpublished reading list, they frighten away many test takers and are among the least frequently taken of CLEP Subject Exams. Conversely, the other two exams in the Composition and Literature category are among the most popular, probably because people who consider themselves educated and intelligent are quite confident in their own powers of analysis and self-expression.

AMERICAN LITERATURE—100 multiple-choice questions based on material covered in a full-year survey course.

The American Literature exam asks questions concerning American literature from colonial through modern times, with emphasis on fiction and poetry. The exam includes questions on particular works, their authors, and their meanings. There are questions on characters and events, on historical settings, and on social import, and you may even be asked who wrote a specific work, what character spoke a certain line, or from what work a passage is excerpted. In addition, many questions require interpretation of poetry and short prose selections reprinted in the exam.

The free-response option entails writing two essays. The first is on an assigned topic, a critical generalization that must be discussed and supported. The second essay is a discussion on your choice of one of two topics, prose or poetry, printed in the test booklet.

ENGLISH LITERATURE—105 multiple-choice questions based on material covered in a full-year survey course.

As with the American Literature exam, the English Literature exam relies heavily on knowledge of specific works from *Beowulf* to the present. Test takers must know authors and their works, styles, literary periods, and literary references. The exam requires heavy analysis of reprinted excerpts and poetry for meanings, moods, and forms.

The free-response option entails two essays. The first essay is based on an excerpt printed in the test booklet. The second essay is to be a discussion of one of two general statements with the test-taker's point of view supported by examples from English literature.

ANALYZING AND INTERPRETING LITERATURE—80 multiple-choice questions based on material taught in a two-semester course on general literature.

Like the examinations in American and English literature, this exam presupposes wide reading with ability to analyze and interpret. Unlike the other two literature exams, it does not require familiarity with specific works. The scope of the exam includes poetry, fiction, nonfiction, and drama; British works, American works, and works in translation; and the Classical period through the twentieth century. The questions are all based on reprinted excerpts and are designed to measure understanding, analysis of elements, interpretation of metaphors, and response to nuances of meaning and style.

The free-response option requires two assigned essays. The first is based on a poem printed in the test booklet; the second requires application of a general literary statement to a work of the test-taker's choice.

FRESHMAN COLLEGE COMPOSITION—90 multiple-choice questions based on material taught in a one-year course on expository writing.

This is a General Exam requiring recognition and application of the fundamentals of standard written English, recognition of styles and techniques, logical development, and use of resource materials. Some questions closely resemble questions on routine tests of English usage and grammar; others are questions based on short passages reprinted in the test booklet.

The free-response option requires a 35-to-40-minute expository essay on a required topic and, in the remaining time, a second essay on one of two topics.

Foreign Languages

The three Foreign Language exams measure knowledge and language skills that a student might be expected to have gained in two years of college study. The material on the exams is so structured that a lower score may signify achievement at the one-year-of-study level. Colleges may, therefore, on the basis of score attained, grant two, three, or four semesters' credit.

Each Foreign Language exam consists of two components. One of these components, called the reading section, is a multiple-choice section consisting of written questions, some short and self-contained, others based on reading passages. The other component is a listening section. In this section, the test taker answers multiple-choice questions on the basis of spoken (taped) statements, conversations, and narratives. The tapes have been prepared by native speakers, some men and some women. In some instances, even the questions are spoken, and the student must choose from the answer choices on the printed page.

The two parts, reading and listening, are scored separately, yielding a reading subscore and a listening subscore. A single total score is also reported. Many colleges will require a certain total score to qualify for credit and a qualifying score on both subtests as indication of overall mastery of the language.

The Foreign Language exams weigh each part as 50 percent of the score. Where the two parts have unequal numbers of questions, all questions on the exam do not have equal value. In this respect, the Foreign Language exams differ from all other CLEP Subject Exams on which all multiple-choice questions carry the same weight.

FRENCH LANGUAGE—LEVELS 1 AND 2—Reading part: 60 minutes, 90 questions; Listening part: 30 minutes, 55 questions.

The reading part measures vocabulary mastery by means of sentence-completion questions requiring the correct word or idiomatic phrase; grammar via sentence-completion questions requiring the correct grammatical form; grammar and vocabulary via word substitutions within a sentence; and reading comprehension with questions about content, meaning, and the effects of structural forms in a passage.

The listening part becomes progressively more difficult. First, the test-taker must choose the picture best represented by a spoken statement. Then come short conversations with printed questions about locale of the conversation, identity of speakers, and subject of the conversation. Finally, there are longer conversations or narratives followed by spoken questions. In this instance, only the answer choices are printed. Conversations, questions, and choices are all in French; directions are in English.

GERMAN LANGUAGE—LEVELS 1 AND 2—Reading part: 60 minutes, 80 questions; Listening part: 30 minutes, 55 questions.

The reading part includes sentence completions both in single sentences and within a short paragraph. The sentence completions are designed to measure vocabulary, mastery of grammatical forms, and manipulation of idiomatic expressions. The reading comprehension questions based on reading passages include questions on content, meaning, structure, and writing style.

The listening part begins with a choice of a picture represented by a spoken statement. The second type of question on the German listening part consists of short conversations. The task of the test-taker is to complete the conversation by choosing the most appropriate next statement. Finally, the test-taker must listen to a lengthy conversation and answer spoken questions based upon it. Of course, conversations, questions, and answer choices are all in German; directions, however, are in English.

SPANISH LANGUAGE—LEVELS 1 AND 2—Reading part: 45 minutes, 70 questions; Listening part: 45 minutes, 70 questions.

The reading part comprises sentence-completion questions and reading comprehension. Some sentence-completion questions are designed to measure vocabulary mastery, and others measure ability to choose the correct grammatical form. Some of the grammar questions include a vocabulary and idiom choice component as well. The reading comprehension questions are based on reading passages. The questions cover content, interpretation, and recognition of the purposes served by certain constructions and figures of speech.

As with the French and German exams, the listening part begins with the task of choosing the picture represented by a spoken sentence. The second segment of the listening part consists of short conversations followed by printed questions and printed choices. The questions seek to determine comprehension of the situation. The third question style in the listening part consists of a fairly long narrative followed by a spoken question. The final question style of the Spanish listening part appears only on the tape. First, directions are given orally on the tape. Then comes a single spoken question followed by four spoken answer choices. The test taker must note which of the four spoken answer choices is most appropriate and mark that letter on the answer sheet. If the test-taker has a reasonable grasp of spoken Spanish, the answers to the questions are fairly obvious. The difficulty lies in concentrating on both the correct answer itself and the letter of that answer.

Science and Mathematics

The six exams in the Science and Mathematics family are precise, technical examinations of specific knowledge and understanding. These exams do not rely on the test-taker's having studied any particular texts or sources but demand true mastery of the full scope of the subject matter and ability to manipulate and reason with this knowledge. It is unlikely that a candidate could be successful with any of the science and mathematics exams without concerted study and guided experience or exposure. Common sense has no part in answering the science and mathematics questions, but creative thinking is an important component of success.

The use of a non-graphing, non-programmable scientific calculator is permitted during the Calculus, College Algebra, and General Chemistry exams.

CALCULUS WITH ELEMENTARY FUNCTIONS—45 multiple-choice questions based on concepts and skills taught in a one-year course.

The Calculus exam presupposes a solid background in basic mathematics, algebra, plane and solid geometry, trigonometry, and analytic geometry. It seeks to gauge understanding of calculus and experience with methods and applications. About 10 percent of the Calculus exam is devoted to elementary functions—algebraic, trigonometric, exponential, and logarithmic. The remainder of the exam is divided about equally into differential calculus and integral calculus.

COLLEGE ALGEBRA—60 multiple-choice questions based on material taught in a one-semester college algebra course.

This is a test of knowledge of basic algebra. It covers topics such as linear and quadratic equations, inequalities, and graphs and includes topics such as the theory of equations and exponential and logarithmic functions. Understanding of algebraic vocabulary, symbols, and notation is taken for granted. About half of the exam is devoted to routine problems to measure algebraic skills; the other half consists of nonroutine problems that require understanding of concepts and application of those concepts and skills.

COLLEGE ALGEBRA—TRIGONOMETRY—63 multiple-choice questions. Part One: 45 minutes, 30 algebra questions; Part Two: 15 minutes, 13 trigonometry questions; Part Three: 30 minutes, 20 trigonometry questions.

This exam is designed to cover material taught in a one-semester course that includes both algebra and trigonometry. The questions within each part reflect the same goals and emphases as those on the separate Algebra and Trigonometry exams. While the two parts are of equal length in both time and number of questions, they are not scored separately. Only a total score is reported; there are no subscores.

TRIGONOMETRY—80 multiple-choice questions based on material taught in a one-semester college trigonometry course.

This exam assumes that a one-semester college trigonometry course concentrates mainly on analytical trigonometry. It further assumes familiarity with both radian and degree measurement and with trigonometric vocabulary and notation. The topics covered include trigonometric functions and their relationships, evaluation of trigonometric functions of positive and negative angles, trigonometric equations and inequalities, graphs of trigonometric functions, and trigonometry of the angle. The greater part of the exam presents routine problems in which students demonstrate basic trigonometric skills. The remaining questions involve nonroutine problems that require an understanding of concepts and their application.

GENERAL BIOLOGY—120 multiple-choice questions based on material taught in a typical one-year college biology course.

The Biology exam gives about equal coverage to the three major broad fields of biology: molecular and cellular biology, organismal biology, and populational biology. The exam is not, however, divided into three sections; questions in these three areas are randomly mingled throughout the examination. The function of the exam is to determine knowledge of facts, principles, and processes as they relate to both plants and animals. The exam also seeks to establish that the test-taker is competent in the lab-science aspects of biology—that is, information gathering, hypothesis construction and measurement, experimental design, and interpretation and generalization of data. To this end, a number of questions are based on experiments and on graphic presentations. There are also questions related to the environment and ecology and to the ethical implications of biological advancements.

GENERAL CHEMISTRY—80 multiple-choice questions based on the material taught in a full-year introductory general chemistry course.

The person who has mastered introductory general chemistry should be able to answer questions showing that he or she knows facts, can apply concepts, and can interpret data relative to the structure and states of matter, reaction types, equations, stoichiometry, equilibrium, kinetics, thermodynamics, descriptive chemistry, and experimental chemistry. Questions on this exam are designed to measure such knowledge through diagrams, equations, and descriptions of experiments and their results. Use of a calculator is permitted for the solving of equations.

Business

The five business-related exams cover an eclectic range of topics from computers through management, accounting, business law, and marketing. Some of these exams clearly presuppose training or work experience in the field being tested. Computer and accounting expertise, for example, can hardly be gained through reading alone; some hands-on experience is required. The other exams can be passed by drawing on knowledge that combines outside reading, some sort of related training or work experience, and a good portion of careful reasoning and common sense.

Many of the questions on the Business exams are of the two-step format, as presented below:

> The Federal Fair Housing Act specifically prohibits discrimination in residential sales on the basis of
>
> I. age.
>
> II. sexual orientation.
>
> III. marital status.
>
> IV. religion.
>
> (A) I only
>
> (B) IV only
>
> (C) I and IV
>
> (D) I, III, and IV
>
> (E) I, II, III, and IV

The correct answer is (B). The Federal Fair Housing Act prohibits discrimination in sales on the basis of race, color, religion, sex, or national origin.

INFORMATION SYSTEMS AND COMPUTER APPLICATIONS—100 multiple-choice questions based on material taught in a typical introductory college-level business course.

This is not a computer exam as such. While the exam does take as a given a general familiarity with information systems and computer applications, it does not raise questions based on specific languages, packages, or products. Questions on the exam are about equally divided between those measuring knowledge of terminology and basic concepts and those testing application of knowledge. Topics covered, without reference to specific products, include hardware, software, systems, programming, user support, information processing, and issues such as intellectual property and privacy rights. The questions clearly presuppose computer literacy and previous experience in computer use.

PRINCIPLES OF MANAGEMENT—100 multiple-choice questions based on material taught in a one-term introductory management course.

The focus of this examination is on the functional aspects of management, though it also asks questions related to the operational aspects of management and to human resources. The examination asks questions requiring knowledge of purposes, functions, and techniques of management; terminology related to management ideas, processes, and techniques; theory and underlying assumptions of concepts of management; and application of knowledge to specific problems. A person who has had experience in the business world, who has done some independent reading, and who reasons clearly should be able to succeed on this examination without formal course work. An in-service course would give an additional advantage.

PRINCIPLES OF ACCOUNTING—78 multiple-choice questions based on content of two semesters of college accounting courses.

Questions on the Accounting exam measure knowledge of both financial accounting and managerial accounting in about the proportion of two thirds to one third. A college may grant one or two semesters of credit depending on the configuration of courses at that college. Answering the accounting questions requires familiarity with accounting concepts and terminology, skill at preparation and use of financial reports, ability to apply accounting techniques to problem situations, and understanding the rationale behind principles and procedures in accounting. Some of the accounting questions involve computations.

Experience, training, or both are needed as qualifying background for success with this exam. The use of a calculator is permitted during this exam.

INTRODUCTORY BUSINESS LAW—100 multiple-choice questions based on content of a one-semester college course.

The bulk of this exam concerns business contracts, their formation, their meaning and applications, and the laws specific to their enforcement. Other questions concern American legal history, legal systems and procedures, and specific laws pertaining to agency and employment, torts, consumer protection, and other areas. About one third of the questions deal with knowledge of basic facts and terms, one third with understanding of concepts and principles, and one third with application of knowledge to specific case problems.

Background for this exam should include reading, experience, and, perhaps, a noncredit course in a subject such as real estate. Common sense and judgment also enter into qualifications for this exam.

PRINCIPLES OF MARKETING—100 multiple-choice questions based on material taught in a one-semester introductory marketing course.

This exam requires basic understanding of markets and marketing. It includes questions on demographics, consumer behavior, the effects and interactions of government regulation, economic trends, effects of advertising, transportation, billing procedures, and related areas. The successful candidate will have a good grasp of the structure of various marketing institutions and will fully comprehend just how the marketing function fits into the business firm and how marketing actions have an impact on the activities and profits of the firm.

Reading, experience, and logical reasoning should all contribute to success on this examination.

CREDITS

Bird in Space, 1925, Constantin Brancusi; © 2001 Artists Rights Society (ARS), New York/ADAGP, Paris

Adam and Eve, 1916–24, Constantin Brancusi; © 2001 Artists Rights Society (ARS), New York/ADAGP, Paris

Oedipus Rex, 1922, Max Ernst; © 2001 Artists Rights Society (ARS), New York/ADAGP, Paris

City Square, 1948, Alberto Giacometti; © 2001 Artists Rights Society (ARS), New York/ADAGP, Paris

Madame Arthur Fontaine, 1904, Edouard Vuillard; © 2001 Artists Rights Society (ARS), New York/ADAGP, Paris

Fountain, 1917, Marcel Duchamp; © 2001 Artists Rights Society (ARS), New York/ADAGP, Paris/Estate of Marcel Duchamp

Heart Mobile, 1947, Alexander Calder; © 2001 Estate of Alexander Calder/Artists Rights Society (ARS), New York

Man with a Violin, 1911–12, Pablo Picasso; © 2001 Estate of Pablo Picasso/Artists Rights Society (ARS), New York

Guernica, Pablo Picasso; © 2001 Estate of Pablo Picasso/Artists Rights Society (ARS), New York

Spitball, 1961, Tony Smith; © 2001 Estate of Tony Smith/Artists Rights Society (ARS), New York

Indefinite Divisibility, Yves Tanguy; © 2001 Estate of Yves Tanguy/Artists Rights Society (ARS), New York

Jane Avril, Henri de Toulouse-Lautrec, French, 1864–1901; Color lithograph, poster, 1899; Gift of the Baldwin M. Baldwin Foundation

Nancy and Olivia, Alice Neel; © The Estate of Alice Neel. Photograph courtesy of Robert Miller Gallery

Women: Sunlight/Moonlight, Sculpture, Roy Lichtenstein; © 2001 Estate of Roy Lichtenstein

How Guenever Made Her a Nun, Aubrey Beardsley; © 2001 Estate of Aubrey Beardsley

NOTES

NOTES

NOTES

NOTES

NOTES

Your everything education destination...
the *all-new* Petersons.com

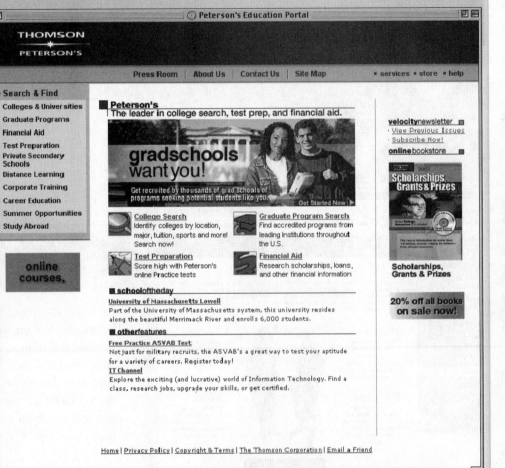

When education is the question, **Petersons.com** is the answer. Log on today and discover what the *all-new* Petersons.com can do for you. Find the ideal college or grad school, take an online practice admission test, or explore financial aid options—all from a name you know and trust, Peterson's.

www.petersons.com

THOMSON
PETERSON'S™